Past and Present Publicatio

Eternal victory

This book is published as part of the joint publishing agreement established in 1977 between the Fondation de la Maison des Sciences de l'Homme and the Press Syndicate of the University of Cambridge. Titles published under this arrangement may appear in any European language or, in the case of volumes of collected essays, in several languages.

New books will appear either as individual titles or in one of the series which the Maison des Sciences de l'Homme and the Cambridge University Press have jointly agreed to publish. All books published jointly by the Maison des Sciences de l'Homme and the Cambridge University Press will be distributed by the Press throughout the world.

Cet ouvrage est publié dans le cadre de l'accord de co-édition passé en 1977 entre la Fondation de la Maison des Sciences de l'Homme et le Press Syndicate of the University of Cambridge. Toutes les langues européennes sont admises pour les titres couverts par cet accord, et les ouvrages collectifs peuvent paraître en plusieurs langues.

Les ouvrages paraissent soit isolément, soit dans l'une des séries que la Maison des Sciences de l'Homme et Cambridge University Press ont convenu de publier ensemble. La distribution dans le monde entier des titres ainsi publiés conjointement par les deux établissements est assurée par Cambridge University Press.

This book is also published in association with and as part of Past and Present Publications, which comprise books similar in character to the articles in the journal *Past and Present*. Whether the volumes in the series are collections of essays – some previously published, others new studies – or monographs, they encompass a wide variety of scholarly and original works primarily concerned with social, economic and cultural changes and their causes and consequences. They will appeal to both specialists and non-specialists and will endeavour to communicate the results of historical and allied research in readable and lively form.

For a list of titles in Past and Present Publications, see end of book.

Eternal victory

Triumphal rulership in late antiquity, Byzantium, and the early medieval West

MICHAEL McCORMICK

Dumbarton Oaks and The Johns Hopkins University

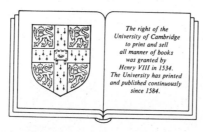

CAMBRIDGE UNIVERSITY PRESS

Cambridge

New York   Port Chester   Melbourne   Sydney

EDITIONS DE LA MAISON DES SCIENCES DE
L'HOMME

Paris

Published by the Press Syndicate of the University of Cambridge
The Pitt Building, Trumpington Street, Cambridge CB2 1RP
40 West 20th Street, New York, NY 10011, USA
10 Stamford Road, Oakleigh, Melbourne 3166, Australia
and Editions de la Maison des Sciences de l'Homme
54 Boulevard Raspail, 57270 Paris Cedex 06

First published 1986
Reprinted 1987
First paperback edition 1990

Printed in Great Britain at the University Press, Cambridge

Library of Congress catalogue card number: 84–19907

British Library Cataloguing in Publication Data
McCormick, Michael
Eternal victory: triumphal rulership in late
Antiquity, Byzantium, and the early medieval West.
(Past and present publications)
1. Triumphs (Ceremonies)—Europe—History
I. Title   II. Series
394'.4'094   GT5030

ISBN 0 521 26180 5 hardback
ISBN 0 521 38659 4 paperback
ISBN 2 7351 0084 7 hardback (France only)
ISBN 2 7351 0347 1 paperback (France only)

To Pants,
In loving memory;
And for Ste Barbara and the Ace of Aces

TM

Contents

Contents

Contents

Foreword

This study began in Belgium. A research topic in the late Nicolas Huyghebaert's Church History Seminar at the francophone University of Louvain grew into a doctoral dissertation. 'Victory and its celebration in the Byzantine empire and the Barbarian Kingdoms, A.D. 476–1000' was directed by my mentor, Léopold Genicot, and defended at the University's Institut d'études médiévales, in May 1979. It benefited from the comments and suggestions of the examining committee: Messrs Robert Bultot, Jacques Fontaine, Léopold Genicot, Nicolas Huyghebaert, Justin Mossay and Guy Muraille.

In the United States, it was substantially expanded and revised. The chronological limits were extended, and its scope evolved in response to the stimulus provided by the two extraordinary institutions I have been privileged to serve. At The Dumbarton Oaks Center for Byzantine Studies (Washington, D.C.), where a number of chapters were first presented as 'Informal Talks', my friends and colleagues provided much insight, support, and wise counsel, in the collegial and enlightened atmosphere fostered by the Director, Giles Constable. My colleagues and teaching duties in the Department of History of The Johns Hopkins University, and particularly the European Seminar, offered a further opportunity to participate in splendid discussion of current historical research concerning a broad range of topics and problems.

Any study of this kind owes a deep debt to libraries and librarians. In Belgium, Father H. Bascour and the library of the Abbaye du Mont-César, the Société des Bollandistes and the Bibliotheek van de Faculteit der Godgeleerdheid (K.U. Leuven) played a decisive role. In America, the incomparable facilities and staff of Dumbarton Oaks left their mark on nearly every page. The reader must know, however, that though this study has been conducted under privileged bibliographical conditions, I decided to limit citations of secondary literature to those titles which seemed, in my judgement, indispensable. In my footnotes, that is, I have been forced to omit many studies which I consulted on various topics.

In one way or another, many friends and colleagues have contributed to this book over the years. Convention urges me to thank those most intimately associated with it. Space forces me to injustice. I am deeply grateful to Léopold Genicot, for the role he has played in my studies and for directing the dissertation out of which this book has grown. John Baldwin, John Callahan, Giles Constable, Nicolas Huyghebaert, and Hubert Silvestre have contributed more than they know through their conversations, counsels and friendship. I owe a lasting debt to Stephen Hadrović, for guiding my first, halting steps in historical studies. Most of these chapters have enjoyed the detailed criticism and insight of Alexander Kazhdan and Nicolas Oikonomides. Others who have read sections and made helpful suggestions include Robert Benson, Averil Cameron, Evangelos Chrysos and Martin Heinzelmann. Finally, I owe an incalculable debt to the enduring encouragement and support of my family, both immediate and extended.

Tonawanda, N.Y.
Thanksgiving, 1983

Note to the paperback edition

The following notes offer additional primary source testimony that I have encountered which may be helpful to users of this book. A few material errors – for knowledge of which I am indebted to reviewers' care – have been corrected silently in the book.[1]

2: the sees of the bishops who wrote to Maurice were in the Lombard territory of Aquileia: H. Berg, 'Bischöfe und Bischofssitze im Ostalpen- und Donauraum von 4. bis zum 8. Jahrhundert', *Die Bayern und ihre Nachbarn*, 1, ed. H. Wolfram and A. Schwarcz (Vienna, 1985), pp. 61–108, here 82–4.

41, n. 22: Evangelos Chrysos has suggested to me that Constantius II's triumphant return to Milan in 355 might be added to this list: Ammianus Marcellinus, *Res gestae* 15, 4, 13, ed. W. Seyfarth *et al.*, 1 (Leipzig, 1978), 45.22–3.

60: Theoderic Strabo's accidental death in 481 seems to have resulted in a state holiday: Jordanes, *Rom.* 436, Mommsen 44.28–9.

70, with n. 123: P. Conte has presented convincing reasons for identifying the island of Kalonymos with Prote, in the Islands of the Princes (Turkish Kenaliada): *Aevum*, 52 (1988), 366.

74–8: for the liturgical mention of a victory celebration over the

[1] At this writing, the following reviews have come to my attention: R. Collins, *English Historical Review*, 104 (1989), 410; P. Conte, *Aevum*, 52 (1988), 362–9; A. Cutler, *Classical World*, 82 (1989), 473–4; M. Heinzelmann, *Francia*, 15 (1987), 1106–7; F. Hockey, *Revue d'histoire ecclésiastique*, 83 (1988), 421–2; P. Lemerle, *Revue historique*, 279 (1988), 185–6; T. C. Lounghis, *Cahiers de civilisation médiévale*, 32 (1989), 169–71; G. Tabacco, *Studi medievali*, ser. 3, 29 (1988), 484–6; U. Treu, *BS*, 50 (1989), 79–81; R. Van Dam, *American Historical Review*, 93 (1988), 1028–9; H. Wolfram, *MIÖG*, 96 (1988), 163–4.

Persians on 12 December: A. Dmitrievsky, *Opisanie liturgits-eskikh rukopisei* I (Kiev, 1895), p. 156.

144: the Bulgar Khan Krum is supposed to have performed the *calcatio* on the metropolitan of Adrianople in 813: *Syn. CPitanum*, Delehaye, 415.4–8.

150–2, with n. 67–8: the following year, Photius referred to Michael III's role in the celebration of 863: *Homilia*, 10, 2, Laourdas, 99.22–100.10. Cf. C. Mango, *The Homilies of Photius Patriarch of Constantinople*, Dumbarton Oaks Studies 3 (Cambridge, Mass., 1958), p. 184; cf. p. 179.

207, n. 88: see *Vita Blasii*, 2 (BHG 278) AASS Nov. 4.658B for a tenth-century occurrence of the term.

233: for another victory endowment, also in the empire's western reaches, see that of Nicephorus I for Patras (Dölger, *Regesten*, no. 365); on which cf. O. Kresten, 'Zur Echtheit des ΣΙΓΙΛΛΙΟΝ des Kaisers Nikephoros I. für Patras', *Römische historische Mitteilungen*, 19 (1977), 15–78, esp. 43–6.

257, n. 120: for evidence of this formula's middle Byzantine social diffusion, see the graffiti of Corinth, ed. B. D. Meritt, *Corinth. Results of Excavations*, 8.1 (Cambridge, Mass., 1931), nos. 200, 205, 212 and 213.

336–7; cf. 259: for more on Clovis' parade and the historical circumstances in which early Germanic leaders experienced and adopted elements of imperial ceremonial, see 'Clovis at Tours, Byzantine Public Ritual and the Origins of Medieval Ruler Symbolism', *Das Reich und die Barbaren*, ed. E. K. Chrysos and A. Schwarcz, Veröffentlichungen des Instituts für Österreichische Geschichtsforschungen, 29 (Vienna, 1989), pp. 155–80.

338–9: on Theudebert's gold issues, see now P. Grierson and M. Blackburn, *Medieval European Coinage*, 1, *The Early Middle Ages* (Cambridge, 1986), pp. 116–17.

375–7: in early 757, Fulrad, abbot of St Denis, collected the keys of the cities 'restored' to Stephen II by Pippin's second Italian campaign and deposited them in the shrine of St Peter: *Lib. pont.*, Duchesne, 1.454.1–12, significantly, an Italian source about a ceremony in Italy. Apparently in 794, John offered symbols of victory after combat near Barcelona to King Louis the Pious and received land in return: MGH *Diplomata Karolinorum*, 1, ed.

E. Mühlbacher *et al*. (1906), no. 179 here 241.40–242.5; cf.
Böhmer-Mühlbacher, *Regesten*, no. 328.
386: the text from the Arles Sacramentary is now edited in 'A New
Ninth-Century Witness to the Carolingian Mass against the
Pagans (Paris, B.N. lat. 2812)', *Revue bénédictine*, 97 (1987), 68–
86.

Abbreviations

AASS	*Acta Sanctorum*, Antwerp, 1643 – 3rd edn, Paris, Rome, Brussels, 1863–.
AB	*Analecta Bollandiana*, Brussels, 1882–.
ACO	*Acta conciliorum oecumenicorum*, ed. E. Schwartz, Berlin, 1914–74.
ANRW	*Aufstieg und Niedergang der römischen Welt. Geschichte und Kultur Roms im Spiegel der neueren Forschung*, ed. H. Temporini and W. Haase, Berlin, 1972–.
BHG	F. Halkin, *Bibliotheca hagiographica graeca*, 3rd edn, Subsidia hagiographica, 8a, Brussels, 1957; F. Halkin, *Auctarium*, Subsidia hagiographica, 47, Brussels, 1969.
BHL	*Bibliotheca hagiographica latina* and *Supplementum*, Subsidia hagiographica, 6 and 12, Brussels, 1898–1901 and 1911.
BS	*Byzantinoslavica*, Prague, 1929–.
Byz.	*Byzantion. Revue internationale des études byzantines*, Brussels, 1924–.
BZ	*Byzantinische Zeitschrift*, Leipzig, Munich, 1892–.
CCL	*Corpus christianorum, series latina*, Turnholt, 1953–.
CFHB	*Corpus fontium historiae byzantinae*, 1967–.
CIL	*Corpus inscriptionum latinarum*, Berlin, 1863–.

CLA	E.A. Lowe, *Codices latini antiquiores. A palaeographical guide to manuscripts prior to the ninth century*, Oxford, 1934–71.
CLLA	K. Gamber, *Codices liturgici latini antiquiores*, 2nd edn, Spicilegium Friburgense, Subsidia, 1, Fribourg, 1968.
CPG	M. Geerard, *Clavis patrum graecorum*, Turnhout, 1974–.
CSEL	*Corpus scriptorum ecclesiasticorum latinorum*, Vienna, 1866–.
DACL	*Dictionnaire d'archéologie chrétienne et de liturgie*, ed. F. Cabrol and H. Leclercq, Paris, 1907–53.
DHGE	*Dictionnaire d'histoire et de géographie ecclésiastiques*, ed. A. Baudrillet, A. De Meyer, E. Van Cauwenbergh, R. Aubert, Paris, 1912–.
Dict. ant.	*Dictionnaire des antiquités grecques et romaines d'après les textes et les monuments*, ed. C. Daremberg and E. Saglio, Paris, 1877–1929.
DOP	*Dumbarton Oaks Papers*, Washington, D.C., 1941–.
FMS	*Frühmittelalterliche Studien*, Münster, 1967–.
GCS	Die Griechischen christlichen Schriftsteller der ersten drei Jahrhunderte, Leipzig, 1897–.
Guilland, *Topographie*	R. Guilland, *Études de topographie de Constantinople byzantine*, Berliner byzantinistische Arbeiten, 37, Berlin, 1969.
ILS	*Inscriptiones latinae selectae*, ed. H. Dessau, Berlin, 1892–1916.
JAC	*Jahrbuch für Antike und Christentum*, Münster-Westfalen, 1964–.
Janin, *Cple byz.*	R. Janin, *Constantinople byzantine. Développement urbain et répertoire topographique*, 2nd edn, Paris, 1964.

Janin, *Églises*	R. Janin, *La géographie ecclésiastique de l'empire byzantin. Le siège de Constantinople et le patriarcat oecuménique: Les églises et les monastères*, 2nd edn, Paris, 1969.
JL	P. Jaffé, S. Löwenfeld et al., *Regesta pontificum Romanorum ab condita ecclesia ad annum post Christum natum MCXCVIII*, Leipzig, 1885–8.
JÖB	*Jahrbuch der österreichischen Byzantinistik*, Vienna, 1951–.
MGH	*Monumenta Germaniae historica*
AA	*Auctores antiquissimi*, 1877–1919.
Capit.	*Capitularia regum Francorum*, ed. A. Boretius and V. Krause, 1883–97.
Conc.	*Concilia aevi Carolini*, ed. A. Werminghoff, 1906–24.
Dipl. stir. Kar.	*Diplomata regum Germaniae ex stirpe Karolinorum*, 1932–60.
Epist.	*Epistolae*, 1887–1939.
Form.	*Formulae Merovingici et Karolini aevi*, 1882.
Poet.	*Poetae latini medii aevi*, 1881–.
SRG	*Scriptores rerum germanicarum in usum scholarum*, 1839–.
SRL	*Scriptores rerum Langobardicarum*, 1878.
SRM	*Scriptores rerum Merovingicarum*, 1884–1951.
SS	*Scriptores*, 1826–1934.
MIÖG	*Mitteilungen des Instituts für österreichische Geschichtsforschung*, Innsbruck, 1880–.
Müller-Wiener, *Bildlexikon*	W. Müller-Wiener, *Bildlexikon zur Topographie Istanbuls*, Tübingen, 1977.
PG	*Patrologia graeca*, ed. J.P. Migne, Paris, 1857–86.
PL	*Patrologia latina*, ed. J.P. Migne, Paris, 1844–64.
PLRE	A.H.M. Jones, J.R. Martindale and J. Morris, *Prosopography of the later Roman Empire*, Cambridge, 1971–.

RAC	*Reallexikon für Antike und Christentum,* ed. T. Klauser, Stuttgart, 1941–.
RE	*Paulys Realencyclopädie der klassischen Altertumswissenschaft,* ed. G. Wissowa et al., Stuttgart, 1893–.
RÉB	*Revue des études byzantines,* Paris, 1946–.
RIC	*The Roman imperial coinage,* ed. H. Mattingly et al., London, 1923–.
SC	Sources chrétiennes, Paris, 1941–.
Settimane	Settimane di studio del centro italiano di studi sull'alto medioevo, Spoleto, 1954–.
TM	*Travaux et mémoires,* Paris, 1965–.
VV	*Vizantiiskii Vremennik,* Leningrad, 1894–.
Wattenbach– Levison, *Geschichtsquellen*	W. Wattenbach and W. Levison, *Deutschlands Geschichtsquellen im Mittelalter. Vorzeit und Karolinger,* Weimar, 1952–.

Introduction: imperial triumph as a historical problem

Der letzte Triumph scheint im J. 302 von Diocletian gehalten zu sein.

J. Marquardt, 1881

Was wissen wir eigentlich von den mittelalterlichen Königen?

P.E. Schramm, 1956

Only a small part of the ritual apparatus of sovereignty was taken over directly by the Germanic kingdoms established in Latin *Romania*.

D.A. Bullough, 1974

To the modern observer, the situation of the Roman empire in the late sixth century appears grim. Barbarian advances, plague and civil strife engulfed the ancient edifice. When a severe uprising rocked Egypt under emperor Maurice (A.D. 582–602), a Roman general named Theodore was dispatched to quell the revolt. Before attacking, he had two recently freed prisoners try to persuade the insurgents to lay down their arms:

Observe all you people who have joined with the rebels: do not war against the general, for the Roman empire is neither enfeebled nor vanquished!

The reported effect was remarkable: a number of dissidents abandoned the revolt and came over to the imperial forces.[1]

---

[1] John of Nikiu, *Chronicle*, tr. R.H. Charles (London, 1916), p. 159, kindly corrected for me on the basis of the Ethiopian by G. Fiaccadori. On the location, J. Maspéro and G. Wiet, *Matériaux pour servir à la géographie de l'Égypte*, Mémoires de l'Institut français d'archéologie orientale, 36 (Cairo, 1914–19), pp. 193–5. The liminary citations are from J. Marquardt, *Römische Staatsverwaltung*, ed. H. Dessau and A. von Domas-

I

Whether or not late Romans actually used this kind of argument may perhaps be questioned. That late Roman writers put such reasoning into their mouths cannot. As Narses supposedly insisted after defeating the Alamannians, eternal victory was the birthright of Rome.[2] The incident could be dismissed if it were isolated or limited to the rhetorical productions of historians and poets. It was not. About the same time, the bishops of Istria wrote to Maurice expressing their belief that they would soon be delivered from the barbarian yoke and returned to the 'freedom' of the 'holy commonwealth' (*sancta res publica*).[3] In far away Arabia, the Koran seemed to expect that a tottering Roman empire would yet snatch victory from the jaws of defeat by the Persians. After the Romans suffered a crushing defeat during the Persian invasion, a tradition immune to imperial censorship claimed that a relative of the Prophet reacted to the news by wagering on Roman victory.[4] At the other end of the world, rumors reached Merovingian Gaul that new, victory-producing saints' relics had come to light in the imperial East.[5] As late as 678, when the Romans made a new treaty with the Arabs, western rulers may have feared that another Byzantine reconquest would follow, for they hastened to request peace treaties with Constantinople.[6] Through the darkest hours of the seventh and eighth

---

zewski, 2nd edn, 2 (reprint, Wiesbaden, 1957), 591 (but cf. *ibid.*, n. 7); P.E. Schramm, 'Herrschaftszeichen und Staatssymbolik', *Herrschaftszeichen und Staatssymbolik. Beiträge zu ihrer Geschichte vom dritten bis zum sechzehnten Jahrhundert, MGH*. Schriften, 13, 3 (Stuttgart, 1956), 1067; and D.A. Bullough, 'Games people played. Drama and ritual as propaganda in medieval Europe', *Transactions of the Royal Historical Society*, ser. 5, 24 (1974), 97–122, here 103.

[2] Agathias, *Historiarum libri v*, 2, 12, 2, ed. R. Keydell, *CFHB*, 2 (Berlin, 1967). 56.4–5; cf. e.g. Corippus, *Iohannidos libri viii*, 2, 381–8 and 4, 344–9, ed. J. Diggle and F.R.D. Goodyear (Cambridge, 1970), 41–2 and 80, and the speech attributed to Justin II during an audience with an Avar envoy, Corippus, *In laudem Iustini augusti minoris* 3, 340–4 and 380–9, ed. Av. Cameron (London, 1976), 71 and 72.

[3] Gregory I, *Registrum* 1, 16a, ed. P. Ewald and L.M. Hartmann, *MGH. Epist.*, 1 (1887). 20.3–4; cf. 18.6–8 and 18.30–5. Cf. F. Lanzoni, *Le diocesi d'Italia dalle origini al principio del secolo VII*, 2, Studi e testi, 35 (Faenza, 1927), 893–4.

[4] Qur'ān, Sūrat al-Rūm, 30:2–4, cited and discussed by A.M.H. Shboul, 'Byzantium and the Arabs: The image of the Byzantines as mirrored in Arabic literature', *Byzantine papers*, ed. E. and M. Jeffreys and A. Moffatt, Byzantina australiensia, 1 (Canberra, 1981), pp. 43–68, here p. 47–8 with n. 32–3.

[5] Gregory of Tours, *Historiarum libri x*, 7, 31, ed. B. Krusch and W. Levison, *MGH. SRM*, 1.1 (1951), 350.6–351.17.

[6] Theophanes, *Chronographia*, A.M. 6169, ed. C. De Boor, 1 (Leipzig, 1883). 356.2–8.

centuries the church and people of Rome prayed ceaselessly for the 'more complete' return of imperial dominion to its former extent.[7] In part, such responses doubtless arose from the usual lag between event and perception.[8] But some part surely came from deep belief in the most potent of Roman myths: the myth of the Roman empire's eternal victory, a myth generated by the unprecedented rise, power and duration of Rome.

If the simple fact of the empire's stupendous growth and power created this belief, imperial authorities of successive eras worked skillfully to maintain it. From the fourth century, as external threats grew more dangerous, foreigners especially were targeted for this message. Imperial legations traveled to 'barbarian' courts to inform them of the emperor's most recent triumphs.[9] To justify the assassination of a barbarian chieftain, two Roman officers could devise no better defense than to claim that the kinglet was

---

F. Šišić, *Provijest Hrvata u vrijeme narodnih vladara* (Zagreb, 1925), pp. 270–1, argues that the treaty was with the Slavic tribes of the Byzantine West, a position accepted by G. Ostrogorsky, *Geschichte des byzantinischen Staates*, 3rd edn (Munich, 1963), p. 104 with n. 4. But that does not exclude, at the very least, the Lombards, who are clearly implicated by Theophanes' use of the word κάσταλδοι, which must be the Lombard *gastald(i)us*: C. Du Cange, *Glossarium mediae et infimae latinitatis*, ed. L. Favre, 4 (Niort, 1885), 40–1; cf. L.M. Hartmann, *Geschichte Italiens im Mittelalter 2*, 1 (Gotha, 1900), 272 with n. 23, pp. 279–80; F. Dölger, *Regesten der Kaiserurkunden des oströmischen Reiches von 565–1453* (Munich, 1924), nos. 204–1, and T.C. Lounghis, *Les ambassades byzantines en Occident depuis la fondation des états barbares jusqu'aux Croisades (407–1090)* (Athens, 1980), pp. 122–3.

[7] *Liber diurnus Romanorum pontificum*, 60, ed. H. Foerster (Bern, 1958), 117.4–17.

[8] N. Reitter, *Der Glaube an die Fortdauer des römischen Reiches im Abendlande wahrend des 5. und 6. Jahrhunderts*, Diss. (Münster, 1900), has collected other testimony on this subject.

[9] Thus in 456 to king Theoderic II: Hydatius, *Chronicon*, 176–7, ed. A. Tranoy, 1, SC, 218 (Paris, 1974). 156; cf. comm., *ibid.* 2, 105; Avitus of Vienne, *Ep.* 46a, whose congratulations to Anastasius I on a victory seem to presume an imperial missive, explicitly referred to in connection with the son of Laurentius: ed. R. Peiper, *MGH. AA*, 6.2 (1883). 76.18–25 (cf. *Ep.* 47, *ibid.* 77.4: 'impletam ... principalis reverentiae iussionem'); only an account of the disastrous campaign of 811 traceable to Michael I's legation can explain the Frankish court's reference to 'multas et insignes victorias in Moesia provincia': *Annales regni Francorum*, a. 812, ed. F. Kurze, *MGH. SRG* (1895), 136; cf. Dölger, *Regesten*, no. 385, and Lounghis, *Ambassades*, pp. 160–1; Theophilus' announcement of a victory against foreign nations to Louis the Pious: *Annales Bertiniani*, a. 839, ed. F. Grat, J. Vieilliard and S. Clémencet, Société de l'histoire de France, 470 (Paris, 1964), 30, on which cf. Dölger, *Regesten*, no. 438. For surviving texts of such victory communiqués, see below, Ch. 5.

undermining foreigners' belief in the emperor's invincibility.[10] Nor was the insistent message of imperial victory confined to envoys and historians. The theme was obligatory for every panegyrist from Pliny to Pisides.[11] Imperial art and ceremony glorified it, the Roman army's passwords and battle cries echoed it.[12] Roman coinage, an ubiquitous and revealing mirror of government thinking, is covered with slogans like 'Eternal Victory' or 'Victory of the Augusti'.[13]

The original expansion and early solidity of Roman power had prepared men's minds to believe in the myth, but a coincidence of constitutional history transformed what might have been a general perception into a fundamental conception. The legacy of the Roman revolution, which grounded the emperor's constitutional power largely in his position as commander-in-chief or *imperator*, lent unique urgency to the message of Roman victory. The ruler's military success confirmed his right to rule.[14] To the constitutional imperative of imperial victory was added a political one, for the ancients were no less sensitive than moderns to the sweet smell of success. That war and a huge military establishment

[10] Agathias, *Hist.* 4, 9, 3, Keydell 134.7–10.
[11] A few examples from many: Pliny, *Panegyricus*, 16–17; *XII panegyrici latini*, 10, (2), 1, 4, ed. R.A.B. Mynors (Oxford, 1964), 244.20; 10 (2), 2, 1, Mynors 245.10; 10 (2), 6, 1, 248.10–11; 11 (3), 4, 3–4, 259.17–25, etc. Themistius, *Oratio 3*, ed. H. Schenkl and G. Downey, 1 (Leipzig, 1965). 60.12–15; cf. Libanius' allusion to imperial victories as a common topic in the panegyrics addressed to Theodosius I: *Oratio 19*, 65, ed. R. Foerster, 2 (Leipzig, 1904). 413.11–17; Procopius of Gaza, *In imperatorem Anastasium panegyricus*, 1, ed. C. Kempen (Bonn, 1918), 1.3–11; Paul Silentiary, *Descriptio sanctae Sophiae*, ed. P. Friedländer, *Johannes von Gaza und Paulus Silentiarius. Kunstbeschreibungen justinianischer Zeit* (Leipzig, 1912), 227.4–16; George Pisides, *Expeditio persica*, 3, 404–27, ed. A. Pertusi, Studia patristica et byzantina, 7 (Ettal, 1959), 134–5.
[12] A. Grabar, *L'empereur dans l'art byzantin. Recherches sur l'art officiel de l'empire d'Orient* (Paris, 1936), pp. 31ff. The use of battle cries or passwords like 'uictoria', 'palma', 'Deus nobiscum' or 'triumphus imperatoris' was counselled by Vegetius, *Epitoma rei militaris*, 3, 5, ed. C. Lang (Leipzig, 1885), 73.14–18; Justinian's armies acclaimed him 'gloriously victorious' (καλλίνικος), e.g. Procopius, *Bella*, 2, 30, 3, ed. J. Haury and G. Wirth, 2nd edn, 1 (Leipzig, 1962). 296.15–17; by the ninth century the accent had shifted, as Byzantine troops shouted 'The cross conquered!': 'Genesius', *Regum libri iv*, 4, 14, ed. A. Lesmüller-Werner and I. Thurn, CFHB, 14 (Berlin, 1978). 66.52–5; *ibid.* 4, 36, 87.35–6.
[13] See, e.g. M. Grant, *Roman history from coins* (Cambridge, 1958), pp. 45–51. For the tetrarchic use of VICTORIA AETERNA AVG and related reverse legends, see the references in *RIC*, 6, 705; cf. *RIC*, 7, 754–8; VICTORIA AVGG etc., *RIC*, 8, 572–3.
[14] J. Gagé, 'La théologie de la victoire impériale', *Revue historique*, 171 (1933), 1–43; see below, Ch. 1.

continuously burdened the empire's later history only enhanced the political appeal of a triumphal style of rulership. Classical civilization's athletic ethos added further impetus to the lionization of the imperial victor, especially since the late antique hippodrome resounded equally with acclamations for the victorious emperor and the triumphant charioteer.[15] Since winning at sports was semantically indistinguishable from military victory (the games themselves were often a gift of imperial munificence), the Roman crowd easily confounded success in the races with the notion of imperial victory.[16] Tens of thousands of voices chanting 'Ni-ka, ni-ka!' created an awesome background for the spectacular self-manifestation of the 'victor and triumphator', as the ruler of the Romans styled himself. And, finally, imperial officials were clever enough to shift the most important rites of imperial power – including victory celebrations – to the vast theater provided by the circus and its fans.

The emperor's perennial victory can be traced across the physical and mental landscape of the late Roman world. Coins, monuments, legal depositions, panegyrics, Sunday services and games – all reflect the ways in which this facet of the imperial idea developed, and the significance it acquired. Above all – and this constitutes the central theme of this study – triumphal ceremonial, propaganda and public display celebrated and confirmed the victorious rulership of the emperor. These ceremonies in particular yield different kinds of insight into the society and government which produced them. A specific performance of a victory celebration can illuminate the organizer's short-term appraisal of the general political situation, for, as we will see, each performance was carefully calibrated to the particular conditions in which power was being exercised. When a ceremony was

---

[15] On the affinity of ancient athletic and military values, H.W. Pleket, 'Games, prizes, athletes and ideology. Some aspects of the history of sport in the Greco-Roman world', *Arena* [= *Stadion. Zeitschrift für Geschichte des Sports und der Körperkultur*], I (1975), 51–89, here 76–8. The linguistic impact of the sporting ethos on a small segment of the imperial age's literary production is outlined by R. Merkelbach, 'Der griechische Wortschatz und die Christen', *Zeitschrift für Papyrologie und Epigraphik*, 18 (1975), 101–48, here 108–36.

[16] J. Gagé, 'Σταυρὸς νικοποιός. La victoire impériale dans l'Empire chrétien', *Revue d'histoire et de philosophie religieuses*, Année 1933, 370–400, here 374ff. On the shout νίκα, A. Cameron, *Porphyrius the Charioteer* (Oxford, 1973), pp. 76–80.

repeatedly performed through the centuries, the historian who collects the scattered evidence and assembles it in its historical order will discover that, for all their continuity, later Roman and Byzantine imperial ceremonies were subject to the relentless law of historical change no less than other facets of human activity. The changes are sometimes evident only when the ceremony is viewed over the long term, but they can provide precious symptoms of wider trends in a society's development. In this regard, the later Roman triumph ceremony and connected customs are particularly enticing. Their expansion and transformations in the 'new' empire of the fourth century can be tracked across seven centuries and more, into the 'Roman' empire of Constantine VII Porphyrogenitus and his successors. What is more – and somewhat paradoxical – the after-effects of the fourth century's renaissance of triumph can be traced beyond the fall of the western empire and deep into the history of the 'successor states' which emerged in the western provinces.

Among the many conditions which conspired in the 'Germanic' kingdoms' coalescence on Roman soil, that of effective political leadership cannot be underestimated. For such a kingdom to survive, the ruler had to exercise leadership over two distinct groups: the newcomers themselves and the Roman society into which they settled. Although it is hard to imagine that the Germanic inheritance was not a significant component in the new-born monarchies' make-up, this element is sometimes exceedingly difficult to grasp.[17] Assimilation and, to some degree, accommodation with local aristocracies were the order of the day.[18] While

---

[17] Given the wealth and antiquity of influence Romans and Germanic groups exercised on one another, it is often very hard to pinpoint the 'Roman' or 'Germanic' character of certain institutions or customs. The debate over the character of the spear as a symbol of authority is a good example: P.E. Schramm, *Herrschaftszeichen und Staatssymbolik*, 2, 497–8 (as modified by *Nachträge*, MGH. Schriften 13a [Munich, 1978], pp. 28–9) and A. Alföldi, '*Hasta–summa imperii*. The spear as embodiment of sovereignty in Rome', *American Journal of Archaeology*, 63 (1959), 1–27 and 'Zum Speersymbol der Souveränität im Altertum', *Festschrift für P.E. Schramm*, 1 (Wiesbaden, 1964), 3–6. For a vigorous statement of the Germanic aspects of rulership in the first generations of the barbarian kingdoms, J.M. Wallace-Hadrill, *Early Germanic kingship in England and on the Continent* (Oxford, 1971), pp. 8ff.

[18] Two recent examples: W. Goffart, *Barbarians and Romans, A.D. 418–584. The techniques of accommodation* (Princeton, 1980) and E.A. Thompson, *Romans and barbarians. The decline of the western empire* (Madison, 1982), esp. pp. 17 and 230ff. Cf.

it seems likely, for instance, that Germanic 'Heerkönigtum' contributed to the newcomers' conceptions of kingship, traces of the
early monarchies' appropriation of traditional Roman forms and
modes of thought are much more distinct.[19] This is all the less
surprising for the mounting evidence of the impact of imperial
iconography and ideas far beyond the empire's ancient boundaries.[20] Whence the growing consensus among scholars that late
Roman ideas and customs of rulership and administration
impregnated the early institutions of barbarian kingdoms.[21] The
afterlife of the imperial ideology of victory opens a new path for
exploring the imperial model's influence on rulership in the new
societies.

But it is not an easy one. Most of the barbarian kingdoms were
short-lived and died a violent death. This scarcely fostered the
generation and preservation of significant amounts of source
material. Ephemeral phenomena like political ceremonies are
particularly poorly documented. Moreover, the progressive
deurbanization of western society diminished the usual late
antique audience for political display, the urban crowd. Over the
centuries this worked profound changes in the ceremonies' setting
and significance. Both factors induce the historian to supplement
the scattered evidence on royal victory ceremonies by seeking out
the old ideology's afterlife and transformations in other settings,
like the early medieval liturgy, inscriptions, panegyrics, acclamations and coinage.

V. Bierbrauer, 'Frühgeschichtliche Akkulturationsprozesse in den germanischen
Staaten am Mittelmeer (Westgoten, Ostgoten, Langobarden) aus der Sicht des
Archäologen', *Atti del 6° congresso internazionale di studi sull'alto medioevo*, 1 (Spoleto,
1980), 89–105.

[19] On the first point, see W. Schlesinger, 'Über germanisches Heerkönigtum', *Das
Königtum. Seine geistigen und rechtlichen Grundlagen*, Vorträge und Forschungen, 3
(Constance, 1956), pp. 104–44, esp. 138ff.

[20] E.g. K. Hauck, 'Von einer spätantiken Randkultur zum karolingischen Europa',
FMS, 1 (1967), 3–93, here, 8–9; H. Vierck, '*Imitatio imperii* und *interpretatio
Germanica* vor der Wikingerzeit', *Les pays du Nord et Byzance (Scandinavie et Byzance)*,
ed. R. Zeitler (Uppsala, 1981), pp. 64–113.

[21] A few examples from many: L. Schmidt, *Geschichte der Wandalen*, 2nd edn (Munich,
1942), p. 156; cf. P. Courtois, *Les Vandales et l'Afrique* (Paris, 1955), p. 243; Hauck,
'Randkultur'; H. Wolfram, 'Gotisches Königtum und römisches Kaisertum von
Theodosius dem Grossen bis Justinian I.', *FMS*, 13 (1979), 1–28, esp. 26: 'Die Regna
auf römischem Boden wurzeln zwar in der Tradition der *externae gentes*, sind aber
lateinische, spätrömische Institutionen'.

To ancient and medieval eyes, most ceremonies were nothing if not obvious. When an ancient writer mentions or describes one, he rarely points out that the event was in fact a symbolic gesture from the repertory of traditional ruler rituals. Attempts to expound the meaning of the symbolic act are just as rare. This calls for a methodology which fits isolated and apparently insignificant facts into the broader cultural and ritual context provided by the study of the customs and conceptions with which late antique and Byzantine society sought, celebrated and glorified military success. Without this interpretive framework, the way the Visigothic king treated the defeated usurper Paul or the chastisement the would-be king of the Lombards inflicted on deacon Seno appear to be isolated instances of bizarre behavior. Viewed against the backdrop of late Roman victory customs, however, the picture alters dramatically and each incident reveals the imperial model's contribution to early medieval kingship. In other words, continuity. Consensus reigns, or is beginning to reign, that substantial areas of continuity underlay, in both East and West, the passage from late antique to early medieval civilization. But within the overall pattern of persisting links, there is many a dialogue between change and continuity and not a few cases of new wine in old jugs. Tracing one cluster of late antique state symbolism will allow us to test a single facet of this continuity. Even more important, though, it will sometimes be feasible to go beyond the observation of continuity – which can conceal resurrection as well as persistence – and ask why Germanic rulers appropriated one or another element and how they changed it. As Schramm emphasized, the borrowing of elements of *Staatssymbolik* is an essentially active process which implies adaptation as much as adoption.[22] This continuous borrowing was generally an affair of kings down to the collapse of Carolingian authority, when new, territorial power centers emerged. That development will furnish a convenient, if not compulsory stopping point for the early medieval West.

In the East, conditions of rulership changed significantly as the great crises of the seventh and eighth centuries worked far reaching transformations in the empire, its society and govern-

---

[22] 'Herrschaftszeichen', pp. 1068–9.

ment.[23] Even as some ritual elements of Byzantine victory celebrations and their monumental setting proclaimed the unshakable continuity of the imperial government with the ancient empire of the Romans, new trends in society and the monarchy conditioned the way they were assembled for specific performances. No account of late antique and Byzantine ceremonial can afford to overlook the unique testimony of Constantine Porphyrogenitus' treatise on imperial rituals. Much remains unclear on the precise value of this tenth-century compilation. The integration of Constantine's information on triumph ceremonies into the framework of their overall development will offer some clarification. This implies that the enquiry into Byzantine victory celebrations will extend down to the end of the tenth century. The most convenient stopping point thereafter is furnished by the end of the Macedonian dynasty to which the Porphyrogenitus belonged. This does not mean that no further victory celebrations were staged in Byzantium or, for that matter, the medieval West. They were. But the transformation of both civilizations and their increasingly divergent paths of development, not to mention the swelling volume of source materials, dictate that the later period be treated on its own merits.

As it stands, the present enquiry will be long enough, for the roots of the late antique and early medieval cult of the ruler's victory reach far back into the classical past, demanding at least cursory consideration of the principate's triumphal celebrations and conceptions. In the fourth century, a unique constellation of factors triggered a renaissance of the idea and ritual expression of triumphal rulership, of a ruler whose essence it was to be victor. Once the historical development of late imperial victory celebrations has been established, individual ceremonies can be used as a window on phenomena like the significance of celebrations over usurpers, performances at Rome and other residences, Christianity's integration into the empire's official symbolism, the dialogue of unity and the division of the empire, or how power and influence were projected within the government. For many centuries, the after-effects of this renewed triumphal ideology lingered on among the heirs to Roman power. The late antique

---

[23] A.P. Kazhdan and A. Cutler, 'Continuity and discontinuity in Byzantine history', *Byz.*, 52 (1982), 44–78.

legacy to Byzantium will be followed through its transformations down to the watershed of the eleventh century. The Ceremony Book and related sources permit a first attempt at uncovering how the palace administration went about the business of organizing an imperial victory celebration, providing a rare insight into the Byzantine government in action. But the capital was not the only stage for imperial display: the message of the emperor's victory was also intended for the bulk of the population, the loyal subjects who lived outside the great late Roman and Byzantine capitals. The role of the church in focusing the public mind on imperial victory and preparing the armies of New Rome for combat is revealing of the temper of the times and offers an important link between eastern and western successor societies. The myth of the later Roman emperor's monopoly on victory celebrations is laid to rest by one aspect of what must be seen as the most prevalent form of *imitatio imperii*, the victory celebrations honoring local commanders. To help assess imperial victory customs' and related conceptions' ramifications in the new kingdoms on the empire's edges, the existence and development of court ceremonial in the Germanic kingdoms which ringed the Mediterranean will require some discussion. Although the historian of similar institutions in half a dozen early Germanic kingdoms is sometimes reduced by the state of the sources to six different kinds of ignorance, the short-lived kingdoms of the Vandals, Burgundians, Ostrogoths, and Lombards each contribute to understanding the destiny and afterlife of the imperial victory ideology. The Visigothic triumph ceremony and other victory customs provide new data on the Hispanogothic elite's intimate familiarity with imperial civiliz-ation as well as on the social context of royal rulership. Finally, the fate of imperial victory customs and conceptions in the kingdom of the Franks will lead from the appropriation of Roman usages by the early Merovingians through the appearance of a liturgy of victory and into the new developments sponsored by the Carolingians, when local offshoots of the old tradition combined with independent innovation and appropriation from the imperial past and present of Byzantine Italy.

Invincible empire: the ideology of victory under the principate

Collective manifestations of joy and relief at the successful conclusion of a military engagement occur throughout human society and throughout history, from the earliest times down to our own V–E and V–J Days of recent memory. In ancient Rome, however, the convergence of a series of unique traditions and historical developments triggered, in the first century before our era, a veritable explosion of victory celebrations and related conceptions. This phenomenon was aptly summarized by Jean Gagé in a famous and influential article on the principate's 'theology' of imperial victory.[1] Despite the dramatic changes in Roman government and society which issued from the crisis of the third century, there is clear continuity between the victory celebrations of the later Roman empire and those of the principate.

It is paradoxical to contrast the attention lavished on the archaic and Republican triumph ceremony with the dearth of thorough studies on the historical development of the same ceremony under the better documented circumstances of the principate. Enough has, however, already been accomplished to sketch provisionally the main lines of the early Roman Empire's most outstanding victory customs. Imperfect though it must be, this sketch will provide the background indispensable to understanding late imperial and Byzantine victory celebrations.

★   ★   ★

In its 'classical' Republican form, the prestigious ceremony of

---

[1] J.Gagé, 'La théologie de la victoire impériale', *Revue historique*, 171 (1933), 1–43. For a critique of the term 'theology': O.J. Brendel, *Gnomon*, 36 (1964), 498–508.

victory, the triumph, was carefully netted in the archaic formalism of Roman religion. Whatever its original nature, the ancient rite seems clearly to display aspects of purification and thanksgiving, associated with the cult of Iuppiter Optimus Maximus and the Capitol.[2] By the days of the waning Republic, however, its religious significance had come to be eclipsed by its political value, a value which is only more evident for the mediocrity of the accomplishments which could sometimes be used to justify the celebration of a triumph.[3] When prominent men engaged in the scramble for power vaunted their *felicitas*, their good fortune or divine favor, as an essential qualification for leadership, what more unequivocal confirmation of *felicitas* could they desire than a resounding military victory, achieved under the proper conditions and sanctioned by the Senate and the gods in the spectacular triumph ceremony?[4] It is perhaps no surprise then that a sharp upswing in Victory cults can be observed at Rome from the third century B.C.[5] The preoccupation with *felicitas* and victories could only have been encouraged by the agonistic conceptions and metaphors of winning at sports which permeated the Hellenistic cultural idiom so highly prized at Rome in the first century B.C.[6]

---

[2] H. Versnel, *Triumphus. An inquiry into the origin, development and meaning of the Roman triumph*, Diss. (Leyden, 1970).

[3] Examples of 'unwarranted' triumphs in the late Republic: E.Pais, *Fasti triumphales populi Romani* I (Rome, 1920), cxi and 269, 283–4.

[4] H. Erkel, *Augustus, Felicitas, Fortuna. Lateinische Wortstudien*, Diss. (Göteborg, 1952), esp. pp. 54–9, with the modifications of C. Brutscher, 'Cäsar und sein Glück', *Museum Helveticum*, 15 (1958), 75–83, here 76–9. On *felicitas* and victory, see R. Combès, *Imperator. Recherches sur l'emploi et la signification du titre d'Imperator dans la Rome républicaine*, Publications de la Faculté des lettres et des sciences humaines de l'Université de Montpellier 26, (Paris, 1966), pp. 208–22 and pp. 408ff, and the penetrating synthesis of J. Gagé, 'Felicitas', *RAC*, 7 (1968), 711–23, esp. 715. Cf. too J. Rufus Fears, *Princeps a diis electus. The divine election of the emperor as a political concept at Rome*, Papers and Monographs of the American Academy in Rome, 26 (Rome, 1977), pp. 90ff and 192ff.

[5] S. Weinstock, 'Victor and Invictus', *Harvard Theological Review*, 50 (1957), 211–47, here 215ff.

[6] Cf. G.W. Bowersock, *Augustus and the Greek World* (Oxford, 1965), pp. 2ff, and A. Momigliano, *Alien wisdom. The limits of Hellenization* (Cambridge, 1975), pp. 12ff on Hellenistic currents at Rome in this period. Some indications on agonistic metaphors in Greek literature will be found in E. Stauffer, ''Aγών', *Theological Dictionary of the New Testament*, tr. G.W. Bromily, I (Grand Rapids, 1964), 134–40, and ''Aθλέω', *ibid.*, 167–8.

Felicitas and the mystique of victory fitted easily into the ideological stock of the Augustan principate and quickly became a significant buttress of the new order. As Gagé demonstrated and many others have confirmed, the essential trait of this mystique was that the emperor's victories demonstrated his aptness for rulership.[7] The central role of imperial victoriousness is easily grasped in light of the military nature of the *imperator*, the military overtones of the *imperium* and the intimate link between possession of the *imperium* and the right to celebrate a triumph.[8] This connection soon led to a new and far-reaching development: the restriction of the triumph to the Augusti or members of their house.[9]

Under the principate, we can observe the forerunners of at least three main aspects of the later Roman emperor's celebration of military success: supplication days, the triumphal parade and victory games. At times of great crisis or success, the Republican Senate had often voted official days of supplication (*supplicationes*) during which the temples were opened and sacrifices performed. *Supplicationes* of thanksgiving came particularly to be associated with the announcement of victory.[10] Like the triumph ceremony with which they are so closely linked, supplication days underwent clear development in the late Republic and principate.[11] Although their religious content never disappeared, it has been suggested that the focus of these services changed. From being propitiatory or expiatory sacrifices focusing on the gods, the *supplicationes* came to center on the prince and his well-being.[12] The rhythm and importance of thanksgiving services appear to

---

[7] 'Théologie', pp. 6ff.

[8] On the military nature of *imperator*: Combès, *Imperator*, pp. 73ff; cf. J. Deininger, 'Von der Republik zur Monarchie. Die Ursprünge der Herrschertitulatur des Prinzipats', *ANRW*, 1, 1 (1972), 982–97. For the link between *imperium* and the triumph, T. Mommsen, *Römisches Staatsrecht* 1 (reprint, Basel, 1952), 115ff and esp. 126ff and 132ff.

[9] Mommsen, *Staatsrecht*, 1, 135–6; cf. 465–7.

[10] The basic study remains L. Halkin, *La supplication d'action de grâces chez les Romains*, Bibliothèque de la Faculté de philosophie et lettres de l'Université de Liège, 128 (Paris, 1958), here pp. 90ff. Cf. too G. Wissowa, *Religion und Kultus der Römer*, Handbuch der Altertumswissenschaft, 5, 4, 2nd edn (Munich, 1912), pp. 423ff, and K. Latte, *Römische Religionsgeschichte, ibid.*, 5, 4 (Munich, 1960), pp. 245–6.

[11] Halkin, *Supplication*, pp. 109ff.

[12] G. Freyburger, 'La supplication d'action de grâces sous le Haut-Empire', *ANRW*, 2, 16, 2 (Berlin, 1978), 1418–39, here 1432.

have declined with the passage of time, even though the latest studies maintain that the rite was preserved as late as A.D. 277.[13]

The core of imperial victory celebrations remained the triumph. A systematic analysis of the development of the ceremony under the empire remains to be written.[14] Of the two main descriptions of this ceremony from the principate, the later concerns the triumph of Aurelian in 274. It is found in the *Scriptores historiae augustae* and today is considered quite implausible.[15] The triumph celebrated by Vespasian and Titus in June of 71 is known, on the other hand, in the detailed and reliable account of Flavius Josephus.[16]

As Josephus tells it, the event can be broken down into three main stages. The first took place outside the *pomerium*, in the Campus Martius area. It was essentially military in nature. The second was the actual *triumphus* or parade from the *porta triumphalis* to the Capitol. The third comprised the religious ceremonies on the Capitol.

The Judaean triumph had already been announced to the

13 Thus Halkin, *Supplication*, p. 129 and Freyburger, 'Supplication', pp. 1428–9. Note however that in both scholars' list of supplications from Septimius Severus to Probus, one is only *implicitly* attested by Herodian (3, 9, 12, ed. C.R. Whittaker, 1 (Cambridge, Mass., 1969), 323–4 (πάσας τε τιμὰς ἐψηφίσατο αὐτῷ) for A.D. 197 while the rest are all derived from the *Scriptores historiae Augustae* (cf. Freyburger, 'Supplication', pp. 1428–9). Should we believe that the *Historia Augusta* is more reliable for victory supplications than it has been shown to be for other ceremonies? Cf. below, n. 15.

14 The only general history of the imperial ceremony is C. Barini, *Triumphalia. Imprese ed onori militari durante l'impero romano* (Turin, 1952). The many descriptions of 'the' triumph ceremony available in the various reference works have, in general, been pieced together from a wide variety of sources spread over several centuries. There is thus no guarantee that such a composite picture actually corresponds to a particular performance of the ceremony. See nonetheless W. Ehlers, 'Triumphus', *RE*, 7A1 (1939), 493–511, here 501ff, and E.W. Merten, *Zwei Herrscherfeste in der Historia Augusta. Untersuchungen zu den pompae der Kaiser Gallienus und Aurelianus*, Antiquitas 4, 5 (Bonn, 1968), pp. 20–8.

15 Merten, *Herrscherfeste*, pp. 101–40.

16 Flavius Josephus, *De bello iudaico*, 7, 118–62, ed. B. Niese and J. von Destinon, *Flavii Iosephi opera* 6 (Berlin, 1894), 586.16–592.4. Illustrations of this ceremony appear on the Arch of Titus; see I.S. Ryberg, *Rites of state religion in Roman art*, Memoirs of the American Academy in Rome, 22 (Rome, 1955), pls. 52–53. For other descriptions of the triumph in classical literature, see the references in Ehlers, 'Triumphus', pp. 501–11.

Roman world with a special commemorative coin issue.[17] Although the Senate had authorized Vespasian and Titus to celebrate separate triumphs, they decided on a joint ceremony. For the event which would open the day's festivities, the army had been led out of the city and drawn up in military array in front of the *Porticus Octaviae*.[18] At dawn, the emperors, clad in traditional purple robes and wearing laurel wreaths, left the Temple of Isis. At the portico, they were met by the Senate, leading officials and Equites. They mounted a tribunal which had been constructed in front of the portico and took their places on ivory seats. The soldiers acclaimed them and Vespasian and Titus performed the 'customary prayers'. After Vespasian made a brief address to the army, the soldiers were dismissed and sent to a traditional banquet furnished by the emperor. Vespasian and Titus proceeded to the *porta triumphalis*, where they had a bite to eat and changed into the triumphal costume.[19]

Now the second phase of the victory celebration could begin. After sacrifices to the deities of the triumphal gate, the parade got underway. So that all would have a chance to see it, the itinerary wound its way to the Capitol through various *theatra*. The parade itself consisted of a tremendous display of luxury items, precious statues of the Roman gods, various beasts and seven hundred richly clad captives who had been selected for their impressive appearance.[20] Then came floats depicting various scenes from the war, followed by the booty. The focal point was formed by the triumphators themselves, introduced by statues of the goddess Victoria. Vespasian and Titus seem to have ridden in triumphal chariots while Domitian rode alongside them on horseback. The parade ended on the Capitol, at the Temple of Iuppiter Optimus Maximus.

The third stage began as soon as the Jewish leader, Simon ben Goria, had been executed in the Forum. Josephus does not describe the sacrifices which made up this part of the ceremony. At their conclusion, the emperors withdrew to the palace. That evening,

---

17 See below, n. 87–8.
18 Josephus, 7, 121–4, Niese–von Destinon, 587.1–15. Cf. S.B. Platner and T. Ashby, *A topographical dictionary of ancient Rome* (London, 1929), p. 427.
19 Josephus, 7, 123–31, Niese–von Destinon, 587.9–588.7.
20 *Ibid.* 7, 138; 589.5–7; cf. 7, 118; 586.16–20.

they celebrated a victory banquet, while general festivities reigned throughout the city.[21]

Josephus' account yields several significant facts. In the first place, it is quite clear that as of A.D. 71, the *adventus* was still quite distinct from the triumphal entry, since they were celebrated within several days of one another.[22] The various phases of the triumph can be distinguished not only by their chronological sequence: each possesses a particular topographical character which can be associated with its intended audience and focus. The first element is military in character. Its audience is the army, Senate and government and it takes place outside the *pomerium*.[23] The second phase of the celebration is directed to the urban population at large and moves through the city: the use of the *theatra* is explicitly linked with the vastness of this audience.[24] The third phase constituted the essential religious transaction of the day and presumably involved a more select audience because of the space limitations of the Area Capitolina.[25] The first three stages lasted so long that Vespasian, then in his sixties, is reported to have uttered a *bon mot* on his fatigue.[26] The final stage in the day's events once again involves a select audience: the guests at the imperial victory banquet, held at the palace. Unfortunately, Josephus is mute on the guest list.

Two obvious points can be made about this kind of staged event under the early principate. It was an urban phenomenon, intended to reach a mass audience. Various elements of the overall audience may be distinguished according to the setting of the varying

[21] *Ibid.* 7, 139–57; 589.8–591.17.

[22] *Ibid.* 7, 119–21, Niese-von Destinon 586.20–587.4 on the *adventus* of Titus at Rome; for that of Vespasian, *ibid.* 7, 68–74, 580.14–581.10. In the present state of our knowledge, it is difficult to fix the date at which the emperor's *adventus* ceased to be celebrated separately from his triumph. This was certainly the case by the fourth century. The problem is complicated by the influence which the triumph ceremony came to exercise on the *adventus*; cf. G. Koeppel, 'Profectio und Adventus', *Bonner Jahrbücher*, 169 (1969), 130–94, on the iconographic evidence, and S.G. MacCormack, 'Change and continuity in late antiquity: the ceremony of the *Adventus*', *Historia*, 21 (1972), 721–52, on the literary evidence.

[23] Cf. Platner–Ashby, *Dictionary*, p. 395.

[24] Josephus, 7, 131, Niese-von Destinon 588.7–9.

[25] Platner–Ashby, *Dictionary*, pp. 47ff. On the sacrifices on the Capitol, see Ehlers, 'Triumphus', p. 510.

[26] Suetonius, *De vita caesarum*, Vespasian, 12, ed. M. Ihm (Leipzig, 1908), 302.32–303.5.

phases of the ceremony. Secondly, the triumph of June 71 was eminently political. It cannot be forgotten that, less than twenty-four months earlier, Vespasian had been hailed as emperor in Egypt while Vitellius enjoyed the purple in the very capital which was now the scene of a great triumph. Jerusalem has been called the 'Flavian Actium' and it was natural that the new usurper and his heir designate should try to maximize their political capital by emphasizing the magnitude of the victory won over the Jewish rebels.

There is a further, related facet of victory celebration on which Josephus is silent. Other sources show quite clearly that, by this date, triumphal games had become a customary element of such celebrations.[27] For instance, various spectacles formed an impressive part of the festivities marking Claudius' British triumph of A.D. 44.[28] In like manner, Domitian celebrated his pseudo-victory over the Dacians not only by a triumphal parade, but also by footraces, military displays in the Circus and mock sea battles.[29]

Roman emperors continued to celebrate their real or imagined victories down to the end of the principate and into the tetrarchic period. Since the evidence concerning the latter is too meager to allow detailed comparison with the renewed ceremonies of the Christian Roman empire, we cannot fail to take into account what is known of victory celebrations of the earlier third century. The unreliability of the *Historia augusta* obliges us to focus on three independently attested state rituals: Septimius Severus' Parthian triumph, the victory celebrations of A.D. 238 and Diocletian's ceremonial swan-song at Rome.

In 198, Septimius Severus dispatched a victory bulletin to the Senate and people of Rome, announcing and perhaps exaggerat-

---

[27] Whether there is any connection between this element of imperial victory celebrations and Mommsen's theory that the *Ludi Romani* were originally part of the archaic triumph ceremony remains an open question. See T. Mommsen, *Römische Forschungen*, 2 (Berlin, 1879), 45ff; cf. G. Wissowa, *Religion*, pp. 452–3 and the criticism of A. Piganiol, *Recherches sur les jeux romains. Notes d'archéologie et d'histoire religieuse*, Publications de la Faculté des lettres de l'Université de Strasbourg, 13 (Strasbourg, 1923), p. 75. According to Piganiol (pp. 83–4, n. 4), the triumphal games may have been an innovation of the late Republic.

[28] Dio Cassius, 60, 23, 4–6, ed. U.P. Boissevain, 2 (Berlin, 1898). 684.26–685.6.

[29] *Ibid.*, 67, 8, 1–2, Boissevain, 3 (Berlin, 1901). 174.10–17.

ing his success against the Parthians at Ctesiphon. The Senate voted 'full honors' and granted Severus the right to bear the victory title *Parthicus maximus*.[30] The actual celebration of the triumph was postponed for four years, when it could be combined with two other public events heavy with political overtones: the marriage of the fourteen-year-old heir apparent Caracalla and the tenth anniversary of Severus' accession. As in 71, the combined festival provided an ideal opportunity for projecting the incipient dynasty's prestige.[31] The celebrations included a ceremonial welcome and triumphal entry, marked by acclamations, sacrifices, festivals and 'victory spectacles' involving wild beast shows. They lasted seven days and entailed the distribution of considerable largess, although the latter seems to have been linked more closely with the anniversary.[32] The next year saw the construction of the triumphal arch which still dominates the Roman Forum.[33]

The celebrations set off by the conclusion of the siege of Aquileia and the assassination of the emperor Maximinus (A.D. 238) afford a rare glimpse into victory practices outside the capital and its traditional ritual framework. The murderers' first act was to send Maximinus' head to the senatorial emperor Clodius Pupienus Maximus, then encamped at Ravenna. All along the way, cities opened their gates and delegations of laurel-bearing citizens greeted the messengers and the head.[34] The arrival of the ghastly symbol at Ravenna and the announcement of Maximinus' troops' recognition of the senatorial emperors were immediately answered by sacrifices and acclamations.[35] When the sacrifices produced favorable omens, Maximus transmitted the head and a report on the 'effortless victory' to Rome. The bearers stuck the token of victory on a pole and proceeded to parade it through the city. An assembly took place in the Circus and large-scale sacrifices

---

[30] Herodian, 3, 9, 12, Whittaker, 1.322. Herodian, who misses few opportunities to criticize Septimius Severus, claims that he undertook the Persian campaign largely because of its potential advantage for his reputation, hitherto based on defeating Roman armies; 3, 8, 9, Whittaker 1.314.
[31] The combination of these holidays is made quite clear by Dio, 77 (Xiphilinus 76), 1, 3, Boissevain, 3.357.12–14.
[32] Herodian, 3, 10, 1–2, Whittaker 1.324–6; Dio, 77, 1, 1–5, Boissevain 3.357.1–358.7, seems to refer to a multiplicity of spectacles. For the largess, see *RIC*, 4, 1, 68–9.
[33] *CIL*, 6, 1, 1033; cf. Kähler, *RE*, 7A1 (1939), 392–3.
[34] Herodian, 8, 6, 5, Whittaker 2.288.   [35] *Ibid.*, 8, 6, 6–7; 2.290.

were undertaken by the coemperor Balbinus, while the magistrates, senators and people rejoiced. Laurel-wreathed messengers hastened to announce the victory to the provinces.[36] Maximus meanwhile headed for Aquileia, where he was met by its citizens as well as emissaries from the towns of Italy. They were dressed in white and bore statues of their gods and any golden crowns that lay to hand, as they showered Maximus with acclamations and flowers.[37] After spending two days making sacrifices in the city, Maximus addressed the pacified army and promised them a substantial largess.[38] Finally, the 'victorious' emperor returned to Rome, where he was met by an *occursus* composed of his imperial colleague Balbinus, Gordian Caesar, the Senate and people. He was received and acclaimed 'like a triumphator'.[39] That these celebrations of 238 have been generally overlooked helps explain how Constantine's triumphal entry of 312 has sometimes appeared puzzling to specialists more familiar with earlier triumphs.

Two generations later, the aging Augusti Diocletian and Maximian marked the culmination of their rule in a composite political extravaganza which included a long-deferred triumph.[40] The celebration at Rome also marked the twentieth anniversary of Diocletian's rule. It may well have been intended to consolidate the prestige of the new tetrarchic system and prepare the population of the capital for the abdication and transition, to which Maximian was bound by an oath sworn in the Temple of Capitoline Jupiter during this very festival.[41]

The slight surviving evidence of the victory celebration focuses on the triumphal parade. The ceremony was a joint one; it is not

[36] *Ibid.*, 8, 6, 7–8; 2.290–2.   [37] *Ibid.*, 8, 7, 2; 2.292–4.

[38] *Ibid.*, 8, 7, 3–7; 2.294–8.

[39] 8, 7, 8; 2.300:... ἥτε σύγκλητος. καὶ ὁ δῆμος. εὐφημοῦντες ὥσπερ θριαμβεύοντα ὑπεδέχοντο. John of Antioch's reading θριαμβεύοντας, if correct, would mean that this triumphal entry was celebrated jointly by the coemperors. This would fit well with the two emperors' collegial exercise of power.

[40] If indeed Eutropius, *Breviarium*, 9, 27, 2, ed. H. Droysen, *MGH.AA*, 2 (1879). 166.19 is correct in attributing it 'ex numerosis gentibus'. As early as 291, Mamertinus had already complimented the Augusti on their habit of delaying their triumph by being ever busy with more victories: *XII pan.*, 11(3), 4, 3, Mynors, 259.17–19. On the celebrations, Barini, *Triumphalia*, pp. 188–9 and esp. W. Ensslin, 'Valerius', *RE*, 7A2 (1948), 2419–95, here 2488–9.

[41] *XII pan.* 6(7), 15, 6, Mynors, 197.17–19; cf. W. Ensslin, 'Maximianus', *RE*, 14 (1930), 2486–516, here 2510. The theory has been attacked but not refuted by G.S.R. Thomas, 'L'abdication de Dioclétien', *Byz.*, 43 (1973), 229–47, esp. 236–44.

unlikely that, in order to concretize an incessant theme of tetrarchic propaganda, the Augusti entered the city in the same vehicle.[42] The parade was impressive. The triumphant emperors' chariot was preceded by *fercula* or hand-carried floats with images of the captives who had been taken from the Persian royal family and which recall the paraphernalia of the Flavians' triumph.[43] Thirteen captured elephants, their drivers and two hundred and fifty horses formed part of the parade, along with other booty taken from the Persians.[44] Although the laconic written sources do not mention it, there is no reason to doubt that Diocletian, a religious conservative, continued the tradition of concluding the triumphal parade on the Capitol, as indeed his panegyrist had assumed he would fourteen years earlier.[45] In different temples, the emperors dedicated the images of the captured Persians as well as thirty-two enemy tunics decorated with pearls.[46] A substantial largess was distributed in the Circus, but it is not known whether this donation was specifically associated with the Vicennalia, the triumph, or both.[47]

Under the principate, then, it is clear that the archaic sacral element of the triumph continued to be dominated and subsumed into its political dimension. Just as the universality of imperial victory ideology came into being at the expense of the historical specificity of particular victories, so the imperial victory feast seemed to be losing some of its link with specific victories, at least insofar as it was now possible to delay the ceremony and schedule it at the emperor's political convenience. Moreover, the triumph's combination with other ceremonies offered the advantage of spreading its traditional prestige and spectacular impact to the more routine extravagances of imperial anniversaries. At a time when the Roman government had to face up to a declining

---

[42] Eutropius, 9, 27, 2, Droysen, 166.20, mentions only one triumphal car: 'ante currum ducti sunt'. In 289, an orator had already expressed his expectation that the Augusti would one day celebrate a triumph in the capital, riding in one chariot: 'uno cupiunt inuehi curru': *XII pan.*, 10(2), 13, 2, Mynors 254.5–7.

[43] Eutropius, 9, 27, 2, Droysen, 166.19–20: cf. W. Ensslin, 'Zur Ostpolitik des Kaisers Diokletian', *Sitzungsberichte der bayerischen Akademie der Wissenschaften, Philos.-hist. Abt.* (1942), I, 52–3.

[44] *Chronographus a. 354*, ed. T. Mommsen, *MGH.AA*, 9 (1892).148.24–8; cf. Cassiodorus, *Chronicon*, ed. T. Mommsen, *MGH.AA*, 11 (1894).150.

[45] *XII pan.*, 10(2), 13, 2, Mynors, 254.6–7.

[46] *Chron. 354*, Mommsen, 148.24–8.

[47] *Ibid.* Cf. *RIC*, 6, 45 for the vicennalia emission.

economic situation, the combination of festivals doubtless reduced the financial outlays which such celebrations would have entailed had they been staged separately. This was all the more inviting since the triumph remained closely connected with a capital events and the emperors had left behind. At the same time, the events of 238 show that long before the reign of Constantine I, victory celebrations of another sort were taking place in the provinces. These were necessarily independent of Rome's sacred topography and followed the person of the triumphant emperor; the pattern would continue into the tetrarchic period. It foreshadows the renaissance of imperial victory festivals in the fourth century.

So much for imperial triumphs down to the early fourth century. But these comparatively rare ceremonies were not the only means by which Roman emperors could magnify and project their victory. Vestment, titulature, monuments, imperial coinage and Roman religion all reflected and refracted different aspects of the imperial ideology of victory. The identification of emperor and victor was externalized and reinforced by customs of imperial costume. Augustus himself wore triumphal dress at festivals and spectacles. His successors continued to extend its use until, in the third century, an opposite development set in, by which the *toga triumphalis* became increasingly identified with consular festivities.[48]

Just as the emperor conveyed an image of his function and qualifications by his choice of public garb, so the names or titles by which he was addressed could mirror varying aspects of imperial ideology. In the first three centuries we find victory titles of two main types: additional personal names or cognomens derived from the names of vanquished peoples (*cognomina devictarum gentium*) and the epithet 'unconquered' (*invictus*; ἀνίκητος).

Cognomens derived from the names of conquered peoples go back to the Republic and were systematized under the early empire.[49] Like the triumph itself, such titles soon came to be restricted to the emperors.[50] These *cognomina* seem to have been

---

[48] So A. Alföldi, 'Insignien und Tracht der römischen Kaiser', *Mitteilungen des Deutschen Archäologischen Instituts, Römische Abteilung*, 50 (1935), 3–158, here 25–43, esp. 32ff.

[49] P. Kneissl, *Die Siegestitulatur der römischen Kaiser. Untersuchungen zu den Siegerbeinamen des ersten und zweiten Jahrhunderts*, Hypomnemata, 23 (Göttingen, 1969), pp. 20ff.

[50] P. Gabinius Secundus (A.D. 41) is the last non-imperial example cited by Kneissl, *Siegestitulatur*, p. 24.

conferred by the Senate, perhaps in connection with the arrival of a victory announcement.[51] Several key moments stand out in their evolution. Until the end of the first century, the emperors used only the title *Germanicus*.[52] Trajan's Dacian victory triggers a new development, which sees the emperor assuming a number of different victory names constructed on the same pattern. By the end of his reign, Trajan appears with the combination *Germanicus, Dacicus, Parthicus*.[53] The development became a trend under Lucius Verus and Marcus Aurelius. The former appears, moreover, to have adopted the victory names *Armeniacus* and *Medicus* for two minor victories. This in turn caused him to innovate by qualifying his *Parthicus* epithet as *maximus*.[54] The whole system flourished under Septimius Severus and his successors, when another lasting innovation occurred: henceforth the victory names were automatically shared by sons, whether they had participated in the campaigns or not.[55] Specific victories now became an inheritable characteristic of the emperors and the precise link with the concrete historical circumstances of a particular victory was loosened. At the same time, the *cognomina devictarum gentium* continued to multiply. Aurelian (270–5) attained a new peak, boasting nine such titles.[56] The tetrarchy extended to the new system of coemperors the principle of shared victory titulature.[57]

The development of *invictus* is not quite as clear. This is largely due to a failure to distinguish 'official' from 'unofficial' usage.[58] Julius Caesar seems to have laid some claim to the epithet. His attachment may well have been inspired by a fascination with Alexander the Great.[59] Augustus, on the other hand, discouraged the use of *invictus* as a formal title. He is, for example, reported to have refused the Senate's request that the epithet *invictus* be

[51] *Ibid.*, p. 181, citing the case of Trajan's title *Parthicus*.
[52] But cf. e.g., *ibid.*, pp. 34 and 36.   [53] *Ibid.*, pp. 69–84.
[54] *Ibid.*, pp. 98ff.   [55] *Ibid.*, p. 185.
[56] *Ibid.*, p. 177.   [57] *Ibid.*, p. 178; cf. below, Ch. 3.
[58] This criticism is particularly valid for the otherwise admirable study of S. Weinstock, 'Victor and Invictus'; cf. his 'Victor, victrix', *RE*, 8A2 (1958), 2485–500. On the necessity of this distinction, see R. Frei-Stolba, 'Inoffizielle Kaisertitulaturen im 1. und 2. Jahrhundert n. Chr.', *Museum Helveticum*, 26 (1969), 18–39, here 18–20, and, in a somewhat different sense, E. van't Dack, 'La papyrologie et l'histoire du Haut-Empire: les *formulae* des empereurs', *ANRW*, 2, 1 (Berlin, 1974), 857–88, here 869ff.
[59] Weinstock, 'Victor and Invictus', pp. 229ff.

attributed to Tiberius.[60] This act may have helped set the pattern
by which the official titulature of the emperors, as it occurs, e.g.,
on the military diplomas, generally avoided *invictus* until well into
the turmoil of the third century.[61] Non-official evidence offers
a contrasting picture. The flattering literary usage of *invictus* is
attested as early as Horace and Ovid.[62] It crops up under Domitian
in Martial and Statius and again in Pliny's panegyric on Trajan (8,
2).[63] Particularly edifying is the evidence from the 'semi-official'
realm of inscriptions which, as Imhof noted, provide a striking
parallel to the geographical spread of the imperial cult.[64] Thus the
earliest epigraphical attestation (ἀνείκητ[ον]) comes from Greek
Asia Minor, in the reign of Trajan.[65] Just as characteristic is the fact
that the first Latin attestation shows up almost a century later and
occurs in Africa. This inscription is associated with Commodus'
self-identification as Hercules Invictus.[66] According to Storch, the
earliest attestations from Rome and Italy come from the reign of
Septimius Severus (193–211) and Caracalla (211–17). But inscriptions with the *invictus* epithet really become common there only
after Severus Alexander (222–35).[67] The slow growth in the
popularity of *invictus* in Latin inscriptions finds an interesting
parallel in the papyrological material from Egypt, where the
Greek equivalent is quite rare. Ἀήττητοϲ does occur, however,
twice in reference to Septimius Severus and Caracalla together and
three times for Caracalla alone.[68]

[60] *Ibid.*, p. 239.
[61] To judge by its absence from the military diplomas down to A.D. 254: cf. H.
Nesselhauf, *CIL*, 16,153, and M. Imhof, '*Invictus* (Beiträge aus der Thesaurusarbeit,
X)', *Museum Helveticum*, 14 (1957), 197–215, here 199. For *invictus* on coins, see
below, n. 69.
[62] Imhof, '*Invictus*', p. 207.
[63] Weinstock, 'Victor and Invictus', p. 214.
[64] On the inscriptions and the problem of imperial tolerance, see Imhof, '*Invictus*',
p. 209.
[65] *Ibid.*, p. 208: ed. T. Ihnken, *Die Inschriften von Magnesia am Sipylos*, Inschriften
griechischer Städten aus Kleinasien, 8 (Bonn, 1978), no. 7, p. 135, dated end of
102–117.
[66] Imhof, '*Invictus*', p. 209; ed. R. Cagnat et al., *Inscriptions latines d'Afrique* (Paris, 1923),
no. 612 from A.D. 191–2. On Commodus' cult of Hercules and this inscription,
Weinstock, 'Victor and Invictus', p. 242.
[67] R.H. Storch, 'The absolutist theology of victory: its place in the late Empire', *Classica
et mediaevalia*, 29 (1972), 197–206, here 200–1.
[68] P. Bureth, *Les titulatures impériales dans les papyrus, les ostraca et les inscriptions d'Égypte*

If it is true that the official consecration of *invictus* as an imperial epithet coincided with its acceptance by the imperial coinage, then the first hint comes from the Orient, on the reverse of coins issued by eastern mints in A.D. 193–4. The title occurs on the obverse of an aureus issued at Rome in 201, i.e., in the reign of Septimius Severus and Caracalla. Again, however, the title only begins to show up with any frequency on obverses from the reign of Aurelian.[69]

The overall pattern is clear: in the first three centuries of the empire, certain reigns emerge as more sensitive to imperial victory epithets. Domitian and Trajan's era is followed by something of a respite under the Antonines, while a renewed increase is observable late in the second century, an increase which culminates in the appearance of *invictus* as an imperial epithet on the coinage. As in coins, so in the use of the *cognomina gentium devictarum*, the reign of Aurelian marks a high point. While it might be thought that this was a most unlikely moment for touting the emperor's victoriousness, the chronological distribution of the evidence suggests a connection with the growth in popularity of the cult of the 'Unconquered Sun', *Sol Invictus*. It is clear, moreover, that the adoption of *invictus* as a regular imperial epithet was a very slow process, pitting innovation against what appears to have been the conservatism of official imperial titulature. It is equally instructive that most of the evidence indicates that the custom of referring to the emperor as *invictus* in a documentary context advanced from the more distant echelons of society toward the emperor and that this practice spread from the Greek East and its Hellenistic traditions to the Latin West.[70]

Among the most eloquent witnesses to the privileged position of the victory ideology in the conceptual underpinnings of the empire are the various monuments which publicized and eternal-

---

(30 a.C.-284 p.C.), Papyrologica bruxellensia, 2 (Brussels, 1964), pp. 98 and 104–5. Note the two isolated occurrences of the same epithet for Vespasian (*ibid.*, p. 38) and Antoninus Pius (*ibid.*, p. 76) as well as the qualification of Julia Domna as μήτηρ ἀνικήτων στρατοπέδων which occurs thrice (*ibid.*, pp. 104–5). Ἀνίκητος is otherwise attested only for Aurelian (twice; *ibid.*, p. 123).

[69] Storch, 'Theology', pp. 201–3.

[70] C. Préaux, *Le monde hellénistique*, 1, Nouvelle Clio, 6 (Paris, 1978), 183–6.

ized the victorious accomplishments of the princes.[71] The several hundred triumphal arches erected under the empire offer the most obvious illustration of this point.[72] Although originally they seem to have been associated with the itinerary of triumphal processions at Rome, it was not long before these arches began to adorn the provinces as well, Romanizing the architectural landscape of the outlying territories and relaying the message of imperial victory.[73] The message could only be reinforced by the reliefs showing triumphal processions which figured prominently on many of these monuments, making the ceremony one of the 'most fully illustrated in art'.[74] At Rome, the victorious campaigns of Trajan and Marcus Aurelius received spectacular and enduring recognition in their columns.[75]

Perhaps the most complete study of a single type of triumphal monument is that which Picard devoted to monumental trophaea; it provides an apt illustration of the development of one facet of triumphal art.[76] From Augustus on, many kinds of monumental trophaea were constructed in the capital, and in the provinces on sites of imperial victories. Precisely in his reign, the same kind of major shift can be observed that we have seen in other domains: the monumental trophy became an imperial prerogative.[77]

In the empire's early centuries, the iconography of these monuments displayed precise local and temporal allusions. Thanks to them, Picard was able to detect a significant change in

---

[71] See J. Gagé, 'Un thème de l'art impérial romain: la Victoire d'Auguste', *École française de Rome. Mélanges d'archéologie et d'histoire*, 49 (1932), 61–92, and, in general, R. Brilliant, *Gesture and rank in Roman art. The uses of gesture to denote status in Roman sculpture and coinage*, Memoirs of the Connecticut Academy of Sciences, 14 (Copenhagen, 1963), pp. 72ff, 93ff, 104ff, etc.

[72] See the chronological listing in W. Kähler, 'Triumphus', *RE*, 7A1 (1939), 373–493, here 467–9.

[73] Thus F. Noack, 'Triumph und Triumphbogen', *Vorträge der Bibliothek Warburg* (1925–6), 147–201, here 162, with n. 5, and 168ff.

[74] See the surviving examples documented and discussed by I.S. Ryberg, *Rites*, pp. 141–62 with figs. 77–89; quotation from p. 141.

[75] See in general G. Becatti, *La colonna coclide istoriata. Problemi storici, iconografici, stilistici* (Rome, 1960), pp. 25ff.

[76] G.C. Picard, *Les trophées romains. Contribution à l'histoire de la religion et de l'art triomphal de Rome*, Bibliothèque des Écoles françaises d'Athènes et de Rome, 187 (Paris, 1957), pp. 232ff.

[77] The last archaeologically attested *trophaeum* cited by Picard is associated with M. Nonius Gallus, who repressed a revolt of the Treviri in 29–28 B.C.: *Trophées*, p. 247.

trophy iconography in 20 B.C., when the restitution of Crassus' *signa* replaced Actium as the dominant manifestation of Augustus' charismatic victoriousness.[78] Thus, too, he could uncover a new shift under Vespasian, reflecting the fact that 'Jerusalem was the Flavian Actium', a development which translated into an upsurge of triumphal art under Vespasian and Domitian.[79] In this domain also, the third century emerges as a critical turning point. On one hand, the dedication of actual *trophaea* monuments seems to end forever after A.D. 220.[80] On the other, the last phase in the history of the Roman trophy, in which it survives as a decorative element of imperial iconography, shares an essential characteristic with other manifestations of victory ideology: *trophaea* tend to lose their specific historical and geographical references and become universal, abstract symbols of imperial victory.[81]

The facet of imperial propaganda which remains most accessible to us today is embodied in the Roman coinage.[82] It was the coinage which relayed to the farthest reaches of the empire the kind of themes embodied in the monuments of the capital and provincial centers.[83] Imperial victory provided, in this area as well, one of the most pervasive of themes, and there exists rich material for a study of victory iconography, of the occasions and motivations for various issues, of the more distant echoes of commemorative or anniversary issues.[84] The goddess Victoria in

[78] *Ibid.*, pp. 274ff.   [79] *Ibid.*, pp. 343–4 and 359–60.
[80] *Ibid.*, p. 474.   [81] *Ibid.*, pp. 469ff.
[82] On the propagandistic aspect of imperial ideology see, int. al., M.P. Charlesworth, 'The virtues of a Roman emperor: propaganda and the creation of belief', *Proceedings of the British Academy*, 23 (1937), 105–33, esp. 108–11. For the propaganda impact of imperial coinage, M. Grant, *Roman history from coins. Some uses of imperial coinage to the historian* (reprint, Cambridge, 1968), pp. 11ff, and *Roman anniversary issues. An exploratory study of the numismatic and medallic commemoration of anniversary years, 49 B.C.-A.D. 375* (Cambridge, 1950), p. xv. Although this aspect of imperial coinage was minimized by A.H.M. Jones, 'Numismatics and history', *Essays in Roman coinage presented to H. Mattingly* (Oxford, 1946), pp. 13–33, esp. 14–16, it has been defended, e.g. by C.H.V. Sutherland, 'The intelligibility of Roman cointypes', *Journal of Roman Studies*, 49 (1959), 46–55; cf. the recent case study of D.H. Evan-Smith, 'Obverse portrait propaganda', *Quaderni Ticinesi. Numismatica e antichità classiche*, 6 (1977), 257–69.
[83] H. St J. Hart, 'Judaea and Rome. The official commentary', *Journal of Theological Studies*, n.s. 3 (1952), 172–98, here 174.
[84] Domitian may have commemorated the victories of Nero Drusus in A.D. 85, while the anniversary of Actium seems to have been remembered in coinage as late as the third century: Grant, *Anniversary issues*, pp. 95 and 58, 88, 100 and 138–9.

her different aspects, trophies, triumphal processions, portrayals of imperial violence or clemency to the vanquished are only a few images which visually summarized the diversity and ubiquity of imperial victoriousness.[85] What remained unintelligible by image alone was clarified or reinforced by inscriptions like DEVICTA IVDAEA, ROMA VICTRIX, TRIVMPHVS PARTHICVS, FORTITUDO AVG. INVICTA, INVICTA VIRTVS and VICT(ORIAE) AETERNAE.[86]

The 'Iudaea capta' series of Vespasian is one of the few which has been studied in some detail and may illustrate for us two important facets of such coinage. VICTORIA AVGVSTI sesterces showing Victory writing on a shield hung on a palm tree and sometimes including a captive, were issued in 'very large numbers' in A.D. 71, along with the IVDAEA CAPTA types.[87] On the evidence of die marks, these coins have been attributed to the spring and summer of that year. This means that they were being circulated *before* the triumph of Vespasian and Titus, in preparation for that event.[88] On the other hand, this same constellation of coins offers a good example of how a provincial mint picked up and translated the imperial theme in the form of a ΙΟΥΔΑΙΑC ΕΑΛ(ωΚΥΙΑC issue.[89]

Although they differ from coinage in nature, significance and survival rate, imperial medallions display a similar concern with Victory and victories right from their earliest stages of development.[90] Second-century medallions allude directly to triumph

---

[85] On *Victoria* see A.R. Bellinger and M.A. Berlincourt, *Victory as a coin type*, Numismatic Notes and Monographs, 149 (New York, 1962), pp. 51ff, and esp. T. Hölscher, *Victoria romana. Archäologische Untersuchungen zur Geschichte und Wesenart der römische Siegesgöttin von den Anfängen bis zum Ende des 3. Jahrhunderts n. Chr.* (Mainz, 1967), pp. 86–7 and 92ff; J. Babelon, 'Le thème iconographique de la violence', *Studies Presented to D.M. Robinson*, 2 (St Louis, 1953), pp. 278–81, and Brilliant, *Gesture*, passim.

[86] *RIC*, 2, 67; 70 and 72; 343; *RIC*, 4, 1, 47; 125 and 234; 108 and 219.

[87] D. Barag, 'The Palestinian *Judaea Capta* coins of Vespasian and Titus and the Era on the coins of Agrippa II minted under the Flavians', *Numismatic Chronicle*, 138 (1978), 14–23, here 17; cf. H. Mattingly, *Coins of the Roman Empire in the British Museum*, 2 (London, 1930), xlv–xlvi.

[88] C.M. Kraay, 'The *Judaea Capta* sestertii of Vespasian', *Israel Numismatic Journal*, 3 (1963), 45–6; Barag, 'Palestinian', p. 18.

[89] Barag, 'Palestinian', p. 14, n. 2 and passim.

[90] J.M.C. Toynbee, *Roman Medallions*, Numismatic Studies, 5 (New York, 1944), pp. 127ff.

ceremonies,[91] while legends like GERMANIA SVBACTA or VICTORIA AVGG are frequent in the largess of Marcus Aurelius.[92] The dominance of military iconography centering on the imperial person which emerges in the third century makes it difficult, even for a specialist, to differentiate between more general issues and types commemorating specific military or ceremonial occasions.[93] Nonetheless, Toynbee has been able to distinguish half a dozen triumphal types between A.D. 239 and 259.[94]

Another powerful channel in the victory ideology of imperial civilization flowed from Roman religion. The cult of Venus Victrix had played a prominent role in the political conflicts of the late Republic.[95] In the coinage of the first and second centuries we find the emperors paying occasional tribute to the victorious aspects of the classical gods of Rome, to Iuppiter Victor, Mars Victor, to Venus Victrix and Minerva Victrix.[96] The Victory of the emperor himself could be honored by the erection of an altar on military parade grounds.[97] Although the cult of the goddess Victoria is well attested in the early empire, in the second and third centuries she grows into a more abstract quality and prepares to make room for new deities.[98] It would appear that the rank and file's enthusiasm for the victorious aspect of the classical gods was growing tepid and it would not be long before new currents flowing into Rome from the East offered them a novel mixture of religious fervor and victory mystique. Whether Commodus

[91] Lucius Verus and Commodus: *ibid.* pp. 84–5; C.L. Clay, 'Roman imperial medallions: the date and purpose of their issue', *Actes du VIIIᵉ Congrès international de numismatique* (Paris, 1976), pp. 253–65 (cf. esp. 255–6) has argued that the bulk of s. II bronze medallions were intended as New Year's gifts. Triumphal issues would then be renewing the memory of a triumph on the next Kalends of January.

[92] Toynbee, *Medallions*, p. 136; on the connection of such gifts with the army: R. MacMullen, 'The emperor's largesses', *Latomus*, 21 (1962), 159–66.

[93] Toynbee, *Medallions*, p. 160.

[94] *Ibid.* It is only natural too that *adventus* medallions be better attested than those associated with imperial victories, for in this period the former was necessarily a more frequent ceremonial occurrence than the latter.

[95] See e.g., Weinstock, 'Victor and Invictus', pp. 229ff.

[96] Weinstock, 'Victor, victrix', pp. 2491–2 and, on victory epithets of the Roman deities in general, *ibid.*, pp. 2494–7.

[97] J. Helgeland, 'Roman Army Religion', *ANRW*, 2, 16, 2 (1978), 1470–1505, here 1496.

[98] Hölscher, *Victoria*, p. 170; cf. pp. 176ff.

displays the influence of his personal cult of Hercules Invictus,[99] or that of the rising Mithraic and solar cults,[100] it is irrefutable that as the solar theology extended its sway over the minds of rulers and ruled alike, it penetrated older and better established cults, whence Sarapis Invictus, etc.,[101] and reached a culmination in Aurelian's enshrinement of Sol Invictus at the heart of Roman religion and the establishment of a calendar feast which is still with us, the *Natalis Solis*, on December 25.[102]

The Roman calendar reveals too how the victory ideology could help impart shape to the civil year. For it was not enough to celebrate a victory at the moment it was achieved. The lasting political significance of victories like that of Actium, Jerusalem, or, for that matter, the Milvian Bridge, and their symbolic value as the opening of a new chapter in the political life of the state, provided a powerful incentive to keep their memory alive in the population, an incentive which was perfectly matched with the antique mentality's proclivity to annual commemorations.[103] Augustus himself set the example by founding anniversary celebrations for Actium.[104] Under Nero, the Senate ordered *feriae* for the days on which a victory was obtained and announced, as well as for that on which the motion was made.[105]

Enough evidence has survived to give a fair idea of the extent to which victory commemorations influenced the overall makeup of the *dies feriati*. We know, for example, of about thirty new festival days introduced between 45 B.C. and A.D.37. While the majority commemorate imperial dedications, *natales*, divinizations and the like, fully one-third perpetuate the memory of victories or

[99] Weinstock, 'Victor and Invictus', pp. 242–3.

[100] Thus the *locus classicus* in F. Cumont, *Textes et monuments figurés relatifs aux mystères de Mithra*, 1 (Brussels, 1899), 181ff; cf. M.J. Vermaseren, *Mithras, the Secret God* (London, 1963), pp. 35–6.

[101] K. Latte, *Römische Religionsgeschichte*, Handbuch der Altertumswissenschaft, 5, 4 (Munich, 1960), pp. 325–53, and esp. Hölscher, *Victoria*, pp. 169–72.

[102] F. Altheim, *Die Soldatenkaiser* (Frankfurt, 1939), pp. 277ff, and H. Usener, *Das Weihnachtsfest*, 2nd edn (Bonn, 1911), pp. 348ff and esp. pp. 358ff.

[103] W. Schmidt, *Geburtstag im Altertum*, Religionsgeschichtliche Versuche und Vorarbeiten, 7, 1 (Giessen, 1908), pp. 1–4. On imperial anniversaries in general, see *ibid.*, pp. 59ff, and esp. P. Herz, 'Kaiserfeste der Prinzipatszeit', *ANRW*, 2, 16, 2, 1135–200.

[104] Dio Cassius, 53, 1, 5, Boissevain 2.414.17–18.

[105] Tacitus, *Annales*, 13, 41, 5, ed. H. Furneaux, 2 (Oxford, 1891), 363.8–11.

triumphs.[106] In fact, the festival calendar grew so rapidly that periodic purges were required under Caligula, Claudius and Marcus Aurelius.[107] Although the details of festival days may indeed have varied from one province to another,[108] it is clear that victory commemorations played a significant role outside of Rome as well and that they thereby helped spread far and wide the message of imperial victory.[109] As the *Feriale Duranum* proves, and as we might well have expected, the Roman army's official calendar did not overlook imperial victory anniversaries.[110] Nor should we forget that decorated festival calendars with victory commemorations were once a prominent feature of the porticoes of Roman cities.[111]

Those who were not directly involved in the victory commemorations of the *dies feriati* could have participated in another, undoubtedly more popular form of victory anniversary: the annual victory games. Here too, the empire followed and built on

[106] A. Degrassi, *Inscriptiones Italiae* 13, 2 (1963), 369.

[107] *Ibid.*, p. 368; cf. Herz, 'Kaiserfeste', p. 1136.

[108] R.O. Fink, A.S. Hoey and W.F. Snyder, 'The *Feriale Duranum*', *Yale Classical Studies*, 7 (1940), 1–222, here 36.

[109] Thus P. Oxy. 705 (A.D. 200–2), in which the author attempts a *captatio benevolentiae* in the petition to the emperors by reminding them of Oxyrhynchus' faithful cooperation in the 'war against the Jews' and of his fellow citizens' annual commemoration of that victory: ed. B.P. Grenfell and A.S. Hunt, *The Oxyrhynchus Papyri* 4 (London, 1904). 165.34–5: καὶ ἔτι καὶ νῦν τὴν τῶν ἐπινεικίων ἡμέραν ἑκάστου ἔτους. πανηγυρίζοντας. According to R.O. Fink, '*Victoria Parthica* and kindred *Victoriae*', *Yale Classical Studies*, 8 (1942), 81–101, here 100, this was a spontaneous, local festival. Cf. the cult-offering listed in a calendar of a temple, perhaps situated at Oxyrhynchus, from the late second or early third century and which commemorates ἐπινίκια of M. Aurelius: P. Oxy. 2553.i.6, ed. E.G. Turner, *Oxyrhynchus Papyri* 31 (London, 1966). 74; cf. 75–6.

[110] Thus, in the early third century, on 28 January, the cohort *XX Palmyrenorum* sacrificed in commemoration of the Parthian victory of Septimius Severus and perhaps of Trajan: P. Dura 54, I.14–16, ed. R. Marichal, *Chartae latinae antiquiores* 6 (Zurich, 1975), no. 309, p. 4.

[111] Thus the fresco state calendar discovered not long ago at Rome under Santa Maria Maggiore: F. Magi, *Il calendario dipinto sotto Santa Maria Maggiore*, Atti della pontificia accademia romana di archeologia, serie 3, Memorie, 11, 1 (Vatican City, 1972), p. 48, assigned the fresco to the fourth century, but arguments for a late second or third-century date have been made by M.R. Salzman, 'New evidence for the dating of the calendar at Santa Maria Maggiore in Rome', *Transactions of the American Philological Association*, 111 (1981), 215–27, and I. Levin, 'A reconsideration of the date of the Esquiline calendar and of its political festivals', *American Journal of Archaeology*, 86 (1982), 429–35.

the Republican tradition concretized in the *Ludi Victoriae Sullianae* or the *Ludi Victoriae Caesaris*. The latter, moreover, are also known to have been observed outside of Rome. They would become the *Ludi Victoriae Caesaris et Claudii* and continue to be celebrated as late as the reign of Trajan.[112] Hadrian too fostered *Ludi Parthici* in honor of Trajan's victory.[113]

This rapid review of victory celebrations and customs under the principate will surely require amplification and correction before a definitive image of early imperial victory feasts and their development can be traced. The evidence at hand suffices nonetheless to indicate the effort devoted to the celebration and magnification of imperial victories and victory for the benefit of the populace. It suggests that imperial victory ceremonies and ideology were propagandized enough to reverberate through Roman society. Yet we might well wonder to what extent the combined organs of imperial propaganda actually bore fruit, whether, in other words, the imperial consciousness of its victorious character ever penetrated beyond the ruling elite of the capital and provinces, and whether such penetration has left any traces at all? The role of the urban population as audience for the most spectacular ceremonies and the development of mass entertainment in connection with imperial success naturally incline us to answer in the affirmative. A few strands of evidence may serve to reinforce this view.

The great poets of the early empire lavished their verses on the triumphs, on the victory monuments and on the victory mystique of their imperial patrons. What more effective way could they have found to ingratiate themselves than to echo the most insistent themes of imperial propaganda?[114] Virgil (*Aen.* 6, 789–859), Statius (*Silv.* 4, 1, 39–43) and Martial (*Epigr. libr.* 8, 65; 9, 101) all sing the imperial song of victory. More significant of the penetration of triumphal themes is the fact that the outward forms

112 Degrassi, *Inscriptiones*, p. 486. Cf. P. Herz, 'Untersuchungen zum Festkalender der römischen Kaiserzeit nach datierten Weih- und Ehreninschriften' (Diss., Mainz, 1975), p. 20, on Claudius' victory anniversary.
113 Dio Cassius, 69, 2, 3, Boissevain, 3.223.3–4. Note the allusion to their suppression after many years.
114 A.M. Taisne, 'Le thème du triomphe dans la poésie et l'art sous les Flaviens', *Latomus*, 32 (1973), 485–504, here 485–91. See too above, on the appearance of the adulatory epithet *invictus* in Ovid and Statius.

of the imperial victory celebration so dominated the general notion of victory that all kinds of mythical victories were described in terms recalling the imperial ceremony. This extension of the triumphal theme goes beyond the triumph of Bacchus to the victory of Jupiter over the Giants and indeed, to Statius' description of Theseus' victory celebration over the Amazons (*Theb.* 12, 519–39).[115] The great poets set the tone for lower orders of littérateurs and the theme of Roman victory became so trite that a gifted satirist could turn it to comic effect. The pompous epic of Petronius' charlatan and sometime versifier Eumolpus opens:

> Orbem iam totum victor Romanus habebat,
> qua mare, qua terrae, qua sidus currit utrumque.
> Nec satiatus erat.
>
> (*Satyricon*, 119)

Beyond such imitative doggerel, beyond the rarefied ambience of literary masterpieces and their audience in the schools, the impact of the imperial ideology of victory can be traced in a number of objects from daily life. It shaped intaglio gems or glass pastes for ringstones and was used to decorate bronze perfume pans. As Vermeule has shown, many of these pieces were directly inspired by specific coin issues.[116] Trophies too find their way not only onto gems, but into lamp decorations.[117] The triumphal procession itself shows up as decoration on the silver cup from Boscoreale.[118]

Another instance of the victory mystique's wide diffusion which reveals the influence of coin imagery comes from archaeological finds from the provinces and, in particular, from the Danube regions. It takes the shape of clay relief plaques and bakers' molds for flat cakes, one of which even has – in addition to the legend VICTORIA AVGVSTI – a baker's label *dulcia*: 'sweet-

---

[115] Cf. Taisne, 'Triomphe', pp. 495ff.
[116] C.C. Vermeule, 'Aspects of Victoria on Roman coins, gems and in monumental art', *Numismatic Circular*, (1958), 3–15 (offprint). Cf. the lead mold reproduced *ibid.*, fig. iv.
[117] Picard, *Trophées*, pp. 335ff and 441–2.
[118] Ryberg, *Rites*, pp. 141ff. On the difficulty of identifying this triumph, T. Hölscher, 'Die Geschichtsauffassung in der römischen Repräsentationskunst', *Jahrbuch des deutschen archäologischen Instituts*, 95 (1980), 265–321, here 281ff.

cakes'.[119] According to Alföldi, most of these plaques and molds would have been used during the imperial holidays of January in the second and third centuries;[120] they appear to offer moving testimony to the local popularity of the *Kaiseridee*.[121] Though the motifs range from an eagle to a gladiatorial contest, a whole series of items focuses on imperial victory. Thus we might imagine cakes showing emperors on horseback, riding down barbarians, triumph processions, Victory writing on a shield and the presentation of barbarian captives to the emperor.[122] Holidays in the hinterland of the *limes* therefore included the offering and distribution of objects and pastries emphasizing the all-encompassing victory of the commander-in-chief.[123] One final example will illustrate how victory ideology extended beyond holidays into the ancient citizen's daily leisure hours, pervading even a late antique game. Although its name and rules remain obscure, the game was played on a board which consisted of six groups of spaces or letters aligned in three rows on stone slabs placed on the floor of public places.[124] The letters usually spelled cheerful messages about gaming or hedonistic slogans like:

VENARI   LAVARI
LVDERE   RIDERE
OCCEST   VIVERE.[125]

'Hunting, bathing, gambling, laughing: that's living!'

[119] A. Alföldi, 'Tonmodel und Reliefsmedaillons aus den Donauländern', *Laureae Aquincenses memoriae Valentini Kuzsinszky dicatae*, 1, Dissertationes pannonicae, 2, 10 (Budapest, 1938), pp. 312–41, here 317. On borrowings from coins: pp. 323 and 329. Sweetcakes for the *Victoria Augusti*: ibid., no. 43, p. 337–8.

[120] *Ibid.*, pp. 314–16; for dates, p. 325, 328–33. Note however that J.W. Salomonson, 'Late-Roman earthenware with relief decoration found in Northern-Africa and Egypt', *Oudheidkundige Mededelingen uit het Rijksmuseum van oudheden te Leiden*, 43 (1962), 53–95 has analyzed a large, related group and assigns them to the fourth and fifth centuries.

[121] Thus Alföldi, 'Tonmodel', pp. 323–4.

[122] See respectively *ibid.*, pls. XLIX, 1 and L, 1 and 3; LI, 1–2 and LIII, 2; LVII, 3; XLVIII.

[123] It is difficult to determine to what extent the molds would have been used for sacrificial pastries (*liba*) or for simple cakes for consumption during festivals. In addition to Alföldi, 'Tonmodel', p. 319, see J. André, *L'alimentation et la cuisine à Rome* (Paris, 1961), pp. 213–18.

[124] In addition to the collections of source materials cited in the following notes, see the comprehensive article of Lamer, 'Lusoriae tabulae', *RE*, 13 (1927), 1900–2029.

[125] M. Ihm, 'Römische Spieltafeln', *Bonner Studien. Aufsätze aus der Altertumswissenschaft Reinhard Kekulé gewidmet* (Berlin, 1890), pp. 223–39, here no. 48, p. 238.

In stark contrast – to modern sensibilities at least – stands a group of gaming boards from Rome and Trier whose datable elements have been associated with the tetrarchy. There the spaces are not spelled out in a humorous vein. Imperial victories mark the progress of players:

PARTHI   OCCISI
BRITT[O]   VICTVS
LVDIT[E]   ROMANI.

'The Parthians have been killed, the Briton vanquished: play, Romans!' The specific reference here may have been Galerius' success in the East and Constantius Chlorus' British victory of 296.[126] From the capital on the northern frontier comes a further instance in which imperial slogans intrude on a popular game, perhaps on the occasion of young Constantine's victories over the Franks and Alamannians:

VIRTVS   IMPERI
HOSTES   VINCTI
LVDANT   ROMANI.[127]

'Vigor of the empire, enemies bound: let the Romans play!' No channel was too modest, no aspect of daily life too remote to trumpet the clearest, most insistent note of imperial propaganda. As we read on another gaming board from the Cimetero di Priscilla in the ancient capital:

At the vanquished foes
Italy rejoices.
Play, Romans![128]

---

[126] C. Huelsen, 'Neue Inschriften', *Mitteilungen des deutschen archäologischen Instituts, Römische Abteilung*, 19 (1904), 142–53, here 142–3.

[127] Ihm, 'Spieltafeln', no. 49, p. 238. Cf. the photograph and commentary by N. Gauthier, *Recueil des inscriptions chrétiennes de la Gaule antérieures à la renaissance carolingienne*, 1. *Première Belgique* (Paris, 1975), 188–9, no. I, 39.

[128] Huelsen, 'Inschriften', p. 143: 'HOSTES VICTOS/ITALIA GAVDET/ [LVDIT]E ROMANI'. Other possible occurrences of the same legend: A. Ferrua, 'Tavole lusorie scritte', *Epigraphica. Rivista italiana di epigrafia*, 8 (1946 (1948)), 53–73, here nos. 44–5, pp. 70–1, Cf. too Ihm, 'Spieltafeln', no. 50, p. 238: '.../ [GENTES] PACATE/ [LVDIT]E ROMANI'.

2

Out of the streets and into the circus: the development of imperial victory celebrations in the later Roman empire

When it has not simply assumed that they disappeared, the conventional wisdom concerning imperial victory celebrations after Diocletian has consisted in two main points. It has presumed that the historical trends apparent in celebrations of the third century continued and prevailed in the Constantinian empire. Because the all-pervasive ideology of victory had crept into so many ceremonies and public attributes of the imperial office, specific celebrations of imperial victories are thought to have declined in historical significance. This was apparently borne out by the 'exhaustive' findings of one specialist that only fourteen victory celebrations are attested for the three centuries between the first Christian emperor and Heraclius.[1] The second main tenet follows from the first: what celebrations there were remained quite stereotyped and revealed little substantive change down to the Byzantine ceremonies of the tenth century.[2]

The following pages will present a quite different view of this facet of the ritual development of the later Roman monarchy. It will become apparent that the 'new' empire witnessed an extraordinary resurgence in the frequency and import of imperial victory festivals. Furthermore, these celebrations' constituent elements will be seen to evidence relentless change in their number, nature and identity within the context of overall

---

[1] J. Kollwitz, *Oströmische Plastik der theodosianischen Zeit*, Studien zur spätantiken Kunstgeschichte, 12 (Berlin, 1941), pp. 63–6; that Kollwitz thought he had approached *Vollständigkeit* is clear from p. 66, n. 4. Cf. for the general characteristics, e.g., H. Wrede, 'Zur Errichtung des Theodosiusobelisken in Istanbul', *Istanbuler Mitteilungen*, 15 (1965), 178–98, esp. 198; cf. Ph. Koukoules, Βυζαντινῶν βίος καὶ πολιτισμός, 2, 1 (Athens, 1948), 55–60.

[2] Kollwitz, *Plastik*, p. 67.

continuity. A critical inventory of rigorously demonstrable imperial celebrations reveals that their frequency was about three times the previous estimate. In terms of their historical development, the late antique ceremonies will appear to fall into three broad phases, stretching from Constantine to Theodosius the Great, from Theodosius' successors to the reign of Anastasius and from Justinian down to the outbreak of iconoclasm. Once these aspects of the ceremony's history will have been established, we will be able to move beyond the bald enumeration of celebrations and evidence to the question of specific celebrations and their contributions to our understanding of the public life of a dying empire.

I. FROM CONSTANTINE I TO THEODOSIUS I

The first phase in the development of later Roman victory celebrations begins with a flurry of festivals. Constantine I celebrated two victories at Trier, early in his reign, in late 306 or early 307 and again in 308 or 310, marking successes over the local barbarians.[3] The festivities in the circus not only entertained the population of his capital with the spectacle of feared barbarians being thrown to the beasts; they were doubtless aimed as well at lending credibility to his usurpation by demonstrating his military ability.[4] But the decisive moment in Constantine's early reign, generally associated with his vision and incipient commitment to Christianity, came in the struggle with his rival Maxentius. The latter's defeat and death outside Rome opened the way for Constantine's triumphal entry the next day. The parade was dominated by the dead emperor's head, raised high for all to see. The festivities included an address to the Senate, spectacles in the victor's presence and the dispatch of victory announcements to the

---

[3] *XII pan.*, 6 (7), 10, 5–6, Mynors, 193.14–19; cf. 6 (7), 12, 3, *ibid.*, 194.26–195.5; Eutropius, *Brev.*, 10, 3, 2, Droysen, 170.20–172.2. Cf. E. Stein, *Histoire du Bas-Empire*, ed. J.R. Palanque, I (Bruges, 1959), 83 with n. 87 (p. 451) and 86 with n. 103 (p. 454), and esp. T.D. Barnes, 'The victories of Constantine', *Zeitschrift für Papyrologie und Epigraphik*, 20 (1976), 149–55, and *Constantine and Eusebius* (Cambridge, Mass., 1981), pp. 29 and 34; Barnes prefers to date the second triumph in 308. Cf. following note.

[4] Thus coinage associated with the second festival calls Constantine *Victor omnium gentium*: *RIC*, 6, 160; cf. Barnes, *Constantine*, p. 29. The ceremony at Deutz recorded on *ILS*, 8937, may refer to one of these victories.

provinces.[5] It has been suggested, moreover, that for the first time, an arriving Roman emperor failed to perform the customary visit to the shrine of the Capitoline Jupiter.[6] The foundation of anniversary games and the erection of commemorative monuments like the Arch of Constantine ensured the event's lasting fame (see fig. 1).[7]

Scarcely two years went by before Constantine could again celebrate a victory over the Germanic barbarians in his northern capital, perhaps in conjunction with his *decennalia*, his tenth regnal anniversary. This triumph, as it was called, again featured the ghastly spectacle of wild beasts tearing barbarian captives to shreds; it may well have included a panegyric and special coin issue.[8] Another victory celebration is not attested until Constantine's defeat of Licinius in 324 and his annexation of the East. These festivities may have coincided with the promotions of Constantius to the rank of Caesar and those of Helena and Fausta to that of Augustae.[9] At any rate, the event was permanently

[5] For a detailed discussion of this ceremony, see below, Ch. 3, 1. For the victory dispatches to the provinces, Nazarius, *XII pan.*, 4 (10), 32, 3–9, Mynors, 167.15–168.11. Among recent studies of this ceremony, see esp. S.G. MacCormack, *Art and ceremony in late antiquity*, The transformation of the classical heritage, 1 (Berkeley, 1981), pp. 33ff with full references.

[6] See below, Ch. 3, 4, pp. 101–2.

[7] The races are attested in the *Chronographus anni 354*, 29 October (*Adventus Divi*), right after 28 October (*Evictio tyranni*), A. Degrassi, *Inscriptiones Italiae* 13, 2 (1963), 257; cf. comm. p. 527. This must be what is meant by *ludi aeterni* in *XII pan.*, 12 (9), 19, 6, Mynors, 285.13–14. For a differing opinion, below, Ch. 3, n. 93. The monuments included that referred to by Eusebius and Rufinus: *Historia ecclesiastica* 9, 9, 10–11, ed. E. Schwartz and T. Mommsen, GCS, 9, 2 (Leipzig, 1908), 832.3–14 and 833.4–9, and the triumphal arch near the Colosseum, on which the essential work remains H.P. L'Orange and A. von Gerkan, *Der spätantike Bildschmuck des Konstantinsbogens*, Studien zur spätantiken Kunstgeschichte, 10 (Berlin, 1939). For the inscription, *ILS*, 1.694. For coinage associated with this victory, *RIC*, 6, 160 and 223, no. 819; cf. *RIC*, 7, 166–7.

[8] Eusebius, *Vita Constantini* (BHG, 361x), 1, 42, 46, ed. F. Winkelmann, GCS, [57] (Berlin, 1975), 39.24–40.3; *XII pan.*, 12 (9), 23, 3, Mynors, 287.26–288.6, called 'hic triumphus', *ibid.* 287.26; on the association of this text with these festivities: E. Galletier, *Panégyriques latins*, 2 (Paris, 1952), 106; *RIC*, 7, 144 and 162–3, n. 2. Cf. Barnes, 'Victories', p. 151.

[9] Socrates, *Historia ecclesiastica*, 1, 8, *PG*, 67.61D (for the superiority of this edn see *CPG*, 6028); cf. Gelasius, *Historia ecclesiastica*, 2, 6, 1, ed. G. Loeschke and M. Heinemann, GCS, 28 (Leipzig, 1918), 45.20–2; Constantine's own reference to it in the letter in Eusebius, *V. Constantini*, 2, 67, Winkelmann 74.26–75.1; cf. too Eusebius, *H.e.*, 10, 9, 7–8, Schwartz 2.902.6–15; *RIC*, 7, 49, n. 6; for the possible promotions see *RIC*, 7, 69–70.

Figure 1. Constantine's triumphal entry into Rome (see pp. 36–7; 51)

commemorated by annual *ludi triumphales*.[10] It is a misfortune that no further details are known of the celebrations, for they seem to have marked a crucial turning point in the development of the monarchy and its ritual apparatus.[11]

The earliest victory celebrations at Constantinople may have occurred after the success of Constantine and his son Constantine II against the Goths, in the winter of 331-2. This at least is what is suggested by one of Constantine's victory titles, a medallion and the identification of the Gothic Column at Constantinople with this occasion.[12] It is also possible that, like the three barbarian successes already noted, the eight other victories over barbarians officially acknowledged by the emperor at the end of his reign were distinguished by triumphal festivities. If so, however, nothing is known about them.[13]

In 343, Constantius II made a partially successful incursion into Persian territory which he celebrated at Antioch.[14] The observances included both a memorable parade displaying the hapless captives and the dispatch of official victory bulletins, known as ἐπινίκια γράμματα or simply ἐπινίκια.[15] They also called for the participation of many bishops from Constantius'

---

[10] *Chronogr. a. 354*, 18–22 September, *Ludi triumphales*, Degrassi 255; cf. comm. pp. 510–11. Note that the battle took place on the *Natalis Traiani*, for whom Constantine was supposed to have a special emulation: *Epitome de caesaribus*, 41, 13, ed. F. Pichlmayr and R. Gründel (Leipzig, 1966), 167.13–14.

[11] See below, Ch. 3, 4.

[12] O. Fiebiger and L. Schmidt, *Inschriftensammlung zur Geschichte der Ostgermanen*, Kaiserliche Akademie der Wissenschaften, Phil.-hist. Kl., Denkschriften, 60, 3 (Vienna, 1917), p. 86, no. 164 (*ILS*, 820); Janin, *Cple byz.*, pp. 85–6; Müller-Wiener, *Bildlexikon*, p. 53. On the medallions, Toynbee, *Medallions*, p. 116, with corrections of *RIC*, 7, 195–6, n. 358; *Excerpta Valesiana*, I, 31, ed. J. Moreau and V. Velkov, 2nd edn (Leipzig, 1968), 9.4–7 and Jerome, *Chronicon*, a. 332, ed. R. Helm, GCS, 4, 2nd edn (Berlin, 1956), 233.6–7; cf. Stein, *Bas-Empire*, I, 129, and Barnes, 'Victories', p. 151.

[13] They are dated and enumerated in Barnes, 'Victories', p. 153.

[14] Theophanes, A.M. 5834, De Boor, 37.11 where the rare technical term ϑριαμβεύω is used. Cf. J.B. Bury, 'Date of the Battle of Singara', *BZ*, 5 (1896), 302–5 and O. Seeck, *Geschichte des Untergangs der antiken Welt*, 4 (Stuttgart, n.d.), 78 and 419.

[15] Athanasius, *Historia Arianorum*, 16, 2, ed. H.G. Opitz, *Athanasius Werke*, 2.1 (Berlin, 1935–41).191.11–15; Libanius, *Oratio* 59, 84, ed. R. Foerster, 4 (Leipzig, 1908).250.14–16. For the date, cf. T.D. Barnes, 'Emperor and bishops, A.D. 324–344: Some problems', *American Journal of Ancient History*, 3 (1978), 53–75, here 67–9. On ἐπινίκια γράμματα, see below, Ch. 5, pp. 190ff.

part of the empire, in what is the first solid and direct evidence of an official role for the Christian church in imperial victory rites.[16] Imperial benefactions to the cities in the area may have been made on this occasion.[17] In any case, the success appears to have been commemorated by annual races.[18]

Magnentius' defeat at the hands of Constantius and his subsequent suicide triggered a series of observances which culminated in the famous visit to Rome five years later. At least one congratulatory legation to the victorious emperor is known from the period immediately following the victory of September 352.[19] The usurper's head was sent around the provinces for the usual ritual display.[20] The official reaction of the ancient capital was summed up by a dedication to the 'restorer of the city of Rome and the world and extinguisher of the pestiferous usurpation, Our Lord Flavius Julius Constantius, Victor and Triumphator, ever Augustus'.[21] Although a number of unrelated victories were officially announced in the capitals and the provinces during Constantius' ensuing stay in the West, there is no explicit record of victory celebrations in his presence before the visit to Rome in 357.[22] At that time, he was able to combine observances for his twentieth anniversary of empire, his *vicennalia*,

---

[16] Athanasius, *loc. cit.*; detailed discussion, below, Ch. 3, 4.

[17] Julian, *Oratio* 1, 17, ed. J. Bidez, 1.1 (Paris, 1932).36.13–21.

[18] Polemius Silvius, *Laterculus*, 31 January, ed. A. Degrassi, *Inscriptiones Italiae*, 13.2 (1963).264; cf. comm. p. 404 and H. Stern, *Le Calendrier de 354. Étude sur son texte et sur ses illustrations*, Bibliothèque archéologique et historique, 55 (Paris, 1953), pp. 83ff.

[19] Thus A. Chastagnol, *La préfecture urbaine à Rome sous le Bas-Empire*, Publications de la Faculté des lettres et sciences humaines d'Alger, 34 (Paris, 1960), p. 422, and *Les fastes de la préfecture de Rome au Bas-Empire*, Études prosopographiques, 2 (Paris, 1962), p. 142. Cf. *CIL*, 6, 1739–42 and *PLRE*, 1, 652, 'Orfitus 3'.

[20] Ammianus Marcellinus, *Res gestae*, 22, 14, 4, ed. C.U. Clark, 1 (Berlin, 1910). 282.17–22, about a fawner who had asked Constantius to be sure to parade Julian's head around as he had that of Magnentius; cf. *PLRE*, 1, 905 'Theodotus 1'.

[21] *ILS*, 731; *CIL*, 6, 1158, raised by Constantius' appointee as Prefect of Rome, Naeratius Caerealis, between 26 September 352 and 8 December 353; cf. Chastagnol, *Fastes*, pp. 135–9, here 137 and *PLRE*, 1, 198 'Cerealis 2'. Another echo of this victory likely comes in an Italian milestone from 352–4; *CIL*, 5, 8073 or *ILS*, 737 'Liberatoribus orbis Romani, conservatoribus rei p. et omnium provincial., dd. nn. Fl. Iul. Constantio Aug. et Fl. Claudio Constantio Caesari'. Cf. too *ILS*, 734; *CIL*, 9, 1117.

[22] On 1 January 357, Themistius referred to the multitude of victory bulletins which had arrived in Constantinople since the emperor's departure for the West: *Oratio* 4, Schenkl and Downey, 1.82.22–6; it is perhaps only rhetoric but cf. Constantius'

with those marking the defeat of Magnentius, almost half a decade after the fact. They comprised a triumphal entry, addresses to the Senate and people, horse races, the reception of delegations with panegyrics from other cities, and a commemorative monument.[23]

A year later, Constantius staged his last recorded victory festival when he took the victory title *Sarmaticus* for the second time and celebrated a triumphal entry into Sirmium.[24] Julian's reign has left no trace of victory celebrations; that of Valens is remarkable only for a new variation on the customary rite for the suppression of a rival emperor, in which the head of the defeated Procopius was sent to the senior Augustus in Gaul.[25] In fact, the slackened pace of recorded victory celebrations was reversed only at a rather unexpected moment: in the aftermath of the crushing defeat at Adrianople.

The Goths' destruction of the Roman army and its commander-in-chief in 378 had a profoundly disturbing effect on contemporaries.[26] It is in this context that we must view the almost frenzied efforts of the highest authorities to magnify even minor successes in subsequent years. Barely a year after Adrianople, victories of the new junior emperor Theodosius I were officially announced at Constantinople on 17 November 379. The official communiqué claimed defeat not only of the Goths, but of the Alans and Huns as well. The report was probably marked by the victory races which were customary in the eastern capital.[27]

---

letter to the Senate of Constantinople on Themistius' behalf, ed. H. Schenkl et al., *ibid.*, 3 (Leipzig, 1974). 122.1–9. During his stay in Italy Constantius dispatched victory bulletins to the provinces for a success won against Persia as well as for those of Julian in Gaul: Ammianus Marcellinus, 16, 12, 67–70, Clark, 1.102.15–103.11.

[23] For a detailed account, see below, Ch. 3, 2. Among recent studies, see esp. MacCormack, *Art and ceremony*, pp. 39–45.

[24] Ammianus Marcellinus 17, 13, 33, Clark, 1.134.11–13; cf. *ibid.*, 17, 13, 25, Clark, 1.132.13–18 and 17, 13, 33, 1.134.5–7; Julian, *Oratio* 5, 8, Bidez, 1.1.226.14–17. Cf. Seeck, *Geschichte*, 4, 273.

[25] Ammianus Marcellinus 27, 2, 10, Clark, 2.1 (Berlin, 1915). 422.13–15; the head had to be returned to the East to convince the defenders of Philippopolis to surrender: *ibid.*, 26, 10, 6, Clark, 2.415.22–416.1. A silver issue at Nicomedia with the legend *Securitas reipublicae* is perhaps related to the defeat of Procopius: *RIC*, 9, 248.

[26] P. Courcelle, *Histoire littéraire des grandes invasions germaniques*, 3rd edn (Paris, 1964), pp. 22ff; cf. F. Paschoud, *Roma aeterna. Études sur le patriotisme romain dans l'Occident latin à l'époque des grandes invasions*, Bibliotheca helvetica romana, 7 (Rome, 1967), p. 15.

[27] This is what Themistius says in 357: at each victory bulletin, the Hippodrome is filled

The same victories were announced in the ancient capital too, where Symmachus informed the Senate and dispatched congratulations to the emperors.[28] The very next year, new victories – this time won by both Augusti – were announced to the population of Constantinople.[29] On 24 November 380, Theodosius staged a triumphal entry into Constantinople, even though in the hostile eyes of Zosimus or his source, the emperor's achievements were much less than billed.[30]

That the psychological need for military success was far from fulfilled even five years after the disaster in Thrace can be measured from Themistius' contorted efforts to portray the Gothic treaty of October 382 and the consulate honoring its chief negotiator as 'victory celebrations' at which even the 'vanquished' Goths participated.[31] Three years later we hear of the city of

---

with chariots; so many holidays have been declared that the citizens need to rest from their rest days: *Or. 4*, Schenkl-Downey, 1.82.22–6. *Consularia Constantinopolitana*, a. 379, ed. T. Mommsen, *MGH. AA*, 9 (1892).243; cf. Marcellinus Comes, *Chronicon*, a. 379, ed. T. Mommsen, *MGH. AA*, 11 (1894).60. On the token character of these successes and those of 380, Seeck, *Geschichte*, 5, 481.

[28] Symmachus, *Ep.* 1, 95, 2, ed. O. Seeck, *MGH. AA*, 6.1 (1883).38.26–9; cf. Seeck, *ibid.*, cxi, and J.F. Matthews, *Western aristocracies and imperial court, A.D. 364–425* (Oxford, 1975), p. 71, with n. 8; p. 75. On victory announcements, see below, Ch. 5, p. 190.

[29] *Cons. Cplitana*, a. 380, Mommsen, *MGH. AA*, 9.243.

[30] Zosimus, *Historia nova*, 4, 33, 1, ed. F. Paschoud, 2.2 (Paris, 1979).296.1–6. In his comm. (pp. 402–3) Paschoud maintains that, for Zosimus, this was not a real triumph; it was so splendid that it resembled a triumph. Aside from the difficulty of distinguishing a triumphal entry which seems like a triumph from a real triumph, the source of this understanding probably lies in the editor's having construed the ὥσπερ of 296.3 with the participial phrase, rather than with the prepositional phrase which it precedes: ... καὶ ὥσπερ ἐπὶ νίκῃ σεμνῇ θρίαμβον ἐκτελῶν.... What Zosimus seems to be saying is that Theodosius entered the capital, celebrating a triumph as if for some magnificent victory; Zosimus is implying that the victory was quite insignificant, as follows from the preceding section: 4, 31, 1ff, *ibid.*, 295.1ff. Cf. Philostorgius, *Historia ecclesiastica*, 9, 19, ed. J. Bidez, GCS, 21 (Leipzig, 1913), 125.7–10; Orosius, *Historia aduersum paganos*, 7, 34, 5–6, ed. C. Zangemeister, *CSEL*, 5 (1882).523.1–3 and Marcellinus Comes, a.380, Mommsen, 61.3–6. On the minor character of the victories, above, n. 27.

[31] *Oratio 16*, Schenkl–Downey, 1.301.16–20; cf. 1.288.6–13 and *Oratio 34*, ed. H. Schenkl, G. Downey and A.F. Norman, 2 (Leipzig, 1971).228.3–5. For an evaluation of the treaty and how different it was from the lyrical effusions of Themistius, Stein, *Bas-Empire*, 1, 194; cf. M. Pavan, *La politica gotica di Teodosio nella pubblicistica del suo tempo* (Rome, 1964), pp. 19ff, and G. Dagron, 'L'empire romain d'Orient au IVe siècle et les traditions politiques de l'Hellénisme. Le témoignage de Thémistios', *TM*, 3 (1968), 1–242, here 103ff.

Rome's reaction to a victory won against the Sarmatians by a general of Valentinian II. The statement to the emperors that the initial victory bulletin was 'confirmed' for the urban population by a triumphal spectacle which included a procession of chained barbarians, hints skillfully at the credibility problem engendered by the cascade of 'successes' that followed one of the gravest defeats in Roman history.[32] The barbarian prisoners were condemned to delight the Roman crowd by their deaths in a gladiatorial show; the City Prefect composed a letter of congratulations to the emperors in which he informed them of the celebrations.[33] Nor was New Rome neglected, for on 12 October 386, Theodosius solemnized the defeat of the barbarian king Odotheus at the hands of the general Promotus by staging a triumphal entry into his capital.[34] The triumph was shared with his son Arcadius, who would have reached the ripe old age of about nine at that time.[35] It seems to have been commemorated by a triumphal column raised in the Forum Tauri.[36]

The clearest expression of the effect of Adrianople comes from a comparison of the frequency of victory celebrations before that disaster and in its aftermath. In the seven decades between the accession of Constantine and the death of Valens, there are twelve explicitly documented victory celebrations or announcements, or less than two per decade. In the first decade after the defeat, the figure leaps to six explicitly attested victory celebrations or announcements. This indicates that the relation between military success or defeat and imperial victory celebrations was more

---

[32] Symmachus, *Relatio 47*, 1, ed. O. Seeck, *MGH.AA*, 6.1 (1883).315.27–9: 'dudum fando acceperat Romanus populus caesorum funera Sarmatarum, at nunc confirmata nuntiorum laetitia spectaculo triumphali'. Cf. 315.29–30: 'vidimus, quae lecta mirabamur...'. On the identity of the general (Bauto?) cited in *Rel. 47*, 2, *ibid.*, 316.2–9, and the date, Seeck, *Geschichte*, 5, 208. The fact that Bauto was consul in 385 (*PLRE*, I, 1959) may suggest that the dating to 384 is preferable nonetheless.

[33] Symmachus, *Rel. 47*, 1, Seeck, 315.25–316.2; cf. *Rel. 47*, 2, *ibid.*, 316.45 and 7–8.

[34] *Cons. Cplitana*, a. 386, Mommsen, 244; cf. Marcellinus Comes, a. 386, Mommsen, 62.1–2; cf. A. Lippold, *Theodosius der Grosse und seine Zeit*, 2nd edn (Munich, 1980), pp. 146–7.

[35] *Cons. Cplitana*, *loc. cit.*; on Arcadius' age, *PLRE*, I, 99, 'Arcadius 5'.

[36] On this column, Janin, *Cple byz.*, pp. 81–2; G. Becatti, *La colonna coclide istoriata. Problemi storici, iconografici, stilistici* (Rome, 1960), pp. 83ff. For the problems in attributing the Louvre sketch to this column, see below, n. 60.

complex than might appear.[37] To the psychological need for success after a crushing defeat ought to be added financial considerations. The frequent association of victory announcements and exceptional tax levies in the form of the *aurum coronarium* suggests an additional motive for the government to multiply its claims to success. It is certainly no accident that in August of 379 Theodosius legislated on the *aurum* offered, among other reasons, for 'res prospere gestae'.[38] This link between victory announcements and exceptional taxes explains why Ammianus Marcellinus alluded to the 'damages' Constantius' victory bulletins entailed for the provinces.[39]

The rituals which attended the repression of Maximus' usurpation were quite spectacular. Shortly after his initial success, Theodosius staged a victorious entry into Emona (mod. Ljubljana) which was described as a 'triumph', and the war's outcome was heralded by a series of ceremonies and public reactions from throughout the empire. But the most memorable festivities occurred during the emperor's visit to Rome, a visit which was timed to coincide with the first anniversary of Maximus' death.[40]

[37] The comparison counts the victory celebrations or announcements of 379, 380 (two: announcement and entry of November), 385, 386, and 389 for the decade from 379 to 389. For the preceding period, the count was established as follows: 306–7, 308–10, 312, ca. 314, 324, 331–2, 343–4, 357, 358–9, as well as at least two victory announcements during Constantius' stay in the West (above, n. 22).

[38] *Codex Theodosianus*, 12, 13, 4, ed. T. Mommsen and P. Krüger (Berlin, 1905), 731.1–6; cf. O. Seeck, *Regesten der Kaiser und Päpste für die Jahre 311 bis 476 n. Chr.* (Stuttgart, 1919), p. 253. On the *aurum coronarium* and its senatorial equivalent, T. Klauser, 'Aurum coronarium', *Gesammelte Arbeiten*, pp. 292–309; J. Karayannopulos, *Das Finanzwesen des frühbyzantinischen Staates*, Südosteuropäische Arbeiten, 52 (Munich, 1958), pp. 141–7.

[39] 16, 12, 69, Clark, 1.103.2–3. See too Ps. Chrysostom, *Comparatio regis et monachi* (*CPG*, 4500), PG, 1.47.390.

[40] On the triumphal *adventus* into Emona, Pacatus, *XII pan.*, 2(12), 37, 1–4, Mynors, 111.17–112.13. Maximus' head appears to have been subjected to a parade of insult and then sent around the provinces: Pacatus, *XII pan.*, 2 (12), 38, 5, Mynors, 113.3–6· and Olympiodorus, apud Photius, *Bibliotheca*, cod. 80, ed. R. Henry, 1 (Paris, 1959). 173.12–16; cf. W. Ensslin, 'Maximus', *RE*, 14 (1930), 2546–55, here 2554, and A. Piganiol and A. Chastagnol, *L'empire chrétien (325–395)* (Paris, 1972), p. 281. Victory announcements were certainly sent to the provinces, for Libanius alludes to one's arrival in Antioch: *Ep.* 866, 2–3, ed. R. Foerster, *Libanii opera*, 11 (Leipzig, 1922).23.2–5. Congratulatory delegations were sent to the victor from various major cities, of which three can be identified with precision: Antioch, Libanius, *Ep.* 878, 1, Foerster, 11.34.3–5. It went in 388 and bore gold crowns; cf. P. Petit, *Libanius et la vie municipale à Antioche au IVe siècle après J.-C.* (Paris, 1955), pp. 418–19. Emesa:

A parade, addresses, largess and a panegyric were all on the agenda.[41] The victory was lastingly enshrined by several monuments in the ancient capital and by the erection of an obelisk in the Hippodrome of the new one.[42] As late as the sixth century, the Roman state continued to mark the defeat of Maximus with an official holiday, as we learn from an offhanded remark of Procopius.[43]

A second threat confronted Theodosius' throne when Eugenius revolted in the West. At first the outcome appeared dubious, so that Theodosius' final victory seemed to many contemporaries little short of miraculous.[44] The usurper's head was displayed to his troops in order that they might recognize their defeat; it was then sent around Italy to convince local forces of the futility of resistance.[45] Again victory bulletins were dispatched, as the reply of Ambrose of Milan testifies. Special thanksgiving masses were celebrated immediately: they constitute the earliest clearly attested Christian victory services performed at imperial demand.[46] Theodosius may have marked the event with a gala visit to Rome; he certainly held victory races at Milan, during which he was overcome by his fatal illness.[47] Paulinus of Nola composed a

---

Libanius, *Ep.*, 846, 1, Foerster, 11.6.24–7.2, which shows that they were a good means of presenting petitions to the emperor (esp. 846, 4, *ibid.*, 7.13–20). Alexandria: patriarch Theophilus had sent gifts with his representative to Rome before the outcome was known. Taking no chances with the vagaries of divine favor, he entrusted him with two letters of congratulations, doubtless so he would be able to convince the winner that his loyalty antedated the outcome.

[41] Cf. below, Ch. 3, 2. For a recent discussion and detailed bibliography, MacCormack, *Art and ceremony*, pp. 50ff.

[42] In Rome, the City Prefect Ceionius Rufius Albinus made a triple dedication to the triple victors Theodosius, Valentinian II and Arcadius: *CIL* 6, 31413–14 and 36959 (cf. *ILS*, 789); cf. Chastagnol, *Fastes*, pp. 233–6 and *PLRE*, 1, 37–8. In Constantinople, the event was marked by the raising of the Obelisk of Theodosius: cf. G. Bruns, *Der Obelisk und seine Basis auf dem Hippodrom zu Konstantinopel*, Istanbuler Forschungen, 7 (Istanbul, 1935), and H. Wrede, 'Errichtung'.

[43] Procopius, *Bella*, 3, 4, 16, Haury, 1.326.3–7. See too below, n. 141.

[44] In addition to the panegyric referred to in n. 48, see Augustine, *De ciuitate Dei*, 5, 26, ed. B. Dombart and A. Kalb, *CCL*, 47 (1955).161.17–22 and Orosius, *Hist. adu. pag.* 7, 35, 11ff, Zangemeister 528.7ff.

[45] Zosimus, *Hist. nova*, 4, 58, 5, Paschoud, 2.2.328.4–9; John of Antioch, *De insidiis*, fg. 79, ed. C. De Boor, *Excerpta historica iussu imp. Constantini Porphyrogeniti confecta*, 3 (Berlin, 1905).119.33–120.3.

[46] Ambrose, *Ep.*, 61, *PL*, 16.1237–8. For detailed discussion, see below, Ch. 3, 4.

[47] The visit to Rome is controversial. It is seemingly referred to by Zosimus, *Hist. nova*,

45

victory oration for the occasion. Although it has not survived, it is known to have insisted on the role of Theodosius' faith and prayers in the battle's outcome.[48] Other observances were held throughout the empire on the local level.[49]

What then were the typical elements associated with imperial victory celebrations between Constantine and Theodosius I? In the imperial presence, they featured triumphal entries and parades, the performance of panegyrics and circus celebrations. In the West, the latter included gladiatorial or beast shows. Chariot races were popular throughout the empire. The suppression of a usurpation usually involved the triumphal parade or display of the enemy's head. In areas beyond the imperial presence, news of the victory was communicated by means of victory dispatches, often accompanied, where relevant, with the display of the enemy's head. Provincial delegations were sent to the emperor; at least some such delegations brought with them the traditional victory gift of the *aurum coronarium*. Imperial victories received enduring commemoration in the form of monuments, of which the most popular in this period were the triumphal column and the triumphal arch. Medallions or special coin issues are also attested. The memory of past successes was perpetuated in public life by means of *ludi aeterni*, holidays and anniversary races held on the dates of great victories. The major celebrations themselves took place in various capital or headquarter cities like Trier, Sirmium, Antioch, Constantinople and Milan, but the sources dwell with greatest delectation on the galas held in Rome. The traditional imperial monopoly of triumph does not appear to have weakened thus far. Finally, the first clear signs of official Christian involvement in the solemnities appear at a rather late date.

4, 59, 1, Paschoud, 2.2.328.19–329.5; Prudentius, *Contra Symmachum*, 1, 408ff, ed. M.P. Cunningham, *CCL*, 126 (1966). 200ff; Theodore Lector, *Historia ecclesiastica, Epitome*, 276–8, ed. G.C. Hansen, GCS, [54] (Berlin, 1971), 85.9–23. Among recent scholars, T.D. Barnes, 'Constans and Gratian in Rome', *Harvard Studies in Classical Philology*, 79 (1975), 325–33, here 330, favors the historicity of the visit, while A. Lippold, *Theodosius*, p. 51, opposes it, pointing out that the chronology of events leaves little room for it.

[48] Jerome, *Ep.*, 58, 8, ed. I. Hilberg, *CSEL*, 54 (1910).537.14–538.12 and Gennadius, *De uiris inlustribus*, 49, ed. E.C. Richardson, Texte und Untersuchungen, 14, 1(Leipzig, 1896), 79.1–4.

[49] John of Antioch, *De insidiis*, fg. 79, De Boor, *Excerpta historica*, 3.120.6–7.

2. FROM THE THEODOSIAN SUCCESSION TO ANASTASIUS

With the passing of Theodosius and the nominal accession of his young sons, the circumstances of the throne experienced no little change. These new conditions could not but have repercussions on the public display of the monarchy and its officers. The Spanish emperor is usually credited with a low opinion of his sons' capacities: hence the tutelage of powerful officials like the Master of Both Services Stilicho in the West and the Praetorian Prefect Rufinus in the East.[50] A later source claims that Theodosius and Arcadius both took measures to ensure that their sons were prevented from accompanying the armies on campaign.[51] Since the emperors could scarcely have ignored the recent disasters of Valens, Maximus and Eugenius, the report fits well with the context. At any rate the fact remains that these emperors did not personally lead their armies, thereby inaugurating a tradition which was to last over two centuries.[52] The new custom was heavy with consequence for victory celebrations, for it meant that imperial triumphal entries were now deprived of their drama. The new style of sedentary emperors residing in Constantinople contributed to making imperial comings and goings rather banal occurrences. However they may have been billed at the time, any entries by emperors into their capital were no longer homecomings from the perils and glories of the front, but merely processions from a suburban palace.[53] Another consequence of the limited capacities or interest of Theodosius' successors was that the old emperor's passing ushered in an era in which the Augusti reigned but did not rule, in which the center stage would be dominated by great bureaucrats, men who naturally sought to match the reality of supreme power with its external trappings and perquisites. A final factor to bear in mind as we review the development of victory celebrations in this period was that the new religion now

[50] Stein, *Bas-Empire*, 1, 226.
[51] John Lydus, *De magistratibus populi Romani*, 2, 11 and 3, 41, ed. R. Wünsch (Leipzig, 1903), 67.6–11 and 130.4–14.
[52] The catalogue of sinister omens with which Theophylactus Simocattes links Maurice's attempt to conduct the army to war against the Avars is probably an expression of the bureaucracy's opposition to direct imperial participation in the war: *Historiae*, 5, 16, 1ff, esp. 2, ed. C. De Boor–P. Wirth, 2nd edn (Leipzig, 1972), 218.7ff.
[53] See below, Ch. 3, n. 58.

became increasingly and irresistibly entrenched in the public life of the state.

Within months of Theodosius' death, the citizens of the eastern capital were confronted with a clear instance of the new political configuration's repercussions on imperial ritual display. The all-powerful position of the Praetorian Prefect of the East came to a swift and brutal end on 27 November 395 as he was assassinated at the young emperor's side, during a review of the troops returning from the campaign against Eugenius. Rufinus' severed head was placed on the end of a spear and paraded into the capital and down its avenues in the ritual insult which had become traditional for an imperial victory over a usurper.[54] What is important for our present purpose is to note that Arcadius himself does not appear to have been threatened, that, although some sources claim such was his intent, Rufinus was never clearly accused of usurpation, and that the victory was not so much that of Arcadius as of one court faction, identified with the Grand Chamberlain (*Praepositus sacri cubiculi*) Eutropius.[55]

These considerations lend credence to Claudian's vitriolic account of what looks very much like a triumphal entry into Constantinople celebrated by the same Eutropius to mark a successful campaign against the Huns. Although it is tinged with satire – the eunuch's parade deserves to be introduced with phallic standards – the description offers a precious glimpse of a victorious general's parade.[56] Eutropius is met by an *occursus* or

---

[54] His association with tax collection as Praetorian Prefect was equally ridiculed, since his hand too was carried around the city by people crying 'Give to the insatiable!' Zosimus, *Hist. nova*, 5, 7, 6, ed. L. Mendelssohn (Leipzig, 1887), 225.7–9; Philostorgius, *H.e.* 11, 3, Bidez, 135.6–11; Jerome, *Ep.* 60, 16, 4, Hilberg, *CSEL*, 54. 570.5–8; Asterius of Amasea, *Homiliae* (CPG, 3260), 4, 9, 1, ed. C. Datema (Leyden, 1970), 43.13–16; Claudian, *In Rufinum* 2, 428–39, ed. T. Birt, *MGH.AA*, 10 (1892).49–50; cf. Rufinus' dream, *ibid.*, 46.327–35.

[55] Thus Jerome pointedly discusses the fate of Rufinus among the *priuatae dignitates*, *Ep.*, 60, 16, 1, Hilberg, *CSEL*, 54.570.2–3, not among the sorry fates of usurpers: 60, 15, 4, Hilberg, 569.16–20; cf. J.B. Bury, *History of the later Roman Empire from the death of Theodosius I to the death of Justinian*, 1 (London, 1923), pp. 112–13; E. Demougeot, *De l'unité à la division de l'empire romain, 395–410. Essai sur le gouvernement impérial* (Paris, 1956), pp. 156–8, doubts very strongly that he even entertained the possibility; A. Cameron, *Claudian, Poetry and Propaganda at the Court of Honorius* (Oxford, 1970), pp. 89–90 is more circumspect, but still doubtful. See too below, Ch. 3, 6.

[56] Claudian, *In Eutropium*, 1, 255–6, Birt, 83.

welcoming delegation, he enters the city, delivers a harangue on his victories and requests the consulate as his reward.[57]

Constantinople's next opportunity for triumphal display occurred when the capital was freed from the perceived menace of the Master of Both Services Gainas and his Gothic garrison. Fravitta, Master of Both Services, seems to have made a triumphal entry into the capital after defeating Gainas.[58] The campaigns which secured the city's safety were commemorated on the narrative reliefs of the triumphal column erected by Arcadius. Unfortunately, the complex and enigmatic designs which are preserved thanks to various early modern sketches of the lost monument still await their definitive study and they cannot yet be fully exploited for our purposes.[59] One scholar has suggested that the reliefs included a conveniently stylized representation of a victory celebration in the Hippodrome.[60] More significant and somewhat less ambiguous is a sequence which, in the Louvre drawing, appears to depict a triumphal entry by an emperor, or,

[57] *Ibid.*, 252–86, Birt, 83–4. Cf. *PLRE*, 2, 441–2.

[58] Eunapius, *De sententiis*, fg. 74, *Excerpta historica*, ed. U.P. Boissevain, 4 (Berlin, 1906).98.7–8: ὁ δὲ Φράβιθος. μάλα φαιδρῶς. καὶ λαμπρῶς. ἐπανῄει ἐπὶ τὴν Κωνσταντίνου πόλιν. In this sort of context, λαμπρῶς. usually means 'with great ceremony'. Thus, for example, Philostorgius' account of the triumphal entry of Theodosius I into Constantinople: *H.e.* 9, 19, Bidez–Winkelmann 125: λαμπρῶς. ἐπὶ τὴν Κωνσταντινούπολιν ἄνεισιν.

[59] The most important work has been done by Kollwitz, *Plastik*, pp. 17ff; G.Q. Giglioli, *La colonna di Arcadio a Costantinopoli* (Naples, 1952), and Becatti, *Colonna*, pp. 151ff. Cf. too R. Grigg, 'Symphonian aeido tes basileias. An image of imperial harmony on the base of the column of Arcadius', *Art Bulletin*, 59 (1977), 469–82.

[60] Becatti, *Colonna*, pp. 237–42. Against Kollwitz, *Plastik*, pp. 21–2 (categorically after a detailed comparison) and Giglioli, *Arcadio*, pp. 15ff, Becatti, *Colonna*, pp. 111ff, claimed that the Louvre drawing (fig. 2–5) must represent a relief from the column of Theodosius. His arguments are based on the minor discrepancies between the various renditions and do not necessarily carry conviction. In addition to the parallels produced by Kollwitz, note, for example, that the crack in spiral 5 of the south side in the Freshfield drawing has removed the head of the first horse (Becatti, pl. 75b); cf. precisely the same accident in the Louvre sketch (*ibid.*, pl. 78b). The real problem would then be that the discrepancies seem to reflect inaccuracies in the various drawings, and it remains unclear which, if any, version is more accurate. Kollwitz argues (*Plastik*, p. 22) that the Louvre sketch misinterpreted an army on the march as a triumphal parade. Actually, the appearance of the camels with bound enemy leaders astraddle argues powerfully for the Louvre artist's faithfulness, since, as is not generally known, camels were frequently used in parades of infamy in late antiquity: see below, n. 62.

perhaps, a Roman commander (figs. 2–5).[61] The parade begins with two mounted officers (?), followed by a group of Germanic barbarians. The latter are easily identified thanks to their distinctive clothing (the men wear pants) and long hair. They are walking with their hands bound behind their backs. They are flanked by Roman soldiers and beasts of burden carrying what appear to be shields and spears, perhaps meant to represent booty from the campaign. Next comes what looks like the commander's group. Inside the gate or triumphal arch there is a horseman holding a spear. The main figure in the group is clearly the horseman who is about to enter the arch: he is distinguished not only by his position, but by the richer caparison of his horse, his raised palm gesture and insignia. He is followed by another horseman similarly decked out, without the insignia. Finally there come three barbarian leaders. They are bound and straddle an animal used in late Roman parades of infamy, the camel.[62] If indeed the Louvre drawing depicts the column of Arcadius and the commander in this parade is to be identified as a Roman general, the scene may represent Fravitta's victorious entry into Constantinople. Otherwise, it either shows a triumphal entry by Arcadius which is not attested in the written sources or refers to quite another event.[63] Whatever the precise identity of the commander in the lost relief, the evidence of the ritual insult to Rufinus and the apparent triumphal entries of Eutropius and Fravitta all indicate that, around the turn of the fourth century, the highest officials of the eastern government came to enjoy honors

---

[61] If the Louvre drawing were reliable for such a small detail, the absence of a diadem from that individual's helmet would be peremptory proof against his imperial status. It is not clear why the prisoners come *after* the victorious commander, usurping the basic rule of later Roman precedence which reserved the last place in any procession for the most important person.

[62] On the spread and use of camels in the Roman empire, E. Demougeot, 'Le chameau et l'Afrique du Nord romaine', *Annales. Économies, sociétés, civilisations*, 15 (1960), 209–47, who missed this function, first attested in the fourth century: Socrates, *H.e.*, 3, 2, *PG*, 67.381C, cf. Sozomen, *Historia ecclesiastica*, 5, 7, 3, ed. J. Bidez and G.C. Hansen, GCS 50, 2nd edn (Berlin, 1960), 202.10–12; John Malalas, *Chronographia*, ed. L. Dindorf (Bonn, 1831), 451.16–21; Procopius, *Bella*, 7, 32, 3, Haury, 2.434.2–6 and *Historia arcana*, 11, 37, ed. J. Haury and G. Wirth, 2nd edn (Leipzig, 1963), 76.14–18; John of Nikiu, 97, 25, Charles, 160.

[63] In this last case, Becatti's suggestion that it shows Theodosius' triumph of 386 would deserve careful scrutiny: *Colonna*, p. 117.

which had long since been considered an imperial monopoly.[64]

Three other victory practices can be associated with the Gainas episode. When Gainas and his Goths first left the capital, their departure and the 'delivery' of the city were marked by thanksgiving services.[65] The final denouement of the affair came, by design or accident, in the midst of the solemn festival of the *vota publica* for the well-being of the ruling emperors. The Hunnic chieftain Uldin defeated and killed Gainas two days before Christmas of 400. On 3 January, the embalmed head of the hated Goth was carried in triumph into the capital and paraded through its streets.[66] Circus spectacles are also reported in connection with this victory.[67]

In the West, the sudden defeat of Gildo, the Master of Both Services *per Africam*, may have offered Honorius' court the occasion for victory observances. The event was certainly commemorated by a number of inscriptions at Rome.[68] Stilicho's Gothic victories at Pollentia and Verona in 402 were celebrated two years later when Honorius and the power behind the throne came to the ancient capital to open the emperor's sixth consulate. The festivities included a triumphal entry, harangue and circus spectacles. They appear to have been memorialized by the last Roman triumphal arch.[69] A close analysis of the ceremonies uncovers evidence of the increasing exaltation of the emperor's status in Rome. It also suggests that there was a profound difference in the perimeters of acceptable ceremonial deportment

---

[64] See below, Ch. 3, 6.

[65] Synesius of Cyrene, *Aegyptii*, 2, 3, ed. N. Terzaghi, *Hymni et opuscula*, 2 (Rome, 1944).118.15–18, on the interpretation of which see below, Ch. 3, 4.

[66] Zosimus, *Hist. nova*, 5, 22, 3, Mendelssohn 243.5–8; Philostorgius, *H.e.*, 11, 8, Bidez–Winkelmann, 139.17–20; Marcellinus Comes, a.401, Mommsen, 66.29–30 *Chronicon paschale*, ed. L. Dindorf (Bonn, 1832), 567.18–19.

[67] Eunapius, *De sententiis*, fg. 72, ed. U.P. Boissevain, *Excerpta historica*, 4 (Berlin, 1906).96.20–97.2. Cf. below, Ch. 3, 3.

[68] Claudian, *De consulatu Stilichonis*, 1, 3–9, Birt, 189, seems to suggest that celebrations were staged at the imperial court. His *De sexto consulatu Honorii*, 366–84, Birt 248–9, may indicate that triumphal celebrations in the prince's presence had been projected at Rome but were never carried out. For the inscriptions: *CIL*, 6.31256, 6.1187 and 1730.

[69] On the triumphal arch, Fiebiger–Schmidt, *Inschriftensammlung*, 25–6, no. 24; cf. Kähler, 'Triumphus', *RE*, 7A1 (1939), 373–493, here 400, no. 43.

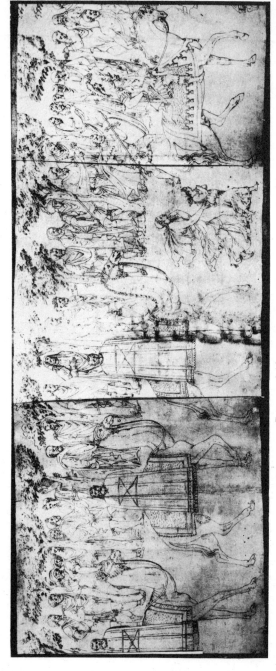

Figure 2. Triumphal procession (see pp. 49–50)

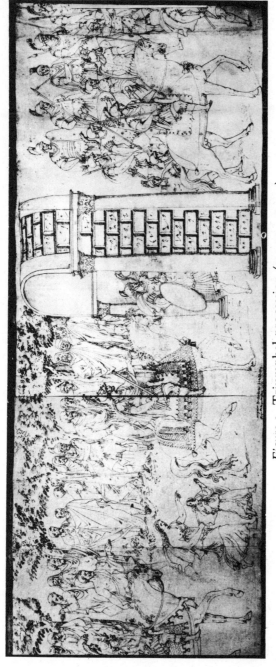

Figure 3. Triumphal procession (see pp. 49–50)

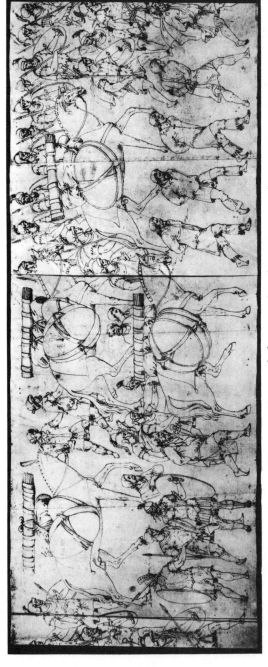

Figure 4. Triumphal procession (see pp. 49–50)

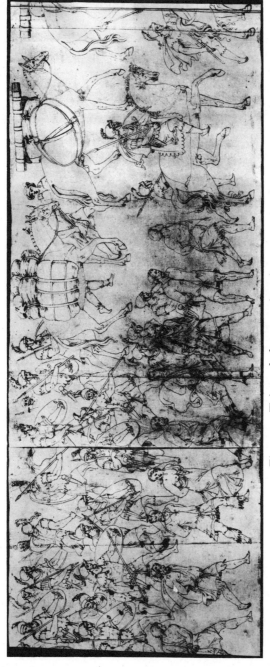

Figure 5. Triumphal procession (see pp. 49–50)

by leading officials of the western empire, in contrast with what we have just observed in contemporary Constantinople.[70]

The prestige of the government in Ravenna cannot have been bolstered by the fall of Stilicho in 408. Two years later, the sack of Rome by Alaric sent shock waves across the Mediterranean. This deeply felt disaster not only triggered the lofty reaction of a City of God: it unleashed a spate of attempts against Honorius' throne. In 411, the head of the usurper Constantine was brought, presumably to Ravenna, whence it may have been dispatched to the provinces.[71] The following year, the grisly relics of the usurpers Jovinus and Sebastian were carried in triumph into the Adriatic capital (fig. 6).[72] Although no record has survived to document the western observances celebrating the murder of the king of the Visigoths, in Constantinople the announcement, on 24 September 415, of his assassination in Spain was treated as a full-fledged imperial victory. It was immediately marked by nocturnal illuminations. The next day, races and a parade hailed the western government's 'victory'.[73] Victory celebrations had now become so indispensable an element of the later Roman government's public display and military success so rare a commodity that even political murders were considered a fitting opportunity to praise the prince's victoriousness.

The capture of Priscus Attalus, one-time usurper and creature of the Visigoths, offered a more promising opportunity for festivities in both parts of the empire. In 415, the prisoner was presented to Honorius and his right hand received token mutilation. This

---

[70] See the detailed account, below, Ch. 3, 2.

[71] *Cons. Cplitana*, a.411, Mommsen, 246. The garbled account in Photius' résumé of Olympiodorus (fg. 19), is not clear: *Bibliotheca*, cod. 80, Henry, 1.173.13–14. Cf. *PLRE*, 2, 316–17.

[72] *Annales Ravennates*, a.412, ed. Bischoff in B. Bischoff and W. Köhler, 'Eine illustrierte Ausgabe der spätantiken Ravennater Annalen', *Medieval Studies in Memory of A. Kingsley Porter*, 1 (Cambridge, Mass., 1939), 125–38, here 127.2–4, illustrated with a picture of three heads (one is their brother Sallustius); *Additamenta ad Prosperum Havniensia*, a.413, ed. T. Mommsen, *MGH.AA*, 9 (1892).300. According to Theophanes, A.M. 5904, De Boor, 81.25–6, the heads were sent to Rome, although the formulation suggests that this is an error for Ravenna. Cf. on these usurpers *PLRE*, 2, 621–2; 971, 'Sallustius 2'; 983, 'Sebastianus 2'.

[73] *Chronicon paschale*, Bonn, 572.8–12; cf. below, Ch. 3, 4.

Figure 6. Display of defeated pretenders' heads (see p. 56)

(see p. 56)

presumably took place at Ravenna.[74] Perhaps a year later, Honorius mounted the last recorded triumphal observances of a Roman emperor in the ancient capital. They included a triumphal entry, during which the hapless pretender was forced to walk in front of Honorius' triumphal chariot.[75] It may have been on this occasion, moreover, that a Roman emperor first incorporated into triumphal ritual the so-called *calcatio colli*, the ancient gesture

[74] Orosius, *Hist. adu. pag.* 7, 42, 9, Zangemeister, 557.9–10; Marcellinus Comes, a.412, Mommsen, 71.3–4, Olympiodorus (fg. 13), apud Photius, *Bibliotheca*, cod. 80, Henry, 1.170.11–13.

[75] Prosper Tiro, *Epitoma chronicon*, a.417, ed. T. Mommsen, *MGH.AA*, 9 (1892).468.

of total victory in which the victor ritually trampled his victim.[76] Perhaps simultaneously with the solemnities in Rome, Ursus, the City Prefect of New Rome, watched over a spectacle ($\vartheta\acute{\epsilon}\alpha\tau\rho ov$) performed in honor of the western emperor's victory in Constantinople on 28 June 416.[77]

On 6 September 421, an important victory over the Persians was announced in the eastern capital. While details of the celebrations are unknown, it is clear that contemporary rhetors vied with one another in composing panegyrics for the occasion. Even the emperor's wife got on that particular band-wagon.[78] It is also distinctly possible that Theodosius II founded anniversary games to commemorate his success.[79] The next year, the Spanish

---

[76] The text of Philostorgius, *H.e.*, ed. Bidez and Winkelmann, 144.9–13 unfortunately has a lacuna at a crucial point, although the phrasing suggests that a *calcatio* was about to be performed. Nicephorus Callistus Xanthopoulos, *Historia ecclesiastica*, 13, 35, *PG*, 146. 1044C–D, actually describes a *calcatio* at this point of his account, which is generally based on Philostorgius. However, Xanthopoulos had the same MS of Philostorgius that has come down to us and Bidez (Philostorgius, *loc. cit.*, apparatus) considered that Xanthopoulos' additional material was conjectural (cf. G. Gentz and K. Aland, 'Die Quellen der Kirchengeschichte des Nicephorus und ihre Bedeutung für die Konstituierung des Textes der älteren Kirchenhistoriker', *Zeitschrift für die neutestamentliche Wissenschaften*, 42 (1949), 104–41, here 119 and 138ff). However, note that Xanthopoulos has material concerning Attalus' appointments that is also lacking in Philostorgius. On the *calcatio* in Roman antiquity, see C. Sittl, *Die Gebärden der Griechen und Römer* (Leipzig, 1890), pp. 106ff, and F.J. Dölger, 'Der Fuss des Siegers auf dem Kopf des Besiegten: Die Siegerstellung Amors', *Antike und Christentum*, 3 (Münster, 1932), 283–4. The *calcatio* seems to have been an iconographical theme before it entered the repertory of imperial triumphal gestures. This is why Shapur is supposed to have contrasted his real *calcatio* of Valerian with Roman pictures: Lactantius, *De mortibus persecutorum*, 5, 3–4, ed. J. Moreau, 1, SC, 39 (Paris, 1954), 83.9–16. Cf. J. Babelon, 'Le thème iconographique de la violence', *Studies presented to D.M. Robinson*, 2 (St Louis, 1953), 278–81, here 278–9, and E. Dinkler-von Schubert, 'Fusstritt', *Lexikon der christlichen Ikonographie*, 2 (1970), 67–9. A recent cross-cultural study of the gesture will be found in E. Neumann, *Herrschafts- und Sexualsymbolik. Grundlagen einer alternativen Symbolforschung* (Stuttgart, 1980), pp. 164ff.

[77] *Chronicon paschale*, Bonn, 573.15–17; cf. *PLRE*, 2, 1192, 'Ursus 3'.

[78] Socrates, *H.e.*, 7, 21, *PG*, 67.784A–B.

[79] Date of announcement: *Chronicon paschale*, Bonn, 579.19–20. Cf. A. Lippold, 'Theodosius II.', *RE*, S. 13 (1973), 971. Referring to the same events, Socrates, *H.e.*, 7, 19, *PG*, 67. 777C–D tells about the famous courier Palladius (cf. *PLRE*, 2, 819–20, 'Palladius 5'), who could get from the Persian front to Constantinople within three days. If this statement was, as seems likely from the context, suggested to Socrates by Palladius' performance in September 421, this would imply that the victory itself was won three days earlier, i.e., 3 September 421. We would then have the explanation for the mysterious *ludi* attested for that date in the Roman state calendar of the mid-

usurper Maximus and his associate Jovinus were brought to Ravenna, where they figured in a triumphal parade which added luster to Honorius' *tricennalia*.[80]

In the half decade following Alaric's sack of Rome, then, we have evidence of four imperial victory celebrations. For the eleven year period between 411 and 422, the total is six, or very nearly the same as in the decade which followed Adrianople. Once again, there appears to be a correlation between severe and widely perceived blows to imperial prestige and intensification in the rhythm of imperial victory celebrations. The more precarious the fortunes of the emperors appeared, the more urgent the need to shore up belief in their invincibility and to proclaim their mediocre successes to the population.

Down to the reign of Honorius, the most distinctive element in western victory celebrations is the emphasis the surviving records place on triumphal entries into the ancient capital, while circus celebrations figured only in a secondary role. Although one may suspect that the situation differed somewhat away from the tradition-bound surroundings of Rome, it is only after Honorius' passing that the first reliable evidence of an important new development occurs. A study of celebrations outside Rome suggests that by this time the circus was already coming to dominate eastern victory observances.[81] It can hardly be a coincidence that the same shift appears to occur in Italy precisely at the outset of the reign of Galla Placidia and the young Caesar Valentinian III. The new rulers of Italy were freshly arrived from the East when the defeated usurper John was brought to them at Aquileia. A victory celebration was held in the city's circus. The traditional parade of infamy was transferred to the arena, where John suffered amputation of a hand and where stage-managed abuse replaced the spontaneous insults of city streets. At Aquileia, it was the professionals of the theater who were entrusted with the

---

fifth century: Polemius Silvius, *Laterculus*, 3 September, Degrassi, 272, cf. comm. p. 506.

[80] *Annales Ravennates*, a. 422, Bischoff, 127; *Chronica Gallica a. 452*, ed. T. Mommsen, *MGH.AA*, 9.656, no. 89; Marcellinus Comes, a.422, Mommsen, 75.12–14; Jordanes, *De summa temporum vel origine actibusque gentis Romanorum*, ed. T. Mommsen, *MGH.AA*, 5.1 (Berlin, 1882).42.7–8, no. 326. Cf. *PLRE*, 2, 745, 'Maximus 7' and 2, 622, 'Iovinus 3'.

[81] See below, Ch. 3, 3.

public ridicule of the unfortunate usurper.[82] It is only fitting that the last recorded victory celebration of the western Roman empire should reveal New Rome's distinctive emphasis on the circus.

Word of John's death reached Constantinople as Theodosius II presided over races in the Hippodrome. In an unprecedented gesture, he interrupted the spectacle, announced the event and immediately organized a thanksgiving procession down the middle of the Hippodrome and out to church, singing hymns of thanksgiving. The emperor himself spent the rest of the day in services.[83]

Thanks no doubt to the poor state of the narrative sources, forty-four years go by before we encounter another record of imperial victory rites. These were staged to mark the demise of Attila's son Dengezich. His head arrived in Constantinople during races in the Hippodrome. The token of victory was paraded down the main boulevard of the capital, the Mese. Later it was set up outside the land walls, in a place called Xylokerkos. The spectacle is said to have attracted huge crowds.[84]

Attempted usurpations supplied the pretext for the next explicitly attested imperial victory celebrations. Those of Zeno's reign publicized the final defeat and execution of his fellow Isaurians Illus and Leontius. In 488, the ancient ritual of the parade of heads into the city was solemnly enacted. In typical Constantinopolitan fashion, it culminated at the Hippodrome in a public display for the spectators and the victorious emperor. Afterwards, the heads were set up at St Conon's in Sycae, where the spectacle once again attracted sizable crowds.[85]

---

[82] Philostorgius, *H.e.*, 12, 13, Bidez, 149.21–4; Procopius, *Bella*, 3, 3, 9, Haury, 1.320.5–9; Olympiodorus (fg. 46), apud Photius, *Bibliotheca*, cod. 80, Henry, 1.187.26–8. Cf. *PLRE*, 2, 594–5, 'Ioannes 6'.

[83] Socrates, *H.e.*, 7, 24, *PG*, 67.792A; cf. John of Antioch, *De insidiis*, fg. 82, De Boor, *Excerpta historica*, 3.27–9.

[84] Marcellinus Comes, a. 469, Mommsen, 90.7–9; *Chronicon paschale*, Bonn 593.3–8; cf. *PLRE*, 2, 354–5; J.O. Maenchen-Helfen, *The world of the Huns. Studies in their history and culture* (Berkeley, 1973), p. 168 for the date.

[85] Malalas, *Chronographia*, Bonn, 389.9–14, cf. the Slavonic version: 15, 3, tr. M. Spinka and G. Downey, *Chronicle of John Malalas, Books VIII–XVIII* (Chicago, 1940), p. 109; Theophanes, A.M. 5980, De Boor, 132.16–18; Marcellinus Comes, a. 488, Mommsen, 93.23–4; John of Antioch, *De insidiis*, fg. 98, De Boor, *Excerpta historica*, 3.139.34–5; *PLRE*, 2, 586–90; 670–1, 'Leontius 17'.

Anastasius I too was forced to confront an Isaurian revolt, the final suppression of which was observed in 498. The heads of the dead rebel leaders, as well as Longinus of Selinus and Indes who had been taken alive, were sent to the capital. Longinus and Indes were decked in chains and paraded down the main avenues of the capital. During the victory races, the Isaurians were marched through the Hippodrome and pushed to the feet of the victorious emperor, who looked on from the imperial box, the *kathisma*.[86] A contemporary observer compared the Hippodrome festivities with Aemilius Paullus' great triumph of 167 B.C., perhaps in part because of Paullus' accomplishment of abolishing the *tributum* thanks to his victory. The comparison is particularly telling because it presupposes, in the minds of contemporary Constantinopolitans, a clear identity between the ancient Roman triumphal parade and the victory celebrations in the fifth-century Hippodrome.[87] In recognition of their contribution to the emperor's success, Anastasius' generals John the Scyth and John Gibbus were honored with back-to-back consulates in 498 and 499.[88] To further publicize his triumph, Anastasius appears to have linked the victory with his fiscal policy by suppressing the detested chrysargyron tax in its honor.[89]

The circumstances surrounding the next recorded victory celebrations in Anastasius' reign recall the lessons of the triumphal activities staged in the aftermath of Adrianople and the sack of Rome. They came hard on the heels of the bloody Trishagion riots in Constantinople, in the midst of the revolt of Vitalian, the

[86] Priscian, *De laude Anastasii imperatoris*, 171–9, ed. E. Baehrens, *Poetae latini minores*, 5 (Leipzig, 1883). 270; cf. 266.50–1; Marcellinus Comes, a.498, Mommsen, 95.6–9; Malalas, *De insidiis*, fg. 37, De Boor, *Excerpta historica*, 3.168.3–5; Evagrius Scholasticus, *Historia ecclesiastica*, 3, 35, ed. J. Bidez and L. Parmentier (London, 1898), 135.8–16; Theophanes, A.M. 5988, De Boor, 139.33–140.7; *PLRE*, 2, 178–9, 'Athenodorus 2', 591, 'Indes', 688–9, 'Longinus 3, 4'. On the date, E. Stein, *Histoire du Bas-Empire*, 2 (Bruges, 1949), 84. On the imperial loge, Janin, *Cple byz.*, pp. 188–9 and R. Guilland, *Études de topographie de Constantinople byzantine*, 1, Berliner byzantinistische Arbeiten, 37 (Berlin, 1969), pp. 462–98.

[87] Priscian, *De laude Anastasii*, 174–7; cf. Plutarch, *Aemilius Paulus*, 38, 1ff.

[88] *PLRE*, 2, 602–3 and 617–18, 'Ioannes 34, 93'.

[89] On the suppression of the *chrysargyron* and its date, Karayannopulos, *Finanzwesen*, pp. 136–7; cf. Stein, *Bas-Empire*, 2, 203–4. Malalas, *De insidiis*, fg. 37, De Boor, *Excerpta historica*, 3.168.5–7, seems to establish the most direct link between the victory and taxes: καὶ μετὰ τὴν νίκην ἔδωκε δωρεὰς πᾶσι τοῖς ὑποτελέσιν τοῖς ὑπὸ τὴν αὐτοῦ βασιλείαν.

Count of Federates and a champion of Chalcedonian orthodoxy against Anastasius' ecclesiastical policies.[90] After a mediocre success which fell far short of deciding the struggle's outcome, Anastasius' generals dispatched a victory bulletin to the capital. This provided the emperor with a badly needed pretext to trumpet his 'victory' by means of a thanksgiving procession to the capital's shrines as well as public spectacles.[91] While these celebrations may have had the effect of calming potential rebels in the city, they did little to ward off the real threat of Vitalian and his army, which were to menace the capital repeatedly before their final defeat in 515. The jubilations with which Constantinople celebrated the contest's conclusion conform to Anastasius' earlier practice. Anastasius himself led a liturgical procession of thanksgiving out of the city's defences to Sosthenion, where the rebellious commander had made his headquarters during the siege.[92] On the other hand, one of the inscriptions honoring the charioteer Porphyrius seems to allude to victory races marking the defeat of Vitalian's naval forces.[93] Beyond the walls of the capital, we hear of one of the last provincial celebrations of an imperial victory. It is highly significant that this celebration is not remembered because of the solemn assembly associated with the arrival of an imperial victory bulletin, circus races, or dancing in the streets.[94] Our sole record of it comes from the sermon which was delivered by Severus of Antioch during the service which commemorated the fall of Vitalian.[95] On the eve of the last phase

[90] Stein, *Bas-Empire*, 2, 177ff; *PLRE*, 2, 1171–6.

[91] John of Antioch, *De insidiis*, fg. 103, De Boor, *Excerpta historica*, 3.144.33–145.1; cf. *PLRE*, 2, 579.

[92] The dating is not completely clear. Marcellinus Comes, a.515, Mommsen, 99.7–10; Malalas, *Chronographia*, Bonn, 405.20–2; cf. Malalas Slav., 16, 3, Spinka–Downey, 117. Cf. A. Chauvot, 'Observations sur la date de l'*Éloge d'Anastase* de Priscien de Césarée', *Latomus*, 36 (1977), 539–50. His suggestion that the *Laus* was written for a victory celebration is interesting but unprovable.

[93] *Anthologia graeca*, 15, 50, 4–6, ed. F. Buffière, 12 (Paris, 1970).152, on which cf. Cameron, *Porphyrius*, p. 128.

[94] For a description of the arrival of an imperial victory bulletin at Antioch in the fourth century, see John Chrysostom, *Homilia 19 in Matthaeum*, *PG*, 57.285; on dancing and exultation, Chrysostom, *Expositiones in Psalmos* (*CPG*, 4413), 7, 15, *PG*, 55.104.

[95] Preserved in the Syriac translation by James of Edessa, among the homilies delivered in 514–15; *Homelia 34* (*CPG*, 7035), ed. and tr. M. Brière, F. Graffin, C.J.A. Lash, *Patrologia Orientalis*, 36 (1972), 430–427; Severus also composed a hymn on Vitalian's defeat, presumably for the same or a related service: *Hymn 262*, 'On Vitalian the

in the late antique development of imperial victory celebrations, the liturgification of victory celebrations was already well under way.

In the course of a century and a quarter, a number of significant trends emerged in imperial victory observances. At the beginning of the period, major celebrations were staged in Rome, Ravenna, Aquileia and Constantinople. By the beginning of the sixth century, imperial victory festivals had become what they would remain for many centuries to come: a monopoly of New Rome. In an age of usurpation, the grisly parade of defeated emperors' heads had become a common occurrence and exerted a profound and sinister impact on the collective psychology of the later Roman population. How else are we to explain that a frenzied mob could murder a heretical monk in the midst of a religious riot, raise his head on a pole and run through the streets of Constantinople screaming vengeance to the 'conspirators against the Trinity'?[96] Or that heads on stakes were perceived as suitable ornament for a late antique 'calendar' (fig. 6)? Nor are we surprised to find a historian assuming that when David killed Goliath, he celebrated his accomplishment by marching into Jerusalem behind the giant's head, raised triumphantly on a pole.[97]

New contours are beginning to shape imperial victory celebrations. As the significance of the triumphal entry recedes, the prominence of circus celebrations increases, reflecting an overall trend in the ritual display of the monarchy and perhaps partly in response to popular taste.[98] Barbarians are no longer fed to the beasts and, by the end of the period, we stop hearing of the erection of triumphal arches. Finally, and most significant for future developments in Byzantium and the barbarian kingdoms, the fifth century witnesses the development and canonization of a

---

Tyrant and on the Victory of the Christ-Loving Anastasius the King' (*CPG*, 7072), ed. and tr. E.W. Brooks, *ibid.*, 7 (1911), 710–11. The sermon explains Evagrius' story that Vitalian later demanded Severus' deposition because of the insulting texts he had written against him; *H.e.* , 4, 4, Bidez–Parmentier, 155.10–13.

[96] Evagrius, *H.e.*, 3, 44, Bidez–Parmentier 146.15–20; Malalas, *Chronographia*, Bonn, 407.16–19; John of Nikiu, *Chronicle* 89, 64, Charles 129.

[97] Malalas, *Chronographia*, Bonn, 426.8–12; cf. 1 Kings 17.54.

[98] See below, Ch. 3, 3.

new form of victory celebration: the liturgical procession of thanksgiving.

3. FROM JUSTINIAN TO THE OUTBREAK OF ICONOCLASM

The final phase in the development of late antique victory practices represents a long period of transition. In some ways, the first signs of a new age are already evident in the reign of Justinian, in the shape of a new infringement on the imperial monopoly of victory or changes in the main audience for victory celebrations. The deepening christianization of society and quickening crises brought added impetus to a phenomenon which did not escape the notice of John the Lydian. Although he claims only to comment on a crisis in the Roman Republic's ancient history, it would have been difficult for a contemporary to miss the point in John's dry observation that the most obvious thing about people who take refuge in liturgical entreaties in time of war is their expectation of defeat.[99] He would not have been surprised by developments in the decades following his death.

The first victory celebrations in Justinian's long reign were perhaps associated with imperial success against the Persians near Dara in 530. John the Lydian was commissioned to compose some kind of account of the operation, and it is not impossible that this account took the form of a panegyric.[100] Whether the victory was honored with races is not known; it was certainly memorialized by an equestrian statue of the emperor dedicated by the Praetorian Prefect Julian. Typically enough for the period, the statue and accompanying inscription were placed in the Hippodrome.[101] In

---

[99] John Lydus, *De magistratibus*, 1, 38, Wünsch, 40.4–9.

[100] *Ibid.*, 3, 28, Wünsch, 116.5–15. The passage is sometimes interpreted as referring to an imperial request to write a history of the war, perhaps because of the apparent allusion in συγγράψαι ... πόλεμον (116.10–11) to Thucydides, 1, 1 (*PLRE*, 2, 613). The entire context, however, concerns panegyrics composed by John, and such a text on Dara would seem to fit equally well here. On the event, Stein, *Bas-Empire*, 2, 288.

[101] The inscription is preserved in the *Planudean Anthology*, 63: *Anthologia graeca*, ed. R. Aubreton and F. Buffière, 13 (Paris, 1980).105. Discussion and further references in B. Croke, 'Justinian's Bulgar victory celebration', *BS*, 41 (1980), 188–95, here 192–3.

the same year, Justinian celebrated a victory won on his behalf by the barbarian king and Master of the Troops Mundo. A spectacle was staged in the Hippodrome which included a parade of the booty and captives, among whom were a Bulgar king.[102] A further dedication inscription was apparently added to the new equestrian monument by the City Prefect Eustathius.[103]

Two years later, Justinian announced the suppression of the Nika uprising and the usurpation attempted by Anastasius' relatives in a victory circular sent to the cities of the empire. Jordanes claims what the missive suggests, that Justinian celebrated the crushing of the revolt as a victory.[104] The evidence is considerably better for the next great ceremony of the reign, when Belisarius' lightning success in Africa resulted in one of the most frequently cited and least understood of late antique triumphs. It began with a novel parade by the victorious general and culminated with the circus celebrations which by now had become the traditional victory festival in Constantinople. In addition to depictions of the ceremony in imperial commissions of both major and minor art, a medallion may have been struck in honor of the reconquest of Africa.[105] During the ceremony,

---

[102] Marcellinus Comes, a.530, Mommsen, 103.7–10 and Theophanes, A.M. 6032, De Boor, 218.31–219.8, clearly derived from a more complete version of Malalas and misdated by ten years: cf. Malalas, *Chronographia*, Bonn, 451.19-22 and esp. W. Ensslin, 'Mundo', *RE*, 16 (1935), 559–60, as well as Croke, 'Bulgar'. Against *PLRE*, 2, 767–8, see B. Croke, 'Mundo the Gepid: from freebooter to Roman general', *Chiron*, 12 (1982), 125–35.

[103] *Planudean Anthology*, 62, *Anthologia graeca*, Aubreton and Buffière, 13.105, with n. 2; cf. Croke, 'Bulgar', pp. 192–4.

[104] Malalas, *Chronographia*, Bonn, 476.22–477.1; *Chronicon paschale*, Bonn, 628.17–20. I am not sure what to make of the similar reference in Theophanes, A.M. 6316, De Boor, 170.24–8, attributed to Justin in A.D. 524. Jordanes, *Rom.*, 364, Mommsen, 47.27–8.

[105] For a detailed discussion of the victory celebration, see below, Ch. 3, 6. For Justinian's magnification of his victories in art, see below, n. 114, 117–18. The only textual evidence for the medallion is the unlikely and late story in Cedrenus, *Synopsis historiarum*, ed. I. Bekker, 1 (Bonn, 1838–9).649.21–4, although it has frequently been assumed that the great half-pound multiple discovered at Caesarea in Cappadocia and stolen and destroyed in 1831 was issued for this occasion. Cf. e.g. W. Hahn, *Moneta Imperii Byzantini. Rekonstruktion des Prägeaufbaues auf synoptisch-tabellarischer Grundlage*, 1 (Vienna, 1973), 46–7, and C. Morrisson, *Catalogue des monnaies byzantines de la Bibliothèque nationale*, 1 (Paris, 1970), 69; cf. 58, with pl. VIII, 1. The history of the piece is laid out in detail in E. Babelon, *Mélanges numismatiques*, 3 (Paris, 1900), 305–43.

Justinian wore the long vestment known as the *loros*. It was probably not the first such association of this garment with an imperial triumph and it was far from being the last, since triumphant Byzantine emperors would still be decked out in its descendant four centuries later (cf. fig. 9, p. 149).[106] Finally, in conformance with well established usage, the victorious general was granted the consulship for the next year.[107]

The premature victory over the Ostrogothic kingdom and the surrender of its king Witigis were not celebrated in the usual arena. The public was excluded, since the special celebration, involving a display of the booty, was held within the confines of the imperial palace. Attendance was restricted to members of the senatorial order. In sharp contrast with the celebrations of six years earlier, no special honors were granted to Belisarius.[108] A similar pattern obtained in August 552, when victory bulletins arrived from Rome, announcing that city's reconquest and the defeat of the Ostrogothic king Totila by the ex-Grand Chamberlain Narses. The news was accompanied by the Gothic king's blood-stained headdress and royal robe. The keys to the city of Rome may have been included in the dispatch. In the presence of the empire's governmental elite, the symbolic objects were solemnly laid at Justinian's feet.[109] It is not unlikely that analogous circumstances

---

[106] John Lydus, *De magistratibus*, 2, 2, Wünsch, 55.27–56.7. On the *loros*, see Schramm, *Herrschaftszeichen und Staatssymbolik*, 1, 25–50 and E. Piltz, 'Insignien, XII. Trabea triumphalis u. Loros', *Reallexikon zur byzantinischen Kunst*, 3 (1978), 428–44.

[107] Procopius, *Bella*, 4, 9, 15–16, Haury, 1.458.10–19.

[108] Procopius, *Bella*, 7, 1, 2–3, Haury, 2.298.2–10. Cf. Stein, *Bas-Empire*, 2, 367.

[109] Malalas, *Chronographia*, Bonn, 486.14–18 and Theophanes, A.M. 6044, De Boor, 228.18–24. For the probability that the keys of Rome were included too, see Procopius, *Bella*, 8, 33, 27, Haury, 2.666.17–19. On the date, A. Lippold, 'Narses', *RE*, S. 12 (1970), 870–89, here 878. Theophanes records that these objects were given to Justinian ἐπὶ σεκρήτου (228.23–4). Anastasius' ninth-century translation has *coram senatu*: ed. C. De Boor, *Theophanis Chronographia*, 2 (Leipzig, 1885). 144.36 (cf. apparatus), suggesting that the present Greek text is slightly corrupt. Σέκρετον in medieval usage can, however, refer to the *Consistorium*: J.B. Bury, *The imperial administrative system in the ninth century*, The British Academy Supplemental Papers, 1 (London, 1911), p. 29 and 83–4. A number of other victory bulletins or symbolic sendings conveyed to Constantinople in the reign of Justinian are known, but any public celebrations they might have occasioned have left no traces: Procopius, *Bella*, 5, 14, 15, Haury, 2.78.3–4 (Rome), cf. 5, 24, 1, Haury, 2.117.24–118.1; 4, 28, 46, Haury, 1.551.13–19 (Roman standards recaptured from Moors); 7, 24, 34, Haury, 2.407.9–12 (second capture of Rome); 8, 14, 43, Haury, 2.564.4–8 (captured Persian standards).

attended the delivery of the last known victory announcements of Justinian's long reign. *Epinikia* letters arrived from Rome with booty and the 'symbols of victory', the keys to the recaptured towns of Verona and Brescia, in November 562.[110]

Although the trend toward a more restricted audience is clear, it was not a monolithic development. Thanks to a tenth-century author's zest for compilation, an official report documents an otherwise unknown triumphal entry late in Justinian's reign.[111] It describes in some detail the ceremony staged to mark the retreat of the marauding Kotrigurs from the suburbs of Constantinople on Monday, 11 August 559.[112] Even though the entry can be shown to be atypical in some of its ritual details, it is of capital importance for two reasons. It is the first explicit proof that emperors had begun to include Christian shrines into their triumphal itineraries. Secondly, it is highly significant that Theophanes – or his source – provides a pretty detailed account of the events leading right up to the triumphal entry and then relegates to silence the ceremonial climax of the emperor's activities that summer.[113] In other words, the document attesting Justinian's triumph of 559 is precisely the exception that proves the rule: ceremonial entries disappear from the narrative sources in the fifth and sixth centuries not because they ceased to occur altogether, but because they lost their appeal to historians.

There can be little doubt that Justinian's reign witnessed a powerful reassertion of the image of the victor emperor. At least

---

[110] Malalas, *Chronographia*, Bonn, 492.17–20; Theophanes, A.M. 6055, De Boor, 237.13–15; cf. on date, Stein, *Bas-Empire*, 2, 610 and 611, n. 1; A. Lippold, *RE*, S. 12, 885.
[111] *On Imperial Expeditions* (Περὶ βασιλικῶν ταξειδίων), ed. J.J. Reiske (Bonn, 1829), 497.13–498.13. The event's date has occasioned some controversy: D. Serruys, 'A propos d'un triomphe de Justinien', *Revue des études grecques*, 20 (1907), 240–4; F. Martroye, 'De la date d'une entrée solennelle de Justinien', *Mémoires de la Société nationale des antiquaires de France*, 69 (1909), 17–41; finally resolved by Stein, *Bas-Empire*, 2, 818–19. On the document's official character: *ibid.*, 819. The atypical itinerary offers powerful additional evidence for Stein's date: see below, Ch. 5, pp. 208ff.
[112] On the historical circumstances, Stein, *Bas-Empire*, 2, 540; J.B. Bury, *History...to the death of Justinian I*, 2, 304–8; and esp. V. Popović, 'La descente des Koutrigours, des Slaves et des Avars vers la Mer Égée: le témoignage de l'archéologie', *Comptes rendus de l'Académie des inscriptions et belles-lettres*, Année 1978, 596–648, here 611.
[113] Theophanes, A.M. 6051, De Boor, 234.3–7.

eight times in the course of his long government, different kinds of celebrations communicated the ruler's victorious qualities to the mass audiences of city streets and circus, as well as to elite onlookers invited into the palace precincts. But the would-be restorer of the Roman world sought also to propagandize his successes by more constant and far-reaching means. The very entrance to the sacred palace was dominated by the Brazen House's great mosaic which amalgamated different victories into the prince's universal triumph.[114] Victory titles redolent of the good old days of the fourth century were trotted out with every new promulgation, as for instance in the constitution *Omnem* of the Digest:

> Emperor Caesar Flavius Justinian Alamannicus,
> Gotthicus, Francicus, Germanicus, Anticus,
> Alanicus, Vandalicus, Africanus, Pious, Fortunate
> Glorious Victor and Triumphator Ever Augustus.[115]

And the texts of the laws echoed the dominant theme to distant audiences: victory was assured for a great Roman emperor with God on his side, a ruler who triumphed over barbarians and through the equity of his laws.[116] The elite who rubbed shoulders with the prince were treated to the same message in even larger doses. At imperial banquets, meals might be served on platters made of Vandal gold and decorated with reliefs of Justinian's triumphs.[117] Even the imperial vestments depicted Roman victory, as the garment Justinian carried to the grave attested.[118]

The troubled years of the later sixth century were not devoid of triumphs. Infringement on the imperial monopoly of victory celebrations occurred in the last years of the reign of Justin II, when the Caesar and heir apparent Tiberius Constantine cele-brated a triumph, most probably on the occasion of a success

---

[114] Procopius, *De aedificiis*, 1, 10, 15–19, ed. J. Haury and G. Wirth, 4 (Leipzig, 1964). 40.20–41.12; see C. Mango, *The Brazen House: a study of the vestibule of the imperial palace of Constantinople* (Copenhagen, 1959), pp. 32–4; cf. MacCormack, *Art and ceremony*, pp. 73–5.

[115] Ed. P. Krüger, *Corpus iuris civilis*, 1 (Berlin, 1928).10.

[116] E.g. *Institutiones*, preface, 1, *ibid.*, no p. Cf. *Cod. Iust.*, 1, 27, 1, 2, *ibid.*, 2 (Berlin, 1929).77, or 1, 27, 2, 1, *ibid.*, 79.

[117] Corippus, *Iust.*, 3, 121–5, Cameron, 64, with comm. 184–5.

[118] *Ibid.*, 1, 272–93, 44–5 with comm. 140–2.

against the Persians in late 576.[119] The principle of imperial
prerogative was soon reasserted by Tiberius himself. As Augustus,
Tiberius 'celebrated a triumph for Maurice's victories', in the terse
but telling formulation of Theophanes. The observances included
special honors for the successful general Maurice, in the form of a
ceremonial reception and, it would appear, his promotion to
Caesar.[120] In 589 or 590, Maurice, now himself emperor, received
a victory dispatch from the Persian front, accompanied by
'symbols of victory' selected from the booty. He ordered a victory
gala which featured circus races and the performance of dances by
the δημοτικοί. As Theophylactus implies, the latter aspect of late
Roman victory celebrations was as familiar to contemporaries of
the fourth through sixth centuries as it is obscure to moderns.[121] In
contrast to these secular festivities, a victory by Maurice's general
Priscus and the subsequent success of Tatimer in 592 were marked
by liturgical services of a novel sort, in the shape of an all-night

[119] The account of this triumph can be pieced together from John of Biclar, *Chronica*,
a.575?, 1, ed. T. Mommsen, *MGH. AA*, 11 (1894).214.7–16, and the palimpsest
provincial chronicle from the late sixth or early seventh century in Vat. reg. lat. 2077
(*CLA*, 1, 115), the *Paschale campanum*, ed. T. Mommsen, *MGH. AA*, 9 (1892).749.
The mention of the twenty-four elephants appears to authorize a connection with
John of Ephesus, *Historiae ecclesiasticae pars III*ᵃ, 3, 2, 48 and 3, 6, 10, tr. E.W. Brooks,
Corpus scriptorum christianorum orientalium, Scriptores syri, series III, 3, *Versio* (Louvain,
1936), 83.24–6 and 229.10–26. The corrected date proposed for the second passage by
A. Dyakanov, *Ioann Efessky i ego tserkovno-istoricheskie trudy* (St Petersburg, 1908), p.
312, squares nicely with Biclar and the *Paschale campanum*. Further discussion of this
ceremony below, Ch. 3, 6.
[120] Theophanes, A.M. 6074, De Boor, 251.31–252.1; cf. Yu. Kulakovsky, *Istoriya
Vizantii*, 2 (Kiev, 1912), 394; P. Goubert, *Byzance avant l'Islam*, 1 (Paris, 1951), 84–6.
[121] Theophylactus Simocattes, *Hist.*, 3, 6, 5, De Boor, 120.20–4 and Theophanes,
Chronographia, A.M. 6080, De Boor, 262.10–14. On the date: J.B. Bury, *A history of
the later Roman Empire from Arcadius to Irene*, 2 (London, 1889), 110; Kulakovsky,
Istoriya, 2, 433–4; E. Honigmann, *Die Ostgrenze des byzantinischen Reiches von 363. bis
1071.*, Corpus bruxellense historiae byzantinae, 3 (Brussels, 1935), p. 27, and M.J.
Higgins, *The Persian War of the Emperor Maurice (586–602)*, 1 (Washington, D.C.,
1939), 73. Theophylactus says that the races and dancing were ὡς εἴθισται
Ῥωμαίοις πανηγυρίζουσιν. That some kind of dancing and related performances
were considered a significant element of triumphal celebrations is shown not only
by Chrysostom's allusion to it (*Expositiones in Psalmos* (*CPG*, 4413), 7, 15, *PG*,
55.104), but by the explicit statement of an anonymous sixth-century treatise on
strategy that circus and theatrical personnel make an important contribution to the
state, particularly in triumphs, when they are charged with leading prisoners
through the circus: Anonymus Byzantinus, Περὶ στρατηγικῆς, 3, 15, ed. H. Köchly
and W. Rüstow, *Griechische Kriegsschriftsteller*, 2 (Leipzig, 1855), 54.

vigil at the Hagia Sophia. The vigil was followed by prayers of supplication on behalf of future victories for emperor Maurice. This part of the service presumably took the form of litanic processions.[122]

The upset of the usurper Phocas in 610 was distinguished by at least two rituals. For the first, the defeated emperor was taken from the palace, stripped of his insignia and brought by boat to Heraclius. With his hands tied behind his back, he was led into the victor's presence. Heraclius remained seated in his throne (σέλ-λιον) and performed the ritual trampling before he ordered Phocas' execution. It is important to note that this part of the ritual was performed on the island of Kalonymos or, perhaps, on board ship; its audience would therefore have been limited to the troops and headquarters staff, as well as prominent officials accompanying the victorious usurper.[123] The second phase of the celebration took place in the capital: the traditional parade of insult to the dead emperor's head. Frequent repetition doubtless had diminished that grisly rite's drawing power and it was performed with a new ferocity that, once again, appears to anticipate later developments.[124] The bodies of the defeated emperor and his leading collaborators were dragged through the streets of Constantinople and consigned to flames in the Forum Bovis.[125]

Heraclius' long struggle against the Persians culminated in a series of spectacular observances, including a triumphal entry

[122] Theophylactus Simocattes, *Hist.*, 6, 8, 8, De Boor, 235.15–21; Theophanes, A.M. 6085, De Boor, 271.8–12. On the incident, Bury, *History...to Irene*, 2, 128–9, and Kulakovsky, *Istoriya*, 2, 457–8. On this type of service, A. Baumstark, *Nocturna laus. Typen frühchristlicher Vigilienfeier und ihr Fortleben vor allem in römischen und monastischen Ritus*, Liturgiewissenschaftliche Quellen und Forschungen, 32 (Münster, 1957), pp. 134–8.

[123] John of Antioch, *De insidiis*, fg. 110, De Boor, *Excerpta historica*, 3.149.27–150.28; Nicephorus, *Breviarium*, ed. C. De Boor (Leipzig, 1880), 4.19–27. I have been unable to identify the island of Kalonymos. If context is any indication, it may have been off the European suburbs of Constantinople: John of Antioch, *loc. cit.*, 3.149.27–150.6. A.N. Stratos, *Byzantium in the seventh century*, (Amsterdam, 1968), 90 places the event on a ship, deducing this probably from the wording of Nicephorus.

[124] John of Antioch, *loc. cit.*, 150.28–32; Nicephorus, *Brev.*, De Boor 4.27–5.7. Similar treatment was inflicted on the body of Bardas Caesar in the ninth century, and perhaps George Maniaces in the eleventh. On the former, 'Genesius', *Reges*, 4, 23, Lesmüller and Thurn, 75.49–51; Theophanes Continuatus, 4, 41, ed. I. Bekker (Bonn, 1838), 206.13–15.

[125] Nicephorus, *Brev.*, De Boor, 5.3–7; *Chronicon paschale*, Bonn, 700.12–13.

which was likely not the first of his reign.[126] The final victory was officially announced in an *epinikia* letter read to the faithful on Pentecost, the fifteenth of May, from the ambo of the Hagia Sophia.[127] The actual return of the emperor took place in 628 or 629. For the first time since Theodosius I, a Roman emperor was truly returning from the front as an undisputed victor; it is not surprising that the event made a great impression on contemporaries, to judge by the account preserved in Theophanes.[128] The ceremony was staged, once again, outside of the city, at the Hiereia Palace, situated on the Asiatic shore of the Sea of Marmara, south of Chalcedon.[129] In view of the distance from the capital, when Theophanes says that 'everyone' (πάντες) went out to meet the emperor, he must mean everyone who counted in his aristocratic eyes. The initial stages of the celebration therefore took place before a more select audience than if it had occurred in the capital.[130] The junior emperor and the patriarch led the welcoming group. The latter's presence was quite remarkable and must be

---

[126] That an *adventus* ceremony was staged to mark Heraclius' return to the capital from Caesarea is revealed by an incident in George, *Vita Theodori Syceotae (BHG*, 1748), 154, ed. A.J. Festugière, *Vie de Théodore de Sykéon*, 1, Subsidia hagiographica, 48 (Brussels, 1970), 125.55–6, in which a paralyzed *comes* of the Excubitors is sufficiently cured to participate in the welcoming ceremonies (ἐξελθὼν ὑπήντησεν τὸν βασιλέα ὑποστρέφοντα). On the date, cf. comm., *ibid.*, 2, 259. Cf. A.N. Stratos, 'La première campagne de l'empereur Héraclius contre les Perses', *JÖB*, 28 (1979), 63–74, here 65–6. There is no specific reference to the ceremony's triumphal character.

[127] F. Dölger, *Regesten*, no. 192; *Chronicon paschale*, Bonn, 727.15–737.17. Cf. below, Ch. 5, pp. 193ff.

[128] Theophanes, A.M. 6119, De Boor, 327.24–328.10. For 628, Bury, *History . . . to Irene*, 2, 245, n. 1; Stratos, *Byzantium*, 1, 240ff; end of 628 or first weeks of 629: A. Pertusi, *Giorgio di Pisidia, Poemi*, 1, Studia patristica et byzantina, 7 (Ettal, 1959), pp. 230–4. Pertusi's identification of the procession of 1 January with the Persian triumph is only hypothetical (Constantine Porphyrogenitus, *De ceremoniis aulae byzantinae*, 2, 28, ed. J.J. Reiske (Bonn, 1829), 628.21–629.12). In favor of the 629 date, A. Frolow, 'La vraie croix et les expéditions d'Héraclius en Perse', *RÉB*, 11 (1953), 88–104, here 104; cf. G. Ostrogorsky, *Geschichte des byzantinischen Staates*, 3rd edn (Munich, 1968), p. 86.

[129] Theophanes, A.M. 6119, De Boor, 328.1–4. Hiereia Palace was one of Heraclius' preferred spots around the capital: Janin, *Cple byz.*, p. 149; cf. pp. 498–9.

[130] The polyvalent concept of λαός in Theophanes would reward a careful study. Cf. below, Ch. 5, n. 27 for an evaluation of one usage. On officials greeting a returning emperor at Hiereia, see the imperial *adventus* memorandum, preserved among the documents appended to Constantine Porphyrogenitus, *On Imperial Expeditions*, Reiske, 495.1–497.13, here 497.3–7. The document is dated to Justinian's reign by

attributed to Sergius' extraordinary role in Heraclius' administration.[131] Constantine III performed the *proskynesis* and embraced
his father, while well-wishers from the city ceased their acclamations and broke into a hymn of thanksgiving. This last act
indicates that the influence of liturgical processions on the old
secular ceremonies of the Roman state was becoming increasingly
pronounced in the seventh century. An escort honored the
emperor with olive branches and lamps.[132] In the capital itself, the
emperor trumpeted his success in customary fashion by parading
captured elephants through the Hippodrome, offering races and
many benefactions – including an annual payment to the Great
Church – during a victory festival which lasted several days.[133]

The era which followed Heraclius' death and experienced the
extraordinary expansion of Islam is exceedingly poor in Byzantine
narrative sources, the mainstay of historians of ceremonial.
Although it may be suspected on the analogy of Adrianople and
the sack of Rome that what minor successes there might have been
were all the more intensely celebrated for the empire's desperate
situation, there is little evidence for them. As a later emperor
would muse, those were times which, so far as Byzantine
historians were concerned, were better consigned to silence.[134]

J.B. Bury, 'The Ceremonial Book of Constantine VII Porphyrogennetus', *English Historical Review*, 22 (1907), 209–27, 417–39, here 439, n. 57.

[131] Theophanes, A.M. 6119, De Boor, 328.4–5. On Sergius' extraordinary role in Heraclius' reign: J.L. Van Dieten, *Geschichte der Patriarchen von Sergios I. bis Johannes VI. (610–715)*, Geschichte der griechischen Patriarchen von Konstantinopel, 4 (Amsterdam, 1972), pp. 3ff and pp. 52ff. On the customary deference of the emperor *vis à vis* the patriarch, O. Treitinger, *Die oströmische Kaiser- und Reichsidee nach ihrer Gestaltung im höfischen Zeremoniell* (Jena, 1938), p. 221. The only other instance in all the triumphal entries we have uncovered down through the eleventh century occurs in the reign of John I Tzimisces.

[132] Theophanes, A.M. 6119, De Boor, 328.2–8. On the use of lamps in imperial ceremonies: J. Gagé, 'Fackel (Kerze)', *RAC*, 7 (1969).154–217, here 180–6.

[133] Nicephorus, *Brev.*, De Boor, 22.20–2; J. Kollwitz, *Plastik*, p. 66, and J. Deér, *Byzanz und das abendländische Herrschertum. Ausgewählte Aufsätze*, Vorträge und Forschungen, 21 (Sigmaringen, 1977), p. 23, both maintain on the basis of this text that Heraclius celebrated a triumphal entry in a chariot drawn by four elephants. This enticing error goes back to Denis Petau's Latin translation of Nicephorus: M. McCormick, *Revue d'histoire ecclésiastique*, 74 (1979), 446.

[134] Constantine Porphyrogenitus, *De administrando imperio*, 21, 31–5, ed. and tr. G. Moravcsik and R.J.H. Jenkins, Dumbarton Oaks Texts, 1, 2nd edn (Washington,

Three quarters of a century pass before another secular celebration is recorded, and that one marks a return to victory observances over internal enemies. On 15 February 706, Justinian II heralded his restoration by parading his rivals, decked in chains, through the streets of Constantinople.[135] Before the races marking his victory, he had the same unfortunates dragged through the Hippodrome and up to his throne, where he trampled each former emperor's neck and the people (δῆμος) intoned – very appropriately, considering his enemies' names – 'You will tread on the lion and the adder, the young lion and the serpent you will trample under foot' (Psalm 90, 13ff).[136] Justinian kept his defeated rivals pinned in this humiliating position all through the first race, after which they were sent to the Kynegion for execution.[137] But the emperor himself would soon experience the vicissitudes of fortune. In 711 he was toppled from the throne a second time. His severed head was carried to the new emperor Philippicus in Constantinople.[138] From there it was sent to the western provinces, which had suffered particularly from Justinian's reprisals at his restoration. After celebrations in Ravenna, the token of defeat was conveyed to Rome.[139]

No one has yet attempted to determine when the ancient state calendar of the Roman empire was finally scrapped. As regards

---

D.C., 1967), 86: Τοῦτο δὲ παρὰ τοῖς ἡμετέροις ἱστορικοῖς οὐ γέγραπται, speaking about the Islamic invasion of Spain and the gradual truncation of the Roman empire from the Goths on. The tradition of conveying the heads of usurpers to the capital continued through the seventh century, although no known text illustrates the celebrations which may have occurred at their arrival. On the usurper and former Exarch of Italy Eleutherius (619), see *Liber pontificalis*, ed. T. Mommsen, *MGH. Gesta pontificum Romanorum* (1898), 168.9–13; cf. Paul Deacon, *Historia Langobardorum*, 4, 3, ed. G. Waitz, *MGH.SRL* (1878), 128.1–5. On the usurper Mezezius and the officials who sided with him, *Liber pontificalis*, Mommsen, 190.6–10. On these uprisings, P. Classen, 'Der erste Römerzug in der Weltgeschichte. Zur Geschichte des Kaisertums im Westen und der Kaiserkrönung in Rom zwischen Theodosius d. Gr. und Karl d. Gr.', *Historische Forschungen für Walter Schlesinger* (Cologne, 1975), pp. 325–47.

135 Theophanes, A.M. 6198, De Boor, 375.6–8. On the date: C. Head, *Justinian II of Byzantium* (Madison, 1972), p. 116.
136 Theophanes, A.M. 6198, De Boor, 375.8–12.
137 Nicephorus, *Brev.*, De Boor, 42.18–19; cf. Theophanes, *loc. cit.*, 375.12–13. On the Kynegion, Janin, *Cple byz.*, p. 376.
138 Nicephorus, *Brev.*, De Boor, 48.11–22.   139 See below, Ch. 6, n. 19.

public commemorative holidays for imperial victories, the last clear reference to the antique system comes in the sixth century.[140] It is quite possible that these holidays were in a state of decadence in the seventh: it is difficult to imagine how a government which suppressed the capital's public bread distributions under the dire pressures of the early seventh century would have financed public holidays for victories of emperors and dynasties which were long since dead.[141] One positive factor which may have contributed to their decadence was the emergence of a new kind of victory commemoration, more in keeping with the spirit of the age.

In the upheavals of the sixth and seventh centuries, late Roman society increasingly sought in supernatural defenses a psychological cushion against the catastrophic events which besieged their civilization.[142] In the hundred years from the 'Avar surprise' to the reign of Leo III, the capital itself would experience major barbarian menaces four times. The supernatural defense of the city, not to mention the morale of its population, was maintained

[140] Procopius, *Bella*, 3, 4, 16, Haury, 1.327.3–7.
[141] Perhaps one of the latest references to a late antique victory anniversary comes in Ps. Sophronius, *Vita Cyri et Ioannis*, 12–14 (*BHG*, 469), *PG*, 87.3.3677–89, here 3685B–8B. Although the date of this text is unclear, it clearly antedates the Islamic conquest of Alexandria. It describes the miraculous power of a turban (μαφόριον) sent to Theodosius I by an Egyptian ascetic, commemorated every year by a public festival called Εἰκόνιον in Alexandria, in which Theodosius' portrait was carried through the city in a parade. If indeed the festival commemorated one of Theodosius' victories, its memory had already grown quite vague: the war involved only 'barbarians' of the 'West' (c. 12, 3685B–C and c. 14, 3687B): cf. Ph. Koukoules, Βυζαντινῶν βίος καὶ πολιτισμός, 2, 1 (Athens, 1948), 44. The old imperial anniversary appears to be more or less subsumed into the celebration of a local holy man's miracle, indicating the kinds of factors which may have been at work to preserve some relics of the old state calendar. The council *in Trullo* (A.D. 691), 62, ed. P.P. Joannou, *Discipline générale antique*, 1.1 (Grottaferrata, 1962), 198.10–200.3, attempted to end paganizing celebrations associated with the old festivals of the *Kalendae*, the Vota and the Brumalia. It is not clear, however, to what extent this measure is relevant to the old state holidays, since the council was obviously aiming at popular observances, and the Vota and Brumalia continued to be celebrated by the palace as late as the tenth century.
[142] N.H. Baynes, 'The supernatural defenders of Constantinople', *AB*, 67 (1949), 165–77, esp. 166: 'This sense of supernatural support must surely have had a profound psychological significance.' Cf. Av. Cameron, 'Images of authority. Elites and icons in late sixth-century Byzantium', *Past and Present*, 84 (1979), 3–35, and P. Goubert, 'Religion et superstitions dans l'armée byzantine à la fin du VIᵉ siècle', *Orientalia christiana periodica*, 13 (1947), 495–500.

with the usual litanies, relic ostentations and services of supplication. What is most remarkable about the four deliverances of
the capital is that, for the first time on record, the patriarch of
Constantinople anchored these events in the collective consciousness of generations to come and in the local cults of the Virgin,
thanks to processions staged every year to commemorate the city's
liberations. The delivery from the Avar surprise, usually dated
617, was still commemorated in the tenth century by a procession
which led from the Hagia Sophia, through the Forum of
Constantine and out the Golden Gate, all the way to the Tribunal
on the Campus Martius of the Hebdomon Palace complex. There,
the eucharistic liturgy was celebrated in the church of John the
Baptist.[143] This ceremony was quite likely an annual reenactment
of a thanksgiving procession performed after the Avar retreat, on
the model of those witnessed, for example, under emperor
Anastasius I. It would have corresponded to the dramatic rituals of
supplication which Heraclius and his trusted supporter, patriarch
Sergius, had organized during the attack itself, at the church of the
Virgin-Jerusalem, just inside the Golden Gate.[144]

The danger of 617 pales in comparison with the gravity of the
capital's situation during the combined Avar and Persian siege
of 626.[145] The Avars' withdrawal was greeted with what appears
to be a kind of spontaneous victory service. According to a
contemporary witness, the patrician Bonus, entrusted with the

[143] For the anniversary of 5 June, *Synaxarium Constantinopolitanum, AASS, Novembris,
Propylaeum* (1902), 729.30–731.5. The procession is described in J. Mateos, *Le
Typicon de la Grande Église*, 1, Orientalia christiana analecta, 165 (Rome, 1962),
306–8. Cf. V. Vasil'evsky, 'Avary, a ne Russkie, Feodor, a ne Georgy', *VV*, 3
(1896), 83–95, and V. Grumel, *Les actes des patriarches*, 1, 1, 2nd edn (Paris, 1972), no.
279. The traditional date was established by N.H. Baynes, 'The date of the Avar
surprise. A chronological study', *BZ*, 21 (1912), 110–28; cf. Ostrogorsky,
Geschichte, p. 79.

[144] On the supplication rites during the attack, see the contemporary description of the
Inventio et depositio vestis B.V.M. in Blachernis (BHG, 1058), ed. C. Loparev, 'Staroe
svidetel'stvo o polozhenii rizy Bogorodichy vo Vlakhernakh v novom istolkovdnii
pritenimel'no k nashestviyu Russkikh na Vizantiyu v 860 godu', *VV*, 2 (1895),
581–628, here 594–5. Against the attribution of this work and *BHG*, 1061 to
'Theodore Syncellus', see H.G. Beck, *Kirche und theologische Literatur im byzantinischen Reich*, Handbuch der Altertumswissenschaft, 12, 2, 1 (Munich, 1959), p. 545.

[145] See in general, F. Barišič, 'Le siège de Constantinople par les Avares et les Slaves en
626', *Byz.*, 24 (1954), 371–95.

administration of the capital in Heraclius' absence, the patriarch and a crowd of citizens went out in front of the Golden Gate and offered up immediate thanksgiving prayers at the sight of the retreating barbarians.[146] Shortly thereafter, a more formal ceremony was organized, in which the junior emperor and the patriarch conducted a procession out of the city to the shrine of the Virgin of Blachernae.[147] The devotion to the Virgin and the appeal to her relics which marked both sieges played a key role in the crystallization of the capital's special cult of Mary, the source of Roman victory.[148] It may have been precisely at this time that the famous Akathistos Hymn was adopted as the classic Byzantine victory ode to the Virgin.[149] According to a liturgical tradition which has found acceptance among scholars, this thanksgiving service included an all-night vigil, during which the Akathistos was sung before a standing congregation.[150] In fact, an all-night vigil fits well with what we have seen of victory celebrations in the late sixth century. Probably as soon as the next year, the event was commemorated by a reenactment of the thanksgiving procession, involving litanic supplications with popular participation and culminating in a eucharistic service at the shrine of the Virgin of Blachernae.[151] According to the liturgical tradition already cited, the Arab sieges of 674–8 and 717–18 witnessed similar ceremonies, including the performance of the Akathistos.[152] At any rate, these

---

[146] *Narratio antiquior miraculi B.V.M. in obsidione* (*BHG*, 1061), 21, ed. L. Sternbach, *Analecta Avarica* (Cracow, 1900), 16.39–17.4.

[147] Nicephorus, *Brev.*, De Boor, 18.24–7.

[148] This development has been clarified by Av. Cameron, 'The Theotokos in sixth-century Constantinople. A city finds its symbol', *Journal of Theological Studies*, n.s. 29 (1978), 79–108 and 'The Virgin's robe: an episode in the history of early seventh-century Constantinople', *Byz.*, 49 (1979), 42–56.

[149] Thus E. Wellesz, 'The *Akathistos*. A study in Byzantine hymnography', *DOP*, 9–10 (1955–6), 143–74, esp. 145–52.

[150] The account (*BHG*, 1063) is preserved in the *Triodion*, for the Saturday of the fifth week of Lent: *PG*, 92.1348D–53B, here 1352B; cf. C.A. Trypanis, *Fourteen early Byzantine cantica*, Wiener byzantinistische Studien, 5 (Vienna, 1968), p. 20.

[151] This is what I conclude from the insistence on διαπαντός in the *Narratio antiquior*, 28, Sternbach, 24.10–15.

[152] *BHG*, 1063, *PG*, 92.1352C–D; cf. Trypanis, *Cantica*, pp. 20–1. For the later siege, see too the poem celebrating the delivery by Theodosius Grammaticus, ed. S.P. Lampros, Ἱστορικὰ μελετήματα (Athens, 1884), 129–32, on the date of which cf. S. Gero, *Byzantine Iconoclasm during the reign of Leo III, with special attention to the oriental sources*, Corpus scriptorum christianorum orientalium, Subsidia, 41 (Louvain, 1973),

victories were still commemorated in the tenth century, the former by a procession from the Hagia Sophia to Blachernae via the Forum of Constantine, the latter by a *pannychis* and procession from the Great Church, through the Forum, out of the city via the Gate of Attalus and back through the Golden Gate and into the church of the Virgin-Jerusalem.[153]

Was the new style of commemoration derived from earlier, lost victory usages at Constantinople? As early as the fifth century, the bishops of Rome celebrated anniversary services for the delivery of their city from the barbarians, and we do know that other annual processions fell into disuse before the composition of the tenth-century Typicon.[154] Nonetheless, the presence there of processions commemorating natural disasters back into the fifth century, combined with the absence of commemorations of events like the deliverance of the city from Gainas' Goths or the attack of the Kotrigurs in 559 – both of which were amply celebrated by the government – suggests that the extension of liturgical commemoration to victories was indeed, for Constantinople, an innovation of the seventh century.[155] What is more, the period in which this kind of commemoration flourished is precisely the century between the Avar surprise and the Arab siege.[156] All this suggests that events of the late sixth and early seventh century created a unique climate which fostered a new development in the venerable custom of victory commemorations and liturgical processions. The shattered confidence of a

---

p. 172. For a homily which patriarch Germanus himself delivered on one of the early anniversaries, V. Grumel, 'Homélie de Saint Germain sur la délivrance de Constantinople', *RÉB*, 16 (1948), 183–205.

[153] Commemoration: 25 June: *Syn. Cplitanum*, Delehaye, 772.8–16; 16 August: *ibid.*, 901.30–904.27. The processions are described in Mateos, *Typicon*, 1.320.1–24 and 1.372.13–374.26 respectively.

[154] Leo I, *Sermo 84*: 'De celebratione diei qua ab Alarico irrupta est Roma', ed. A. Chavasse, *CCL*, 138A (1973).525–6; R. Janin, 'Les processions religieuses à Byzance', *RÉB*, 24 (1966), 69–88, here 70–1.

[155] Fifth-century disasters still celebrated at Constantinople in the tenth century included the fall of ashes of 472 (Mateos, *Typicon*, 1.90.22–8; cf. Marcellinus Comes, a.472, Mommsen, 90.18–21); and the earthquake of A.D. 480, apparently celebrated in Mateos, *Typicon* (25 October), 1.44.24–46.1. Cf. V. Grumel, *La chronologie*, Traité d'études byzantines, 1 (Paris, 1958), p. 478.

[156] These are the only such processions reported by Janin, 'Processions'.

besieged population was transferred, at least temporarily, from imperial invincibility to the victory-giving Virgin.[157]

CONCLUSION

After a rapid review of the facts, it is clear that our understanding of late antique victory celebrations is due for revision. Quantitatively, their number far surpasses what previous studies have suggested. The true measure of the resurgence of imperial victory festivals in the Christian Roman empire emerges only from a comparison with what went before. The best available study of classical celebrations down to the fourth century counts only eight triumphal galas between A.D. 150 and 306.[158] Even if we were to double that number to allow for gaps in Barini's results and the less abundant evidence of the earlier period, the comparison with the century and a half following Constantine's accession is telling. Documented victory celebrations under the new empire numbered nearly twice as many in the same period of time: twenty-seven. The establishment of the Christian Roman empire entailed a decisive increase in triumphal ceremonies, a kind of renaissance of triumph.

Qualitatively, it is equally clear that the notion of a substantially unchanging 'Byzantine' ceremony must be jettisoned. There is no such thing as a 'typical' late Roman or Byzantine triumph ceremony. Emphasis shifts from triumphal parades through the city to parades through the Hippodrome, from beast spectacles to horse races, from grandiose mass demonstrations to more secluded,

---

157   It is interesting to note that the Synaxary of the tenth century does not appear to have commemorations relating to sieges of the recent past, for example, Krum's attacks on Constantinople in 813 and 814, the siege of Thomas the Slav in 821–2, the Russian attack of 860 (see below) or the attacks of Symeon of Bulgaria in 913 and 924. The Synaxary's notice for 25 June τῶν Σαρακηνῶν καὶ τῶν 'Ροῦν ἡ ἔλευσις. καὶ λιτὴ ἐν Βλαχέρναις. occurs only in the MS Patmos, John Theologos, 266 (s.X): *Syn. Cplitanum*, Delehaye, 769.41–2. Even if 'Ροῦν does mean 'Ρῶς, this could well be the exception that proves the rule, because the anniversary commemoration appears to have been joined to the preexistent one for the Arab siege. Against H. Grégoire and P. Orgels, 'Les invasions russes dans le Synaxaire de Constantinople', *Byz.*, 24 (1954), 141–5, see C. Mango, *The Homilies of Photius, Patriarch of Constantinople*, Dumbarton Oaks Studies, 3 (Washington, D.C., 1958), p. 81, n. 27.

158   C. Barini, *Triumphalia. Imprese ed onori militari durante l'impero romano* (Turin, 1952), pp. 203–4.

aristocratic gatherings, from celebrations over internal enemies to those over external ones. And, the direction of change
is not irreversible. The steady progress of Christian elements is
unmistakable. As new rites appear, old ones fall away. Triumphal
arches disappear after the fifth century, triumphal columns
somewhat later.[159] The issue of special gold ceremonial multiples
or medallions comes practically to a close.[160] The timing of
celebrations does not appear to have any clear relation with the
stage of an emperor's reign (e.g., many more celebrations early
on); it does display irrefutable – if surprising – links with the
decline of imperial military fortunes. Victory ceremonies cannot
be viewed as agents of historical change. They must, however, be
recognized as symptoms of change. Against the general backdrop
of the historical trends in their development, we may now turn to
the problem of certain specific celebrations and their impact on the
public life of the late antique state.

---

[159] Thus Justinian's reconstruction of Theodosius' column in the Augustaeum: Janin,
Cple byz., pp. 74–6.
[160] P. Grierson, *Catalogue of the Byzantine coins in the Dumbarton Oaks Collection and in
the Whittemore Collection*, 2, 1 (Washington, D.C., 1968), 9.

3

Imperial victory celebrations and the public life of the later Roman state

Although a rapid review of all known imperial victory celebrations and their essential characteristics has yielded a clearer picture of the broad trends and stages of their development, it is far from exhausting the evidence which specific celebrations provide on particular moments in the life of the later Roman monarchy and its public display. For the historian of late antique ritual, it is important to clarify the precise ceremonial content of celebrations at Rome and to address the thorny question of what relation these rituals bore to developments outside the *Urbs*. For the historian of religion and the imperial idea, the connection between the emperors' new theology and military success would seem implicit in a slogan like 'By this sign conquer!' and the stories attached to it. Yet the positive contribution of Christianity to victory celebrations was anything but swift and obvious. For the historian of late Roman government, an analysis of specific ceremonial events can shed light on the practice and propaganda of the monarchy and its officers. But first we need to consider one of the more durable myths about late antique victory celebrations, namely that some observances were true triumphs and others were not, particularly insofar as barbarians and usurpers were concerned.

I. USURPERS AND BARBARIANS

With disarming confidence, modern historians have not infrequently pronounced a particular victory festival to be a 'real triumph', an 'ovation', or indeed, not a triumph 'in the proper sense', as though the sham of senatorial approval in the preceding century or the old legalistic conditions had any real significance to the authoritarian monarchs and triumphators of the Constantinian empire.[1] One of the most influential contributions to this way of thinking has come from the characterization with which Ammianus Marcellinus opened his oft-cited description of Constantius' triumphal visit to Rome in 357.

While in the East and in Gaul these matters were arranged as well as was possible under the circumstances, Constantius was itching to visit Rome and celebrate without cause a triumph for Roman blood, as though the temple of Janus had been closed and all enemies overthrown after the destruction of Magnentius.[2]

It is clear that in some conservative circles, it remained fashionable to express resentment over the celebration of victories in civil war.[3] Yet it has been observed that this particular judgement and others like it are but another instance of Ammianus' hostility to Constantius and a specific example of his tendency to judge and condemn contemporaries against the presumed standards of the good old days.[4] Even if the evidence were overlooked from the victory celebrations of A.D. 238, it is undeniable that fourth-

---

[1] E.g. Kollwitz, *Plastik*, pp. 64 and 65; cf. above, Ch. 2, n. 30, and next n.

[2] Ammianus Marcellinus, 16, 10, 1–2, Clark, 1. 84.9–17: 'Haec dum per eoas partes et Gallias pro captu temporum disponuntur, Constantius quasi cluso Iani templo stratisque hostibus cunctis, Romam uisere gestiebat, post Magnenti exitium absque nomine ex sanguine Romano triumphaturus. nec enim gentem ullam bella cientem per se superauit, aut uictam fortitudine suorum conperit ducum, uel addidit quaedam imperio, aut usquam in necessitatibus summis, primus uel inter primos est uisus, sed ut pompam nimis extentam, rigentiaque auro uexilla, et pulchritudinem stipatorum ostenderet, agenti tranquillius populo, haec uel simile quicquam uidere, nec speranti umquam nec optanti...'. Among the most useful discussions of this passage for our purposes, see R. Laqueur, 'Das Kaisertum und die Gesellschaft des Reiches', *Probleme der Spätantike. Vorträge auf dem 17. deutschen Historikertag gehalten* (Stuttgart, 1930), pp. 1–38, here 33–6; A. Alföldi, *Die Kontorniaten. Ein verkanntes Propagandamittel der Stadtrömischem Heidnischen Aristokratie in ihrem Kampfe gegen das Christliche Kaisertum*, 1 (Budapest, 1943), 50ff; J.A. Straub, *Vom Herrscherideal in der Spätantike*, Forschungen zur Kirchen- und Geistesgeschichte, 18 (Stuttgart, 1939), pp. 175ff; R. Klein, 'Der Rombesuch des Kaisers Konstantius II. im Jahre 357', *Athenaeum*, n.s. 57 (1979), 98–115, esp. 99ff, according to whom the occasion was both the victory over Magnentius and recent successes against the barbarians; according to MacCormack, *Art and ceremony*, p. 41, 'no triumph took place'.

[3] Thus Claudian, in a speech put in Roma's mouth, laments the fact that imperial triumphs at Rome, in recent memory, had all celebrated civil wars: *VI cons.*, 393–406, Birt 249.

[4] See, e.g. Straub, *Herrscherideal*, pp. 177–82 and 'Konstantins Verzicht auf den Gang zum Kapitol', *Historia*, 4 (1955), 297–313, here 299–300. G. Sabbah, *La méthode*

century emperors had little difficulty celebrating success over rivals.[5] Indeed, it is possible to go even further, for Ammianus' judgement flies in the face of facts: the rituals which have left the widest echo in surviving records are precisely those which trumpeted the fall of usurpers.[6] That this is not due to an accident of source preservation is suggested by the imposing number of commemorative inscriptions and monuments associated with these victories, and comforted by the relatively frequent provincial congratulatory delegations to the victorious emperor.[7] Such a legation was not merely an opportunity to present the traditional golden crown, wish the emperor well and solicit favors for one's hometown and friends. It was also – and perhaps especially – a vital means of assuring the victor of a city's unswerving loyalty, particularly if that loyalty had been compromised during the struggle.[8] In much the same way dedications referring to victories in civil war provided a particularly ostentatious celebration of a locality's loyalty.[9]

As devastating as the barbarian incursions may have been to the particular regions they afflicted, it is easy to forget that they remained a localized phenomenon. Except perhaps for the months and years immediately following Adrianople – when the frequency of victory celebrations over barbarians surged upwards – few fourth-century emperors would have been justi-

---

d'Ammien Marcellin. Recherches sur la construction du discours historique dans les Res gestae (Paris, 1978), pp. 300–8, goes so far as to see in the 'unjustified triumph' a general theme in Ammianus' historical outlook; he thinks that Julian's *Letter to the Athenians* influenced Ammianus' account.

[5] In addition to the celebrations of 325 and 395 discussed in Ch. 2, see below, nn. 15–20.

[6] This is particularly true of the celebrations of 312, 352–7, 388–9, and 394–5.

[7] This seems to be the sense of Nazarius, *XII pan.*, 4, 32, 5, Mynors, 167.22–4 for A.D. 312. On the delegation which included Themistius' panegyric of 357, see Dagron, 'Thémistios', pp. 20–1 and 205–12. Cf. too above, Ch. 2, n. 23. For Theodosius' victory over Maximus, we know of legations from Antioch and Emesus: Libanius, *Ep.* 878, 1, ed. R. Foerster, *Opera*, 11 (Leipzig, 1922). 34.3–5 and *Ep.*, 846, 1, Foerster, 11.6.24–7.2, on which see P. Petit, *Libanius*, pp. 418–19; as well as Alexandria: Socrates, *H.e.*, 6, 2, *PG*, 67.664A-B; cf. Sozomen, *H.e.*, 8, 2, 17, Bidez–Hansen, 352.14–18. For the victory of 394: Ambrose, *Ep.*, 61, 4, *PL*, 16.1237–8. See too following n. and, for the third century, the celebrations of 238, above, Ch. 1.

[8] Thus the presumed legation of Orfitus on behalf of the Senate of Rome after Magnentius' defeat: Chastagnol, *Fastes*, p. 142.

[9] E.g. *ILS*, 688–91, etc. Roman milestones would probably reward a study from this point of view, e.g. *ILS*, 693 or 737.

fied in feeling that the Germanic invasions threatened their throne and the very existence of their empire. An imperial rival, on the other hand, was a more dangerous foe and a deeper threat to a nascent dynasty.[10] The stakes went far beyond the tax revenues of the most prosperous province and called into question the loyalties of millions of citizens, loyalties which were constantly forced into display, tested and sometimes compromised in dozens of details of daily life: during regnal holidays, in liturgical commemorations, in the presence of the imperial portraits, dating a document to a particular consulate and even accepting payment in a particular coin.[11] Politically, then, the need to elicit and provide evidence of unshaken or restored allegiance was particularly acute in the wake of a civil war. It is this need which underlies the extraordinary significance attached to celebrations over imperial rivals in this period: the imperial victory festival rendered manifest the renewed fabric of loyalty between ruler and ruled. What then are we to make of Ammianus' statement? To Roman readers of his own generation, the implicit criticism must have seemed clear and cutting, coming as it did in a work which was published almost contemporaneously with an event which it does not mention: the trip of Theodosius I to Rome to celebrate the destruction of a usurper.[12]

[10] The point is clearly made in quite another context by W. Goffart, 'Rome, Constantinople and the Barbarians', *American Historical Review*, 86 (1981), 275–306, here 282–3 and 295.

[11] The political implication of consular recognitions is amply exploited by T.D. Barnes, *Constantine*, pp. 30ff and *passim*. On coins, *ibid.*, p. 76. On portraits, H. Kruse, *Studien zur offiziellen Geltung des Kaiserbildes im römischen Reiche*, Studien zur Geschichte und Kultur des Altertums, 19, 3 (Paderborn, 1934), pp. 17ff. See in general, below, Ch. 6, 1.

[12] On the date of composition of this section of the *Res gestae*, as well as Ammianus' attitude toward Theodosius, E.A. Thompson, *The historical work of Ammianus Marcellinus* (Cambridge, 1947), pp. 18–19; cf. e.g. R.C. Blockley, *Ammianus Marcellinus. A study of his historiography and political thought*, Collection Latomus, 141 (Brussels, 1975), p. 15. It is probably no coincidence that the epitome of Valerius Maximus, *Facta et dicta memorabilia*, composed by Julius 'Paris' in the late fourth or fifth century (cf. *PLRE*, 1, 667) drops the section of the chapter *De iure triumphandi* (Valerius Maximus, 2, 8, 7, ed. C. Kempf (Leipzig, 1888), 96.18–97.17) which explains that triumphs are not granted for civil wars: Julius Paris, ed. *ibid.*, 496–7. Cf. however the later (?) epitome of Januarius Nepotianus (cf. A. Lippold, *Kleine Pauly*, 4 (1972), 64) in which the section continues to occur, ed. Kempf, *loc. cit.*

2. IMPERIAL VICTORY RITUALS: EVIDENCE FROM ROME

A well-known remark by an eastern observer of the fourth century refers to the eternal city as the 'capital of trophies'.[13] Like most of their contemporaries, the authors of our sources continued to attach to the ancient capital an importance out of all proportion with Rome's real political, strategic or economic significance.[14] This bias is reflected in the evidence, and, while we may decry the negligence of contemporaries in recording details of the far more numerous victory celebrations staged in the empire's new capitals, we cannot afford to overlook the valuable information associated with the visits to Rome by Constantine I, Constantius II, Theodosius I, and Honorius.

Contemporaries viewed all these visits as comprising victory celebrations. Ironically, the most immediately obvious consecration of a victory is the one visit which has the least claim to official recognition of its triumphal character. From the name of the state holiday which continued to mark the event four decades later, it is manifest that Constantine's entry into Rome in 312 was commemorated as an *adventus*, even though the triumphal arch erected to honor the event is called an 'arcus triumphis insignis'.[15] It is just as clear that contemporaries associated with the prince had little trouble touting the defeat of a Roman army as suitable material for a victory celebration, for that is how they presented the events of 28 October 312.[16] That Constantius' *vicennalia* festivities in 357 entailed a victory celebration is patent from

---

[13] Themistius, *Or.*, 3, 42b, ed. Schenkl–Downey, 1.60.15.

[14] See e.g. Paschoud, *Roma aeterna*, pp. 9ff, 159ff, etc., and on Greek authors, J. Palm, *Rom, Römertum und Imperium in der griechischen Literatur der Kaiserzeit*, Acta regiae societatis humaniorum litterarum Lundensis, 57 (Lund, 1959), pp. 84ff.

[15] *Chronographus a. 354*, De Grassi, 257, where 28 October is designated *Evictio tyranni* and 29 October, *Adventus Divi*, and celebrated with 24 races; cf. comm., *ibid.*, 527. It is worth noting, however, that the defeat of Licinius is commemorated in the same place with *Ludi triumphales*: 18 September, *ibid.*, 255; cf. 510–11. For the inscription on the Arch of Constantine: *ILS*, 694.

[16] Thus Eusebius, *H.e.*, 9, 9, 9, Schwartz, 2.830.23–4, ἐπὶ Ῥώμης μετ' ἐπινικίων εἰσήλαυνεν (cf. Rufinus' translation, Mommsen, *ibid.*, 831.17–18: 'urbem Romam triumphaturus ingreditur'); cf. Eusebius, *V. Constantini*, 1, 39, 1, Winkelmann, 36.3; Nazarius, *XII pan.*, 4 (10), 30, 5, 31, 1–2, and 32, 1, Mynors, 166.14–17, 166.18–25 and 167.11–12. Note that a year after the event, the anonymous panegyrist applies the term to the ridicule inflicted on Maxentius' head: *ioci triumphales*, *XII pan.*, 12 (9), 18, 3, Mynors, 284.22.

Ammianus' polemic; Themistius too states outright that Constantinople was not jealous of the emperor's decision to celebrate the victory festival in old Rome before doing so in the new one. His contemporary testimony is seconded by the inscription of the obelisk erected in the Circus Maximus at Constantius' command.[17] The timing of Theodosius' trip to coincide with the first anniversary of Maximus' final defeat – a state holiday in its own right – in itself suggests that the visit of 389 included victory observances. The suggestion is borne out by explicit contemporary evidence.[18] Finally, the association of Stilicho's Gothic victories with Honorius' visit to Rome to assume the consulate in 403–4 is equally distinct.[19]

Descriptions of the four events focus on the ceremonial entry and triumphal parade; only passing allusion is made to the spectacles and other activities which accompanied the visits. This is in line with both earlier tradition and the contemporary situation, in that visits by the emperor to Rome had become so rare and observances surrounding an emperor's arrival in any city had grown into one of the great state ceremonies of late antiquity.[20] It is worthwhile to define the common characteristics of these celebrations.

On one occasion, the victory was announced shortly before the ceremony but the report was not believed until Maxentius' head was held high for all to see.[21] When circumstances permitted, the preparations for the ceremony must have been costly and time-consuming.[22] To the man in the street, their most obvious

[17] Above, n. 2; Themistius, *Or.*, 3, Schenkl–Downey 1.60.26–61.3; *ILS*, 736.1–4 and 20–4, as well as the later evidence of Sozomen, *H.e.*, 4, 8, 1, Bidez–Hansen, 147.7ff.
[18] Pacatus, *XII pan.*, 2 (12), 46, 1, Mynors, 119.24–5; cf. Rufinus, *H.e.*, 11, 17, Mommsen, 2.1022.16–17 and Socrates, *H.e.*, 5, 14, *PG*, 67.601A and Sozomen, *H.e.*, 7, 14, 7, Bidez–Hansen 319.13–16.
[19] Thus Prudentius, *Contra Symmachum*, 2, 721–8, ed. M.P. Cunningham, *CCL*, 126 (1966), 236 and Claudian, *VI cons.*, 580, Birt, 256 and esp. 395–6, p. 249. Cf. Stein, *Bas-Empire*, 1, 248–9; E. Demougeot, *De l'unité*, pp. 286–7 and Cameron, *Claudian*, pp. 180–1.
[20] MacCormack, *Art and ceremony*, pp. 18ff and 39ff.
[21] Thus Zosimus, *Hist. nova*, 2, 17, 1, Paschoud, 1.88.29–89.1.
[22] In 312, Constantine probably found the city already decorated, since Maxentius had just celebrated his regnal anniversary: *RIC*, 6, 16ff. Theophanes, A.M. 5802, De Boor, 1.14.11–15 does however claim that the Romans decorated their city for the ceremony. According to Ammianus Marcellinus, 16, 10, 4, Clark, 1.85.1, the

element would have been the festive decking out of the city's avenues with flowers, tapestries and precious objects, the *coronatio urbis*.[23] The area of approach used by the imperial party is unambiguous only for the ceremonies of 312 and 404. Claudian's description of the latter shows welcoming crowds stretched out to the Milvian Bridge and situates it along the Via Flaminia.[24] The site of the battle of the Milvian Bridge along with the Arch of Constantine's depiction of the entry at the Arch of Domitian on the Campus Martius (cf. fig. 1, p. 38), as well as what is known of Constantius' itinerary, imply that the same route was followed in 312 and 357.[25] This suggests that the parades passed through the Campus Martius and presumably, down the Via lata to the Forum.[26]

Outside the city, the imperial party was met by the Senate of Rome, distinguished officials and the people. Only in the case of Constantine do we actually hear of a senatorial escort into Rome. Honorius refused to allow the senators to precede his chariot.[27] The imperial segment of the parade possessed a distinctly military character, since the emperor himself was surrounded by an escort of sumptuously uniformed heavy cavalry; in 403–4 they wore

---

preparations for Constantius' triumphal *adventus* were extensive and expensive. On this aspect of victory celebrations, see Ch. 5.

[23] Prudentius, *Contra Symmachum*, 2, 726–8, Cunningham, 236. Cf. below, Ch. 5, pp. 205ff.

[24] Claudian, *VI cons.*, 534–46, Birt, 254.

[25] On the identification of the topographical details of the Constantine relief: L'Orange–von Gerkan, *Bildschmuck*, pp. 77–80. On Constantius' approach via Ocriculum, Ammianus, 16, 10, 4, Clark, 1.85.1–4; cf. G. Radke, 'Viae publicae romanae', *RE*, S. 13 (1973), 1417–1686, here 1549ff.

[26] Cf. Platner–Ashby, *Dictionary*, pp. 230ff and 564.

[27] Lactantius, *De mort. pers.*, 44, 10, Moreau, 1.127.34–6; *XII pan.*, 12 (9), 19, 1, Mynors, 284.26–8; Nazarius, *XII pan.*, 4 (10), 31, 1, Mynors, 166.18–19; Eusebius, *H.e.*, 9, 9, 9, Schwartz, 830.23–832.3. Constantius was met near the city and welcomed by the Senate, some of whose members displayed effigies of their patrician ancestors: Ammianus Marcellinus, 16, 10, 5, Clark, 1.85.4–7; Claudian, *VI cons.*, 554–9, Birt, 254–5, claims that Honorius' gesture showed him to be a citizen rather than a lord, thus fulfilling expectations of imperial deportment during visits to Rome (cf. Cameron, *Claudian*, pp. 382–3). Unless this means that he granted them precedence by preceding them, the ceremonial content of this gesture is not clear; certainly late antiquity identified the act of walking immediately in front of a riding ruler with the humiliation of a captive: thus Attalus' position in the triumph of 416, above, Ch. 2, p. 57, or the humiliation inflicted on Galla Placidia by king Segeric in 415 (*PLRE*, 2, 987): Olympiodorus, fg. 26, apud Photius, *Bibliotheca*, cod. 80, Henry, 1.176.17–20.

gilded armor and scarlet silk uniforms.[28] Like the highly visible
imperial purple, this combination of colors would have greatly
aided onlookers in picking out the imperial party in the long
cortege.[29]

In 312, the nature of the victory being celebrated was
unmistakably identified by Maxentius' head, carried high on a
lance. As the gruesome spectacle passed by, it was subjected to
abuse, to political horse-play and to mock acclamations, allowing
the population to deliver itself of the very different behavior they
must have exhibited to their dead ruler but hours earlier.[30] In 388,
the imperial party was preceded by hand-carried floats (*fercula*),
which probably followed the tradition in vigor down to the
beginning of the century and offered displays relating to Theodosius' victories. One contemporary description of these floats
mentions pictures of captured cities and signs identifying the
defeated enemies.[31]

In keeping with the new symbolism of autocracy, the later
Roman emperor rode seated in a triumphal vehicle worked with
gold and decorated with jewels. Most descriptions use the
traditional word *currus*, but the relief of the Arch of Constantine
(fig. 1, p. 38) and Ammianus Marcellinus prove that a four-
wheeled vehicle, a *carpentum*, was now standard.[32] Tradition
expected that the emperors' rare visits to Rome be enlivened by a
few odd gestures of his civility, a living archaism, harkening back

[28] Ammianus Marcellinus, 16, 10, 6–8, Clark, 1.85.7–22; Claudian, *VI cons.*, 564–77, Birt, 255.
[29] This technical reason for the great value attached to purple in periods of ceremonial development is often overlooked. It must have been so obvious to the everyday experience of late antique ritual that contemporaries rarely refer to it: Cassiodorus, *Variae*, 1, 2, 2, ed. Å. Fridh, *CCL*, 96 (1973). 10.13–16.
[30] *XII pan.*, 12 (9), 18, 3, Mynors, 284.21–3 and 19, 1, 284.24; Nazarius, *XII pan.*, 4 (10), 31, 5, Mynors, 167.7–8. Cf. the role of the usurper's head in the observances of A.D. 238.
[31] Pacatus, *XII pan.*, 2 (12), 47, 3, Mynors, 120.6–7. Cf. the description of such floats in Ambrose of Milan's comparison of Christ's *via dolorosa* to a triumphal procession: *Expositio euangelii secundum Lucam*, 10, 109–11, ed. M. Adriaen, *CCL*, 14.4 (1957). 376.1019–377.1054, based on sermons delivered in 377–8 (Adriaen, p. vii).
[32] Ammianus Marcellinus, 10, 16, 6, Clark, 1.85.10–12; Claudian, *VI cons.*, 551 and 579, Birt, 254 and 255; Prudentius, *Contra Symmachum*, 2, 731, Cunningham, 236. On imperial vehicles, see W. Weber, 'Die Reliquienprozession auf der Elfenbeintafel des Trierer Domschatzes und das kaiserliche Hofzeremoniell', *Trierer Zeitschrift für Geschichte und Kunst des Trierer Landes*, 42 (1979), 135–51, here 140–7.

to the days of the first citizen.[33] Even Constantius, whose rigid hieratic posture throughout the parade has become practically a *topos* among modern writers on the fourth-century monarchy, condescended to throw some crumbs of consideration to the Roman crowd during the games.[34] Theodosius I actually stepped down from his carriage and walked a ways. Thanks to a contemporary exegesis of this symbolic gesture, we know that it was meant to convey to onlookers Theodosius' mastery of a contemporary ideal: the emperor triumphs in his personal, ethical conduct as much as in his military practice.[35] A similar construction was placed on Honorius' treatment of the Senate during his parade.[36] Clearly, contemporary witnesses pinned more and more significance on such ceremonial details, even as they became rarer and rarer.

The triumphal parade halted in the Forum Romanum. Both Constantius and Theodosius paid homage to the city's traditions by addressing the Senate first, in the Curia, and then speaking to a wider assembly of the people from the *rostra*.[37] In 403–4, Honorius seems only to have spoken from the *rostra*, depriving the Senate of the private address traditionally delivered by earlier emperors.[38] If the swelling of senatorial ranks in the late fourth century combined with the small size of the Curia caution against reading too much into this departure from custom, another innovation shows why it had become necessary to ritualize even the emperor's rare demonstrations of civility.[39] The Arch of Constantine's relief of the address from the Tribunal depicts an erect emperor, delivering his harangue on his feet. A century later,

---

[33] Cf. Straub, *Herrscherideal*, pp. 187ff, and MacCormack, *Art and ceremony*, p. 42.

[34] Ammianus Marcellinus, 16, 10, 13–14, Clark, 1.86.12–20.

[35] Pacatus, *XII pan.*, 2 (12), 47, 3, Mynors, 120.6–8.

[36] See above, n. 27.

[37] Ammianus Marcellinus, 16, 10, 13, Clark, 1.86.15: 'adlocutus nobilitatem in curia, populumque ⟨e⟩ tribunali'. Pacatus, *XII pan.*, 2 (12), 47, 3, Mynors, 120.6. Constantine addressed the Senate *in curia*, but it is not clear if he did so as part of the triumphal parade: *XII pan.*, 12 (9), 20, 1–2, Mynors, 285.19–26; cf. the relief referred to below, n. 40.

[38] Claudian, *VI cons.*, 587–94, Birt, 256.

[39] On the increase of the size of the Senate at Rome, A.H.M. Jones, *The later Roman Empire: a social, economic, and administrative survey*, 1 (Norman, 1964), 527, where the size is estimated as comparable to that of Constantinople, i.e. ca. 2,000 members. On the Curia: Platner–Ashby, *Dictionary*, pp. 143ff.

the symbolism of autocracy had so progressed that when Honorius spoke to the nobility of Rome from the same spot, he remained majestically seated in an ivory throne.[40]

The prominence of the Capitoline sacrifices in the triumph ceremonies down to 312 and the muteness of the sources have led to a general consensus among scholars that Constantine avoided this pagan religious act and thereby inaugurated a new era in the public ceremonies of the Roman state. In fact, one of the most striking features of all the accounts of victory celebrations held at Rome is their religious neutrality, a trend which, for the later decades of the fourth century at least, is at odds with developments outside the ancient capital. The religious ambiguity of victory celebrations at Rome is a significant aspect of the emergence of Christian rituals of victory, and deserves detailed consideration.[41]

After the emperor's address, the last leg of the parade took place. The ruler was escorted along the Via sacra and into the palace, to the applause and acclamations of onlookers.[42] In 312, the emperor wore the military service outfit (fig. 1); nearly a century later, the emperor donned a triumphal *trabea*, a costume which was equally appropriate to the occasion's triumphal and consular character.[43] It is not clear whether the distributions of largess attested in 312 and 389 and intentionally foregone in 403–4 were specifically connected with the victory observances.[44] At any rate, the festivities continued with shows and spectacles in the circus, at which the victorious emperor himself presided.[45] All of

---

[40] Illustrated L'Orange–von Gerkan, *Bildschmuck*, pl. 15a; cf. discussion, pp. 80ff. Claudian, *VI cons.*, 587–96, Birt, 256. This evidence tends to confirm Cameron's analysis of the attitude of Claudian and Stilicho toward the Senate: *Claudian*, pp. 379ff.

[41] See below, section 4.

[42] Claudian, *VI cons.*, 603–10, Birt, 256–7; cf. *XII pan.*, 12 (9), 19, 3, Mynors, 285.4–7; Ammianus Marcellinus, 16, 10, 13, Clark, 1.86.15–16.

[43] For 312, cf. L'Orange–von Gerkan, *Bildschmuck*, pp. 74–5. Cf. Claudian, *VI cons.*, 561–4, Birt, 255. On the *trabea triumphalis*, above, Ch. 2, n. 106.

[44] For 388: *Cons. Cplitana*, a. 389, Mommsen, 245; Marcellinus Comes, a. 389, Mommsen, 62.14–15; cf. *RIC*, 9, 132, no. 160, and pp. 112–13, for coinage possibly connected with the *congiarium*. For the omission of largess in 403–4, Claudian, *VI cons.*, 603–10, Birt, 256–7; cf. Cameron, *Claudian*, pp. 384–5. The distribution of largess is depicted on the Arch of Constantine: L'Orange–von Gerkan, *Bildschmuck*, pl. 17; cf. comm. pp. 89ff.

[45] 312: *XII pan.*, 12 (9), 9, 6, Mynors, 285.12–14; 357: Ammianus Marcellinus, 16, 10,

the ceremonies were important enough to receive lasting commemoration in monumental form: the Arch of Constantine, the
Obelisk of the Circus Maximus, statues to the *Extinctor tyrannorum*
and, for Honorius, the raising of the last triumphal arch in Roman
history.[46]

Comparison of the content of fourth-century victory celebrations at Rome with those of the principate reveals fundamental continuity coupled with highly significant innovation.
Many major elements of the ceremony of A.D. 71 are indeed
present: a ceremonial entry and welcome, a victory parade, games
and commemorative monuments. The fact that fourth-century
triumphal parades appear to have unfolded in approximately the
same urban theater and followed roughly the same itinerary must
have been a powerful factor working for superficial continuity.
In its flexible scheduling and combination with other ritual observances, however, the late antique ceremony showed its indebted-
ness to the third century. Its unique character is now underscored
by three main developments. The late antique ceremony accentuated imperial majesty. Now the triumphator entered Rome
seated; by 404 he addressed the city's elite from the same posture.
The gap between ruler and ruled was now so wide that even
imperial displays of civility were becoming ritualized and staged.
Secondly, the ceremony's military character had become more
pronounced. Due to the fusion of the emperor's ceremonial entry
or *adventus* with the triumphal parade, the ceremony no longer
began in the Campus Martius area, but at a greater distance from
the city, where Senate and people welcomed the ruler. Gone was
the distinction between the specifically military and civil phases of
the ceremony, symbolized by the emperor's dress and symbolic
gestures. The whole parade had now taken on a more military
character, in keeping with the progressive militarization of society
at work in the fourth century. Just as the ceremony began in a
different way and in a different place, so the topographical climax
of the parade shifted slightly to the East. In the third characteristic
development, the procession skirted the Capitol, ignored the

13–14, Clark, 1.86.16–20; no information for 388; 403–4, Claudian, *VI cons.*,
611–39, Birt, 257–8.
[46] Cf. above, Ch. 2, nn. 7, 23, 42, and 69. On Honorius' arch, cf. too below, nn. 168–9.

Temple of Jupiter and stopped at the Forum, thereby enhancing the ceremony's religious ambiguity. While the largely pagan Senate endured the abandonment of the imperial sacrifice to Jupiter, the decision to make the Curia the new focal point of the celebration could only have caressed senatorial self-awareness and help ward off senatorial disaffection with the new order. The new importance of the ceremony's senatorial stage coheres well with the policy of Constantine I and his successors toward the imperial Senate.[47]

3. IMPERIAL VICTORY RITUALS: NON-ROMAN EVIDENCE

Thanks to the detail of their descriptions and their familiarity to scholars, the four great ceremonies at Rome have dominated the modern image of victory celebrations in the fourth and fifth centuries.[48] Yet they constitute less than a quarter of the total number of celebrations securely attested in this period. Developments outside the ancient city's tradition-bound atmosphere provide complementary insight into the ceremony's evolution in the fourth century.

There is some evidence to suggest that the triumphal entry remained the most outstanding facet of imperial victory celebrations in several other performances. For example, the sparse notices relative to the observances of Constantius II at Sirmium and Theodosius I at Constantinople in 386 hint that the triumphal entry dominated those occasions.[49] The triumphal parade on the Louvre drawing (figs. 2–5, pp. 52–5) provides concordant evidence. But the bulk of surviving testimony points to a growing tendency in another direction.

As early as Constantine's first victory celebrations in his northern capital of Trier, it was the victory spectacles staged in the arena that captured the attention of panegyrist and chronicler alike. Several times early in his reign, Constantine used barbarian captives for gladiatorial games which featured a parade of captives into the arena rather than the triumphal march through the

---

[47] M.T.W. Arnheim, *The senatorial aristocracy in the later Roman empire* (Oxford, 1972), pp. 49ff.
[48] Thus Kollwitz, *Plastik*, pp. 63–5; cf. MacCormack, *Art and ceremony*, pp. 53ff.
[49] Above, Ch. 2, pp. 41 and 42.

capital's streets.[50] That a similar celebration would have been conceivable in mid-century Gaul is implied by Libanius' praise of Julian's decision to forego the pleasure of displaying a prostrate barbarian king to the very citizens he had once menaced.[51] In the second half of the century, victory celebrations in the emperor's absence manifestly hinged on sporting extravaganzas. According to Themistius, every victory bulletin arriving in New Rome was heralded with races.[52] In the West, Symmachus organized a more traditional gladiatorial show and parade of captives for a victory of Valentinian II.[53] The very fact that Constantius raised a victory monument in the Circus Maximus shows that, even in the ancient capital, it was impossible to remain insensitive to the creeping assimilation of imperial military victory and the cult of sporting success. To judge by the scenes of barbarian submission portrayed on the base of the Theodosian Obelisk and a reference to circus celebrations in connection with the Gainas affair, the triumphal entry must have been experiencing serious competition from triumphal circus spectacles by the close of the fourth century.[54]

Constantinople preserved and strengthened this development by staging races and a theater spectacle for western victories in 415 and 416.[55] It is therefore no surprise to find the eastern candidates for the western throne celebrating their victory with a parade in the circus, only ten years later.[56] For the next two centuries, the Hippodrome would be the central scene of nearly all secular celebrations of imperial victory. Does this signify that the new kind of circus victory celebration entirely supplanted the old triumphal entry? One recent study has suggested that, in the fifth century, the imperial *adventus* temporarily disappeared from the customs of the court at Constantinople, due to the residence of the emperors in that city and their failure to participate in campaigns.[57] But the argument from silence is a dangerous one,

[50] Above, Ch. 2, pp. 36ff.   [51] Libanius, *Or.*, 18, 66, Foerster, 2.264.15–18.

[52] Themistius, *Or.*, 4, Schenkl–Downey, 1.82.22–3.

[53] Symmachus, *Rel.*, 47, 1, Seeck, 315.27–316.2.

[54] On the Obelisk reliefs, G. Bruns, *Obelisk*, pp. 40ff; A. Grabar, *L'empereur dans l'art byzantin*, p. 65; Wrede, 'Errichtung', p. 197; Eunapius, *De sententiis*, fg. 72, Boissevain, *Excerpta historica* 4.96.20–97.2.

[55] Above, Ch. 2, pp. 56ff. Cf. below, section 5.   [56] Above, Ch. 2, p. 59–60.

[57] MacCormack, *Art and ceremony*, p. 68.

particularly in eras as poor in detailed records as the fifth century, and a cogent case can be made for the survival of the imperial *adventus* ceremony.[58] We cannot therefore be confident that the triumphal entry entirely disappeared from the Constantinopolitan historical experience until Justinian's triumph of 559. If it did survive, however, its significance was eclipsed by the more popular celebrations staged in conjunction with great sporting events. One possible motive for this shift in emphasis was the decline in drama inherent to a situation in which the emperor routinely entered and left his capital for holidays, but never accompanied the army to the frontier.[59]

How can this transformation of the setting of the imperial victory festival be explained? If the purpose of all imperial ceremonial was ultimately to project a certain image of the monarchy, it followed that the best stage for such projection would be the one most likely to affect significant sectors of the population. As the stupendous growth of American football's popularity attests in our own time, tastes in spectator sports change. Such a change appears to have been at work precisely in

---

[58] One motive alleged for the ceremony's disappearance is that 'Eastern emperors of the fifth century rarely left Constantinople'. While it is true that emperors now avoided direct participation in military campaigns and long tours through the provinces, it cannot be forgotten that the *villeggiatura* life-style of Roman society (e.g. J.P.V.D. Balsdon, *Life and leisure in ancient Rome* (New York, 1969), pp. 196ff) certainly survived among Constantinople's elite, as is evidenced by the development and frequentation of suburban palaces: Janin, *Cple byz.*, pp. 138ff. The strength of the link between imperial parades and imperial sojourns in the suburbs is shown by the semantic shift which accompanied the adoption of Latin *processus* into late Greek, where it means 'imperial trip outside the walls' or 'villeggiatura'. Cf. G.W.H. Lampe, *A Patristic Greek Lexicon* (Oxford, 1961), p. 1153, s.v. πρόκενσος, to which unique attestation may be added a mass of occurrences, including *Chron. pasch.*, Bonn, 702.10–13, 16–18, 19–21; *Vita Danielis stylitae* (BHG, 489), 55 and 65, ed. H. Delehaye, *Les saints stylites*, Subsidia hagiographica, 14 (Brussels, 1923), 54.19 and 64.11; Eustratius, *Vita Eutychii* (BHG, 657), 24 and 66, PG, 86.2301C and 2349A; George, *Vita Theodori Syceotae* (BHG, 1748), 97, Festugière, 79.5–8; cf. Theophanes, A.M. 6289, De Boor, 471.7–8, etc. Particularly noteworthy is the apparent Grecism of Marcellinus Comes, a. 507 and 512, Mommsen 97.1–2 and 98.4, 'in processibus'. Finally, ceremonial entries by emperors are still attested at Constantinople in the first half of the fifth century: see e.g. below, Ch. 5, n. 100. That they were quite familiar to that city's faithful is indicated by the patriarch Proclus' reference to the ceremony, *Homilia 9*, 1–4 (CPG 5808), PG, 65.772B–776D.

[59] Above, Ch. 2, p. 47.

the fourth and fifth centuries, when the eastern regions of the empire became increasingly enamored of Roman-style chariot races.[60] In one sense, then, the shift in the setting of victory celebrations corresponded to an effort to capitalize on developments in popular sporting tastes. These developments must have been clearly recognized and seized upon, for the trend of victory celebrations to coalesce with great sporting events forms but a specific instance of a more general tendency to focus imperial display on the circus. This trend could only have been reinforced by the security problems generated by significant organized movements through the streets of a capital increasingly rife with riot.[61] From this point of view, too, the circus offered clear advantages. While the size of the stadium and the popularity of the bait ensured a large audience for imperial display, its architectural configuration favored 'crowd control', if that is the proper term for the kind of massacre attested during the Nika revolt. Moreover, the strength and situation of the imperial *kathisma* guaranteed the security of the emperor during the shows and provided a safe escape route into the Great Palace.[62] It is thus not surprising that even as solemn an act as the investiture of new emperors shifted to Constantinople's Hippodrome in the second half of the fifth century.[63] So too acts of obvious political impact, like the burning of tax registers under Anastasius I.[64] By the next century, the imperial official in charge of ceremonies could contrast the modern form of imperial investiture, prevalent since the 'invention' of imperial circus rituals, with the 'ancient' one, in use down to the middle of the fifth century.[65] Hand in hand with

---

[60] Thus A. Cameron, *Circus Factions. Blues and Greens at Rome and Byzantium* (Oxford, 1976), pp. 216–18. A thorough study of the late antique circus is a pressing need.

[61] Thus Anastasius is reported to have created precedent by ordering the City Prefect to participate in all processions, in order to ensure public order and his own safety: Theodore Lector, *H.e.*, 469, Hansen, 139.16–19; cf. Theophanes, A.M. 5999, De Boor, 150.1–4.

[62] On these aspects of the Kathisma, R. Guilland, *Topogr.*, 1, 467.

[63] On imperial coronations in the Hippodrome from 473 on: Treitinger, *Oströmische*, pp. 10ff.

[64] Cameron, *Circus*, p. 172.

[65] Constantine VII Porphyrogenitus, *De Cer.*, 1, 91, Bonn, 417.7–9: καὶ ταῦτα [i.e. accession *adventus*] ἡ ἀρχαιότης. νῦν δὲ ἐπενοήθη καὶ ἐν τῷ ἱππικῷ τὰς ἀναγορεύσεις γίνεσθαι. This section is almost certainly drawn from a lost treatise by Peter the Patrician: Stein, *Bas–Empire*, 2, 728 with n. 3.

the new emphasis on circus celebrations, it has been suggested, the imperial government increasingly assumed the expenses of running the circus and its shows.[66] It is clear, at any rate, that in the sixth century, and perhaps as early as the fifth, circus personnel assumed direct responsibility for the details of managing imperial victory shows. Little wonder that a sixth-century strategic thinker could justify this group's positive contribution to society on precisely these grounds.[67]

In the absence of limpid and detailed evidence, it is not easy to give a thorough account of the content of the victory celebrations which were now occurring in the imperial circus; it is, however, possible to piece together the main lines of what must have been their most common elements. In a sense, any circus event in the emperor's presence entailed some non-specific reiteration of victory ideology, thanks to the ubiquitous character of that ideology. Any spectacle staged before the emperor would naturally have begun with an acclamation of greeting to the prince.[68] A common greeting like 'May you conquer, O Augustus!' aptly set the stage for a display of imperial victoriousness.[69] In the first century of the Christian empire, military drills and even mock battles featuring a soldier's salute to the emperor appear to have been popular.[70] Late in the sixth century, Tiberius

---

[66] Thus Cameron, *Circus*, pp. 217ff. Not all the evidence points in the same direction and the problem requires further study: cf. J. Gascou, 'Les institutions de l'Hippodrome en Égypte byzantine', *Bulletin de l'Institut français d'archéologie orientale*, 76 (1976), 185–212.

[67] Anonymus Byzantinus, 3, 15, Köchly and Rüstow, 54. Their responsibility as early as 425 may be inferred from Procopius' reference to the torments inflicted on the defeated usurper John by theater personnel (παρὰ τῶν ἀπὸ σκηνῆς), if that allusion is not based on an anachronistic assumption: *Bella*, 3, 3, 9, Haury, 1.320.7–9.

[68] Thus Claudian, *VI cons.*, 612–17, Birt, 257, provides an early example.

[69] The best example is in the famous 'Circus dialogue' preserved in Theophanes, A.M. 6024, De Boor, 181.34–184.1, here 182.1. On the phrase itself, see Cameron, *Porphyrius*, pp. 77–9 and 248.

[70] Claudian, *VI cons.*, 621–39, Birt, 257–8 and Vegetius, *Epit.*, 2, 23, Lang, 57.5–8. On the general content of circus spectacles see L. Friedländer in J. Marquardt, *Römische Staatsverwaltung* 3, 3rd edn (Darmstadt, 1885), 504ff. Ph. Koukoules, Βυζαντινῶν βίος καὶ πολιτισμός, 2 (Athens, 1949), 7ff. R. Guilland, 'Études sur l'Hippodrome de Byzance. VI. Les spectacles de l'Hippodrome', *BS*, 27 (1966). 289–307, and O. Pasquato, *Gli spettacoli in S. Giovanni Crisostomo. Paganesimo e Cristianesimo ad Antiochia e Costantinopoli nel IV secolo*, Orientalia christiana analecta, 201 (Rome, 1976).

and Maurice reminded the populace of Constantinople of past victories over the Persians by beginning all circus shows with a parade of elephants captured in the East: the beasts were driven into the Hippodrome and up to the imperial box, where, like any vanquished barbarian, they stopped and bowed to the emperor. Then they made the sign of the cross with their trunks. After their performance, the emperor rewarded them with presents and they left the arena, having reminded the audience of past imperial victories and confirmed their late antique belief in pachyderm intelligence.[71]

Shows specifically related to imperial victories, or events construed as such, included offshoots of the *fercula* of the triumphal parade. One occurred during the observances marking the defeat of Gainas, when a City Prefect assembled in the middle of the stadium a lot of tablets showing fleeing barbarians with a hand appearing out of the clouds. To make the message perfectly clear, the pictures included legends like 'The hand of God driving away the barbarians' or 'Barbarians fleeing God'. In the eyes of a pagan like Eunapius such a spectacle deprived the emperors and soldiers of their due and was as stupid as it was vulgar. But then there is no reason to think of Eunapius as a typical racing fan.[72]

General probability and medieval custom suggest that the political element of sporting extravaganzas preceded the actual races themselves, for why would ardent fans hang around when the action was over?[73] Perhaps most commonly, the victory show took the form of a parade. Sometimes the spectacle merely entailed transferring a street spectacle to the arena, as for example in 425 when the brutal parade of infamy and mutilation were inflicted on the usurper John, in the circus at Aquileia.[74] Of the various parades displaying captives, some may have been derived from the gladiators' cortege of antiquity, as in fourth-century victory shows, while others evolved out of the triumphal parade and included a cortege of live rebel leaders or heads on poles, along

---

[71] John of Ephesus, *H.e.*, 3, 2, 48, tr. Brooks, 84.2–13. For the late antique belief in elephants' intelligence: Cassiodorus, *Variae*, 10, 30, 3, Fridh, 412.23–413.31.
[72] Eunapius, *De sententiis*, fg. 72, Boissevain, *Excerpta historica* 4.96.20–97.2. On the problems posed by this account, below, n. 167.
[73] The medieval custom is clear from *De cer.*, 2, 20, Bonn, 615.4–15.
[74] Above, Ch. 2, p. 59–60.

with displays of booty.[75] Captive enemy leaders would be driven to the feet of the emperor, who was enthroned in the imperial box. They would be forced to prostrate themselves before the victorious ruler and, where such an act was appropriate, ritually stripped of their insignia.[76] If the story is reliable, Honorius may well have ritually trampled the vanquished usurper Attalus during such a spectacle.[77] At any rate, Cassiodorus was familiar with this gesture and associated it with victory shows in the circus.[78] Whatever symbolic gestures of victory and defeat may have been in use in the Hippodrome, they must of necessity have been highly visible and easy to grasp, even from a distance, in the absence of modern means of communication and explanation such as are found in today's stadiums.

What was the origin of this ritualized presentation of a defeated enemy leader to the supreme commander of the Roman empire? After a victory and capture of enemy leaders, it had been a common custom in the army to present them to the victorious emperor, standing or seated on a throne on a tribunal, in the presence of the troops. When the captive had attempted usurpation, he was ritually stripped of his imperial insignia before being forced to perform the *proskynesis* to the victorious prince. It is quite likely that the army supplied the model for the analogous rite in circus victory spectacles.[79]

---

[75] The phrasing of *XII pan.*, 12 (9), 23, 3, Mynors, 287.26–288.6 suggests the influence of the gladiatorial parade which opened such contests; cf. e.g., G. Lafaye, 'Gladiator', *Dict. ant.* 2, 2 (1896), 1563–99, here 1593ff. For the parade of captives or rebels' heads, see the fifth- and sixth-century spectacles recorded for Zeno, Anastasius and Justinian, above, Ch. 2.

[76] Priscian, *Anastas.*, 171–3, Baehrens, 270: 'Ipse locus . . ./et uinctos oculis domitosque tyrannos/ante pedes uestros mediis circensibus actos'; Procopius, *Bella*, 4, 9, 12, Haury, 1.457.22–4. That such a spectacle may already have figured in fourth-century victory celebrations is suggested by Libanius' mention of Julian's refusal to display Chnodomar κύπτοντα to those who the barbarian had despoiled; instead he sent him along to Constantius II: Libanius, *Or.*, 12, 49, Foerster, 2.27.1.

[77] See above, Ch. 2, n. 76.

[78] Cassiodorus, *Variae*, 3, 51, 8, Fridh, 134.55–7: 'Spina infelicium captiuorum sortem designat, ubi duces Romanorum supra dorsa hostium ambulantes laborum suorum gaudia perceperunt', in the course of his description of the circus and its parts.

[79] The scene of the presentation of a captive to the emperor is depicted on at least one third-century medallion (Gordian): F. Gnecchi, *I medaglioni romani*, 2 (Milan, 1912), 92, with pl. 105, 9. Perhaps the best known ritual divestiture in the fourth century was that of Vetranio by Constantius II: Socrates, *H.e.*, 2, 28, *PG*, 67.276A; Sozomen, *H.e.*

An enigmatic theater spectacle staged in Constantinople to mark the defeat of Attalus might have illuminated the circus shows, especially since the theater's influence on Hippodrome productions has recently been reemphasized.[80] But nothing is known of this spectacle's content, except that it did not likely resemble classical drama which, by this time, was a thing of the past.[81] Thanks to the fulminations of contemporary preachers, we can dimly perceive a continuing tradition of mime and panto-mime, with variety shows of music, dancing and varying degrees of obscenity, rather along the lines of modern burlesque or vaudeville.[82] That classical theater sometimes reflected weightier political themes and recent 'news' events is well known, but that this tradition surely continued into late antiquity is not common knowledge.[83] In fact, it is not impossible that the modern notion of late Roman theater as a breeding ground for sensual deprava-tion and civil disturbance is, to a large degree, the product of the professional deformations of our ecclesiastical sources. Beyond the general improbability that burlesque reviews could have wholly avoided allusions to contemporary institutions, politics and even news events, there is specific evidence nearly contemporary with Attalus' defeat which shows that soldiers, for example, liked to stage skits ridiculing the imperial court during New Year revelries which were inspired by contemporary theater and recalled the

---

4, 4, 2–3, Bidez, 142.7–15; Zosimus, *Hist. nova*, 2, 44, 3–4, Paschoud 1.117.1–13. Other examples of the presentation of captives: Valens and Procopius: John of Antioch, *De insidiis*, fg. 76, De Boor, *Excerpta historica*, 3.116.2–6, cf. Philostorgius, *H.e.*, 9, 5, Bidez, 118.1–3; Theodosius and Maximus and Eugenius: Socrates, *H.e.*, 5, 14, *PG*, 67.600C and 5, 25, 653A; Sozomen, *H.e.*, 7, 24, 7, Bidez, 338.12–14; Zosimus, *Hist. nova*, 4, 46, 2–3, Paschoud, 2.2.314.23–315.10; Claudian, *Panegyricus de quarto consulatu Honorii*, 81–6, Birt, 153, etc.

[80] Cameron, *Circus*, pp. 214ff.

[81] The evidence is reviewed by H.A. Kelly, 'Tragedy and the performance of tragedy in late Roman antiquity', *Traditio*, 35 (1979), 20–44.

[82] Chrysostom is a particularly well-tapped source on the subject: A. Vogt, 'Le théâtre à Byzance et dans l'Empire du IVe au XIIIe siècles. I. Le théâtre profane', *Revue des questions historiques*, 59 (1931), 257–96 (esp. pp. 16ff of the offprint); G.J. Theocharidis, *Beiträge zur Geschichte des byzantinischen Profantheaters im IV. und V. Jahrhundert*, Λαογραφία, Παράρτημα, 3 (Thessalonica, 1940); B.H. Vandenberghe, 'Saint Jean Chrysostome et les spectacles', *Zeitschrift für Religions- und Geistesgeschichte*, 7 (1955), 34–46 and Pasquato, *Spettacoli*, passim.

[83] For political shows in the classical period: Balsdon, *Life and leisure*, pp. 272ff; cf. Cameron, *Circus*, pp. 171ff.

antics of the depraved *stupidi* of mime.[84] Shows inspired by news events reached even into distant provinces, as is demonstrated by the chance survival of a fifth- or sixth-century list of props for a series of sketches. The last piece on the list is called 'the [show] of the Goths'. It involved the representation of a river, a tribunal – suitable therefore for the appearance of a general or commander-in-chief in a submission or related scene – and costumes of Gothic men and women.[85] Its last editor believes that the props were intended for a reenactment of the crossing of the Danube by the Goths in 376, but the props could lend themselves to any number of related scenarios.[86] Clearly, on the basis of these analogies, it is not at all impossible that the theater show of 416 included material more immediately germane to Attalus' defeat than a simple song and dance variety show.

Outside of Rome, circus victory spectacles were gaining in significance in the course of the fourth century. By the next century, they would entirely eclipse the old triumphal parade through the city. Once again, in other words, developments in the provinces outstripped those in Rome and foreshadowed future trends. If the kinds of spectacles which now celebrated imperial victory were not in themselves radically new, two of their characteristics were. Parades or rituals associated with city streets and military camps were now being transferred to the closed, controlled environment of the circus and staged in conjunction with sporting events. The harnessing of popular enthusiasm combined with the emergence of a well-oiled mechanism for pro-government displays in the circus produced a vast and successful forum for mass communication, adaptable to a whole range of imperial ceremonies. Secondly, the emperor ceased to appear as a direct participant in parades of victory, just as he no longer figured directly in the campaigns leading up to the celebration. He becomes the distant, impassive cause, focus, and goal of the campaign and its symbolic conclusion, the victory parade. He was no longer directly implicated in the miasma of war and bloodshed,

---

[84] Asterius of Amasea, *Hom.* 4, 7, 1ff, Datema, 41.31–42.2.

[85] P. Berol. 13927, ed. I. Cazzaniga, 'Note marginali al papiro berlinese 13927 (V–VI sec. d. C.). Un inventario di oggetti necessari per rappresentazioni sceniche', *Studi classici e orientali*, 7 (1958), 7–19, here 10.ii.22–6: [Show] ζ′ εἰς τὸ τῶν Γότϑων.

[86] *Ibid.*, pp. 16–17.

no longer immediately involved in the cascade of defeats, but remained the source and end of victories accomplished through the agency of his generals. Side by side with the new secular form of victory celebrations, there emerged new religious rites of victory, and it is to this problem that we must now turn.

4. THE CHRISTIANIZATION OF IMPERIAL VICTORY CELEBRATIONS

The enduring consequences of Constantine the Great's religious proclivities have made the problem of his conversion, and its repercussions on the style and content of Roman government, one of the great subjects of historical controversy. Modern scholars have focused on the process of Constantine's conversion and the earliest public display of his new loyalties in areas like legislation and *Staatssymbolik*.[87] At the same time, the personal commitment of the ruler and his sons to the 'religion of bloodless sacrifice' did not automatically entail a total transformation of government and society; inevitably, the christianization of the monarchy and its officers spanned many decades.[88] In this context, the question of how and why the monarchy christianized its public self-expression is an essential one. Historians of art have, in many respects, led the way in uncovering this fundamental rethinking of the official visual symbolism of the state.[89] Recent efforts have revealed how profitable such an enquiry can be if it is extended to the monarchy's ritual symbolism.[90]

Although victory observances were only one element in the panoply of imperial ceremonial, the reconstruction of the process of their christianization affords insight into the actual implement-

---

[87] E.g. N.H. Baynes, *Constantine the Great and the Christian Church*, 2nd edn (London, 1972); A. Alföldi, *The Conversion of Constantine and Pagan Rome*, tr. H. Mattingly (Oxford, 1948); H. Dörries, *Das Selbstzeugnis Kaiser Konstantins*, Abhandlungen der Akademie der Wissenschaften in Göttingen, philol.-hist. Kl. 3.34 (1955); and H. Kraft, *Kaiser Konstantins religiöse Entwicklung*, Beiträge zur historischen Theologie, 20 (Tübingen, 1955).

[88] A process which is graphically illustrated by R. von Haehling, *Die Religionszugehörigkeit der hohen Amtsträger des Römischen Reiches seit Constantins I. Alleinherrschaft bis zum Ende der Theodosianischen Dynastie (324–450 bzw. 455 n.Chr.)*, Antiquitas, 3, 23 (Bonn, 1978).

[89] E.g. Kollwitz, *Plastik*, pp. 50ff.

[90] E.g. MacCormack, *Art and ceremony*, pp. 93ff.

ation of the new symbolism of empire. Even though the first decades of this process are partially obscured by the disproportionate importance attributed to the somewhat atypical celebrations staged at Rome, enough is clear to allow us to discern two phases: first, the neutralization of the pagan cult aspect of imperial celebrations, which introduced a kind of creeping christianization. The latter culminated in the second phase, which witnessed the emergence of specifically Christian victory rites.

By almost all accounts, Constantine's commitment to his new religion was inextricably bound up in his own understanding of his military success, in his 'vision' before the battle for Rome, in the Christian God's promise of victory: *hoc signo uinces*.[91] That morning, his soldiers bore the Christian symbol into battle on their shields, and there is little likelihood they changed their decoration for the triumphal entry into the capital the next day.[92] In an ingenious study of the event, Straub surmised that Constantine broke ancient tradition by refusing to perform the sacrifice to the Capitoline Jupiter which was customary on such occasions.[93] Even if the hypothesis is impossible to verify, it seems clear that the break with Capitoline tradition was accomplished by the time of Constantine's vicennalia in Rome, at the latest.[94] Thanks to

---

[91] E.g. Dörries, *Selbstzeugnis*, pp. 243ff. Cf. Barnes, *Constantine*, p. 43.

[92] *Ibid.*, p. 48.

[93] J. Straub, 'Konstantins Verzicht', arguing from the unthinkableness of a pagan sacrifice for a devotee of Christianity and from what he considers the significant omission of the description of a visit to the Capitol in the panegyric of 313 and the same rhetorician's intriguing remark that some dared complain that Constantine had entered the palace too quickly: *XII pan.*, 12 (9), 19, 3, Mynors, 285.4–6. Although most specialists now follow Straub's hypothesis (e.g. Barnes, *Constantine*, p. 44), F. Altheim launched an aggressive and unanswered attack on the theory: 'Konstantins Triumph von 312', *Zeitschrift für Religions- und Geistesgeschichte*, 9 (1957), 221–31. His arguments do not convince: he assumes with no evidence that the ritual elements of a triumph must have been the same in 312 as in the first century B.C. and recognizes in the 313 panegyrist's use of terms like *numen* and *ludi aeterni* irrefutable references to the cult of Jupiter. *Numen*, however, is an exceedingly common expression in the panegyrics (T. Janson, *A Concordance to the Latin Panegyrics* (Hildesheim, 1979), pp. 485–7), while the expression *ludi aeterni* more likely refers to the 'eternal' victory games founded to mark the success. On the other hand, Straub's use of the argument from silence is not altogether reassuring. Were we to assume, for the sake of hypothesis, that Constantine had indeed yielded to tradition and performed the customary visit to the Capitol, would it have been politic for the panegyrist of 313 to remind him of it? Cf. following n.

[94] F. Paschoud, *Cinq études sur Zosime* (Paris, 1975), pp. 24ff, argues for 315.

Constantine's innovation and its observance by his successors, imperial victory celebrations at Rome appear strangely neutral in the midst of an empire whose ideology increasingly relied on its religious content. Even though Christian symbols would have been visible on the shields of troops marching in the triumphal parade from 312 on, even though the emblems of Christianity would have enjoyed a position of prominence on the imperial standards displayed during subsequent visits to Rome – as Prudentius gloats on one occasion – there is no indication that the elimination of the pagan content of imperial victory celebrations was quickly matched by the introduction of a Christian substitute.[95] As late as 389, a panegyric delivered at Theodosius' triumph in Rome gave no hint that the victorious emperor marched under a Christian standard.[96]

The explanation for this unlikely ambiguity must be sought in the historical context of the four ceremonies. One factor was surely the ceremonial traditionalism already detected in victory observances at Rome, in itself due in part, no doubt, to the fact that the majority of the city's elite remained staunch and conservative pagans.[97] If, moreover, modern historians are correct in associating the timing of imperial visits to Rome with thaws in the prince's anti-paganism, it would have made little sense for the visiting emperor to offend his audience's sensitivities by ostentatiously replacing the venerated Capitoline shrine with a Christian ersatz.[98] Furthermore, a significant part in

[95] This is not to say, of course, that in the course of their stay emperors systematically shunned Christian shrines or that Christianity would have been totally excluded from other aspects of the celebration. On the other hand, there is simply no evidence for the incorporation of a Christian sanctuary into the itinerary of the triumphal parade at Rome, along the lines of the Capitoline ritual. For Prudentius' speech, put in the mouth of Theodosius I and addressed to Roma: *Contra Symmachum*, 1, 464–6, Cunningham, 202.

[96] See the observations on this aspect of Pacatus in S.G. MacCormack, 'Latin prose panegyrics: Tradition and discontinuity in the later Roman empire', *Revue des études augustiniennes*, 22 (1976), 29–77, here 62–4. Cf. however below, n. 114 for a Christian element in a coin associated with the event.

[97] See e.g. A.H.M. Jones, 'The social background of the struggle between Paganism and Christianity', in *The conflict between paganism and Christianity in the fourth century*, ed. A. Momigliano (Oxford, 1963), pp. 17–37, esp. 31.

[98] Thus Chastagnol, *Préfecture*, pp. 424–5, on the visit of 357; cf. *ibid.*, p. 441, on the visit of 389, and p. 445 for that of 403–4.

the orchestration of the first day's festivities would have fallen to the City Prefect. He served not only as a privileged link between the people of the capital and the prince, but was also responsible for the maintenance of public order in the streets and the overall organization of spectacles.[99] In fact, during the celebrations of 312, 357 and 389, the urban prefecture was occupied by a pagan.[100] It is likely that this was just as true of Honorius' visit in 403–4.[101] Although the new triumph was devoid of pagan ceremonial elements, it is probable nonetheless that the pagan ascendancy in the urban prefecture on all these occasions helped preserve what was left of the old ceremony from Christian accretions.

But it has already been observed that ceremonies staged at Rome were not always in step with developments in the provinces. The years surrounding the defeat of Licinius seem to have been particularly fertile in ceremonial innovation: it was then that the diadem was introduced into the repertory of imperial insignia and an organized ceremonial corps, the silentiaries, first appears.[102] From precisely the same period stems an innovation in Constantine's titulature which reflects the development of his Christian loyalties. A new epithet of victory replaced the imperial epithet *invictus*, the solar connotations of which seem beyond question and would scarcely have escaped contemporaries accustomed to celebrate the festival of the Unconquered Sun every 25 December. This honorary title of *victor* was to dominate official usage down to Heraclius' revamping of the whole system.[103]

---

99 *Ibid.*, pp. 254ff and 279ff.
100 Annius Anullinus (27 October–29 November 312): Chastagnol, *Fastes*, pp. 45–7; in 357: Orfitus, *ibid.*, p. 144; cf. *Préfecture*, pp. 424–5, and von Haehling, *Religionszugehörigkeit*, pp. 373–4; in 389: Rufius Albinus, Chastagnol, *Fastes*, pp. 234–5; cf. von Haehling, *Religionszugehörigkeit*, pp. 393–4.
101 Of the two known City Prefects between 403 and 407, Postumius Lampadius was definitely a pagan, while the religious background of the other is unknown: Chastagnol, *Fastes*, pp. 260–1; cf. von Haehling, *Religionszugehörigkeit*, p. 401. On pagan dominance of the prefecture in this period: Chastagnol, *Préfecture*, p. 445.
102 The diadem begins to show up on the gold coinage in 324 (*RIC*, 7, 43–6) or 325: M.R. Alföldi, *Die Constantinische Goldprägung. Untersuchungen zu ihrer Bedeutung für Kaiserpolitik und Hofkunst* (Mainz, 1963), p. 104. The silentiaries appear as a group in a law assigned to 328: O. Seeck, 'Silentiarius', *RE*, 3A (1929), 57–8, here 57.
103 G. Rösch, ᾿Ονομα βασιλέως. *Studien zum offiziellen Gebrauch der Kaisertitel in spätantiker und frühbyzantinischer Zeit*, Byzantina vindobonensia, 10 (Vienna, 1978),

Although it has been maintained that the new epithet accentuated Constantine's relation with the Christian God and thereby assumed positive religious overtones,[104] it is difficult to see what distinctively Christian content the word *victor* possessed in the 320s. In fact, the abandonment of the solar connotations of the honorary epithet *invictus* can be compared more accurately to the religious ambiguity of Roman victory celebrations: the element most offensive to Christians was replaced with a new epithet which need grate on neither new nor old believers.[105]

Whether Constantine introduced any distinctly Christian elements into victory celebrations outside Rome in the rest of his reign cannot now be determined, but the fact that Eusebius is reduced to presenting Constantine's convocation of the Nicaean Council as his thank-offering to the Christian God for the defeat of Licinius suggests that there was not much to discuss in the way of Christianity at the actual victory celebrations.[106] Aside from victory observances, however, one event hints at another, less controversial channel for incipient christianization: the public participation of the representatives of the Christian church in imperial festivities. One of the earliest such occasions was a magnificent state banquet, apparently held as part of the vicennalia

---

pp. 45–6, 78–9; and the important contribution of A. Chastagnol, 'Un gouverneur Constantinien de Tripolitaine: Laenatius Romulus, *Praeses* en 324–326', *Latomus*, 25 (1966), 539–52, here 543–9, which dates the introduction certainly between 10 December 323 and 8 November 324, and probably to the immediate aftermath of the victory.

[104] Thus Rösch, *Kaisertitel*, p. 79.

[105] It is noteworthy in this respect that Eusebius, *V. Constantini*, 2, 19, 2, Winkelmann, 56.4–6, who is ready to see a Christian symbol under every Constantinian bush, specifically links the invention of the new title only with the emperor's 'victory granted from God over all enemies': ταύτην γὰρ αὐτὸς αὐτῷ τὴν ἐπώνυμον κυριωτάτην ἐπηγορίαν εὕρατο τῆς ἐκ θεοῦ δεδομένης αὐτῷ κατὰ πάντων ἐχθρῶν τε καὶ πολεμίων νίκης εἵνεκα, in a phrase which is *added* to the material taken over from *H.e.*, 10, 9, 6, Schwartz, 900.24–902.4.

[106] Eusebius, *V. Constantini*, 3, 7, 2, Winkelmann, 85.2–5, whence the expression is picked up by the church historians, e.g. Socrates, *H.e.*, 1, 8, *PG*, 67.61B. The 'victory feast' referred to at *V. Constantini*, 3, 14, Winkelmann, 88.17–18, seems to be a metaphorical usage connected with the resolution of the Easter controversy which Eusebius has just narrated: ὧν δὴ πραχθέντων, δευτέραν ταύτην νίκην ἄρασθαι εἰπὼν βασιλεὺς κατὰ τοῦ τῆς ἐκκλησίας ἐχθροῦ ἐπινίκιον ἑορτὴν τῷ θεῷ συνετέλει.

celebrations and coinciding with the council of Nicaea.[107] Eusebius' gushing account of this honor – 'you might almost have seemed to visualize an image of Christ's kingdom' – emphasizes its novelty for the flattered episcopate. The institution of imperial banquets was an important classical legacy to late antique society; invitations to them were highly prized and offered the emperors an opportunity to achieve much the same goals as a public ceremony, but in circumstances more befitting the select nature of the participants. What the audience of such an event lacked in numbers, it surely made up in influence.[108] Although direct attestation for victory banquets in this period has yet to emerge, the kind of gala dinner associated with the Flavian triumph of 71 was still around early in the fourth century. Given the importance of various kinds of state banquets in the late empire – an importance which could only have increased with the emergence of the privileged bureaucratic caste – it would seem likely that ceremonial dinners continued to be served in connection with the triumphs of the Constantinian empire.[109]

The first known public participation of representatives of the Christian community in imperial victory celebrations may have

---

[107] Eusebius, *V. Constantini*, 3, 15, 1–16, Winkelmann, 88.19–89.13; Theophanes, A.M. 5816, De Boor, 22.28–30; cf. K. Baus and E. Ewig, *Handbuch der Kirchengeschichte*, 2, 1 (Freiburg, 1973), 28–9.

[108] See in general Treitinger, *Oströmische*, pp. 101ff as well as following n.

[109] For the triumphal banquet of 71, see above, Ch. 1. For a banquet which seems to be associated with the triumph of Diocletian in 303, Peter Patrician, *De sententiis*, fg. 185, Boissevain, *Excerpta historica*, 4.270.6–8. The best source on imperial banquets is quite late, Philotheus' *Cleterologium* (a handbook for imperial *maître d's*) from A.D. 899: ed. N. Oikonomides, *Les listes de préséance byzantines des IXe et Xe siècles*, Le monde byzantin (Paris, 1972), 81–235. Evidence on the institution prior to iconoclasm is quite scattered; it includes the usurper Maximus' banquet at which Martin of Tours participated, Sulpicius Severus, *V. Martini* (*BHL*, 5610), 20, 2ff, ed. J. Fontaine, SC, 133–5 (Paris, 1967–9), here 1.296; Theodosius I is supposed to have increased imperial banquet expenditures: Zosimus, *Hist. nova*, 4, 28, 1, Paschoud, 2.2.291.6–14; Justinian cancelled a Christmas banquet in the Hall of the Nineteen Couches as part of the public mourning for an earthquake: Theophanes, A.M. 6050, De Boor, 232.4–6, and of course had Vandal gold made into a banquet service, above Ch. 2; banquets for the empire's elite were included in Maurice's marriage celebrations: Theophylactus Simocattes, *Hist.*, 1, 10, 12, De Boor, 59.3–4; an example of Justinian II's fabled cruelty was that he ordered his enemies to be executed at the end of state banquets: Theophanes, A.M. 6198, De Boor, 375.19–20; Philippicus celebrated a banquet in the Zeuxippos with the elite on the Saturday before Pentecost: *ibid.*, A.M. 6205, De Boor 383.5–9, etc.

been linked with such an occasion. The festival held at Antioch in 343 in honor of Constantius II's Persian success included some unspecified activity which required the presence of the bishops from his territory who were meeting at Serdica.[110] At least this is what the bishops claimed, for they used the arrival of an imperial victory bulletin as an 'ignoble pretext', in the words of one highly prejudiced observer, for avoiding an uncomfortable ecclesiastical confrontation.[111] Although the incidental context in which this mention crops up fails to specify why the bishops were needed at the emperor's court, it is plain that the announcement must have comprised some kind of invitation to the celebrations. In light of what is known about Constantine's vicennalia, it is not impossible that the bishops may also have been expected to appear at a victory banquet.[112]

In the reign of Theodosius I, the christianization of the government, its personnel and its symbolism marked a new and definitive advance.[113] Although no major Christian elements are apparent in Theodosius' victory parade and other observances at Rome in 389, a rare gold *solidus* associated with the visit and struck in the ancient capital displays on its reverse a vota shield topped by the *chrismon*, so that the legend reads GLORIA – R ☧ O – MANORUM, between helmeted figures of Roma and Constantinopolis.[114]

The usurpation of Eugenius gave new focus to paganism's vital forces in the West. At the same time, an unbending Theodosius struck ever deeper at the old religion. For contemporaries, it was easy to visualize the political and military confrontation of the eastern and western governments as a struggle between the ancient deities of Rome and the new God from the East. The ideological element was clearly present at the battle of Cold River, fought in

[110] See above, Ch. 2, p. 39–40.
[111] Athanasius, *Historia Arianorum*, 16, 2, Opitz, 191.12–15.
[112] It is not clear whether there is a connection between the flight of the eastern bishops and the canon promulgated by the Council of Serdica requiring bishops resident along the main routes of the empire to check whether bishops traveling to the imperial court had actually received an official invitation, the stated intention being to repress trips 'propter desideria et ambitiones': *Concilium Serdicense*, 7, ed. C.H. Turner, *Ecclesiae occidentalis monumenta iuris antiquissima*, 1.2.3 (Oxford, 1930), 470.26–7.
[113] E.g. Lippold, *Theodosius*, pp. 132ff.   [114] *RIC*, 9, 132, no. 60; cf. pp. 112–13.

the shadow of Nicomachus Flavianus' huge statues of Jupiter, when the western army's standards opposed Hercules to the eastern army's *labarum*.[115] Theodosius' preparations for war involved more than logistics. For the first time on record, the Roman emperor himself participated in the new form of public devotion which was then sweeping the cities of the East: he celebrated liturgical processions of supplication with priests and people, going from shrine to shrine to beseech divine intervention on behalf of his army.[116] One of his first measures after the victory was to order special thanksgiving services for his success, as is proven by the obsequious answer of Ambrose:[117] 'Other emperors order the preparation of triumphal arches or other ornaments of triumph at the first taste of victory. Your clemency' – Ambrose is about to ask mercy for Eugenius' supporters – 'prepares a sacrifice for God and desires bishops to celebrate an offering and thanksgiving service to the Lord.'[118] The novelty of Theodosius' directive is underscored by Ambrose's need to explain exactly how he performed the special thanksgiving Mass, and an interesting description it is:

Even though I am unworthy and unequal to such a duty and to the solemnity of such prayers (*vota*), yet I will write you what I did. I carried your Piety's letter with me to the altar, I placed it on the altar, I held it in my hand when I offered the sacrifice, so that your faith spoke with my

[115] See e.g. H. Bloch, 'A new document from the last pagan revival in the West', *Harvard Theological Review*, 38 (1945), 199–244, here 235–9, and 'The pagan revival in the West at the end of the fourth century', *The conflict between Paganism and Christianity*, pp. 193–218, here 200–1. Recently J. Szidat, 'Die Usurpation des Eugenius', *Historia*, 28 (1979), 487–508, has sought to emphasize the non-religious factors in the conflict, but this need not in itself invalidate the struggle's ideological overtones.

[116] Rufinus, *H.e.*, 11, 33, Mommsen, 2.1037.1–6, confirmed in part by Sozomen, *H.e.*, 7, 24, 2, and 8–9, Bidez, 337.14–19 and 338.15–23, where we learn that Theodosius, as he was setting out for the West and the war, stopped at the chapel of St John the Baptist in the Hebdomon palace complex, to pray for victory. Cf. W. Ensslin, 'Die Religionspolitik des Kaiser Theodosius d. Gr.', *Sitzungsberichte der Bayerischen Akademie der Wissenschaften*, Phil.-hist. Kl. (1953), H.2., here pp. 84–6.

[117] *Ep.*, 61, *PL*, 16.1237–8, datable to September 394: J.R. Palanque, *Saint Ambroise et l'empire romain. Contribution à l'histoire des rapports de l'église et de l'État à la fin du quatrième siècle* (Paris, 1933), pp. 548–9; cf. pp. 286ff on the circumstances.

[118] *Ep.*, 61, 4, *PL*, 16.1238A: 'Alii imperatores in exordio victoriae arcus triumphales parari jubent, aut alia insignia triumphorum: clementia tua hostiam Deo parat, oblationem et gratiarum actionem per sacerdotes celebrari Domino desiderat.'

voice and the letter of the emperor discharged the function of the bishop's offering.[119]

This extraordinary association of Theodosius' victory bulletin with the altar and performance of the Mass by the bishop of Milan was clearly intended to render manifest the unique intention of the special thanksgiving which Theodosius had demanded, as well as the extraordinary position of the emperor in the fourth-century church.[120] And this from the man who first denied the Roman emperor the right of approaching and remaining by the altar.[121] That the bishop's presence was required as well for the victorious emperor's triumphal arrival in Milan is clear from the *Vita Ambrosii*, which notes that the bishop managed to get to the city on the eve of Theodosius' entry.[122] Any doubts privileged onlookers may have had on the Christian content of the emperor's victory and its celebration were dispelled by the lost panegyric, in which Paulinus of Nola emphasized that the emperor conquered more by faith and prayer than by force of arms.[123] Paulinus' emphasis was more than an expression of the conflict's religiously charged atmosphere. A sense of the incongruity of religious celebrations for the massive bloodshed which had purchased the legitimate emperor's victory persisted, for, as Ambrose informs us, after the battle Theodosius abstained from communion until he had satisfied himself that he continued to enjoy divine favor.[124]

[119] *Ep.*, 16, 5, *PL*, 16.1238A: 'Etsi ego indignus atque impar tanto muneri et tantorum votorum celebritati: tamen quid fecerim scribo. Epistolam pietatis tuae mecum ad altare detuli, ipsam altari imposui, ipsam gestavi manu, cum offerrem sacrificium, ut fides tua in mea voce loqueretur, et Apices Augusti sacerdotalis oblationis munere fungerentur.'

[120] The vocabulary here seems to recall the offertory procession; cf. R. Johanny, *L'eucharistie, centre de l'histoire du salut chez saint Ambroise de Milan*, Théologie historique, 9 (Paris, 1968), pp. 60–5. On the veneration of the altar in the second half of the fourth century: F.J. Dölger, 'Die Heiligkeit des Altars und ihre Begründung im christlichen Altertum', *Antike und Christentum*, 2 (Münster, 1930), 161–83, esp. 165 and 182–3; for the history and diversity of the offerings which could be laid on the altar: J.A. Jungmann, *The mass of the Roman rite: its origins and development*, tr. F.A. Brunner, 2 (New York, 1955), 10–26.

[121] E.g. Treitinger, *Oströmische*, p. 136.

[122] Paulinus, *V. Ambrosii* (BHL, 377), 32, ed. M. Pellegrino, Verba seniorum, n.s. 1 (Rome, 1961), 96.1–2.

[123] Gennadius, *De uiris inl.*, 49, Richardson, 79.1–4; cf. Jerome, *Ep.*, 58, 8, ed. I. Hilberg, *CSEL*, 54 (1910). 537.14–538.12.

[124] Ambrose, *De obitu Theodosii*, 34, ed. O. Faller, *CSEL*, 73 (1955). 371–401, here

The consciousness of the miasma of bloodshed in the late fourth century reveals the complexity of the mental world into which Christian victory services were born and helps explain why Christian writers attached such weight to the theme of the emperors' 'bloodless victory'.[125]

The tradition which emerged under Theodosius the Great flourished under his successors. The expulsion of the Goths from Constantinople was marked not only by circus celebrations which emphasized the bloodless nature of the 'victory', but also by thanksgiving services which may have owed something to the personal involvement in the crisis of a particularly influential patriarch, John Chrysostom.[126] The celebrations which hailed at Constantinople the murder of Athaulf also included an element whose Christian character has gone unrecognized. According to the Paschal Chronicle, the festivities were twofold: first a *lychnapsia* or lamp-lighting and, on the morrow, circus races.[127] The custom of lighting lamps around the entrance to public and private buildings for private festivities or public holidays was deeply entrenched in ancient society; on the latter occasion it was condemned and avoided by Christians, according to Tertullian.[128] In the fourth century, the term could still have decidedly

---

388.7–389.10. See the interesting comm. on this and the following point in F. Heim, 'Le thème de la "victoire sans combat" chez Ambroise', *Ambroise de Milan. XVIᵉ centenaire de son élection épiscopale*, ed. Y.M. Duval (Paris, 1974), pp. 267–81, here 266–7. On the necessity of purification before communion in Ambrose's thought, Johanny, *L'eucharistie*, pp. 188ff.

[125] Heim, 'Thème', *passim*.

[126] For the emphasis on the bloodless nature of the victory in the circus celebrations, see the passage of Eunapius, cited above, n. 72. The evidence for thanksgiving services comes in Synesius of Cyrene, *Aegyptii*, 2, 3, Terzaghi, 2.118.15–18: ἐκκλησία δὴ πρώτη περὶ τὸν ἱερέα τὸν μέγαν, καὶ πῦρ ἱερὸν ἥπτετο, καὶ εὐχαὶ χαριστήριοι μὲν ὑπὲρ τῶν διαπεπραγμένων, ἱκετήριοι δὲ ὑπὲρ τῶν πεπραξομένων. It is generally admitted today that the 'high priest' of the story is to be identified with Arcadius (cf. e.g. C. Lacombrade, *Synésios de Cyrène. Hellène et chrétien* [Paris, 1951], pp. 105 and 109, n. 35). The parallel passage adduced from Plutarch by Terzaghi (*Isis et Osiris*, 46, 369E: ἐδίδαξε δὲ τῷ μὲν εὐκταῖα θύειν καὶ χαριστήρια, τῷ δ'ἀποτρόπαια καὶ σκυθρωπά) only reinforces this interpretation by pointing up the Christian resonances of Synesius' vocabulary in his transformation of his source. On Chrysostom's role, C. Baur, *Der heilige Johannes Chrysostomus und seine Zeit*, 2 (Munich, 1930), 106ff.

[127] See above, Ch. 2, p. 56.

[128] See in general J. Toutain, 'Lucerna', *Dict. ant.*, 3, 2 (Paris, 1904), 1320–39, here

pagan overtones.[129] Could this custom have survived unchanged in the strongly Christian capital on the Bosphorus? In fact, a fifth-century source uses the word as a synonym for the Christian liturgical office of *lychnikon*.[130] More likely, in the present context, however, is the identification of the Chronicle's 'lamp-lighting' with a Christian fascination with public illuminations which was gaining ground in the East in precisely these decades, a fascination which is all the more understandable for the fact that public street lights still lay in Constantinople's future.[131] Thus, in order to combat the nefarious influence of Arian night rallies, Chrysostom, with the help of empress Eudoxia (400–4), orga-nized torchlight parades, the main attraction of which consisted of cross-shaped silver candle holders – paid for out of the empress' pocket – and hymn singing, in which members of the empress' *cubiculum* played a proven role.[132] That such torchlight pro-cessions were associated with the custom of *lychnapsia* is demon-strated by events of 22 June 431. According to Cyril of Alexandria, the whole city of Ephesus was anxiously awaiting the pronounce-ment of the assembled bishops concerning Nestorius. At word of his condemnation and deposition, the population began to acclaim the council and praise God that His enemy was laid low. When the bishops left the church of the Virgin, they were escorted by rejoicing citizens carrying lights; women led the way, swinging censers, 'and there was great rejoicing and lamp-lighting (*lych-napsia*) in the city'.[133] Since the festive illuminations of Friday, 24 September 415, fall squarely in the midst of the new fashion, it

---

1336–7; Juvenal, 12, 89ff. Tertullian, *Apologeticum*, 35, 1–5, esp. 4, ed. E. Dekkers, *CCL*, 1 (1954). 145.15–16 defends Christians from accusations of lèse-majesté because of their refusal to decorate and light up their doorsteps on imperial holidays; cf. *Ad uxorem*, 2, 6, 1, ed. E. Kroymann, *ibid.*, 390.1–6.

129 *Chronographus a. 354*, 12 August, Lychnapsia, Degrassi, comm. 494.

130 Lampe, *Patristic Greek Lexicon*, p. 816, s.v.

131 Probably instituted in 438–41: G. Dagron, *Naissance d'une capitale. Constantinople et ses institutions de 330 à 451*, Bibliothèque byzantine, Études, 7 (Paris, 1974), p. 269 with n. 1.

132 Socrates, *H.e.*, 6, 8, *PG*, 69.689A–C; cf. *PLRE*, 2, 242, 'Brison'. At about the same date, a torchlight procession and *pannychides* are attested in connection with the return of the consul and Praetorian Prefect Aurelian: Synesius, *Aegyptii*, 2, 4, Terzaghi, 2.122.14.

133 Cyril of Alexandria, *Ep.* 25, ed. E. Schwartz, *ACO*, 1.1.1 (1927). 118.5–10.

would appear likely that this celebration also participated in the new Christian character of the old custom. The races staged the next day provided the secular counterpart to the Christian observances of the eve.

The next specifically Christian victory rites came in 425. When Theodosius II learned of the defeat of the usurper John, he interrupted the races which were already in progress and organized a thanksgiving procession which culminated in the performance of prayers for the rest of the day at an unspecified church.[134] Here unrelated secular festivities were interrupted to allow the liturgical celebration to take place. Once again, the Christian victory rite is independent of and parallel to the older secular celebrations, much like the thanksgiving Mass of Ambrose and the other instances just examined. That this distinction was not an accident is shown by John of Antioch's account of Anastasius' victory celebrations after the first insignificant defeats inflicted on Vitalian. When he received the victory bulletin, Anastasius organized a procession of thanksgiving and victory spectacles.[135] In other words, specifically Christian victory rites appear to have developed independently of more secular festivities like the triumphal parade and circus show.

Did the secular celebrations of triumphal parade and circus spectacles begin at this time to feature Christian ritual elements as well? The first recorded instance of an imperial triumph parade which incorporated a public visit to a Christian shrine comes from late in the reign of Justinian.[136] In the religiously charged atmosphere of the early seventh century, additional liturgical elements worked their way into the emperor's triumphal entry, and the synthesis of the old Roman parade and the new Christian rituals was complete.[137]

5. THE DIVISION OF THE EMPIRE AND THE COLLEGIALITY OF VICTORY

The physical vastness and the diversity of the menaces which weighed upon it led more than once to the empire's division into

[134] Above, Ch. 2, n. 83.   [135] Above, Ch. 2, n. 91.   [136] Above, Ch. 2, n. 112.
[137] During Heraclius' triumph: above, Ch. 2, p. 72.

areas controlled by mutually recognized imperial colleagues. In theory, the fundamental unity of the Roman world persisted unchallenged. In practice, the ideal of imperial unity corresponded to a reality ranging from outright war to close cooperation, even though many facets of public life, like citizenship, coinage and consular nominations, offered compelling grounds for coordination between the empire's *partes*. Under these conditions, imperial victory ideology stands out as a specific manifestation of the more general notion of imperial unity. The image of collegial victoriousness which can be won from developments of the fourth and fifth centuries forces recognition of subtle variations on this theme and brings nuance to certain aspects of imperial policy and its public projection in this turbulent era.[138]

One path for exploring the problem is opened by imperial triumphal titles derived from the names of conquered peoples. As has already been noted, under the tetrarchy, these titles reflected the unity of the imperial institution in victory: coemperors shared the same *cognomina* derived from their colleagues' successes.[139] After an initial period in which he continued to observe this principle, Constantine broke new ground. The emperor and his sons ceased sharing each other's titles automatically.[140] Constantius II pursued and extended this policy during his independent rule, for he denied Caesar Julian the usage of victory titles

[138] On the theory and practice of imperial unity, see in general E. Kornemann, *Doppelprinzipat und Reichsteilung im Imperium Romanum* (Leipzig, 1930); A.H.M. Jones, *Later Roman Empire*, 1, 325–6; S. Mazzarino, *Stilicone. La crisi imperiale dopo Teodosio* (Rome, 1942), pp. 80ff; J.R. Palanque, 'Collégialité et partages dans l'empire romain aux IVe et Ve siècles', *Revue des études anciennes*, 46 (1944), 47–64, 280–98; Demougeot, *De l'unité, passim* and for the later period, W.E. Kaegi, Jr, *Byzantium and the decline of Rome* (Princeton, 1968), pp. 3ff, and W.N. Bayless, *The political unity of the Roman Empire during the disintegration of the West, A.D. 395–457* (Diss. Brown Univ. 1972), (Ann Arbor, 1980).
[139] See above, Ch. 1, n. 57.
[140] T.D. Barnes, 'Imperial campaigns, A.D. 285–311', *Phoenix*, 30 (1976), 174–93, here 176 and 191–3, and 'Victories', p. 150, which have superseded this aspect of E. Ferrero, 'Constantinus I', *Dizionario epigrafico di antichità romane*, 2nd edn, 2, 1 (1961), 637–55. Kneissl, *Siegestitulatur*, pp. 178–9 (cf. too p. 182 on sons' titles in s. III), sees no break with tetrarchic traditions under Constantine and his sons, a view which is rightly opposed by Rösch, *Kaisertitel*, pp. 54–5 and pp. 79ff. This evidence counters Kornemann's view (*Doppelprinzipat*, pp. 130–1) that the regime of Constantine and his sons was a clear-cut family version of the Diocletianic tetrarchy.

corresponding to his successful expeditions.[141] Only after Julian assumed full power could he adopt the triumphal titles *Germanicus, Alamannicus, Francicus* and *Sarmaticus*.[142]

The accession of Valentinian I included, at the army's demand, the reestablishment of a more genuinely collegial power-sharing agreement.[143] It entailed a resurrection of the conceptions of collegial victory in vogue at the beginning of the century, a restoration embodied in the common victory *cognomina* of Valentinian, Valens and Gratian.[144] Under Theodosius and his successors, the elaborate system of victory epithets seems to slide into a state of suspended animation, during which the choice of epithets became quite stereotyped and its occurrence exceedingly rare and unsystematic.[145] Several times more before the conquest of Constantinople in 1204, the old titles would be resurrected by emperors nostalgic for the trappings of the Roman empire, but in each case, the reanimated title system seems *sui generis*, spurred by considerations specific to the moment and the ruler.[146]

The decline of these titles in the late fourth century was foreshadowed by a sinking rate of attestation which had set in under Diocletian.[147] Among the factors in their decadence were the excesses of the age – an earlier inscription had even called Probus (A.D. 276–82) 'real Gothic [victor], real Germanic [victor]' – and perhaps, the emergence of the notion of the emperor as universal conqueror, *victor omnium gentium*.[148] But two further considerations which have not found their way into discussions of the problem go a long way toward explaining the old titles' decline.

Insofar as they are representative of what has been identified as a 'pacifist' current of opinion, the utterances of a philosopher,

---

141 Rösch, *Kaisertitel*, pp. 81–2.
142 Kneissl, *Siegestitulatur*, p. 179; Rösch, *Kaisertitel*, p. 83.
143 Jones, *Later Roman Empire*, I, 139.
144 Kneissl, *Siegestitulatur*, pp. 178–9; Rösch, *Kaisertitel*, pp. 84–5.
145 Rösch, *Kaisertitel*, pp. 85 and 92ff.
146 In addition to attestations under Marcian and Anastasius (Rösch, *Kaisertitel*, pp. 92ff), the title was particularly favored by Justinian (*ibid.*, pp. 101ff) and, much later, Manuel I Comnenus: A.A. Vasiliev, *The Goths in the Crimea*, Mediaeval Academy Monographs, 11 (Cambridge, Mass., 1936), pp. 140–5.
147 Kneissl, *Siegestitulatur*, pp. 178–9.
148 Probus, from *CIL*, 2, 3738, cited by Kneissl, *Siegestitulatur*, pp. 167 and 177; on the second point, Rösch, *Kaisertitel*, p. 53.

publicist and urban prefect like Themistius are naturally subject to caution when they touch on military themes.[149] Nonetheless his evident dislike for the old triumphal titles throws light on attitudes toward them in precisely the period when they disappear from inscriptions.

To Themistius' mind, and that of Pacatus as well, these titles conjured up images of the Republican past. This suggests that, to contemporary ears, *Germanicus* and the like had a distinctly archaic ring.[150] The philosopher-politician nonetheless calls the epithets imperfect, because they are contingent: they require an outbreak of barbarian madness before they can be used truthfully. This typical example of late antique bluster deftly hints once again at the credibility problem of imperial victories in the second half of the fourth century.[151] The way in which Themistius refers to the titles implies that they were not generally used when addressing the prince in person, or even in acclamations, since he mentions not 'users' or 'speakers' but those who *write* the triumphal titles.[152] In his opinion, the negative nature of the titles, attributed after all to those who destroy a people or a region, was not much re-commendation either.[153] On the one hand, Themistius defends a less warlike policy by urging emperors to imitate heavenly attributes associated with *philanthropia*; on the other, he attempts to infuse a new, positive content into the term *Gothicus*, arguing from the attributes of the Greek gods that such a title may be more fitting to a people's savior than to its destroyer.[154] Themistius' pronouncements on the subject suggest that, in some circles at least, the old victory titles were hard to reconcile with the new,

---

[149] Cf. Dagron, 'Thémistios', pp. 92ff.

[150] Thus Themistius, *Or.*, 10 (I or II.370: Dagron, 'Thémistios', p. 22), Schenkl–Downey, 1.213.1–8; cf. Pacatus, XII pan., 2 (12), 5, 4, Mynors, 86.1–8, who suggests that if the custom of attributing triumphal titles to *Romani duces* had survived into the age of Theodosius the Great's father, the Theodosian house would have enjoyed more such titles than now existed *in annalium scriniis*. With the words 'si eius saeculo mos ille uixisset' (Mynors, 86.1), Pacatus is referring implicitly to the limitation of the titles to the emperors.

[151] *Or.*, 6 (IV.364: Dagron, 'Thémistios', p. 21), Schenkl–Downey, 1.118.14–15.

[152] *Ibid.*: καὶ ἅμα εἰ μὴ παρακινοῖεν οἱ βάρβαροι ψεύδεσθαι γράφοντας ἀναγκαῖον.

[153] *Or.*, 10, Schenkl–Downey, 1.213.6–8.

[154] *Or.*, 6, Schenkl–Downey, 1.118.10–12; *Or.*, 10, *ibid.*, 213.8–15; *Or.*, 15 (congratulatory speech to Theodosius I on his barbarian victories of 379–80: Dagron, 'Thémistios', p. 23), *ibid.*, 279.21–9.

more positive attitude toward the Germanic barbarians, who were just then finding positions of prestige and influence in the higher strata of Roman society.[155] The extent to which Themistius' thought on the subject may have influenced his imperial pupil Arcadius is not, on the other hand, clear.

If changing attitudes lessened the significance attached to the old victory *cognomina* in some circles, specific historical circumstances probably precipitated their sclerosis. At first glance, it would appear paradoxical that one of the least militaristic political figures of the era should oppose titles which, according to conventional wisdom, were conferred by the very Senate for which Themistius was such an avid recruiter.[156] The answer is that, by the reign of Constantius II at the latest, the conferral of such titles was no longer left to the Senate. As we learn from Ammianus Marcellinus' account of Constantius' second assumption of the title *Sarmaticus*, the attribution of the victory *cognomina* was now exclusively in the hands of the army.[157] Since the successors of Theodosius I kept far from the field in times of military activity, the army lost all opportunity for such acclamations, and the victory titles lapsed into a kind of obsolescence.

Even as the decline of *Germanicus* and the like close down one path to uncovering the theory and practice of the collegiality of victory after Adrianople, others open up. In this era, for example, even the minor victories of one Augustus were announced in the great cities of his colleague's domain. Thus the successful skirmishes of Theodosius in 379 were announced in both capitals: from Constantinople, there survives a historical record of the

---

[155] Cf. Dagron, 'Thémistios', pp. 98ff. Note the resentment which such titles could still provoke in Germanic rulers of the sixth century: Ennodius of Pavia, *Panegyricus*, 17, ed. F. Vogel, *MGH. AA*, 17 (1885). 203–14, here 213.5–9 (cf. below, Ch. 7); Agathias, *Historiae*, 1, 4, 3, Keydell, 14.6–9 (below, Ch. 9); cf. F.H. Tinnefeld, *Kategorien der Kaiserkritik in der byzantinischen Historiographie von Prokop bis Niketas Choniates* (Munich, 1971), p. 42.

[156] Kneissl, *Siegestitulatur*, pp. 181ff.

[157] Ammianus Marcellinus, 17, 13, 25, Clark, 1.132.14–15: '...Constantius... militarique consensu, secundo Sarmaticus appellatus, ex uocabulo subactorum...'. Cf. Constantius' speech to the troops, *ibid.*, 17, 13, 33, Clark, 1.134.5–7: 'postremo ego quoque hostilis uocabuli spolium prae me fero, secundo Sarmatici cognomentum, quod uos unum idemque sentientes, mihi (ne sit adrogans dicere), *merito tribuistis*', with not the slightest allusion to senatorial confirmation.

announcement, while a letter of Symmachus refers to the announcement to the Roman Senate and requests that the western emperors Gratian and, probably, Valentinian II be informed of his joy at 'their' victories.[158] The Valentinian system remained in force for several decades. In 385, for instance, Symmachus wrote a letter of congratulations on the accomplishments of one of Valentinian II's generals. True to the traditions of the age, the note is addressed to the whole college of emperors; the victory is considered their common accomplishment.[159]

Victory monuments tell the same story. Early in the century, the city of Rome had erected a triumphal arch dedicated to the sole avenger of the Republic.[160] Eight decades later, the exigencies of collegial victory imposed a different pattern. Now the City Prefect would commemorate Theodosius the Great's victory over another emperor by raising *three* statues of the co-emperors in the Forum. To express the community of victory – a victory due entirely to the efforts of Theodosius – what easier or more tactful way than to repeat the same inscription three times, changing only the name to fit the Augustus whose statue adorned the base?

To the extinguisher of tyrants and author of public security, Our Lord Theodosius [viz. Valentinian/Arcadius], eternal and fortunate ever Augustus, Ceionius Rufus Albinus....[161]

---

[158] *Cons. Cplitana*, a.379, Mommsen, 243; Symmachus, *Ep.*, 95, to Syagrius, who would have been Gratian's *Magister officiorum* at that time (*PLRE*, 1, 862–3, 'Fl. Syagrius 3' and Seeck, *Regesten*, p. 250; against Seeck's redating of *Cod. Theod.* 7, 12, 2a: *PLRE, loc. cit.*), Seeck, 38.27–9. On the identification of the victory, *ibid.*, cxi.

[159] On the collegiality of address of official communications, Jones, *Later Roman Empire*, 1, 325. Here: Symmachus, *Rel.*, 47, 1, Seeck, 315.25–316.9; address: 315.25–7; common accomplishment: 'Bellorum...*vestrorum* gloriosus exitus', 315.25; the commander was 'divinae clementiae *vestrae* fretus auspiciis...' 316.3; cf. 316.7: '...sit *vobis* frequens usus ac facilis laurearum...'. On the identity of the commander, Seeck, *Untergang*, 5, 208. Note that *Cons. Cplitana*, a.380, record the announcement of victories of both Augusti (*amborum augustorum*), i.e. of Gratian and Theodosius, leaving the child Valentinian II out of the picture. Naturally the simple language of the *Fasti* should not be pressed here, for it lacks the legal precision of official communications. The expression emphasizes rather that both active emperors actually won separate victories, minor though they may have been.

[160] *ILS*, 694.

[161] *CIL*, 6, 31413–14, 36959, here 36959: 'Extinctori tyrannorum ac publicae securitati⟨s⟩ auctori d.n. Theodosio perpetuo ac felici semper Augusto, Ceionius

The death of Theodosius and the installation of his sons as rulers of the empire's twin halves has usually been taken as the beginning of the end of Roman unity, a division which was scarcely bridged in the years following Alaric's sack of Rome.[162] Recent studies have argued that the situation was more complex; they find confirmation in the collegiality of victory.

The public stance of imperial harmony on which the Theodosian succession rested was sorely tested by Gildo's revolt against the western government, in which Constantinople had played no little part. As troubled as relations might have become between the two administrations, Stilicho's mouthpiece was ever cautious to confine his criticism to those who influenced Honorius' brother from behind the throne.[163] No sooner had the matter been settled to the western government's satisfaction and relief than Stilicho's publicist trumpeted the restoration of the '*complete* harmony of the brothers'.[164] The victory monument raised in the Roman Forum to eternalize this success eternalized as well the emperors' *plena concordia*, since it espouses the mutually shared nature of the victory. The seeming unlikeliness of this dedication only reinforces the view that the decision to erect the monument reflects the western government's eagerness to normalize relations with Constantinople after the denouement.[165]

The same public position of full harmony is mirrored in the East by the monumental celebration of the Goths' expulsion from Constantinople and the final defeat and death of Gainas. The spiral

Rufius Albinus, v.c., praef. urbi iterum vice sacra iudicans, d.n.m.q. eius'. On Albinus, Chastagnol, *Fastes*, pp. 233–6; cf. *PLRE*, 1, 37–8. We might be tempted to draw differing conclusions about the attitude in Constantinople from the fact that the Latin hexameters on the base of the Obelisk of Theodosius, erected on the same occasion, mention only Theodosius and his issue: *ILS*, 821. However, this is a poetic text, and Valentinian II does appear to figure in the relief itself, according to G. Bruns, *Der Obelisk*, p 71.

162 E.g. Demougeot, *De l'unité*, pp. 566ff; cf. Palanque, 'Collégialité', pp. 289–90.
163 Cameron, *Claudian*, pp. 51–4.
164 Claudian, *De bello Gildonico*, 1, 4–5, Birt, 54: 'Concordia fratrum/Plena redit'.
165 Cameron, *Claudian*, pp. 110–11; cf. p. 52. For the inscription, *CIL*, 6, 1187 and 31256: 'Imperatoribus invictissimis felicissimisque dd. nn. Arcadio et Honorio. fratribus senatus populusque. Romanus vindicata rebellione et Africae restitutione laetus'. Note however that two Roman dedications to Stilicho for the same occasion give no hint of shared glory: *CIL*, 6, 1730 and 'Revue des publications épigraphiques', *Revue archéologique* (1926), no. 124.

relief of the triumphal column put up in New Rome indulged in artistic, or rather political license, by showing both Honorius and Arcadius celebrating the defeat of the Germanic faction.[166] This fact reinforces the possibility that the report of spectacles in the circus in honor of Gainas' defeat is accurate in situating the show in the ancient capital.[167] If it is correct, these celebrations are the first indication that, under the Theodosian system, the joint nature of imperial victories was marked in the territory of the victor's colleague in more effective and expensive fashion than had previously been the case. Such a new policy did not, however, imply a retreat from the more traditional, monumental embodiment of the collegiality of victory, as is clearly shown by the last Roman triumphal arch set up in the ancient capital. This arch, which was visible down to the Renaissance on the west bank of the Tiber by the Ponte S. Angelo, commemorated the Gothic victories of Honorius and Stilicho, celebrated in the triumph of 404.[168] It was put up a year later and dedicated to the 'most clement, most fortunate, world-wide victors, Our Lords, Arcadius, Honorius and Theodosius'.[169]

The evidence on joint celebration of Ravenna's victory over the usurper Fl. Claudius Constantinus is ambiguous.[170] Four years

---

[166] Becatti, *Colonna*, pp. 237–42; cf. Mazzarino, *Stilicone*, pp. 88ff.

[167] Eunapius, *De sententiis*, fg. 72, Boissevain, *Excerpta historica*, 4.96.20–97.2. The text has ἐν Ῥώμῃ at 96.20. For Rome: *PLRE*, 2, 1222, 'Anonymous 13'; for Constantinople: B. Baldwin, '"Perses": A mysterious Prefect in Eunapius', *Byz.*, 46 (1976), 5–8, and MacCormack, *Art and ceremony*, p. 11. The assimilation 'Rome' = 'New Rome' seems somewhat arbitrary in this context since elsewhere Eunapius calls Rome and Constantinople by their proper names, e.g. fg. 52, Boissevain 87.23 and fg. 74, 98.8, or fg. 80, 102.19–20. L. Cracco Ruggini, *Simboli di battaglia ideologica nel tardo ellenismo* (1972), was not available to me.

[168] *ILS*, 798, or *CIL*, 6, 1196; cf. Fiebiger–Schmidt, *Inschriftensammlung*, no. 24, pp. 25–6, and W. Kähler, 'Triumphbogen', *RE*, 7A, 400, no. 43.

[169] Fiebiger–Schmidt, *loc. cit.*: 'Imppp. clementissimis felicissimis toto orbe victoribus, ddd. nn⟨n⟩. Arcadio Honorio Theodosio Auggg. ad perenne indicium triumpho⟨rum⟩, quod Getarum nationem in omne aevum doc⟨u⟩ere exti⟨ngui⟩, arcum simulacris eorum tropaeisque decora⟨tum⟩ senatus populusque Romanus totius operis splendore...'.

[170] *Cons. Cplitana*, a.411, Mommsen, 246, has simply 'his conss. Constantini tyranni in conto caput adlatum est XIIII. kal. Octobr.'. If the failure to specify the place to which the head was brought is not due to a textual accident, it would mean that the entry refers to Constantinople and attests a head parade there; it is not however impossible that Ravenna was meant (thus *PLRE*, 2, 316–17).

later, however, East Rome saluted the western government's 'victory' over Athaulf with considerable panache, since the news triggered the festive lamp-lighting discussed above, as well as circus races. The pattern holds in 416, as evidenced by the theater show honoring Honorius' defeat of Attalus.[171] That this kind of joint celebration survived at least as late as 425 is shown by the decision of Theodosius II to hold a liturgical procession and thanksgiving services for the defeat in the West of John the usurper.[172] Finally, if it is true that the unidentified festival of 3 September in the calendar of Polemius Silvius corresponds to the commemoration of the younger Theodosius' victory over the Persians in 421, this could only mean that the western court continued to reciprocate the eastern government's public projection of collegial victory through Ravenna's annual state holidays, even into the darkest hours of the western Roman empire's final agony.[173]

Throughout the fourth and fifth centuries, then, the shared nature of victory and its celebration manifested and reflected the vicissitudes of the conception of the collegiality of imperial rule. Constantine's new family monarchy abandoned the tetrarchic system of common victory titles, while Valentinian's restoration of a collegial system of government brought with it a return to the old conception of joint victoriousness. The conception thrived under Theodosius the Great and experienced a new and unexpected development in the years following his death.

Set against what is known of the regional rivalries of the period, the public projection of imperial unity to the populations of Constantinople and Rome is, in itself, vital evidence both of the governments' will to maintain solidarity in the face of events and of their belief in the desirability of establishing or reinforcing their populations' belief in that solidarity. This in itself tells us that contemporary perceptions and evaluations of the situation of the empire and its constituent parts were, in these years, somewhat more complex than is sometimes claimed.

---

[171] Above, Ch. 2, p. 58.   [172] Above, Ch. 2, p. 60.
[173] Above, Ch. 2, n. 79. Cf. too the evidence of the coinage presented by Kaegi, *Decline*, pp. 23ff.

6. VICTORY CELEBRATIONS AND THE THRONE

At the same time that imperial victory celebrations could be used to communicate the political message of the underlying unity of imperial power, they could also serve to project and publicly define the relations between the monarch and lesser centers of power. In a society where all eyes were bracketed on the throne, in which an individual's status and social prestige soared or plummeted according to his standing *vis-à-vis* the emperor, great significance could be attached to little gestures. In the context of the collegiality of victory, attention has already been drawn to Constantius' reluctance to see Julian Caesar using the triumphal titles to which his victories might have entitled him. There can be little doubt that the reason lay in Constantius' obsessive fear of competition from his young nephew. For example, unlike other emperors, Constantius' victory bulletins sometimes failed even to mention the role played by his generals in battles which took place far from his presence.[174] Julian's frequent victory dispatches from the front and Constantius' refusal to grant him due credit only encouraged the courtiers who sneered to imperial laughter at the 'little victor' (*victorinus*), a cruel pun on both Julian's subordinate status to Constantius, who of course bore the official title *Victor*, and the Caesar's short stature – 'the yakking mole', as some disgruntled soldiers called him.[175] That Julian's subordinate and precarious position was driven home and publicly displayed is only underscored by the fact that Constantius never allowed Julian to celebrate, or even join in Constantius' celebrations of the Caesar's successes in Gaul. Julian felt strongly that he was in fact entitled to joint celebration with the emperor and his bitterness hangs heavy in his own account of the slight.[176]

---

[174] Ammianus Marcellinus, 16, 12, 69, Clark, 1.103.1–2. That other emperors cited their generals can be deduced not only from Ammianus' remark, but also from Symmachus, *Rel.* 47, 2, Seeck, 316.2–9.

[175] Rösch, *Kaisertitel*, p. 80; G.W. Bowersock, *Julian the Apostate* (Cambridge, Mass., 1978), pp. 12–13.

[176] Julian, *Ad Athenienses*, 8, ed. J. Bidez, *Oeuvres complètes* 1.1 (Paris, 1932). 226.6–17. Julian first emphasizes that he had played by the rules: οὐκ ἐφϑόνησα τοῦ κατορϑώματος. Κωνσταντίῳ; even though he could not celebrate a triumph by himself (καίτοι εἰ μὴ ϑριαμβεύειν ἐξῆν), he could have executed his captive Chnodomar and deprived Constantius of the glory of displaying a live enemy king. He then reminds his audience of Constantius' denial of a joint celebration: Συνέβη

In this instance, the slight lay in Constantius' denial to Julian of a privilege frequently granted to the heir apparent, a favor which explains the seeming incongruity of a child concelebrating the outcome of a military campaign, as though he had played some significant part in it. Constantine himself seems deliberately to have associated the fourteen- or fifteen-year-old Caesar Constantine II with observances of a victory over the Goths.[177] In the same manner, Theodosius honored the defeat of the Greutungs jointly with his cotriumphator and heir apparent, the child Arcadius, who would have been about nine years old in 386.[178] He later took his four-year-old son Honorius along for the victory festival held at Rome in 389. The trip to Rome was the first official meeting between the population and elite of the ancient capital and the boy who was destined to be their Augustus, even as the nominal ruler of the West, Valentinian II, remained far to the North and out of the picture in distant Trier.[179] Some years later, Claudian asserted that the child had played a prominent, if passive, role in the ceremonies, seated in his father's lap.[180] That Honorius' presence was meant to make a political point regarding Theodosius' plans for the future has been deduced by more than one scholar.[181] The distribution of significant largess was a standard and obvious effort to influence in this direction the pockets, if not the hearts and minds, of the Roman population. A rare bronze issue from the mint of Rome bears the slogan 'The Hope of the State'. The formula was customarily associated with heirs to the throne and has been linked with Honorius' presence in the eternal city; the distribution of such coins coupled with a 'Most Noble Boy' sitting in the triumphator's lap was a message of unmistakable clarity to

---

τοίνυν, ἐμοῦ μὲν ἀγωνισαμένου, ἐκείνου δὲ ὁδεύσαντος. μόνον . . . οὐχ ἡμᾶς, ἀλλ᾽ ἐκεῖνον θριαμβεῦσαι (all around this passage, he uses the first person singular when speaking of himself alone). This appraisal, minus the bitterness, is echoed by Libanius in 363: *Or.*, 12, 49, Foerster, 2.26.15–27.6 and again in *Or.*, 18, 66–7, Foerster, 264.15–265.12.

[177] Above, Ch. 2, p. 39.
[178] Above, Ch. 2, p. 43.
[179] Cf. Seeck, *Untergang*, 5, 227.
[180] Claudian, *VI cons.*, 53–68, Birt, 237–8; cf. *Cons. Cplitana*, a.389, Mommsen, 245; cf. W. Ensslin, 'War Kaiser Theodosius I. zweimal in Rom?', *Hermes*, 81 (1953), 500–7, here 500; and Lippold, *Theodosius*, p. 39.
[181] Thus Seeck, *Untergang*, 5, 227; *RIC*, 9, 112–13.

the mass of onlookers not privy to Theodosius' inner counsels.[182]
In much the same fashion, Honorius was hurriedly summoned
from the East to participate in the victory celebrations over
Eugenius, even as his father's health waned.[183] At his arrival in
Milan, Honorius, now aged ten, participated in a parade which
Claudian links with Eugenius' defeat.[184] The child ruler joined his
father for the victory celebration staged in the Milanese circus and,
when Theodosius was overcome by his fatal illness at lunch,
Honorius presided over the rest of the day's doings by himself.[185]
In each case, the obvious aim was to present to an expectant
population a future heir to the throne and to the imperial
monopoly of victory. The words of a contemporary propagandist
accurately summed up the intent of children's participation in such
ceremonies:

> Prospera Romuleis sperantur tempora rebus
> In nomen ventura tuum. Praemissa futuris
> Dant exempla fidem....[186]

The succession for which the population had been prepared by
Theodosius' triumphs introduced a new phase in late Roman rule
when the emperors reigned but did not govern.[187] From the
splendor of their imperial isolation, the Augusti emerged only to
perform the essential symbolic acts of a ceremonial monarchy,
while the reality of power was fought over by the great courtiers,
civil servants and military men of the era.[188] It was not only the
reality, but also the trappings of power which leading officials of
the eastern court arrogated unto themselves. Rufinus' assassination and the concomitant victory of Eutropius' faction in
governmental infighting were heralded as though Rufinus had

---

[182] *RIC*, 9, 133, no. 63; cf. p. 113.
[183] Thus Socrates, *H.e.*, 5, 26, *PG*, 67.653C.
[184] Claudian, *Panegyricus de tertio consulatu Honorii*, 126–41, Birt, 146, esp. lines 128–30: '...cum te genitoris amico/Exceptus gremio mediam veherere per urbem/Velaretque pios communis laurea currus!' delivered less than a year after the event.
[185] Socrates, *H.e.*, 5, 26, *PG*, 67.653C.
[186] Claudian, *IV cons.*, 619–21, Birt, 173, on the first consulate of Honorius, then aged two, which coincided with his father's victory and triumph over the Greutungs.
[187] Stein, *Bas-Empire*, 1, 225.
[188] See Synesius of Cyrene's complaints concerning Arcadius' isolation: *De regno*, 14, ed. Terzaghi, 2.29.8ff, confirmed by the crowds which flocked to see Arcadius on one of his rare public appearances in the city: Socrates, *H.e.*, 6, 23, *PG*, 67.732A-B.

actually usurped the purple and Arcadius had actually defeated him. Eutropius and Fravitta seem to have celebrated splendid triumphal entries into the capital, in honor of their military expeditions. Thus too the City Prefect dominated the victory celebrations for the defeat of Attalus in 416.[189] All of this reveals a remarkable flexibility in the perimeters of public acceptability of symbolic deportment by leading officials in late fourth- and early fifth-century Constantinople. After a new series of emperors who ruled as well as reigned, this wide measure of privilege had manifestly come to an end, since the scant honor conceded to Belisarius could be hailed as an unprecedented achievement. Perhaps the old strictures had begun to be reasserted as early as the anger of Theodosius II one day in the Hippodrome, when the crowd acclaimed the building activities of the great Urban and Praetorian Prefect Cyrus with the shout, 'Constantine founded it, Cyrus renewed it', an incident which is reported to have triggered the official's fall.[190]

Just as interesting as this evidence on the ebullient, open character of government and society in Constantinople at the turn of the fourth century are the contrasting developments in the ancient capital. There too great officials like Stilicho dominated, enjoying positions which seemingly compared to those of the mandarins of the eastern court, as well as the kind of ceremonial perquisites appropriate to imperial dignitaries. But their public display fell short of the appropriation of imperial ritual which characterized contemporary New Rome. Thus the celebrations of Stilicho's victories sound a more moderate note. Why else would Claudian conclude a description of how glorious Stilicho's triumphal parade *would have been*, had he but desired to celebrate it in the ancient way?[191] But Stilicho was above all that: according

---

[189] *Chron. pasch.*, Bonn, 573.15–17; cf. *PLRE*, 2, 1192, 'Ursus 3', and above, p. 58. A. Lippold, 'Theodosius II.', *RE*, S. 13 (1973), 961–1044, here 968, presumes that the emperor was present; yet it would seem unlikely that the imperial presence would be passed over in silence while that of a high official was emphasized. It is interesting to compare this incident with evidence of lasting ceremonial innovation introduced during and because of the childhood of Theodosius II: John Lydus, *De magistratibus*, 2, 9, Wünsch, 64.11–18.

[190] Malalas, *Chronographia*, Bonn, 361.19–362.4. On the incident, cf. Dagron, *Naissance*, pp. 270–2.

[191] Claudian, *De consulatu Stilichonis*, 3, 14–25, Birt, 221.

to Claudian, he preferred to celebrate his triumph in men's minds, a statement which scarcely veils Claudian's habitual technique of creating virtue out of necessity.[192] When it came right down to celebrating Stilicho's great victories at Pollentia and Verona, the best he could hope for in the ancient capital was the privilege of *consessus vehiculi*, of riding with the emperor in his triumphal car:

> Tunc tibi magnorum mercem Fortuna laborum
> Persolvit, Stilicho, curru cum vectus eodem
> Vrbe triumphantem generum florente iuventa
> Conspiceres....[193]

In the ancient capital, custom called for stricter adherence to the old conventions of public behavior and imperial perquisites. In the new city, and, indeed, the new society of upwardly mobile civil servants, there was, for a brief time in the fifth century, less tradition and fewer entrenched censors to check the new elite's hunger for outward signs of prestige and power. Just as it was a western bishop who first imposed limits on the eastern emperor's accustomed freedom of movement within the sacred space of the Christian sanctuary, so western society stood ever more scrupulously by the recognized ritual prerogatives of imperial office, even as the western empire began its long slide into oblivion. The contrast in the ritual behavior of the two *partes'* highest officials is symptomatic of the emerging differences in the societies that shaped them.

By the sixth century, a different tone prevailed in Rome on the Bosphorus. Procopius' Secret History testifies to the efforts of Justinian and Theodora to impose new codes of deportment on the empire's great officials, a testimony which is seconded by developments like Justinian's ambivalent attitude toward the ordinary consulate or the abandonment of the elaborate rituals of the imperial law courts.[194]

---

[192] *Ibid.*, 3, 26–9, Birt, 221–2: 'Sed non inmodicus proprii iactator honoris/Consul, Roma, tuus. Non illum praemia tantum/Quam labor ipse iuvat; strepitus fastidit inanes/Inque animis hominum pompa meliore triumphat'. On virtue and necessity in Claudian's technique, see e.g. Cameron, *Claudian*, p. 385.

[193] Claudian, *VI cons.*, 578–81, Birt, 255–6.

[194] Procopius, *Anec.*, 15, 13–17 and 30, 21–6, Haury, 3.1.95.19–96.12 and 184.19–185.23; Stein, *Bas-Empire*, 2, 461ff, on Justinian's motives; John Lydus, *De magistratibus*, 2, 116, Wünsch, 71.24ff.

Against this background occurred one of the most widely cited and misapprehended victory celebrations of the period: the 'last "Roman" triumph' – the celebration by Justinian of Belisarius' reconquest of Africa. Scholarly evaluations of this event have ranged from cautious paraphrase of Procopius' rather enigmatic account to fantastic effusions which reconstruct the event on the basis of the medieval ceremonies staged four hundred years later, or blithely impose on the sixth-century event legal conceptions from the first century before Christ.[195]

Procopius, and historians who have followed him, made much of the uniqueness of the honor granted his hero. The celebration described by Procopius consisted essentially of a parade in two stages. First came a victory parade from Belisarius' house – presumably within the city and therefore excluding a triumphal entry like those attributed to successful commanders a century earlier – through the main boulevard of the city, doubtless still scarred by the great destruction of the Nika revolt, and into the Hippodrome. The second stage was the familiar and traditional triumphal parade of booty and captives down the middle of the Hippodrome.[196] Only the first element appears new, and only it could be presented as a restoration of ancient Roman custom; it alone deserves the qualification of 'Belisarius' triumph'. In fact, no other late antique authors familiar with the facts – including an eyewitness like John the Lydian – even approach the modern proclivity to view the whole celebration as 'Belisarius' triumph'. At most, Belisarius is mentioned for his role in capturing Gelimer and presenting him to the emperor at victory celebrations; at the least, his role is passed over in silence.[197]

---

[195] For this ceremony as the last Roman triumph, Av. Cameron's comm. to Corippus, *Iust.*, p. 119. Bury, *Later Roman empire . . . to the death of Justinian*, 2, 139 paraphrases Procopius closely, as do Stein, *Bas-Empire*, 2, 320 – who fails to distinguish Belisarius' parade from the Hippodrome proceedings – and L. Schmidt, *Geschichte der Wandalen* (Munich, 1942), pp. 141–2 – who places Theodora in the *kathisma* without any textual evidence. L.M. Chassin, *Bélisaire, généralissime byzantin (504–565)* (Paris, 1957), pp. 81–4 takes the ceremonial cake with his extravagant liberties with the evidence; Kollwitz, *Plastik*, p. 65 identifies this ceremony as an *ovatio*. Cf. too the discussion in MacCormack, *Art and ceremony*, pp. 74–6.

[196] Procopius, *Bella*, 4, 9, 3, Haury, 1.456.7–13.

[197] Thus John Lydus, *De magistratibus*, 2, 2, Wünsch, 56.1–6, mentions that it was customary for Roman emperors to wear the *loros* whenever they celebrated triumphs over captive kings (ὅταν ἐπὶ βασιλεῦσιν αἰχμαλώτοις θριαμβεῦσαι) and

Why was Belisarius granted what Procopius considered a unique honor? Several factors certainly contributed to creating a situation favorable for such a gesture on the part of the emperor. Politically speaking, Belisarius enjoyed the influence both of his own personality on the emperor and of the intimate friendship between his wife and the empress.[198] In another sense, such an honor could be construed as a fitting reward for his own contribution to the expedition which brought such plentiful riches, lands and future taxes to the empire. Not only was the general supposed to have been granted unique authority at the campaign's outset; like other generals of his age, he helped to man and finance his expeditions out of his own pocket.[199] Generals were known to contribute from their own funds to entice prime candidates into the ranks even of imperial units. Belisarius' two thousand private retainers played an essential military role; moreover, he is recorded to have gone so far as to replace the horses and arms his troops lost in battle, surely a substantial outlay.[200]

These factors helped to create the conditions in which a new departure in victory ceremonial could occur. But as so often happens in the history of ceremonies, the apparent innovation of Belisarius' triumphal parade through the streets of Constantinople was precipitated by the immediate political context of the

---

proves it by citing the case of Gelimir. Cf. 3, 55, Wünsch 144.19–25 (the subject of the sentence is Justinian). See too Jordanes, *Getica*, 171, ed. T. Mommsen, *MGH. AA*, 5.1 (1882). 102.16–21: 'nam mox Iustiniani imperatoris ultio in eum apparuit et cum omne genus suum opibusque ... Constantinopolim delatus per virum gloriosissimum Belisarium ..., magnum in circo populo spectaculum fuit seraque suae paenitudinis gerens cum se videret de fastigio regali deiectum ...'. Jordanes, who insists on Belisarius' contribution (cf. 172, p. 103.1) still calls this victory 'triumphus Iustiniani imperatoris a deo sibi donatus' (*ibid.*, 103.3); cf. too 307, p. 136.25–137.2. See also Marius of Avenches, *Chronica* a.534, 2, ed. T. Mommsen, *MGH.AA*, 11.235; Zachary Rhetor, *H.e.* 9, 17, tr. E.W. Brooks, *Corpus scriptorum christianorum orientalium*, Scriptores Syri, 3.2 (1924). 91.29ff; Corippus, *Ioh.*, 3, 17–22, Diggle and Goodyear, 47; Malalas, *Chronographia*, Bonn, 478.22–479.3 which fails even to mention Belisarius.

[198] Stein, *Bas-Empire*, 2, 285.

[199] On Belisarius' powers: Bury, *Later Roman Empire ... to the death of Justinian*, 2, 127; Stein, *Bas-Empire*, 2, 312, and J. Durliat, 'Magister militum–στρατηλάτης dans l'Empire byzantin (VIᵉ-VIIᵉ siècles)', *BZ*, 72 (1979), 306–20, here 308.

[200] Stein, *Bas-Empire*, 2, 312–13; Jones, *Later Roman Empire*, 1, 666–8; Belisarius supplies horses and arms: Procopius, *Bella*, 7, 1, 8, Haury, 2.299.8–13.

moment. His return to the capital had taken place under a cloud of suspicion. According to Procopius, unnamed officials had levied muffled accusations of intended usurpation against the popular and spectacularly successful young general. Less than thirty months after he nearly lost the throne to the Nika upheaval and usurpation attempt, Justinian must have taken the charges quite seriously.[201] However, in a way that is unclear today, suspicion was quickly dispelled or silenced and Justinian proceeded to publish his confidence in his general to the bureaucracy, the capital's population and the world at large, by granting him an honor loudly touted as unprecedented. But the victory observances did more than underscore the emperor's renewed confidence in Belisarius: the conqueror of Africa performed two symbolic gestures whose significance could not have escaped officials and onlookers familiar with the minute details of public ritual deportment. In his parade through the city he was not allowed the use of a horse or public vehicle; rather, he walked humbly, like any commoner.[202] Any spectator who failed to grasp the fundamentally subordinate status of even so exalted a personality as Belisarius when he walked in procession to the Hippodrome would certainly have gotten the point at the next stage in the parade. There, the massed spectators were treated not only to ritual divestiture of the Vandal king in front of the imperial box and the obvious symbolic gesture of his forced full prostration before the seated emperor: they also witnessed the reverence of the general for his emperor, as he too performed the *proskynesis*, 'seeing that he was a suppliant of the emperor'.[203] The

---

[201] Procopius, *Bella*, 4, 8, 1ff, Haury, 1.452.1ff; cf. B. Rubin, 'Prokopios v. Kaisareia', *RE*, 23, 1 (1957), 273–599, here 419.

[202] Procopius, *Bella*, 4, 9, 3, Haury, 1.456.9–10: οὐ τῷ παλαιῷ μέντοι τρόπῳ, ἀλλὰ πεζῇ βαδίζων ἐκ τῆς οἰκίας τῆς αὐτοῦ.... That this crimp on Belisarius' ceremonial style was the principal element lacking for a real, old-fashioned triumph is evidenced by Procopius' description of Belisarius' consular procession, which, in contrast to the victory celebration, was a triumph κατὰ...τὸν παλαιὸν νόμον, *Bella*, 4, 9, 15, Haury, 1.458.11–13: ἐς ὑπάτους γὰρ προελθόντι οἱ ξυνέπεσε φέρεσθαί τε πρὸς τῶν αἰχμαλώτων καὶ ἐν τῷ δίφρῳ ὀχουμένῳ to throw booty to the crowd. Moving about the city on foot was not something exalted personalities engaged in without a motive deeper than lust for exercise. Note too Procopius' description of the parade-like character of Belisarius' daily trips from his house to the Forum: *Bella*, 7, 1, 5–6, Haury, 2.298.20–299.1.

[203] Procopius, *Bella*, 4, 9, 12, Haury, 1.457.22–458.2.

imperial subject as suppliant was a notion rooted in the bureaucratic procedures of the empire; the term (ἱκέτης) used by Procopius occurs in rescripts and serves as the technical designation for a petitioner.[204] The attitude of prosternation offered explicit recognition of an emperor's exalted status; in return for the suppliant's gesture of loyalty, imperial authority could intervene in the routine affairs of the provincial administration on his behalf. To the officials, subjects and representatives of foreign powers present that day in the Hippodrome, Belisarius' gesture could be construed as a clear public statement on where he stood regarding rumors of schemes against the throne.[205]

The external form of the ceremony honoring Belisarius was a variation on one of the basic building blocks of late Roman secular and religious ceremonial, the procession. In this instance, it is clear that the organizers drew their inspiration from the most prestigious ritual then available to the secular elite, the consular procession, which likewise began at the consul's home and could end at the circus.[206] The rite inflicted on Gelimer had a different background. As has already been pointed out, this ritual divestiture of a defeated leader had been associated with the army in the fourth century. Today it was transferred from the camps to the city, from the military audience of a victorious army to the urban audience of Constantinople. The fact that the ceremony culminated in the divestiture and forced *proskynesis* must have sent shivers down the spine of any Gothic onlookers. For this gesture was not intended to obliterate the distinctions between an emperor's subjects and his enemies. On the contrary, it signaled to any who had not yet grasped Justinian's approach to the barbarian kingdoms that the Vandal ruler was not regarded as an independ-

---

[204] For ἱκέτης as technical term, see three rescripts of ca. A.D. 551: J. Maspero, *Papyrus grecs d'époque byzantine*, 1.1 (Cairo, 1910), no. 67024, p. 54.12 and 19; no. 67026, p. 59.4, 6, 14 and 18 and no. 67028, p. 61.6 and 9.

[205] For the Persian ambassador's presence, see Zachary Rhetor, *H.e.*, 9, 7, tr. Brooks, 2.91.29–32.

[206] A good example of the great prestige still attached to this ritual in the first half of the sixth century comes from Boethius, *Philosophiae consolatio*, 2, prosa 3, 8, ed. L. Bieler, CCL, 94 (1957). 22.22–30 where the imprisoned aristocrat muses on the sudden reverse of fortune which had cast him into prison after enjoying the spectacle of two sons' consulate. On consular processions, Corippus, *Iust.*, Cameron, 194–5 and 201–2, with all necessary references.

ent sovereign. He was but a defeated usurper, a rebel against the Roman order.[207]

Procopius' description of the victory celebration of 534 reveals a composite ceremony whose constituent elements are easily identifiable within late Roman society's repertory of public ritual. The external forms of the processions were typically late antique. Yet Procopius presents the whole extravaganza as a unique restoration of ancient Roman tradition, a great leap backward of some six centuries.[208] Although some have been quick to perceive *Kaiserkritik* in Procopius' assertion,[209] is it not more likely that he is echoing the original, official interpretation of this staged event? After all, Justinian is well known for his insistence that his reign was essentially a return to the good old days of ancient lore. What more effective way to innovate in victory ritual than by staging what was billed as a return to the pristine traditions of ancient Rome? This interpretation is only strengthened by the consideration that the chief officer for imperial ceremonial at the time of Belisarius' parade was none other than Tribonian, a lawyer deeply imbued with the splendors of Roman antiquity.[210] At any rate, after the innovation of the celebration of 534, Belisarius was allowed to celebrate his victory in more customary fashion, by assuming the consulate. In so doing, he enjoyed the traditional reward bestowed on victorious generals as recently as the reign of Anastasius.[211]

At first glance, the celebration of a triumph by Caesar Tiberius in the reign of Justin II appears related to the kind of development signaled by Belisarius' parade. In actuality, the parallel is misleading. Even the most exalted general was scarcely on the same footing as a general who bore the title of Caesar and the presumption of being the heir apparent. The precise circumstances are decisive on this score. Roman operations on the Persian frontier had been very unsuccessful, involving disasters at Antioch and Apamaea as well as the fall of Dara in 573 and the torching of Melitene in 575, followed by failed negotiations with the

[207] Cf. MacCormack's differing appraisal, *Art and ceremony*, p. 76.
[208] *Bella*, 4, 93, Haury, 1.456.9–10.   [209] Rubin, 'Prokopios', p. 420.
[210] T. Honoré, *Tribonian* (London, 1978), pp. 57 and 246.
[211] Procopius, *Bella*, 4, 9, 15, Haury, 1.458.10–15. Cf. above, Ch. 2, p. 61.

Persians.[212] In the capital, the emperor's progressive insanity was an open secret. In moments of semi-lucidity, he was trotted out before the bureaucracy for promotions; for the benefit of the general population, he was carried to the circus shows, but was unable to stay beyond the morning spectacles.[213] Whether or not the triumph of 576 took place during a period in which Justin was unfit for public appearance, the sight of the successful general and designated successor presiding over victory celebrations featuring splendid Persian booty must have been reassuring to the population. The Caesar was in control, both of the throne and of the rather battered mystique of imperial victory.[214]

The preceding pages have attempted to clarify a few of the ways in which imperial victory celebrations were enmeshed in the public life and mentality of late imperial society. The obsession with usurpation, the unrealistic fascination of a decaying former capital, the vital dynamism of developments in the provinces are all reflected in this one facet of the ritual apparatus of late antique monarchy. The manner in which imperial victory celebrations projected the unity of the empire – a fundamental tenet of a dying world's political creed – as well as manifested the interrelations of power close to the throne, reveals the complex political message contained in these ceremonies. The detailed consideration of specific ceremonies indicates an important methodological point. Even more significant than revered traditions or imitation of the past to the characteristics of each celebration, it would seem, was the precise political and social configuration of the moment. With these lessons in mind, we may turn to the medieval inheritance of late Roman triumphal traditions.

---

[212] See e.g. N.H. Baynes, *Cambridge Medieval History*, 2 (Cambridge, 1913), 272ff. Cf. J. Kulakovsky, *Istoriya Vizantii*, 2 (Kiev, 1912), 366ff.
[213] John of Ephesus, *H.e.*, 3, 3, 6, tr. Brooks, 95.18–26.
[214] On this celebration, above, Ch. 2, pp. 68–9.

4

The development of imperial victory celebrations in early medieval Byzantium

Victory celebrations from the advent of iconoclasm down to the great watershed of the eleventh century offer a complex picture. Superficial continuity combines with deep change, long lapses of darkness are interrupted by brief bursts of light. Even a cursory examination reveals the undying influence of the precedents set by the later Roman state, beginning with the central role of military victory in the imperial idea and its ritual expressions.[1] Familiar from late antiquity are the triumphal entries, supplication and thanksgiving processions, spectacles involving races and commemorative coin issues associated with real or imagined imperial success. Contemporary observers were well aware of these connections, as is clear from the conscious links they make between celebrations of their own day and those of ancient Rome.[2] More significant – because less subject to the 'distorting mirror' of the Byzantine literary vision – is the recourse medieval

---

[1] A late eleventh- or early twelfth-century Arab observer went so far as to state: 'When [the king] has fought an enemy and come back in triumph and victory, his rank and position in the kingdom grow. If, however, he has been defeated and proved too weak, he is dismissed from kingship...': V. Minorski, 'Marvazi on the Byzantines', *Annuaire de l'Institut de philologie et d'histoire orientales et slaves*, 10 (1950), 455–69, here 460. Cf. Treitinger, *Oströmische*, pp. 169ff, and H. Hunger, *Prooimion. Elemente der byzantinischen Kaiseridee in den Arengen der Urkunden*, Wiener byzantinistische Studien, 1 (Vienna, 1964), pp. 73ff.

[2] Constantine VII compares his grandfather's triumph of 873 to those of the ancient emperors of glorious Rome: Theoph. Cont., 5, 40, Bekker, 271.4–5; on this kind of literary conceit in the *Vita Basilii*: R.J.H. Jenkins, 'The classical background of the *Scriptores Post Theophanem*', *DOP*, 8 (1954), 11–30. Cf. the pointed, implicit comparison between Camillus' triumph and that of Tzimisces (below, n. 171) and the influence of Procopius on a description of Nicephorus Phocas' triumph (below, n. 142).

organizers of ceremonies had to antique sources when devising their modern staged events: the dossier on triumphal entries assembled by Constantine VII Porphyrogenitus reaches back to the sixth century for its source material.[3]

The continuity, then, of Byzantium's early medieval victory celebrations with those of late antiquity is evident. But continuity does not imply identity. It would in fact be more accurate to think of the enduring traditions of the later Roman empire's public life as constituting a kind of ceremonial repertory, from which the rulers of medieval Byzantium could select and assemble the elements they favored for the ceremony of the moment. Like the use of classical *spolia* in medieval monuments, for all the identity of constituent elements, the resulting whole is surprisingly novel.

Victory celebrations were not, of course, the only occasion on which imperial victoriousness impinged on medieval Constantinople's public life. Annual religious observances like the great processions for the liturgical year's central feasts filled the streets with well organized chants for imperial victory, while the secular celebrations of the Hippodrome fused sporting success with military victory. When an eighth-century emperor addressed the crowd, his opening words were 'My fortune has conquered!'[4] But, without question, the most central and influential projection of imperial victory occurred in the elaborate celebrations of military success organized ad hoc.

Broadly speaking, victory observances in the years stretching from the resurgence of the empire under the iconoclasts down to the transformations of the eleventh century display three particularly important trends: first, an intensification of developments launched in the sixth and seventh centuries, including an increasing liturgification of the ceremony, a recurrent association of victory with the cult of the Virgin, as well as an initial tendency toward increased selectivity of audience; second, the dissolution of

---

[3] *Imperial Expeditions*, Bonn, 497.14–498.13.
[4] For the acclamations chanted during imperial processions on feast days see Constantine VII Porphyrogenitus, *De ceremoniis aulae byzantinae*, 1, 3, ed. A. Vogt, 1 (Paris, 1935).36.17–20 (Epiphany); 1, 4, 1.38.20–1 (Easter); 1, 5, 1.42.9–11 (Easter Monday), etc. For the assimilation of sporting to military victory in Hippodrome acclamations, see, e.g. *De cer.*, 1, 78, ed. A. Vogt, 2 (Paris, 1939).128.5–9. For the emperor's boastful address: Stephen Deacon, *Vita et miracula Stephani iunioris*, (BHG, 1666), *PG*, 100.1137A.

the ancient imperial monopoly of victory; and third, a sporadic growth and decline in the frequency of imperial victory celebrations. With regard to this last point, if the chronological distribution of victory celebrations were plotted on a horizontal line, the result would be not an even or partially even pattern, but several clusters of ceremonies. The clustering appears significant and offers precious insight into the ritual's historical nature and development. Perhaps, it might be objected, the pattern is due merely to the fact that victory celebrations naturally occurred in periods of success and expansion. Even were we to forget, however, the lessons of late antiquity, we would then have to expect that the triumphs of imperial military policy in the tenth century would have triggered more frequent celebrations before and after the third quarter of that century. But such does not seem to have been the case.

On the other hand, the representativeness of the evidence might be called into question. For example, arguments from silence are less than convincing in the obscurity of the eighth century. While we may hope, however, that further research will bring to light new celebrations, only massive shortcomings in the evidence would alter the fundamental picture for the ninth and tenth centuries. Furthermore, the one opportunity the sources afford for verifying their representativeness yields a positive result. The historiographical and hagiographical sources allow the conclusion that, notwithstanding the formal assertion of Theophanes' continuators, Theophilus celebrated two triumphs.[5] This conclusion is fully borne out by evidence from the tenth-century palace milieu: to the highly privy knowledge of the emperor who compiled the technical treatise On Imperial Expeditions, Theophilus celebrated two triumphs.[6] This comforts the assumption that the evidence assembled here is sufficiently representative to warrant consideration of the causes of the sporadic nature of victory celebration in the ninth through eleventh centuries.

---

[5] This is clearly the meaning of the words: '... ἡττητό τε ἀεὶ καὶ οὐ κατὰ βασιλέα ὑπέστρεφεν': Theoph. Cont., 3, 2, Bonn, 87.7–8. For the narrative evidence on these triumphs, below, nn. 52 and 61–5.

[6] *Imp. Exp.*, Bonn, 507.22–508.1: ἰστέον δὲ καὶ τοῦτο, ὅτι πάλιν ἐκ δευτέρου ἐξελθόντος.... This account is completely independent of the surviving narrative sources for the reign of Theophilus.

I. TRIUMPHS OF CONSTANTINE V

In victory celebrations as in so many other areas, the years following the deliverance of Constantinople in 718 are a mystery. The first recorded triumph came early in the reign of Leo's son and successor, Constantine V. It honored his successful resumption of power after the usurpation of his sister's father-in-law, the *curopalates* and Count of Opsikion, Artabasdus, whose eminent position in the state derived from the decisive role he had once played in Leo III's rise to power.[7] The grisly relic of imperial restoration was no longer set up outside the walls: to certify to the capital's population that the usurpation was over, the head of one of the rebel's chief supporters was hung for three days from the Arch of the Milion, the milestone situated in the monumental heart of Constantinople.[8] Like Justinian II's return to power some forty years earlier, Constantine marked his victory with the traditional horse races, apparently staged in the great Hippodrome.[9] The races were preceded by the public humiliation of the vanquished usurper, his sons and their friends. The parade of infamy was transplanted to the arena. The defeated were led through the Diippion – a detail which seems to have conveyed particular scorn – and marched along the race track.[10] The patriarch Anastasius, judged guilty of collaborating with the

[7] On the revolt, Ostrogorsky, *Geschichte*, pp. 137–9; A. Lombard, *Constantin V, empereur des Romains* (Paris, 1902), pp. 26–30; W.E. Kaegi, Jr, *Byzantine Military Unrest, 471–843. An Interpretation* (Amsterdam, 1981), pp. 214ff. For Artabasdus' career, R. Guilland, 'Le curopalate', Βυζάντινα, 2 (1970), 187–249, here 198–9; seals: G. Zacos and A. Veglery, *Byzantine Lead Seals*, 1, 2 (Basel, 1972), no. 1741 with further references.

[8] Theophanes, A.M. 6235, De Boor, 420.16–18. On the Milion, Janin, *Cple byz.*, pp. 103–4; R. Guilland, *Topographie*, 2, 28–31; the report of its archaeological discovery: N. Fıratlı–T. Ergıl, 'Divanyolu *Milion* sondajı', *Istanbul Arkeoloji Müzeleri Yilliği*, 15–16 (1969), 199–212 (Eng.: 208–12); Müller-Wiener, *Bildlexikon*, pp. 216–18.

[9] Theophanes, A.M. 6235, De Boor, 420.27–421.1; cf. the translation by Anastasius Bibliothecarius, ed. De Boor, *ibid.*, 2.275.4–5; Nicephorus, *Brev.*, De Boor, 62.14–16.

[10] On the Diippion, see esp. C. Mango, 'Le *Diippion*. Étude historique et topographique', *RÉB*, 8 (1950), 152–61; cf. Janin, *Cple byz.*, pp. 342–3 and Guilland, *Topographie*, 1, 393–410, esp. 394–5. The infamy associated with the Diippion is implied by Germanus' prophecy of 729: Theophanes, A.M. 6221, De Boor, 407.29–408.18. On the late antique and medieval parade of infamy, the basic study is Ph. Koukoules, "Η διαπόμπευσις κατὰ τοὺς βυζαντινοὺς χρόνους.', *Byzantina Metabyzantina*, 1, 2 (1949), 75–101.

usurper, was part of the same sorry spectacle: he had been publicly beaten and was paraded through the arena, seated backward on an ass.[11]

Twice in his reign, Constantine celebrated success over the Bulgarians with a triumphal entry.[12] The costly victory of 30 June 763, over the khan Teletz, was honored by a dual observance.[13] Concerning the ceremonial entry, Theophanes or his source points out, as though the detail were noteworthy, that Constantine entered the city fully armed, accompanied by the army. The parade featured proof of the victory in the form of Bulgarian prisoners yoked to wooden shackles.[14] Some elements of the late antique organizational apparatus for such ceremonies were still – or at least, once again – functional, since Constantine was acclaimed en route by the 'demes' and the execution of the prisoners was entrusted to individuals identified as πολῖται and δημόται of the colors, i.e. πολῖται and members of the factions in their eighth-century incarnation.[15] The success was further heralded by races

---

[11] Theophanes, A.M. 6235, De Boor, 420.27–421.2. It is interesting to note that Nicephorus, *Brev.*, leaves Anastasius' humiliation to silence.

[12] Concerning the triumphal entry of late 773 next to nothing is known; Theophanes' account suggests that it may have included a harangue in which Constantine called the operation the 'noble war': Theophanes, A.M. 6265, De Boor, 447.23–6. On the campaign, Ostrogorsky, *Geschichte*, p. 141, Lombard, *Constantin V*, pp. 54–5. For A.M. 6257 (= A.D. 765), Theophanes describes the public humiliation of monks and the parade of infamy and execution of 19 officials from the highest ranks of government in association with races held on 21 and 25 August respectively (De Boor, 437.25–438.21; Nicephorus, *Brev.*, De Boor, 74.1–21). The parades were clearly in the tradition of the political use of the Hippodrome (cf. Theophanes, 438.3–4: they were paraded 'as though they had been plotting evil things against the emperor'). In the present state of research, it is not clear whether these races were connected with possible celebrations marking the disastrous campaign from which the emperor had returned on 19 July (Theophanes 437.25), whether they were specifically staged for the occasion, or whether these dates corresponded to public holidays in the lost state calendar of the iconoclast emperors. It is at any rate an excellent example of the political use Constantine V made of the circus and which is further evidenced by the *V. Stephani iunioris*, PG, 100.1136C–7A.

[13] On the conflict: Lombard, *Constantin V*, p. 47ff; V. Zlatarski, *Istoriya na pervoto bŭlgarsko tsarstvo*, I, 1 (Sofia, 1918), 214; S. Runciman, *A history of the first Bulgarian empire* (London, 1930), p. 38; V. Beševliev, *Die protobulgarische Periode der bulgarischen Geschichte* (Amsterdam, 1981), pp. 214–15; Nicephorus I, *Antirrheticus*, 3, 72, PG, 100.505A–9A, emphasizes the carnage on both sides.

[14] Theophanes, A.M. 6254, De Boor, 433.10–14; cf. Nicephorus, *Brev.*, De Boor, 69.16–21.

[15] *Ibid.* Cf. the commentary in Cameron, *Circus*, pp. 302–4; note however (cf. *ibid.*,

which served as the setting for another parade displaying the booty recovered in the campaign.[16]

Constantine was not content to publicize his victories in the short term. To a degree which does not appear to have been attempted by his father, he sought to perpetuate their memory in lasting monuments. Although direct evidence of his contribution to the iconography of victory has yet to emerge, his efforts are documented by his warmest enemies. The Acts of the second ecumenical council of Nicaea in 787 refutes the 'blasphemous' acclamations in praise of the orthodoxy of Constantine and his son Leo, shouted by the bishops of the iconoclast synod of 754. According to the deacon Epiphanius, the bishops should have used more suitable texts, honoring the emperor for his victories. Constantine's military successes were obviously familiar to all, as Epiphanius reminds his audience, thanks to the number of monumental depictions of them still around:

Rather, they should have declared their [the emperors'] acts of courage, their victories over enemies, their subjugation of barbarians, which many [artists] have depicted in pictures and in murals, to preserve the record of events, inciting beholders to affection and zeal....[17]

The extent to which the monumental and ceremonial celebration of his successes explains Constantine's extraordinary reputation in the next generation can no longer be determined. Yet it is

---

p. 304) that the tenor of Theophanes' account seems to situate acclamations during the triumphal entry, not the 'triumphal games', which are mentioned only by Nicephorus.

[16] Nicephorus, *Brev.*, De Boor, 69.23–7. The booty included two great golden basins of 800 lbs each. They had been cast in Italy and found their way into barbarian hands. Lombard, *Constantin V*, p. 47 (cf. p. 101), mistranslates δημοσιεύειν (in this context it means 'display' not 'confiscate') and wrongly concludes that the basins were set up as victory monuments.

[17] *Concilium Nicaenum II*, actio 6, ed. J.D. Mansi, *Sacrorum conciliorum nova et amplissima collectio*, 13 (Florence, 1767), 356B: ἔδει μᾶλλον αὐτοῖς τὰς ἀνδρείας τούτων ἐξειπεῖν, τὰς κατὰ τῶν πολεμίων νίκας, τὰς βαρβαρικὰς ὑποπτώσεις, ἅς ἐν εἰκόσι καὶ διατοίχοις εἰς μνήμην ἐξηγήσεως πολλοὶ ἐστηλογράφησαν, τοὺς ὁρῶντας πρὸς πόθον καὶ ζῆλον ἕλκοντες· τὴν τοῦ ὑπηκόου περιποίησιν, τὰς βουλάς, τὰ τρόπαια, τὰς κοσμικὰς συστάσεις, τὰς πολιτικὰς καταστάσεις, τὰς τῶν πόλεων ἐπανορθώσεις. αὗται ἀξιεπαίνετοι βασιλεῦσιν εὐφημίαι, αἵτινες καὶ πᾶν τὸ ὑπήκοον προσκαλοῦνται εἰς εὔνοιαν. The tradition of acclaiming the emperors at councils was an old one, but explicit victory acclamations are rare, e.g. Council of Constantinople (553), actio VI, ed. J. Straub, *ACO*, 4.1 (1971). 182.9–10.

noteworthy that this most denigrated of Byzantine rulers – the Copronymus, as future generations would call him – was remembered as the bulwark of the state in the dark hours of the early ninth century.[18] Surely his own efforts were not without influence on the creation of popular belief reflected by an incident during the siege of Constantinople in 812. While the population thronged to the Church of the Holy Apostles to attend the supplications against the besieging Bulgarians, some participants took advantage of the confusion, pried open the gates leading to the imperial tombs and threw themselves on Constantine's sarcophagus: 'Rise up!' they cried, 'Save the collapsing state!' Some went so far as to claim they had seen him ride out of his tomb to defeat the barbarians.[19]

2. AN AGE OF GENERALS: VICTORY CELEBRATIONS IN THE LATE EIGHTH CENTURY

Like the short reign of Leo IV itself, the ceremony honoring a Byzantine success against the Arabs in 778 seems couched in obscurity: it is thought to have taken place in conjunction with the ancient festival of Maiumas, it was celebrated far from downtown Constantinople and, most significant of all, it marks a distinct departure from the old imperial monopoly of victory. The campaign which it celebrated involved the combined forces of the Thracesion, Anatolikon, Bucellarion, Armeniakon and Opsikion military districts or themes, under the command of the *strategoi* Michael Lachanodracon, and the Armenians Artabasdus, Tatzates, Baristerotzes and Gregory son of Muselakios, respectively.[20]

The Byzantine forces attempted to besiege Germanicia and also engaged with apparent success the forces commanded by Thumama ibn Wali. According to the Arabic sources, the operations involved a 'summer' raid of A.H. 161, i.e., 9 October

---

[18] On the substantial increase in the literary vilification of Constantine's character in the course of the ninth century: S. Gero, *Byzantine iconoclasm during the reign of Constantine V*, Corpus scriptorum christianorum orientalium, Subsidia, 52 (Louvain, 1977), pp. 58, 164–5 and 169–75.

[19] Theophanes, A.M. 6305, De Boor, 501.3–12.

[20] *Ibid.*, A.M. 6270, De Boor 451.12–17; cf. P. Speck, *Kaiser Konstantin VI. Die Legitimation einer Fremden und der Versuch einer eigenen Herrschaft*, 1 (Munich, 1978), 92–4 and esp. 2, 438, n. 341–2a for seal evidence on these commanders.

777–27 September 778 A.D. Such raids were conventionally launched from 10 July to 8 September.[21] Notwithstanding, then, the common error which connects the victory celebration with the ancient festival of Maiumas and, by inference, the month of May, this ceremony must have taken place in late summer.[22] Its site was the Sophianae Palace on the Asiatic shore of the Bosphorus, generally localized at the modern Çengelköy.[23] The setting indicates that, like the first observances honoring Heraclius' return from the Persian war, the proceedings were not primarily intended for the urban population of the capital. They were directed rather at the theme commanders, their troops and whatever officials had followed the emperors on the Asiatic villeggiatura. They involved the seven-year-old coemperor Constantine VI and a largess to the troops. This last fact lends support to Grierson's observation that a new coin type issued in gold and copper at Constantinople must be associated with the event. The new type's obverse shows both emperors wearing military garb and seated on a lyre-backed throne (fig. 7); it may well have been intended as a depiction of the celebration itself.[24] As the emperors watched from their throne, the theme commanders staged a

---

[21] Theophanes, A.M. 6270, De Boor, 451.11–24. Cf. G. Weil, *Geschichte der Chalifen*, 2 (Mannheim, 1848), 98 with n. 1–2. The relevant passages of al Tabari and ibn Wadhih are tr. E.W. Brooks, 'Byzantines and Arabs in the time of the early Abbasids', *English Historical Review*, 15 (1900), 728–47, here 735; on the summer campaigns, *ibid.*, 730; R.J. Lilie, *Die byzantinische Reaktion auf die Ausbreitung der Araber. Studien zur Strukturwandlung des byzantinischen Staates im 7. und 8. Jhd.*, Miscellanea byzantina Monacensia, 22 (Munich, 1976), pp. 167 and 181.

[22] Modern scholars have often followed Theophanes' editor's lead and have understood A.M. 6270, De Boor, 451.26, ποιήσας Μαϊουμᾶν as 'spent the festival of Maioumas', which would imply a chronological contradiction in Theophanes' date of 6270: cf. Preisendanz, 'Maioumas', *RE*, 14, 1 (1923), 610–12, here 611; L. Robert, 'Epigraphica XI. Inscription de Nicée', *Revue des études grecques*, 49 (1936), 9–14, here 12, n. 3; Speck, *Konstantin VI.*, 1, 94. Anastasius correctly translates 'facta maioma', Theophanes, De Boor, 2.299.18, and so should we. Rather than resurrecting a festival which disappeared 200 years earlier, the expression ποιεῖν μαϊουμᾶν ought to be taken in its ordinary Middle Byzantine sense, 'distribute largess', an interpretation which fits the context very well. For this sense of μαϊουμᾶς, see Philotheus, *Cleterologium*, Oikonomides, 133.12 (tr. 'primes'); cf. *Imp. Exp.*, Bonn, 488.2 and 491.6.

[23] Janin, *Cple byz.*, pp. 153 and 489; Guilland, *Topographie*, 2, 80–120, esp. 85–6.

[24] P. Grierson, *Catalogue of the Byzantine coins in the Dumbarton Oaks Collection and in the Whittemore Collection*, 3, 1 (Washington, 1973), 325, 329–30, 333–4.

Figure 7. Gold *nomisma* of Leo IV and Constantine VI (enlarged; see p. 138)

ceremony in which they, and not the emperors, played the key role.[25]

One clue to the comprehension of this staged event lies in the identity of its principal actors, the *strategoi*. By 778, the theme 'system' had long since emerged in its classic form, with all its consequences for the substantial decentralization of the empire's military establishment. Joined with the gradual subsumption of civil administration by the military, the decentralization naturally enhanced the position of the themes as relatively autonomous power centers within the fabric of Byzantine government.[26] This development is amply attested by the fact that it was the theme commanders and their troops who lay at the heart of most of the revolts and usurpations from the late seventh down to the early ninth century: indeed, it is often to this very phenomenon of revolt that the earliest mention of various themes is due.[27] The

[25] Theophanes, A.M. 6270, De Boor, 451.25–7: ὁ δὲ βασιλεὺς ποιήσας μαϊουμᾶν ἐν Σοφιαναῖς ἐκάθισεν ἐπὶ σένζου μετὰ τοῦ υἱοῦ αὐτοῦ, καὶ οὕτως ἐθριάμβευσαν οἱ στρατηγοὶ τὰ ἐπινίκια. As Theophanes' phrasing indicates, it was the commanders who celebrated the victory feast.

[26] From the extensive bibliography, see esp. J. Karayannopulos, *Die Entstehung der byzantinischen Themenordnung*, Byzantinisches Archiv, 10 (Munich, 1959), and R.J. Lilie, '"Thrakien" und "Thrakesion". Zur byzantinischen Provinzorganisation am Ende des 7. Jahrhunderts'. *JÖB*, 26 (1977), 7–47.

[27] Partial list in Lilie, '"Thrakien"', p. 23; see now Kaegi, *Unrest*, p. 173ff.

theme commanders' position in the political equation peaked in times of vacillation or transition in the Great Palace, as for instance, when Artabasdus revolted at the outset of Constantine Copronymus' independent rule.[28] Certainly the reign of Leo IV, who apparently suffered from poor health, was another such moment.[29] The *strategoi*'s role in the political configuration of his rule has no better illustration than Theophanes' detailed account of the ritual forms imposed on the decision to bypass Leo's stepbrothers and elevate his infant son to the purple as coemperor and successor designate. Leo began by embarking on serious expenditures on behalf of the theme armies and the tagmata. When this initiative had had its desired effect (ὅθεν κινηθέντες, says Theophanes), *all* the theme commanders entered the city with great military retinues and began publicly petitioning Leo to raise his son to the throne. It is difficult to avoid the impression of a political quid pro quo in these events.[30]

Before acquiescing to the generals' request, Leo insisted that they and other leading elements of society should furnish written copies of oaths sworn by relics of the true cross and deposit them on the altar of the Hagia Sophia. The oaths were intended to satisfy the emperor that they would never support an emperor 'outside of Leo and Constantine and their seed', a patent reference to Leo's half-brothers.[31]

Two and a half years later, the theme commanders and their troops gathered in the Asiatic suburbs of Constantinople to celebrate a major victory. In light of the foregoing, the ceremony's unusual character becomes comprehensible. The *strategoi* and their soldiers were rewarded for their victory – and, we may suppose, their continued loyalty. The commanders then staged some kind of triumphal parade in front of the coemperors

[28] *Ibid.*, e.g. pp. 236ff.

[29] On Leo's health, Grierson, *Coins*, 3, 1, 325.

[30] Theophanes, A.M. 6270, De Boor, 449.11–19. Cf. Ostrogorsky, *Geschichte*, p. 147, who tends to see this event in almost Hegelian terms, as an instance of the progress of a certain principle of undivided rule and primogeniture, rather than an expression of a short-term, political *rapport des forces*; more sensibly, Speck, *Konstantin VI.*, 1, 73ff; cf. too A. Christophilopoulou, Ἐκλογή, ἀναγόρευσις καὶ στέψις τοῦ βυζαντινοῦ αὐτοκράτορος. (Athens, 1956), pp. 81–2.

[31] Theophanes, A.M. 6268, De Boor, 450.19–451.23. That the precautions were fully justified is shown, inter alia, by the attempted plot of Caesar Nicephorus in the month following Constantine's coronation: *ibid.*, 23–6.

they had sworn to uphold. In a place safely quarantined from the city itself, the theme commanders played out the central role in a ceremony which, circumstances suggest, glorified as much their loyalty to a faltering emperor and his child successor as their military success in the East. Viewed in its political context, the ceremony casts a shaft of light on an obscure moment in the eighth century. Twenty-four months later, Leo was dead and the theme commanders would be called upon to live up to their oaths.

The next recorded victory celebration occurred in Irene's regency, after the commander's return to Constantinople in January 784. It followed spectacularly unsuccessful campaigns in Asia Minor the preceding year, and the fact that it honored an incursion into the Peloponnesus seems significant in light of Irene's Athenian origins.[32] This time the festivities featured horse races, the precise setting of which is not specified.[33] Again, the celebrations' central figure seems not to have been the regent or her son: rather, they focused on the campaign's commander, Stauracius, influential palace eunuch, patrician and logothete of the Oxys Dromos.[34] His identity is the telling difference with respect to the theme commanders' triumph of 778. It has been observed that, under Irene, command of Byzantine forces on campaign usually went to individuals drawn from outside the ranks of the professional military.[35] The reason the ceremonial spotlight and effective high command shifted away from professionals like the theme and tagmatic commanders is not hard to find. In the course of her rule, Irene faced an extraordinary number of conspiracies and revolts, most of which could be traced to officers of the theme or tagmatic armies.[36] In its glorification of

[32] Theophanes, A.M. 6275, De Boor, 456.24–457.2. Cf. P. Lemerle, *Philippe et la Macédoine orientale à l'époque chrétienne et byzantine*, Bibliothèque des Écoles françaises d'Athènes et de Rome, 158 (Paris, 1945), p. 122; D.A. Zakythenos, Ἡ βυζαντινὴ Ἑλλάς, *392–1204* (Athens, 1965), pp. 45–6 and 55; A. Bon, *Le Péloponnèse byzantin jusqu'en 1204*, Bibliothèque byzantine, Études, 1 (Paris, 1951), pp. 42–3 and Speck, *Konstantin VI.*, 1, 123–6.

[33] Theophanes, A.M. 6276, De Boor, 457.4–6.

[34] On the office, R. Guilland, 'Les logothètes. Études sur l'histoire administrative de l'empire byzantin', *RÉB*, 29 (1971), 31–70. For Stauracius' career, *ibid.*, p. 47; cf. R. Guilland, 'Patrices de Léon III à Michel II', *Byz.*, 40 (1970), 317–60, here 333–4.

[35] Lilie, '"Thrakien"', pp. 17–18.

[36] See e.g. Speck, *Konstantin VI.*, 1, 120ff, 215ff and 285ff and the account in Kaegi, *Unrest*, pp. 216ff.

Stauracius, whose condition excluded him from the purple, the ceremony of 784 clearly reflects Irene's policy of command appointments.

That her fears were founded is underscored by the next victory celebration, which marked the successful suppression of a revolt by the powerful Armeniakon theme. Campaigns of 791 and 792 had ended in no appreciable success against the Arabs and outright disaster against the Bulgarians.[37] In late 792 a conspiracy on behalf of Caesar Nicephorus was uncovered. Implicated in it were the tagmata and Alexius Musele, a former commander of the Armeniakon theme. The news of his punishment and that of Constantine VI's relatives provoked an uprising in the Armeniakon.[38] The rebels defeated the first punitive expedition sent against them. In 793, Constantine led an army drawn from the other themes against the insurgents. They were defeated by treachery on Pentecost (26 May). After the execution of the ring-leaders, the victorious young emperor staged a triumphal entry into the capital through the Blachernae Gate, on Monday, 24 June 793. He was preceded by one thousand Armeniakon rebels who had had the words 'Armeniakon plotter' inscribed on their faces.[39] Disfigurement was a profoundly resonant theme in the period and forms the negative counterpart to the early Byzantine fascination with the human face, a fascination which was embodied in the cult of icons and official portraits of all kinds and which continually crops up in ritual humiliation.[40] Criminals had

---

[37] Theophanes, A.M. 6284, De Boor, 467.16 and A.M. 6284, 467.33; cf. Speck, *Konstantin VI.*, 1, 243ff.

[38] Theophanes, A.M. 6285, De Boor, 468.23–5; cf. Speck, *Konstantin VI.*, 1, 246, and on Alexius, R. Guilland, 'Patrices de Léon III', p. 330.

[39] Theophanes, A.M. 6285, De Boor, 469.11–14. On these events, Speck, *Konstantin VI.*, 1, 249–50. On the Blachernae Gate, Janin, *Cple byz.*, p. 285; Janin, *Églises*, p. 161ff, on the shrine.

[40] Thus for example the famous *mandylion* relic focused on the *face* as the image of Christ: Av. Cameron, *The sceptic and the shroud* (Inaugural Lecture, King's College, London [n.d., p.]), pp. 8ff. For imperial portraits, Kruse, *Studien*, whose evidence could easily be augmented. On the portraits of patriarchs and their functions in churches of the fifth and sixth centuries: Theophanes, A.M. 6004, De Boor, 155.24–8, and esp. John of Ephesus, *H.e.*, 3, 1, 11, tr. Brooks 7.13–15; 3, 1, 36, *ibid.*, 32.13–14; 3, 2, 27, *ibid.*, 66.25–67.17; 3, 2, 34, *ibid.*, 73.3–6; cf. Constantine I's statement on the human face in his law forbidding disfigurement of criminals condemned to quarries: *Cod. Theod.*, 9, 40, 2 (= *Cod. Iust.* 9, 47, 17), Mommsen–Krüger, 501.4–5.

their faces blackened for the parade of infamy, iconodule monks had satirical verses tattooed into their foreheads and, as is well known, physical disfigurement was considered sufficient grounds for disqualification from the throne – at least it was down to Justinian II.[41]

What is the significance of Constantine's deviation from custom in eschewing the traditional setting for triumph, the Golden Gate, and shifting the whole ceremony a few kilometers to the north? A connection with the Blachernae shrine comes immediately to mind and, in fact, Theophanes supplies the key to the enigma when he takes the unusual step of specifying the ceremony's precise date. Constantine's entry through the Blachernae Gate took place on the eve of the great procession celebrated at the nearby shrine to commemorate the Virgin's deliverance of the city in 678.[42] Because imperial triumphal entries had associated Christian shrines with their itinerary since the sixth century, it is difficult to avoid the conclusion that the willful departure from custom in 793 reflected a skillful tailoring of the ceremony to the capital's liturgical life and an effort to link Constantine's victory in civil war, the commemoration of an earlier success and the cult of the Virgin. Coming from the grandson of the enemy of the Theotokos, this last aspect must have been perceived as a particularly eloquent statement of the dynasty's new religious policy.[43] By its last recorded celebration, the Isaurian dynasty had returned in a way to the first, in which Leo III celebrated the Virgin's relic for saving her city from the Arab siege of 718.

---

[41] On the Graptoi brothers, e.g. Ostrogorsky, *Geschichte*, p. 175; for the blackening of criminals' faces, Koukoules, 'Διαπόμπευσις.', pp. 86–7.

[42] Above, Ch. 2, pp. 76–7.

[43] On Constantine V as the enemy of the Theotokos, Gero, *Constantine V*, pp. 146ff. Janin, *Églises*, pp. 161ff, knows of no other evidence for a particular cult of the Blachernae church and its relics on the part of Constantine VI. Another instance in which Constantine VI associated his military success with a saint's day comes from the provinces. After defeating the Arabs on the feast of John Theologus (8 May), Constantine visited the saint's shrine at Ephesus and granted the saint's fair a remission of customs duty of 100 lbs of gold: Theophanes, A.M. 6287, De Boor, 469.27–470.1. On 8 May: *Synaxarium Cplitanum*, Delehaye, 663–4; on Byzantine commercial fairs and the cult of saints. S. Vryonis, Jr, 'The panēgyris of the Byzantine saint: a study in the nature of a medieval institution, its origin and fate', *The Byzantine Saint*, ed. S. Hackel, Studies Supplementary to Sobornost, 5 (London, 1981), pp. 196–226.

3. AMORIAN TRIUMPHS

Of the four victory celebrations recorded under the Amorian dynasty, the first offers an excellent link with the eighth century, in that it marked the last great uprising of the themes, the revolt of Thomas the Slav. The observances comprised three main phases, beginning with the scene of Thomas' betrayal at Adrianople in October 823.[44] Its audience was the army and whatever officials had joined Michael II for the siege of Thomas' stronghold.[45] In their presence, Thomas suffered the ritual of defeat: he was presented to the emperor and forced to perform the *proskynesis*. To signify to all onlookers the totality of his victory, Michael performed the ritual trampling of his defeated rival (fig. 8). By this time the *calcatio* was perceived as an ancient rite typical of the imperial dignity. Its impact on the Byzantine imagination was so strong that, as tenth-century historians correctly observed, ritual trampling had worked its way into all kinds of unexpected social contexts.[46] After the *calcatio*, the terrible penalty of double amputation was inflicted on the unfortunate insurgent, and he underwent the ritual parade of infamy, seated backward on an ass, an animal unfitting to his station, and pleading for mercy from the 'true emperor'.[47] The distinctive feature of this savage observance

---

[44] On the revolt, A.A. Vasiliev, *Byzance et les Arabes*, ed. and tr. H. Grégoire and M. Canard, Corpus bruxellense historiae byzantinae, 1–2 (Brussels, 1935–68), here 1, 22ff, and P. Lemerle, 'Thomas le Slave', *TM*, 1 (1965), 255–97.

[45] On the army's presence, John Scylitzes, *Synopsis historiarum*, ed. I. Thurn, *CFHB*, 5 (Berlin, 1973), 40.60.

[46] Theoph. Cont. 2, 19, Bonn, 69.11–16:... περισχόντες αὐτὸν λαμβάνουσί τε διὰ χειρῶν καὶ προσάγουσι τῷ ἐχθρῷ. ὁ δὲ τὸ δόξαν πάλαι τοῖς βασιλεῦσι καὶ εἰς συνήθειαν ἤδη ἐλθὸν πρῶτον τελέσας καὶ ὑποκάτω θεὶς τῶν ποδῶν, ἀκρωτηριάζει τοῦτον καὶ πόδας καὶ χεῖρας ἀπαρράσσει αὐτοῦ, ἐπὶ ὄνου τε θεατρίζει πᾶσι, τοῦτο μόνον ἐπιτραγῳδοῦντα ἐλέησόν με ὁ ἀληθῶς βασιλεῦ. Cf. 'Genesius', 2, 8, Lesmüller-Werner and Thurn, 31.49–54, and esp. George the Monk, *Chronicon*, ed. C. De Boor, 2 (Leipzig, 1904).797.11–14, which looks to be the source of Theoph. Cont.'s phrasing. For a few from many non-imperial uses of the gesture in the period: Theoph. Cont., 3, 13, Bonn, 102.19–103.2; Theosterictus, *Vita Nicetae* (*BHG*, 1341), 37, *AASS*, Aprilis 1 (1865).xxv; Ignatius, *Vita Nicephori patriarchae* (*BHG*, 1335), ed. C. De Boor, *Nicephori ... opuscula historica* (Leipzig, 1880), 204.7–11; Sabas, *Vita Joannicii* (*BHG*, 935), ed. J. Van Den Gheyn, *AASS*, Nov. 2.1 (1894).373A–B; *Synaxarium Cplitanum*, Delehaye, 22 January, 415.4–8.

[47] The development of bodily mutilation as a penalty in Roman law is problematic and little attested in the normative texts, perhaps because the degree and type of mutilation were determined by custom or the prosecuting magistrate. On the

Figure 8. Michael II's triumph over Thomas the Slav (see pp. 144–6)

was its setting. Unlike eighth-century victories over imperial rivals, Thomas' parade of infamy was not staged in the capital's streets or the Hippodrome. The reason must be sought in the character of Thomas' revolt. Even though imperial propaganda was at considerable pains to amplify the massive participation of foreign infidels in Thomas' army, Lemerle has shown that this account was meant to conceal Thomas' great success and popularity with the Byzantine army. The staging of the first observance in front of the reunited troops was clearly intended to impress upon them the completeness of Thomas' failure and perhaps to facilitate the mopping-up operations which lay ahead.[48]

The campaign was concluded by the emperor's triumphal entry into Constantinople and victory races, in which Michael displayed his clemency – or recognized the social forces he was up against – by imposing only a ritualized humiliation on some of the former rebels. Their sole punishment was to be paraded through the Hippodrome in derision, with their hands bound behind their backs and seated on asses.[49] At least one literary work marked the occasion.[50]

Michael's son and successor Theophilus staged two victory festivals whose contents are well known thanks to the chance survival of convergent but independent documents. The ceremonies' dates are controverted. The first has traditionally been assigned to 831, but a recent review of the evidence has suggested that 837 may be more suitable. In the former case, the triumph would have publicized some minor successes which had followed a long string of imperial reverses.[51]

---

development of such penalties see T. Mommsen, *Römisches Strafrecht* (Leipzig, 1879), pp. 981ff, and B. Sinogowitz, *Studien zur Strafrecht der Ekloge* (Athens, 1956), pp. 18ff.

[48] On the role of army in the revolt, Lemerle, 'Thomas', pp. 286ff, 289–90 and 295.

[49] Theoph. Cont., 4, 20, Bonn, 71.15–20; 'Genesius', 2, 9, Lesmüller-Werner, 32.75–80; John Zonaras, *Epitome historiarum*, 15, 23, 33, ed. T. Büttner-Wobst (Bonn, 1897). 347.7–13.

[50] Ignatius, deacon and *skevophylax* of the Hagia Sophia, is recorded to have composed a work in iambs, Τὰ κατὰ Θωμᾶν: Souda, *Lexicon*, ed. A. Adler, 2 (Leipzig, 1931).608.2–3.

[51] For the traditional dating: Vasiliev–Canard, *Arabes*, 1, 103–5; cf. J. Rosser, 'Theophilus' Khurramite policy and its finale: the revolt of Theophobus' Persian troops in 838', Βυζαντινά, 6 (1974), 265–71, esp. 266. If the date of 831 were accepted,

The first phase of the ceremony once again focused on a triumphal entry. The bald phrase of the narrative sources 'he returned to the imperial city with splendid victory' contrasts with the detailed contemporary record preserved in Constantine Porphyrogenitus' treatise On Imperial Expeditions.[52] As was by now typical, the observances included two ceremonial welcomes. The first took place in the Asiatic suburban palace of Hiereia and was socially exclusive: it was limited to the highest officials of the government, the Augusta and male members of the senatorial order resident in Constantinople.[53] There the emperor and his welcomers spent a week awaiting preparations for the gala in the capital. When the time was up and the prisoners expected for the triumphal procession had still not arrived, an additional three-day waiting period took place, during which the court was transferred to the European suburban palace of St Mamas (mod. Beşiktaş).[54]

When all the preparations were finally complete, a triumphal procession of soldiers bearing the booty and leading prisoners began the main festivities in the capital. The emperor, the Caesar and heir apparent Alexius Musele and the imperial party followed in a separate group.[55] Ceremonial receptions were organized at the Golden Gate and along the parade's itinerary from that gate to the Arch of the Milion, via the great Middle Avenue or Mese.[56]

---

recent imperial reverses would have included the fall of Crete and the two failed attempts to retake it, the ongoing loss of Sicily (Palermo falling in the summer of 831), and the death of Theophilus' son and heir in 830 or 831 (Grierson, *Coins*, 3, 1, 412). However, W. Treadgold, 'The chronological accuracy of the *Chronicle* of Symeon the Logothete for the years 813–845', *DOP*, 33 (1979), 159–97, has cast strong doubts on the traditional dating and suggests that this triumph actually took place in 837: p.178; cf. p. 172. This leaves open, however, the problem of the second triumph, traditionally associated with 837: cf. below, n. 61.

[52] Theoph. Cont., 3, 23, Bonn, 114.21–22: καὶ μετὰ νίκης λαμπρᾶς πρὸς τὴν βασιλεύουσαν ἐπανέρχεται...; cf. *Imp. Exp.*, Bonn, 503.17–507.22.

[53] On Hiereia, localized at modern Fenerbahçe, see Janin, *Cple byz.*, pp. 148–50. The deduction that only male members of the senatorial order participated in the first *adventus* ceremony is based on the fact that their wives were granted permission to join them only later: *Imp. Exp.*, Bonn, 504.14–16.

[54] *Imp. Exp.*, Bonn, 504.16–18; Janin, *Cple byz.*, p. 141; pp. 473–4.

[55] *Imp. Exp.*, Bonn, 505.7–19.

[56] *Imp. Exp.*, Bonn, 505.19–506.8. That at least one other ceremonial reception took place inside the city can be deduced not only from prevailing custom (cf. below, Ch. 5, p. 212ff); the *synkletos* appears with the emperor in the final stretch of the parade

After prayers at the Hagia Sophia, the emperor received the homage of the 'city community' and delivered an account of his campaign from a special platform set up in front of the Brazen House, the cupola of which was appropriately adorned with mosaics of an earlier emperor's triumphs.[57] The next and following days were enlivened with an extravagant series of audiences, promotions and largess. The vast scope of the promotions handed out to commemorate the triumph is revealed by the Imperial Expeditions' statement that they affected officials from the rank of imperial *mandatores* all the way up to the patricians, that is, almost the entire range of the imperial title system.[58]

The festival also featured equestrian shows; they included a second performance of the army's triumphal parade of booty and captives and, perhaps in addition to races, the earliest known joust of the Middle Ages.[59] Theophilus further sought to publicize his

---

and they are distinguished from those who actually entered the city with the emperor: *ibid.*, 506.8–13. On the Mese: Guilland, *Topographie*, 2, 69ff.

[57] *Imp. Exp.*, 507.1–9; J.B. Bury, *A History of the eastern Roman empire from the fall of Irene to the accession of Basil I (A.D. 812–867)* (London, 1912), p. 128, n. 4, offers this translation of πολίτευμα τῆς πόλεως (*Imp. Exp.*, Bonn, 507.4–5); in actuality, its tenth-century meaning may be more restricted: cf. Theoph. Cont., 5, 18, Bonn, 239.4–8. On these decorations of the Brazen House, above, Ch. 2, p. 68.

[58] *Imp. Exp.*, Bonn, 507.15–19. For the use of ἀντίληψις in reference to promotions in the hierarchy of state dignities, Philotheus, *Cleterologium*, Oikonomides, 87.4, 7 and 11; 93.10–11 and esp. 189.11–14, on the distribution of dignities at a great banquet in the Triklinos of Justinian; cf. too 221.21–4. To gauge the significance of the promotions, we need only compare the account of *Imp. Exp.*, Bonn, 507. 16–18: ... καὶ προετέθησαν ἀντιλήψεις πλεῖσται ἀναβιβαζόμεναι ἀπὸ τῆς τῶν βασιλικῶν μανδατόρων ἀξίας μέχρι τῆς κυριωνύμου πατρικιότητος (cf. J.J. Reiske, comm., *De ceremoniis*, 2 (Bonn, 1830), 593–4), with the list of state dignities from 842–3 in the *Uspensky Tacticon*, ed. Oikonomides, *Listes de préséance*, 47.11–63.7. This shows that the promotions distributed for this triumph covered almost the entire range of major positions in the title-dignity system, i.e. it affected some 190 dignitaries or groups of dignitaries in all.

[59] *Imp. Exp.*, Bonn, 507.19–20; Theoph. Cont., 3, 23, Bonn, 115.5–116.8. The latter's reference to this ceremony as the 'domestic's triumph' (*ibid.*, 115.5–6: ἐπεὶ γοῦν ἐν τῷ τῶν ἵππων ἀμιλλητηρίῳ ὁ τοῦ δομεστίκου θρίαμβος ἐτελεῖτο ...) raises the tantalizing possibility that in the early ninth century, celebrations in the Hippodrome were particularly associated with the domestic. It cannot be ruled out, however, that the expression is an anachronism, induced by the Phocades' ascendancy in victory celebrations of the tenth century. The identity of the Domestic of the Scholes at the time of this campaign is not clear. For the period, R. Guilland, *Recherches sur les*

Figure 9. Copper *follis* of Theophilus (enlarged; see pp. 148–9)

success, it has been suggested, with a new issue of copper coins. On them, the emperor was depicted in the *loros* and wearing the ancient triumphal headdress known as the 'tufa' (fig. 9). The reverse legend certainly fitted the occasion: 'You conquer, O Augustus Theophilus'.[60]

Another, very similar ceremony was staged either to honor Theophilus' pillage of Zapetra in 837 or at an unspecified date thereafter.[61] Again the celebration entailed an intermediary stay in the Asiatic suburbs, this time in the new Arab-style palace of Bryas.[62] The triumphal entry took substantially the same form as Theophilus' first one, except that, this time, the emperor ordered all the city's children to come out to welcome him with flower wreaths.[63] Again horse contests were held; this time Theophilus is reported to have done something which would have been

---

institutions byzantines, 1, Berliner byzantinistische Arbeiten, 35 (Berlin, 1967), pp. 436–7, cites only Manuel Armenios.

[60] Grierson, *Coins*, 3, 1, 413. Theophilus did indeed wear a *tufa* during the triumphal entry, but not the *loros*, naturally enough, since it is hard to imagine how one would wear this full-length gown on horseback: *Imp. Exp.*, Bonn, 505.9–14 with *scholion*, *ibid.*, line 22.

[61] Vasiliev–Canard, *Arabes*, 1, 137–41; cf. however above, n. 51.

[62] Georgius Continuatus, *Theophilus*, 14, ed. I. Bekker (Bonn, 1838), 798.21–4. Cf. G. Moravcsik, *Byzantinoturcica*, 1, Berliner byzantinistische Arbeiten, 10 (Berlin, 1958), 269–72; Symeon Magister, ed. Bekker, (Bonn, 1838), *Theophilus*, 11, 634.17–20. On Bryas, Janin, *Cple byz.*, p. 146.

[63] *Imp. Exp.*, Bonn, 508.2–5; if the traditional dating is scrapped, perhaps there was a connection with the birth of Michael III in 840; cf. C. Mango, 'When was Michael III Born?' *DOP*, 21 (1967), 253–8.

unimaginable for his late Roman predecessors: he himself led the first race and, unsurprisingly, crowned his military success with a sporting victory.[64] The booty displayed during the festivities included gold, silver and a host of Saracen captives.[65]

In addition to the light they shed on the organizational aspects of early medieval triumphs, the records of these celebrations evidence a couple of significant trends. Special ceremonies are staged involving special audiences, in that the traditional triumphal parade through the city and the victory races are flanked by a series of more private festivities for the senatorial order and the bureaucracy at large. Secondly there may have been some movement away from the fusion of civil and military elements which was typical of the late antique triumphal parade. Although Theophilus and the Caesar wore military garb throughout the procession, the imperial party may have been more clearly distinguished from the rest of the army, for it began its parade only after the troops had entered the city.[66]

Later sources give Michael III no direct role in the successful campaign which triggered the last victory celebrations of the Amorians (863). This is flatly contradicted by the Arabic sources and probably stems from the hostility of Basil I's descendants toward their forebear's victim.[67] The theme commanders celebrated a splendid triumphal entry into the capital, which may have included the presence of Michael III, although his participation is not explicitly attested.[68] Prominent in the procession was the

---

[64] Georg. Cont., *Theophilus*, 14, Bonn, 798.23–799.3; Sym. Mag., *Theophilus*, 11, *ibid.*, 634.19–22.

[65] *Passio XLII martyrum Amoriensium* (BHG, 1209), ed. V. Vasil'evsky and P. Nikitin, 'Skazaniya o 42 amoriiskikh muchenikakh i tserkovnaya sluzhba im', *Zapiski imperatorskoi akademii nauk, otdelenie istoricheskikh nauk i filologii*, ser. 8, 7, 2 (St Petersburg, 1905), 40.24–42.1.

[66] *Imp. Exp.*, Bonn, 505.7–18.

[67] Vasiliev–Canard, *Arabes*, 1, 251, citing Tabari; cf. G. Huxley, 'The emperor Michael III and the battle of Bishop's Meadow (A.D. 863)', *Greek, Roman and Byzantine Studies*, 16 (1975), 443–50.

[68] Cf. preceding note. Sym. Mag., Bonn, 666.10–12; cf. Georg. Cont. [= redaction A], Bonn, 825.6–7, and ed. E. Muralt, *Georgii Monachi Chronicon* [= A], (St Petersburg, 1859), 734.5–6, and Georg. Cont. [= redaction B], ed. V.M. Istrin, *Khronika Georgiya amartola v drevnem slavyanorusskom perevode*, 2 (Petrograd, 1922), 9.28–9 (on the two redactions of Georg. Cont., Moravcsik, *Byzantinoturcica*, 1, 269–72). Cf. *Vita Antonii iunioris* (BHG, 142), *additamentum*, 15, ed. F. Halkin, 'S. Antoine le Jeune et Pétronas, le vainqueur des Arabes', *AB*, 62 (1944), 187–225, here 220.1–4. In addition

display of the defeated emir's head and those of many of his followers. If the theme commanders dominated the ceremony, they were led by a member of the imperial house, the patrician Petronas, maternal uncle of Michael III and brother of the regime's éminence grise, the Caesar Bardas. In addition to his overall responsibility for the operation, Petronas seems to have been *strategos* of the Thracesion theme at the time.[69] His contribution was particularly honored in a special reception by Michael III and the senatorial order; he was promoted to the rank of *magistros* and, it would appear, the Domesticate of the Scholes.[70]

The second stage of the celebrations was again dominated by the theme commanders and took place in the Hippodrome.[71] Acclamations which may have been composed for this occasion are preserved in the Ceremony Book and offer insight into the tenor of public utterances framed for such celebrations. They consisted of two quadruple invocations and closed with a wish for the stability of Michael's position and that of the Augustae.[72] The

---

to Petronas, the only other commander identified by name is Nasar, *strategos* of the Bucellarion. Also participating in the operations and presumably the celebrations were the *strategoi* of the Armeniakon, of Colonea, Paphlagonia, Anatolikon, Opsikion, Cappadocia, the *kleisurarchs* of Seleucia and Charsianon and the *strategoi* of Thrace and Macedonia. This list, broken down by the directions from which the various units approached the Arabs, comes from Theoph. Cont., 4, 25, Bonn, 181.9–20. In his comm. on this passage, H. Gelzer, *Die Genesis der byzantinischen Themenverfassung* (Leipzig, 1899), pp. 99–100, proposed emending 'Colonea' (Theoph. Cont., Bonn, 181.12) to 'Chaldia'. This is certainly wrong because, as Gelzer has not observed, the author of Theoph. Cont. or his source *respected the precedence* of the theme commanders as he enumerated each group's composition. Theoph. Cont.'s listing of units attacking from the North runs Armeniakon (third in *Uspensky Tacticon* and Philotheus), Bucellarion (sixth in both), Colonea (absent in *Uspensky*; ninth in Philotheus) and Paphlagonia (eighth in *Uspensky*; tenth in Philotheus). Chaldia, on the other hand, ranks eleventh in *Uspensky* and thirteenth in Philotheus (ed. Oikonomides, 49 and 137–9).

69 Cf. *V. Antonii iun., add.*, 14, Halkin, 218.8–9 and, in general, R. Guilland, 'Patrices des règnes de Théophile et de Michel II', *Revue des études Sud-Est européennes*, 8 (1970), 593–610, here 597–8.

70 *V. Antonii iun., add.*, 15, Halkin, 230.4–5. On Petronas' dignities: Guilland, 'Patrices de Théophile', p. 598.

71 Georg. Cont. [B], Istrin, 9.28–9: οἱ δὲ στρατηγοὶ . . . ἐθριάμβευσαν ἐν τῷ ἱππικῷ; cf. Georg. Cont. [A], Muralt, 734.6, and Bonn, 825.7.

72 *De cer.*, 1, 78 (69), Vogt, 2.136.13–23: ῎Ακτα ἐπὶ μεγιστάνῳ ἀμηρᾷ ἐν πολέμῳ ἡττηθέντι καὶ ἀναιρεθέντι; for the attribution and date: J.B. Bury, 'The Ceremonial Book of Constantine Porphyrogennetos, II', *English Historical Review*, 87 (1907),

opening invocations insist three times on the role of God in procuring victory and once on the divine source of imperial authority.[73] The emperor is hailed as the embodiment of the 'success of the Romans', the courage of his army and the instrument of his enemies' fall. If the ascription is correct, it reveals a truly bipolar ceremony: the ceremonial action fell to the victorious commanders while the texts saluted the young emperor as the ultimate instrument of Roman victory.[74]

4. THE LEGITIMATION OF BASIL I

The dark events of the night of 24 September 867 were not long concealed from the inhabitants of Constantinople. As a usurper who had achieved power by the most repellent means, with no great family or professional connections to buttress his position, Basil I could only have been expected to seek in the repertory of imperial ideology demonstrative evidence for the aptness of his rule. Whence his forged Armenian genealogy; whence too, it is likely, political festivals for his putative successes. Omens of victoriousness early attached themselves to the Basil legend. The story of the babe Basil finding shelter in an eagle's shadow had obvious classical and late antique antecedents which connected it with victory.[75] Even more significant is the unexplained coincidence, propagated no later than the funeral oration of Leo VI on his father, according to which the Macedonian peasant first entered the imperial city via the middle portal of the Golden Gate, which was normally opened only for triumphs.[76]

According to Constantine VII, God distinguished the very first day of Basil's independent rule by causing it to coincide with the arrival of news of a great victory and the deliverance of a great

---

417–39, here 434; cf. his *History... accession of Basil I*, p. 177, n. 3, and Huxley, 'Emperor', p. 450.

[73] *De cer.*, I, 78 (69), Vogt, 2.136.15–17.

[74] *Ibid.*, 136.17–20.

[75] Theoph. Cont., 5, 5, Bonn, 218.2–219.15; cf. G. Moravcsik, 'Sagen und Legenden über Kaiser Basileios I.', *DOP*, 15 (1961), 61–126, here 83–5.

[76] Ed. A. Vogt and I. Hausherr, 'Oraison funèbre de Basile Ier par son fils Léon VI le Sage', *Orientalia christiana*, 26 (1932), 5–79, here 50.16–24 where its triumphal symbolism is explicitly mentioned. Constantine VII echoes the same story in the *Vita Basilii*: Theoph. Cont., 5, 9, Bonn, 223.8–10; cf. Moravcsik, 'Sagen', p. 93.

number of Christian prisoners.[77] As the very first public act of his independent rule, Basil decided to stage a procession to the Hagia Sophia to thank God for the victory and for his sole control of the throne, a celebration which implied divine, or at least patriarchal sanction.[78] En route back to the palace, Basil availed himself of the traditional means of garnering favor by throwing coins to onlookers lucky or important enough to be standing nearby.[79]

The positive political effects which may have attended the triumph Basil celebrated in 879 were quickly dissipated by the sudden death of the co-star of that ceremony and heir apparent. It is not perhaps coincidence that within the year the decision was made to stage another liturgical celebration of victory, this time to dramatize the successes of the imperial fleet commanded by Basil Nasar, against Arab detachments in Italian waters.[80] The quantity of olive oil captured by Nasar was so enormous that its sale triggered a steep, if temporary, slide in the price of that staple of

---

[77] Theoph. Cont., 5, 29, Bonn, 256.8–12. Constantine's vagueness about the precise occasion for the victory celebration and the absence of this detail from other historians may suggest that he invented the story to buttress the theology of usurpation exemplified in his account of Basil's reign. It is just as possible, however, that the usurper, like so many of his predecessors, merely seized on some minor success and inflated it into an epoch-making victory at a politically propitious moment. One possible candidate, suggested to me by A.P. Kazhdan, would be a minor success against the revolt of Symbatius, which came to an end in the first year of Basil's independent rule. Cf. A.P. Kazhdan, 'Iz istorii vizantiiskoi khronografii X v. 1. O sostave tak nazyvaemoi "khroniki prodolzhatelya Feofana"', *VV*, n.s., 19 (1961), 79–96, here 88. Another possibility would be a success related to the Frankish emperor Louis II's campaigns in southern Italy: cf. J. Gay, *L'Italie méridionale et l'empire byzantin depuis l'avènement de Basile Ier jusqu'à la prise de Bari par les Normands (867–1071)*, Bibliothèque des Écoles françaises d'Athènes et de Rome, 90 (Paris, 1904), pp. 72–5.

[78] Theoph. Cont., 5, 29, Bonn, 256.12–15: πρόοδον οὖν ὁ βασιλεὺς ἐπὶ τὸν μέγαν τοῦ θεοῦ ναὸν τὸν τῆς ἐκείνου σοφίας ἐπώνυμον ποιησάμενος, καὶ τὰς περὶ πάντων ὁμοῦ εὐχαριστίας αὐτῷ ἀποδούς... Scylitzes, Thurn, 132.28–31, describes the procession and largess but leaves out the reason.

[79] Theoph. Cont., 5, 29, Bonn, 256.15–20; cf. Scylitzes, Thurn, 132.28–31.

[80] Theoph. Cont., 5, 65, Bonn, 305.13–15; cf. Scylitzes, Thurn, 155.46–156.64; P. Schreiner, *Die byzantinischen Kleinchroniken*, 2, CFHB, 12 (Berlin, 1977), 109–10, and *Vita Elias iun.* (BHG, 580), 25, ed. G. Rossi Taibbi, *Vita di sant'Elia il Giovane*, Testi e monumenti, Testi 7 (Palermo, 1962), 38.495–9. On the expedition: Gay, *Italie*, pp. 111–14 and H. Ahrweiler, *Byzance et la mer. La marine de guerre, la politique et les institutions maritimes de Byzance aux VIIe–XVe siècles*, Bibliothèque byzantine, Études, 5 (Paris, 1966), p. 113.

cooking and lighting fuel at Constantinople.[81] Such a development could only produce a favorable impact on the capital's general population.

Of spectacular triumphal entries and related observances, it would appear that Basil celebrated two, both in the 870s.[82] The first celebration seems to evidence the kind of political image-making already referred to. It was organized in connection with Basil's personal direction of an expedition against Samosata, Zapetra and Melitene (Malatya) in 873. The emperor was successful against the first towns but suffered a defeat at Melitene. Two years earlier, he had already returned to the capital in humiliation and, following Lemerle, it is easy to grasp the political motive behind his decision to conclude the campaign of 873 with a quick incursion into Paulician territory to take the sting out of his failure.[83] Basil's second triumph marked his personal direction of a campaign against Germanicia and Adata, during which Tefrike also fell to Byzantine forces; it may be dated to the autumn of 879.[84] As far as can be determined today, both festivities assumed the same general shape and may conveniently be treated together.

[81] Scylitzes, Thurn, 155.52–156.53.

[82] It was formerly believed that Basil celebrated a triumph in 872 to celebrate the fall of Tefrike, one in 873 after a campaign against Melitene and Samosata and a final one in 878 or 879, after an expedition against Germanicia. The rubric 'The victorious return from campaign of Basil, the Christ-loving emperor' (*Imp. Exp.*, Bonn, 498.14–15) was supposed to indicate that the author had combined two similar ceremonies in this account. This view was challenged by N. Oikonomides, *Listes de préséance*, p. 350 and n. 355–6, who suggested that the fall of Tefrike actually took place in 879, a view confirmed by P. Lemerle, 'L'histoire des Pauliciens d'Asie mineure d'après les sources grecques', *TM*, 5 (1973), 1–144, here 103, 104–8, further demonstrating that Constantine VII's *V. Basilii*, c. 37–40, combined two separate campaigns to camouflage Basil's initial failure.

[83] Lemerle, 'Pauliciens', p. 105; E. Honigmann, *Die Ostgrenze des byzantinischen Reiches von 363 bis 1071*, Corpus bruxellense historiae byzantinae, 3 (Brussels, 1935), pp. 58–60; Vasiliev–Canard, *Arabes*, 2, 1, 43–7.

[84] On the expedition, *ibid.*, pp. 79–94; Lemerle, 'Pauliciens', pp. 105–8. The ceremony was dated 878 by Lemerle on the basis of the conclusion of F. Halkin, 'Trois dates historiques précisées grâce au Synaxaire', *Byz.*, 24 (1954), 14–17, that Basil's son Constantine, who participated in this ceremony, died on 3 September 879, and since the campaign was terminated because of the approach of winter (Theoph. Cont., 5, 48, Bonn, 282.9–10). V. Grumel, 'Quel est l'empereur Constantin le Nouveau commémoré dans le Synaxaire au 3 septembre?' *AB*, 84 (1966), 254–60, argues that the Constantine in question is more likely Constantine IV. If this obstacle is removed, Canard's traditional date would seem preferable. Cf. however P. Karlin-Hayter, *Byz.*, 36 (1966), 624–6.

Before returning to the capital in 873, Basil staged a special ceremony for the troops, in which valorous soldiers were rewarded and promoted before retiring to winter quarters.[85] The celebrations in the capital concentrated on the triumphal entry: unlike those of the Amorians, neither of Basil's triumphs is known to have been extended with circus shows. On both occasions, Basil began his triumphal entry by crossing over from the Asiatic suburbs to the Hebdomon. In 879, he was welcomed there by representatives of every generation of city-dwellers, decked out with floral wreaths, and by the entire senatorial order resident in the capital.[86] The emperor prayed at a shrine which he held in special esteem, the church of St John the Baptist-in-Hebdomon.[87] In 873, the parade led from the Hebdomon to the Hagia Sophia via the Golden Gate; the itinerary was punctuated by the victory acclamations of the demes.[88] The more circumstantial account from 879 indicates an intermediate phase: the emperor, accompanied by the heir, Constantine the younger, and preceded by the Senate and people (λαός) of the city and 'ordinary banners', rode down the paved road leading to the Golden Gate, as far as the

[85] Theoph. Cont., 5, 40, Bonn, 271.1–2; cf. Scylitzes, Thurn, 137.55–6; in 879, the event was staged at Midaion, the fourth-ranking town of the Opsikion theme, on the great strategic road east of Dorylaeum on the Tembris, perhaps to be localized at Karadja Eyuk (Theoph. Cont., 5, 49, Bonn, 283.22–284.2); cf. J.A. Cramer, *A geographical and historical description of Asia Minor*, 2 (Oxford, 1832), 20–1; W.M. Ramsay, *The historical geography of Asia Minor* (reprint, Amsterdam, 1962), p. 239, and Constantine VII, *De thematibus*, 4, 29, ed. A. Pertusi, Studi e testi, 160 (Vatican City, 1952), 69.

[86] In 873, the Hebdomon is referred to only by Scylitzes, Thurn, 137.56–7; for 879, *Imp. Exp.*, Bonn, 498.17–499.2; in the second account, it is not clear what exactly the *Eria* is: διεπέρασεν ἐπὶ τὰ Ἡρία ἐν τῷ Ἑβδόμῳ (498.17–18). Reiske's Latin tr. tacitly emends the text, and, following a *scholion*, identifies τὰ Ἡρία as ἡ Ἰερεία, probably on the analogy of 504.13; cf. Janin, *Églises*, p. 414. The identity of τὰ Ἡρία remains problematic.

[87] *Imp. Exp.*, Bonn, 499.2–3. On Basil's restoration of this church: Theoph. Cont., 5, 94, Bonn, 340.6–10; cf. Janin, *Églises*, p. 413. It should be emphasized that neither Scylitzes nor the detailed description of *Imp. Exp.* breathes a word about the ancient *palace* of the Hebdomon, which had been destroyed by Krum at the beginning of the century. Janin, *Cple byz.*, p. 140, argues that it must have been rebuilt, 'comme on le voit par le *Livre des cérémonies* décrivant le triomphe des empereurs' (no reference given). The only relevant reference is at 496.14 which concerns the early Byzantine period. The evidence of victory celebrations does not therefore support a reconstruction of this palace in the ninth century.

[88] Theoph. Cont., 5, 40, Bonn, 271.2–9; cf. Scylitzes, Thurn, 137.55–60.

monastery of the Virgin of the Abraamites. There the emperors prayed and rested while the triumphal cortege was drawn up.[89] As under the Amorians, the parade had two distinct segments. The first soon got under way down the triumphal route to the Brazen House and the Palace, displaying the booty and captives taken in the campaign.[90] Shortly thereafter, the emperors themselves donned military attire and started their own parade. First they were greeted by the demes chanting victory acclamations somewhat similar in inspiration to those attributed to the celebration of 867. Just outside the Golden Gate, they encountered the eparch and the patrician and *praipositos* Baanes.[91] This parade too traveled down the Mese, which had been specially adorned for the occasion. Before reaching the Forum of Constantine, the parade stopped over half a dozen times for acclamations.[92] At the Forum, the emperors dismounted and paid a visit to the shrine of the Virgin-in-the-Forum, where they were greeted by the patriarch Photius.[93] After prayers there, a new phase began: the emperors changed out of their military uniforms and put on silk robes and chlamydes. In what is clearly an innovation with respect to earlier ninth-century usage, they walked through the Forum behind the great golden processional cross of the emperors and various standards. This procession led them down the final segment of the Mese and into the Hagia Sophia, where a eucharistic liturgy was performed.[94] In addition to the new, non-military segment of the triumphal parade, a further innovation occurred during the service in the Hagia Sophia, according to Basil's grandson. In the course of the thanksgiving services, the usurper was ceremoniously crowned

---

[89] *Imp. Exp.*, Bonn, 499.5–9. On the Abraamites': Janin, *Églises*, pp. 4–6.

[90] *Imp. Exp.*, Bonn, 500.1–2.

[91] *Imp. Exp.*, Bonn, 500.3–501.17. I am assuming that the ἀπομονεύς of 501.13 is identical with the διέπων of 503.7–8; cf. Theophilus' entry, *ibid.*, 506.2. On Baanes' career, R. Guilland, 'Patrices des règnes de Basile Ier et de Léon VI', *BZ*, 63 (1970), 300–17, here 301; cf. his *Institutions*, 1, 353–4; 361. Possible candidates for the unnamed eparch: V. Laurent, *Le corpus des sceaux de l'empire byzantin*, ed. N. Oikonomides and W. Seibt, 2 (Paris, 1981), nos. 1002–6.

[92] *Imp. Exp.*, Bonn, 501.19–502.2, and *scholion* 502.22–3. Cf. below, Ch. 5, p.212ff, for a detailed discussion.

[93] Another Basilian foundation: Janin, *Églises*, pp. 236–7; *Imp. Exp.*, Bonn, 502.2–7.

[94] *Imp. Exp.*, Bonn, 502.2–18. That they walked can be deduced from the account's failure to mention their remounting; cf. 500.15–17 and the account of Nicephorus Phocas' imperial *adventus* of 963, *De cer.*, 1, 96, Bonn, 439.6–9.

with the 'crown of victory' by Photius: the visible sign of his authority and his victory was publicly conveyed to him by the head of the church. The explanation for this unusual ceremony is likely to be found in the circumstances of Basil's seizure of power. The only explicit ecclesiastical sanction of his authority had come in the original ceremony of his elevation to the purple by his benefactor and victim Michael III and in the usual services at the Hagia Sophia, starting with the thanksgiving procession of 25 September 867, for, according to the specialist of imperial investitures, no new coronation had attended the usurpation.[95] Since venerable tradition had long associated crowns and victory, the triumphs of 873 and 879 may well have seemed apt moments for a new public display of the church's approval of the upstart emperor's authority.[96]

The celebration that began with the bureaucracy ended with it as well. A full-scale banquet (κλητώριον μέγιστον) was set out in the Triklinos of Justinian. The guest list seems to have concentrated on the senatorial order.[97] Once again, the distribution of largess appears to have been accompanied by promotions.[98]

Basil's successor Leo VI likely staged at least two major victory celebrations. The second marked a defeat of the Saracens on the upper Euphrates, probably in the autumn of 901.[99] Arethas of

---

[95] Theoph. Cont., 5, 40, Bonn, 271.7–10 and 5, 49, 284.2–5. On Basil's investiture, Christophilopoulou, 'Εκλογή, p. 92; cf. however, 'Genesius,' 4, 29, Lesmüller-Werner and Thurn, 80.92–3 which appears to suggest otherwise.

[96] On crowns and victory in this period, see e.g., J. Deér, 'Der Ursprung der Kaiserkrone', *Byzanz und das abendländische Herrschertum. Ausgewählte Aufsätze*, Vorträge und Forschungen, 21 (Sigmaringen, 1977), p. 38.

[97] *Imp. Exp.*, Bonn, 502.19–21. The guests received βεστομιλιαρήσια, which N. Oikonomides has suggested to me should be understood as miliaresia from the imperial Vestiarium. The interpretation fits well with the fact that the director of the Vestiarium, the protovestiarios, was in charge of gifts given to dignitaries at palace functions: Guilland, *Institutions*, 1, 217 with n. 4, p.288.

[98] *Imp. Exp.*, Bonn, 503.13–16: ἐπανιόντι τοίνυν τῷ βασιλεῖ ἀπὸ τοῦ φοσσάτου ἀντιλήψεις. πλεῖσται καὶ δωρεῶν παροχαὶ πᾶσιν κατὰ τὸ δυνατὸν τοῖς. τε μετ' αὐτοῦ καὶ τοῖς ἐν τῇ πόλει ἐδίδοντο. Note the distinction of ἀντιλήψεις. from δωρεῶν παροχαί and cf. the usage of ἀντίληψις in Philotheus, referred to above, n. 58.

[99] See Vasiliev–Canard, *Arabes*, 2, 1, 117–18 and R.J.H. Jenkins, B. Laourdas and C.A. Mango, 'Nine Orations of Arethas from Cod. Marc. Gr. 524', *BZ*, 47 (1954), 1–40, here 14–15.

Caesarea alludes to the great quantity of plunder and the wealth which the distribution of booty brought to the army, 'enough to suffice for an entire lifetime of comfort', in the speech he delivered at a banquet in honor of 'the most illustrious triumph ever celebrated'.[100] If Arethas may be taken literally, Leo must have celebrated another triumph between 886 and 901.[101] There is little direct evidence on victory celebrations in the reign of Romanus Lecapenus, a fact which may seem surprising in view of his shaky status as a usurper and of the accomplishments of Byzantine arms in the East. The narrative sources' reticence is probably due in part to the circumstance that they view Lecapenus' reign through the eyes of Constantine Porphyrogenitus' restoration to power in 945. That some victories were indeed celebrated in the period is arguable on more than general grounds. A chance allusion in Theophanes Continuatus' story of the Arab renegade Abū Ḥasafs suggests that Lecapenus celebrated at least one triumph for an eastern victory. The story also demonstrates that commanders of field forces came to the capital to participate in triumphal parades.[102] Furthermore, the medieval erosion of the imperial monopoly on victory continued under Lecapenus, for there is evidence of a victory celebration in honor of the eunuch patrician Theophanes, who forced the Russians to retreat from Constantinople in 941.[103] The festivity resembled that accorded Petronas nearly a century before. It seems to have involved a triumphal return, a splendid ceremonial reception and a promotion, in this case to the office of *parakoimomenos*. That such a great honor was granted Theophanes fits well with the important role he played in

---

[100] Arethas, *Opera minora*, ed. L.G. Westerink, 2 (Leipzig, 1972).31–4; for the occasion, cf. the title: 31.1–2; citations: 31.17–20.

[101] Arethas, *loc. cit.*, 31.19–20: θρίαμβος, πάλιν ὑμῖν.

[102] Theoph. Cont., 6, 24, Bonn, 415.10ff, esp. 416.8–11; cf. Georg. Cont., Bonn, 907.13–16; Istrin, 57.3–6. The precise chronology of the defection of Abū Ḥasafs and Aposalath to John Curcuas is not clear. On the Arabic evidence: M. Canard, *Histoire de la dynastie des H'amdanides de Jazîra et de Syrie*, 1, Publications de la Faculté des lettres d'Alger, 2, 21 (Paris, 1953), 733–5, as revised in Vasiliev–Canard, *Arabes*, 2, 1, 268–9.

[103] Theoph. Cont., 6, 39, Bonn, 425.23–426.2, and the practically identical accounts of Georg. Cont., Istrin, 61.32–4, and Muralt, 843.20–2. On Theophanes, Guilland, *Institutions*, 1, 181–2 and esp. 219–20.

Lecapenus' administration and his closeness to the imperial family.[104]

5. HIGH TIDE OF TRIUMPH: 956–72

In two decades, tenth-century Constantinople witnessed as many victory celebrations as are known to have occurred in the preceding 150 years. The earliest recorded triumph of Constantine VII came some ten years after his accession to real power. It represents clear-cut innovation and deserves careful scrutiny.

The short-term military backdrop to the staged event of 956 was a gloomy one. Three years earlier, the scourge of Byzantine Anatolia, Sayf ad-Daula, emir of Aleppo, had inflicted heavy casualties on the Byzantine army and, more particularly, on the Phocas clan: the patrician Leo Maleinus had been killed, the Domestic of the Scholes Bardas Phocas, himself married to a Maleina, had been wounded and his son Constantine, *strategos* of Seleucia, had fallen captive and suffered the humiliation of being paraded through the streets of Aleppo.[105] This was a severe blow to the prestige of a family whose support and high visibility in military affairs were essential to the restoration of Constantine.[106] In October 954, Sayf inflicted another disaster and again casualties ran heavy among the aristocrats, reaching two more Phocades: the domestic's son-in-law and grandson.[107] This defeat triggered Bardas' dismissal and in 954 or 955, the domesticate passed into the hands of his son Nicephorus. The change in command did not produce immediate results, since Byzantine forces suffered further humiliations in late 955 and again, in the spring of 956, when Romanus, son or brother-in-law of John Tzimisces, fell.[108] In what appears to have been a very secondary operation related to this defeat, Nicephorus' brother, the patrician Leo Phocas,

---

[104] For example, Theophanes played a highly visible role in the wedding of Maria Lecapenus and Peter of Bulgaria: *ibid.*, p. 182.

[105] On these events, known chiefly through Arabic sources, Vasiliev–Canard, *Arabes*, 2, 1, 348–51. On the wife of Bardas Phocas and Constantine, C. Loparev, 'Opisanie nekotorykh grecheskikh zhitii svyatykh', *VV*, 4 (1897), 337–401, here 360–1.

[106] A. Rambaud, *L'empire grec au Xe siècle. Constantin Porphyrogénète* (Paris, 1870), p. 39.

[107] Vasiliev–Canard, *Arabes*, 2, 1, 353; cf. I. Djurić, 'Poroditsa Foka', *Zbornik radova*, 17 (1976), 191–296, here 251.

[108] Vasiliev–Canard, *Arabes*, pp. 354–7.

captured Sayf's cousin Abu'l 'Ašā'ir.[109] The Porphyrogenitus and his supporters both badly needed some sign of military success. The result was a spectacularly innovative ceremony. In it, Constantine VII performed the ancient ritual trampling of an enemy leader, last attested 125 years earlier at the conclusion of the desperate struggle against Thomas the Slav (fig. 8, p. 145).[110] The fact that the celebration involved the rare *calcatio* of a high-ranking Arab in an unspecified location of the capital are precious clues to a detailed knowledge of the ceremony.

Scholars have long recognized that many of the descriptions contained in Constantine Porphyrogenitus' ceremonial compilation are based on accounts of actual performances.[111] Moreover, it has been shown that in the absence of contradictory evidence like obsolete titles or inappropriate numbers of emperors or empresses, it must be assumed that these descriptions were derived

---

[109] *Ibid.*, p. 358.

[110] Scylitzes, Thurn, 242.22–4. It might be noted that Scylitzes' account exaggerates the victory's scope and insists not on Abu'l 'Ašā'ir's command responsibility, but on his blood connection with Sayf: Scylitzes, Thurn, 241.18–20; cf. Vasiliev–Canard, *Arabes*, 2, 1, 358. It is difficult to determine what, if any, relation there might be between this incident and the testimony on the slightly later captivity (962–6) of the poet and half-Greek Abū Firās al-Ḥamdāni, tr. R. Dvorak, *Abû Firâs, ein Arabischer Dichter und Held . . . Mit Iaâlabî's Auswahl aus seiner Poësie* (Leyden, 1895), pp. 100–1, who claims that all Arab prisoners—himself excepted, as a token of the emperor's personal esteem—suffered the *calcatio* in a place called B'ṬŪM (=Hippodrome?). This testimony is not borne out by that of other Arab prisoners, e.g. A.A. Vasiliev, 'Harun-ibn-Yahya and his description of Constantinople', *Seminarium konda-kovianum*, 5 (1932), 149–63. On Abū Firās, H.A.R. Gibbs, 'Abû Firās al-Ḥamdāni', *Encyclopaedia of Islam*, 1 (1960), 119–20.

[111] Impressive proof for this theory was advanced in G. Ostrogorsky–E. Stein, 'Die Krönungsordnungen des Zeremonienbuches. Chronologische und Verfassungsge-schichtliche Bemerkungen', *Byz.*, 7 (1932), 185–233, here 185–90, where they prove that the normative text for the installation of a new patriarch (*De cer.*, 2, 14) was drawn from the historical account of the installation of the patriarch Theophylactus on 2 February 933, contained *ibid.*, 2, 38. The adaptation consists essentially of the reduction of all verbs to the present tense and the suppression of personal names; the interpolation or suppression of material which is relevant or irrelevant to a normative source; updating of obsolete titles, etc. The fact that 2, 14 was derived from 2, 38 proves too that, no matter what Constantine VII himself says about using only oral sources for Book 2 (Bonn, 516.11–17), the second book does in fact utilize written documents. On the date of this part of Book 2, Bury, 'Ceremonial Book', p. 222.

from the *most recent performance* of a rite prior to the work's compilation.[112]

Book 2, chapter 19 of the Ceremony Book describes a ritual attested only once in the seven hundred years surveyed here: the *calcatio* of a captive Arab emir. Furthermore, this section of the Ceremony Book was compiled between 957 and 959. In other words, *De ceremoniis*, 2, 19, was written down, at the latest, two and a half years after the ritual humiliation of Abu'l 'Ašā'ir; at the earliest, the transcription could have taken place within months of the event. The conclusion is inescapable: *De ceremoniis* 2, 19 is based on this event.

The image won of this ceremony is a vivid one. Initial ceremonies inside the Great Palace complex open it early in the morning; they involved the veneration of Constantine Porphyrogenitus by members of the senatorial order and personnel of the Chamber (*kouboukleion*) and the formation of a procession.[113] The cortège went to the Hagia Sophia for a thanksgiving service, including the chanting of Marian hymns deemed appropriate to a victory festival.[114] Next, the emperor and patriarch progressed to the Forum of Constantine in separate processions. The emperor stopped and remained standing at the top of the steps by the marble base of a cross set up at the foot of the Porphyry Column, while the patriarch entered the tiny shrine of Holy Constantine.[115] Arab prisoners were lined up facing the emperor; triumphal officials (οἱ ἐπινικάριοι) held them by the hand, as soldiers (ταξεῶται) brought forth their captured spears and standards.[116] A *psaltes* then intoned a victory ode inspired by

---

[112] F. Dölger, rev. of Ostrogorsky–Stein, 'Krönungsordnungen', in *BZ*, 36 (1936), 145–57, here 149.

[113] *De cer.*, 2, 19, Bonn, 607.18–608.18.

[114] *Ibid.*, 608.18–609.7. The author cites as appropriate examples: Προστασία φοβερά, E. Follieri, *Initia hymnorum ecclesiae graecae*, vols. 1–5bis, Studi e testi, 211–15bis (Vatican City, 1960–6), here 3, 366; Ἐπὶ σοὶ χαίρει, *ibid.*, 1, 515; Τεῖχος ἀκαταμάχητον, *ibid.*, 4, 40; Τῇ ὑπερμάχῳ στρατηγῷ τὰ νικητήρια, *ibid.*, 4, 139–40.

[115] *De cer.*, 2, 19, Bonn, 609.9–18. On the Column: Janin, *Cple byz.*, pp. 77–80; Müller-Wiener, *Bildlexikon*, pp. 255–7; on the shrine, Janin, *Églises*, p. 306; and esp. C. Mango, 'Constantine's Porphyry Column and the Chapel of St. Constantine', Δελτίον τῆς χριστιανικῆς ἀρχαιολογικῆς ἑταιρείας, 10 (1980–1), 103–10.

[116] *De cer.*, 2, 19, Bonn, 609.18–610.2.

Moses' Victory Canticle (Exod. 15, 1–18), while other *psaltai* and the assembled crowd (ὁ λαός) answered in responsorial fashion.[117] When they finished singing, a delegation consisting of the Logothete of the Drome,[118] the Domestic of the Scholes, the *strategoi* who had participated in the expedition, i.e., Nicephorus Phocas and, presumably, John Tzimisces, among others, as well as the turmarchs and leading officials (μετὰ τῶν τουρμαρχῶν καὶ μεγάλων ἀρχόντων) of the eastern themes, led Abu'l 'Aša'ir to the triumphant emperor and placed him under the imperial feet, even as the protostrator pushed the emperor's lance against the captive's neck. Simultaneously, the other prisoners fell flat on their faces, the Byzantine soldiers turned the Islamic standards on their heads and the *psaltes* intoned the *prokeimenon* or responsorial psalm 'What God is great like our God? Thou art the God who works wonders' (Ps. 76 [77], 14, 15).[119] To devout onlookers, the selection of this text must have enhanced the solemn character of the occasion. Thanks to the cathedral services of the Great Church, it would have been familiar to the crowd from some of the liturgical year's leading feasts: vespers of Christmas Day, Easter Sunday, Low Sunday, Pentecost and, most significantly, from the procession and eucharistic service of 16 August, commemorating the Virgin's delivery of Constantinople from the Arab siege of 718.[120] Once again, the Virgin was recognized for her decisive intervention against the infidel enemies of the Byzantine empire.

As the service continued, divine succor was implored with the Great Rogation, chanted as far as the very appropriate line 'cast every enemy under the emperor's feet'; the spectators rejoined with forty Kyrie eleisons and the patriarch concluded with the

---

[117] *Ibid.*, 610.2–5.
[118] Identity unknown; for a prosopographical list, see R. Guilland, 'Les logothètes. Études sur l'histoire administrative de l'Empire byzantin', *RÉB*, 29 (1971), 5–115, here 53–6; cf. Laurent, *Corpus*, 2, 208, no. 430. The reason for the military's participation in the ceremony is obvious; that for the logothete's, less so. It may have been due to his general responsibility for foreign affairs or for foreign dignitaries during their stay in the empire; Scylitzes attests that, ritual humiliation aside, Abu'l 'Aša'ir was well treated in captivity : Thurn, 241.23–4.
[119] *De cer.*, 2, 19, Bonn, 610.6–611.4.
[120] *Typicon*, Mateos, 1.158.11–12; 2.96.9–10; 2.108.22–3; 2.138.22–3 and 1.374.19–20.

appropriate prayer.[121] Abu'l 'Ašā'ir and his companions were then marched off backwards, their faces still turned toward the emperor and his lieutenants. Four groups came forward and took up their customary positions near Constantine: the *demotai* of the two factions, members of the Arithmos or Vigla (one of the units entrusted with the defense of the Palace), the oarsmen of the Imperial Vessel and the *psaltai*.[122] At a sign from the *praipositos*, Joseph Bringas, these groups broke into a great four-part acclamation, beginning with the customary wishes for long life followed by invocations of Christ, hailing the continual growth of the empire of the Romans and ending with protestations of loyalty. This was the same acclamation used by the army on the occasion of victory celebrations or imperial largess.[123] The ritual concluded with a declamation of the Polychronion and, as in his grandfather's very different triumph in the preceding century, the emperor retired to the Virgin's Forum shrine. There Constantine removed the elaborate *loros* he had worn during the ceremony, got on a horse and rode back to the palace.[124]

This particular kind of imperial victory celebration involved no triumphal entry: it was tailor-made for an emperor who habitually resided in Constantinople. Yet it avoided as well the traditional circus setting. By its fusion of the liturgical thanksgiving service with a very political triumphal ritual, the ceremony of 956 marks a new peak in the liturgy's impact on imperial victory

---

121 *De cer.*, 2, 19, Bonn, 611.4–9. On the Μεγάλη ἐκτενή see *Typicon*, Mateos, 2, 293, L. Clugnet, *Dictionnaire grec–français des noms liturgiques en usage dans l'Église grecque* (Paris, 1895), pp. 45–6, and G.P. Μπεκατῶρος, 'Αἴτησις', Θρησκευτικὴ καὶ ἠθικὴ ἐγκυκλοπαιδεία, 1 (1962), 1117–20, here 1119. Various texts are printed in F.E. Brightman, *Liturgies Eastern and Western* (Oxford, 1896), 362.30ff, and esp. J. Goar, *Euchologion, sive rituale Graecorum*, 2nd edn (Venice, 1730), pp. 32–3.

122 *De cer.*, 2, 19, Bonn, 611.9–15. On *demotai*, see R. Guilland, 'Études sur l'Hippodrome de Byzance, IX. Les factions au Xe siècle: Leur organisation', *BS*, 30 (1969), 1–17, here 6–7; cf. Oikonomides, *Listes*, p. 326 and below, Ch. 5, pp. 223–5. On the *Arithmos*, Oikonomides, *Listes*, pp. 331–2; cf. Guilland, *Institutions*, 1, 563–87; on the oarsmen, Constantine VII, *De adm. imp.*, 51, 1ff, Moravcsik–Jenkins, 246; cf. *Comm.*, pp. 195ff. On the site's layout, Mango, 'Porphyry Column', pp. 106–7.

123 *De cer.*, 2, 19, Bonn, 611.16–612.13; on Bringas, Guilland, *Institutions*, 1, 183. With slight variants, the same acclamation occurs at *De cer.*, 2, 43, Bonn, 649.11ff, where the rubric identifies it as 'Acclamation acclaimed by the army during victory celebrations and triumphs. Note that the same acclamation is sung also by the army when some munificence or *maimas* is given to them by the emperor.'

124 *De cer.*, 2, 19, Bonn, 612.14–17.

rituals. The public phase of the observances began in the 'people's church', the Hagia Sophia; even the most secular element, the ritual humiliation of Sayf's cousin, took place in the presence of the patriarch; its character was decisively informed by the broad role assigned to liturgical elements in its ritual make-up: hymn-singing, a litany and a *prokeimenon* associated with some of the great feasts of the Constantinopolitan ecclesiastical calendar.

The reason which induced the appropriate officials to shift this ceremony out of the more traditional setting of the Hippodrome is not known. But several factors help explain why the Forum of Constantine could be viewed as a suitable alternate site. As the Typicon of the Great Church makes abundantly clear, the Forum of Constantine was one of the most important stational pivots in the processional liturgy of the capital.[125] The Forum and more particularly the shrine of the Virgin located there had played an important role in the triumphs of Constantine's grandfather, a fact of which the Porphyrogenitus was certainly aware, since he himself recorded it in the Imperial Expeditions.[126] In a way Constantine's solemn procession *to* the Forum was the counterpart of the final leg of his grandfather's triumphal parade, a solemn procession *from* the Forum. As a site, the large, open character of the Forum combined with the raised platform of the column's base must have afforded excellent conditions for assembling a crowd and performing symbolic gestures within easy view.[127] Finally, the growth of commerce in the ninth and tenth century was contributing to make this site one of the city's chief commercial gathering places. A reason given for the construction of the Virgin's-in-the-Forum was to provide a religious center for the merchants who flocked to the Forum.[128] By the middle of the tenth century, the Forum of Constantine and the last stretch of the Mese leading to the Hagia Sophia were assuming their definitive character as Constantinople's bazaar.[129] It is difficult to avoid the

[125] It is the most frequently mentioned monument in the *Typicon*: *Typicon*, Mateos, 'Index topographique', 2, 273, s.v. Φόρος.
[126] *Imp. Exp.*, Bonn, 602.2–14.
[127] See the cross-section of the monument's former state in Müller-Wiener, *Bildlexikon*, p. 256, and esp. Mango, 'Porphyry Column', p. 108, fig. 1.
[128] Janin, *Églises*, pp. 245–6.
[129] The rent contracts exhumed by N. Oikonomides throw vivid light on the commercial activities of the Forum in 957–9: 'Quelques boutiques de Constan-

impression that by deciding to stage his victory celebration in its midst and paying homage to the merchants' shrine, Constantine or his ceremonial officers were not indifferent to the impact it might have on the sector of the population particularly associated with that area of the cityscape.

The nature of the military's representation in the triumph of 956 shows significant development since the early Byzantine period. As in Belisarius' parade four centuries earlier, the commander of the armies still leads the enemy leader to the emperor's feet. Now, however, the Domestic of the Scholes is not alone: in addition to the Logothete of the Drome, he is accompanied by the theme commanders. They in turn are escorted by their ranking subordinates. The ceremonial role of the military has become a *collegial* one, in which the commanders and their subordinates participate as a group, projecting for all to see their solidarity as an organizational and social unit. This development becomes even more eloquent when we fit what faces we can to the anonymous titles of the Ceremony Book's account. The recent reverses of the Phocades at Sayf's hands were surely more evident to contemporaries than they are to us.[130] The effect on the crowd must have been sensational when they saw two or more Phocas kinsmen leading the feared Sayf's relatives to the Porphyrogenitus' feet. By the same lights, it becomes clearer why Abu'l 'Ašā'ir was treated royally after the purely symbolic humiliation in the Forum, for Sayf's treatment of Greek prisioners is reported to have improved markedly soon after these events.[131]

Twice more Constantine celebrated victories over the Saracens. For reasons that are not clear today, both observances shifted back to the more traditional site and featured parades in the Hippodrome. The first took place in September or October of 956 and marked the victory of Basil Hexamilites, patrician and *strategos* of

tinople au Xe s.: Prix, loyers, imposition (*cod. Patmiacus 171*)', DOP, 26 (1972), 345–56; cf. Guilland, *Topographie*, 2, 73ff.

130 See for example the attitude toward Sayf betrayed by the late tenth-century *V. Pauli* (BHG, 1474), 28, ed. H. Delehaye, 'Vita S. Pauli junioris in Monte Latro', AB, 11 (1892), 19–74; 136–81, here 74:...ἀλλὰ καὶ ἡνίκα γοῦν πρὸς τὸν ἐν Σαρακηνοῖς περιώνυμον, δῆλος δὲ οὗτος ἅπασι ἐξ ὀνόματος Χαμβδᾶς...; on the date of this text, *ibid.*, pp. 11–12.

131 Vasiliev–Canard, *Arabes*, 2, 1, 360.

the Cibyrraeot theme, over an Islamic fleet from Tarsus.[132] The
second occurred in late 958 or 959 and hailed the defeat of Naǧa al
Kasaki by John Tzimisces and his joint operation against Samosata
with the regime's éminence grise, the *parakoimomenos* Basil
Lecapenus.[133] In all probability, one of these celebrations served as
the model for the ceremony described in the Ceremony Book, 2,
20.[134] This ritual has a more archaic flavor than the triumph of the
Forum: it takes place in the traditional setting of the Hippodrome
and is relatively free of liturgical elements. It was integrated into
the general ceremonial for imperial appearances in the Hippodrome and associated with foot or horse races.[135] It featured the
ancient parade of captured arms, booty, flags, prisoners and horses
and camels. They were led around the track and lined up facing
the emperor. The same performers intoned the same acclamation
as was used in the Great Forum. As they sang it, the Arabs fell on
their faces and soldiers turned the captured banners upside
down.[136] Even though centuries before Justinian II had used it in
this setting, the *calcatio* is conspicuously absent from this performance, offering a precious indication that this ritual was an
optional element from the repertory of imperial ceremonial, to be
trotted out as the captives' status and circumstances dictated.

The Phocades were again at the center of the ceremonial stage
after Leo Phocas' victory over Sayf on 8 November 960. Leo
seems to have been granted a triumphal entry; like Petronas a
century earlier, he was received with great splendor by the
emperor; he was allowed to stage a parade of booty and captives in

---

[132] Theoph. Cont., 6, 29, Bonn, 452.20–453.19; cf. Vasiliev–Canard, *Arabes*, 2, 1, 360;
E. Eickhoff, *Seekrieg und Seepolitik zwischen Islam und Abendland. Das Mittelmeer
unter byzantinischer und arabischer Hegemonie (650–1040)* (Berlin, 1966), p. 326.

[133] Theoph. Cont. 6, 44, Bonn, 461.19–462.4; cf. Vasiliev–Canard, *Arabes*, 2, 1, 362–4.

[134] *De cer.*, 2, 20, Bonn, 612.21–615.15. One hint that the model may have been the
ceremony of 956 comes from the instructions for the arrangement of the parade, in
which the positioning of horses or camels is couched in hypothetical terms, as
though none had figured in the account on which the chapter is based and as one
might expect for a naval engagement, 613.7–8: καὶ εἰ μὲν εἰσιν ἵπποι ἢ καὶ κάμηλοι
ἵστανται ὄπισθεν τῶν δεσμίων...; cf. 614.8–11 where the various elements of the
parade are each described as getting underway, and there is no mention of captured
animals.

[135] *De cer.*, 2, 20, Bonn, 612.21; cf. 614.2–5 and 615.14–15.

[136] *Ibid.*, 614.7–615.4.

the Hippodrome. Leo and his fellow soldiers were rewarded as well with various, unspecified promotions.[137]

The reconquest of Crete by Nicephorus Phocas was an event of capital importance for the entire eastern Mediterranean basin.[138] Nicephorus appears to have expected the honors of a triumph, for he earmarked certain spoils and captives for the ceremony as soon as he had stormed Chandax in March of 961.[139] Back in the capital, the news was greeted with a thanksgiving service.[140] Like his brother two years before, Nicephorus was magnificently received by Romanus II when he returned to Constantinople that spring or summer.[141] One account indicates that the ceremony was inspired by Procopius' description of Belisarius' triumphal progress. Phocas was allowed to stage a triumphal

---

[137] On the expedition, Canard, *Dynastie*, 1, 800ff; Honigmann, *Ostgrenze*, pp. 85–6. For the victory celebrations, Theoph. Cont., 6, 4, Bonn, 480.10–12; Leo Deacon, *Historiae*, ed. C.B. Hase (Bonn, 1828), 23.24–24.6; Scylitzes, Thurn, 250.59–61; Zonaras, 16, 23, 12–13, Büttner-Wobst, 492.1–5.

[138] Ahrweiler, *Byzance et la mer*, pp. 114–15; Eickhoff, *Seekrieg*, pp. 341–3.

[139] Leo Deacon, 2, 8, Bonn, 27.6–10.

[140] Sym. Mag., Bonn, 759.19–20.

[141] Sym. Mag., Bonn, 759.20: μετ'οὐ πολύ; Nicephorus was back on the eastern front in late 961: Canard, *Dynastie*, p. 805. The sources are at odds about this ceremony. Scylitzes and derivative sources state that Nicephorus was not allowed to enter the capital in 961: Scylitzes, Thurn, 252.19–21; Zonaras, Büttner–Wobst, 492.6–8; Michael Glycas, *Annales*, ed. I. Bekker (Bonn, 1836), 566.17–21. Scylitzes' account of the triumph of 963 seems to imply that Nicephorus was celebrating his Cretan and Syrian victories simultaneously: Thurn, 254.59–60. But Leo the Deacon describes two separate ceremonies and Sym. Mag. places the Cretan triumph under Romanus II, who was dead by the time of the Syrian triumph. The authority of the latter sources seems preferable: Sym. was following the lost last part of Theoph. Cont., written shortly after the events, while Leon, writing in 992, drew on largely independent and reliable sources (Moravcsik, *Byzantinoturcica*, pp. 500–2; cf. 541–2 and 398–9). N.M. Foggini, apud Leo Deacon, Bonn, pp. xxxiv–xxxv, G. Schlumberger, *Un empereur byzantin du dixième siècle: Nicéphore Phocas* (Paris, 1890), p. 99, n. 1, and N.M. Panagiotakes, Θεοδόσιος ὁ διάκονος καὶ τὸ ποίημα αὐτοῦ "Ἅλωσις τῆς Κρήτης, Κρητικὴ ἱστορικὴ βιβλιοθήκη, 2 (Heraklion, 1969), p. 36 with n. 94 and pp. 38–9, all accept the historicity of the 961 triumph. One explanation for the confusion is suggested by Sym. Mag.'s insistence that Nicephorus came to Constantinople in 961 at the express order of Romanus II: Bonn, 759.21: κελεύσει τοῦ βασιλέως πρὸς τὴν πόλιν εἰσῆλθεν. For 963, Scylitzes or his source appears to echo Sym. Mag. when he insists that Nicephorus entered the capital by the express order of Theophano, while Bringas *once again* tried to prevent this: Thurn, 254.47–9: εἴσεισιν ὁ Φωκᾶς, Νικηφόρος, κελεύσει τῆς δεσποίνης, τοῦ Ἰωσὴφ καθάπαξ καὶ πάλιν κωλύοντος, ἐν Κωνσταντινουπόλει. This suggests that Scylitzes' source may have dwelled on Bringas' efforts to thwart the triumph of 961, whence Scylitzes' notion that Phocas was actually forbidden to enter the capital.

parade of the captive Saracens, all clad in white, from his own house to the Hippodrome. Like Justinian's general, he was obliged to forego the use of a horse or vehicle and celebrate his triumph on foot.[142] The parade featured the traditional order of booty followed by prisoners. Onlookers were deeply impressed and Nicephorus, in recognition of his services, was promoted to the dignity of *magistros* and entrusted once again with the domesticate in the East.[143]

Two years later, Romanus was dead and a shaky regency struggled to settle its authority.[144] Into the vacuum rode none other than the conqueror of Crete, crowned with fresh laurels from his attack on Aleppo.[145] A millennium after Augustus had sought to strip Roman generals of the triumph's prestige and an easy springboard to power, history was turning full circle. That contemporaries perceived Nicephorus' projected celebration in this light is implied by Joseph Bringas' effort to halt Phocas' visit to the capital in April of 963.[146] Nicephorus is supposed to have already resolved on revolution when he made his entry into the city.[147] He pointedly reminded the populace of his past success by once more displaying booty from Crete in the Hippodrome parade. His piety and its contribution to his victories were emphasized by the appearance among the spoils of a precious relic of John the Baptist.[148] According to a contemporary observer, the public glorification of this latest success only deepened Phocas' hold on the popular imagination.[149] Within two months, his troops had proclaimed him Augustus from his family stronghold in Cappadocia.

---

[142] Sym. Mag., Bonn, 759.20–760.1. Perhaps this condition was imposed by Bringas, whose position would have allowed him to intervene in such matters. Sym. Mag.'s wording and terseness (cf. esp. 760.4–6) suggest that he is using Procopius via an intermediary source, probably Theophanes, A.M. 6026, De Boor, 199.18–200.12.

[143] Leo Deacon, 2, 8, 9, Bonn, 28.13–29.5; Sym. Mag., Bonn, 760.1–2.

[144] Ostrogorsky, *Geschichte*, p. 247; Guilland, *Institutions*, 1, 183; Schlumberger, *Nicéphore*, pp. 262ff. Bringas feared, for instance, that the deposed Stephen Lecapenus (924–45) might yet attempt a power-play: Scylitzes, Thurn, 255.66–72.

[145] Canard, *Dynastie*, pp. 805–17.

[146] Scylitzes, Thurn, 254.48–9; cf. above, n. 141.

[147] Leo Deacon, 2, 11, Bonn, 31.23.

[148] *Ibid.*, 32.1–2, suggests a triumphal entry: εἰσελάσαντι δὲ εἰc. τὸ Βυζάντιον καὶ κατ-άγοντι τὸν θρίαμβον. Phocas enjoyed a ceremonial reception by the people and senatorial order: *ibid.*, 32.6–10; cf. Scylitzes, Thurn, 254.49–52.

[149] Leo Deacon, 2, 11, Bonn, 32.10–14.

It is little wonder that the usurper general's solemn entry into Constantinople should recall, in more than one detail, the triumphal entries of earlier autocrats. The initial acclamations, which were surely the product of feverish composition and rehearsal, would have been quite appropriate to a triumph:

> ...Welcome, Nicephorus who has routed the enemy's regiments!
> Welcome, Nicephorus who has sacked the enemy's cities!
> Welcome, most courageous victor, ever august!
> Welcome to you, through whom the pagans have been subjugated!
> By you vanquished Ismael has been struck with terror![150]

Following the precedent set by Basil I and the Forum triumph of 956, the church of the Virgin-in-the-Forum marked a key transition in the parade.[151] That the usurper consciously exploited his image as a winner protected by the Virgin is underscored by a fact whose significance has not generally been appreciated. In an age when the date of imperial investiture was superstitiously calibrated to the liturgical year, when popular belief invested certain days with deep and mysterious potency, Nicephorus alone chose August 16 for his entry and coronation.[152] The liturgical feast of the Virgin's victory over the Arab besiegers of Constantinople, the same feast which had contributed so much to Nicephorus' first victory celebration as Domestic of the Scholes, was a fitting anniversary of accession and was surely meant to set the tone for the reign of the 'pale death of Saracens'.

Precisely two years later, further evidence of the divine favor accompanying the usurper's arms could be trumpeted. On the two hundred and forty-seventh anniversary of the deliverance of Constantinople from the Arabs and the second anniversary of Nicephorus' coronation, the Byzantine army occupied Tarsus, long a source of great danger for the East.[153] Nicephorus II could not fail to capitalize on this success and October witnessed his triumphal entry into the city. The army's cross-standards which had been lost to the Arabs of Tarsus at the century's outset were

---

[150] *De cer.*, I, 96, Bonn, 438.15–19: καλῶς ἦλθες, Νικηφόρε, ὁ τροπωσάμενος φάλαγγας πολεμίων· καλῶς ἦλθες, Νικηφόρε, ὁ πορθήσας πόλεις ἐναντίων· καλῶς ἦλθες, ἀνδριώτατε νικητά, ἀεισέβαστε, καλῶς ἦλθες, δι' οὗ ὑπετάγησαν ἔθνη. διὰ σοῦ Ἰσμαὴλ ἡττηθεὶς κατεπτώθη...
[151] *Ibid.*, 439.4–7.   [152] See, e.g., Treadgold, 'Accuracy', pp. 166–7, n. 34.
[153] Canard, *Dynastie*, p. 823.

recovered and set up as special dedication objects in the Hagia Sophia. The public was gratified with races and victory spectacles.[154] To enshrine the memory of his success, Nicephorus revived the tradition of victory monuments. He had the bronze gates of fallen Tarsus and Mopsuestia gilded. The ones he displayed on the new fortifications he was constructing around the Great Palace; the others added a modern triumphal note to the iconography of one of the key architectural settings for triumphal ritual, the Golden Gate.[155]

The bold but treacherous assassination plot which brought Tzimisces the purple also brought him serious liabilities. He alienated the powerful Phocades, whose reaction would erupt in revolt less than a year after his accession.[156] Just as serious were his difficulties with the patriarch Polyeuctus, who exacted from the usurper a humiliation one scholar has rated a 'Byzantine Canossa'. To obtain ecclesiastical sanction, Tzimisces was forced to separate himself from Theophano, the source of his power.[157] His continued need for a firm seat for his rule is evidenced too by his marriage into the Macedonian dynasty, via the respectable if homely daughter of Constantine VII.[158] Against this unsettled backdrop came word of renewed difficulties on the Bulgarian frontier.

The campaign itself was presented in such a way as to emphasize the divine favor which is supposed to have attended it. Although there is some discrepancy in the actual dates, Scylitzes and Leo Deacon consciously connect the most important battles with the feast days of the military saints George and Theodore Stratelates.[159] Imperial success was ascribed to their patronage: a

---

[154] Leo Deacon, 4, 14, Bonn, 61.1–11; Scylitzes, Thurn, 270.35–7.
[155] Scylitzes, Thurn, 270.37–44; cf. Zonaras, 16, 25, 8–9, Büttner-Wobst, 502.18–503.9. For the identification of the Acropolis with the Great Palace fortifications, Guilland, *Topographie*, 1, 341ff.
[156] G. Schlumberger, *L'épopée byzantine à la fin du dixième siècle*, 1 (Paris, 1896), 127ff; cf. F. Dölger, *Regesten*, no. 732.
[157] Ostrogorsky, *Geschichte*, p. 243.
[158] Schlumberger, *Épopée*, 1, 78–9.
[159] Scylitzes, Thurn, 300.65–6 (battle on St George's day); *ibid.*, 308.17–19 (battle on St Theodore's day); cf. Leo Deacon, 9, 8, Bonn, 152.11–12. Cf. Runciman, *Bulgarian Empire*, p. 212, n. 1, and F. Dölger, 'Die Chronologie des grossen Feldzuges des Kaisers Johannes Tzimiskes gegen die Russen', *BZ*, 32 (1932), 275–92, here 287–90, whose chronology has been followed here.

miraculous storm occurred, there were reports of St Theodore's personal participation in combat, and a visionary appearance in Constantinople of the Virgin and St Theodore guaranteed the celestial credibility of the imperial parricide.[160] While still in the field, John himself consecrated his victory to the saints by celebrating special victory services in honor of St George and by transferring to Theodore an ancient prerogative of imperial sovereignty: one of the captured towns was renamed Theodoro-polis.[161] That this atmosphere of supernatural support and the apparent subordination of imperial prestige to the cult of the saints was no accident in Tzimisces' policy is confirmed by the triumphal entry into Constantinople which concluded the campaign (fig. 10).[162]

Leo the Deacon and John Scylitzes provide interlocking accounts of this event which are quite likely derived from the same lost source.[163] They reveal a ceremony so closely related to the description of the Imperial Expeditions that it is difficult to rule out some direct influence of that compilation.[164] Yet comparison of the entry of 971 with the Expeditions uncovers several glaring and

---

[160] Scylitzes, Thurn, 308.10–309.25.

[161] St George: *ibid.*, 300.65–6; on the new name: *ibid.*, 309.29–33; cf. Leo Deacon, 9, 12, Bonn, 158.1–2. On the custom of a sovereign renaming a site after himself in late antiquity and the early Middle Ages, see in general L. Musset, 'Les villes baptisées du nom d'un souverain au haut moyen âge (Vᵉ–Xᵉ siècles)', *Revue du moyen âge latin*, 25–34 (1978), 27–38; Tzimisces had exercized the same prerogative for himself, renaming the Bulgarian capital 'Ioannoupolis': Scylitzes, Thurn, 298.9–10; Leo Deacon, 8, 8, Bonn, 138.16–19.

[162] Another bogus miracle which involved the supernatural legitimacy of Tzimisces' usurpation was the discovery in a senatorial garden of a stele with a couple's portrait and the acclamation-legend: 'To the Christ-loving John and Theodora, many years!' Even then, some cynics considered the discovery to be a contrivance by the *synkletikos* to gain imperial favor: Scylitzes, Thurn, 303.62–73.

[163] Leo Deacon, 9, 12, Bonn 158.3–159.9, and Scylitzes, Thurn, 310.54–69; in addition to some overlaps, each source provides elements lacking in the other. This tends to confirm, for this section, the hypothesis of M. Syuzyumov, 'Ob istochnikakh L'va D'yakona i Skilitsy', *Vizantiiskoe obrozrenie*, 2 (1916), 106–66, that both authors used a common source for non-ecclesiastical events of this period. Cf. below, n. 172, for an apparent discrepancy, and n. 171 for definite traces of a common source's allusion to Plutarch.

[164] Thus the insistence on Tzimisces' reimbursement for the gifts of victory crowns and *skeptra*: Leo Deacon, 9, 12, Bonn, 158.8–10; cf. *Imp. Exp.*, Bonn, 501.16–17 and the description of the decoration of the Mese; Leo Deacon, Bonn, 158.16–20 and *Imp. Exp.*, Bonn, 499.9–15 with *scholion*.

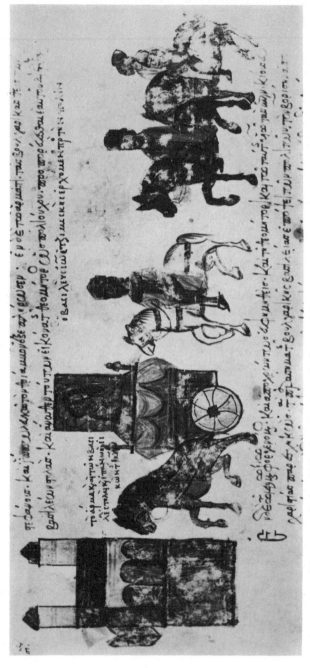

Figure 10. John Tzimisces' triumphal entry into Constantinople (see pp. 171–4)

highly significant innovations. Thus, the composition of the official welcoming party outside the Golden Gate was enhanced by the presence of the new patriarch, Basil I Scamandrenus. The only comparable instance in which the patriarch so honored a victorious emperor went back to the unique cooperation of Heraclius and Sergius during the Persian war.[165] Of Basil himself, nothing is known, except that he was regarded as John's pliable creature and was deposed after a short patriarchate.[166] His coming out of the city to join the other dignitaries was an extraordinary concession to the emperor; as such, it was a powerful statement of the new patriarch's reversal of Polyeuctus' hostility toward the controversial monarch.[167] The second innovation was the presentation of a triumphal wagon to Tzimisces and the request that he ride it to the 'accustomed' triumph.[168] Tzimisces refused to do so; instead, he set in it the captured icon of the Virgin and the Bulgarian imperial regalia (fig. 10).[169] By the tenth century, there was of course nothing at all customary about such a wagon for imperial triumphs. A clear understanding of the organization of such celebrations, whose slightest details were regulated by the appropriate officials, precludes assent to the sources' suggestion that this was a spontaneous innovation which could have caught the emperor by surprise.[170] In fact, John celebrated the triumphal entry as was customary, riding on a white horse behind the new element, a wagon decked out with the icon and Bulgarian spoils. The physical juxtaposition of the emperor, icon and captive regalia was clearly not coincidental. Not only did it allow John to

---

[165] See above, Ch. 2, pp. 71–2.
[166] V. Grumel, *Regestes*, 1, 2, 228: 'Textes et mentions font défaut'. Cf. L. Bréhier, *DHGE*, 6 (1932), 1127–9, here 1128.
[167] On the general deference owed by the Byzantine emperor to the patriarch in this period and its limits, Treitinger, *Oströmische*, pp. 221ff. On precedence and who met whom where, below, Ch. 5, pp. 210–11. The nature of the *synodos* which accompanied Basil is less clear. See B. Stephanides, 'Die geschichtliche Entwicklung der Synoden des Patriarchats von Konstantinopel', *Zeitschrift für Kirchengeschichte*, 55 (1936), 127–57, here 133–4, and, particularly, J. Darrouzès, *Recherches sur les ὀφφίκια de l'Église byzantine*, Archives de l'Orient chrétien, 11 (Paris, 1970), p. 53.
[168] Scylitzes, Thurn, 310.55–7; Leo Deacon, 9, 12, Bonn, 158.6–8: ... οὐ προσεπιβῆναι τοῦτον ἠξίουν, καὶ τὸν νενομισμένον καταγαγεῖν θρίαμβον.
[169] *Ibid.*, 158.6–14; Scylitzes, Thurn, 310.55–62.
[170] Cf. below, Ch. 5, p. 223. Historians have sometimes been insufficiently circumspect in their appraisal of the story e.g. Schlumberger, *Épopée*, 1, 175–6.

emphasize the divine favor manifested in his victory: it enabled the emperor to make a spectacularly ostentatious act of humility. A clue that John's contemporaries construed the ceremonial arrangement in precisely this way is concealed in a hitherto unnoticed classical allusion apparently shared by both sources: the description of John's chariot is borrowed from Plutarch's *Camillus*, in which the Roman's fabled arrogance was revealed by his use of the triumphal chariot.[171]

The third innovation with respect to ninth-century entries is significant on a different score, for it reveals how ancient ceremonies constantly incorporated and assimilated more recent ritual developments. The segment of Tzimisces' triumphal entry staged in the Forum is much more developed than had been the case in the ninth century. Not only was the emperor acclaimed there as in earlier entries. Now this segment was the scene of thanksgiving hymns to the Virgin and, before the eyes of the assembled *politai*, the great symbolic act of the captive Bulgarian tsar's ritual divestiture was enacted.[172] The influence of Constantine VII's triumph over Abu'l 'Aṣā'ir is patent. As was customary, the triumphal parade came to an end with a service in the Hagia Sophia.[173]

To commemorate and express his gratitude for the victory, John fulfilled a vow he had made at the campaign's outset and undertook a reconstruction of the ancient monumental setting for one station in victorious entries, the Chalke or Brazen House, which now became the church of the Savior of the Chalke.[174] By

---

[171] Scylitzes, Thurn, 310.55–7: ... τέθριππον ὄχημα λευκοπώλων [var. λευκοπῶλον] ἔχοντες ἡτοιμασμένον πάνυ διαπρεπῶς καὶ τούτου ἐπιβάντα ἀξιοῦντες θριαμβεῦσαι...ὁ δὲ μηδὲν σοβαρὸν ἐθέλων...; Leo Deacon, Bonn, 158.6–7: ἦγον δὲ καὶ χρυσοκόλλητον λευκόπωλον ἅρμα· οὗ προσεπιβῆναι τοῦτον ἠξίουν; cf. Plutarch, *Camillus*, 7, 1: ... εἴτε ὑπὸ τῶν εὐδαιμονιζόντων αὐτὸν εἰς ὄγκον ἐξαρθεὶς καὶ φρόνημα νόμιμον καὶ πολιτικῆς ἀρχῆς ἐπαχθέστερον, τά τε ἄλλα σοβαρῶς ἐθριάμβευσε καὶ τέθριππον ὑποζευξάμενος λευκόπωλον ἐπέβη καὶ διεξήλασε τῆς 'Ρώμης....

[172] Scylitzes, Thurn, 310.62–6. Leo Deacon skips this element and appears implicitly to situate the divestiture in the Great Palace: 158.20–3. Preference here must go to Scylitzes' quite explicit localization of the event in the Forum.

[173] Scylitzes, Thurn, 310.66–9; cf. Leo Deacon, Bonn, 158.20–3.

[174] Janin, *Églises*, pp. 529–30; Müller-Wiener, *Bildlexikon*, p. 81. Mango has provided strong arguments for identifying the church with the Ottoman Arslanhane, including the reference to Scyths in the fragmentary commemorative inscription κατὰ Σκυθῶν ἔπνευσας θερμὸν ἐν μάχαις witnessed by Thomas Smith (*Opuscula*

one account, too, there was an implicit link between the victory celebration and the remission of the *kapnikon* tax and the first issue of the anonymous series of copper coinage.[175]

Tzimisces staged another triumphal entry in late 972 or 973, in honor of the conquest of Nisibis (12 October 972). It too focused on the Forum and the last leg of the Mese and included a spectacular display of booty.[176]

In less than two decades, Constantinople had witnessed as many victory celebrations as are known to have occurred in the preceding century and a half. This sudden spasm of triumphs cannot be laid solely at the feet of the sources' survival or the chronology of Byzantine feats of arms. Although a complete explanation would require a much fuller understanding of developments of ninth- and tenth-century history than is yet available, two salient contributory factors are already evident.

The first comes from the mouth of the Porphyrogenitus himself. Looking back on the past of court usages, Constantine characterized the era preceding his reign as one of decay and disorganization in the rituals which alone distinguished the imperial *taxis* from private life.[177] His purpose in compiling the Ceremony Book was to restore neglected traditions and transmit them to his successors.[178] Constantine himself viewed his own exercise of power as a turning point in this history. There is no little irony in the fact that the author of the work which has most influenced the modern notion of an unchanging Byzantium,

(Rotterdam, 1716), p. 121, cited by Mango, *Brazen House*, p. 167). The last four words reinforce his conclusion, since a strange wind played a miraculous role in the victory: Scylitzes, Thurn, 308.10–12.

175 *Ibid.*, 311.74–8; cf. Dölger, *Regesten*, nos. 741–2; G. Ostrogorsky, *Die ländliche Steuergemeinde des byzantinischen Reiches im X. Jahrhundert* (reprint, Amsterdam, 1969), p. 52. Grierson, *Coins*, 3, 1, 634–5, esp. n. 5, rejects the apparent, implicit link with the triumph.

176 Leo Deacon, 10, 2, Bonn, 163.1–9; cf. Canard, *Dynastie*, pp. 840–1, and esp. M. Canard, 'La date des expéditions mésopotamiennes de Jean Tzimiscès', *Annuaire de l'Institut de philologie et d'histoire orientales et slaves*, 10 (1950), 99–108, esp. 107.

177 *De cer.*, 1, praef., Vogt, 1.1.7–11: Πολλὰ γὰρ οἶδε τῷ μακρῷ χρόνῳ συναπολήγειν, ὡς ἐν αὐτῷ πραχθέντα καὶ ὑπ'αὐτοῦ δαπανώμενα, μεθ'ὧν καὶ τὸ μέγα χρῆμα καὶ τίμιον, ἡ τῆς βασιλείου τάξεως ἔκθεσίς τε καὶ ὑποτύπωσις, ἧς παροραθείσης καί, οἷον εἰπεῖν, ἀπονεκρωθείσης... and *ibid.*, 1.16–2.1.

178 *Ibid.*, 2.8–9:... πατρίων ἐθῶν παρεωραμένων παράδοσιν τοῖς μεθ' ἡμᾶς ἐνσημήνασθαι....

frozen in time, should have undertaken his task with an anguished cry against the relentless changes imposed by history, ever working to transform the imperial and senatorial 'orders' (τάξεις).[179]

But was Constantine's effort at renewing the symbolic display of empire successful?[180] The rush of victory rites just examined seems to suggest so. True, part of the spurt can be ascribed to a second factor, namely that two usurpers, who needed the legitimacy conferred by military success, followed Constantine's son on the throne. But a direct connection between ceremonial reform and the Ceremony Book appeared in the identification of Constantine's first recorded victory celebration with the general protocol for a triumph in the Forum. That the transformation of ceremonial renewal into documentary guidelines bore fruit is indicated by the discovery of a second early manuscript of the treatise, an unexpected testimony to the interest awakened by such a technical document.[181] The fact that the Ceremony Book continued to be revised in the reigns of Romanus II and Nicephorus Phocas strongly suggests that it was indeed being consulted and influencing ceremonies of those years.[182] There are even grounds for suspecting the impact of one of the Constantinian compilations on a victory festival staged by John Tzimisces. These observations need to be tested against the history of a broad range of ceremonies before it can safely be concluded that the ceremonial renewal attempted by Constantine VII and embodied in the Ceremony Book and allied records was in fact effective and triggered at least two decades of ritual renewal. But the evidence of one small sector from the panoply of imperial ceremonial appears to point in that direction.

The Nisibis triumph of 972 marks the end of a remarkable

[179] *De cer.*, 2, praef., Bonn, 516.1–5, esp. 3–5:... μεταπιπτόντων πάντως, καὶ μεταβαλλομένων ταῖς, κατὰ καιροὺς, τῶν πραγμάτων μεταποιήσεσι καὶ τῶν τάξεων....

[180] In addition to the compilation of the Ceremony Book, further evidence of Constantine's preoccupation with this sector comes from his renewal of the imperial robes and regalia (Theoph. Cont., 6, 15, Bonn, 447.1–2), and his restoration of the Obelisk in the Hippodrome (Müller-Wiener, *Bildlexikon*, p. 65).

[181] Cf. C. Mango and I. Ševčenko, 'A New MS of the *De caeremoniis*', DOP, 14 (1960), 247–9.

[182] Bury, 'Ceremonial Book', pp. 217–21.

spate of victory celebrations which began late in Constantine VII's reign and came to an end in the long regency of Basil Lecapenus. This long interruption is only known to have been broken two or three times by Basil II, who does not appear to have been overly attached to the splendors incumbent on the imperial office.[183]

Basil and, in all likelihood, his brother and coemperor Constantine VIII celebrated a triumphal entry to signal the defeat on 13 April 989 of the dangerous usurpation led by Bardas Phocas.[184] The pattern conforms in general to that of other tenth-century triumphal entries. The parade seems to have reached its high point in the area between the Forum of Constantine and the Arch of the Milion.[185] In keeping with the occasion, Phocas' head was publicly displayed and insulted, while the aristocratic Melissenus and Mesanyktes clans endured the humiliation of seeing members of their families paraded on asses, preceded by heralds proclaiming their crime, as the cortege headed through downtown Constantinople.[186] To further publicize his triumph and express his gratitude for the Virgin's aid in this desperate struggle, Basil issued a commemorative coin which alluded to her succor.[187]

---

[183] Michael Psellus, *Chronographia*, ed. E. Renauld, 1 (Paris, 1926), Basil II, 31, 19.17–20.29.

[184] Schlumberger, *Épopée*, 1, 684ff, Ostrogorsky, *Geschichte*, pp. 248–52; Djurić, 'Poroditsa', p. 280. The participation of Constantine VIII is quite plausible, since the coruler accompanied Basil on the campaign and even claimed to have killed the usurper himself: Scylitzes, Thurn, 337.67, and Psellus, Basil II, 16, Renauld, 1. 11.17–19. Cf. too the entry of ca. 996, below, n. 189.

[185] Scylitzes, Thurn, 338.34–5; on the localization of the 'agora' in such contexts, Guilland, *Topographie*, 2, 69 and esp. 73ff.

[186] Scylitzes, Thurn, 338.34–5; Yahya-ibn-Sa'id of Antioch, *Histoire*, tr. A.A. Vasiliev, *Patrologia orientalis*, 23 (1932), 426. Scylitzes names Theodosius Mesanyktes, perhaps to be identified with the youth ἐκ τῆς τῶν Ἀνατολικῶν γῆς who led the assault on the walls of Prethslava some twenty years earlier: Leo Deacon, 8, 6, Bonn, 135.17–20. The man by the same name who was involved with ἄλλοι πολλοὶ τῶν ταγματικῶν ἀρχόντων in a plot against Michael the Paphlagonian may have been a descendant (Scylitzes, Thurn, 412.81–7). Scylitzes also names Theognostus Melissenus. The latter's brother, who held the dignity of *magistros* and had been entrusted with Philippopolis and Antioch, was spared the humiliation of appearing in the parade since he had urged his brother to refrain from insulting Basil's imperial dignity during the final battle. On Leo's career: D.A. Zakythenos, 'Μελέται περὶ τῆς διοικητικῆς διαιρέσεως ἐν τῷ Βυζαντινῷ κράτει', 'Επετηρὶς τῆς ἑταιρείας τῶν βυζαντινῶν σπουδῶν, 18 (1948), 42–62, here 60, and V. Laurent, 'La chronologie des gouverneurs d'Antioche sous la seconde domination byzantine', *Mélanges de l'Université S. Joseph*, 38 (1962), 221–54, here 232.

[187] P. Grierson, 'A misattributed miliaresion of Basil II', *Zbornik radova*, 8 (1963),

Another great series of ritual observances marked the successful outcome of the years of war against the Bulgarians.[188] Before returning to the capital, Basil made a triumphal progress through the conquered territories and traveled to Athens, where he celebrated special thanksgiving services to the Virgin in the Parthenon.[189] The victory celebration in Constantinople took place in the first half of 1019, since the patriarch Sergius was still alive at the time.[190] The triumphal entry seems to have been quite in keeping with contemporary tradition. Basil entered the city through the great middle portals of the Golden Gate, wearing the *tufa* and driving before him noble Bulgarian captives, including the wife of John Vladislav and David, archbishop of the Bulgars. The parade ended at the Hagia Sophia where a service of thanksgiving hymns took place and Basil refused to fulfill his vow to remit the *allelengyon* in honor of the victory.[191]

6. THE CELEBRATION OF VICTORY UNDER THE LAST MACEDONIANS

Modern assessments of the three decades between the passing of Basil II and the death of Theodora have varied radically, from assumptions of utter decadence to appreciations of tentative innovation. Whatever the value judgement, most will agree that it was an era of uneasy transition, on the eve of the great

---

111–16; cf. *Coins*, 3, 2, 600, 611, 631, with pl. 47, 19.1–4. Basil had ridden into this battle, clutching an icon of the Virgin: Psellus, *Chronographia*, Basil II, 16, Renauld, 1.10.3–5.

[188] Scylitzes, Thurn, 358.88–92 and 364.80–2. Cf. Schlumberger, *Épopée*, 2, 398–410, and Bon, *Péloponnèse*, p. 81.

[189] Basil and Constantine VIII were expected to make a victorious entry into the capital ca. 996 after a campaign in which they deserved the titles σκυθικὸς ὥσπερ δὴ καὶ ἀνταρκτικός as we learn from two letters of Leo Syncellus and metropolitan of Synades, *ep.* 53 and 54, ed. J. Darrouzès, *Épistoliers byzantins du Xe siècle*, Archives de l'Orient chrétien, 6 (Paris, 1960), 205.11–12 and 208.5–10, and 209.20–3, 210.42–3 and 69–70. The triumph of 1001 mentioned by Schlumberger, *Épopée*, 2, 199–200 (cf. Grierson, *Coins*, 3, 2, 606) is a ghost ceremony of which I have found no trace in the sources.

[190] Grumel, *Regestes*, 1, 2, 239.

[191] Scylitzes, Thurn, 364.88–365.98. The famous miniature of a triumphant Basil II in Venice, B. Marc. gr. 17, f.iii recto, has usually been associated with this victory: e.g., A. Grabar, *L'empereur dans l'art byzantin*, pp. 86–7. A. Cutler, 'A Psalter of Basil II (Part II)', *Arte Veneta*, 31 (1977), 9–15, here 10ff, has challenged this identification.

transformations ushered in by the Comneni. It witnessed at least five major victory celebrations. Although for most of them the evidence is reduced to a bald mention of unusual facts, like the humiliation of the defeated usurper Theophilus Eroticus, who was dressed in women's clothes and paraded through the Hippodrome, it is clear that the celebration of victory had lost little of its earlier prestige.[192] Thus Romanus III Argyrus eagerly anticipated that a triumph would conclude his ill-starred efforts in the East and went so far as to order the fabrication of the triumphal crowns needed in the ceremony.[193] Michael IV celebrated a triumphal entry at great personal and political cost, reversing the previous policy of concealing his fatal illness. Indeed, not long before the disaster at Manzikert, Romanus Diogenes staged a celebration whose propagandistic intents were hardly matched by his military results.[194]

The victory celebrations about which we are best informed occurred in the 1040s. At this turning point in the monarchy's history, it is symbolically significant that both observances marked the defeat of internal enemies. Shortly before his death on 10 December 1041, Michael IV staged a triumphal entry to honor his victory over the Bulgarian uprising led by Peter Deljan. The defeat of the Bulgarians must have been a welcome relief to a government whose head of state was incurably ill and which had confronted two serious conspiracies, a terrible drought and a fire

[192] This Hippodrome celebration took place in 1043 to publicize the defeat of the revolt of Theophilus, *strategos* of Cyprus: Scylitzes, Thurn, 429.13–17. In the same year, Monomachus seems to have celebrated a triumphal entry in honor of the repulse of a Russian attack on Constantinople: Psellus, *Chronographia*, Constantine IX, 96, Renauld, 2.12.1–13. Psellus also reports that Constantine celebrated the 'greatest triumph ever heard of' after the defeat of Leo Tornicius in 1047: *ibid.*, 123, Renauld, 2.29.13–16. Scylitzes says that the captured rebels were dishonored with a parade through the business district of the Mese, while the speech of John Mauropous delivered at the victory celebration shows that thanksgiving services were celebrated not in the Hagia Sophia but in the church of St George Tropaiophorus: Scylitzes, Thurn, 442.81–5, and Mauropous, *Opus* 186, ed. P. de Lagarde (Göttingen, 1882), 178–95, here 195, no. 73. Cf. J. Lefort, 'Rhétorique et politique. Trois discours de Jean Mauropous en 1047', *TM*, 6 (1976), 265–303, here 272ff. A victory celebration seems also to have marked Isaac Comnenus' defeat of the Pechnegs in 1059: Psellus, *Chronographia*, Isaac, 70, Renauld, 2.127.20–5.

[193] Psellus, *Chronographia*, Romanus III, 7, Renauld, 1.36.18–22. Cf. below, Ch. 5, p. 212.

[194] Psellus, *Chronographia*, Romanus IV, 13, Renauld 2.159.8–11; cf. 14, p. 159, 1–5.

which had devastated the capital only a year earlier.[195] The ceremony was a double one: the defeated and disfigured rebel leaders were paraded through the city during Michael's triumphal entry and once again in the Hippodrome, when foot and horse races were held in tribute to the victory.[196] The decision to celebrate a traditional parade was made only with reluctance, for until the ceremony, Michael's entourage had been at pains to conceal his dwindling health. Whatever their calculations, a contemporary spectator could only conclude that a transition of power was at hand.[197]

The choice of a new emperor for the Porphyrogenita in 1042 was not easily made and it is not therefore surprising that the first year and a half of Constantine Monomachus' reign saw no less than three victory celebrations.[198] Of these, one is well enough attested to reward a careful examination. In it, the full legacy of the silent appropriation of elements of imperial ceremonial by army commanders is clearly manifested.

The unexpected defeat of the usurper George Maniaces at the hands of the loyalist army led by the eunuch *sebastophorus* Stephen Pergamenus triggered a series of celebrations in whose organization the visibly relieved Monomachus played a leading part.[199] Following ancient tradition, Stephen dispatched the awful symbol of victory to Constantine IX, so that the usurper's head could be paraded through the streets of Constantinople and prove to the

[195] Schlumberger, *Épopée*, 3, 310–11; N. Skabalonovich, *Vizantiiskoe gosudarstvo i tserkov v XI veke* (St Petersburg, 1884), pp. 33ff.
[196] Michael Attaleiates, *Historia*, ed. I. Bekker (Bonn, 1853), 10.10–15; Psellus, *Chronographia*, Michael IV, 49–51, Renauld, 1.82–3; Scylitzes, Thurn, 414.46–7. Schlumberger, *Épopée*, 3, 308, n. 3, interpreted Attaleiates' account to mean that Michael celebrated both a horseback and foot parade for the occasion. Foot races had been associated with triumphs in the Hippodrome since the mid-tenth century at the latest (*De cer.*, 2, 20, Bonn, 612.21) and were used no later than the late ninth century for imperial anniversaries: Philotheus, *Cleterologium*, Oikonomides, 217.33.
[197] Psellus, *loc. cit.*, 51, Renauld, 1.83.4–8. Cf. his graphic description of Michael's funereal appearance in this ceremony: 50, Renauld, 1.82.1–8.
[198] Psellus, *Chronographia*, Constantine IX, 18, Renauld, 1.126.1–11.
[199] Skabalanovich, *Gosudarstvo*, pp. 58ff; Schlumberger, *Épopée*, 3, 450–6. On Maniaces, R. Guilland, 'Patrices du règne de Constantin IX Monomaque', *Zbornik radova*, 13 (1971), 1–25, here 10–12; on Stephen, R. Guilland, 'Le sébastophore: ὁ σεβαστοφόρος', *RÉB*, 21 (1963), 199–207, here 201–2.

population the battle's outcome.[200] Constantine ordered the performance of victory services and had the head attached to the top of the Hippodrome, whence it would be visible to all.[201]

Uncharacteristically, the decision to celebrate a triumph was made only at the last minute, when the general and his army had already arrived outside the walls. It took place sometime between March and July 1043.[202] The itinerary focused on Constantinople's bazaar, i.e. the area from the Forum to the Arch of Milion.[203] Since the organization of the parade was directly in the hands of Constantine, there can be no doubt about the ceremony's acceptability to the throne. The loyalist forces opened the parade. First came lightly armed troops, moving as an unorganized crowd. Next came the heavy cavalry, fully armed and, unlike the light troops, observing strict military order. Behind them came representatives of the rebel's army; their heads had been shaven in disgrace and they were seated backward on asses; their necks were draped with dung or other refuse. This last refinement appears novel and may have been in retaliation for Maniaces' reported treatment of the imperial envoy Pardus.[204] Even in public humiliation, the Byzantines observed the rules of precedence: the dead usurper's head, held aloft on spear, closed the

---

[200] Scylitzes, Thurn, 428.92–3: καὶ τῷ μὲν βασιλεῖ ἄγγελος ἐπέμφθη κομίζων τὰ εὐαγγέλια τῆς νίκης. Scylitzes omits the head sending and passes directly to the triumphal entry:... εἴσεισι δὲ μεθ᾽ ἡμέρας τινὰς καὶ ὁ Στέφανος τὴν κεφαλὴν ἄγων τοῦ Μανιάκη καὶ τοὺς κρατηθέντας ἐν τῷ πολέμῳ· [. ed.] καὶ διὰ μέσης τῆς Πλατείας θριαμβεύσας.... Cf. Psellus, *loc. cit.*, 86, Renauld, 2.6.6–8. The performance of the traditional head parade can be deduced from *ibid.*, 87, Renauld, 2.7.15–16: ἐφ᾽οἷς ἡ τοῦ τυράννου δὶς ἐθριαμβεύετο κεφαλή, where the head is referred to as having been paraded a second time. Clearly Psellus assumes that the reader knows what happened when a usurper's head was brought into the capital. Renauld's labored construction of the fastening of the head to the Hippodrome as 'une première manière de triomphe', *ed. cit.*, 2. 7, n. 3 is therefore unnecessary.

[201] Psellus, *loc. cit.*, Renauld, 2.6.7–12.

[202] *Ibid.*, 87, Renauld, 2.6.1–4. Maniaces had crossed over to Dyrrachium in February and by July, Stephen was in disgrace: Skabalanovich, *Gosudarstvo*, pp. 58–9.

[203] Gregory Abū'l Faraj (Bar Hebraeus), *Chronography*, tr. E.A. Wallis Budge, I (Oxford, 1932).201; Scylitzes, Thurn, 428.95:... καὶ διὰ μέσης τῆς Πλατείας θριαμβεύσας, on which topographical term see Guilland, *Topographie*, 2, 75.

[204] Psellus, *loc. cit.*, 87, Renauld, 2.7.6–15; Scylitzes, Thurn, 428.96–7; Gregory, Wallis Budge, 201, for the descriptions of the parade. On Pardus, Guilland, 'Constantin IX', pp. 14–15. According to the well-informed William of Puglia, Maniaces had filled Pardus' nose, ears and mouth with *stercus equinum*: *La geste de Robert Guiscard*, I, 486–90, ed. M. Mathieu (Palermo, 1961), 124.

parade of his defeated followers.[205] For any onlooker who failed to grasp the significance of this brutal display, heralds marched with the parade, crying 'These are the just reward of everyone who rebelleth against the king [i.e. emperor].'[206] After the imperial guards, in the very place which ancient custom and recent usage reserved for the emperor himself, spectators saw the victorious eunuch, splendid in his array and riding the traditional white horse (fig. 11).[207] Bringing up the rear was another unit of imperial guards.[208] The parade reached its culmination near the old goal of triumphal parades, now converted into the church of the Chalke.[209] The emperor watched in pomp from its forecourt; seated beside him to either side, in an obvious statement of the nature and source of Constantine's joint rule, were the two purple-born empresses Zoe and Theodora. After the procession and appropriate acclamations, Constantine rode off in ceremony to the palace.[210]

Although there is no evidence that Stephen Pergamenus' triumph set a decisive new precedent – considering how quickly he attempted to convert his triumphal prestige into the purple, we

---

[205] The head was accompanied by some unspecified element of the usurper's σχῆμα: Psellus, *loc. cit.*, Renauld, 2.7.15–17; cf. Scylitzes, Thurn, 428.95–6.

[206] Gregory, *loc. cit.* Although infrequently attested, heralds seem customarily to have preceded the parade of infamy, crying a rather formulaic statement of exemplary punishment; cf. Agnellus, *Liber pontificalis ecclesiae Ravennatis*, 141, ed. A. Testi Rasponi, *Rerum italicarum scriptores*, 2.3 (Bologna, 1924).371.1–4, and Nicetas Choniates, *Historia*, ed. J.A. Van Dieten, *CFHB*, 11, 1 (Berlin, 1975).131.10–14.

[207] Psellus, *loc. cit.*, 87, Renauld, 2.7.17–21. The axe-bearers of lines 17–18 seem to be the Varangians, *ibid.*, n. 5: cf. 1.118.5–6 with n. 3, 2.95.9–10 and 97.33–6 and S. Blöndal–B.S. Benedikz, *The Varangians of Byzantium* (Cambridge, 1978), p. 104. Perhaps the ῥαβδοῦχοι are to be identified with the Manglabitai, on which see Oikonomides, *Listes*, p. 328. It should be noted that here, as elsewhere, Psellus' formulation is not without ambiguity for the modern reader: 7.18–21: πολύ τι πλῆθος προϊόντες τοῦ τῶν στρατευμάτων ἡγεμονεύσαντος, καὶ ἐπὶ πᾶσιν ἐκεῖνος ἐπίσημος καὶ ἵππῳ καὶ τῇ στολῇ, καὶ ἐπὶ τούτῳ τὸ δορυφορικὸν ξύμπαν. It might seem that this ἐκεῖνος refers to the ἐκεῖνος which occurs at 7.5 and is the subject down to line 15 and that Constantine himself rode in triumph, an error made by Schlumberger, *Épopée*, 3, 455. Renauld's translation is, however, certainly correct. In c. 88, we read that the empresses sat next to Constantine at Chalke while they watched the triumph (7.5–6). Furthermore, Scylitzes' account, which contains elements not found in Psellus (localization of the parade, color of Stephen's horse) clearly has Stephen in the place of honor: Thurn, 428.93–7. Cf. too Attaleiates, Bonn, 19.22–20.1.

[208] Psellus, *loc. cit.*, Renauld, 2.7.20–21: τὸ δορυφορικὸν ξύμπαν.

[209] Mango, *Brazen House*, pp. 152–3.   [210] Psellus, *loc. cit.*, 88, Renauld, 2.7.1–8.

Figure 11. Triumph of Stephen Pergamenus over George Maniaces (see pp. 180–2)

should expect the contrary – it seems significant that the emperor's place should be taken precisely by a member of the group recently identified by Lemerle as distinctive and typical of the innovative trends then at work in Byzantine government and society, the all-powerful minister of state.[211] For a fleeting moment, the *sebastophorus* enjoyed the pinnacle of power and unlimited credence with the emperor, before he was cast down in utter disgrace for a plot against the throne.[212] The ceremony honoring Pergamenus' victory over Maniaces affords at last unmistakable evidence of the symbolic contours assumed by a successful imperial lieutenant's assimilation of imperial victory prerogatives. In a medieval society, there was no place for the systematic exclusion or curbing of the elite implicit in the classical doctrine of the imperial monopoly of victory.

Imperial victory celebrations did not come to an end with the Macedonian dynasty. On the contrary, the militarist tendencies of the revamped Comnenian style of government would provide ample opportunity for new and innovative victory celebrations and honors. But the great social transformations under way in the eleventh century meant that the context and content of these celebrations would, of necessity, adapt to new circumstances and make of them a subject worthy of a specialized study. While their analysis may well shed light on the conditions of later Byzantine government and society, it is not indispensable to a provisional assessment of imperial victory celebrations of the late antique and early medieval period.

CONCLUSION

The preceding review of victory celebrations down to the eleventh century indicates that, like their late antique ancestors, the triumphal observances of early medieval Byzantium underwent no little change, with respect to their content, structure, setting and participants. It is important to remember that, even

---

[211] P. Lemerle, *Cinq études sur le XIᵉ siècle byzantin* (Paris, 1977), 260–3. In the Escurial or Oikonomides Tacticon, the Sebastophorus ranks extremely high, second of those who do not dine at the emperor's table and ahead of all the *magistroi* and patricians: ed. N. Oikonomides, *Listes*, 263.10.

[212] On Stephen's influence, Attaleiates, Bonn, 20.1–3.

though many elements, like the solemn entry, parade and head display or thanksgiving services remained the same, medieval victory celebrations did experience historical development leading to profound and significant transformations.

Perhaps the single most striking facet of this change is the repeated emergence of non-imperial participants as the central focus of the ceremony, a phenomenon which seems to contradict the conventional wisdom on the Byzantine monarchy. It is often assumed that the Byzantine emperor was, in practice, the absolute autocrat he claimed to be in theory.[213] The history of medieval victory celebrations paints a differing picture, one in which the leading role oscillates between the emperor himself and his military commanders and reflects, to a greater or lesser extent, the dominant element in the power equation of the moment. When, for example, the theme commanders emerge as the decisive power-brokers of empire under Leo IV, this fact is mirrored by the content of the celebration of imperial victory. In the tenth century, it is the Domestic of the Scholes who lays claim to ceremonial preeminence while the great theme commanders are reduced to playing a collegial second fiddle. Under Irene in the eighth century and Constantine Monomachus in the eleventh, it is a palace eunuch chosen from outside the ranks of the traditional military elites who dominates the celebration of victory. The short-term balance of political forces in the palace is vividly revealed to us, in much the same way as it was intended to be revealed to contemporaries. But the full significance and explanation of these patterns must await future clarification of the evolution of Byzantine society in the dark age.

Historical change extends much further than these details of ceremonial organization and is often all the more revealing of developments in the general conditions of Byzantine existence for its unconscious character. For instance, although the basic itinerary of the triumphal parade through Constantinople varied rather little, texts of the ninth century and earlier tend to localize the parade in the Middle Avenue, in the Mese. In the late tenth and

[213] Cf. A.P. Kazhdan, 'O sotsial'noi prirode vizantiiskogo samoderzhaviya', *Narody Azii i Afriki*, 6 (1966), 52–64 and H.G. Beck, *Das byzantinische Jahrtausend* (Munich, 1978), pp. 46ff.

eleventh century, the same route begins to be referred to as the 'Market'. Although the physical location of the ceremony remains constant, the manner in which contemporaries perceived it has undergone an important transformation that cannot be without relation to the resurgence of commercial activity at Constantinople.[214]

In the three and a third centuries between the defense of Constantinople in 718 and the death of Constantine IX, we have encountered some thirty-two victory celebrations, or an average of about one celebration per decade. The average span between celebrations would be even greater if we were to factor out the clusters of 956–72 and the 1040s. If this evidence is reliable, the rhythm of imperial victory celebrations appears to have slackened, in comparison with their dynamic development in late antiquity.

Usurpations too occupy a smaller part of the picture in the medieval period. Of course, very important celebrations heralded the defeats of Artabasdus, Thomas the Slav or George Maniaces. But the frequency of major celebrations for the suppression of opposition (less than one-third the attested celebrations) seems distinctly lower than in late antiquity. By their content and character, usurpation celebrations provide a counterproof to the positive evidence of the aristocracy's desire to be seen in honorable positions in honorable parades. The humiliation of appearing in public, shaved and defiled, riding backward on an ass, must have been an extraordinary one for the scions of the great families of Byzantium since, on more than one occasion, it *replaced* the death penalty. In the eighth century, the punishment for revolt or close association with revolt was often capital.[215] No later than the ninth century, a new trend begins to appear. After suppressing the revolt of Thomas the Slav, Michael II decided that the humiliation of featuring in his triumph and exile were punishment enough for the most guilty of Thomas' supporters.[216] Thus too no further

---

[214] *Imp. Exp.*, Bonn, 497.20, 500.1, 502.12; cf. 505.9: μέσον τῆς πόλεως; Leo Deacon, 9, 12, Bonn, 158.17, situates the triumph of 971 in the Mese, while that of 972 is διὰ τῆς ἀγορᾶς (10, 2, Bonn 163.6). Triumph of 989: Scylitzes, Thurn, 337.35; Gregory, loc. cit.

[215] Thus the executions which attended the attempted usurpation of 719: cf. Kaegi, *Unrest*, pp. 211–12, or that of nineteen high officials under Constantine V: above, n. 12.

[216] Above, p. 146.

punishment was meted out to Maniaces' followers who figured in Stephen's triumphal parade.[217] Another example is the ritual humiliation of the usurper Theophilus Eroticus. After being paraded in the Hippodrome in women's clothing, he had his property confiscated and was simply 'dismissed'.[218] It is probably no accident that eleventh-century sources distinguish carefully between stages of alienation and resistance toward the monarch, between *apostasia* (defection) and *tyrannis* (usurpation) or that the tenth-century compiler of the Ceremony Book included a document on the proper procedure for imperial pardons of Slavic defectors.[219] That there remained borders which could not be crossed is demonstrated not only by the execution of would-be usurpers in this period: if the defection of Andronicus Ducas does not seem to have triggered far-reaching repression, the usurpation of his son resulted in massacre.[220] But an incident from the revolt of Bardas Phocas shows how flexible these borders had become. As the imperial army faced off with the insurgent forces, Leo Melissenus is supposed to have tried to stop his brother Theognostus from piling unseemly abuse and insults on the emperors they were about to combat. Basil II is supposed to have witnessed the incident from afar. After the collapse of the revolt and the capture of the Melisseni, the ring-leaders of the usurpation attempt were paraded through Constantinople, with the sole exception of Leo Melissenus. Although he had fought against the emperor and lent his support to an imperial rival, he had done so within the bounds of behavior acceptable to that fabled smasher of aristocratic fortunes and was spared the public humiliation of the parade of infamy.[221] In other words, in more than one instance of usurpation attempts from the ninth century on, the aristocracy

---

[217] Gregory, *loc. cit.* Cf. Scylitzes continuatus, ed. I. Bekker, 2 (Bonn, 1839).270.13–16 on the μανιακᾶτοι who afterwards served the empire.

[218] Scylitzes, Thurn, 429.13–17. I do not know why the editor has taken ἀπέλυσε (line 17), 'dismissed', to mean that Monomachus executed him (*ibid.*, 518, *sub nomine*).

[219] *De cer.*, 2, 37, 'Περί τινων ἀποστατησάντων καὶ πάλιν δουλωθέντων, πῶς ἐδέχθησαν παρὰ τοῦ βασιλέως.', Bonn 634.9–635.6; on the date, Bury, 'Ceremonial Book', p. 213. Mauropous, *Opus*, 186, 3, Lagarde, 178. Cf. Psellus, *Chronographia*, Constantine IX, 98, Renauld, 2.14.6–12.

[220] D.I. Polemis, *The Doukai. A contribution to Byzantine prosopography* (London, 1968), p. 20 and p. 24 with n. 18.

[221] See above, n. 186.

seems to have enjoyed almost a kind of 'right to resistance' which is strikingly 'medieval' in character.[222]

The circumstances in which triumphs were staged provide some information useful to evaluating one aspect of their significance to Byzantine rulers. Although a number of celebrations marked real and important successes, at the very least two were staged to celebrate victories of a dubious sort.[223] We may suspect that there were others among the celebrations whose significance is not easy to assess with accuracy. It is at any rate clear that in medieval Byzantium, as in the later Roman empire, victories and victory celebrations did not always go hand in hand, and that such celebrations could owe as much to the political requirements of the moment as to any real military significance of the operations they honored.

Finally, if we are to attempt to classify major victory celebrations according to the period in a reign in which they occurred, another pattern emerges. A sizable proportion (eleven of thirty-two) of imperial victory celebrations were celebrated within the first three years of the beginning of a given emperor's actual exercise of power. This seems to suggest that emperors were particularly eager to celebrate victories early in their reign, at a time when such ceremonies could make their greatest contribution to establishing the new emperor's reputation and political clout.[224]

---

[222] Cf. the classic study of F. Kern, *Gottesgnadentum und Widerstandsrecht im früheren Mittelalter. Zur Entwicklungsgeschichte der Monarchie*, 2nd edn (Münster, 1954).

[223] Basil's triumph of 873 and Constantine VII's in 956. Other possible instances would be Theophilus' first triumph, if the traditional date is maintained, and Stauracius' celebration.

[224] Triumphs of 743, 775, 823, 965, 971, 972, the three victories celebrated in 1043 and those of Isaac I and Romanus IV. If the traditional date were maintained, the first triumph of Theophilus would have to be added.

5

Organizing a Byzantine triumph

A Byzantine triumph was not undertaken lightly. The spectacular ceremony mobilized a small army of street cleaners, clergymen, senators, poets, prisoners and spectators, while the performance itself blocked the capital's main thoroughfares for the better part of a day. No attempt has yet been made to uncover the hidden mechanisms which assured the smooth functioning and optimal efficacity of an early Byzantine staged 'event'.[1] To do so is to attempt to assemble a picture of how the Palace as an institution went about the serious business of exalting the monarchy and its officers.[2]

Although the source material on any aspect of the Byzantine monarchy prior to the eleventh century is exasperatingly thin, the situation is probably least dismaying for imperial ceremonial. The triumph was a 'non-catalogue' ceremony, i.e., a staged event which did not recur at fixed intervals. It naturally tended therefore to leave fewer documentary traces than ceremonics which

---

[1] The sole possible exception is the excellent work of D. Th. Belyaev, 'Ezhednevnye priemy Vizantiiskikh tsarei i prazdnichnye vykhody ikh v khram sv. Sofii v IX–XI vv.', *Zapiski imperatorskago russkago arkheologicheskogo obshchestva*, n.s. 6 (1893), i-xlvii and 1–199. The other parts of his monumental study, 'Obzor glavnykh chastei Bol'shago Dvortsa Vizantiiskikh tsarei', *ibid.*, n.s. 5 (1893), 1–200, and 'Bogomol'nye vykhody vizantiiskikh tsarei v gorodskie i prigorodnye khramy Konstantinopolya', *Zapiski klassicheskogo otdeleniya imperatorskago Russkago arkheologicheskago obshchestva*, 4 (1906), 1–189 are less useful in this respect.

[2] 'The Palace' (Τὸ παλάτιον) is sometimes used in the Byzantine period to designate the whole institutional complex surrounding the monarchy. See for example the litany, ed. B. Capelle, 'Le *Kyrie* de la messe et le pape Gélase', *Revue bénédictine*, 46 (1934), 126–44, here, 131, no. 6.

took place every few weeks or even yearly.[3] However, routine characterized ancient bureaucracies no less than modern ones, and precious evidence can be derived from procedures followed in other ceremonies to flesh out our image of the organization of Byzantine victory celebrations. Moreover, the usages of the later Roman empire can sometimes be adduced, if not to furnish positive indications on medieval practice, then at least to allow a measure of our ignorance of the latter.

The very first step in the process which led to the celebration of a triumph was the announcement of a victory. Next to nothing is known about the 'media', the diffusion of official news in the Byzantine empire.[4] It is clear, however, that just as the Palace sought to conceal or delay bad news, so it seems to have attempted to spread word of its success.[5] In Republican and early imperial Rome, the laurel-draped letter or *litterae laureatae* was the traditional form assumed by victory bulletins dispatched to the capital.[6] The tradition was very much alive under the tetrarchy and carried over into the early Byzantine era, even though the laurel festoons seem to disappear after the fifth century.[7] Often the

---

[3] For this use of the term κατάλογος, see, e.g. *De cer.*, 1, 78 (69), Vogt, 2.118. 1–2 (cf. app. ad locum). An excellent illustration of the tendency of recurring ceremonies to dominate record-keeping is provided by Philotheus' Banquet Treatise or *Cleterologium* of September 899, which emphasizes that it is intended for use in the regularly recurring celebrations involving state banquets, ed. Oikonomides, *Listes*, 225.5–9.

[4] For the classical period, see W. Riepl, *Das Nachrichtenwesen des Altertums mit besonderer Rücksicht auf die Römer* (Leipzig, 1913), pp. 322ff, 387ff, etc.

[5] In 312, Maxentius suppressed at Rome reports of Constantine's victories in northern Italy: *XII pan.*, 12 (9), 15, 1, Mynors, 281.25–6. Theodosius II temporarily silenced news of Honorius' death in order to make the necessary arrangements: Socrates, *H.e.*, 7, 23, *PG*, 67.789A. In 602, Maurice attempted to conceal the news of Phocas' usurpation by staging races and having heralds make only a partial disclosure of the facts: Theophylactus Simocattes, *Hist.*, 8, 7, 8, De Boor, 296.20–4; cf. Theophanes, A.M. 6094, De Boor, 287.9–12. In the ninth century, Michael III was famous for eliminating the signal lights warning of an Arab attack, so as not to discourage the *politai* from attending his race performances: *Imp. Exp.*, Bonn, 493.10–19; cf. P. Lemerle, *Le premier humanisme byzantin. Notes et remarques sur enseignement et culture à Byzance des origines au Xᵉ siècle*, Bibliothèque byzantine, Études, 6 (Paris, 1971), p. 155 with n. 29.

[6] A. von Premerstein, 'Litterae laureatae', *RE*, 12 (1925), 1014; L. Halkin, *Supplication*, pp. 80–7.

[7] S. Mazzarino, '"Annunci" e "publica laetitia": L'iscrizione romana di Fausto e altri testi', *Antico, tardoantico ed èra costantiniana*, 1 (n. p., 1974), pp. 229–50; M. McCormick, 'Odoacer, Emperor Zeno and the Rugian victory legation', *Byz.*, 47 (1977), 212–32, here 218–19. To the evidence assembled there, add, for the Tetrarchy,

bulletins were accompanied by objects captured in battle, the 'symbols of victory', destined to be laid at the feet of the supreme commander and ultimate victor.[8] In late antiquity, the bulletin and its symbols of success became so deeply identified with victory itself that an impatient emperor could send to the field and demand symbols of victory from a slow-moving general.[9] The symbols themselves served a dual purpose. On the one hand, they allowed the local commander to recognize publicly the emperor's monopoly of victory and to reassure Constantinople that he would not use his success as a springboard to the purple.[10] On the other, this time-honored military custom supplied tangible proof of the victory. As an exasperated general retorted to soldiers upset when he dispatched booty to emperor Maurice, 'What other witnesses to your accomplishments will you be able to produce [in Constantinople]?'[11] A society accustomed to increasing victory celebrations generated by decreasing success demanded proof of the victories which were publicly announced to it.

Imperial officers continued to produce victory bulletins well into the Middle Ages and it has been suggested that the content and tone of these documents must have left a deep imprint on the

---

XII pan., 11 (3), 7, 1, Mynors, 261.14–16 (*laurea*) and 8 (5), 5, 2, Mynors, 228.5–6, on victory messengers expected at Trier. For victory bulletins of Constantine and his successors, *XII pan.*, 7 (6), 14, 1, Mynors, 214.4–7; Eusebius, *H.e.*, 9, 9, 12, Schwartz, 832.18–21; Claudian, *De bello gildonico*, 1, 10–13, Birt, 545; John of Antioch, *De insidiis*, fg. 103, De Boor, *Excerpta historica*, 3.143.10–12 and Heraclius' reports to the capital mentioned by Theophanes, A.M. 6116, De Boor, 312.29–313.2, in addition to the documents mentioned in Chs. 2 and 3 above.

[8] McCormick, 'Odoacer', 218 with n. 28. Further evidence on the custom occurs in Theodosius' prayer for his son, Claudian, *III cons.*, 33–8, Birt, 142; Procopius, *Bella*, 5, 14, 15, Haury, 2.78.3–4; cf. 5, 24, 1, *ibid.*, 117.24–118.1 and again 7, 24, 34, *ibid.*, 407.9–12 (commander and keys of Rome); *ibid.*, 4, 28, 46, Haury 1.551.13–19 and 8, 14, 43, 2.564.4–8 (recaptured Roman and Persian standards). That such objects were laid at the emperor's feet is suggested by Ammianus' acerbic remark that the assassinated Gallus' shoes were thrown at Constantius' feet as though they were the spoils of a Persian king: 15, 1, 2, Clark, 1.38.10–11; cf. Theophanes, A.M. 6044, De Boor, 228.18–24, on which see McCormick, *loc. cit.*

[9] Justin II sent a messenger requesting the keys of Nisibis to hasten the siege of that city: Evagrius, *H.e.*, 5, 9, Bidez–Parmentier, 204.20–5.

[10] McCormick, 'Odoacer', 217–18. Similar reassurance seems to be implied by the circumstances of Aristomachus' trip to Constantinople after his success in Nubia under Maurice: John of Nikiu, 95, 14–15, tr. Charles, 153.

[11] Theophylactus Simocattes, *Hist.*, 6, 7, 12–16, De Boor, 233.28–234.18.

surviving historical records.[12] The victory communiqués which Constantine V sent to Constantinople during his Bulgar wars could still be consulted by the patriarch Nicephorus several decades later.[13] By 809, events had so eroded imperial credibility that Nicephorus I was forced to swear to the accuracy of victory dispatches claiming that he was celebrating Easter in the camp of the defeated Bulgarian khan.[14] Five years later, Leo V circulated to all towns and territories an official report of his defeat of Krum at Constantinople.[15] In the heyday of his usurpation, Thomas the Slav sent out victory bulletins which his ultimate victor would qualify as falsifications. Forgeries or not, they did succeed in bringing the rebel additional support.[16] Victory bulletins continued to arrive in the capital down to the twelfth century.[17]

The fashion in which an imperial victory bulletin was communicated to the public had not continued unchanged since ancient times. Under the Roman Republic, generals' *litterae laureatae* were first read to the Senate and only later published to the general population in a *contio*.[18] This differentiation of audience was preserved in the Constantinian empire: in the second half of the fourth century, the Senates of Rome and Constantinople continued to hear victory bulletins from the commander-in-chief, read to them by the City Prefect or his equivalent.[19] In the provinces, the situation may have been somewhat different. For instance, at

---

[12] V. Beševliev, 'Die Botschaften der Byzantinischen Kaiser aus dem Schlachtfeld', Βυζαντινά, 6 (1974), 78–83; cf. McCormick, 'Odoacer', 219, n. 30. Later evidence shows that, in the twelfth century, the Logothete of the Dromos was entrusted with the composition of victory letters, but it would be unwise to extrapolate from this instance to earlier usage: Michael Italicus, *Op.*, 40, ed. P. Gautier, Archives de l'Orient chrétien, 14 (Paris, 1972), 232–4 with n. 4; cf. too 248.8. I owe this reference to the kindness of R. Browning.

[13] Nicephorus, *Antirrheticus*, 3, 72, *PG*, 100.508B-C.

[14] Theophanes, A.M. 6301, De Boor, 485.12–14; Dölger, *Regesten*, no. 369. A similar report must be what Theophanes had in mind when he castigated Nicephorus for announcing (ἐκήρυττε), in July 811, the great role of Stauracius in the initial, successful engagements on the eve of his great defeat: Theophanes, A.M. 6303, De Boor, 490.18–21.

[15] Dölger, *Regesten*, no. 392; cf. Beševliev, 'Botschaften', p. 75.

[16] Theoph. Cont., 2, 16, Bonn, 63.18–64.1; cf. Genesius, 2, 6, Lesmüller-Werner and Thurn, 29.72–7.

[17] See above, n. 12.

[18] Halkin, *Supplications*, pp. 83–7.

[19] That ἐπινίκια γράμματα were read to the senators of Constantinople is implicit in Constantius' reference to their expectation that this was what they were going to hear

Antioch around 390, John Chrysostom's listeners were familiar with a ceremony in which all elements of the population together listened to imperial victory bulletins.[20] It took place in a *theatron*. While the imperial words were being read, leading dignitaries, governors, city council and people remained standing and observed the strictest silence. Any disruption of the ceremony with unsolicited noise was punishable by death for insult to the imperial majesty. The assembly was concluded with acclamations and in this way parallels procedure for most imperial announcements.[21]

The one piece of early medieval evidence on the physical context for the public delivery of victory bulletins is tantalizing in its suggestion of the primacy of the sacred: Heraclius' surviving report from the Persian front was read from the ambo of the Hagia Sophia on Sunday, 15 May 628.[22] At first glance, the announcement's timing – 15 May was Pentecost in that year – and the extraordinary role of patriarch Sergius in the imperial government might seem to suggest that this was an unusual derogation from contemporary custom. Over a century earlier, the setting for important imperial announcements appears to have varied according to their content: churches were used for doctrinal or ecclesiastical communications, civil buildings for less religious matters.[23] In the sixth century, this changed. Justinian's

---

when Justinus, probably proconsul of Constantinople, read them the notification of Themistius' promotion, in the letter preserved among the latter's works: ed. Schenkl–Downey Norman, 3.122.6–9; cf. *PLRE*, 1, 489, 'Iustinus 2'. In 379, Symmachus read an imperial victory bulletin to the Roman Senate, *Ep.*, 1, 95, Seeck, 38.20 and esp. 27–9; cf. Chastagnol, *Préfecture*, p. 68. For a description of the reading of an imperial letter to the Constantinopolitan Senate, Themistius, *Or.*, 2, Schenkl–Downey, 1.31.8–17.

20 *Hom. XIX in Matth.*, *PG*, 57.285. For the date, cf. H. Musurillo, 'John Chrysostom's Homilies on Matthew and the Version of Annianus', *Kyriakon. Festschrift Johannes Quasten*, 1 (Münster, 1970), 452–60, here 454.

21 *PG*, 57.285; cf. Jones, *Later Roman Empire*, 2, 722–3.

22 *Chron. pasch.*, Bonn, 727.9–14.

23 Thus in 475–6, an imperial *asecretis* read *mandata* of personal and doctrinal content from the ambo of old Hagia Sophia: *V. Danielis stylitae* (*BHG*, 489), 84, Delehaye, 79.1–19. For other instances of imperial communication of religious content read in churches: Theophanes, A.M. 6005, De Boor, 158.8–10 and 159.5–8; Evagrius, *H.e.*, 3, 13, Bidez–Parmentier, 110.11ff. In A.D. 484, on the other hand, the first reading of Verina's proclamation of the usurper Leontius was given in Antioch's Praetorium: Malalus Slav., 15, Spinka–Downey, 107.

novel on the provincial administration was to be displayed at church entrances and copies of imperial edicts were dispatched to various episcopal sees.[24] That the reading of Heraclius' victory bulletin in the Hagia Sophia conformed to contemporary custom is confirmed by an Armenian historian, who mentions that the same emperor had ordered that another important political document be read to the patriarch and grandees of Constantinople in 'the House of God', presumably the Hagia Sophia.[25] And so, in Byzantium's dark age, the 'Great Church' came to serve as the natural point of assembly and public communication in times of crisis. Thus the usurper Leontius raised what may have been a standard cry in his era, sending heralds to shout 'All Christians to the Hagia Sophia!' in each of the city's regions. The citizenry assembled at the Baptistery, where the uprising against Justinian II was revealed.[26] In the middle of the eighth century, the false news of Constantine V's demise and the accession of Artabasdus was announced to the *laos* assembled in the galleries of the Hagia Sophia.[27] The pattern was not, however, irreversible, since, by the eleventh century at the latest, important imperial announcements were being read in the Forum.[28]

It is not easy to characterize the content and character of a kind

[24] R. Scott, 'Malalas and Justinian's Codification', *Byzantine Papers*, Byzantina australiensia, 1 (Canberra, 1981), 12–31, esp. 16 and 19.

[25] Sebeos, *Histoire d'Héraclius*, 26, tr. F. Macler (Paris, 1904), 80.

[26] Theophanes, A.M. 6187, De Boor, 369.12–16. A similar assembly earlier in the seventh century is recorded by Sebeos, *Hist. Hér.*, 32, Macler, 105.

[27] Theophanes, A.M. 6233, De Boor, 415.2–12. I am not sure how to resolve the ambiguity inherent in an eighth-century usage of the word λαός. The localization in the galleries suggests that it may have been a select audience. On the galleries of the Hagia Sophia and some of their functions, T.F. Mathews, *The early churches of Constantinople: architecture and liturgy* (University Park, 1971), pp. 128ff. A rough estimate of the galleries' theoretical maximum capacity might be attempted on the basis of the usable floor space, which Robert L. Van Nice and John Wilson were kind enough to calculate for me. The result was 2867 m² for all three galleries together. Allowing a very generous 1 m² per person (part of the galleries were reserved for imperial use: cf. Mathews, *Early churches*, pp. 133–4), the λαός which listened to the announcement could have numbered around 3000 persons. For the measurements of the galleries on which these conjectures are based, see R.L. Van Nice, *Saint Sophia in Istanbul: An Architectural Survey* (Washington, D.C., 1965), pl. 2.

[28] For ceremony announcements, see below; for the reading of an important imperial communication in the Forum in 1042, Dölger, *Regesten*, no. 848. A few indications on the publication of Byzantine laws are given by F. Dölger–J. Karayannopulos, *Byzantinische Urkundenlehre* (Munich, 1968), pp. 71ff.

of document which has rarely been preserved, but a few salient points are worth mentioning.[29] To set the tone, the bulletins typically began with a biblical citation or two.[30] Heraclius' missive carries this the farthest. It starts with a wholesale quotation of Psalm 99 and proceeds to trumpet the fall of the impious in language and imagery which reverberate with allusions to the Psalter.[31] There follows a relatively precise narration of the facts, including frequent references to dates, places and personal names.[32] Such accounts were anything but immune to propagandizing, as is shown by Nicephorus I's oaths on the truthfulness of his *epinikia* and the same emperor's efforts to portray his son and heir as the mainspring of victory, as well as by Lemerle's analysis of Michael and Theophilus' loose handling of the truth in 824.[33] To judge by the surviving document of 628, the style in which seventh-century emperors announced their victory was relatively straightforward and accessible to a popular audience. Unlike the

[29] In addition to Heraclius' letter, Dölger, *Regesten*, no. 192, see the letter of 824 announcing the defeat of Thomas the Slav to the Frankish emperor Louis the Pious (Dölger, *Regesten*, no. 408), ed. A. Werminghoff, *MGH. Conc.*, 1.2 (1908), 475–80 and the controverted letter of John Tzimisces to Ashod (Dölger, *Regesten*, no. 750), preserved in Matthew of Edessa, tr. E. Dulaurier, *Chronique de Matthieu d'Edesse (962–1136)*, Bibliothèque historique arménienne (Paris, 1858), 16–23; cf. C. Kuchuk-Ioannesov, 'Pismo imperatora Ioanna Tsimiskhiya k armyanskomyu tsaryu Ashotu III.', *VV*, 10 (1903), 91–101, here 93–101, and P.E. Walker, 'The "crusade" of John Tzimisces in the light of new Arabic evidence', *Byz.*, 47 (1977), 301–7.

[30] Dölger, *Regesten*, no. 192, cites James 1.17, Proverbs 8.15–16 and Isaiah 45.13 as the editor noted: *ed. cit.*, 475.33–6; no. 750, tr. Dulaurier, 16, seems to allude to Psalm 97 (98).1 or perhaps Acts 2.11 as well as Romans 11.33.

[31] *Regesten*, no. 192, Bonn, 727.15–21: Psalm 99 (100); 727.21–728.2: cf. Psalm 95 (96). 11–12; 728.6: Psalm 108 (109).15; 728.7–8: cf. Psalm 30 (31).19; 728.10: Psalm 9.6, etc. It might be noted that Dometianus' homily on the recapture of Martyropolis, preserved in Theophylactus Simocattes, *Hist.*, 4, 16, 23, De Boor, 187.5–6, alludes to Psalm 95 (96).11–12 in much the same fashion as Heraclius' victory bulletin.

[32] In addition to *Regesten*, no. 192, Bonn, 728.12–734.9; *Regesten*, no. 408, Werminghoff, 476.6–478.8; *Regesten*, no. 750, tr. Dulaurier, 17–23. This particular point is confirmed by an anecdote in the *Vita Symeonis stylitae iunioris (BHG, 1689)*, 187, ed. P. van den Ven, *La vie ancienne de S. Syméon Stylite le jeune*, Subsidia hagiographica, 32, 1 (Brussels, 1962), 165.16–21: *epinikia* which arrived at Antioch within the week bore out the saint's prophecy of a Roman victory over Alamundar down to the day and hour.

[33] On sworn *epinikia*, above, n. 14. I presume that an imperial victory bulletin was the means by which Nicephorus ἐκήρυττε the initial success of the invasion of Bulgaria as due to the εὐτυχία καὶ εὐβουλία of Stauracius (Theophanes, A.M. 6303, De Boor, 490.18–21). For the propagandistic version of Thomas the Slav's uprising, Lemerle, 'Thomas le Slave', p. 258.

language of the elite, this early Byzantine victory bulletin did not avoid military jargon or Latinisms.[34]

Little information is available on any kind of imperial decision-making in the early Middle Ages. A number of less than successful campaigns conducted by the emperors themselves seem not to have included triumphs.[35] If a major victory celebration was not an automatic by-product of an imperial expedition, the staging of such a celebration required a conscious decision. That this decision was made at the highest level of government is suggested both by general ceremonial practice and specific evidence for victory celebrations. Thus, even for routine annual processions to the Hagia Sophia, it was the emperors themselves who formally ordered the ceremony's organization.[36] The triumphs of Theophilus and Michael IV imply that this was no less true of victory celebrations.[37] For the triumph of an imperial general, the ruler's

[34] On the social connotations of the avoidance of loan-words, M. McCormick, 'Greek hagiography and popular Latin in late antiquity: the case of *Biberaticum – βιβερατικόν*', *American Journal of Philology*, 102 (1981), 154–63, here 158–9. Among jargon or Latinisms in Heraclius' letter: καστέλλιον (Bonn, 728.21); ἄπληκτον (729.16; 730.11); παλάτια (729.23); ἐκστράτευμα (730.8); οἱ τῆς σκούλκας (730.12); ἀδσηκρῆτις Περσῶν (730.14), etc.

[35] Thus for Constantine V: Theophanes, A.M. 6257, De Boor, 437.24–5: εἰσῆλθεν ἀδόξως ἐν τῇ πόλει. This may be the implication as well, ibid., A.M. 6266, 448.4: μηδὲν ποιήσας. Constantine VI returned to the capital as a fugitive after an unsuccessful effort against the Bulgarians in 792, ibid., A.M. 6284, 467.33. This would also appear to be the meaning of Theophanes' expression for Nicephorus I's return after a futile Bulgarian campaign: ὑπέστρεψε ἄπρακτος, ibid., A.M. 6299, 482.25–9. Ἄπρακτος seems here to be the antonym of ἔμπρακτος, used in the context of a triumphal entry, e.g., Constantine V's triumph of 773, ibid., A.M. 6265, 447.24: ὑπέστρεψε θριαμβεύσας ἐν τῇ πόλει, καὶ ἔμπρακτος εἰσελθών.... Theophilus, for all his campaigns, seems to have celebrated only two triumphs: cf. above, Ch. 4, p. 133. The hostile author of Theoph. Cont., 3, 2, Bonn, 87.1–8, distorts this to suggest that he never celebrated a triumph, the imperial act par excellence: ἀλλ' ἥττητό τε ἀεὶ καὶ οὐ κατὰ βασιλέα ὑπέστρεψεν. For recent findings that Basil I did not celebrate as many triumphs as campaigns, above, Ch. 4, p. 154, n. 82.

[36] *De cer.*, 1, 1, Vogt, 1.3.11–12: εἶτα κελεύουσιν τούτους [the *praipositoi*] οἱ δεσπόται ἄγεσθαι ἐπὶ τὸν αὔριον πρόκενσον. Cf. Belyaev, 'Priemy', pp. 21–2.

[37] Thus Theophilus is explicitly stated to have commanded (διορίσατο, ἐκέλευσε) the senators and their wives to remain with him until he staged his victorious entry. He later ordered the children of Constantinople to welcome him during his second triumph (προσέταξεν; *Imp. Exp.*, Bonn, 504.12 and 14; 508.3). The level of debate is indicated for Michael IV's Bulgarian triumph by Psellus' statement that until then (τέως), Michael's counselors had attempted to conceal his fatal illness καὶ βουλὴν ἐποιοῦντο περὶ καταστάσεως, to avoid a revolution: *Chronographia*, Michael IV, 51,

command may well have been even more indispensable.[38]

The decision to celebrate a triumph probably fell into two stages. Sometimes, even before he set out on a campaign, an emperor might make the determination that he would, if at all possible, celebrate a triumph. This would explain Basil I's afterthought of an incursion into Paulician territory in 873.[39] That Constantine VII intended to stage a triumphal entry is suggested by his compilation of the treatise On Imperial Expeditions, complete with dossiers on how other emperors celebrated their triumphs. Romanus III Argyrus is known to have ordered the manufacture of a victory crown even before leaving the capital for a campaign into Asia Minor.[40] The final decision must, however, have been made shortly before the event.

Regularly recurring ceremonies like annual processions or catalogue banquets received the green light from the emperor on the day before their performance.[41] Considering the complexity of the ceremony, the number of participants and the fact that it involved an area of the city which witnessed imperial ceremonies only occasionally, the final go-ahead for a triumphal entry would of necessity have been given at least that far in advance.[42]

Renauld, 1.83.4–7. This section follows immediately the account of Michael's triumph. Although Renauld takes κατάστασις to mean 'l'administration', it is not impossible that it refers to the ceremony itself.

[38] For Nicephorus Phocas' triumphs of 961 and 963, the sources emphasize that the ruler explicitly ordered the general to enter the city; by implication, this would appear to apply to the celebration of the triumph as well: above, Ch. 4, n. 141 and esp. Sym. Mag., Bonn, 759.20–3. Explicit evidence to this effect is offered by Psellus' account of Stephen's triumphal entry of 1043: *Chronographia*, Constantine IX, 87, Renauld, 2.6.3–4: ὁ αὐτοκράτωρ θρίαμβον δεῖν ἔγνω ἐπὶ τοῖς τροπαίοις κατάγειν.

[39] Above, Ch. 4, n. 154.

[40] Above, Ch. 4, n. 193.

[41] Written orders for annual processions were issued on the day preceding the procession: *De cer.*, 1, 1, Vogt, 1.3.12–4.6. Further evidence for arrangements made on the eve of the ceremony in Belyaev, 'Priemy', p. 22, n. 2; cf. pp. 40–1.

[42] Theophilus had anticipated a delay of up to seven days between his arrival in the Asiatic suburbs of the capital and the arrival of the captives destined to appear in his parade; in actuality, the prisoners' late arrival added three days to his schedule: *Imp. Exp.*, Bonn, 504.11–18. From Psellus, we know that Constantine IX waited until the last minute and the arrival of the victorious army at the walls before deciding to grant a triumphal entry to the *Sebastophorus*, although the precise time frame is not given: *Chronographia*, Constantine IX, 87, Renauld, 2.6.1–4. Nicephorus Phocas' first ceremonial entry into the capital seems to have occurred two or three days after his brother took control of the city and order was restored: *De cer.*, 1, 96, Bonn,

The great early medieval ceremonies of enthronement and promotion were customarily timed to coincide with the most prestigious feasts of the political and liturgical calendar, days like Christmas, Easter, Pentecost, Autokratoria and even the anniversary of the delivery of Constantinople from the Arabs.[43] The rare indications on the precise date of victory celebrations hint that emperors sometimes tried to link their own triumphs with dates hallowed by church observance. Thus Constantine VI celebrated his triumphal entry of 794 on the eve of the great festival of Blachernae which commemorated the role of the Virgin's relic in defending the capital over a century earlier. In this instance, the ceremony's timing explains its unique itinerary.[44]

Whatever the date of imperial victory celebrations, the Byzantines followed Roman custom which fixed the main events of public life early in the morning.[45] The great annual processions to the Hagia Sophia – and, by implication, the coronations and promotions associated with them – got started very early in the day.[46] So too the triumph in the Forum, which was staged early in the morning.[47] In 559, Justinian's triumphal entry began shortly after dawn, in the day's first hour.[48] Although there is no explicit record of the time at which early medieval triumphal entries got underway, several factors argue for an early start here as well.

437.17–438.5. The material arrangements for such a ceremony were of course very much like those of the triumphal entry.

[43] For other examples, Treadgold, 'Accuracy', pp. 166–7, n. 34. For the timing of bureaucratic promotions ὡς ἐκ θεοῦ τὴν ψῆφον λαμβάνουσαι in the Chrysotriklinos under Leo VI, see Philotheus, *Cleterologium*, Oikonomides, 85.28–30. On Nicephorus II's coronation date, Ch. 4, p. 169. In addition to the prestige and, perhaps, good fortune associated with those days, it is not unlikely that the leading provincial officials came to the capital for the great holidays, thereby increasing the size and quality of the governmental audience for such events. See, e.g. Michael and Theophilus, Dölger, *Regesten*, no. 408, Werminghoff, 476.33–4.

[44] Above, Ch. 4, p. 143. On the other hand, there is no evidence of special motives for Constantine IX's celebration of the defeat of Tornicius on 29 December 1047 or Justinian's triumph on 11 August 559.

[45] Balsdon, *Life and Leisure*, p. 24. The point is made precisely for imperial entries by the *adventus* of Titus, probably at Alexandria, on 25 April 71 at 7 a.m.: P. Oxy. 2725, ed. L. Ingrams et al., *The Oxyrhynchus Papyri*, 34 (London, 1968), 127–9.

[46] Belyaev, 'Priemy', p. 41. In the sixth century, for instance, Tiberius was promoted Caesar in the morning: John of Ephesus, *H.e.*, 3, 3, 5, tr. Brooks, 95.7.

[47] *De cer.*, 2, 19, Bonn, 607.18.   [48] *Imp. Exp.*, Bonn, 497.6.

Imperial *adventus* covered the same itinerary in much the same way and are known to have begun in the morning.[49] *A contrario*, imperial entries which took place at other times of the day were singled out and evidence a non-ritualistic character.[50] Finally, the length and complexity of the ceremony practically enjoined an early start whenever feasible.

Insuring the widest possible publicity for a ceremony meant announcing it to the city's population.[51] Oral or written announcements were by nature ephemeral and have vanished with hardly a trace.[52] Thanks only to bureaucratic prescription is it known that written orders (μανδᾶτα) were issued to various governmental offices informing them of a ceremony on the eve of its performance.[53] Certainly rumor or intentional 'leaks' had a hand in spreading the word on more than one occasion. Informal news of Leo VI's impending participation in his father's Elias Day procession of 886 electrified the city's population and brought them out in droves. No Constantinopolitan needed to be told that it meant Leo's restoration as heir designate to the throne.[54] But this was hardly typical and the Palace would not likely have left the publicity for its ceremonies to chance.

It is well known that verbal announcements of dates, times and

---

[49] Thus the solemn entry of Nicephorus II on 16 August 963: *De cer.*, 1, 96, Bonn, 438.4.

[50] Thus the violent recapture of Constantinople by Constantine V: Theophanes, A.M. 6235, De Boor, 420.11–12: ἄφνω παραταξάμενος τῇ δείλῃ διὰ τοῦ χερσαίου τείχους τὴν πόλιν παρέλαβεν, or Leo V's entry after his usurpation at the Hebdomon; it took place at midday and avoided the Golden Gate: *ibid.*, A.M. 6305, 502.25–6: καὶ μεσούσης ἡμέρας . . . διὰ τῆς Χαρσίου πόρτης εἰσέρχεται καταλαβὼν τὰ βασίλεια.

[51] The only work done on announcements until now comes from liturgists: T. Klauser, 'Festankündigung', *RAC*, 7 (1969), 767–85, and F. Cabrol, 'L'annonce des fêtes', *DACL*, 1, 2 (1907), 2230–41.

[52] See for example the reflections of Klauser, 'Festankündigung', pp. 773–4; 779–80; 784.

[53] E. g. *De cer.*, 1, 1, Vogt, 1.3.12–21. Cf. the references collected by Belyaev, 'Priemy', p. 22, n. 2, and the office of the patriarchal referendary, entrusted with liturgical messages for the Palace: Darrouzès, *Recherches*, pp. 373–4.

[54] *Vita Theophano imp.* (*BHG*, 1794), 19, ed. E. Kurtz, 'Zwei griechische Texte über die hl. Theophano, die Gemahlin Kaisers Leo VI.', *Zapiski imperatorskoi akademii nauk*, s. 8, *po istor.-filol. otdeleniyu*, 3, no. 2 (St Petersburg, 1898), 13.12–14 and 13.18–23. For the date, R.J.H. Jenkins, 'The chronological accuracy of the "Logothete" for the years A.D. 867–913', *DOP*, 19 (1965), 91–112, here 101–3. Another, comparable instance is Corippus' account of how 'Fama' spread word of Justin II's accession: *Iust.*, 1, 298ff, Cameron, 45.

places were part and parcel of late antique liturgical practice.[55] In fifth-century Constantinople, an emperor could easily order the patriarch to announce details of an upcoming relic translation.[56] Imperial ceremonies too were announced in advance. The announcement seems to have taken the form of an imperial order.[57] In 602, for example, Phocas dispatched the *asecretis* Theodore to the Hagia Sophia. There he mounted the ambo and delivered to the population the usurper's order ($\pi\rho\acute{o}\sigma\tau\alpha\gamma\mu\alpha$) that they go out to the Hebdomon Palace for his coronation.[58] Under Constantine V, the crowd who watched the ritual humiliation of the patriarch Constantine was convoked in the Hagia Sophia by imperial command.[59] In the eleventh century, the inauguration of Michael V as Caesar was announced in advance, perhaps by heralds. A little later, an Arab visitor remarked on the public announcement of Hippodrome festivities by criers on the day preceding the gathering.[60] These general announcements appear to have been intended for the population at large, since more specific means were at hand for alerting the city's governmental and commercial elite. Imperial ritual had long since institutionalized the involvement of two highly significant social groups, the members of the senatorial order or *synkletikoi* and the city's guilds.

Senatorial rank brought to its holders substantial privileges and perquisites; in return, members of the order were considered bound to the emperor by special ties which ran deeper than those of society at large.[61] Senatorial dignity entailed the highly prized

[55] See e.g. Klauser, 'Festankündigung', p. 780.

[56] *V. Danielis stylitae* (*BHG*, 489), 58, Delehaye, 56.21–5. Klauser, 'Festankündigung', p. 782 on κατηγοριάρης (= κατογυριάρης) is unfounded: Darrouzès, *Recherches*, p. 237.

[57] Belyaev, 'Priemy', pp. 40–1, is the sole treatment of this problem available to date and it concerns only the notification of palace institutions treated in *De cer.*, 1, 1.

[58] Theophylactus Simocattes, *Hist.*, 8, 10, 1–3, De Boor, 302.20–303.1; cf. Theophanes, A.M. 6094, De Boor, 289.10–13.

[59] *Ibid.*, A.M. 6259, De Boor, 441.11–13 (ἐκ διαταγῆς βασιλικῆς).

[60] Psellus, *Chronographia*, Michael IV, 23, Renauld, 1.67.4–6: Δημοτελῆ γοῦν ἑορτὴν προκηρύξαντες καὶ τοὺς ἐν τέλει ξύμπαντες εἰς τὸν ἐν Βλαχέρναις συνηθροικότες ναόν. It is not impossible that προκηρύσσω is being used metaphorically. Criers for the Hippodrome: Minorski, 'Marvazi', p. 461.

[61] The best treatments are A. Christophilopoulou, Ἡ σύγκλητος εἰς τὸ Βυζαντινὸν κράτος, Ἐπετηρὶς τοῦ ἀρχείου τῆς ἱστορίας τοῦ ἑλληνικοῦ δικαίου, 2 (Athens, 1949);

right of participating in imperial processions and ceremonies.[62]
The constant reference to the senatorial order in the Ceremony
Book offers convincing evidence of the *synkletikoi*'s indispensable
role in imperial ritual. Indeed, scholars have obstinately neglected
the fact that for its author, the book was essentially a 'Treatise on
Imperial and Senatorial Ceremonial'.[63] In the Middle Ages, the
distinction between right and obligation was a fine one and, as we
learn from the tenth-century Life of Euthymius, attendance at
imperial ceremonies was not left to the senatorial pleasure. When
the newly appointed patriarchal *syncellus* had failed to show up at
regular court ceremonies for some time, the imperial minister
Stylianus Zaoutzes is supposed to have sent him a written
warning:

Apparently, father, it has escaped Your Holiness' notice that you too are
now a dignitary of the realm (ὅτι βασιλικοῦ ἀξιώματος. καὐτὸς.
μέτοχος. γέγονας.) and that you, just like those of us who are enrolled

---

H.G. Beck, *Senat und Volk von Konstantinopel. Probleme der byzantinischen Verfassungs-geschichte*, Sitzungsberichte der Bayerische Akademie der Wissenschaften, Philos.-hist. Kl. (Munich, 1966), no. 6, and the brief but excellent observations of P. Lemerle, *Cinq études*, pp. 287ff. A thorough social and institutional history of the *synkletos* is badly needed. The notion of the special ties between *synkletikoi* and the emperor comes through clearly in the words put into the mouth of Leo III by the ninth-century author of the *Passio X martyrum* (*BHG*, 1195), *AASS Aug.*, 2 (1735). 434–7, here 442D (same ref. in 3rd edn), when that emperor is depicted as reprimanding the members of the elite who were involved in the riot over the Chalke icon: Ἔδει μὲν ὑμᾶς. ὡς. ἅτε ἐν ὑπεροχῇ γένους. καὶ ἀξιωμάτων ὄντας, μὴ οὕτως. μετὰ τῶν ἀγοραίων καὶ ἀγροίκων ἑαυτοὺς. ἐκκαταμῖξαι καὶ στάσιν τοσαύτην ἐμποιῆσαι τῇ πόλει, ἔτι μὲν καὶ ἀντάρτας. τῆς. ἐμῆς. βασιλείας. γενέσθαι. On the document and its date: I. Ševčenko, 'Hagiography of the Iconoclast Period', *Iconoclasm*, ed. A. Bryer and J. Herrin (Birmingham, 1977), pp. 113–31, here 114 with n. 6, and esp. C. Mango, *Brazen House*, pp. 116–17.

[62] The great importance to contemporary minds of participation in ceremonies is evidenced by a letter in which Theodore Studite consoles the *spatharius* Eudocimus, who was depressed by his loss of sight, which precluded his participation in imperial processions: at least, writes Theodore, this should preserve him from the company of fornicators and wrongdoers! *Ep.*, 2, 185, *PG*, 99.1569B. See also the efforts of the cleric Ktenas to buy his way into the dignity of protospatharius and its concomitant ceremonial obligations: Constantine VII, *De adm. imp.*, 50, 236–56, Moravcsik-Jenkins, 244, and *Commentary*, pp. 194–5; cf. P. Lemerle, '*Roga* et rente d'état aux Xᵉ–XIᵉ siècles', *RÉB*, 25 (1967), 77–100, here 79–80.

[63] *De cer.*, 2, Praef., Bonn, 516.1: Ὁ περὶ τῆς. βασιλικῆς. καὶ συγκλητικῆς. τάξεως. λόγος. For an overview of senatorial participation in imperial rituals, Christophilopoulou, Σύγκλητος., pp. 111–20; cf. Belyaev, 'Priemy', *passim*.

with you in the sacred Senate, must not fail to participate in the regular ceremonies. Do not persist in mocking the Empire with this prolonged retirement, showing your contempt for the rulers themselves....[64]

This obligation clarifies why the authors of various accounts of triumphal entries simply presuppose the *synkletikoi*'s general participation in ceremonies of welcome and victory. It is understandable that a late antique bureaucrat had once taken the trouble to specify the various alternatives open to members of the senatorial order for discharging their duty of participation in imperial entries.[65] The manner in which senators were convoked cannot have differed greatly from that attested for other ceremonies.[66]

If the senatorial order resident in the capital was *ipso facto* intimately involved in a triumph, the ecclesiastical elite of the provinces, at least, needed explicit authorization to enter the capital and participate in the ceremony. Thus, late in the tenth century, Leo, the metropolitan of Synades wrote to his colleagues and the emperor in Constantinople, expressing his eagerness to reach the city, witness and perhaps even eulogize the triumph of Basil and his brother. To do so, however, required imperial authorization (τὸ τῆς εἰσελεύσεως ἐνδόσιμον); as the bishop bitterly complains, it was not forthcoming and Leo was stuck in Pylae with the pigs intended for the tables of Constantinople.[67] Even in the event that he would miss the ceremony, Leo hoped to learn its details from more fortunate colleagues.[68]

---

[64] *Vita Euthymii* (BHG, 651), 4, ed. P. Karlin-Hayter, Bibliothèque de Byzantion, 3 (Brussels, 1970), 23.16–22, whose translation I have adapted somewhat. The crucial passage is:...καὶ καθάπερ ἡμεῖς, οἱ σὺν σοὶ τῇ ἱερᾷ συγκλήτῳ καταλεγέντες, οὕτως, καὶ σὺ ὀφείλεις, τοῦ μὴ καθυστερεῖν τῶν ἐκ τύπου προελεύσεων. μήτε τῇ ἡσυχίᾳ ἐπὶ πολὺ προσκαρτερῶν καταπαίζῃς τῆς βασιλείας, καταφρονῶν καὶ αὐτῶν τῶν βασιλευόντων. The requirement probably goes at least as far back as Justinian's novella on the Senate (A.D. 537): *Novellae Iustiniani*, 62, 1, 3, ed. R. Schoell and P. Krüger, *Corpus iuris civilis*, 3 (Berlin, 1928). 333.9–10, referring to circus games and *conventus*. See too Themistius' insistence on the special obligation of the Senate of Constantinople to celebrate imperial holidays: *Or.*, 4, Schenkl–Downey, 1.78.21–6.

[65] *Imp. Exp.*, Bonn, 495.1–497.13, dated to Justinian's reign by Bury, 'Ceremonial Book', p. 439, n. 57.

[66] See Belyaev, 'Priemy', p. 23, n. 1. It is noteworthy that in the reports appended to *Imp. Exp.*, their participation is so taken for granted that it is stated without explanation: Bonn 498.20–499.1 and 504.5–6.

[67] *Ep.*, 53 (to members of the Holy Synod) and 54 (to Basil II), Darrouzès, 205–10.

[68] *Ep.*, 54, Darrouzès, 210.67–71.

Like many of the monarchy's rituals, participation in an imperial triumph was mostly an affair for men. The sexual segregation which had crept into late Roman life and which, by the sixth century, was regarded as characteristic of Constantinople's upper crust, is underscored by the glaring absence of women – captives aside – from triumphal processions and attendant ceremonies.[69] Thus, the senators who went out to Hiereia to greet the triumphant Theophilus were unaccompanied by their wives. It was only when the emperor decided to keep his magnates with him that the ladies were summoned to join the court. The motivation for this order is revealing: it was intended to allow the wives to be with the Augusta, not their husbands.[70] The reason is that in early medieval Byzantium, the public lives of the ladies of the elite generally revolved around the ceremonial life of the empress, while that of their husbands turned on the activities of the emperor.[71] The rare exceptions to this principle are readily

---

[69] On sexual segregation, see L. Bréhier, *La civilisation byzantine*, 2nd edn (Paris, 1970), pp. 19 and 21; cf. J. Grosdidier de Matons, 'La femme dans l'empire byzantin', *Histoire mondiale de la femme*, ed. P. Grimal, 3 (Paris, 1967), 11–43, here 27–8; some indications on empresses and ceremonial, *ibid.*, pp. 22–3; on the segregation of women at games and spectacles in ancient Rome, Balsdon, *Life and leisure*, pp. 258–9. Describing the reaction of the population of Constantinople during the earthquake of 557, Agathias observes that social order was completely overturned to the point that women mingled freely with men – and not just lower class types either: *Hist.*, 5, 3, 7, Keydell, 167.16–23.

[70] *Imp. Exp.*, Bonn, 504.14–16: ἐκέλευσε δὲ [ὁ βασιλεὺς] καὶ τὰς γυναῖκας τῶν συγκλητικῶν ἐξελθούσας τῆς πόλεως διάγειν σὺν τῇ αὐγούστῃ ἐκεῖσε.

[71] This is why, for example, Theophanes adds the extremely rare detail that the elite of Constantinople went out to greet Irene, the fiancée of Leo IV, *with their wives*: A.M. 6261, De Boor, 444.15–19. This parallel ceremonial life of the women of the Byzantine elite is rooted in the attitudes of late antiquity. Thus, it is apparent that the empress did not participate in the baptismal procession of Theodosius II: Mark,,*Vita Porphyrii* (*BHG*, 1570), 47 and 48, ed. H. Grégoire and M.A. Kugener (Paris, 1930), 39.15–40.23; cf. the embarrassment of the senatorial ladies of the sixth century, caught between their duty of associating with the wife of the new Caesar Tiberius and the Augusta Sophia's jealousy: John of Ephesus, *H.e.*, 3, 3, 8, tr. Brooks, 98.12–20. Women, with the exception of the ζωστὴ πατρικία are absent from the imperial banquet guest lists of the ninth and tenth centuries: Philotheus, *Cleterologium*, Oikonomides, 95.22–97.6 etc. The special relationship between an empress and the senatorial ladies is emphasized by the words Michael II is supposed to have put into the mouth of his own magnates: οὐ γάρ ἐστιν οἷον.... γυναικὸς ἄνευ...βασιλέα τε ζῆν καὶ τὰς ἡμετέρας στερεῖσθαι γαμετὰς δεσποίνης καὶ βασιλίδος.. Theoph. Cont., 2, 24, Bonn, 78.14–16. It is worth observing that on her promotion the ζωστὴ πατρικία distributed *sportulae* to the *wives* of patricians and

explicable in terms of the particular circumstances. That the imperial sisters sat side by side with Constantine IX during the triumph over Maniaces was due not to custom, but to Constantine's constitutional debt to them as the source of his authority.[72]

The senatorial order was not the only element of the city's population directly implicated in imperial ceremonies. In late antiquity, the municipal guilds had played a role in representing the populace and turning out a crowd for imperial ceremonies.[73] This certainly held for triumph ceremonies, as Justinian's celebration of 559 shows. The streets were so packed his horse could scarcely move forward. This is less a token of the aging emperor's popularity than the efficiency of the City Prefect's office at turning out the corporations for a public display of loyalty.[74] It is unclear whether all the guilds continued to play the role of official spectator-participant in the early medieval triumph, although they certainly appeared in other ceremonies.[75] The only group

---

theme commanders: *De cer.*, 1, 59 (50), Vogt, 2.65.28–66.5. Cf. the audience of the Augusta in the gallery of the Hagia Sophia, involving only the wives of various state dignitaries: *De cer.*, 1, 9, Vogt, 1.61.10–62.1.

[72] Cf. above, Ch. 4. p. 182. Naturally the general ceremonial segregation of women did not hold in exceptional circumstances, like the regency of Irene (cf. e.g. Theophanes, A.M. 6291, De Boor, 474.6–11 for her Easter Monday procession or A.M. 6295, 477.3–6 for the implication that she had presided over banquets with patricians) or Theodora, widow of Theophilus (banquet for the feast of Orthodoxy, attended by the clergy: Theoph. Cont., 4, 11, Bonn, 160.16–161.17).

[73] According to J.P. Waltzing, *Étude historique sur les corporations professionnelles chez les Romains depuis les origines jusqu'à la chute de l'Empire d'Occident*, 1 (Louvain, 1895), 425, and 2 (1896), 180–7, the *collegia* actually participated in triumph ceremonies of the third century, but his evidence comes from the *Scriptores historiae augustae*, which is not reliable for that period.

[74] *Imp. Exp.*, Bonn, 498.2–7. Note that the corporations come right after the Prefect's office. Cf. the similar evidence of Corippus' description of Justin II's consular procession, *Iust.*, 4, 68, Cameron 75, where the *vulgus* is 'divisum in turmas atque in sua corpora', rightly interpreted by Cameron, 196.

[75] The guilds were represented – again in association with the eparch's office – at the solemn procession from the Great Palace to the Hagia Sophia: *De cer.*, 1, 1, Vogt, 19.16–18. That they were there as a kind of official crowd is suggested by Liutprand's vivid description, for this is surely the identity of the 'throng of merchants and ignoble persons': Liutprand of Cremona, *Legatio*, 9, ed. J. Becker, *MGH. SRG*, (1915), 80.19–23. They also turned out for the festivities occasioned by the visit of Arab emissaries under Constantine VII: *De cer.*, 2, 15, Bonn, 579.8–12, where there seem to have been more than six of them. Cf. S. Vryonis, Jr, 'Byzantine

which may have participated directly in imperial triumphal processions was the rather higher status organization of notaries: in the early tenth century, this guild was obligated to take part in various imperial ceremonies at the eparch's behest. Failure to do so entailed the stiff fine of a third of a nomisma, of which half went to the eparch's office and half to the delinquent notary's colleagues.[76] This last detail discloses the extent to which participation in an imperial ceremony was a question of group prestige.[77] Equally revealing is the fact that this fine is only slightly higher than the one for failing to attend a colleague's funeral procession.[78]

If they may have played a lesser role in producing and re-presenting the crowd, the early medieval guilds followed in the footsteps of their classical predecessors in another area, the decoration of the capital for the emperor's ceremonial progress. This festive decking out of city streets with greenery and other ornaments (*coronatio*; στεφάνωσις) was deeply rooted in the millenary usages of Mediterranean civilization.[79] Just as private citizens festooned their homes for weddings and births, so whole cities were decorated for the great religious and civil festivals of

ΔΗΜΟΚΡΑΤΙΑ and the guilds in the eleventh century', *DOP*, 17 (1963), 289–314, here 300, as well as the more exceptional events referred to *ibid.*, pp. 294–5. It is not impossible that guilds were present in the πολίτευμα which expressed its loyalty to Theophilus in front of the Brazen House during that emperor's first triumph.

76 *Book of the Eparch*, 1, 4, ed. J. Nicole, repr. I. Dujčev, Τὸ ἐπαρχικὸν βιβλίον (London, 1970), 16.9–14. The ceremonies are referred to rather vaguely as ἐν βασιλικῷ προκένσῳ ἢ ἱπποδρόμῳ ἢ συλλόγῳ ἢ προσκλήσει τοῦ ἐνδοξοτάτου ἐπάρχου, εἴτε ἐν οἱαδηπότε ἄλλῃ συνάξει. Cf. A. Stöckle, *Spätrömische und byzantinische Zünfte. Untersuchungen zum sogenannten ἐπαρχικὸν βιβλίον Leos des Weisen*, Klio. Beiträge zur alten Geschichte, 10 (Leipzig, 1911), p. 18.

77 The identification of τοῖς ἐν τῷ συλλόγῳ (*Book of the Eparch*, Nicole, 16.14) as 'colleagues' seems unanimous: Nicole, *ibid.* and p. 136; Freshfield, *ibid.*, p. 225, and M. Syuzyumov, *Vizantiiskaya kniga Eparkha* (Moscow, 1962), p. 47. The notion that failure to appear at an imperial ceremony was as much an infringement on the peer group as on the eparch's authority closely parallels information about a seventh-century lay confraternity in Constantinople, in which a member who had failed to attend a confraternity ceremony for the feast of John the Baptist faced a fine imposed by the organization's treasurer: *Miracula Artemii* (*BHG*, 173), 18, ed. A. Papadopoulos-Kerameus, *Varia graeca sacra* (St Petersburg, 1909), 20.4–21.27. Note that the vocabulary describing the confraternity's ceremony is borrowed from imperial ritual.

78 *Book of the Eparch*, 1, 26, Nicole, 22.6–13.

79 R. Turcan, 'Les guirlandes dans l'antiquité classique', *JAC*, 14 (1971), 92–139, here 94.

antiquity, including, in particular, Roman triumphs.[80] Although some rigorists had originally opposed Christian participation in these rites, they were no more successful here than elsewhere at alienating the new religion from the old society.[81] Indeed, by late antiquity, the custom had spilled out of private and public secular use and into the decoration of churches.[82] Among the many occasions on which the capitals of the later Roman empire were adorned with wreaths, lights, silk veils and silver and gold decorations were consular processions, imperial accessions, *adventus*, baptisms and marriages.[83] The guilds seem to have played no little role in these preparations.[84] Although the record is, as usual, blank for the Byzantine dark age, the tradition survived or at least revived. Thus, the tenth-century guilds of silk and silver merchants were charged with the decoration of the Tribounalion between the Great Palace and the Hagia Sophia.[85] A clue to how the system worked comes from a detailed palace memorandum on the decoration of the Great Palace complex for a visit of emissaries

---

[80] *Ibid.*, 108–24.
[81] E.g. Tertullian, *De corona*, 13, 8–9, ed. A. Kroymann, *CCL*, 2 (1954). 1062.51–1063.1, or *De idololatria*, 15, 7–8, ed. A. Reifferscheid and G. Wissowa, *ibid.*, 1116.18–2 (sic). Cf. K. Baus, *Der Kranz in Antike und Christentum. Eine religionsgeschichtliche Untersuchung mit besonderer Berücksichtigung Tertullians*, Theophaneia, 2 (Bonn, 1940), pp. 66ff with further references.
[82] R. Turcan, 'Girlande', *RAC*, 11 (1981), 1–23, here 18–19.
[83] E.g. Chrysostom, *Homiliae in Kalendas*, 3, *PG*, 48.956–7; Claudius, *In Rufinum*, 2, 339–42, Birt, 46, *Cons. Stilich.*, 2, 397–407, Birt, 217 and *IV cons.*, 643–8, Birt, 258; Proclus, *Homilia 9*, *PG*, 65.773A (*CPG*, 5808); Corippus, *Iust.*, 3, 62–7, Cameron 62 and 4, 74–89 and 206ff, Cameron 75–6 and 79; Mark, *V. Porphyrii*, 47, Grégoire–Kugener, 39.3–7; Evagrius, *H.e.*, 6, 1, Bidez–Parmentier, 221.1–23; Theophylactus Simocattes, *Hist.*, 1, 10, 1–12, De Boor, 57.4–59.5.
[84] Cf. e.g. J. Marquardt, *Das Privatleben der Römer*, 2nd edn (Leipzig, 1886), p. 586; the actual participation of the guilds in decorating the city is evidenced by the *signa collegiorum* among the adornments of the streets through which Constantine I passed early in his reign: *XII pan.*, 5 (8), 8, 4, Mynors, 181.4–9 and confirmed by the decorations set out in front of the *ergasteria* of Antioch to celebrate the clemency of Theodosius I after the Statues riot: Chrysostom, *Hom. 21 in statuas*, 4, *PG*, 49.220. From *Hom. in Kalendas 1*, *PG*, 48.954, it would appear that the *ergasteria* used this as an opportunity to advertise their wares.
[85] *De cer.*, 1, 1, Vogt, 1.9.9–13. Cf. Vryonis, 'Guilds', p. 300, and Stöckle, *Zünfte*, p. 32. Contradictory identifications of the nature of this monument in Belyaev, 'Priemy' p. 75, and Janin, *Cple byz.*, p. 112: according to the former, it was a kind of square; for the latter, a hall.

from Tarsus on 31 May 946.[86] This document indicates that it was the City Prefect who actually organized the decoration with material supplied by the guilds.[87]

The eparch was in charge of the preparations (τὰ προεισόδια) for a triumphal entry insofar as they involved decorations and the like. The ornaments were arranged along the entire triumphal route, from the Golden Gate to the Arch of the Milion.[88] Although there is no direct proof that the guilds provided some of the decorations for Middle Avenue on these occasions, their subordination to the City Prefect and the circumstance that their shops appear to have been grouped by trade, i.e. by guild, along part of the triumphal itinerary suggest that this may have been the case; decorations were certainly supplied by those who lived along the avenue.[89] The preparations also included cleaning the street and strewing it with flowers; perhaps too sawdust was sprinkled on the least savory spots of the imperial path.[90] With the combined floral decorations of branches of sweet-smelling laurel, rosemary and myrtle wreaths and lattices decked with brocades and chandeliers, it is no surprise that the medieval observer could compare the heart of the city with a huge Greek marriage trellis (παστάς). The triumph procession constituted a treat for the beleaguered Byzantine nose as well as the eye.[91]

---

[86] Appended to *De cer.*, 2, 15, Bonn, 570.11–592.19; for the date and circumstances, Vasiliev–Canard, *Arabes*, 2, 1, 314–15.

[87] *De cer.*, 2, 15, Bonn, 572.14–18: ... τὸ τριβουνάλιον ἐξώπλισεν ὁ ὕπαρχος. κατὰ τὸ εἰωθὸς. τῆς. προελεύσεως. ἀπό τε βλαττίων ἁπλωμάτων καὶ σενδὲς. καὶ ἀπὸ ἔργων χρυσῶν καὶ χειμευτῶν καὶ ἀναγλύφων ἀργυρῶν, δηλονότι τῶν ἀργυροπρατῶν ταῦτα παρεχόντων.

[88] The eparch's responsibility is clearly stated in two of the reports on triumphal entries appended to *Imp. Exp.*, Bonn, 499.9–15, 502.21–503.2 (Basil I) and 505.3–7 (Theophilus). To my knowledge, the use of the term προεισόδια for the preparations for an *adventus* is first attested in Psellus, *Chronographia*, Constantine IX, 19, Renauld, 1.127.11. It is certainly older, however, as Theodore Studite's metaphorical use of the word shows: *Ep.*, 2, 12, *PG*, 99.1153A.

[89] Guilland, *Topographie*, 2, 70; cf. p.73. Scylitzes, Thurn, 417.8–9.

[90] *Imp. Exp.*, Bonn, 499.14–15 and 503.1–2. Street-cleaning, sawdust and flower treatment were standard operating procedure for imperial processions: *De cer.*, 1, 1, Vogt, 1.3.21–4.6. This was naturally no innovation of the medieval period: Proclus, *Hom.* 9, *PG*, 65.773A.

[91] On the use of these plants, *Imp. Exp.*, 499.10–11. The comparison with the marriage trellis is made in a gloss on this passage: *ibid.*, 499.20–1. So too Leo Deacon, *Hist.*, 9, 12, Bonn, 158.16–20, compares Middle Avenue during Tzimisces' triumph of 971 to

Would the guilds have had sole responsibility for supplying decorations? The analogy of other ceremonies suggests otherwise, at least as far as the Palace is concerned. The 946 memorandum demonstrates that for a particularly impressive festival, the Palace mobilized resources in precious objects like silver-plated chains and chandeliers, hangings and so on, from several sources. These included not only the various halls, treasuries and chapels of the Great Palace complex itself, but also different churches and social welfare institutions like hospitals and old-age homes.[92] The way in which these items were collected is revealed by an anecdote in the contemporary Life of Empress Theophano (*ob.* 893). To decorate the palatine church of Elias for the ceremonies honoring that prophet's feast day, the official in charge dispatched a subordinate to the church where the appropriate decorations were kept. In this case, the stenographer and *candidatus* Myron was entrusted with the task and obviously was accompanied by helpers. The *proestōs* of the Holy Apostles' handed over the required material and it was sent to the appropriate place.[93] This procedure, however, relates only to the adornment of the Great Palace itself, and the extent to which it may have been followed for areas outside the palace precincts is not clear.

Although the triumphal route's general outline was dictated by the urban landscape and detailed by custom, circumstances occasionally compelled change. Thus the itinerary of Justinian's

---

a bridal chamber, δίκην θαλάμου. On the nature and Hellenistic origin of the παστάς, see C. Vatin, *Recherches sur le mariage et la condition de la femme mariée à l'époque hellénistique*, Bibliothèque des Écoles françaises d'Athènes et de Rome, 216 (Paris, 1970), pp. 211ff.

[92] *De cer.*, 2, 15, Bonn, 570.18–582.19 lists the following institutions as sources: Sts Sergius and Bacchus, the Nea, *xenones*, *gerokomia* and *ekklesiai* in general (572.8–9 and 22–3), Blachernae, the Chrysotriklinos, the Virgin of Pharos, the imperial Phylax, the oratories of St Peter and St Theodore ἐν τῷ Παλατίῳ, Holy Apostles', St Demetrius τοῦ Παλατίου and the Vestiarium τοῦ Καριανοῦ.

[93] *V. Theophano*, 25, Kurtz, 17.20–31. On Myron's dignity which, if it was low in the overall palatine hierarchy, was still nothing to sneeze at, see R. Guilland, 'Le titre de candidat, *candidatus*, ὁ κανδιδᾶτος.', *Polychronion. Festschrift F. Dölger* (Heidelberg, 1966), pp. 210–25. Myron should be added to his prosopographical list, *ibid.*, p. 216. That Myron was assisted can be deduced from the fact that the decorations collected from the Apostles' were sent along (προπέμπει), while he himself took care of Theophano's veil: *V. Theophano*, 25, Kurtz, 17.28. On St Elias', see Janin, *Églises*, pp. 136–7.

triumph of 559 was largely atypical, in that it stretched from the Gate of Charisius along the upper segment of Middle Avenue, with the major sanctuary being the Holy Apostles', rather than starting at the Golden Gate and perhaps ending with a visit to the Hagia Sophia.[94] The reason for this change was the terrible earthquake of December 557 which resulted, it would appear, in serious damage along the lower Middle Avenue and the collapse of the Great Church's dome in the summer of 558.[95] Similarly, although doubtless for other motives, Leo V seems to have made his entry of 813 via the Gate of Charisius.[96] Such exceptions aside, however, the City Prefect and population could not but have been aware of the great portico-lined boulevard of triumphal tradition, the lower and central Middle Avenue, which stretched from the city's ceremonial entrance at the Golden Gate to its monumental heart, via the major public squares.[97] If, however, street patterns and buildings defined the route in more or less permanent fashion,

---

[94] *Imp. Exp.*, Bonn, 497.13–498.13. That the normal triumphal itinerary already began at the Golden Gate at this date is assured not only by the existence of that lavish monument, but also by the fact that the author of the report just cited alludes to a change in the ceremony because the emperor had *not* entered through the Golden Gate: *ibid.*, 498.9–11.

[95] Hagia Sophia: Müller-Wiener, *Bildlexikon*, p. 86; for damage to the Middle Avenue area associated with this earthquake see R. Naumann, 'Neue Beobachtungen am Theodosiusbogen und Forum Tauri in Istanbul', *Istanbuler Mitteilungen*, 27 (1976), 117–41, here 132.

[96] Theophanes, A.M. 6305, De Boor, 502.25–26, Χαρσίου being the reading accepted by De Boor from codd. Vat. gr. 978, Monac. gr. 391 and particularly Anastasius Bibliothecarius, *ibid.*, 2.339.29. Χαρσίου (a collateral form of Χαρισίου: cf. Janin, *Cple byz.*, p. 281) is certainly, given custom, the *lectio difficilior* and must be preferred to the Χρυσῆς of Par. gr. 1711, a MS characterized by revisions and interpolations (*ibid.*, 2.517ff). The reason for this textual excursus is that Theophanes' contemporary (it was written down probably within months of the event: Moravcsik, *Byzantinoturcica*, I, 531) testimony flatly contradicts tenth-century historiography, which describes in semi-legendary terms a typical *adventus* via the Golden Gate, with a welcome by the *synkletikoi* at St John Stoudios: 'Genesius', I, 4, Lesmüller-Werner and Thurn, 5.70–6.87 and Theoph. Cont., I, 9, Bonn, 18.18–19.9. Whether the tenth-century account was a fabrication of that period or goes back to a propagandizing account favorable to Leo V is not clear. Perhaps the entry took place via the Gate of Charisius because of the presence there of partisans of the usurper; cf. e.g. *Scriptor incertus de Leone Armenio*, ed. I. Bekker (Bonn, 1842), 340.9–12. Cf. too Ignatius' *V. Nicephori* (BHG, 1335), De Boor, 163.13–14, written after 842 (Ševčenko, 'Hagiography', p. 123).

[97] D. Th. Belyaev, 'Bogomol'nye vykhody', pp. 1–56; Janin, *Cple byz.*, pp. 36–7; Guilland, *Topographie*, 2, 69–79; Dagron, *Naissance*, pp. 98–102; Müller-Wiener, *Bildlexikon*, pp. 269–70.

the emperor's stops along that route, i.e. the points at which he met various representative groups, were subject to innovation.

In the eyes of the Constantinopolitan aristocracy, the most meaningful of the ritual encounters which studded the triumphal route was that of the emperor and the officials entrusted with the city and palace in his absence. Although these officials customarily left the capital to meet a homecoming emperor as soon as he approached the area, they later returned to the city before him to stage the ritual welcome, during which the emperor received the customary 'gifts' of a laurel wreath and a gold crown.[98] The encounter usually took place in the presence of the senatorial order. In the early Middle Ages this second, city greeting habitually occurred at the entrance to the city, generally the Golden Gate.[99] This had not always been the case, however, for, on at least some occasions, it had been customary for City Prefects and senators of the fifth and sixth centuries to welcome the emperor and offer him the traditional presents inside the city, at the Forum of Theodosius (Forum Tauri).[100] Even earlier, it would seem, this kind of ritual encounter was associated with the Forum of Constantine.[101] In other words, with the passage of time, the point of ritual encounter between the emperor, his

[98] Thus *Imp. Exp.*, Bonn, 497.3–7; cf. 504.4–6; 505.3–7 and 506.1–3.

[99] *Imp. Exp.*, 497.16–18 (A.D. 559); 501.12–16 (Basil I); 506.1–4 (Theophilus); Leo Deacon, *Hist.*, 9, 12, Bonn, 158.4–10, and Scylitzes, Thurn, 310.54–8 (A.D. 971); Scylitzes, Thurn, 364.88–365.90 (Basil II); Psellus, *Chronographia*, Michael IV, 50, Renauld, 1.82.1–2. Cf. the *adventus* of Constantine IX, *ibid.*, Constantine IX, 19, 1.126.1–127.13 (note, however, that the passage is corrupt; N.H. Baynes' suggestion in *Gnomon*, 12 (1936), 360 must be dismissed, since the Long Walls were far too distant for this theory: Janin, *Cple byz.*, pp. 262–3). Cf. too the tenth-century version of Leo V's entry, in which he was greeted by the Count of the Walls outside the City: Theoph. Cont., 1, 8, Bonn, 17.6–18 and the more explicit version of 'Genesius', 1, 3, Lesmüller-Werner and Thurn, 4.45–8.

[100] Thus, on Saturday, 30 September 416, Theodosius returned to Constantinople from Heraclea and received the gold crown κατὰ τὴν συνήθειαν from Ursus, the City Prefect and the Senate, ἐν τῷ Θεοδοσιακῷ φόρῳ: *Chron. pasch.*, Bonn, 574.1–5. The *adventus* memorandum attached to *Imp. Exp.* identifies this place less ambiguously: Bonn, 496.17–497.1: ...ἐπαντοῦσιν αὐτῷ ἐν τῷ φόρῳ Θεοδοσίου τῷ καλουμένῳ ταύρῳ...; cf. Guilland, *Topographie*, 2, 57. On the Forum Tauri, Janin, *Cple byz.*, pp. 64–8; Müller-Wiener, *Bildlexikon*, pp. 258–65 and esp. Naumann, 'Neue Beobachtungen'.

[101] *De cer.*, 1, 91, Bonn, 414.13–17. Scholars still occasionally assume that this passage is part of the historical report of the coronation of Leo I in A.D. 457 (e.g. Dagron, *Naissance*, p. 102, n. 1), but Bury, *History of the later Roman empire...to the death of*

prefect and his senate shifted outward from the Column of Constantine toward the city limits. Now in the ancient world, the distance one advanced outward to greet an arriving person was calibrated – and commonly considered – to mark the honor in which that person was held.[102] In this light, the outward shift of the point of ritual encounter symbolized the relationship of the senatorial order to the purple. Even as the point of encounter moved outward, however, the gift-giving which characterized the meeting underwent profound change: it became an exchange.

The Byzantine wreath offerings at the Golden Gate harken back to the Hellenistic and Roman custom of greeting an arriving or victorious sovereign with a golden wreath known as the *aurum coronarium*.[103] By the fourth century, this voluntary contribution had long since become compulsory; it developed into two kinds of payments of which the senatorial version, known technically as

---

Justinian, 1, 312, n. 2, and Treitinger, *Oströmische*, p. 10, n. 9 (cf. *BZ*, 39 (1939), 197) already were able to detect the heterogenous nature of 412.18 to 417.12. It is not impossible that this section antedates the completion of the Theodosian Walls, since the only gate mentioned and ceremonially distinguished is called simply ἡ πόρτη (416.17) and is located between the Helenianae Palace – now localized outside the Constantinian rampart – and the Forum of Constantine. On Helenianae, see V. Tiftixoglu, 'Die Helenianai nebst einigen anderen Besitzungen im Vorfeld des frühen Konstantinopel', *Studien zur Frühgeschichte Konstantinopels*, Miscellanea byzantina Monacensia, 14 (Munich, 1973), pp. 49–120, here 50–4.

102 Note Augustus' obvious pride on this point: *Res gestae diui Augusti*, 12, 1. Some of the best evidence concerns emperors and holy persons. Thus, early in the fifth century, Melania was greatly honored by the empress who first came out to greet her in the palace's portico and then made her sit with her on the throne: Gerontius, *Vita Melaniae iunioris* (*BHG*, 1241), 12, ed. D. Gorce, SC, 90 (Paris, 1962), 148; cf. *BHL*, 5885, ed. M. Rampolla del Tindaro, *Santa Melania giuniore, senatrice romana* (Rome, 1905), 9.31–10.2. This attitude survived well into the Middle Ages: after a two-and-a-half-year absence, Euthymius was welcomed at the palace by Leo VI, outside the Silver Gate, as his biographer carefully notes: *V. Euthymii*, 4, Karlin-Hayter, 21.20–3. The key to understanding the authors' attentiveness to this detail is provided by John Lydus, *De magistratibus*, 2, 9, where the great prestige of the Praetorian Prefecture is demonstrated by the fact that all the leading palace officials came forth beyond their own thresholds to greet the Prefect and that the emperor himself, or at least the emperor's portrait, left the palace to go forth with him: Wünsch, 63.22–64.18. Particularly illuminating in this respect is the emphasis the papal legates of 519 laid on the distance outward from Constantinople that exalted persons of the court came to greet them during their *adventus* (the tenth milestone); *Collectio avellana*, 167 and 223, ed. O. Günther, *CSEL*, 35.2 (1898). 619.2–11 and 683.6–15.

103 T. Klauser, 'Aurum coronarium', pp. 298–309.

the *aurum oblaticium*, disappeared prior to the compilation of the Justinianic Code.[104] Although the triumph's gold wreaths have been identified with the latter, it is clear that unlike the *oblaticium*, they survived as a ritual element and were transformed in the process.[105] From a compulsory 'gift', the wreaths developed into an element of ritual exchange. In return for them, the arriving emperor offered his officials cash equal or beyond the objects' value. In other words, by the sixth century, the senatorial order had freed itself of a real financial burden even as they maintained a ritual homage. The fact that medieval emperors immediately, publicly reimbursed the welcomers emphasized that imperial behavior toward the senatorial elite was bound and limited by custom.[106] By the eleventh century, even procurement of the wreath seems to have been assumed by the emperor.[107]

The meeting of senatorial order and emperor was but one of many ritual encounters staged along the triumphal boulevard. The antiquity of the system is clear. Thus, one of the rare glimpses we catch of the founder of New Rome in his capital reveals him riding on horseback down Middle Avenue and meeting petitioners when returning from a *prokensos*.[108] The custom of choruses greeting the arriving emperor with festive acclamations at various stations (κατὰ τόπους) along the road was quite familiar to Constantinopolitans before the middle of the fifth century.[109] Through the centuries, occasional mention is made of some monument by which the emperor passed, but the only complete picture of triumphal stations comes from 879, when Basil I enjoyed two ceremonies outside the walls and stopped for ten receptions (δοχαί) between the Golden Gate and the Great

---

[104] Karayannopulos, *Finanzswesen*, pp. 141–7; Jones, *Later Roman Empire*, 1, 430–1.

[105] Karayannopulos, *Finanzwesen*, pp. 142–4; but cf. W. Ensslin, *Zur Frage nach der ersten Kaiserkrönung durch den Patriarchen und zur Bedeutung dieses Aktes im Wahlzeremoniell* (Würzburg, 1947), pp. 22–3.

[106] That the crowns continued to be given in late antique imperial arrivals and triumphs is clear from the *Adventus* memorandum (*Imp. Exp.*, 496.19–497.3). Cf. *ibid.*, 501.12–17, and Leo Deacon, 9, 12, Bonn, 158.8–10.

[107] Psellus, *Chronographia*, Romanus III, 7, Renauld, 2.159.8–11.

[108] Letter of Constantine I, Socrates, *H.e.*, 1, 34, *PG*, 67.168B–C; cf. Sozomen, *H.e.*, 2, 28, 5–9, Bidez–Hansen, 19.19ff; Gelasius, *H.e.*, 3, 18, 4, Loeschke–Heinemann, 180.12–15.

[109] Thus in Proclus, patriarch of Constantinople, *Hom.* 9, 2, *PG*, 65.773A: ... χοροὺς ἐγκωμίων κατὰ τόπους συνυφαίνουσιν ...

Church.[110] After the initial welcome at the Hebdomon and a visit to St John Baptist's in-the-Hebdomon, the first stage of the ceremony ended by the side of the paved road leading to the Golden Gate, at the monastery of the Virgin of the Abraamites, just outside the wall. The visit expressed Basil's veneration for that shrine, its icon and its monastic community, which had played a prominent role in the struggle against Theophilus' iconoclast policies.[111] Moreover, the halt afforded the princes a moment of rest and allowed them to change from their purple riding caftans (σκαραμάγγια) into military uniforms. In the meantime, the military parade was drawn up and started down Middle Avenue.[112] The first reception took place as the emperors left the shrine. They were acclaimed by both factions, decked out with gold-striped garlands on their brows (στεφάνια σημεντέϊνα), tunics (καμίσια) and flower wreaths around their necks; in their hands they carried handkerchiefs. The demarchs wore their 'victory cloaks' (τὰ νικητικὰ αὐτῶν σαγία).[113] The first acclamation they chanted was a hymn of welcome and thanksgiving:

Glory to God who has returned our own Lords to us victoriously!
Glory to God who has exalted you, emperors of the Romans!
Glory to you, O most holy Trinity, because we have seen that our own
  Lords have conquered!
Welcome, O conquering, most courageous Lords![114]

[110] In addition to the station at the Forum of Theodosius discussed above, cf. Phocas' entry of 602, via the Golden Gate and the Troadesian Porticoes (*Chron. pasch.*, Bonn, 693.20–4; cf. Janin, *Cple byz.*, p. 93) or the dubious account of Leo's welcome at St John Stoudios in 'Genesius', I, 4, Lesmüller-Werner and Thurn, 5.70–3, and Theoph. Cont., I, 9, Bonn, 18.19–21. As pointed out above, Justinian's triumph of 559 is not typical and cannot serve as a point of comparison.

[111] Janin, *Églises*, pp. 4–6. Small wonder that Theophilus snubbed the sixth-century foundation during his first triumphal entry and preferred to rest in a tent pitched in the meadow of the Kombinostasion: above, Ch. 4, 3.

[112] *Imp. Exp.*, 499.5–500.3. The precedent was followed by Nicephorus Phocas in 963: *De cer.*, I, 92, Bonn, 438.

[113] *Imp. Exp.*, 500.16–501.3.

[114] *Ibid.*, 500.3–7: δόξα Θεῷ τῷ ἀποδόντι ἡμῖν μετὰ νίκης τοὺς ἰδίους δεσπότας· / δόξα Θεῷ τῷ μεγαλύναντι ὑμᾶς, αὐτοκράτορες Ῥωμαίων / δόξα σοι, παναγία τριάς, ὅτι εἴδομεν νικήσαντας τοὺς ἰδίους δεσπότας· / καλῶς ἤλθετε νικήσαντες, ἀνδριώτατοι δεσπόται. The δόξα Θεῷ formula seems to have been traditional in triumphal acclamations of the ninth and tenth centuries; cf. the two texts Δόξα Θεῷ τῷ

This was followed by further, unspecified victory acclamations and, as the procession got under way, the factions intoned military-flavored processional chants.[115]

The first station inside the city was about 1.5 km down the lower Middle Avenue at a monument known as the Sigma. This was probably a crescent-shaped portico marked by a column bearing the statue of Theodosius II.[116] After the reception, the parade turned left and marched perhaps another half kilometer to the Exakionion, which seems to have been a lofty column situated just outside the Constantinian wall.[117] The parade then entered the Constantinian city and continued about 650 m to the Forum of Arcadius or Xerolophos, a square surrounded by porticos and distinguished by the great triumphal column of Arcadius.[118] Once the acclamations were completed, the parade again got underway, making no further stops until it reached the Forum of the Ox, the Bous, which was probably to the west of the modern Aksaray.[119] The next segment took the parade to the Capitol, which Naumann has tentatively associated with the grandiose

---

Δεσπότη πάντων and Δόξα Θεῷ τῷ συντρίβοντι πολεμίους, in *De cer.*, 1, 78 (69), Vogt 2.135.22–136.23.

[115] *Imp. Exp.*, 501.7–9: καὶ λοιπὰ ἐπευφημήσθησαν νικητικά, καὶ ἀπελατικοῖ στρατηγικοὶ ἐλέχθησαν. On this term, for which the various dictionaries are of no avail, see J. Handschin, *Das Zeremonienwerk Kaiser Konstantins und die sangbare Dichtung* (Basel, 1942), pp. 8–9 and 108, n. 1.

[116] The following account is based on *Imp. Exp.*, 501.19–502.2 and 502.22–3. On the Sigma, Janin, *Cple Byz.*, pp. 424–5. It was above the monastery of Peribleptos, i.e. the modern Sulu manastir; this allows an approximate measurement of the parade's first segment. Cf. Müller-Wiener, *Bildlexikon*, pp. 200–1.

[117] Janin, *Cple byz.*, pp. 351–2; Guilland, *Topographie*, 2, 62–5; Dagron, *Naissance*, p. 100. The rough estimate of the distance is based on the possibility that the Exakionion was near the Isakapi Mescidi: Müller-Wiener, *Bildlexikon*, p. 118.

[118] Janin, *Cple Byz.*, pp. 71–2; 439–40; Guilland, *Topographie*, pp. 59–62; Müller-Wiener, *Bildlexikon*, pp. 250–3. *Imp. Exp.* does not specify where in this large square the reception was staged, although the Ceremony Book mentions stations at the 'first arch', in the 'middle of the Forum', and 'across from St Callinicus': *De cer.*, 1, 26 (17), Vogt, 1.98.12–18 and 1, 8, *ibid.*, 51.16–17. Despite Guilland, *Topographie*, 1, 434, the relationship of these places is not clear. Perhaps the αὐτίκα of 501.20 is meant to imply that there was no stop at mid-Forum. The approximate distance estimate is based on Isakapi Mescidi and the Column of Arcadius.

[119] Janin, *Cple Byz.*, pp. 69–71; Müller-Wiener, *Bildlexikon*, pp. 253–4. The suggestion that the Bous was west of Aksaray comes from R. Naumann, 'Der antike Rundbau beim Myrelaion und der Palast Romanos I. Lekapenos', *Istanbuler Mitteilungen*, 16 (1966), 199–216, here 210. Perhaps there was some connection with the remains of

circular structure known as the 'Myrelaeum'. In any event, the Capitol cannot have been far from there.[120] Nearby, the ceremony again came to a halt at the intersection of the upper Middle Avenue with the main boulevard, at a place marked by a column surmounted by a cross and the embracing 'Tetrarchs' which are familiar to modern visitors to San Marco's.[121] From there, the procession moved to the Forum Tauri, its triumphal column and the Arch of Theodosius, about half a kilometer from the round building.[122] The next stop took place at the Artopolia or Bakers' Quarter, known for its porticos, its column with a cross, and an arch, which may have been the precise site of this station.[123] Finally the parade arrived at the large, circular, portico-lined Forum of Constantine, which was dominated by its great porphyry column.[124] At the Forum, Basil and his son dismounted and were met by the patriarch and his retinue outside Basil's foundation of the Virgin-in-the-Forum.[125] Again a church served

---

what has been called a triumphal arch, uncovered just south of the wall around Murat paşa Camii in 1956: cf. F. Dirimtekin, *Ayasofya Müzesi Yilliği*, 1 (1959), 19 and fig. 11; J. Lafontaine, 'Fouilles et découvertes à Istanbul de 1952 à 1960', *Byz.*, 29–30 (1959–60), 339–86, here 374, and R. Janin, 'Constantinople byzantine. Découvertes et notes de topographie', *RÉB*, 21 (1968), 256–69, here 256. If so, this stretch of the parade would have measured about half a kilometer.

120 Naumann, 'Rundbau', p. 211; cf. too R. Naumann, *Anatolian Studies*, 17 (1967), 30–1. C.L. Striker, *The Myrelaion (Bodrum Camii) in Istanbul* (Princeton, 1981), pp. 14–15, rejects the identification, but the last word has yet to be said.

121 Janin, *Cple Byz.*, p. 410; Müller-Wiener, *Bildlexikon*, pp. 266–7. Cf. Naumann, 'Rundbau', pp. 209–10, on the discovery of the missing foot of this group in the rubble by the round building and its potential implication that the Philadelphion was not as far from this site as is generally thought. Concerning the Capitol theory, it must be noted that the account of the 559 triumph clearly places the Capitol right by the intersection of the two Middle Avenues, i.e. the Philadelphion: *Imp. Exp.* 497.19–21 and 498.5–6. Even if the Philadelphion were half way down the Mese toward the Forum Tauri, it would only have been about 225 m from the round building.

122 Janin, *Cple Byz.*, pp. 64–8 and 81–2; Guilland, *Topographie*, pp. 56–9; Müller-Wiener, *Bildlexikon*, pp. 258–65; R. Naumann, 'Neue Beobachtungen'.

123 Janin, *Cple Byz.*, p. 315. Other itineraries halt ἐν τῷ φουρνικῷ i.e. the arch (derived from Latin *fornix*: cf. the Arch of the Milion, etc.; *De cer.*, 1, 5, Vogt, 1.45.5 etc.): *De cer.*, 1, 8, Vogt, 1.51.28.

124 Janin, *Cple Byz.*, pp. 62–4; Müller-Wiener, *Bildlexikon*, pp. 255–7. The Forum of Constantine is about 750 m from the Arch of Theodosius, which was at the western end of the Forum of Theodosius. If the Arch of Artopolia were about halfway between them, it would have been at most ca. 325 m from either.

125 *Imp. Exp.*, 502.2–5; cf. Janin, *Cple Byz.*, pp. 236–7.

a multiple purpose. It was a meeting point, it offered an opportunity to pay public homage to a shrine – and indirectly, perhaps, to the merchants associated with it – and it allowed the princes to change from their military uniforms into civilian garb, consisting of purple *divitisia*, *kampagia* sandals and gold-threaded capes.[126] Still dismounted, they walked in procession, following the great gilded and bejeweled ceremonial cross and various standards, until they came to the Milion Arch and then went into the Hagia Sophia.[127] The return to the Great Palace observed the usual ceremonial for solemn processions.[128]

What does this review of the stations used in 879 reveal about ceremonial development of the period? First, it makes clear that regular spacing of stations was quite secondary to other factors in their selection. Segments of the parade vary from ca. 1.5 km down to around 300–225 m or less, with several seeming to have been spaced at about half a kilometer.[129] It is difficult to avoid the impression that the difference in frequency and intervals between stations of the Theodosian sector (two stations in ca. 2 km) and the Constantinian city (seven stations in ca. 3 km) cannot be disassociated from the very different population densities of the two sectors.[130] The comparison of the stations of 879 with those attested for imperial processions of the tenth century is also instructive (see Table 1).

With two exceptions (the Sigma and the Capitol), the stations used by Basil I correspond to stations in the repertory of potential reception sites indicated by the Ceremony Book. That the Sigma does not show up in the latter is likely due to its excentric location.[131] The replacement of the Capitol by the Amastrianum

---

[126] *Imp. Exp.*, 502.6–9. On *divitisia* and *chlamydes*, Grierson, *Coins*, 3, 1, 117–20; on the former, cf. Belyaev, 'Priemy', pp. 50–7. For *kampagia*, Oikonomides, *Listes*, p. 167, n. 115. On the merchant presence in the Forum, above, Ch. 4, p. 164.

[127] *Imp. Exp.*, 502.5–17.

[128] *Ibid.*, 502.17–19; cf. *De cer.*, 1, 1, Vogt, 1.1ff.

[129] It follows that there is no clear pattern of distances which would help situate unidentified points.

[130] D. Jacoby, 'La population de Constantinople à l'époque byzantine: un problème de démographie urbaine', *Byz.*, 31 (1961), 81–109, esp. 105–7; cf. Dagron, *Naissance*, p. 524.

[131] The Sigma is attested as a liturgical station in the tenth-century *Typicon*, Mateos, 1.10 (2 September).

is more intriguing, but unclear.[132] In the Ceremony Book's list of stations, there appear several stations not attested in 879 yet clearly on the triumph's itinerary, like the Modius, Praetorium and various points around the Milion – Hagia Sophia – Brazen House complex. This, along with discrepancies between the Ceremony Book's lists themselves, points up how incorrect it is to presume unswerving adherence to millenary traditions in the locations of stations.[133] This in itself shows what other evidence confirms, namely that custom did not dictate the selection of stations, even if it may have defined the margins of choice.[134]

The nature of these sites reflects an element typical of Constantinople's urban landscape: seven of the ten would have been visible from afar thanks to their characteristic columns.[135] It would be a mistake to explain this fact by the triumphal connotations of some of the columns, for many of the same sites figure prominently in non-triumphal ceremonies.[136] The choice of these stations may have been more closely linked with the urbanistic function of these columns, if it may be presumed that the example of old Rome influenced that of the new one. There, such columns were erected at junctures between new city quarters and old ones, to allow travelers between city sectors constantly to get their bearings.[137] While the details of settlement patterns in Constantinople and how they might relate to the location of monumental columns remain unclear, what is known about the latter lends credence to this possibility: the key stopping points of the parade coincided with key landmarks.[138]

---

[132] Note that although the Capitol is absent from the tenth-century stational lists of the Ceremony Book (Table 1), it is still cited in the *Typicon*, Mateos, 1.366.20 (10 August).

[133] Guilland, *Topographie*, 1, 434: 'L'emplacement des stations, ayant été fixé par la tradition, est immuable.' To explain such divergencies as appear from our Table 1, Guilland invokes the 'très incorrecte' text of *De cer.* and a copyist who was likely ignorant of Byzantine affairs. On the basis of these absurd assumptions, Guilland corrects the text wherever his theses require.

[134] See below on the *praipositos'* selection of station sites.

[135] Sigma, Exakionion, Xerolophos, Philadelphion, Forum Tauri, Artopolia and Forum of Constantine.

[136] See Table 1.

[137] W. Gauer, 'Die Triumphsäulen als Wahrzeichen Roms und der Roma secunda und als Denkmäler der Herrschaft im Donauraum', *Antike und Abendland*, 27 (1981), 179–92, here 183–4.

[138] Thus the Exakionion seems to have marked the end of the old Middle Avenue at the

Table 1. *Comparison of stations of the triumph of 879 and the station lists of the Ceremony Book*

879	*De cer.*, 1, 26 (17), Vogt, 1.97.30–99.13 From St Mocius	*De cer.*, 1, 8, Vogt, 1.51.4–52.13 From Pege (cf. Guilland, *Topographie*, 1, 228)	*De cer.*, 1, 5, Vogt 1.43.4–45.16 From Holy Apostles'	*De cer.*, 1, 10, Vogt 1.74.14–75.27 From Holy Apostles'
1. Golden Gate				
2. Sigma	Different Route	Different Route	(Stations 1–3)	(Stations 1–3)
3. Exakionion	1. St Mocius	1. Outside arch of Portico?		
4. Xerolophos	2. Exakionion	2. Aqueduct with water		
	3. Monetai	3. St Mocius	Upper Middle Avenue	Upper Middle Avenue
	4. First arch of Xerolophos	4. Exakionion		
	5. Middle of Xerolophos	5. Xerolophos		
5. Bous	6. Bous	6. Bous		
6. Capitol	7. Amastrianon	7. Amastrianon		
7. Philadelphion	8. Philadelphion	8. Philadelphion	4. Philadelphion	4. Philadelphion
	9. Modios			5. Modios

Lower Middle Avenue

218

8. Tauros	10. Tauros	9. Tauros	5. Tauros	6. Tauros
9. Artopolia	11. Artopolia	10. Arch of Artopolia	6. Arch of Artopolia	7. Artopolia
10. Forum	12. Forum	11. Forum	7. Forum	8. Forum
[via Milion]	13. Praetorium	12. Praetorium	8. Praetorium	9. Plakaton of Milion
	14. Milion	13. Arch of Milion	9. Arch of Milion	
	15. Marmaroton of Milion	14. A bit further	10. Somewhat past Arch	10. Zeuxippos
[Hagia Sophia]	16. Zeuxippos	15. A bit further	11. Further	11. Brazen House
	17. Brazen House			

What precisely took place at the stations? The report of 879 merely states that 'in the named places, receptions (δοχαί) of the factions (τῶν μερῶν) and acclamations (εὐφημίαι) took place', presuming that readers of such a technical document were familiar with procedure on this point.[139] One clue comes from the description of the first station at the Abraamites'. After Basil and his son had 'received' them, i.e. acknowledged some symbolic gesture, like a *proskynesis*, the combined factions acclaimed them. The entire group then moved off toward the Golden Gate, with the factions leading the way. There, they stopped, took up position in front of the gate and the sovereigns were again acclaimed in similar fashion by the same groups.[140] Since no new elements beyond the location of the next stations are mentioned, the text implicitly suggests that a similar procedure was observed at the next station.[141] The account of Theophilus' triumph specifically states that the factions greeted the emperor (ὑπήντησαν) as was customary for a festive procession (ὡς ἐπὶ ἑορτασίμου προκένσου).[142] In fact, the Ceremony Book's account of *dochai* on just such occasions confirms the implicit suggestion of the triumph reports. At each station, the faction salutes the emperor, sings the appropriate acclamation and then escorts the emperor to the next station, chanting fitting texts, if the emperor so desires.[143]

Now that the parade's ritual content is clearer, it is possible to offer a rough estimate of how long it might have lasted. The

---

Constantinian ramparts; the Sigma was the point at which the outbound traveler had to turn right to reach the Golden Gate; Justinian's column marked the Augustaeum Square and the monumental heart of the city.

[139] *Imp. Exp.*, 502.22–3.

[140] *Ibid.*, 500.16–501.18.

[141] Indeed, this may explain why the notice emphasizes that the emperors entered the great middle portal of the Golden Gate διϱγευόμενοι (501.19). Aside from the initial statement that the emperors were preceded by the Senate and people from the Hebdomon and the references just examined, no mention at all is made of their escort, although we can be sure that the central segment of the triumphal parade consisted of more than the emperor and his son. By the same token, we hear of Theophilus' escort of Senate and *cubiculum* only when the parade reached the Milion, where it is specified that these groups dismounted: *ibid.*, 506.8–16.

[142] *Ibid.*, 506.5–6.

[143] *De cer.*, I, 10, Vogt, 1.74.14–75.27 and I, 26 (17), Vogt, 1.97.30–99.17. Cf. Guilland, *Topographie*, I, 426–7.

distance from the Golden Gate to the Hagia Sophia is about 5.5 km, i.e. a little over an hour's walk at a normal pace, which would be quite a bit faster than a parade usually moves. It is difficult to imagine that the stopping, performance of acclamations, rearrangement of the faction in front of the parade and starting up again of the procession could have been accomplished in less than twenty minutes at every stop.[144] The halt at the Virgin-in-the-Forum, involving as it did the welcome of the patriarch, a visit to the shrine and the changing of the emperors' vestments, must have taken considerably longer. We may thus conservatively estimate that these operations alone required about two hours. Considering that the military section of the parade got underway while the emperor was still resting in the Abraamites', it is difficult to conceive of such a parade lasting less than four hours, even before the service in the Hagia Sophia. If we remember that the first ceremony of the day had taken place at the seventh milestone from the city, we can readily grasp why Basil headed for the Banquet Hall of Justinian as soon as the service was over: he and his hungry escort had performed very close to a full day's work.

It has already been noted that the city side of the victory parade fell under the jurisdiction of the eparch. The further question of which official was in charge of the actual organization of the triumph is as important as it is difficult. Although the practical absence of any preliminary work on the institutional underpinning of imperial rituals necessarily limits us to a partial, incomplete view, one important fact stands out: here, as elsewhere, long-term changes in the competence and organization of the Palace were the rule, not the exception.

In virtue of his authority over the guards and other personnel of the palace, the Master of the Offices was the key figure in the public life of the later Roman court. His responsibility for audiences and the like contributed powerfully to making him the empire's leading ceremonial official.[145] This situation is clearly

---

[144] Cf. *Imp. Exp.*, 501.9: ἔμπροσθεν περιπατούντων τῶν δύο μερῶν.

[145] A.E.R. Boak, 'The Master of the Offices in the Later Roman and Byzantine Empire', *Two studies in later Roman and Byzantine administration* (New York, 1924), pp. 1–160, here 92ff and 98ff; M. Clauss, *Der magister officiorum in der Spätantike (4.-6. Jahrhundert)*, Vestigia, 12 (Munich, 1980), pp. 64–72. Prosopographical lists from

mirrored by Peter the Patrician's lost treatise on the history and duties of that post, the surviving fragments of which are the single most significant source on imperial ceremonial of the fifth and sixth centuries.[146] In fact, the general grounds for attributing the arrangement of the triumphal parade to the *Magister officiorum* are confirmed for the sixth century, since the essential decisions on the organization of Justinian's triumph are specifically attributed to his Master in the report preserved in the Imperial Expeditions.[147] The stages and dates at which the Master was stripped of these functions are obscured by the darkness of the seventh and eighth centuries. Yet it is clear that developments here parallel the general trend of an era which saw an increasing reliance on domestic or private institutions of the palace at the expense of the great mandarins of the later Roman civil service. Bury has adduced evidence suggesting that the office suffered its greatest losses before the end of the reign of Leo III. It seems likely, however, that as late as 769 the Master was still sharing with his eventual successor some competence in the field of ceremonies.[148]

By the time of Basil's triumph in 879, power in ceremonial matters had passed into the hands of the *praipositos* or Chamberlain, the descendant of the late Roman *praepositus sacri cubiculi*.[149] In the late ninth and early tenth century, the Chamberlain was the primary giver of cues during imperial ceremonies, in effect managing the ritual appearances and encounters of the sovereign,

---

320 to 527 in *PLRE*, 1, 1059–61 and 2, 1257–8. Cf. Clauss, pp. 139ff. For the period after Justinian, see Boak, 'Master', p. 151; cf. Laurent, *Corpus*, 2, 669 with no. 1195.

[146] On Peter Patrician's Περὶ πολιτικῆς. τάξεως, 'published' between 548 and 552, see Stein, *Bas-Empire*, 2, 728.

[147] A detail of Justinian's welcome which obviously represents a derogation from custom (shouting of τὸ θριαμβευτάλιον by an *admissionalis* at the Palace's entrance) is specifically identified as a decision of the Master of Offices: *Imp. Exp.*, Bonn, 498.9–10: οὕτω γὰρ συνεῖδεν γενέσθαι ὁ μάγιστρος....

[148] Bury, *Administrative system*, pp. 29–33; cf. Boak, 'Master', pp. 99–100. The evidence for 769 is from the appearance of the *magistros* side by side with the *praipositos* in *De cer.*, 1, 52 (43), Vogt, 2.26–9, esp. 27.13 and 28.3. On the date of this text: C. Diehl, *Études byzantines* (Paris, 1905), pp. 293–306; for 769: G. Ostrogorsky, *Byzantinische Jahrbücher*, 7 (1930), 20.

[149] See, in general, J.E. Dunlap, 'The office of the Grand Chamberlain in the later Roman and Byzantine empires', *Two studies*, pp. 162–324; Oikonomides, *Listes*, p. 300, and Guilland, *Institutions*, 1, 333–80. For an overview of the *praipositos'* involvement in imperial ceremonies, *ibid.*, pp. 343–8; cf. Belyaev, 'Priemy', *passim*.

and he seems even to have been entrusted with the operations of the Hippodrome.[150] Did this general ceremonial competence extend to the aspects of the triumphal parade not covered by the eparch's urban jurisdiction? Once again, the reports appended to the Imperial Expeditions allow a specific and positive answer. In 879, it was the *praipositos* – and not, therefore, the emperor or victorious generals – who defined the actual order and arrangement of the triumphal parade. It was he who stage-managed the ritual encounter of the victorious emperor and the governmental elite, the *synkletikoi*.[151] That it was now the *praipositos* who determined the locations of the stations and the ceremonies performed by what were still called the 'factions' in the late ninth century is a token of the extent to which the latter institution had become wedded to the palace bureaucracy.[152] Even the cheers of greeting for the triumphant emperor could not be left to chance. Indeed, spontaneity was so little appreciated that when it occurred, it was apt to frighten an emperor half out of his wits.[153] Thus, as the 879 report specifically states, the text of the victory acclamations too fell under the responsibilities of the *praipositos*.[154]

This point raises an important issue in the medieval history of the factions. It has been presumed that the *poietai* and *melistai* referred to in Philotheus' *Cleterologium* were in charge of the composition of acclamations.[155] The existence of some kind of part-time post of this nature fits well with the obvious fact that many acclamations are tailored to very precise circumstances. New circumstances required new texts, or at least the adaptation of old ones.[156] If the traditional assumptions about the duties of the factions' poets are as well founded as they appear to be, the

---

[150] A few from many examples in Guilland, *Institutions*, I, 343–4. For the Hippodrome, the key text is the mutilated final chapter of *De cer.*, 2, 56 (cod. '57'), Bonn, 807. Cf. Bury, 'Ceremony Book', pp. 219–21.

[151] *Imp. Exp.*, Bonn, 503.2–5: ...τὴν δὲ τῆς προελεύσεως τάξιν καὶ ἀπαντὴν τῆς συγκλήτου...ὁ πραιπόσιτος διωρίσατο.

[152] *Ibid.*., 503.3–5.

[153] Thus Basil himself was startled and almost abandoned the Elias Day procession when the crowd broke out in an unexpected 'Glory to God' at the sight of Leon VI in the cortege: *V. Theophano*, 19 Kurtz, 13.24–30; cf. comm. p. 56, n. 20.

[154] *Imp. Exp.* 503.3–4: ...καὶ τῶν μερῶν τὰς ἐπινικίους φωνὰς...διωρίσατο.

[155] *Cleterologium*, Oikonomides, 123.31 and 125.3 and 161.7, where they are listed together; cf. *ibid.*, p. 326.

[156] See the triumphal acclamations cited above, n. 114, or the acclamation obviously

statement from 879 that the *praipositos* Baanes was in charge of poems must mean that he was in charge of the *poietai*. This in turn implies that the factions were *subordinate to the praipositos* at this date. Guilland has studied the problem. While he admits that there were contacts between the factions and the *praipositoi*, he categorically denies that the former were in any way subordinated to the latter, chiefly on the grounds of his interpretation of the last two chapters of the present state of the Ceremony Book.[157] He is indeed correct in asserting that in the breakdown of sums distributed to various personnel from the customary payments conveyed to the *praipositoi* by newly promoted patricians, the members of the factions, including *poietai* and *melistai*, are listed separately from the group designated as ἡ τάξις τοῦ ἱπποδρομίου.[158] He is quite wrong, however, in claiming, on the basic of the rubric to the Ceremony Book's last chapter (Περὶ συνηθειῶν τῶν πραιποσίτων ἐν τῇ τάξει τοῦ ἱπποδρομίου), that that mutilated regulation refers exclusively to the same group as the one designated by the words τάξις τοῦ ἱπποδρομίου in the section on patricians' customary payments, and therefore does not include the factions.[159] Notwithstanding the chapter's rubric, Guilland failed to notice that the personnel being paid in *De cer.*, 2, 56, are *taxeis politikai* and not the simple members of the *taxis* or personnel of the Hippodrome referred to in 2, 55. On the other hand, when the *praipositoi* paid the *taxeis politikai* their salary (ῥόγα), they used two sets of records: their own, which listed the members of the *taxeis* by name, and written certifications (ἀσφάλεια) that the members of the *politikai taxeis* had indeed performed their service. The latter are provided by none other

---

tailored to Nicephorus II cited in Ch. 4, n. 150, as well as the liturgical parallel of the 'new *troparia*' referred to in the thanksgiving service, *De cer.*, 2, 19, Bonn, 609.8–9. Obviously, composing poems for imperial ceremonies was not a full-time job. Thus, as early as the seventh century, a deacon of the Hagia Sophia had been able to combine his church post with that of Poet of the Blues: *Miracula Artemii* (*BHG*, 173), 21, Papadopoulos-Kerameus 25.19–20.

[157] R. Guilland, 'Études sur l'Hippodrome de Byzance. IX. Les factions au Xe siècle: leur organisation', *BS*, 30 (1969), 1–17, esp. 11 and 13.

[158] *De cer.*, 2, 55, Bonn, 798.19–799.16. The poets and *melistai* of each faction receive six miliaresia each: 799.5–8; cf. 802.14–16 and 804.3–4. The τάξις τοῦ ἱπποδρομίου is listed *ibid.*, 799.17–800.6, etc.

[159] 'Factions', pp. 12–13; *De cer.*, Bonn, 807.1–33.

than the *chartoularioi* or record-keepers *of the two factions* (οἱ τῶν δύο μερῶν χαρτουλάριοι), i.e., the same officials who are listed as the second of the seven classes of faction personnel subordinated to the *demarchoi* in Philotheus' *Cleterologium*.[160] Clearly, these salaries, paid by the *praipositoi*, from their own records, in their own houses and with funds drawn from the imperial financial office of the *eidikos logos*, can only mean that at the date treated by the last chapter of the Ceremony Book and probably by the time of the 879 triumph at the latest, the factions were, at least in certain aspects of their activity, subordinate to the *praipositos* and paid employees of the state bureaucracy.[161]

In arranging the parade, the *praipositos* was assisted by the Master of Ceremony (ὁ ἐπὶ τῆς καταστάσεως), the silentiaries and the entire *cubiculum*.[162] The *praipositos* himself is identified by name in the case of the 879 triumph; he was none other than the great Baanes, perhaps Basil's most trusted and influential lieutenant, the man who had represented the emperor at the council of 869 and who, while the emperor was absent on campaign, enjoyed almost vice-regal authority.[163]

The decisive roles played by the late Roman Master of the Offices and by the early medieval *praipositos* have a significant feature in common. In both instances, the organization of the triumph ceremony fell to perhaps the highest, most powerful official of the empire of their days. That they, and no one lesser, were charged with the arrangement of the imperial end of the triumphal parade makes abundantly clear, if further illustration were required, the importance ceremonial in general and triumphs in particular assumed in the eyes of the imperial palace.

---

[160] *De cer.*, 2, 56, Bonn, 807.19–20; cf. *Cleterologium*, Oikonomides, 123.28–125.7 and *De cer.*, 2, 55, Bonn, 799.2 and 803.21–804.1 (eight miliaresia), where they are also listed among the personnel of the factions (μέρη).

[161] *De cer.*, 2, 56, Bonn, 807.14–20: τὸ γὰρ ἀκρόστιχον τῆς ῥόγας τῶν πολιτικῶν τάξεων τοῦ ἱπποδρομίου ἐλάμβανον οἱ πραιπόσιτοι ἐκ τοῦ εἰδικοῦ λόγου, ἔχοντες παρ' ἑαυτοῖς ἐν κώδηξιν τὰς τάξεις κατ' ὄνομα καὶ ἐν τῷ οἴκῳ αὐτῶν ἐρόγευον, λογαριάζοντες ἕκαστον μὴ ἀμελῶς διακεῖσθαι πρὸς τὴν δουλείαν αὐτοῦ, καθὼς οἱ τῶν δύο μερῶν χαρτουλάριοι μετ' ἐγγράφου ἀσφαλείας τούτους ὑπεδείκνυον.

[162] *Imp. Exp.*, 503.5–6.

[163] Guilland, *Institutions*, 1, 353–4; cf. his 'Contribution à la prosopographie de l'empire byzantin. Les patrices', *BZ*, 63 (1970), 300–17, here 301. The *Imp. Exp.* states: διέπων τὴν ἐκ προσώπου τοῦ βασιλέως δουλείας ἀρχήν, 503.8.

But the ceremonial power concentrated in the *praipositos'* hands seems already to have been slipping from his grasp less than a century after Baanes' performance of 879.[164] At present, it is not clear who, if anyone, succeeded *ex officio* to the *praipositos* as the chief organizer for ceremonies.[165] What is clear is that, as late as the reign of Constantine IX, the arrangement of the triumphal parade was important enough to be looked after by the emperor in person.[166]

Nor is it clear whether the role of the Protonotary of the Dromos in the triumphs from the 950s which are outlined in the Ceremony Book is related to the decline of the *praipositos*. In both cases, the Protonotary is in charge of the parade of prisoners; in the triumph in the Hippodrome, he arranged the whole parade. What has changed with respect to the arrangements of 879 is that now, the military possessed veto power over these arrangements. As the Ceremony Book explicitly records, before the *praipositos* can give the cue for the show to begin, the Domestic of the Scholes and relevant military officers have the right of inspecting the parade and making what changes they see fit, *after* the Protonotary had finished his arrangements.[167]

The modern historian cannot remain indifferent to the economic aspects of these ceremonies. Calculations of the Byzantine budget have proven irresistible to more than one generation of scholars. But it must be recognized that we do not know what part of the budget was eaten up by ceremonial expenses in general or what the cost of one early medieval triumph

---

[164] Thus Belyaev, 'Priemy', pp. 21–2, observing the appearance of ὁ παραδυναστεύων between the *praipositos* and the emperor in ceremonial affairs, described in *De cer.*, 2, 2. Cf. too on this passage H.G. Beck, 'Der byzantinische Ministerpräsident', *BZ*, 48 (1955), 309–38, here 331, n. 1.

[165] According to Guilland, in the twelfth century, these functions came to rest in the hands of the Protovestiarites, assisted by the πριμικήριος τῆς αὐλῆς: 'Études sur l'histoire administrative de l'empire byzantin. Le protovestiarite', *Rivista di studi bizantini e neoellenici*, n.s. 4 (14; 1967), 3–10, and *Institutions*, 1, 303–4. The title *praipositos* disappears altogether toward the end of the eleventh century: Oikonomides, *Listes*, p. 300.

[166] Psellus, *Chronographia*, Constantine IX, 7, Renauld 2.6.4–7.11, who uses this fact as a pretext for dwelling on the emperor's sense of theatricality.

[167] *De cer.*, 2, 19, Bonn, 609.21–610.2; 2, 20, Bonn, 613.2–614.2, esp. 613.18–19: καὶ εἴ τι ἂν εὕρωσιν ἐλλειπὲς τῆς τοῦ πρωτονοταρίου τοῦ δρόμου στάσεως, ἐπιδιορθοῦνται . . .

may have been. But cost they did. Back in the later Roman empire, triumphs had been considered an expensive affair. So much so, in fact, that a reformer had felt the need to warn against the excessive expenditures they entailed.[168] Although even this very general kind of evidence is lacking for the victory celebrations of early medieval Constantinople, it is possible to identify some certain or highly probable areas of expenditure triggered by triumphs of the ninth or tenth centuries.

The texts from this period clearly attest the emperor's payment for the triumphal crown offered to him by the City Prefect.[169] Nothing is known about possible remuneration of participants in the parade, nor is there evidence of direct payments to the factions solely for their performance of the triumphal ceremony.[170] It is not impossible that they enjoyed some kind of pleasant favors: for example, in the ninth century, it was customary to fill certain fountains or basins outside the palace complex with honeyed wine, pistachios and almonds, for the benefit of the factions or other performers in imperial receptions.[171] Certain participants in some imperial processions received gratuities for their role, but it is not known whether this custom extended to triumphs.[172]

A greater dent in the imperial pocket may have been made when the triumphal festivities included a eucharistic service in the Hagia Sophia. The hold of this great building on the modern imagination inclines us to forget how rarely the emperors of the

---

[168] Anonymous, *De rebus bellicis*, 1, 1, ed. R. Ireland, *De rebus bellicis*, 2, B.A.R. International Series, 63 (Oxford, 1979), 5; cf. Ammianus Marcellinus, 16, 10, 4, Clark, 1.85.1. The papyri would probably reward study from this viewpoint. See e.g. the purchase order for a rug for the *adventus* of a *dux* in A.D. 352 in P. Oxy. 1431, ed. B.P. Grenfell and A.S. Hunt, *The Oxyrhynchus Papyri*, 12 (London, 1916). 89–90.

[169] Above, p. 212.

[170] The last chapter of *De cer.* does not specify the frequency of payments. At payment the *praipositos* takes into account that the beneficiaries have not been found wanting in regard to their duties, as attested by the written certifications provided by the factions' *chartularii*: Bonn, 807.14–20.

[171] This is described in what seems to be an extract from an unknown imperial ceremony book inserted in Theoph. Cont. 3, 43, Bonn, 142.1–6. It is confirmed by the testimony of Harun Ibn Yahya, tr. A.A. Vasiliev, 'Harun-ibn-Yahya and his description of Constantinople', *Seminarium kondakovianum*, 5 (1932), 149–63, here 156–7.

[172] Thus, Philotheus reports payments to the imperial tailors, gold weavers and goldsmiths εἰς τὰ πρόκενσα, Oikonomides, 133.8–12; cf. transl. *ibid.*, 132.

early Middle Ages attended services there, little more than half a dozen times per year.[173] The imperial reluctance to use the church 'of the common people' as an outside observer of the ninth century called it, becomes a good deal more understandable if we recall that emperors were expected to make a significant gift each time they attended eucharist there.[174] In the tenth century, the recommended sum was ten lbs of gold.[175] Furthermore, the emperor was expected to distribute purses of gold to the archdeacon, ushers (ὀστιάριοι), choirmasters (ψάλται), and unspecified poor people (οἱ πένητες.), as well as the sacristans.[176]

Byzantine triumphs of the ninth and tenth centuries do not generally appear to have been accompanied by the indiscriminate throwing of coins to the crowd. On the contrary, what general largess there was took place within the confines of the palace. In 879, the recipients were members of the senatorial order who were paid in what the text calls 'vestomiliaresia', i.e. silver coins presumably from the imperial *Vestiarium*.[177] We have no idea how much cash went into this kind of largess. What evidence there is concerns other occasions and may usefully be tabulated as shown in Table 2.

This list does not, of course, allow us to draw any quantitative conclusions regarding imperial expenditures on largess to the *synkletikoi* during triumphal festivities of the ninth century. It does,

---

[173] Cf. e.g., Belyaev, 'Priemy', pp. 37–8.

[174] *De cer.*, 1, 1, Vogt, 1.14.20–1. Ibn Yahya refers to the Hagia Sophia as the church 'of the common people', doubtless as distinguished from the more opulent – and select – ambience of the smaller sanctuaries within the Great Palace complex: Vasiliev, 158, cf. 156–7.

[175] As is evidenced by a *scholion* on the passage of *De cer.*, 1, 1, just cited: Vogt, 1.14, app.: Ἰστέον ὅτι ὀφείλει ἔχειν τὸ ἀποκόμβιον χρυσοῦ λίτρας ιʹ. . . . The rest of the gloss is partly mutilated and has given rise to several slightly different restitutions. It is quite clear, however, that the damaged section bears only on the proper way of dividing up the sum of 10 lbs if more than one emperor happens to be present at the service: cf. [I.] Hausherr, in A. Vogt, *Le livre des cérémonies. Commentaire* (Paris, 1935), pp. 64–6, and V. Grumel, 'Comment reconstituer la scolie du *De ceremoniis*, l. I, c. 1 (éd. Vogt, p. 14)', *Échos d'Orient*, 35 (1936), 237–9.

[176] *De cer.*, 1, 1, Vogt, 1.14.7–13. It is not clear whether the sum paid to the *psaltai* was intended to be distributed further among the singers. It is not impossible that the choir was paid after every performance. This seems to be the implication of *Vita Georgii Amastridos* (BHG, 668), 15, ed. V.G. Vasil'evsky, *Trudy*, 3 (St Petersburg, 1915), 29.11–30.1.

[177] *Imp. Exp.*, 502.21. The identification was suggested to me by N. Oikonomides.

Table 2. *Imperial largess associated with state ceremonies of the ninth century*

1. Coronations (all sums in gold unless otherwise noted)
   811: Michael I
       50 lbs to the patriarch
       25 lbs to the 'clergy'[178]
       ? to the Senate and army (τὰ στρατεύματα)[179]
   811 (Christmas): Theophylactus (junior emperor)
       Precious liturgical furnishings to the Hagia Sophia
       25 lbs to the patriarch
       100 lbs to the 'holy (ἐναγής) clergy'[180]
   821 or 830 (Whitsunday): coronation and marriage of Theodora to coemperor Theophilus
       15 lbs to the patriarch
       15 lbs to the 'clergy'
       50 lbs to the Senate[181]
   899: (customary sum for a *basileus* who becomes *autokrator*)
       100 lbs to 'the Great Church'
       100 lbs to the 'whole Senate and *kouboukleion* etc.'
       1000 *miliaresia* (?) for each *tagma* and group of *offikia*[182]
   899: (customary sums for a junior emperor)
       One-half of the preceding[183]
2. Other occasions
   Brumalia of the emperor (899):
       20 lbs to *synkletikoi*, wide range of dignitaries and palace personnel[184]

---

178 Theophanes, A.M. 6304, De Boor, 493.32–3: καὶ ἐδωρήσατο τῷ πατριάρχῃ χρυσίου λίτρας ν´ καὶ τῷ κλήρῳ κε´. I suppose the latter refers to the clergy of the Hagia Sophia, since the preceding sentence describes the coronation there.

179 *Ibid.*, 493.33–494.1.

180 *Ibid.*, 494.28–33. Same presumption concerning the clergy. The figure seems quite out of line with the others.

181 *Vita Theodorae imperatricis* (*BHG*, 1731), ed. W. [= V.E.] Regel, *Analecta Byzantino-Russica* (St Petersburg, 1891), 5.19–25; cf. Grierson, *Coins*, 3, 1, 387. On the date, Treadgold, 'Accuracy', pp. 173–4.

182 Philotheus, *Cleterologium*, Oikonomides, 99.5–8: . . . καὶ τῇ συγκλήτῳ πάσῃ σὺν τοῖς τοῦ κουβουκλίου καὶ λοιποῖς χρυσοῦ λίτρας ρ´ καὶ χιλιάδας διαφόρους μιλιαρησίων ἑκάστῳ τάγματι καὶ ὀφφικίων τῇ συστάσει. Oikonomides prefers to translate the phrase more loosely: 'and many thousands of miliaresia to each tagma . . .'.

183 *Ibid.*, 99.13.

184 *Ibid.*, 223.28–9; detailed breakdown of beneficiaries (drawn up in response to controversy provoked by unnamed dissatisfied dignitaries) and exemplary sums, *ibid.*, 225.10–16. Additional payments not taken into account in this sum are made to rowers of the imperial *dromonia*, whose largess was increased by Constantine VII,

Table 2.   (*Contd.*)

Brumalia of the coemperor (899):
    10 lbs to the same beneficiaries
Brumalia of the empress (899):
    8 lbs to the same beneficiaries[185]
Anniversary of power (*autokratoria*) of Leo VI (899):
    16 lbs to the same beneficiaries, minus the lower officials, palace
    personnel and dignitaries as specified[186]

---

however, furnish some idea of the varying orders of magnitude of imperial munificence to the Byzantine governmental elite on different ceremonial occasions of the period.

One area of expenditure for which no evidence is available is the cost of the circus spectacles marking triumphs. However, it seems likely that, compared with late antique races, costs were lower in the early medieval period. On one hand, the number of races staged in a medieval celebration appears to have declined considerably, i.e. to about eight from the later Roman custom of up to twenty-four.[187] On the other, the Ceremony Book indicates that in the tenth century at least, foot races were – perhaps increasingly – substituted for horse races.[188] Since acquiring and maintaining the horses likely constituted the single greatest expense in circus racing, any such substitutions implied considerable savings for the imperial treasury.[189]

    De cer., 2, 18, Bonn, 601.10–19. The same emperor is reported to have consolidated all three Brumalia largesses into one lump munificence of 50 lbs: *ibid.*, 607.1–14.

[185] *Ibid.*, 223.29–225.4.

[186] *Ibid.*, 221.31–222.3. Those excluded from this largess, as well as from the unspecified (16 lbs?) amount for the coronation anniversary (στέψιμον) are listed *ibid.*, 229.18–231.2. Excluded are the chartularii of the *sekreta*, the notaries, personnel of the Vestiarium, table servants (ὑπουργίαι) and dignitaries 'of the City'.

[187] Guilland, *Institutions*, 1, 573.

[188] *De cer.*, 2, 20, Bonn, 612.21.

[189] On the cost of circus races and the maintenance of the stables, Petit, *Libanius et la vie municipale*, pp. 136–9, and esp. the important study of J. Gascou, 'Institutions de l'Hippodrome'.

6

A distant echo: victory celebrations in the imperial provinces

The links between the later Roman capital and the provinces form a subject whose importance is not diminished by the contraction of urban life outside the imperial city in the seventh century.[1] The study of state rituals has largely been confined to those of the capital and little heed has been paid to their echo in the provinces. This is somewhat problematic from the point of view of imperial propaganda's broader effectiveness since, even if the empire's elite were indeed concentrated in the capital, no emperor could conceive a viable rule which failed to convince the provinces that 'the emperor established in Constantinople was always victorious', which failed to harness the provinces' resources of men, money, and material to the imperial nerve center.[2]

Provincial ceremonial also illuminates the Byzantine impact on the barbarian kingdoms. The trend towards concentration of imperial victory celebrations in Constantinople has already been observed. If the imperial city were the only source of western

---

[1] For a recent panorama of the archaeological evidence from the main towns in the transitional period at the end of antiquity, see C. Bouras, 'City and village: urban design and architecture', *JÖB*, 31, 2 (1981), 611–53; for a case study of one area's passage from provincialism to separatism, A. Guillou, *Régionalisme et indépendance dans l'empire byzantin au VIIe siècle. L'exemple de l'exarchat et de la Pentapole d'Italie*, Studi storici, 75–6 (Rome, 1969); on the problem of province and capital, I. Ševčenko, 'Constantinople viewed from the eastern provinces in the middle Byzantine period', *Harvard Ukrainian Studies*, 3/4 (1979–80), 712–47, and J. Herrin, 'Realities of Byzantine provincial government: Hellas and Peloponnesos, 1180–1205', *DOP*, 29 (1975), 253–84.

[2] The quotation is from Cecaumenus' advice to his children to shun plots against the emperor hatched in the provinces and offers eloquent testimony on the penetration of eleventh-century victory ideology: ed. G.G. Litavrin, *Sovety i rasskazy Kekavmena* (Moscow, 1972), 268.8–13; cf. 248.13–250.13; cf. comm. pp. 558–9.

familiarity with Byzantine court customs, this would imply a drastic narrowing of potential channels of influence, limited essentially to travelers to the East. But from the fifth century to the ninth, the western successor societies were close to or even contiguous with provincial outposts of the Byzantine empire. That it was these frontier provinces which funneled the greatest continuous Byzantine influence into the new kingdoms has more than general probability in its favor. Obolensky has shown that they were among the most dynamic factors in early medieval cultural exchange. His findings are only reinforced by Grierson's conclusion that far from serving as a truly international medium of exchange, Byzantine money – and bronze coinage at that – durably filled this role only in zones contiguous with the empire.[3]

Even though the capital dominates the extant evidence, enough scraps have survived to warrant exploring the tenor of public life in the imperial provinces. The dearth of material means that, at this stage, the exploration must be more tantalizing than complete. Nonetheless, three main ways in which the imperial ideology impinged on the awareness of the empire's towns and settlements can be distinguished: the bonds between provincials and their distant sovereigns, the impact of the church and army on provincial life and, finally, the ceremonial life of local officialdom.

I. TIES THAT BIND

The fourth-century monarchy's itinerant character had guaranteed many provincials the opportunity of directly beholding their ruler and his imperial splendor and participating in his rituals. Even small towns emulated the great capitals in the preparations and festivities marking ceremonies like the imperial *adventus*.[4] But solemn entries and departures were not the only imperial rites staged on the road. The exigencies of the moment meant, for

---

[3] D. Obolensky, 'Byzantine frontier zones and cultural exchanges', *Actes du XIVe Congrès international des études byzantines*, 1 (Bucharest, 1974), 302–14; P. Grierson, 'Coinage and money in the Byzantine empire, 498–ca. 1090', *Moneta e scambi nell'alto medioevo*, Settimane, 8 (Spoleto, 1961), pp. 411–53, here 447–53.

[4] MacCormack, *Art and ceremony*, pp. 17ff. For small towns, see the anecdote on Caesar Julian's passage through ἐν τῶν πολιχνίων in Socrates, *H.e.*, 3, 1, PG, 67.373B.

example, that even the assumption of the consulate could occur far from the main imperial residences and, as has been seen, victory celebrations followed the same pattern.[5] Down to the eleventh century, the western empire's collapse and the restriction of the eastern court to Constantinople and its environs sharply reduced such occasions, especially as far as the western provinces were concerned. In 688, Justinian II seems to have made a visit to Thessalonica which perhaps included a triumphal entry as well as a victory endowment for St Demetrius.[6] Further west, another exception was Constans II's stay in Italy (663–8), which naturally implied a displacement of the monarchy's ritual apparatus, exemplified by Constans' *adventus* into Rome.[7] Even if legitimate emperors were rare birds in Byzantine Italy, however, the region spawned an impressive array of usurpers from Eleutherius in the seventh century to Maniaces in the eleventh, and pomp commensurate with their ambition must have surrounded each of them. Between 619 and 787, for instance, Byzantine Italy and Africa witnessed no fewer than nine temporarily successful usurpations, more than one every other decade.[8]

Even in the traveling monarchy's heyday, direct contact with the monarchy and its ceremonies must have affected far fewer citizens than the usual displays of loyalty which were entrenched in everyday life. Quite a number of them survived into the seventh and eighth centuries.[9] Provincial centers publicly manifested

---

[5] Thus the consulate of Jovian at Ancyra in 364: Seeck, *Regesten*, p. 214; or of Ausonius at Bordeaux in 379: Matthews, *Western aristocracies*, p. 72.

[6] Ed. J.M. Spieser, 'Inventaires en vue d'un recueil des inscriptions historiques de Byzance', *TM*, 5 (1973), 145–81, here 156–9, with bibliography. Cf. Dölger, *Regesten*, no. 258. However, G.J. Theocharides, 'Justinian II. oder Basileios II.? Eine neue Losung zu älteren Problem', *Byz.*, 46 (1976), 75–118, has offered serious grounds for relating the famous St Demetrius fresco to Basil II's triumphal entry into Sirmium.

[7] *Lib. pont.*, Mommsen, 186.9–187.13.

[8] P. Classen, 'Der erste Römerzug in der Weltgeschichte. Zur Geschichte des Kaisertums im Westen und der Kaiserkrönung in Rom zwischen Theodosius d. Gr. und Karl d. Gr.', *Historische Forschungen für Walter Schlesinger* (Cologne, 1974), pp. 325–47, here 336–7.

[9] P.E. Schramm, 'Die Anerkennung Karls des Grossen als Kaiser. Ein Kapitel aus der Geschichte der mittelalterlichen Staatssymbolik', *Historische Zeitschrift*, 172 (1951), 449–515, here 465–6, and J. Deér, 'Die Vorrechte des Kaiser in Rom', *Zum Kaisertum Karls des Grossen. Beiträge und Aufsätze*, ed. G. Wolf, Wege der Forschung, 38 (Darmstadt, 1972), pp. 30–115, here 89ff.

loyalty to a new sovereign with ceremonies and acclamations honoring the arrival of his official portrait; traces of the custom survive from sixth-century Egypt, seventh-century Italy and even unspecified areas in the eighth century.[10] Like rituals marked the distribution of locks of child emperors' hair to provincial officials in the seventh century and later.[11]

The promulgation of imperial laws and the announcement of public rejoicing (*gaudia publica, laetitiae publicae*) were another occasion on which the central government of late antiquity reached out to the provincial population. It was very much in the central government's interest to diffuse news of its successes to distant areas, for the perception of a weakened throne could easily trigger regional disturbances. This is seen for instance in the Italian uprising of 718, which coincided with reports of the great siege of Constantinople.[12] The abuses of messengers or local officials who demanded gratuities before announcing imperial victories or the like had resulted in a series of fourth-century laws.[13] Both the custom and the abuse were still around in the sixth century, when Justinian adapted the early legislation and set a maximum fee for announcements.[14] In some form, provincial victory communiqués persisted into the ninth century.[15] As we have seen, the

[10] Thus Dioscorus' panegyric on Justin II (P. Cair. II.67183), ed. E. Heitsch, *Die griechischen Dichterfragmente der römischen Kaiserzeit*, 1, Abhandlungen der Akademie der Wissenschaften in Göttingen, Philol.-hist. Kl. 3, 49 (Göttingen, 1961), 128–9, on which cf. H. Kruse, *Studien*, pp. 41–2; the report on the adoration and acclamation of Phocas' portrait inserted in Gregory I's correspondence: *Registrum*, Appendix 8 (formerly 13, 1), ed. D. Norberg, *CCL*, 140A (1982).1101. That the custom survived in the eighth century follows from the appeal made to it in the acts of the second Council of Nicaea (787), *actio 2*, ed. J.D. Mansi, *Sacrorum conciliorum nova et amplissima collectio*, 12 (Florence, 1766). 1067A.

[11] 684–5 at Rome: *Lib. pont.*, Mommsen, 204.1–3. Cf. the account of the child emperor's first haircut and the distribution of his locks to various officials, *De cer.*, 2, 23, Bonn, 620.20–622.17. Leo VI's locks were immediately given to, among others, the commanders and officers of the Anatolikon and Cappadocian themes, *ibid.*, 622.1–17; cf. Treitinger, *Oströmische*, pp. 105–8.

[12] Leo III's announcement to the western provinces that the empire had not yet fallen to the Arabs was considered a crucial factor in the collapse of the usurpation of Basil and Sergius in 718: Theophanes, A.M. 6210, De Boor, 398.6–17.

[13] *Cod. Theod.*, 8, 11, 2–4, Mommsen–Meyer, 406–7, esp. 8, 11, 3, dated 13 February 369. For actual diffusion of victory bulletins, above, Ch. 2, p. 41n22, and 5, p. 192–3. We catch a glimpse of messengers bearing the good news of the birth of an heir in Mark, *V. Porphyrii*, 44, Grégoire–Kugener 37.6–8.

[14] *Cod. Iust.*, 12, 63, 1–2, Krüger, 487.4–8.   [15] Above, Ch. 5, n. 16.

announcements could precipitate local celebrations of the emperor's success.[16] In fourth-century Antioch, the reading of imperial victory bulletins was a rather impressive affair. Provincial celebrations of imperial victories continued more or less unbroken down to the reign of Anastasius I.[17] Theophanes' account of Leo III's *sacra* to the population of the West indicates that similar rituals were not unknown two centuries later.[18] They likely occurred sporadically in the subsequent period, for as late as the eighth century, Ravenna celebrated the traditional parade of mockery when the head of Justinian II was carried in from the capital.[19] Contrary to fourth-century custom, by this date the provincial display of a defeated tyrant's head was limited to a region which had particularly suffered at his hands.[20]

Acclamations, which often touted imperial victory, remained an indispensable element of public life in the provinces no less than in the capital.[21] The ideology of imperial victory insinuated its way too into other, less obvious, civic activities. Perhaps the most striking were the solemn legal oaths imposed on citizens in situations as diverse as tax declarations, court testimony, confirmation of contractual agreements of sale, service, donation, loan, etc., or as a means of proof in private documents.[22] A victory epithet like 'all-conquering' or 'invincible' often accompanied the imperial title in the oath formula's invocation of the emperor's name.[23] Because such oaths were meant to inspire awe, the concepts a citizen invoked in swearing plumbed the core of the

[16] Above, Ch. 2, pp. 62.
[17] Thus the liturgical service for the defeat of Vitalian attested by Severus' homily delivered on that occasion, above, Ch. 2, n. 95. Procopius of Gaza seems to allude to another celebration staged in Gaza for a victory of the same emperor: *In imp. Anast. pan.*, 1, Kempen 1.3–6.
[18] For Antioch, see above, Ch. 5, n. 20–1; for Leo III, above, n. 12.
[19] See the anecdote concerning the parade at Ravenna preserved in Agnellus, *Liber pontificalis ecclesiae Ravennatis*, 142, ed. O. Holder-Egger, *MGH. SRL* (1878), 371.15–25.
[20] Cf. Theophanes, A.M. 6203, De Boor, 381.5–6, and Nicephorus, *Brev.*, De Boor, 47.22–3.
[21] See in general T. Klauser, 'Akklamationen', *RAC*, 1 (1950), 216–33.
[22] E. Seidl, *Der Eid im römisch-ägyptischen Provinzialrecht*, 2, Münchener Beiträge zur Papyrusforschung und antiken Rechtsgeschichte, 24 (Munich, 1935), 59ff.
[23] From Egyptian documents of s.iv–vii: τοῦ τὰ πάντα νικῶντος δεσπότου, Seidl, *Eid*, pp. 6–12; τῶν ἀνικήτων βασιλέων, ibid., 6; καλλινίκων αἰωνίων Αὐγούστων, ibid., 7, n. 5, etc. Concordant testimony from Italian papyri: J.O. Tjäder, *Die nichtliterari-*

later Roman psyche: oaths were sworn by the emperor's genius (τύχη), by his safety and permanence, by God the *pantokrator*, by the holy and consubstantial Trinity and, very frequently, from the reign of Diocletian down to the collapse of Roman rule in Egypt and the end of the evidence, by the victory of the Roman emperors.[24] This kind of oath cannot help but recall the ubiquitous reverse of contemporary coinage 'Victory of the Augusti'.[25]

Victory ideology's prominence in the legal catchwords of provincial practice may have encouraged its permanence in the epistolary etiquette of private and public communications addressed to the throne by the upper crust of town and country.[26] Well-wishing for the emperor which concluded a letter to a member of the capital's ruling circles might even echo the phraseology of public oaths.[27] Epithets reminiscent of official victory titles were used by subjects in addressing letters to the ruler.[28] Appeals to imperial victory abounded in the customary

---

schen lateinischen Papyri Italiens aus der Zeit 445–700, I, Acta instituti romani regni Sueciae, 4°, 19 (Lund, 1955), 304.30–2, no. 13: 'et salutem invictissimi principis obtestans Romanum gubernantis imperium' (4.iv.553); cf. *ibid.*, 240.21, no. 8 (17.vii.564); 348.44–6, no. 20 (ca. 600).

[24] Other concepts: Seidl, *Eid*, pp. 5–12. Oaths by the imperial victory occur among surviving formulas of the tetrarchy, Constantine II and colleagues, Honorius, Theodosius II, Valentinian III and Marcian, Leo I, Anastasius, Justin I, Justinian, Justin II, Tiberius II, Maurice, Phocas and Heraclius and Constantine III: K.A. Worp, 'Byzantine imperial titulature in the Greek documentary papyri: the oath formulas', *Zeitschrift für Papyrologie und Epigraphik*, 45 (1982), 199–223, here 223.

[25] See, e.g., A.R. Bellinger, *Catalogue of the Byzantine Coins in the Dumbarton Oaks Collection...*, I (Washington, D.C., 1966), 381 (16 entries); P. Grierson, *ibid.*, 2, 2 (Washington, D.C., 1968), 721 (29 entries).

[26] Seidl, *Eid*, pp. 44–7, considers the numerous petitions in fifth- and sixth-century papyri which make entreaties 'by God Almighty and the piety and victory of our lord Fl. Leo, Eternal Augustus' etc. which were clearly inspired by the oaths, evidence of later Romans' frivolous attitude toward the oath formulas. It is just as possible that the borrowing was intended to lend gravity to their petitions.

[27] Patriarch John of Jerusalem to the patriarch of Constantinople (518) concludes with a statement on his church's prayers [ὑπὲρ] νίκης. καὶ διαμονῆς. τοῦ εὐσεβεστάτου καὶ γαληνοτάτου ἡμῶν βασιλέως, ed. E. Schwartz, *ACO*, 3 (1940). 78.36–7. Cf. the like formulas in Seidl, *Eid*, pp. 9–12.

[28] A few examples from many: bishops assembled at Antioch to Jovian (νικητῇ Αὐγούστῳ), Socrates, *H.e.*, 3, 25, *PG*, 67.453A; cf. Sozomen, *H.e.*, 6, 4, 7, Bidez–Hansen, 241.12–14; church of Egypt to Leo I (νικητῇ, τροπαιούχῳ καὶ Αὐγούστῳ), Evagrius, *H.e.*, 2, 8, Bidez–Parmentier, 56.31–2; bishops of Asia to

well-wishing which opened or closed communications with the throne. The formulas show a certain variety, ranging from the hope that the emperor will trample the barbarian tribes underfoot to the desire that his triumph here on earth be equalled by that in the afterlife.[29] Ceremonies, acclamations, oaths and epistolary politeness helped instill imperial victory into the ideological content of provincials' relations with their emperor. But these diverse acts of secular public life were not the only forum in which the public mind focused on the Roman emperor's victory.

2. GOD AND COUNTRY

Even in the centuries before the empire's conversion, Christians had prided themselves on their scrupulous fulfillment of the Pauline injunction to pray to their God on behalf of their rulers.[30] After Constantine, this aspect of Christian discipline only grew in significance. And so it was that the church and its public worship came to provide an enduring and frequent forum in which the average Roman subject voiced his loyalty to the emperor. When the last priest of the imperial cult had died and the last sporting event had been staged in the local circus, the church continued to function and relay the imperial idea. From the fourth century on,

Basiliscus and Marcus (αἰωνίοις, νικηταῖς, Αὐγούστοις), *ibid.*, 3, 5, Bidez–Parmentier, 105.1–3. The usage of the papal chancellery is reflected by the *Liber diurnus*, Foerster, 181.2–4; cf. Pope Martin I to Constans II in 649 (JL, 2062): νικητῇ τροπαιούχῳ, ed. J.D. Mansi, *Concilia*, 10 (Florence, 1764). 789D.

[29] A mass of documents contain such expressions and offer fertile soil for research into attitudes toward the imperial office. A few examples: bishops of Lydia to Leo I, ed. E. Schwartz, *ACO*, 2.5 (1936).57.17–19; bishops of Cappadocia Secunda to same, *ibid.*, 79.4–8; bishops of Galatia Prima to same, *ibid.*, 93.3–5; Severus to Justinian, Zachary Rhetor, *H.e.*, 9, 16, tr. Brooks, 2.90.2–4; bishops of Syria Secunda to same, ed. Schwartz, *ACO*, 3 (1940).31.35–9; Gregory I, *Reg.*, 5, 30, Norberg, 296.4–297.8; *ibid.*, 6, 16, 386.38–44; *ibid.*, 7, 6, 452.2–453.6; *ibid.*, 13, 32, Norberg, 1033.18–19; Martin I to Constans II (JL, 2062), ed. Mansi, *Concilia*, 10.796D–797A; bishops of Africa to same, *ibid.*, 925E–928A; cf. too, *ibid.*, 976A–B and 1001D. The custom survived into the Middle Ages, e.g., Theodore Studite to Michael II, *Ep.*, 2, 86, *PG*, 99.1332B.

[30] 1 Timothy, 2, 1–2. Melito of Sardes, Tertullian and Origen confirm the observance of this precept in the pre-Constantinian church: L. Biehl, *Das liturgische Gebet für Kaiser und Reich. Ein Beitrag zur Geschichte des Verhältnisses von Kirche und Staat* (Paderborn, 1937), pp. 30–3; cf. O. Michel–T. Klauser, 'Gebet II. (Fürbitte)', *RAC*, 9 (1976).1–36, here 33.

the regular performance of public prayers for the emperor and for his victory must have been a common experience in the daily life of the provinces and capitals.[31] The political nature of this act is illuminated by Chrysostom's implication that public prayers for the emperor were not necessarily the sincerest form of loyalty display, an implication that would be echoed by Theodore Studite centuries later.[32]

Much work remains to be done before the history of the Orthodox liturgy's social function gains a solid footing. Yet this aspect of public life cannot be ignored. Prayer for the emperor was of course common to province and capital alike. In the provinces, however, the absence of the imperial court's constant pageantry, of the physical immediacy of its ceremonies and personnel, lent public prayer a greater part in shaping the subjects' conception of their ruler and his activities. The growing role of sixth-century churches in diffusing imperial decrees and communiqués underscores this function of the local church as a focal point for provincials' interaction with the imperial government. For the bulk of the lay population, the eucharistic liturgy constituted the most familiar and frequented church service. The modern-day service books of the Orthodox church preserve several prayers which graphically illustrate the place accorded the emperors and their victory in the religious life of Byzantine society. The diptych section of the Liturgy of St Basil commemorates the emperors by borrowing from the vocabulary of the Old Testament. It entreats the Lord to:

[31] The many references to such prayers in post-Constantinian patristic literature could, by themselves, form the basis of a monograph. Most refer, in a general way, to prayers for the well-being of the emperor and empire. Thus the 'customary prayers' Arius was eager to perform on behalf of Constantine I (*CPG*, 2027), *Ep.* apud Socrates, *H.e.*, 1, 26, *PG*, 67.152A; cf. e.g. Constantine's requirement of such prayers: Eusebius, *V. Constantini*, 4, 14, 1–2, Winkelmann, 125.12–18, etc. Some emperors certainly considered them a source of victory, as Zeno stated in his *Henoticon*, ed. E. Schwartz, *Codex Vaticanus gr. 1431, eine antichalkedonische Sammlung aus der Zeit Kaiser Zenos*, Abhandlungen der bayerischen Akademie der Wissenschaften, Philos.-philol. und hist. Kl., 32, 6 (1927), 53.1–9; cf. Acacius' letter to Peter of Alexandria on the *Henoticon* (*CPG*, 5991), ap. Zachary Rhetor, *H.e.*, 5, 11, tr. Brooks, 1.164.2–6.

[32] Chrysostom, *Hom. 21 in statuas*, 3, *PG*, 49.218, stating that it is easier to subjugate a city by fear and enjoy its public prayers than to win it over by affection and enjoy its citizens' private prayers; cf. Theodore Studite, *Ep.*, 1, 4, *PG*, 99.921C–D, in which he protests that he continues to commemorate the emperor in the liturgy and to pray for him in *both* public and private.

Remember...our most pious and faithful emperors...shelter their heads on the day of battle, strengthen their arm, raise their right hand, confirm their empire, subjugate unto them all the barbarian peoples who want war, grant them deep and lasting peace.[33]

Although the early history of such texts is far from clear, the unanimity of the various liturgies as they are known today argues strongly for the antiquity of the Mass prayers for imperial victory.[34] The convergent testimony of the eastern liturgies is seconded not only by an early manuscript of the Liturgy of Chrysostom, but by one of the most venerable of liturgical documents, a potsherd bearing the prayers of intercession in a script which may go back to the fourth or fifth century.[35] When the exarch of Ravenna was notified of a new pope's election, the announcement stressed the bishop-elect's eagerness to pour forth prayers 'for the life and safety and perfect victories' of the Byzantine emperors, so that God might grant 'the great victor emperors' multiple success, making the *respublica* triumph over the barbarians and restoring the earlier extent of the Roman empire'.[36] Besides, a related development is evinced by the western liturgies. The city of Rome included in some of its services prayers which sound much like their eastern cousins:[37]

---

[33] P.N. Trempelas, Αἱ τρεῖς λειτουργίαι κατὰ τοὺς ἐν Ἀθήναις κώδικας, Texte und Forschungen zur byzantinisch-neugriechischen Philologie, 15 (Athens, 1935), 185–6 (allusions to Psalms 139.8; 46.4; 67.31 and Ezekiel 30.25).

[34] Thus the Liturgy of Chrysostom, ed. Trempelas, 58.11–59.2: 'cast down under their feet every enemy and hostile power'; cf. the Syrian Liturgy of St James, Brightman, 55.12–19: 'Remember O Lord, our most pious and Christ-loving emperor, the pious and Christ-loving empress, the whole palace and their army and their celestial succor and victory'; cf. Liturgy of St Mark, *ibid.*, 128.8–21.

[35] J. Mateos, 'Évolution historique de la liturgie de saint Jean Chrysostome', *Proche-Orient chrétien*, 20 (1970), 98–122, here 100, reports a prayer for the emperors and the success of the imperial army in Grottaferrata, Γ. β. VII (s.ix-x). For O. Tait-Petrie 415 and other witnesses, see J. Van Haelst, 'Une ancienne prière d'intercession de la liturgie de Saint Marc', *Ancient Society*, 1 (1970), 95–114, here 100, cf. 109–10; J. Gascou, *Bulletin de l'Institut français d'archéologie orientale*, 76 (1976), 188, n. 1, suggests that the document may be some what later than the s.iv-v date advanced by Van Haelst.

[36] *Lib. diurn.*, 60, Foerster, 117.5–17.

[37] See in general G. Tellenbach, *Römischer und christlicher Reichsgedanke in der Liturgie des frühen Mittelalters*, Sitzungsberichte der Heidelberger Akademie der Wissenschaften, Philos.-hist. Kl. 1934–5, 1 (Heidelberg, 1934), 9.

O God, who dominates all kingdoms by thy eternal empire, bend the ears of thy mercy to the prayers of our humility and assist the princes of the Roman realm that, by thy tranquility and power they might ever be victors with clemency.[38]

Or:

Let us also pray for our most Christian emperor, that our God and Lord may subjugate to him all barbarian peoples, for our lasting peace.[39]

Both texts would find favor with later celebrants and entered the common stock of the Romanized liturgy of the medieval West. And, although they were perhaps less familiar to the general population, it should not be forgotten that the empire's monasteries sent up daily prayers for the emperor and his victory in the liturgy of the hours.[40] Incomplete though it is, this brief review suggests the important role played by the regular, ongoing services of the empire's churches in focusing, for a brief moment every week, the average citizen's awareness on the empire's leadership and its victory.

But the church did not confine itself to incorporating prayers for victory over the barbarians into its Sunday services. As has

[38] *Ibid.*, 61: 'Deus, qui regnis omnibus aeternis dominaris imperio, inclina ad preces humilitatis nostrae aures misericordiae tuae, et Romani regni adesto principibus, ut tua tranquillitatem clementer tua sint semper virtute victores.'

[39] *Ibid.*, 52: 'Oremus et pro christianissimo imperatore nostro, ut deus et dominus noster subditas illi faciat omnes barbaras nationes ad nostram perpetuam pacem.' Cf. also *ibid.*, 53. The enduring prestige of the traditional Latin prayers for imperial victory at Rome during the crises of the seventh century explains the proud note of the *Lib. pont.*, Mommsen, 198.8–13, describing how the bishop of Porto celebrated a public, Latin Mass in the Hagia Sophia on 21 April 681, at which 'omnes unianimiter in laudes et victoriis piissimorum imperatorum idem Latine vocibus adclamarent'.

[40] Thus the prayer for the emperor's victory over the barbarians which still occurs in the introduction to the Orthros office (= western Matins), after Psalms 19 and 20: Τὸ μέγα ὡρολόγιον, ἀκολουθία τοῦ ὄρθρου, ed. M.I. Saliveros (Athens, n.d.), 63: εὔφρανον ἐν τῇ δυνάμει σου τοὺς πιστοὺς βασιλεῖς ἡμῶν, νίκας χορηγῶν αὐτοῖς κατὰ τῶν πολεμίων...; cf. the next prayer:...καὶ χορήγει αὐτοῖς οὐρανόθεν τὴν νίκην; cf. E. Amand de Mendieta, *Mount Athos. The garden of the Panhagia*, Berliner byzantinistische Arbeiten, 41 (Berlin, 1972), p. 294. Although the origins of these and similar prayers is not yet known, monastic prayer for the well-being of the state is very ancient. See, e.g., on Anastasius' and Justinian's appreciation for the prayers of the monks of Palestine, Cyril Scythopolitanus, *Vita Sabae* (BHG, 1608), 51 and 72, ed. E. Schwartz, Texte und Untersuchungen 49, 2 (Leipzig, 1939), 143.6–9 and 174.24–175.4; cf. the early tenth-century evidence of the *V. Euthymii*, 5, Karlin-Hayter 31.7–9.

already been observed, special services staged by the patriarchs of Constantinople helped sustain the city through the great sieges of the seventh and eighth centuries; Photius, among others, maintained the tradition in the next century.[41] It has not often been noticed, however, that the capital's supplications of divine aid against the barbarians manifest a phenomenon which had emerged earlier in the empire's provinces. Several centuries before, bishops had devised local measures to martial their cities' spiritual strength through the difficult days of enemy attack. Insight into such observances is yielded by the sermons Maximus, bishop of Turin, delivered during an invasion of Italy in the opening years of the fifth century.[42] When his city was threatened, Maximus ordered city-wide fasts in imitation of the Ninivites of old. The fasts were obviously accompanied by prayer services of some sort. Not only was prayer more effective than arrows in wounding barbarians at long range, it offered better hope of victory.[43] 'With these weapons [prayer, chanting, fasting, mercy], the Christians are wont to vanquish their enemies, with these weapons they defend the city's ramparts.' As Maximus would emphasize, the fasts of his flock destroyed the spiritual and carnal enemies of the Christians and ensured the success of the Roman army.[44]

This kind of spiritual defence of the empire's cities was by no means restricted to Italy. Similar ceremonies can be traced back to the ancient Roman *lustratio urbis* and the liturgical procession around the walls of a besieged city was practiced in late antique Gaul and Spain.[45] At the beginning of the sixth century, the

[41] Photius, *Hom.*, 3, 1, and 4, 5, ed. B. Laourdas, Παράρτημα, Ἑλληνικά, 12 (Thessalonica, 1959), 31.31–32.4, 37.21–3 and 48.20–5.
[42] A. Mutzenbecher, *CCL*, 23 (1962).xxxv, n. 1, suggests 393 (Eugenius), 401–2 (Alaric), 406 (Radagaisus) or 411 (Athaulf). The references to barbarians in sermons 83, *ibid.*, 339.13, and 86, 353.74, seem to militate against Eugenius. P. Courcelle, *Histoire littéraire des grandes invasions germaniques*, 3rd edn (Paris, 1964), p. 33, n. 2, gives no reason for his identification with Alaric.
[43] *Sermo* 81, 4, Mutzenbecher, 334.72; *ibid.*, 3, 333.60–1 and 334.81. On the biblical inspiration, Y.M. Duval, *Le Livre de Jonas dans la littérature chrétienne grecque et latine*, 2 (Paris, 1973), 545; *sermo* 83, 1, Mutzenbecher, 339.20–2; cf. *sermo* 85, 3, 350.71–2.
[44] *Sermo* 86, 1, Mutzenbecher, 352.11–14: 'His enim telis,... solent aduersarios suos uincere christiani, his armis ciuitatis moenia custodire.' Cf. *ibid.*, 4, 353.72–5; *sermo* 69, 4, Mutzenbecher, 290.92–291.97.
[45] This ancient ceremony has attracted the attention of historians of religion, e.g.

bishop of Tella brought encouragement to the troops defending his Mesopotamian city. He blessed them, sprinkled them and the wall with holy water and distributed communion.[46] When an approaching Persian army terrified the citizens of Apamea, they begged their bishop to break with custom and stage a procession. They wanted a public showing of the city's precious relic of the true cross, which was normally shown to the population only one day a year. The unusual ostentation worked: a miracle occurred which restored the population's courage and helped them come to terms with the invader; a commemorative picture was duly set up in the church where the miracle had happened.[47] In much the same way, the citizens of Thessalonica turned to St Demetrius during the sieges of the sixth and seventh centuries and a dream instructed their pastor that they would survive, if only they all shouted 'Kyrie eleison' together.[48] As archbishop John himself explained, the Thessalonians' reliance on supernatural means to obtain victory did not detract from their intelligence or courage, since a Christian was really victorious only when victory was accomplished 'with God'.[49]

The organized supplication of divine aid against barbarian incursions was a lasting feature of life in the Byzantine provinces. In February 601, Pope Gregory I wrote the bishops of Sicily, requiring that they stage compulsory public litanies directed

---

P. Saint-Yves, *Essais de folklore biblique* (Paris, 1923), pp. 185ff, and M. Eliade, *Traité d'histoire des religions* (Paris, 1964), p. 313. On the Roman lustration, G. Wissowa, 'Amburbium', *RE*, 1, 2 (1894), 1816–17, and, in general, W. Pax, 'Bittprozession', *RAC*, 2 (1951), 422–9, and *idem*, 'Circumambulatio', *RAC*, 3 (1955), 143–57.

[46] Joshua Stylite, *Chronicle*, 58, tr. W. Wright (Cambridge, 1882), 48.

[47] Procopius, *Bella*, 2, 11, 16–20, Haury–Wirth 1.200.15–201.8, and Evagrius, *H.e.*, 4, 26, Bidez–Parmentier, 173.1–31. The same mentality was at work in the remarkable sermon by Dometianus at the services honoring the Roman reoccupation of Martyropolis later in the century: Theophylactus Simocattes, *Hist.*, 4, 16, 1–26, De Boor, 183.26–187.20.

[48] The citizens and archbishop prepared for barbarian assault by making a tearful prayer to God; one defender shot a stone with the saint's name written on it, to marvelous effect: *Miracula Demetrii* (BHG, 516z–523), 187, 204–6 and 256; cf. the reference to Demetrius, 'invincible ally' at 216, ed. P. Lemerle, *Les plus anciens recueils des miracles de S. Démétrius et la pénétration des Slaves dans les Balkans*, 1 (Paris, 1979), 177.24–30; 186.33–187.25; 214.33–215.10 and 194.1–2 respectively.

[49] John of Thessalonica, *Miracula Demetrii* (BHG, 499–516), 164–5, ed. Lemerle, 158.6–26.

against the 'incursions of barbarian savagery'.[50] Similar services in
times of military crisis were still being staged in the eternal city in
the eighth and ninth centuries.[51] In the Cibyrraeot theme, on the
southern coast of Asia Minor, fasting and supplications were
regarded as a most effective weapon against Arab attack in the
ninth century.[52] To these local initiatives must be added the long-
standing custom of ordering special services across the empire for
special needs: Licinius and Maurice are supposed to have done so in
response to personal crises, while from the tenth century administrative correspondence survives showing how the imperial
government imposed special prayers on monastic communities
during important expeditions.[53] The chance mention of supplications in historical records affords no sense of how common a
feature they must once have been in the empire's provincial life.
But the fact that this kind of service is foreseen in the appropriate
liturgical repertories provides a strong indication that their
performance was not infrequent.[54] As the empire's cities prayed

[50] JL, 1821, *Reg.*, II, 31, Norberg, 919.2–920.13.
[51] Fasting and litanies organized by Gregory II during Rome's struggle against
Eutychius, *Liber pontificalis*, ed. L. Duchesne, I (Paris, 1886). 406.21–6. Another
instance is probably attested *ibid.*, 442.17–443.1, on which see M. McCormick, 'The
liturgy of war in the early Middle Ages: crisis, litanies and the Carolingian
monarchy', *Viator*, 15 (1984), 1–23, here p. 18. For the ninth-century service, see
below, Ch. 9, n. 115.
[52] *Vita Antonii iunioris* (*BHG*, 142), 15–16, ed. A. Papadopoulos-Kerameus, Συλλογή
παλαιστινῆς καὶ συριακῆς ἁγιολογίας, I, Pravoslavnyi Palestinskii sbornik, 57 (St
Petersburg, 1907), 197.8.
[53] Licinius: Eusebius, *V. Constantini*, I, 57, 3, Winkelmann, 45.5–7 (illness); Maurice:
Theophanes, A.M. 6094, De Boor, 284.21–285.1 (sin). The tenth-century war
services are recorded in the correspondence of Symeon Magistros and Logothete of
the Drome: *Epp.* 83 and 88, ed. J. Darrouzès, *Epistoliers byzantins du Xe siècle*, Archives
de l'Orient chrétien, 6 (Paris, 1960), 146–7 and 149. I owe this last reference to the
kindness of N. Oikonomides. Cf. H. Ahrweiler, 'Un discours inédit de Constantin
VII Porphyrogénète', *TM*, 2 (1967), 393–404, here 395, n. 10.
[54] Thus the list of Gospel readings contained in Vat. pal. lat. 46 (s. ix), which reflects
Roman usage of the seventh century, has texts to be read at services 'In commotione
gentium': ed. T. Klauser, 'Ein vollständiges Evangelienverzeichnis der römischen
Kirche aus dem 7. Jahrhundert, erhalten im Cod. Vat. Pal. lat. 46', *Gesammelte
Arbeiten*, pp. 5–20, here p. 18. For a similar Greek service and prayers whose dates
remain to be determined, see, e.g., Goar, *Euchologion*, 641ff (ἀκολουθία εἰς
ἐπέλευσιν βαρβάρων); the prayer attributed to Macarius of Philadelphia, *ibid.*,
645–6, and the anonymous εὐχὴ ἐπὶ ἐπιδρομῆς βαρβάρων, *ibid.*, 646–7; cf. Sp.
Zerbos, Εὐχολόγιον τὸ μέγα περιέχον τὰς τῶν ἑπτὰ μυστηρίων ἀκολουθίας, 5th edn
(Venice, 1885), 561ff. Another indication in the same direction may well be Justinian,

and fasted to obtain divine aid against attackers, so they thanked the divinity when their prayers were heard and enemies suffered defeat. Since human nature is more prone to ask than to thank, it is probably no accident that the evidence for supplications outweighs that for thanksgiving services. Still, such services were celebrated, possibly at a very early date.[55]

While the bishops of a tottering empire maintained their menaced cities' morale by putting God on their side, the armies of Rome scarcely remained immune to the general population's need for spiritual insurance against defeat. The sanctimonious religious trappings of medieval armies and the notion of crusade are familiar, if paradoxical, aspects of the civilizations which grew out of the later Roman matrix, but the extent to which later institutions and customs derive from the attitudes and superstitious practices of the Christian Roman army has not yet been fully perceived.[56] The research accomplished to date has yielded three basic conclusions regarding the army's liturgical activities. Constantine and Licinius introduced collective monotheistic prayer services staged by and for the army; sooner or later this innovation was matched by the establishment of a regular chaplains' organization for Sunday services.[57] Second, the great crises on the eastern front sparked an intensification of military religious practices in the late sixth and early seventh centuries.[58]

Novella (= *Corpus iuris civilis*, 3), 123, 31–2, Schoell–Kröll, 617.6–28, which forbids litanies celebrated without the approval of the local clergy and involves local military and civilian authorities in repression of disturbances to them.

[55] Maximus' treatment of the theme of thanksgiving for God's benefactions at the end of *Sermo* 72, 3, Mutzenbecher, 302.54–303.79, is not clearly related to the preceding paragraphs. The anonymous *Miracula Demetrii* (*BHG*, 516z–523), 192 describe how, after repulsing a sea attack, the Thessalonians ran to the church of St Demetrius and intoned a hymn of thanksgiving to their hero: Lemerle, 178.30–179.3. Cf. John, *Miracula Demetrii* (*BHG*, 499–516), 161–2, Lemerle, 157.20–158.2, and the litany of thanksgiving organized by Pope Zachary after successful negotiations with the Lombards in 742: *Lib. pont.*, Duchesne, 1.429.5–7.

[56] The best overall treatment remains C. Erdmann, *Die Entstehung des Kreuzzugsgedankens* (Stuttgart, 1935); see too the very useful account of A.M. Koeniger, *Die Militärseelsorge der Karolingerzeit. Ihr Recht und ihr Praxis*, Veröffentlichungen aus dem kirchenhistorischen Seminar München, 4, 7 (Munich, 1918).

[57] Barnes, *Constantine and Eusebius*, p. 48; cf. Koeniger, *Militärseelsorge*, pp. 21–2, n. 2.

[58] P. Goubert, 'Religion et superstitions dans l'armée byzantine à la fin du VIe siècle, *Orientalia christiana periodica*, 13 (1947), 495–500.

Third, the Byzantine armies of the ninth and tenth centuries displayed a preoccupation with religious rituals which is considered typically medieval.[59]

While there seems no question that the Christian trappings of Roman armies increased in the sixth century, their roots go back much farther. It is not, however, easy to distinguish between a commander's personal, private activities and services involving the troops. Eusebius, for instance, reports that the bishops who Constantine had invited on his projected last campaign against the Persians went the emperor one better by enthusiastically promising to fight with him. Their weapons would be prayers of supplication to the Lord. But it is not clear that such supplications would have involved the army, had the expedition actually taken place.[60] Another area in which personal initiatives fostered an early infusion of Christian sacrality into Roman military life was the cult of relics. According to Ambrose of Milan and the fifth-century church historians, Constantine himself had had relics incorporated into his war helmet and his horse's harness.[61] Although the story itself may be legendary, it shows that the army's concern with relics needed explanation just two generations after the great emperor's death. That relics were in fact treasured by campaigning Roman officers follows from the versified jibes Claudian addressed at a superstitious Master of the Cavalry.[62]

The Roman army's participation in highly organized liturgical observances aimed at securing victory can be traced farther back into the sixth century than is commonly believed. Even before the great crises of the late 500s, the armies of Justinian were equipped

---

[59] A. Heisenberg, 'Kriegsgottesdienst in Byzanz', *Aufsätze zur Kultur- und Sprachgeschichte vornehmlich des Orients Ernst Kuhn zum 70. Geburtstage am 7. Februar 1916 gewidmet* (Breslau, 1916), pp. 244–57, and J. Vieillefond, 'Les pratiques religieuses dans l'armée byzantine d'après les traités militaires', *Revue des études anciennes*, 37 (1935), 322–30.

[60] Eusebius, *V. Constantini*, 4, 56, 2–3, Winkelmann, 143.24–144.1. Other possible personal initiatives, *ibid.*, 2, 12, 2, Winkelmann, 53.21–5; Orosius, *Hist.*, 7, 36, 5, Zangemeister, 534.4–9; cf. 7, 36, 8, 535.6–8 and probably Corippus, *Ioh.*, 8, 294–9, Diggle, 176.

[61] Ambrose, *Or. ob. Theod.*, 47–8, Faller, 396.1–397.13; cf. Socrates, *H.e.*, 1, 17, *PG*, 67.120B–C; Sozomen, *H.e.*, 2, 1, 9, Bidez–Hansen, 40.15–20; Gelasius, *H.e.*, 3, 7, 8, Loeschke–Heinemann, 146.24–31.

[62] Claudian, *Opera minora*, 50 (77), Birt, 340; cf. *PLRE*, 2, 581–2, 'Iacobus 1'.

with a well-developed set of spiritual measures for strengthening the troops and winning God's favor and victory.[63] From then on, the army's liturgical preparation for battle and thanksgiving for success appear to have entered into Byzantine military routine. By the turn of the century, the subject was deemed worthy of discussion in an eminently practical handbook for Roman commanders, Maurice's *Strategicon*. This development emphasizes the extent to which the liturgy's growing impact on imperial triumphs was but one facet of a more general trend, by which the sacred extended its sway over various aspects of public life, and particularly that of the military.

What then did a Justinianic army do to ensure its victory? The best account comes from Corippus. It may be somewhat atypical. Since it concerns a battle which occurred on some kind of holy day, the description may place unusual emphasis on the eucharistic element in the army's service.[64] At dawn, the army began to set up a field chapel in the central sector of the camp reserved for officers.[65] In hierarchical order, the officers and troops brought their war standards to the shrine.[66] The participants were divided into choruses and sang 'sweet hymns'. When the commanding officer reached the chapel's threshold, the onlookers began to wail and cry and the assembly broke into a prayer entreating divine forgiveness.[67] The commander got down on his knees and bowed low, weeping and praying:

Look upon the Romans at last, look, O highest God, and succor them, O holy Father, and with your power, I beseech you, smash the proud

[63] In addition to the evidence cited in the following notes, Procopius' presentation of commanders' exhortations to their troops before combat suggests that, as early as the 530s, measures were taken to propitiate God by both the Romans and their Arian adversaries: e.g. Procopius, *Bella*, 4, 1, 20, Haury–Wirth, 1.442.21–3; 4, 3, 32, 1.428.4–9; cf. *Bella* 3, 19, 11, 1.393.1–3 and 8, 30, 1–2, 2.647.25–648.3. Narses' efforts to propitiate God and the Virgin before battle were already legendary after half a century: Evagrius, *H.e.*, 4, 24, Bidez–Parmentier, 171.13–18, and their memory was still alive in Italy 200 years later: Paul Deacon, *Hist. Lang.*, 2, 3, Bethmann–Waitz, 74.1–2.
[64] Sunday or some other feast day: Corippus, *Ioh.*, 8, 213–4, Diggle, 173; cf. 8, 254–5, Diggle, 174.
[65] *Ibid.*, 8, 318–21; 324–8, Diggle, 177. [66] *Ibid.*, 321–3, Diggle, 177.
[67] *Ibid.*, 328–36, Diggle, 177–8.

pagans. Let the peoples recognize you alone as Lord and powerful, while you crush the enemy and save your own kind by battle![68]

Officers and troops alike joined in the tearful supplications. The priest offered communion on behalf of the Romans and blessed the commander. The eucharist was pleasing to God: it sanctified and purified the Roman race before their battle with the barbarians.[69] The pre-battle service took place in a penitential atmosphere; officers organized the supplications of victory for the sanctification of the troops and their standards; communion was distributed. The general picture finds support in the better known testimony of Maurice's military handbook. There too the prayers before battle are celebrated in camp, where the army's priests, commander and officers take the lead in performing the Roman army's litany of supplication, 'Kyrie eleison'. As each unit moves off to combat behind their newly blessed standards, they sing out the battle chant 'Nobiscum Deus' three times. Only Corippus' eucharistic element is lacking.[70]

As the empire's military fortunes sank in the late sixth century, Roman commanders sought out new and more potent relics for their armies and rumors of the victory-producing relics discovered in the East spread to the West. Although no early liturgical manuscripts have come to light documenting in detail the army's *profectio bellica* ceremony of the late sixth or seventh century, it must have looked like the ancestor it was of the ceremony reported by Leo the Deacon, to which we will return shortly. The army and the emperor marched behind the imperial battle standard, a gilded war cross containing a relic of the true cross.[71] The old standbys were reinforced by the newer cult of sacred images. Thus emperor Maurice's brother-in-law seized

[68] *Ibid.*, 348–52, Diggle, 178: 'respice iam tandem Romanos, respice, summe,/ atque pius succurre, pater, gentesque superbas/ frange, precor, uirtute tua: dominumque potentem/ te solum agnoscant populi, dum conteris hostes/ et saluas per bella tuos'.
[69] *Ibid.*, 357–69, Diggle, 179; the account is interrupted by a lacuna.
[70] Mauricius, *Strategicon*, 2, 18, 2, ed. G.T. Dennis, *CFHB*, 17 (Vienna, 1981). 138.13–140.21; cf. 7, B, 16, Dennis, 260.8–10. On the blessing of standards 7A, 1, 232.1–4. Cf., too, 8, 2, 1, 278.2–4, on the confidence instilled by such measures.
[71] Theophylactus Simocattes, *Hist.*, 5, 16, 11, De Boor, 220.1–3; cf. Frolow, *Relique*, p. 183. Maurice sought relics for the well-being of the army: John, *Miracula Demetrii*, 51, Lemerle, 89.11–14, as did Philippicus, his brother-in-law: Evagrius, *H.e.*, 1, 13, Bidez–Parmentier, 23.12–16. For rumors of victory relics, see Introduc-

upon the developing devotion to icons to bolster the confidence of an army campaigning against the Persians, and Heraclius followed suit.[72] Mango's suggestion that the rejection of icons in the eighth century was connected with the cult of military success fits well with this evidence. In the post-iconoclastic period, the Byzantine army painted saints' portraits on their shields and a tenth-century emperor could ride into battle clutching an icon of the Virgin.[73]

Religious observances helped structure other key moments in the life of the later Roman army, for instance when it set out against the enemy or initiated a new phase of operations.[74] Heraclius may have been mindful of the disastrous consequences of a predecessor's order that the army winter at the front when he commanded that the field army be 'purified' (ἀγνίζειν) for three days, presumably through fasts and prayers, before he discovered divine advice that the troops should winter in Albania.[75] The army of Italy's official seal proclaimed its need for divine assistance.[76] And a ninth-century Neapolitan source mentions the blessing performed on Byzantine troops of the eighth century.[77]

The later Roman army's liturgical practices set the tone for the armed forces of medieval Constantinople. While the content is similar, the services themselves appear to have grown more

tion. On the veneration of the cross by the Byzantine army, see N. Thierry, 'Le culte de la croix dans l'empire byzantin du VIIᶜ siècle au Xᶜ dans ses rapports avec la guerre contre l'infidèle. Nouveaux témoignages archéologiques', *Rivista di studi bizantini e slavi* (= *Miscellanea Agostino Pertusi*), 1 (1980), 205–28.

[72] Theophylactus Simocattes, *Hist.*, 2, 3, 4–8, De Boor, 73.24–74.17. Cf. Theophanes, A.M. 6078, De Boor, 255.13–19, George Pisides, *Expeditio persica*, 1, 139–51, Pertusi, 91; cf. *ibid.*, 2, 85–7, Pertusi, 101, and his *Heraclias*, 1, 218, Pertusi, 250.

[73] C. Mango, 'Historical Introduction', *Iconoclasm*, ed. A. Bryer and J. Herrin (Birmingham, 1977), pp. 1–6, here 2–3. Cf. W.E. Kaegi, Jr, 'The Byzantine armies and iconoclasm', *BS*, 27 (1966), 48–70, on the complexity of military attitudes, and Thierry, 'Culte', pp. 226–8. Portrait of St John on the shields of Petronas' army: Theoph. Cont., 4, 25, Bonn, 180.21–181.2. On Basil II's use of an icon in battle, above, Ch. 4, p. 178, n. 187.

[74] E.g. Theophylactus Simocattes, *Hist.*, 5, 16, 7, De Boor, 217.7–11.

[75] Theophanes, A.M. 6114, De Boor, 308.12–17. For the meaning of ἀγνίζειν here, see below, n. 82.

[76] G. Zacos and A. Veglery, *Byzantine Lead Seals*, 1, 1 (Basel, 1972), 583–4, no. 807: 'Deus adiuta/ exerchitus Italiae'.

[77] *Gesta episcoporum Neapolitanorum*, 36, ed. G. Waitz, MGH. SRL (1878), 421.44–422.3.

extensive and frequent.[78] Ninth-century armies were supposed to perform litanies on the eve of battle.[79] Leo the Deacon offers an allusive description of a *profectio bellica* by Tzimisces. The emperor 'raised the cross-standard', prayed for divine favor at the Chalke shrine and continued to the Hagia Sophia, where he beseeched God to send an angel of victory 'who would walk in front of the army and straighten its path'. Then the emperor participated in a liturgical procession to the Blachernae shrine and the final service.[80] A campaigning army's activities in the tenth century included nightly hymns, litanies, and up to one hundred kyries. Failure to perform this duty was to be treated harshly and unrepentant shirkers were beaten, demoted and subjected to the parade of infamy with shaven head.[81] Paradoxical though it seems from a purely military perspective, the army was supposed to celebrate a three-day fast culminating in communion just before battle.[82] The tradition of blessing the standards and performing litanies before engaging the enemy remained in honor into the middle Byzantine era, and a tenth-century emperor's communication to the troops refers to the new power they will enjoy thanks to the archsacred relics he has dispatched to sanctify the army.[83] To precisely this period has been assigned one of the rare texts of a battle service which has come to light.[84]

[78] Vieillefond, 'Pratiques religieuses', p. 324.

[79] Leo VI, *Tactica*, 14, 1, ed. R. Vári, 2.1 (Budapest, 1922).126–7.

[80] Leo Deacon, *Hist.*, 8, 1, Bonn, 128.1–129.8. Cf. the very similar language of Visigothic and Frankish *profectio bellica* services, discussed below, Chs. 8 and 9. On the angel of victory, Kantorowicz, 'King's Advent', pp. 55–6.

[81] Nicephorus, *Praecepta militaria*, ed. Yu. A. Kulakovsky, *Strategika imperatora Nikifora*, Zapiski imperatorskoy akademii nauk, ser. 8, po istor.-filol. otdeleniyu, 8, 9 (St Petersburg, 1908), 20.22–21.3. On the author: A. Dain, 'Les stratégistes byzantins', *TM*, 2 (1967), 317–92, here 370.

[82] Nicephorus, *Praec. mil.*, Kulakovsky, 21.4–17, explaining the means by which the army is 'purified'.

[83] Cf. the military treatise known as Παρεκβολαί, 44, 36, ed. J.A. de Foucault, *Strategemata* (Paris, 1949), 114. For the dispatch of relics from the capital to the troops, see Constantine VII, *Contio ad duces exercitus orientalis*, 8, ed. R. Vári, 'Zum historischen Exzerptenwerk des Konstantinos Porphyrogennetos', *BZ*, 17 (1908), 75–85, here 83.20–31. Note that among the 'symbols of Christ's passion' sent to the army, the emperor refers to 'the god-bearing shroud (τῆς θεοφόρου σινδόνος)'. This unnoticed reference should be added to the dossier of the shroud of Turin controversy.

[84] A. Pertusi, 'Una acolouthia militare inedita del X secolo', *Aevum*, 22 (1948), 145–68, here 148–9 for date.

Byzantine commanders were certainly alive to the positive impact of such services on their troops' morale, but we would be victims of our modern mentality if we left at that the explanation of this development.[85] Thanks to the antique and medieval conviction that God intervened continuously, directly and explicably in human affairs, the ethical and theological purity of an army were usually considered no less essential to success than its professional competence and size, a view which was only comforted by the Bible (e.g., 2 Chronicles 14; Psalm 117). As early as Eusebius, Christians stressed the ruler's efforts to ensure the moral purity of victorious armies.[86] Beyond the imminence of violent death and the notion that war resulted from sin, this assumption of the moral underpinnings of victory elucidates the penitential atmosphere which dominates the army's pre-combat services as well as the notion that fasting was a useful preparation for battle. This explains Heraclius' insistence that his troops refrain from evil.[87] A century later, Leo III's *Ecloga* expressly stated that:

Those who go out to war against the enemy must protect themselves from every evil word and deed and keep their mind on God alone.... For 'it is not on the size of the army that victory in battle depends, but strength comes from God'.[88]

The attitude was quite widespread. Narses halted an imminent engagement with the Franks and Alamannians because a Herul auxiliary had murdered one of his servants and the Roman general considered it impious to fight before expiating that miasma, even at the risk of sowing discord in his own ranks.[89] As an imperial

---

[85] E.g. Nicephorus, *Praec. mil.*, Kulakovsky, 21.16–17.

[86] *V. Constantini*, 1, 8, 2, Winkelmann, 18.16–17.

[87] Theophanes, A.M. 6113, De Boor, 304.11–13; cf. Pisides, *Exp. pers.*, 2, 191–205, Pertusi, 106–7.

[88] Leo III, *Ecloga* 18, 1, ed. L. Burgmann, Forschungen zur byzantinischen Rechtsgeschichte, 10 (Frankfurt, 1983), 244.946–50: Τοὺς ἐξερχομένους εἰς ἐχθροὺς ἐπὶ πολέμῳ φυλάξαι δεῖ ἑαυτοὺς ἀπὸ παντὸς πονηροῦ ῥήματος καὶ πράγματος καὶ πρὸς μόνον τὸν Θεὸν τὸν νοῦν αὐτῶν ἔχειν... οὐκ ἐν πλήθει γὰρ δυνάμεως νίκη πολέμου, ἀλλ᾽ ἐκ Θεοῦ ἡ ἰσχύς.

[89] Agathias, *Hist.*, 2, 7, 2–5, Keydell, 49.6–26. By the same token, the Roman army's defeat by the Persians could be ascribed to the murder of Gubazes: *ibid.*, 3, 8, 2, Keydell, 92.34–93.4; cf. the reference put in the mouth of another leader of the Lazi: 3, 10, 2, 95.19–23. The same attitude is evident in the way Theophanes interprets a Roman commander's orders to his troops not to disturb farmers' labors: Theo-

subject in Italy noted, since God was on the side of the just, heavy casualties in the Roman army could only be attributed to its sins.[90] A soldier on the disastrous campaign of 811 resisted a rich woman's bedroom eyes, since yielding would have been a sin even if he weren't on the razor's edge because of the expedition, 'justice' being 'the arms of war'.[91] By the same token, St Elias the Younger's suggestions for improving the moral deportment of Byzantine sailors were credited with victory over the Arabs early in the tenth century.[92] The military handbooks prove that this attitude was not a hagiographer's peculiarity.[93]

When sanctified armies prepared for combat against 'infidel' troops by staging litanies, fasting and communicating, it was perhaps only another step to conclude that death in battle was a special kind of religious sacrifice or even a form of martyrdom. Nicephorus Phocas' unsuccessful efforts to win martyrs' honors for his dead warriors is not infrequently cited as proof that the Byzantine church opposed such notions. While this may be true, it is often forgotten that the information derives from a very hostile source and that the attitudes of the church's leading figures were not necessarily those of society at large.[94] As a matter of fact, the idea that death in battle against the infidel brought with it eternal life was not a new one in Byzantium. Heraclius himself is supposed to have exhorted his troops with that very promise.[95] The same soldiers to whom Phocas promised martyrdom may well have heard similar words from Constantine VII only a few years

---

phanes, A.M. 6078, De Boor, 255.7–10, on the basis of Theophylactus Simocattes, *Hist.*, 2, 2, 5, De Boor, 72.18–20.

[90] *Lib. pont.*, Mommsen, 183.18–21.

[91] *Vita Nicolai Studitae* (*BHG*, 1365), *PG*, 105.893D–896A.

[92] *Vita S. Elias iunioris* (*BHG*, 580), 43, Rossi Taibbi, 64.866–66.900

[93] Leo VI, *Tactica*, 14, 1, Vári 2.1.126; Nicephorus, *Praec. mil.*, Kulakovsky, 21.7–13.

[94] Scylitzes, *Nicephorus II*, 18, Thurn, 274.62–5, in the list of Nicephorus' evil deeds. On the Orthodox tradition's deeply rooted antagonism to the notion of a 'holy war', see V. Laurent, 'L'idée de guerre sainte et la tradition byzantine', *Revue historique du Sud-Est européen*, 23 (1946), 71–98.

[95] Theophanes, A.M. 6114, De Boor, 307.11–12: οὐκ ἔστιν ἄμισθος ὁ κίνδυνος, ἀλλ᾿ αἰωνίου ζωῆς πρόξενος. Cf. another speech reported *ibid.*, A.M. 6115, De Boor, 310.26–311.2: θύσωμεν οὖν τῷ θεῷ ἑαυτοὺς ὑπὲρ τῆς τῶν ἀδελφῶν ἡμῶν σωτηρίας, λάβωμεν στέφος μαρτύρων, ἵνα καὶ ὁ μέλλων ἡμᾶς χρόνος ἐπαινέσῃ καὶ ὁ θεὸς τοὺς μισθοὺς ἀποδώσῃ.

before.[96] Even the church's attitude was not devoid of ambiguity. The liturgy of tenth-century Constantinople continued to commemorate the casualties from the disastrous Bulgarian campaign of 811, although it is fair to add that the commemoration notice explains that some of the troops refused to abjure Christianity before their deaths.[97]

As elsewhere, the army's thanksgiving services after battle are referred to less frequently than its supplication rites. Constantine I is supposed to have thanked the Christian God for his success on the spot and Roman commanders are depicted in a similar light in the sixth century.[98] The army's participation in post-combat services is explicitly attested under Heraclius.[99] A ninth-century emperor recommended that thanksgiving be the first item on the army's agenda after a successful engagement. Only then should the commander reward outstanding soldiers and punish bad ones.[100] By the time the 'Military Instructions' were composed, hymn-singing services after a successful engagement were so deeply embedded in the Byzantine army's routine that a military theorist could stress their secondary value as a means of preventing victorious troops from headlong pursuit of retreating enemies and potential ambush.[101]

3. LITTLE CAESARS

Because the pioneering studies of Alföldi and Kantorowicz on ancient and medieval rituals of government concentrated on the monarchy, subsequent work has by and large neglected the significant hoopla which attended the public acts of lesser

---

[96] The emperor vowed to kiss their bodies, wounded for Christ, 'like martyrs' members' (ὡς μαρτυρικὰ μέλη), in the *Contio ad duces*, 8, Vári 83.17.

[97] *Syn. Cplitanum*, 26 July, no. 10, Delehaye, 846.4–848.9.

[98] Eusebius, *V. Constantini*, 1, 39, 3, Winkelmann, 36.8–11; cf. Procopius, *Bella*, 8, 33, 1, Haury 2.661.20–4 and Corippus, *Ioh.*, 1, 99–109, Diggle, 7.

[99] Pisides, *Exp. pers.*, 3, 276–80, Pertusi, 128; cf. Theophanes, A.M. 6113, De Boor, 306.1–5 and the thanksgiving services for the Virgin's help in victory at Bebdarch: *ibid.*, A.M. 6118, 321.22–5.

[100] Leo VI, *Tactica*, 16, 2, PG, 107.90B.

[101] Στρατηγικὰ παραγγέλματα, 47, de Foucault, 118. For the actual performance of such services see, e.g., Tzimisces' victory over the Russians, Scylitzes, Thurn, 300.65–7.

officials.[102] In fact, flamboyant symbolic gestures permeated all levels of these societies: imperial rituals were but the apex of a ceremonial pyramid which extended down to the lower classes.[103] In the provinces as in the capital, prominent and not so prominent officials reveled and quibbled over their ritual perquisites. All eyes were bracketed on the emperor in this society, and the throne's public rituals served as the standard by which lesser magistrates' ceremonies were measured and modeled. As a late antique observer noted, every Roman official was an emperor in miniature and the impact of the ruler's custom could be felt in very different spheres.[104] Thus the patriarch of Constantinople had an assistant whose title of *kastresios* bore inappropriate military connotations, while a seventh-century Greek confraternity adopted the Latin technical vocabulary of imperial ritual for devotions to their patron saint.[105]

The movements of government officials through their cities reflected contemporary aristocratic values and reminded the public of their exalted status, as embodied in the size of their official or unofficial escort of retainers, subordinates, bodyguards and assorted hangers on.[106] This kind of informal parade survived

---

[102] One exception is J.H.W.G. Liebeschuetz, *Antioch. City and imperial Administration in the later Roman empire* (Oxford, 1972), pp. 208ff.

[103] See M. McCormick, 'Analyzing imperial ceremonies' *JÖB*, 35 (1985), 1–20.

[104] Themistius, *Or.* 8, Schenkl–Downey 1.176.24–177.2; cf. Claudian, *IV cons.*, 299–300, Birt, 161: 'componitur orbis/Regis ad exemplum'.

[105] On the *kastresios*, see V. Laurent, *Le corpus des sceaux de l'empire byzantin*, 5, 1 (Paris, 1963), 103–4; on the derivation from the emperor's *comes castrensis*, H.G. Beck, *Kirche und theologische Literatur im byzantinischen Reich*, Handbuch der Altertumswissenschaft, 12, 2, 1 (Munich, 1959), p. 118; for the borrowing of ὀψικεύω, see *Miracula Artemii* (*BHG*, 173), 18, Papadopoulos-Kerameus, 21.6.

[106] In 411, Synesius of Cyrene refers to a parade (πομπή) of Anysius, dux Libyarum: *Ep.* 77, ed. A. Garzya (Rome, 1979), 136.2–3; *PLRE*, 2, 108, 'Anysius 1'. According to Procopius, an official's escort customarily bore no weapons other than swords when they were in town: *Bella*, 4, 28, 8, Haury–Wirth 1.546.9–11. Ps.-Chrysostom, *Comparatio regis et monachi* (*CPG*, 4500), *PG*, 47.387 recognized the impact on the public of officials' glittering escorts replete with splendid vehicles, heralds and guards. Great dignitaries would forgo the honors of escort as an ostentatious sign of humility. Thus the governor of Egypt Nicetas when he went to make apologies to the patriarch of Alexandria: Leontius Neapolitanus, *Vita Ioannis Eleemosynarii* (*BHG*, 886), 12, ed. H. Gelzer (Freiburg, 1893), 25.4–8. John Vincomalus, monk and retired Master of the Offices, used to return from visits to the palace escorted–up to his monastery's door–by the pomp befitting his station. Once inside the monastery, he changed into monastic garb and went about his humble duties in

through the crises of the seventh and eighth centuries and flourished in the aristocratic milieux of medieval Constantinople.[107] Like
their uniforms and insignia, the highest officials' vehicles were
distinctive of their particular function and subject to imperial
sanction.[108] Admission to the audiences of provincial officials was
broken down into precisely graduated series reminiscent of the
imperial court's *vela* or entrées; they could even be codified in
charter-like form.[109] The appearance of a high official triggered
elaborate symbolic gestures of greeting and obeisance like genuflec-
tion while favored suppliants were allowed to kiss his hand.[110] Just
as for the emperors themselves, local elites marked the arrivals and
departures of V.I.P.s with elaborate ceremonies of welcome and
farewell, provincial renditions of the imperial *adventus* and *profectio*
rites, the ritual content of which could be finely shaded to express the
precise degree of awe and fear appropriate to different ranks.[111]

---

the kitchen or stable: Theodorus Lector, *H.e.*, 387, Hansen, 109.7–12. Showy
retinues of sycophants were avidly assembled by wealthy citizens: Chrysostom,
Homilia in Kalendas, 3, *PG*, 48.957.

[107] Thus the high official and lord father of the anonymous author of *V. Theophano*, 26,
Kurtz, 18.20–1, is depicted returning home after a day at the office, accompanied by
his 'customary procession' (μετὰ τῆς συνήθους προελεύσεως αὐτοῦ) around 900.
Cf. e.g. Theoph. Cont., 5, 9, Bonn, 225.1–7, on an aristocrat's efforts to build up his
retinue and, in general, the insightful essay of H.G. Beck, *Byzantinische Gefolg-
schaftswesen*, Bayerische Akademie der Wissenschaften, philos.-hist. Kl., Sitzungsberichte (1965), 5.

[108] E.g. Dagron, *Naissance*, p. 269; *Cod. Theod.*, 14, 12 (*Cod. Iust.* 11, 20),
Mommsen–Krüger, 789; Themistius, *Or.* 31, Schenkl–Downey–Norman,
2.189.22–4; Synesius of Cyrene, *Ep.* 127, Garzya, 218.5–6, etc. On the illustrations
of insignia, P.C. Berger, *The insignia of the 'Notitia Dignitatum'* (New York, 1981).
Insignia of provincial authorities seem to have become more impressive with time.
Thus a ninth-century *ek prosopou* of the Cibyrraeot theme wore a uniform, a 'tiara'
and carried a staff: *V. Ant. iun.*, 18, Papadopoulos-Kerameus, 199.17–21.

[109] Thus the fourth-century *ordo salutationis* for audiences of the *consularis* of Numidia,
A. Chastagnol, *L'Album municipal de Timgad*, Antiquitas, 3, 22(Bonn, 1972), 75–81.

[110] Hand or foot-kissing of officials: Claudian, *Ruf. II*, 442–5, Birt, 50; Corippus, *Ioh.*,
4, 309–11, Diggle, 78; 7, 234–5, Diggle, 153. In medieval Constantinople, it was
customary to genuflect before high officials: Gregory, *Vita Basilii iunioris* (*BHG*,
263), 3, *AASS*, Mart. 3 (1865). 20*D. Hand-kissing was carried over to Christian
bishops, e.g. Paulinus, *V. Ambrosii*, 4, Pellegrino, 54.4–56.6; cf. *ibid.*, 9, 62.14–16
and 64.5–6.

[111] Liebeschuetz, *Antioch*, pp. 208–9. Julian tried to regulate the participation of pagan
priests in local *adventus* of officials: *Ep.* 84 (49), Bidez, 1.2, 2nd edn (Paris, 1960).
146.12–20. Cf. Libanius on his own conduct: *Or.*, 2, 7, Foerster, 1.241.7–12. For

Like their imperial counterparts, these provincial rituals occasioned panegyrics and acclamations.[112] The field army also used similar ceremonies to honor the arrival or departure of ranking officers.[113]

An earlier chapter has shown how, in the new capital of Constantinople, high officials managed to arrogate temporarily some elements of the prestigious imperial triumph ceremony. One wonders whether, despite the imperial monopoly of victory, the *imitatio imperii* was pursued on this level and in this manner, far from the watchful – and jealous – eyes of the court and monarch. Although the evidence is far from plentiful, there is enough of it to provide a clear yes and not a few ceremonial details.

In 373, Flavius Theodosius, Master of the Cavalry and father of the later emperor of the same name, was sent to Africa to suppress a usurpation undertaken by the Moor Firmus. Theodosius marked his victory by staging a ceremony which looks very much like a triumphal entry into the Mauretanian city of Sitifis, his headquarters, to the applause and acclamations of the various orders of

---

adventus and *profectio* of various officials: Joshua Stylite, *Chronicle*, 100, tr. Wright 75–6 (A.D. 506), and, in the early seventh century: Theophylactus Simocattes, *Hist.*, 7, 2, 17–19, De Boor, 249.8–20 and 7, 3, 3–4, 249.27–250.5; John of Nikiu, 97, 8, tr. Charles, 158. Such ceremonies continued to be observed in later years. Thus the absence of the customary rituals at the customary spot is cited as proof that an exarch came to Rome surreptitiously: *Lib. pont.*, Mommsen, 211.7–9, while the ceremonial for the exarch served as the model for Charlemagne's *adventus* in 774: *Lib. pont.*, Duchesne, 1.497.4–5; cf. the arrival of the *monostrategos* at Ravenna, Agnellus, *Lib. pont. Rav.*, 137, Holder-Egger, 368.6–11. For the customary *adventus* of a ninth-century governor of the Cibyrraeot theme, *V. Ant. iun.*, 10, Papadopoulos-Kerameus, 193.25–31. The final point is nicely illustrated by Gregory of Nyssa's use of social rank differentiations as expressed in the τιμαί of dignitaries to elucidate honors rendered to the Father and Son: *Contra Eunomium*, I, 333, ed. W. Jaeger, *Opera*, I, 2nd edn (Leyden, 1960), 125.26–126.7.

[112] Acclamations: Liebeschuetz, *Antioch*, pp. 209ff. Some fragmentary examples of occasional poetry for local officials survive in the papyri: Heitsch, *Dichterfragmente*, 120–4, no. 36 (a s.v *profectio* of the *dux Thebaidos*?) and the collection of Dioscorus' panegyrics on local officials for various occasions, *ibid.*, 129–47, nos. 42.2–22. Dioscorus' constant recycling of his poems suggests just how banal such occasions were.

[113] For instance, new commanders of the late sixth century were customarily welcomed by their officers and troops three miles from camp. They were expected to dismount and walk between the ranks, displaying their good will: Theophylactus Simocattes, *Hist.*, 3, 1, 6–7, De Boor, 110.28–111.8. The army might also stage an *occursus* for a Roman client ruler: Agathias, *Hist.*, 3, 15, 3, Keydell, 103.21–5.

citizens.[114] Shortly thereafter, the victorious general was executed in murky circumstances.[115]

The senior Theodosius' victory celebration was not an isolated incident in late Roman provincial life. Between 368 and 377, Flavius Saturninus appears to have held some kind of celebrations at Seleucia. They honored the general's success against Isaurian bandits.[116] A little later, Synesius of Cyrene expected that the commander of his region's Roman forces would someday celebrate the triumphal parade for a Libyan victory and on that occasion, he hoped, the officer would ride the horse Synesius had given him.[117] The successful field operations of Justinian's era have left a few traces of triumphal celebrations mounted by local commanders returning to their headquarters. Solomon celebrated a triumphal entry into Carthage in 534 and a like ceremony was staged by John about a decade and a half later.[118] Narses did as

114 Ammianus Marcellinus, 29, 5, 56, Clark, 519.2–3: '... Sitifim triumphanti similis redit, aetatum ordinumque omnium celebrabili fauore susceptus'. Cf. too the following n. On Sitifis in this period and its use as Theodosius' headquarters, C. Lepelley, *Les cités de l'Afrique romaine au Bas-Empire*, 2 (Paris, 1981), 497ff and 502–3, n. 25. On Theodosius, *PLRE*, 1, 902–4, 'Theodosius 3'.

115 See A. Demandt, 'Der Tod des älteren Theodosius', *Historia*, 18 (1969), 598–625, and A. Lippold, 'Kaiser Theodosius d. Gr. und sein Vater', *Rivista di storia dell' Antichità*, 2 (1972), 196–200. It is not impossible that Theodosius' self-decreed honor may have played a role in the accusations against him, whence Ammianus' ginger wording and, perhaps, Ambrose's striking description: *Or. ob. Theod.*, 53, Faller, 399.5–6: '... qui *patrem* eius *triumphatorem occiderant*'.

116 This is suggested by the fifth-century *Miracula Theclae (BHG*, 1718), 28, ed. G. Dagron, Subsidia hagiographica, 62 (Brussels, 1975), 364.34–40; on the date, *ibid.*, pp. 116–18.

117 *Ep.*, 37 (40), Garzya 49.4–5: '... καὶ ὅταν κατάγῃς ἐπὶ τῷ Λιβυκῷ τροπαίῳ πομπὴν ἐπινίκιον; cf. 49.6. *PLRE*, 2, 1186, 'Uranius 1' suggests that this individual may not have been the dux Libyarum at all, but an otherwise unknown landowner and that the allusion to a victory parade is but a joke. This is quite hypothetical and, as these pages make clear, there is no need to explain away a non-imperial victory celebration at that time and place.

118 Procopius, *Bella*, 4, 12, 56, Haury 1.470.13–15: οὕτω τε Ῥωμαῖοι μὲν ξὺν πάσῃ τῇ λείᾳ ἐς Καρχηδόνα ᾔεσαν, τὴν ἐπινίκιον ἑορτὴν ἄγοντες. On the date and circumstances, A. Nagl, 'Solomon', *RE*, 2, 5 (1927), 941–6, here 942; Schmidt, *Wandalen*, p. 145. Cf. the Roman army's entry with booty and the captive Esdilasa after the second victory over the Moors, which, even if it is not so unambiguously described, must have been of the same order: Procopius, *Bella*, 4, 12, 29, Haury, 1.475.7–8. Corippus' *Ioh.* originally may have contained three descriptions of provincial triumphs (cf. *Ioh.*, 1, 6–7, Diggle, 3); 6, 56–103, Diggle, 115–17; a second triumphal entry with Carcasan's head high on a pole (the Moor's misunderstanding

much at Rome around the same time. Clearly the triumphal entry into local headquarters was prized by Roman commanders of the sixth century. A further variation consisted in the solemn entries of generals into newly conquered towns, attested for Belisarius at Syracuse.[119]

The somber years of the Arab invasion did not snuff out local victory celebrations. A Sardinian commander's dispatch of the 'symbols of victory' to the capital, commemorated by a triumphal inscription assigned to the seventh century, must have been connected with some kind of victory celebration at a late antique building in Porto Torres.[120] In 641, the exarch Isaac staged the ancient parade of a defeated rebel's head into Ravenna and had it set up in the circus.[121] In the eighth century, the city revolted against the central government and defeated the *monostrategus* sent against it by Constantinople. The successful Ravennate forces were not inventing a new ceremony when they marked their victory by celebrating a litanic procession through the city's streets to the church of Saints John and Paul, on whose feast day the battle had occurred. In typical late antique fashion, the streets were decked out with expensive hangings for the occasion.[122] Local

of an oracle, in a scene swiped from Claudian), 6, 167–76, Diggle, 119 (cf. the fulfillment, 6, 184–7, Diggle, 120) and the future triumph referred to near the poem's mutilated end, 8, 502–3, Diggle, 184.

[119] Agathias, *Hist.*, 2, 10, 7, Keydell, 54.15–17; cf. 2, 11, 1, 55.6–9, and A. Lippold, 'Narses', *RE*, S.12 (1970), 870–89; here 884. Another such entry may lurk behind the verbiage of Theophylactus Simocattes, *Hist.*, 1, 7, 6, De Boor, 53.7–11, on Commentiolus' victory over the Slavs near Adrianople. Belisarius at Carthage and Syracuse: Procopius, *Bella*, 3, 20, 1, Haury, 1.396.11–19, 21, 399.5–22 and 5, 5, 18, 2.27.19–24.

[120] Ed. A. Taramelli, *Notizie degli scavi* (1928), 256–9; cf. *Notizie degli scavi* (1931), 111–14: A. Solmi, 'L'iscrizione greca di Porto Torres del secolo VII', *Studi di storia e diritto in onore di Enrico Besta per il XL anno del suo insegnamento*, 4 (Milan, 1939), 337–49, and S. Mazzarino, 'Su un'iscrizione trionfale di Turris Libisonis', *Epigraphica*, 2 (1940), 292–313; cf. L. Durliat, 'La lettre L dans les inscriptions de l'Afrique byzantine', *Byz.*, 49 (1979), 156–74, here 158; generally assigned to Constans II or Constantine IV. The introductory formula Νικᾷ ἡ τύχη τοῦ βασιλέως καὶ τῶν Ῥωμαίων echoes a form traditional in both imperial and circus acclamations: *De cer.*, 1, 92, Bonn, 425.10–11 (coronation of Anastasius I), or the opening of Constantine V's address in the Hippodrome: Stephen, *V. Steph. iun.*, *PG*, 100.1137A. Cf. Cameron, *Porphyrius*, pp. 76–9.

[121] *Lib. pont.*, Mommsen, 178.17–179.7. For the date, Classen, 'Römerzug', p. 342. Purely provincial display of the defeated enemy's head was no seventh-century innovation: cf. Marc. Comes, *Chron.*, a. 497, Mommsen, 95.1–2.

[122] Agnellus, *Lib. pont. Rav.*, 153, Holder-Egger 337.19–22.

victory celebrations continued to be staged under the Macedonian dynasty. Philetus Synadenus once expressed his regret that he could not participate in the welcome ceremony for the victorious general Nicephorus Uranus and, half a world away, Byzantine Bari witnessed a captured rebel's parade of infamy.[123]

What did these provincial triumphs look like? The only detailed description comes from Byzantine Africa. It suggests that the provincial ceremony was very much a miniature version of the old fourth-century triumphal entry, decked out with Christian elements. The fully armed troops and their victorious commander entered the local capital in parade. They were greeted by citizens waving palm and laurel branches, acclaiming the emperor.[124] The parade included captives with 'inscripta fronte', some kind of accusatory *tituli* which recall the facial markings of the vanquished Armeniakon rebels of 793.[125] The prisoners were placed on camels; they might be overshadowed by the display of a defeated leader's head, raised high on the traditional lance.[126] The parade culminated at a church. While the prisoners were displayed to the populace, the commander entered the sanctuary, escorted by the army's standards. Here a public thanksgiving offering might be made for God's just decision in favor of Roman arms, and a service concluded the celebration.[127]

CONCLUSION

The study of governmental rituals in the provinces adds another dimension to the historical development of imperial ceremonial in late antiquity and the early Middle Ages. On one hand, the local echo of imperial victories which the provinces had contributed

---

[123] Ed. J. Darrouzès, *Épistoliers*, 256.12–14; Lupus Protospatharius, *Annales*, a. 1021, ed. G.H. Pertz, *MGH.SS*, 5 (1844).57.23–4.

[124] Corippus, *Ioh.*, 6, 56–76, Diggle, 115–16.

[125] *Ibid.*, 77–96, Diggle, 116. Cf. above, Ch. 4, p. 142.

[126] Corippus, *Ioh.*, 77–96, Diggle, 116; cf. 6, 169–76, Diggle, 119, and 184–7, Diggle, 120.

[127] *Ibid.*, 6, 97–103, Diggle, 116–17. Victory offerings in a provincial context seem to be attested as early as Saturninus: *Miracula Theclae*, 28, Dagron, 363.37–40. They too flourished in the Middle Ages, e.g. the gift of Nasar Basileios to the church of Methone after his defeat of an Arab fleet in 881: Theoph. Cont., 5, 63, Bonn, 304.12–15.

since the days of Augustus did not cease in late antiquity. On the other, there can be no doubt that, within their own jurisdictions, local commanders imitated imperial victory celebrations. Both of these phenomena constituted a significant part of imperial ceremonial's overall impact on late Roman society. For the medieval future, the church's role was heavy with consequence, since its contribution was both constant and enduring. Throughout the empire, prayers for the Roman emperor and his victory were offered on a regular basis and came to be considered a touchstone of a territory's political identity.[128] This fact should not be overlooked when one considers the vigor and even vehemence with which emperors intervened in the theological disputes of the fifth through ninth centuries. In times of crisis, local ecclesiastical instances organized emergency services to obtain divine aid. The local services set a precedent which the capital itself would follow and develop in the great siege ceremonies of the seventh century. The Roman army followed society at large by adapting similar practices to its own needs and fashioning a kind of Christian spirituality of war, thereby anticipating the religious trappings of the feudal armies of medieval Europe. At the same time that these considerations help identify the impact of imperial rites within the empire, they suggest that the channels by which the empire's *Staatssymbolik* influenced the new entities growing up in its margins were quite a bit wider than sometimes imagined. It is time to turn to those new societies of the early medieval West, to determine what impact the celebration of Roman victory may have had on the public expression of rulership in the barbarian kingdoms.

---

[128] E.g. Deér, 'Vorrechte', pp. 89ff.

7

Ephemeral empires: triumphal rulership in barbarian Africa, Burgundy and Italy

If the study of rulership among pre-invasion Germanic peoples must often rely on little more than educated guesses, the picture becomes somewhat clearer once the new rulers supplanted imperial authority within the Roman empire. Even so, our knowledge is not without shadows and even yawning gaps. The ephemeral character of most of the new political entities – a life span of some three-quarters of a century for the Tolosan Visigoths and the Ostrogoths, roughly a hundred years for the Vandals in Africa, half that for the second Burgundian kingdom, two centuries for the Toledan Visigoths and the Lombards – stands in stark contrast to the millenary existence of the eastern Roman empire. The amount of source material they generated and which has been preserved is not large. The earliest monarchies' Arianism cancelled as well the ecclesiastical and liturgical evidence from which we might have expected valuable clues and which might otherwise have stood the best chance of surviving the kingdoms' collapse.

Matters are complicated by the absence of a scholarly consensus on the existence or extent of a ritual apparatus of sovereignty inspired by that of the new rulers' former commander-in-chief, the Roman emperor. This dictates an approach different from that followed in tracing the development of late antique victory celebrations and their destiny in Byzantium. Whereas the concern of Roman and Byzantine society with ceremonial needed no demonstration, it is prudent to establish a context for the scattered data on the antique victory ideology's afterlife in the barbarian kingdoms. This requires reviewing, however briefly, what evidence each successor society has left on the adoption of a royal

ceremonial and, where possible, its adaptation. It implies as well
that the scholarly net must be cast wider than before, to catch even
the most fugitive refractions of imperial victory conceptions and
customs in the new, obscure world which was emerging out of the
rubble of the Roman empire.

I. THE KING'S TRIUMPHAL MAJESTY IN VANDAL AFRICA

As with the other northern newcomers to the Mediterranean, the
royal institution of the ethnic conglomerate lumped under the
name 'Vandals' is usually reckoned to have had Germanic, tribal
roots. The royal title itself testified to this origin, for the ruler of
Carthage was not the 'King of Africa' but the 'King of the Vandals
and the Alans'. In the conquest era, the monarchy was pretty
firmly held in the hands of the Hasdingi clan.[1] In Africa, Vandal
kingship experienced development in the direction of late Roman
absolutism.[2] The ruler of Carthage was referred to as *D.n. rex*,
'Our Lord King', in a fashion directly inspired by imperial usage.[3]
He used a royal throne and built audience halls.[4] The imperial
purple distinguished his garb from that of his subjects and in the
reign of king Gunthamund (484–96), the prince's name, along
with an imperial-style portrait, began to appear on local currency
of silver and copper.[5]

Archaeology and texts agree that the conquerors of Africa soon
succumbed to the seduction of the later Roman life-style.[6] An

[1] H. Wolfram, *Intitulatio I. Die lateinische Königs- und Fürstentitel bis zum Ende des 8. Jahrhunderts*, MIÖG, Ergänzungsband, 21 (Graz, 1967), pp. 79–87; cf. his 'The shaping of the early medieval kingdom', *Viator*, 1 (1970), 1–20, here 2ff. For a recent overview, F.M. Clover, 'Carthage and the Vandals', *Excavations at Carthage, 1978, conducted by the University of Michigan*, 7 (Ann Arbor, 1982), 1–22, esp. 3.
[2] Schmidt, *Wandalen*, p. 156, and C. Courtois, *Les Vandales et l'Afrique* (Paris, 1955), p. 243.
[3] Courtois, *Afrique*, p. 243, n. 5.
[4] Procopius, *Bella*, 3, 20, 21, Haury 1.399.21–2; cf. 4, 9, 4, 456.14; *Anthologia Latina*, nos. 203 and perhaps 215, ed. F. Bücheler and A. Riese, 1.1 (Leipzig, 1894), 176 and 182–3.
[5] If we may suppose that the purple gown which was stripped from the captive Gelimir was actually a Vandal garment: Procopius, *Bella*, 4, 9, 12, Haury 1.457.22–3. For the coinage: W. Hahn, *Moneta Imperii Byzantini. Rekonstruktion des Prägeaufbaues auf synoptisch-tabellarischer Grundlage*, 1, Österreichische Akademie der Wissenschaften, Philos.-hist. Kl., Denkschriften, 109 (Vienna, 1973), 94–5; pl. 42, 1ff.
[6] Clover, 'Carthage', pp. 7ff and 13ff.

experienced Byzantine observer described their sixth-century descendants as the most luxury-loving people he had ever encountered. The Vandals' passion for the baths, banquets, fine cuisine, silk clothing, theater and circus shows, dancers, mimes and garden estates testified to their assimilation of the late antique aristocrat's way of life.[7] Yet it would be a mistake to conclude that the new monarchy immediately shed all signs of its alien identity. In the second generation after the settlement, both barbarians and Romans who were associated with the royal palace wore the distinctive dress of the Germanic overlords, even when attending orthodox religious services.[8]

There are grounds for suspecting that the new rulers went beyond the appropriation of one or another emblem of imperial power and modeled elements of their public deportment on that of the emperors. Special, richly decorated vehicles appropriate to a queen are mentioned among the booty Belisarius paraded at Constantinople.[9] King Huniric (477–84) imitated and irritated the emperors by dubbing the coastal town of Hadrumetum with his own name – an act which the reconquering emperor would be quick to eradicate, when he rebaptized Unuricopolis as Iustiniana.[10] The Arian persecution included some form of the parade of infamy.[11] The poems of the Latin Anthology reinforce eastern testimony on the popularity of circus spectacles in Vandal Carthage, although it is not clear who funded them nor whether they served as the drawing card for the kind of political

[7] Procopius, *Bella*, 4, 6, 6–9, Haury, 1.444.3–16.
[8] Victor of Vita, *Historia persecutionis africanae prouinciae*, 2, 8–9, ed. M. Petschenig, CSEL, 7 (1881). 27.2–13.
[9] Procopius, *Bella*, 4, 9, 4, Haury 1.456.13–15; cf. Schmidt, *Wandalen*, p. 157. It should be noted, however, that this passage concerns mostly plunder which the Vandals had taken from the imperial palace in Rome (Procopius, *Bella*, 4, 9, 5, 1.456.20–1) and it is not altogether clear that here βασιλέως refers to the Vandal ruler rather than the Roman emperor.
[10] *Notitia prouinciarum et ciuitatum Africae*, ed. M. Petschenig, CSEL, 7 (1881), here 127, no. 107. On the document, C. Courtois, *Victor de Vita et son oeuvre. Étude critique* (Alger, 1954), pp. 91ff; cf. Procopius, *De aedificiis*, 6, 6, 7, Haury–Wirth, 4.182.6. Hadrumetum was the capital of Byzacena and, despite the poor epigraphic evidence, not likely a monohippic town: Lepelley, *Cités*, 2, 261–4. On this custom, see L. Musset, 'Les villes baptisées du nom d'un souverain au haut moyen âge (Ve–Xe siècles)', *Revue du moyen âge latin*, 25–34 (1978), 27–38, here 31.
[11] Victor, *Hist. pers.*, 2, 9, Petschenig, 27.14–16.

spectacles favored in Constantinople.[12] King Thrasamund's court (496–523) celebrated the regnal anniversary in sufficiently traditional manner to require the production of Latin panegyric.[13]

Some form of victory celebrations must be added to the Hasdingi's royal rituals. One poet's gushing over 'victrix Carthago' or another's enthusiasm for the Vandals' 'triumph-bearing wars' indicate that the old ideology of victory had not lost its literary and political potency under the new regime. Even more interesting, the first formula points to the adaptation of the old notions to express the new regional sentiment fostered by the establishment of independent political authorities in the western provinces.[14] A piece of government correspondence seems to document the ritual dimension. A victory bulletin sent to the last king by his brother Tzazo is preserved in Procopius; it announces the outcome of an expedition against the rebellious governor of Sardinia.[15] Although Belisarius' secretary would surely have subjected the Vandal document to a stylistic revision which went beyond the exigencies of translation, its contents cannot be dismissed as pure fabrication.[16] Procopius very likely held Tzazo's

---

[12] Clover, 'Carthage', pp. 10–11.

[13] Florentinus, *In laudem regis*, *Anth. lat.* no. 376, Bücheler–Riese, 1.1.288–9. A sixth-century writer may have imagined that Geiseric entered Carthage in triumph at the very outset of the Vandal era: Ferrandus of Carthage, *Vita Fulgentii* (*BHL*, 3208), ed. G. Lapeyre (Paris, 1929), 11: 'rex Gensericus memoratam Carthaginem victor invadens'.

[14] Florentinus, *Laud. reg.*, *Anth. lat.* no. 376, Bücheler–Riese 1.289.29, 'victrix Carthago triumphat'; Dracontius, *Satisfactio*, 21–2, ed. F. Vollmer, *MGH.AA*, 14 (1905).114.

[15] Schmidt, *Wandalen*, pp. 135–6; H.J. Diesner, 'Vandalen', *RE*, S.10 (1965), 957–92, here 970.

[16] Both P. Classen, 'Kaiserreskript und Königsurkunde. Diplomatische Studien zum römisch-germanischen Kontinuitätsproblem', *Archiv für Diplomatik*, 1 (1955), 1–87 and 2 (1956), 2–115, here 2, 5 and Wolfram, *Intitulatio I.*, pp. 80–2, were troubled by the document's undiplomatic character and tended to minimize Procopius' reliability, suggesting that the Vandal documents he cites might even be rhetorical inventions. Yet Classen notes one document's surprising accuracy in the unusual formulation of the address (2, 5, n. 20) and Wolfram explains Procopius' precision in Tzazo's use of the title as an effort to flaunt his knowledge of Vandal politics and terminology (*Intitulatio I.*, p. 81). B. Rubin, 'Prokopios von Kaisereia', *RE*, 23, 1 (1957), 273–599, here 414, believes the content to be substantially authentic (cf. e.g. *ibid.*, 433, for another probable use of a documentary source). Taken together, these views suggest that while the form may be Procopius', he could well have preserved the gist of the documents.

letter in his hands, for the Vandal messengers sailed blithely into Carthage just after the imperial army had occupied the city.[17] It begins:

Know, O King (βασιλεῦ) of both Vandals and Alans, that the usurper Godas has perished after falling into our hands, that the island is again subject to your rule, and celebrate the victory festival.[18]

The turn of events meant that this success would never be celebrated by the Vandal kings, but Tzazo's message suggests that some kind of victory celebrations were staged in Vandal Africa. The expectation of the king's brother that the letter would trigger a victory celebration could only have been founded in the knowledge that such celebrations were part of the Vandal kings' public exercise of power. An allusion by Dracontius points in the same direction, suggesting that triumphal entries remained a familiar element of public life in the fifth century.[19]

Like other aspects of royal *Staatssymbolik*, Vandal victory celebrations may have drawn on the Roman ideological and ritual repertory. Communications between the kings and their subjects seem to have been modeled on those between contemporary emperors and Romans; like them, they featured typical elements of imperial triumphal etiquette. The arenga of one of two surviving documents issued by king Huniric's chancellery opens with the words: 'It is a recognized characteristic of the virtue of triumphal and royal majesty to turn evil counsels against their authors.'[20] If the king's majesty is royal, it is also – and

---

[17] Procopius, *Bella*, 3, 24, 5–6, Haury, 1.410.17–24.

[18] *Ibid.*, 3, 24, 3, 410.10–13: Γώδαν ἀπολωλέναι τὸν τύραννον, ὑπὸ ταῖς ἡμετέραις γεγονότα χερσί, καὶ τὴν νῆσον αὖθις ὑπὸ τῇ σῇ βασιλείᾳ εἶναι, ὦ Βανδίλων τε καὶ Ἀλανῶν βασιλεῦ, ἴσθι καὶ τὴν ἐπινίκιον ἑορτὴν ἄγε. The last four words are not metaphorical: cf. *Bella*, 4, 12, 56, Haury, 1.470.14–15.

[19] To be effective, *Satisf.*, 203–4, Vollmer, 124 ('"me pugnante" comes [dicit] "victor ab hoste redis"') presupposes that Vandal kings celebrated some sort of triumphal entry after a campaign.

[20] 'Triumphalis et maiestatis regiae probatur esse uirtutis mala in auctores consilia retorquere', apud Victor, *Hist. pers.*, 3, 3, Petschenig, 72.19–20. For the diplomatic aspect of the documents preserved in Victor, R. Heuberger, 'Vandalische Reichskanzlei und Königsurkunde im Vergleich mit verwandten Einrichtungen und Erscheinungen', *MIÖG*, Ergänzungsband, 11 (1929), 76–113, here 93ff, and Classen, 'Kaiserreskript', 2, 3–5. It ought to be pointed out that this use of the genitive of characteristic (not noted by R. Pitkäranta, *Studien zum Latein des Victor Vitensis*,

especially – triumphal, for the rhetorical figure used in the Latin deliberately emphasizes the triumphal character of Vandal rulership even more than its royal nature.[21] Coinage reflects a similar tendency. The kingdom's early issues continue to display the old imperial Victory types, but this may be due more to mint routine than conscious decision.[22] More significant is king Thrasamund's introduction of a Victory type on copper issues.[23] An independent voice confirms that contemporaries perceived the triumphal element in Thrasamund's rule. Between his first and second exile (A.D. 515–17), bishop Fulgentius of Ruspe answered a pamphlet by Thrasamund with an anti-Arian theological treatise dedicated to the king himself.[24] The Catholic bishop applied flattering epithets of the imperial victory ideology to the Germanic ruler who had revived the victory coinage, and he did so in a place where they could scarcely be missed: the treatise's opening words.[25] The poets who praised Vandal kings could not fail to hail their great victories against marauding Moors and other reprobates.[26] Dracontius even went so far as to adapt the theme of bloodless victory to king Gunthamund (484–96), who received triumphs from God through the battles of his general Ansila, a

---

Commentationes humanarum litterarum, 61 (Helsinki, 1978), pp. 39–43, but discerned by Petschenig, p. 158, s.v. 'genetiuus qualitatis') is a regular feature of Late Latin bureaucratese, and particularly of arengas. Cf. Cassiodorus, *Variae*, 2, 7, Fridh, 61.3; 2, 9, 1, Fridh, 61.3–4; 2, 16, 1, 67.2–3; 3, 5, 2, 100.9–10, etc. This is additional evidence for the authenticity of the acts quoted by Victor.

21 The schema is a + xb and the figure a kind of hyperbaton, intended to distinguish the first word of the clause: L. Arbusow, *Colores rhetorici. Eine Auswahl rhetorischer Figuren und Gemeinplätze als Hilfsmittel für Übungen an mittelalterlichen Texten*, ed. H. Peter, 2nd edn (Göttingen, 1963), pp. 80–1.

22 Hahn, *Moneta*, 1, 93.

23 *Ibid.*, 1, 94; cf. *Moneta*, 3 (Vienna, 1981), 60.

24 *Ad Trasamundum regem*. For the date, M. Schanz et al., *Geschichte der römischen Litteratur*, 4.2, Handbuch der Altertumswissenschaft, 8 (Munich, 1920), 528.

25 Ed. J. Fraipont, *CCL*, 91 (1961).97.1–2: 'Triumphalibus tuis sensibus, piissime rex, nequaquam crediderim obliuione subtractum...'. The triumphal theme seems to have been particularly resonant at that moment, for Fulgentius returns to it in his conceit on the king's desire to acquire more space for the mind than the kingdom: *ibid.*, 99.101–7. For Thrasamund's reading of the treatise, Ferrandus, *V. Fulgentii*, 21, Lapeyre, 103.

26 Dracontius, *Satisf.*, 21–3, Vollmer, 144; cf. Florentinus, *Anth. lat.*, no. 376, 28–36, Bücheler–Riese, 1.1.289.

notion which is a far cry from the Germanic conception of
Heerkönigtum.[27]

Perhaps the most moving testimony of the victory ideology's
continued life comes from a humble wooden tablet discovered in
the area of Djebel Mrata, on the Vandal kingdom's southern
reaches.[28] In the private diplomatic use of a dowry contract
established on 17 September 493 (?), the date is given as 'Year nine
of the Lord Most Unvanquished King'.[29] The expression is
probably not pure formula, since it does not recur in the thirty odd
documents uncovered with the contract. By its distance from the
capital and its private origin, Albertini Tablet no. 1 provides
precious evidence that a Roman frontier milieu found nothing
unthinkable about decking out a barbarian king with one of the
most prized and familiar epithets of the imperial dignity.

2. VICTORY CUSTOMS IN THE KINGDOM OF
THE BURGUNDIANS

The Burgundian kingdom flourished briefly in eastern Gaul
before it was absorbed by the Merovingians in the course of the
sixth century.[30] The monarchy's relations with the Roman
church and population were generally harmonious and even
cordial.[31] If we consider that king Gundobad (ca. 474–516) was
the nephew of Ricimer, patrician and Master of Both Services,
that Gundobad enjoyed the same dignity, had served in the same
capacity in Gaul and Italy and indeed that he had himself disposed
of one emperor and created another, traces of a deep Roman
imprint on the outward manifestations of his kingship will not
come as a surprise.[32] One king, for example, is known to have

[27] Dracontius, *Satisf.*, 211–14, Vollmer, 124; cf. Schlesinger, 'Heerkönigtum', esp.
  p. 122.
[28] *Tablettes Albertini. Actes privés de l'époque vandale (fin du Ve siècle)*, ed. C. Courtois et
  al. (Paris, 1952), pp. 189ff; Courtois, *Afrique*, p. 218.
[29] 'Anno nono domini inuictissimi regis xii kalendas octobres…', *Tab. Alb.*, 1,
  Courtois, 215.1.
[30] See in general L. Schmidt, *Geschichte der deutschen Stämme bis zum Ausgang der
  Völkerwanderung. Die Ostgermanen*, 2nd edn (Munich, 1934), pp. 129ff.
[31] E.g. L. Musset, *Les invasions: les vagues germaniques*, Nouvelle Clio, 12 (Paris, 1965),
  pp. 114–15.
[32] *PLRE*, 2, 524–5.

played a role in a church dedication, an event which lent itself to ritualized participation in the imperial tradition.[33] The Burgundian army practiced the triumphal display of a vanquished leader's head and at least one king seems to have staged a triumphal entry into Vienne.[34] This fits the testimony of Avitus, bishop of that city (*ob.* 518), who alluded to the victory panegyric he would deliver when king Sigismund returned from what he hoped would be a successful campaign against the Franks.[35] Naturally victory wishes were not lacking in such circumstances.[36] Avitus himself prayed for the king's triumph and he implies that this was the duty of every orthodox Christian. Whether this entailed special public services for the king's victory is not clear.[37] Here as elsewhere in the imperial provinces, the cult of saints spilled over into the supernatural defense of the threatened city.[38] Given that next to nothing is known about the internal history of the second Burgundian monarchy, the evidence is not unimpressive. These Germanic kings surely availed themselves of some of the victory customs of imperial civilization.

3. TRIUMPHAL IDEOLOGY IN OSTROGOTHIC ITALY

Scholars are in rare unanimity that there is little certainty regarding Odoacer's legal position in the Roman scheme of things.[39] His frequent use of the non-Roman title *rex* and his

---

[33] M. McCormick, *Revue d'histoire ecclésiastique*, 82 (1977), 661.

[34] Heads: Agathias, *Hist.*, 1, 3, 5, Keydell, 13.12–18, and Gregory of Tours, *Hist.*, 3, 6, Krusch–Levison, 103.6–7; triumphal entry: Godigisel after his and Clovis' defeat of his brother Gundobad: Gregory of Tours, *Hist.*, 2, 32, Krusch–Levison, 79.3–5: 'Godigisilus vero, obtenta victuria ... cum pace discessit Viennamque triumphans, tamquam si iam totum possiderit regnum, ingreditur'. Cf. *PLRE*, 2, 516, 'Godigisel 2'.

[35] *Ep.*, 45, Peiper, 74.30–1.

[36] Avitus, *Ep.*, 91, Peiper, 99.12–14; *Ep.*, 45, 74.28 as well as the passage from *Ep.* 92 cited in the following note.

[37] *Ep.*, 92, Peiper, 99.18–22. Note that *Ep.*, 85, indicates that the Catholic liturgy of Burgundy included prayers for the king on, I should think, the Vigil of Easter: Peiper, 95.10–13.

[38] C. Perrat and A. Audin, 'Alcimii Ecdicii Aviti Viennensis episcopi homilia dicta in dedicatione superioris basilicae', *Studi in onore di Aristide Calderini e Roberto Paribeni*, 2 (Milan, 1957), 433–51, here 449.4–451.17.

[39] On Odoacer in general, *PLRE*, 2, 791–3. For an overview of different opinions on

refusal to don the purple robes of supreme authority or other royal insignia, even as he sought Constantinopolitan approval for his acts, underline the ambiguity of his situation.[40] Among the means the former member of the imperial guard used to ferret out emperor Zeno's recognition was the dispatch of the customary 'symbols of victory' to the commander-in-chief, a ploy which met with partial success.[41]

The kingdom established by his assassin was to prove shorter-lived than that of the Vandals. The personality and long reign of its founder so dominate the history of the Ostrogothic state that Theoderic's background deserves some consideration when the impact of royal victory on the public projection of his power is examined. As the son of an Arian king and his Catholic concubine – the latter accompanied her son to Italy and was active in 496, while her presence at a crucial moment was still a matter for panegyrical comment a decade later[42] – Theoderic was probably predisposed to seek accommodation with the vast majority of his subjects. The forty-year-old conqueror of Italy had hardly escaped exposure to the social values and mores of the later Roman elite. Born in the ruins of Roman Pannonia, he had spent more than half his youth at court in Constantinople, in the midst of the imperial government's burgeoning ritual apparatus. The last decade of his life before the invasion of Italy had been punctuated by negotiations, ruptures and rapprochements with the eastern throne. He rose to the state dignity of patrician, obtained two appointments as Master of Both Services in the Presence (476/7–8; 483–7) and was adopted as emperor Zeno's 'son' according to Germanic custom. In 484 he reached the summit of Roman aristocratic ambition, the consulate, for which, favor of favors, the Roman taxpayer picked up the tab.[43]

---

the 'constitutional position', Thompson, *Romans and barbarians*, pp. 65ff and 274–5, n. 13ff.

[40] On *rex* see, e.g., McCormick, 'Odoacer', pp. 212–13. For his refusal of the purple: Cassiodorus, *Chron.*, no. 1303, Mommsen, 159.

[41] McCormick, 'Odoacer', pp. 217ff.

[42] *PLRE*, 2, 400, 'Erelieva'. Her status as concubine is expressly stated by Jordanes, *Get.*, 269, Mommsen, 128.2. Ennodius of Pavia depicts Theoderic addressing not his troops, but his mother just before a fateful confrontation with Odoacer: *Panegyricus*, 43, Vogel, 208.16ff.

[43] The sources for this account are assembled in *PLRE*, 2, 1077–81, 'Theodericus 7'; for

Yet even such a long and intimate involvement with New Rome did not imply complete assimilation. Contemporary Italians could not mistake the conqueror's 'foreign', heretical brand of Christianity, with its divine scripture in a barbarian tongue, nor could they miss the distinctively non-Roman identity projected by the Amal's official portraits.[44] Like his successors, Theoderic wore long hair and a close-cropped moustache, aspects of personal grooming which were emblematic of the barbarian.[45] In fact, as Gothic displeasure over the excessive romanization of his heir suggests, for Theoderic to have ignored his power base in the *exercitus Gothorum* might well have proved suicidal.[46] By inclination, then, as well as calculation, Theoderic was condemned to strike a delicate balance between the armed occupying minority of his own kind and the Italian majority. The latter was dominated by a wealthy and influential aristocracy who, less than two decades before, had yet been accustomed to an imperial court in their midst, who had enjoyed the favors of Theoderic's predecessor and who continued to express their eminent position in society and government with all the traditional perquisites and ceremonial of the later Roman ruling class.[47] How could the new outsider

---

a more detailed treatment, W. Ensslin, *Theoderich der Grosse*, 2nd edn (Munich, 1959), pp. 7–57.

[44] On Ulfila and the preservation of the Gothic language among Visigoths and Ostrogoths, H. Wolfram, *Geschichte der Goten von den Anfängen bis zur Mitte des sechsten Jahrhunderts. Entwurf einer historischen Ethnographie* (Munich, 1979), pp. 83ff and 257–60.

[45] See the analysis of Theoderic's portrait on his signet ring or the so-called Senigallia coin by P.E. Schramm and W. Berges, *Herrschaftszeichen und Staatssymbolik*, 1, 219ff. His successor Athalaric is shown with the same hairstyle and a kind of gown which does not seem to conform to the canons of imperial costume: W.F. Volbach, *Elfenbeinarbeiten der Spätantike und des frühen Mittelalters*, Kataloge vor- und frühgeschichtlicher Altertümer, 7, 3rd edn (Mainz, 1976), no. 31, with pl. 16. The same must presumably have been true of the statues or other images of Theoderic at Rome which Boethius' widow was accused of having smashed: Procopius, *Bella*, 7, 20, 29, Haury, 2.389.15–20.

[46] Gothic dissatisfaction with Athalaric's lack of proper barbarism: Procopius, *Bella*, 5, 2, 6–17, Haury, 2.11.5–12.19.

[47] Stein, *Bas-Empire*, 2, 41ff and 120ff; A. Chastagnol, *Le Sénat romain sous le règne d'Odoacre. Recherches sur l'épigraphie du Colisée au V*ᵉ*siècle*, Antiquitas 3, 4°, 3 (Bonn, 1966), pp. 52ff. For the great significance still attached to spectacular ceremonies like the accession to the ordinary consulate: Boethius, *Phil. consol.*, 2, 3, 8, Bieler,

project his authority to this audience without recourse to traditional Roman ritual?

Unlike Odoacer, Theoderic probably adopted the sacred purple in his public dress, although he generally eschewed the insignia of empire.[48] As one of his officials noted, the imperial color served a very practical purpose in public ritual, in addition to its symbolic value.[49] Theoderic's palace in Ravenna was likely designed with an eye to ceremonial functions: it must have contained an audience hall in which the Master of Offices stage-managed senatorial encounters with the king in much the same fashion as in contemporary Constantinople.[50] Nor could the palace have lacked impressive banquet facilities, for Theoderic consciously organized and exploited such occasions to enhance his policy of prestige.[51]

If the Gothic king skillfully avoided overt acts of usurpation, his own official pronouncements were not above borrowing slogans like '*humanitas*' from imperial propaganda in a way that implied

---

22.22–30. Cf. Cassiodorus, *Var.*, 3, 39, 1–2, Fridh, 124. For the continued prestige of official vehicles, *ibid.*, 6, 3, 2, Fridh, 226.1–10 and 6, 4, 6, 229.34–5.

[48] Ensslin, *Theoderich*, p. 156 (cf. Wolfram, *Goten*, p. 381) believed that Theoderic wore a diadem, but the evidence he cites, Cassiodorus, *Var.*, 1, 42, 4, Fridh, 46.21–47.25, is clearly metaphorical if the syntax is properly understood: B.H. Skahill, *The syntax of the Variae of Cassiodorus*, Studies in medieval and renaissance Latin, 3 (Washington, D.C., 1934), p. 74. Ennodius, *Pan.*, 14, Vogel, 205.7 seems no less metaphorical. Nor are crowns depicted on the portraits of the first Gothic kings (above, n. 45). This fits with Procopius, *Bella*, 5, 1, 26, Haury, 2.8.8–9. On the other hand, the contemporary *Vita Caesarii Arelatensis* (*BHL* 1508–9), 36, by Cyprian, Firminus, Viventius, Messianus and Stephen, ed. G. Morin, *S. Caesarii episcopi Arelatensis opera omnia*, 2 (Maredsous, 1942).310.21–6, clearly states that Theoderic removed some kind of headgear (*deposito ornatu de capite*) when he greeted the holy man. There was at any rate a change in policy during the Byzantine invasion, since Totila's bejeweled headdress was sent to Justinian as the symbol of victory: above, Ch. 2, p. 66.

[49] Cassiodorus, *Var.*, 1, 2, 2, Fridh, 10.13–16; cf. M. McCormick, 'Analyzing imperial ceremonies', *JÖB*, (in press).

[50] The controversy generated by E. Dyggve, *Ravennatum palatium sacrum. La basilica ipetrale per ceremonie. Studi sull'architettura dei palazzi della tarda antichità*, Archaeo-logisk-kunsthistoriske meddelelser 3, 2 (Copenhagen, 1941), and pretty well laid to rest by G. De Frankovich, *Il Palatium di Teodorico a Ravenna e la cosidetta 'architettura di potenza'* (Rome, 1970), and F.W. Deichmann, *Ravenna. Hauptstadt des spätantiken Abendlandes*, 2, 1 (Wiesbaden, 1974), 143ff, does not affect this general conclusion, since it is independently confirmed by literary evidence: Cassiodorus, *Var.*, 6, 6, 2, Fridh, 231.10–12. Cf. following n.

[51] Cassiodorus, *Var.*, 6, 9, 7–8, Fridh, 237.56–238.67.

his own exalted status.[52] Indeed, Theoderic explicitly argued that the superiority of his rule compared with other barbarian kings could be measured by the degree to which he imitated the emperor in Constantinople. His own regime he characterized as Roman and a worthy replacement for the barbarism which had prevailed, for instance, prior to his annexation of Gaul.[53]

One way in which Gothic rulers revealed their *humanitas* to the Roman population was through expenditures for spectacles. Theaters were restored at royal expense.[54] State revenues helped finance at least some spectacles and salary the performers, while Theoderic's official correspondence more than once betrays a shrewd understanding of the political benefits he expected from such largess.[55] As they had in the old days, king Theodahad's (534–6) circus races and theater shows included displays of civic sentiment and loyalty to the regime in the form of acclamations.[56] There is no reason to suppose they were an innovation of that brief reign.

In addition to the official portraits, other equally traditional means projected Theoderic's authority to the masses and elites. There has been speculation that a victory celebration was the

---

[52] M. McCormick, *American Journal of Philology*, 102 (1981), 346. Cf. R.M. Honig, *Humanitas und Rhetorik in spätrömischen Kaisergesetzen* (Göttingen, 1960).

[53] Cassiodorus, *Var.*, 1, 1, 3 (Theoderic to Anastasius I), Fridh, 9.18–20; *ibid.*, 3, 17, 1, Fridh, 109.3–9. Cf. *Var.*, 1, 6, 1–2, 17.2–5 and 3, 16, 3, 109.1–6, where the 'Romanus princeps' seems to be Theoderic.

[54] *Exc. Val.*, 60, Moreau–Velkov, 17.12–15, and, at Pavia, *ibid.*, 71, 21.1–2. Cf. his *cubiculum* funding the restoration of the Theater of Pompey: Cassiodorus, *Var.*, 4, 51, 3 and 12, Fridh, 177.14–17 and 179.78–82, and the inscription commemorating Athalaric's reconstruction of seats at Pavia in 528–9: *ILS*, 829.

[55] Cassiodorus, *Var.*, 1, 20, 1–4, Fridh, 28.3–29.33 and *Var.*, 1, 30, 1, Fridh, 36.5–9. Pantomimes paid by City Prefect: *Var.*, 1, 33, 2, 39.8–40.2; charioteers by Praetorian Prefect, *Var.*, 2, 9, 2, 62.6–16, and 3, 51, 1, 133.5–12. Theoderic via Cassiodorus recognizes using the shows to promote a feeling of 'beatitudo temporum' (*Var.*, 3, 51, 12–13, 135.84–93) and to ensure that the crowd ('conuentus uester') be 'pacis ornatus' (*Var.*, 1, 31, 1, 37.2–38.6). The thought of showing up an eastern rival does not seem foreign to Theoderic's considerations in rewarding an eastern charioteer: *Var.*, 3, 51, 1, Fridh, 133.8–12. On the sociology of this kind of munificence: P. Veyne, *Le pain et le cirque. Sociologie historique d'un pluralisme politique* (Paris, 1976), pp. 701ff.

[56] Procopius, *Bella*, 5, 6, 4, Haury, 2.28.22–29.2, where the terrified Theodahad's offer to allow acclamation of Justinian before the king during spectacles is presented as an important concession in the negotiations with the imperial envoy Peter Patrician. The implication is that such was not the case at that time.

setting for Ennodius' panegyric on the king; it is at any rate clear that various state festivals were enhanced with the traditional speeches of praise.[57] Perhaps most startling is the implication that the traditional and popular New Year's *vota* festivities for the emperor's well-being were diverted to the benefit of the new barbarian king.[58]

All this suggests that Theoderic and his successors adopted some of the rituals of power which the native population had come to expect from their lords. Even though the records are rare, a couple of state ceremonies revolving around the king are explicitly attested, although only one of them is knowable in any detail. Notwithstanding a persistent tradition in modern scholarship, however, there is no direct evidence for the triumphs which Theoderic is often said to have celebrated at Rome and Ravenna.[59]

---

[57] The hypothesis that the panegyric was intended for a victory celebration was formulated by H. Hasenstab, *Studien zu Ennodius. Ein Beitrag zur Geschichte der Völkerwanderung* (Munich, 1890), pp. 46–7, but it is impossible to verify. Cassiodorus is known to have given a panegyric on Theoderic prior to his appointment as Quaestor in 507 (*PLRE*, 2, 266), another on Eutharic Cilliga at Rome in 519 (*ibid.*, p. 268), and again, it would appear, for the marriage of Witigis and Matasuntha, and may have written more: *Var.*, praef. 11, Fridh, 5.73–4 and D.M. Cappuyns, 'Cassiodore', *DHGE*, 11 (1949), 1349–1408, here 1364–5.

[58] Cassiodorus, *Var.*, 6, 7, 2, Fridh, 233.14–17.

[59] E.g. Hasenstab, *Ennodius*, pp. 46–7; Wolfram, *Goten*, pp. 358 and 382. The mistake derives from the difficult popular Latin of the *Exc. Val.* Thus the account of Theoderic's *tricennalia* celebrations at Rome, *Exc. Val.*, 67, 'Per tricennalem triumphans populo ingressus palatium', Moreau, 19.23–4, where there is no indication that the anniversary coincided with a victory celebration and it is incorrect to assign the old technical meaning to *triumphare*. So too in the second passage: *Exc. Val.*, 80, Moreau, 23.8–9: 'Ergo Theodoricus dato consulatu Eutharico Romae et Ravennae triumphavit.' Here the deceptively simple syntax appears to mean that Theoderic celebrated a triumph at Rome and Ravenna, when Eutharic received the consulate. But it is clear from Cassiodorus' *Chronicle*, composed for that very occasion, that Theoderic was *not* present at the celebrations at Rome: *Chron.* 1364, Mommsen, 161, where 'patris' is used loosely of Eutharic's father-in-law. The inescapable conclusion is that Eutharic is the subject of 'triumphavit'. In fact, the explanation for 'Theoderic' in the nominative is that the anonymous author no longer fully understood the ablative absolute; this confusion conforms to his usage in other passages. This example of the phenomenon must be added to those noticed by J.N. Adams, *The text and language of a Vulgar Latin chronicle (Anonymus Valesianus II)*, Bulletin of the Institute of Classical Studies, Supplement 36 (London, 1976), p. 99. 'Triumph' occurs elsewhere in the weakened meaning of a 'splendid parade', e.g., Jordanes, *Rom.*, 348, Mommsen, 45.7–8: 'Consulis ordinarii triumphum ex publico dono peregit'; cf. Jordanes, *Get.*, 289, Mommsen, 132.16–17.

The festivities which marked Theoderic's thirtieth anniversary of kingship are the best known of his state ceremonies. The old warp of the fourth-century literary imagination continued to prevail two hundred years later, for the accounts of the anniversary are dominated by the king's state visit to Rome. He received the honors of an *adventus*, publicly displayed his benevolence toward St Peter and his latter-day representative, and staged a parade through the city. Like the imperial processions which manifestly inspired it, this parade wound its way to the Roman Forum. There the king delivered a speech to the applause of senate and people, and followed up with another parade into the ancient imperial palace. The whole extravaganza was capped by circus races and royal gifts to the city and population.[60]

Even in the absence of explicit records of Ostrogothic victory celebrations, it is clear that the old imperial victory conceptions found new life under the Amal king. It could scarcely have been otherwise in a political regime which justified the Gothic army's occupation of Italy and its riches by the king's success in defending the country from (other) barbarians.[61] An impressive trace of this theory occurs in an inscription which records repairs to the Curia of the Roman Senate and whose respectful stance toward Anastasius and reserve toward Theoderic suggests that it may have been erected during a period of entente with the East. The king's royal title is conspicuous by its absence. Instead, the inscription invokes both of 'Our Lords', Anastasius, 'Perpetual Augustus' and Theoderic 'Most Glorious and Triumphal Gentleman'.[62] As in an

---

[60] See in general G. delle Valle, 'Teoderico e Roma', *Rendiconti della Accademia di archeologia, lettere e belle arti, Napoli*, n.s. 34 (1959), 119–76, here 162ff; Stein, *Bas-Empire*, 2, 133–4; Ensslin, *Theoderich*, pp. 107ff. The main sources are *Exc. Val.*, 65–7, Moreau, 19.14–20.2, and Ferrandus, *V. Fulgentii*, 9, Lapeyre, 55–6. On the Golden Palm, Platner–Ashby, *Dictionary*, p. 382. On the honors Totila could expect from St Benedict, Gregory I, *Dialogi*, 2, 14, and 3, 6, ed. A. de Vogüé 2, SC, 260 (Paris, 1979), 180.1–27; cf. 3, 6, 1, 276.1–5. Less well known is the account of Theoderic's initial *adventus* into Ravenna preserved in the ninth-century *Lib. pont. eccl. Rav.*, 39, of Agnellus, Holder-Egger, 303.20–304.1. According to Holder-Egger, this passage derives from the lost sixth-century chronicle of bishop Maximian (*ibid.*, p. 272; cf. Wattenbach–Levison, *Geschichtsquellen*, p. 429), and, as he notes, the account jibes with Procopius, *Bella*, 5, 1, 24, Haury, 2.7.23–8.2.

[61] E.g. Cassiodorus, *Var.*, 7, 3, 3, Fridh, 263.26–9; 8, 3, 4, 303.24–7; 9, 19, 4, 370.18–20; 10, 14, 1, 397.6–9; cf. *ibid.*, 2, 398.18–19.

[62] *Année épigraphique* (1953), no. 68; cf. A. Bartoli, 'Lavori nella sede del senato romano

273

important inscription of Odoacer at Rome, the royal dignity is omitted; here it is replaced by an ad hoc title, obviously derived from the old victory ideology.[63] The same theme recurs in the literary vestiges of relations between the king and his Romans. Thus Ennodius expresses precious paradox at the sight of Theoderic's 'war-potent right hand, full of famous triumphs', turning to the more serene pleasures of gardening.[64] The squabbles surrounding pope Symmachus' election provided grist for the triumphal mill: the king's intervention concludes the 'wars' of the opposing factions and directs the 'fortunate army' of the church 'to triumph', i.e. resolution of the schism.[65]

Royal victory looms even larger in panegyric. Ennodius' praise begins with the prince's valor: his victories are countless, he has known as many triumphs as wars. The mere sight of the Goth on the battlefield suffices to vanquish his enemies.[66] The victories which stud Theoderic's path are so frequent that they have become everyday occurrences.[67] For the 'most unvanquished' king, adulthood is nothing other than the 'maturity of triumphs'.[68] To judge by the surviving fragments of Cassiodorus' lost panegyrics relevant to Theoderic, that ambitious civil servant was no less insistent than Ennodius in demonstrating that the Gothic king lived up to the imperial ideal of triumphal rulership.[69] 'Bravo, untiring triumphator!' says Cassiodorus; the king's military exploits restored the weary limbs of Rome and returned ancient blessedness to the modern age. Theoderic has revived Rome's historic grandeur by returning Gaul to its sway and, echoing the official line no less than Virgil, Cassiodorus hails the

---

al tempo di Teoderico', *Bullettino della Commissione archeologica comunale di Roma*, 73 (1949–50), 77–88: 'Salvis dominis nostris Anastasio perpetuo augusto et gloriosissimo ac triumfali viro Theoderico...'; cf. *PLRE*, 2, 480, 'Florianus 4'. If 'Florianus 4' is identical with 'Florianus 2' (*ibid.*), the inscription would date from 507–18.

[63] Cf. McCormick, 'Odoacer', p. 213.
[64] *De horto regis*, Vogel, 214.1 (no. 264).
[65] *In Christi signo*, Vogel, 319.3–4 (no. 458).
[66] *Pan.*, 5–6, Vogel, 203.27–204.4.
[67] *Pan.*, 6, Vogel, 204.5–6.
[68] In a precious expression for 'in the course of your life': *Pan.*, 23, Vogel, 206.6: 'Inter vitae tirocinia et triumphorum maturitatem...'; *invictus* theme: *Pan.* 10 and 31, Vogel 204.26 and 207.12.
[69] For the relation with Theoderic, L. Traube, *MGH.AA*, 12 (1894), 463, n. 1.

king for curbing the haughty foreigners with his supreme power (*imperium*).[70] The ideology of victory offered the arsenal of Gothic propaganda a potent weapon.

Theoderic, at least, had some claim to these triumphs. But the ruler's victory was as obligatory under the new kings as it had been under the Caesars. Many years after his paeans on Theoderic, Cassiodorus addressed a letter to the Senate, informing it of his promotion to Praetorian Prefect. He used the opportunity to sketch a kind of mini-panegyric on the next generation of Amal rulers, king Athalaric and his mother Amalasuntha. Even for an experienced propagandist, glorifying the military triumphs of a sickly fifteen-year-old was no easy task. The resourceful bureaucrat seized upon a related theme which expressed the new values of a Christian society: he praised the young king not for his military victories but for his great ethical and moral triumph.[71] Unfortunately for the Ostrogoths, the incompleteness of Athalaric's ethical victory was revealed the following year when he died of debauchery.[72]

Next comes lavish praise for Amalasuntha, her linguistic and literary accomplishments and her excellent discretion, which of course had brought Cassiodorus to office. He integrates her into the imperial tradition by a comparison with the great Galla Placidia: indeed, the Gothic queen was greater because Amalasuntha's Germanic army remained strong and terrified the enemy – an implicit criticism of fifth-century policy.[73] Against the wishes of the eastern prince, that army had once again made the Danube 'Roman'.[74] On the eve of war, the king of the Franks had succumbed to sickness 'for the triumph of our princes'.[75] The Burgundian chose to remain whole by obedience rather than suffer loss by resisting, for the safest defense against the Goths was to lay down one's arms. The new values protrude again: thanks to

---

[70] *Orationum reliquiae*, ed. L. Traube, *MGH.AA*, 12 (1894). 466.14–21; *ibid.*, 466.10–11: 'frenat superbas gentes imperio' (cf. *Aen.*, 1, 523). Note that Cassiodorus' creative citation of Virgil (cf. McCormick, *American Journal of Philology*, 102 (1981), 346) substitutes 'imperium' for Dido's 'iustitia'.
[71] *Var.*, 11, 1, 4, Fridh, 422.26–423.34.
[72] J.R. Palanque, 'Athalaric', *DHGE*, 4 (1930), 1294–5.
[73] *Var.*, 11, 1, 10, Fridh, 424.68–70. [74] *Ibid.*, 10–11, 424.71–81.
[75] 'In triumphum principum nostrorum', *ibid.*, 12, Fridh, 424.81–92.

divine felicity, Amalasuntha conquers all without a struggle.[76]

But was this insistence on royal victory confined to the rarefied ambience and audience of panegyrics? The Life of Epiphanius, for instance, offers a tantalizing parallel to the Vandal dowry contract when it shows Romans using the epithets *invictus* and *invictissimus* during meetings with barbarian kings: Epiphanius does so in direct reference to Theoderic himself.[77] Even more significant is the use eminent Romans made of the victory ideology in public statements connected with political and diplomatic competition between Ravenna and Constantinople.

From 497 to 504, relations between the Gothic regime and Anastasius were relatively good.[78] Then Theoderic annexed Sirmium (504). Hostilities ensued and the situation took a turn for the worse when the Byzantine-inspired alliance of Franks and Burgundians defeated and killed Theoderic's Visigothic ally and son-in-law, Alaric II.[79] The concession of a state dignity to the Frankish king and an imperial fleet's attack on southern Italy rounded off the reverse to the Ostrogothic system of alliances. Although the Ostrogothic army's success helped contain damage to Theoderic's prestige, relations with Constantinople remained in a very bad way until the treaty of 510.[80] Even then, full reconciliation had to await the accession of Justin I and the settlement of the Acacian schism.[81]

Perhaps in the spring of 507 and certainly between 504 and 508, Ennodius, a man of distinguished social and intellectual background, delivered his Panegyric on Theoderic. Coming at such a critical time, any public demonstration of aristocratic Roman support must have been very welcome.[82] Ennodius' insistence on

---

[76] *Ibid.*, 13, 424.92–100.
[77] *V. Epiphanii*, 125, Vogel, 100.6; cf. 155, Vogel, 103.31–2; 185, 107.29 as well as 179, 106.36.
[78] Following Stein, *Bas-Empire*, 2, 115 and 138; cf. Ensslin, *Theoderich*, pp. 77ff; P. Lamma, *Oriente e occidente nell'alto medioevo. Studi storici sulle due civiltà* (Padua, 1968), pp. 33–4.
[79] Stein, *Bas-Empire*, 2, 146–9.
[80] *Ibid.*, pp. 149–52.
[81] *Ibid.*, pp. 224ff. On the schism and Anastasius' policy, P. Charanis, *Church and state in the later Roman empire. The religious policy of Anastasius the First, 491–518* (Madison, 1939).
[82] For the date, see J. Sundwall, *Abhandlungen zur Geschichte des ausgehenden Römertums* (Helsinki, 1919), pp. 42–3. Sundwall's conclusion that *Pan.* was orally delivered at

Theoderic's all-encompassing victory has already been noted and it fits well with the difficult military situation of the time. An even more direct allusion to the international scene bursts out of the panegyrist's protest against an unnamed person's assumption of the imperial victory epithet *Alamannicus*. The words are not Theoderic's own, but Ennodius was not so foolish as to sing praises displeasing to his king. They shed light on how the king could be viewed by his Roman subjects and how he may have viewed himself.

Quid! Frustra maiores nostri divos et pontifices vocarunt, quibus sceptra conlata sunt. singulare est actibus implere sanctissimum et veneranda nomina non habere. rex meus sit iure Alamannicus, dicatur alienus. ut divus vitam agat ex fructu conscientiae nec requirat pomposae vocabula nuda iactantiae, in cuius moribus veritati militant blandimenta maiorum.[83]

The swipe at the emperor in Constantinople is barely concealed. 'The naked names of pompous ostentation' are the imperial victory and piety epithets which, in Anastasius' case, included precisely the title *Alamannicus* as well as *pontifex*.[84] Since Theoderic had just assured the protection of the Alamanni who had fled into Rhaetia and perhaps had reaffirmed his claim to that territory, he was more entitled to the epithet 'Alamannic' than an emperor who took the name without any direct involvement.[85]

Ravenna in Theoderic's presence on the occasion of some celebration (and not necessarily Hasenstab's triumph) is not refuted by Schanz's summary considerations, *Geschichte*, 4, 2, 138, with n. 7.

[83] *Pan.*, Vogel, 213.5–9. The reference to the 'fruit of conscience' seems like a literary allusion, to Pliny, *Ep.*, 1, 8, 14, or perhaps more likely to Macrobius, *Commentarii in Somnium Scipionis, 2,* 10, 2, ed. I. Willis, *Opera*, 2 (Leipzig, 1970).124.26–7: 'virtutis fructum sapiens in conscientia ponit, minus perfectus in gloria...'. I find the judgement of F. Vogel (*MGH.AA*, 7.xvii–xviii) and Ensslin (*Theoderich*, pp. 139–40) on the identity of *rex alienus* more convincing than that of M. Reydellet, *La royauté dans la littérature latine de Sidoine Apollinaire à Isidore de Séville*, Bibliothèque des Écoles françaises d'Athènes et de Rome, 243 (Rome, 1981), pp. 173–4.

[84] Thus in a letter from Anastasius I to the senate of Rome dated 28 July 516 and preserved in the *Collectio Avellana*, 113, Günther, 2.506.20–3.

[85] The question of the occupation of Rhaetia is complicated. See Stein, *Bas-Empire*, 2, 147–8 with n. 1, Ensslin, *Theoderich*, p. 136, F. Beyerle, 'Süddeutschland in der politischen Konzeption Theoderichs des Grossen', *Vorträge und Forschungen*, 1 (Constance, 1955), 65–81 and H. Ditten, 'Zu Prokops Nachrichten über die deutschen Stämme', *BS*, 36 (1975), 1–24, here 15ff.

In some sense, Ennodius' plaint reflects the essential dilemma of the Gothic king perceptively recognized by Procopius: imperial prerogative and accepted custom barred the way to recognition of what Theoderic really represented.[86] And it should be stressed that Ennodius and his audience could not have found the imperial titulature totally repugnant: in almost the same breath, the panegyrist referred to those 'naked names of ostentation' as *veneranda nomina*. The very bitterness of the outburst shows how seriously Theoderic and his supporters took the usages of imperial victory titulature.

Ennodius' testimony is deepened and reinforced by wholly independent evidence from a senatorial project to drain part of the Pomptine Marshes and repair the Appian Way. A remarkable inscription commemorated the work:

Our Lord, the most Glorious and Celebrated King Theoderic, Victor and Triumphator, ever Augustus, Born for the good of the state, Guardian of Freedom and Propagator of the Roman Name, Tamer of the Foreigners, has happily restored, God willing, to public use and the security of travelers, the route and area of the Appian Way's Nineteen-Mile stretch which had been inundated by the adjacent marshes under all previous princes. Caecina Mavortius Basilius Decius, of the Decii stock, most famous and illustrious gentleman, ex-City Prefect, ex-Praetorian Prefect, ex-Ordinary Consul, patrician, zealously perspiring in the task enjoined him and happily devoted to the proclamations of the most clement Prince has restored them to a very ancient dryness quite unknown to the forefathers, for the perpetuation of the glory of such a lord, by means of many new channels which drain the water into the sea. Ḝ ['Palm and Laurel,' i.e. 'Victory!'].[87]

---

[86] Procopius, *Bella*, 5, 1, 29, Haury, 2.9.1–2.
[87] *CIL*, 10, 6850–2; *ILS*, 827; Fiebiger–Schmidt, no. 193, cited here: 'Dominus noster gloriosissimus adque inclytus rex Theodericus, victor ac triumfator, semper Augustus, bono rei publicae natus, custos libertatis et propagator Romani nominis, domitor gentium, Decennovii viae Appiae, id est a Tripontio usque Tarricinam, iter et loca, quae confluentibus ab utraque parte paludibus per omnes retro principes inundaverant, usui publico et securitate viantium, admiranda propitio Deo felicitate restituit: operi iniuncto naviter insudante adque clementissimi principis feliciter deserviente praeconiis ex prosapie Deciorum Caecina Mavortio Basilio Decio viro clarissimo et inlustri, ex praefecto urbi, ex praefecto praetorio, ex consule ordinario, patricio, qui ad perpetuandam tanti domini gloriam per plurimos, qui ante non, albeos deducta in mare aqua ignotae atavis et nimis antiquae reddidit siccitati. Ḝ.' For

This precious document has been roundly dismissed as quite atypical, a product of senatorial wishful thinking.[88] Such characterizations may be admissable from a constitutional perspective, but the inscription's significance alters considerably in the light of contemporary political developments. The royal letters 'imposing' the task on Decius – in return for which the senator received title to the recovered land – date from 507–11 and it is likely that this holds for the inscription as well.[89] The emphasis laid on the road repairs and the role Terracina played in the war with Constantinople indicate the continuing significance of the Appian Way in the infrastructure of Gothic Italy and suggest that it remained a well-traveled highway.[90] The senatorial wishful thinking of the commemorative inscription was certainly not placed under a bushel, since the inscription, which seems to have been set up on the Via Appia near Terracina, was chiseled in at least three or four copies, a sure sign that it was intended to be seen and make an impression.[91] The project was undertaken by a scion of the illustrious Decii family who held very high and delicate office, including the praetorian and urban prefectures under Odoacer. His family history and position suggest that he would have been identified with that king's policy of favoring the senatorial aristocracy in return for political support.[92] His probable brothers both had been consuls and also held urban and praetorian prefectures under Odoacer, while his nephews enjoyed high rank and the consulate under Theoderic, including Theodore in 505 and Importunus in 509.[93] In other words, we see here a leading member of the senatorial aristocracy engaged in an important – and profitable – enterprise for the common weal, raising conspicuous monuments to his own accomplishment and

---

the monogram. H.I. Marrou, 'Palma et Laurus', *Mélanges d'archéologie et d'histoire. École française de Rome*, 58 (1941–6), 109–31, esp. 119.

[88] E.g. Ensslin, *Theoderich*, p. 155; A.H.M. Jones, 'The constitutional position of Odoacer and Theoderic', *Journal of Roman Studies*, 52 (1962), 126–38, here 128.

[89] Cassiodorus, *Var.*, 2, 32 and 33, Fridh, 79–81.

[90] G.Radke, 'Viae publicae Romanae', *RE*, S.13 (1973), 1417–1686, here 1519–20; cf. Procopius, *Bella*, 5, 1, 1–2, Haury, 2.51.1–20.

[91] *CIL*, 10, 6850–2. No measurements given.

[92] *PLRE*, 2, 349 'Decius 2'; Cf. Chastagnol, *Sénat*, pp. 98–9.

[93] *PLRE*, 2, 217–18, 'Basilius 12' and '13'; 2, 1097–8, 'Theodorus 62', and 2, 592; cf. Chastagnol, *Sénat*, pp. 83–4.

the barbarian king. Against a backdrop of recent or ongoing
diplomatic and military confrontation with New Rome, Decius
publicly threw his lot in with the king, hailing him as *rex* and
Augustus and adopting for him the old imperial triumphal couplet
of 'Victor and Triumphator' and the epithet 'Tamer of
Foreigners'.[94] The whole was topped off by the circus monogram
emblematic of victory, which was appropriate for a family known
as the official patrons of the Green faction.[95] As the king himself
declared, the 'eyes of all' were on this project, a concrete symbol of
the collaboration of senate and king at a time when dissension
might have courted disaster.[96] Nor was it only Decius who was
implicated in the undertaking: a senatorial commission had
inspected the site and set out markers proclaiming the senatorial
role; the organizer had been invited to take on associates to share
both the costs and rewards.[97] The commemorative inscriptions
proclaimed to Latium the political colors of Decius and, echoing
the regime's own self-justification, laid heavy emphasis on the
king's victorious qualities. Despite their radically different formulation, therefore, these signs continue and broaden the line
of development outlined by the description of Theoderic as
'Triumphal Gentleman' at the Curia.[98]

One more time the Roman senate trotted out the terms of the
victory ideology to make a political point in the troubled relations
between Constantinople and Italy. The envoys Anastasius dis-

94 For 'domitor gentium [barbararum]' see e.g. Vegetius, *Mil.*, 2, praef., Lang, 33.11.
Cf. the very similar expressions used of the senate in *Epistulae theodericianae variae*, 9,
ed. T. Mommsen, *MGH.AA*, 12 (1894).392.2: 'Domitori orbis, praesuli et reparatori
libertatis senatui...'.
95 The patronage (*patrocinium*) had been exercised by Decius' probable brother; between
507–11 it was transferred to this man's heirs, Decius' nephews Albinus and Avienus:
Cassiodorus, *Var.*, 1, 20, 3, Fridh, 29.19–22 (cf. *PLRE*, 2, 217, 'Basilius 12').
96 Cassiodorus, *Var.*, 2, 33, 2, Fridh, 81.22–4: 'Intuere quippe omnium ora atque oculos
in te esse conuersos: respice serenitatis nostrae suspensa iudicia.'
97 *Ibid.*, 2, 32, 4, Fridh, 80.23–31; cf. 33, 2, Fridh, 81, and the boundary marker
discovered in the nineteenth century: *ILS*, 8956.
98 Another example of Theoderic's assumption of imperial attributes which may date
from this period and which parallels the decision of the Vandal king is the naming of a
site in 'Alamanorum patria', Theodericopolis, attested by the Anonymous Ravennate, *Cosmographia*, which seems to preserve some data from the Ostrogothic period:
ed. J. Schnetz, *Itineraria romana*, 2 (Leipzig, 1940), 61.6. Cf. F. Staab, 'Ostrogothic
geographers at the court of Theodoric the Great: A study of the sources of the
Anonymous Cosmographer of Ravenna', *Viator*, 7 (1976), 27–64.

patched to Rome in 516 seem to have been charged with enlisting the senate's aid in reestablishing peace in the church and improving relations between Italy and the empire.[99] The emperor's request of *senatus suus* posed a delicate diplomatic dilemma. In theory, his position as emperor put him into direct relation with the senate of old Rome. In reality, it was the Ostrogothic king who was master of the city. By a subtle combination of victory epithets, the 'Our Lord' title and the subordinate rank of son to father, the senate's reply paid lip service to imperial ascendancy while reminding Anastasius – still engaged in a difficult war with Vitalian, the champion of orthodoxy – of Roman realities.

Si prima semper est, *imperator inuicte*, a regentibus supplicum spectata deuotio, si solo gratia dominorum conciliatur obsequio, indubitanter agnosces, sacrae iussionis oracula quanta senatus uestri fuerint gratulatione suscepta, maxime cum ad hoc et animus *domini nostri inuictissimi* regis Theoderici *filii uestri* mandatorum uestrorum oboedientiam praecipientis accederet....[100]

The king is qualified with epithets which were not inappropriate to the imperial dignity, for he is 'Our Lord' and 'Most Unvanquished'. One cannot but observe that Theoderic is *invictissimus* in the superlative, whereas the supreme triumphator rates only the positive degree. The sole indication of the Ostrogoth's subordination to the emperor comes in the *filius vester* epithet. The senate's carefully crafted letter uses the terminology of victory to insinuate Theoderic's de facto local superiority over the emperor, even as the adoptive sonship and the royal title denote de iure inferiority. As the document itself recognizes, Theoderic had acquiesced to the emperor's request of the senate. This is tantamount to saying the senators' reply had Ravenna's stamp of approval.[101]

It is clear that members of the senatorial aristocracy made liberal use of the concepts and tokens of imperial victory in their public dealings with the barbarian rulers of their country. In so doing, they echoed the ruler's self-justification as it was advanced by his spokesmen. But are there any other traces of efforts by Theoderic to transmit this vision of a victorious kingship to the population?

---

[99] Stein, *Bas-Empire*, 2, 189ff. Anastasius' letter is in *Coll. Avell.*, 113, Günther, 2.506–7.
[100] *Coll. Avell.*, 114, Günther, 2.508.4–11.
[101] Cf. Stein, *Bas-Empire*, 2, 190.

As interpreted by the mosaic of San Apollinare Nuovo, the façade of the palace at Ravenna was decorated with statues or mosaics. It is not coincidental that they represent the personification of Victory.[102] For Theoderic – or at least his mint master – speaks directly to us on a gold medallion bearing his portrait and traditionally associated with the *tricennalia* celebrations at Rome.[103] The obverse legend reads REX THEODERICVS PIVS PRINC IS. The last group of letters has generated some controversy but it is most commonly resolved either as *Princ(eps) i(nvictus) s(emper)* or *Princ(eps) i(nvictu/nvictissimu)s*, the same victory epithet which other contemporaries used for Theoderic.[104] The unconquered king is portrayed in military dress, holding a Victory skipping on a globe. There is no mistaking the reverse message. A skipping Victory is wreathed with a royal title which corresponds to the senatorial evidence: 'King Theoderic, Conqueror of the Foreigners'.[105] Furthermore, similar themes are reflected in Theoderic's official correspondence, which contains more than one trace of concepts like princely victory and most fortunate armies.[106] While the prince's letters and heavy gold medallions targeted a more elite audience, broader segments of the population were not forgotten. As in the imperial provinces, the message of the new order's victory was propagated to the masses on the kingdom's silver and bronze coinage. As in Vandal Africa, the local coinage testifies to the marriage of growing regional loyalties and victory ideology:

---

[102] B. Thordemann, 'Was wissen wir von den Palästen zu Ravenna?', *Acta archaeologica*, 37 (1966), 1–24, here 13–15, and Deichmann, *Ravenna*, 2, 1, 143.

[103] V. Bierbrauer, *Die ostgotischen Grab- und Schatzfunde in Italien*, Biblioteca degli Studi medievali, 7 (Spoleto, n.d.), pp. 292–3; E. Bernareggi, 'Il medaglioni d'oro di Teodorico', *Rivista italiana di numismatica e scienze affini*, ser. 5, 17 (1969), 98–106, arguing for a later date, against which see F.W. Deichmann, *BZ*, 64 (1971), 291, who does, however, accept the 'invictissimus' resolution. Cf. too Hahn, *Moneta*, 1, 83.

[104] Bernareggi, 'Medaglioni', pp. 98–9; cf. e.g. Bierbrauer, *Schatzfunde*, p. 293.

[105] 'REX THEODERICVS VICTOR GENTIVM.'

[106] The army or an expedition can be routinely characterized as 'felicissimus', or the like, e.g. Cassiodorus, *Var.*, 5, 10, 1, Fridh, 190.2–3, 5, 32, 1, Fridh, 217.1; 5, 36, 1, 210.5; 11, 16, 4, 445.21. This is in keeping with contemporary Constantinopolitan usage, e.g. Justinian, *Novella, Appendix constitutionum dispersarum*, 7, 18, Schoell-Kröll, 3.801.40; *ibid.*, 9, 803.29 and 34; echoes of the victory ideology: Cassiodorus, *Var.*, 4, 32, 1, Fridh, 163.5–7; 8, 9, 6, 308.48 (concerning the late Theoderic, 'inuictus'); 11, 1, 10–13, 424.68–100.

the slogan ROMA INVICTA was calculated to appeal to peninsular sentiment.[107] Prayers for the king's success were expected of Italian prelates.[108] Early evidence of centrally organized nationwide fasts and prayer services in time of emergency also occurs under the Ostrogoths.[109] King Theodahad may even have ordered supplication services at Rome during the Byzantine invasion, but we do not know whether his command was carried out.[110]

The prominence of the king's unyielding victory in the political ideology and practice of Ostrogothic Italy has left unmistakable traces, despite the scarcity of direct evidence on the public ceremonies with which Theoderic expressed his rulership. But there is also one use of an element of the old victory conceptions that hints at new development. As we have observed, the later Roman idea of imperial victory tended to emphasize the emperor's monopoly of the quality which gave military success. Another view crops up in Jordanes' work 'On the Origin and Deeds of the Goths', written in A.D. 551 in an area controlled by Constantinople.[111] Jordanes' relative unoriginality with respect to his source material and the abundance of victory motifs found in his work may indicate that the latter go back to his main source, Cassiodorus' lost History of the Goths, which was composed at Theoderic's request.[112] The Goths' 'prehistory' is characterized by a succession of victories which were a kind of prefiguration of their later history. The almost typological relation between the tribe's ancient and recent history is exemplified by a remark concerning an archaic victory over the Vandals: '... and, at that time already, they subjugated their [*sc.* the Ulmerugi's] neighbors, the Vandals, and added them to their victories'.[113] The Goths as an ethnic unit were invested with the quality of victory. This explains

---

107 Hahn, *Moneta*, I, 85ff and 89ff.
108 Cassiodorus, *Var.*, 8, 8, 2, Fridh, 307.14–18.
109 *Ibid.*, 11, 3, 3, Fridh, 428.14–20 ('To various bishops', A.D. 533).
110 *Ibid.*, 10, 17, 2, Fridh, 400.19–21 ('To the Roman people', A.D. 535; cf. 10, 18, 1, 400.5–410.7 'To the Roman Senate', A.D. 535).
111 Wattenbach–Levison, *Geschichtsquellen*, pp. 76–7.
112 *Ibid.*, pp. 70–2 and 77.
113 *Get.*, 26, Mommsen, 60.11–12: '... eorumque vicinos Vandalos iam tunc subiugantes suis applicavere victoriis'. Other examples of 'prehistoric' Gothic victories: *Get.*, 28, Mommsen, 61.1–4; 47, 66.15–16; 49, 67.6–11; cf. 100, 83.20–2.

why Ennodius could point to the presence of *other* victors in the king's following, an observation which would not have been very politic if it had been pronounced at court in contemporary Constantinople.[114]

4. LOMBARD KINGSHIP AND VICTORY

No sooner had Byzantine Italy begun to recover from the hardships imposed by imperial reconquest and the Goths' dogged resistance than a new menace appeared on the scene, when the Lombards abandoned their recent settlement in Pannonia and invaded northern Italy.[115] They soon showed themselves a more lasting force than either the Goths or the imperialists, establishing a kingdom and duchies which were destined to dominate the peninsula's northern and central territories for over two hundred years. Yet the narrative sources for the kingdom's history are exceedingly thin; they are not backed up by significant amounts of archival material until the eighth century. Particularly severe is the lack of reliable narrative for the final decades of the monarchy's development, on the eve of the Carolingian conquest.[116] Nor are there any liturgical manuscripts which represent the kingdom's royal rites prior to the Frankish take-over.[117]

---

[114] Ennodius, *Pan.*, 69, Vogel, 211.31–2: 'diu vicisti in universis congressibus ⟨tuis⟩, nunc incipiens in obsequio habere victores'. Cf. *ibid.*, 83, 213.18–19, on the renewal of the 'victricia agmina' of Goths. On the role of the royal following in Ostrogothic government and society, Ensslin, *Theoderich*, pp. 173–5; Wolfram, *Goten*, pp. 362–6; T.S. Burns, *The Ostrogoths. Kingship and society*, Historia, Einzelschriften, 36 (Wiesbaden, 1980), pp. 107ff, but cf. on the limitations of Gothic ethnic awareness in Italy, G. Vetter, *Die Ostgoten und Theoderich*, Forschungen zur Kirchen- und Geistesgeschichte, 15 (Stuttgart, 1938), p. 27, and Burns, *Ostrogoths*, pp. 125–6.

[115] On the migration see J. Werner, *Die Langobarden in Pannonien. Beiträge zur Kenntnis der langobardischen Bodenfunde vor 568*, 1, Bayerische Akademie der Wissenschaften, Philos.-hist. Kl., Abhandlungen, n.F. 55 (Munich, 1962), pp. 13ff.

[116] Cf. e.g. R. Schneider, *Königswahl und Königserhebung im Frühmittelalter. Untersuchungen zur Herrschaftsnachfolge bei den Langobarden und Merowingern*, Monographien zur Geschichte des Mittelalters, 3 (Stuttgart, 1972), p. 6.

[117] K. Gamber, 'Ein oberitalienisches Sakramentarfragment des M-Typus', *Sacris erudiri*, 13 (1962), 367–76, voiced the hypothesis that the last two prayers of the 'Mass against the pagans' in Vatican, B. apost. Vat. lat. 337, flyleaves (s. ix according to Gamber, *CLLA*, 809) were original compositions which went back to the independent Lombard kingdom. But they are most likely related to contemporary Frankish texts: see below, Ch. 9, n. 99.

The circumstances of the Lombard settlement differed greatly from those of the Vandals, Burgundians and Ostrogoths. On one hand, the Lombards established themselves in an area where the social, economic and administrative structures of Roman civilization had suffered severe dislocation during the Gothic wars.[118] On the other, the Lombards, unlike their predecessors, were relative newcomers to the seductions of Mediterranean civilization. They lacked the long tradition of imperial service or conflict which had familiarized other groups with Roman institutions and attitudes. To be sure, the Lombards' archaeological traces reveal contacts with the subroman civilization associated with the Merovingians and, even in the Pannonian period, the elite were hardly immune to the attraction of Roman luxury goods.[119] But by and large, the savage and alien character of the Lombards impressed even experienced barbarian watchers.[120] For both reasons, assimilation of Roman values and customs as well as cooption by local subroman society appear to have progressed more slowly. The newcomers were in no hurry to jettison all sense of their ancient customs and identity. Victory banquets in the form of saga-style drinking bouts, the custom of requiring one's son to obtain arms from the king of another tribe, the expectation that the queen pour the wine for her husband's band of trusty warriors, all are attested for the sixth century and their memory was vivid in the mind of Paul Deacon two hundred years later.[121]

Nonetheless, once they settled in the heartland of the old Roman empire, it was impossible for the Lombards to escape the spell cast by a decaying but superior material civilization. If social fusion

---

[118] On the devastation of Italy, Stein, *Bas-Empire*, 2, 616ff. Cf. P. Llewellyn, *Rome in the dark ages* (London, 1971), pp. 78ff.

[119] Werner, *Langobarden*, 1, 131ff and 106–7, on Mediterranean luxury items from a princely grave of the Pannonian period.

[120] Limited Roman influence on the Lombards prior to 568: Schmidt, *Ostgermanen*, pp. 611–12; on their savagery, *ibid.*, p. 592.

[121] Paul Deacon, *Hist. Lang.*, 1, 23, Bethmann–Waitz, 61.8–10 (on such banquets in early Germanic society, cf. Tacitus, *De Germania*, 22); *Hist. Lang.*, 1, 23, 61.11–13 and 1, 24, 62.9–12; cf. E. Eichmann, 'Die Adoption des deutschen Königs durch den Papst', *Zeitschrift der Savigny-Stiftung für Rechtsgeschichte, Germanistische Abteilung*, n.F. 37 (1916), 291–312, here 295–6, and K. Hauck, 'Formes de parenté artificielle dans le haut moyen âge', *Famille et parenté dans l'Occident médiéval*, Collection de l'École française de Rome, 30 (Rome, 1977), pp. 43–7, here 45; *Hist. Lang.*, 3, 30, 109.14–16, cf. *Beowulf*, 620ff, ed. C.L. Wrenn, 3rd edn (London, 1958), 121.

had to await the eighth century, the seventh saw the new settlers increasingly assimilate the language and religion of the local population.[122] Their incomplete control over the peninsula surely contributed to the impact of Byzantine provincial culture on the newcomers. Once installed in Italy, the Lombards entered into more or less permanent conflict of varying intensity with the armed forces of Ravenna. In the middle of the seventh century, the Lombards had even to confront an imperial army led by the Roman emperor in person. Military competition could only have produced a greater familiarity with the operational style and practices of the Byzantine army.[123] Moreover, in times of war and peace alike, early medieval frontiers were not exactly impermeable. When duke Arichis of Benevento (594–640/1) sent his son to the court of king Rothari (636–52), he is supposed to have traveled via Ravenna.[124] King Aistulf had to promulgate specific legislation against any official (*iudex*) or freeman (*arimann*) who might have dealings with the Romans during the final war against Ravenna. The implication is that such contacts were an ongoing affair at both levels of Lombard society, war or no war.[125] Archaeology confirms the documents here: Lombards appear to

---

[122] E. Sestan, 'La composizione etnica della società in rapporto allo svolgimento della civiltà in Italia nel secolo VII', *Caratteri del secolo VII in Occidente*, 2, Settimane, 5 (Spoleto, 1958), 649–77; cf. R. Buchner, *ibid.*, 1, 316–17 and esp. J. Jarnut, *Prosopographische und sozialgeschichtliche Studien zum Langobardenreich in Italien (568–774)*, Bonner historische Forschungen 38 (Bonn, 1972), p. 426, and J. Werner, 'Stand und Aufgaben der frühmittelalterlichen Archäologie in der Langobardenfrage', *Atti del 6° congresso internazionale di studi sull'alto medioevo*, 1 (Spoleto, 1980), 27–46. Lombard Arianism has traditionally been cited as a factor separating the two groups but this has recently been called into question: S.C. Fanning, 'Lombard Arianism reconsidered', *Speculum*, 56 (1981), 241–58. Another factor was likely the ramifications of the empire's 'eternal victory', for many Roman citizens considered the Lombard settlement just another in a long series of troublesome but short-term disruptions in imperial administration: C. Diehl, *Études sur l'administration byzantine dans l'Exarchat de Ravenne (568–751)*, Bibliothèque des Écoles françaises d'Athènes et de Rome, 53 (Paris, 1888), pp. 10–11.

[123] See in general Diehl, *Exarchat*, pp. 197ff; cf. G.P. Bognetti, 'L'influsso delle istituzioni militari romane sulle istituzioni longobarde del sec. V e la natura della *fara*', *Atti del congresso internazionale di diritto romano e di storia di diritto*, 4 (Milan, 1953), 167–210.

[124] Whence the rumor that the crafty Romans had him drugged, for he seems not to have been right in the head: Paul Deacon, *Hist. Lang.*, 4, 42, Bethmann–Waitz, 134.23–5.

[125] Aistulf, *Leges*, 4, ed. F. Bluhme, *MGH.Leges*, 4 (1868).196.18–197.3.

286

have acted as middlemen, exporting Egyptian bronzeware and Ravennate gold coinage north of the Alps.[126]

Some degree of social differentiation marked Lombard attitudes toward late Roman civilization. The monarchy in particular seems to have led the way in aggressively appropriating elements of the host culture. As early as the first generations in Italy, royal marriages with the Merovingians and Thuringians constituted a first step in this direction.[127] When the prefect Longinus' pleas of love finally prevailed over the Lombard queen Rosamunda, she could find no more propitious moment for murdering her unfortunate lover, the royal *cubicularius* Helmechis, than while he relaxed in a Roman bath. Even were we to dismiss the story as legend, it unquestionably seemed natural, scarcely two generations later, to imagine the murder-suicide in an institution emblematic of Roman civilization.[128] It was no accident that the one place in the upper echelons of Lombard society which appears to have admitted a meaningful proportion of Romans was the royal entourage.[129] By the eighth century, the royal chancellery was adopting more and more elements which smacked of the imperial administration. Close links with Constantinople in the final years of the kingdom's existence are suggested by the young ruler Adelchis' decision to take refuge there, after Charlemagne conquered Pavia.[130]

The attitude of Lombard rulers towards the trappings of monarchy offers fresh insight into the elite's appropriation of some

---

[126] Werner, *Langobarden*, I, 17–18.

[127] See the marriages cited in Schneider, *Königswahl*, pp. 17, 19, and 22.

[128] *Origo gentis Langobardorum*, 5, ed. G. Waitz, *MGH.SRL*, (1878), 5.6–10, composed under king Rothari (636–52): cf. Wattenbach–Levison, *Geschichtsquellen*, p. 207. Schmidt, *Ostgermanen*, p. 595, considers the detail to be legendary. The story implies adaptation, as well as adoption, of Roman customs, for there would have been little point to Helmechis' and Rosamunda's affair if Lombard *cubicularii* were of the same condition as those of the eastern court.

[129] Jarnut, *Langobardenreich*, p. 411.

[130] C. Brühl, 'Zentral- und Finanzverwaltung im Franken- und im Langobardenreich', *I problemi dell'Occidente nel secolo VIII*, I, Settimane, 20 (Spoleto, 1973), pp. 61–94 and 169–85, and 'Purpururkunden', *Festschrift H. Beumann* (Sigmaringen, 1977), pp. 3–21, esp. 9–10, on the chancellery. On Adelchis and the Byzantine involvement: P. Classen, 'Karl der Grosse, das Papsttum und Byzanz. Die Begründung des karolingischen Kaisertums', *Karl der Grosse. Lebenswerk und Nachleben*, I (Düsseldorf, 1965), 537–608, here 555–6.

facets of late Roman civilization. The early decision to reside in a capital city may have stimulated the development of royal ceremonial. Although their choice at first wavered among Verona, Milan and Pavia, the kings finally settled on the last city.[131] Of potential areas of enquiry, only Lombard accessions have been thoroughly studied to date. The scarcity of evidence bars forever a full understanding of these rites, but Schneider has detected bits of differing ceremonies.[132] Their variety probably means that accession ceremonies evolved in the course of the kingdom's history. To judge by its setting, the earliest known royal accession ceremony may well have drawn heavily on imperial ritual. In July 604, king Agilulf's son Adalvald was raised (*levatus est*) to the royal dignity in the circus at Milan, in the presence of the king and the legates of Theudebert II, king of Austrasia, whose daughter was affianced to Adalvald.[133] A century later, coronations had moved to a more sacral zone; at least one included investiture with a lance which perhaps bore a banner, and the accession of Luitprand may have included an enthronement ceremony.[134] Some kind of ceremonial display and customary deportment distinguished royal audiences granted to foreign ambassadors.[135] The *adventus* rite appears to have been practiced by Lombard kings, but it is difficult to specify Roman ritual's impact on this ceremony from Paul Deacon's jejeune descriptions.[136] Historical topography and Lombard building activity reinforce the narrative sources' hints that ceremonial enhanced key moments in the life of the monarchy. From the

---

[131] E. Ewig, 'Résidence et capitale pendant le haut moyen âge', *Spätantikes und fränkisches Gallien*, 1, Beihefte der *Francia*, 3 (Munich, 1976), pp. 362–408, here 373ff; P. Vaccari, 'Pavia nell'alto medioevo', *La città nell'alto medioevo*, Settimane, 6 (Spoleto, 1959), pp. 151–92, and esp. D.A. Bullough, 'Urban change in early medieval Italy: the example of Pavia', *Papers of the British School at Rome*, 34 (1966), 82–130, here 90–2 and 94–5.

[132] Cf. Schneider, *Königswahl*, p. 260; H. Fröhlich, 'Studien zur langobardischen Thronfolge von den Anfängen bis zur Eroberung des italienischen Reiches durch Karl den Grossen (774)' (Diss. Tübingen, 1980), was not available to me.

[133] Paul Deacon, *Hist. Lang.*, 4, 30, Bethmann–Waitz, 127.9–11; cf. Schneider, *Königswahl*, pp. 33–5.

[134] *Hist. Lang.*, 6, 55, 184.19–23; cf. Schneider, *Königswahl*, pp. 55ff.

[135] Paul Deacon, *Hist. Lang.*, 6, 35, Bethmann–Waitz, 76.27–9; cf. *ibid.*, 3, 30, 109.6–8 concerning audiences at the Bavarian court.

[136] Paul Deacon, *Hist. Lang.*, 3, 30, Bethmann–Waitz, 110.3–9 and 5, 39, 159.6–11.

monarchy's early days, there may have been an implicit connection between the Hebdomon palace complex in the European suburbs of Constantinople with its chapel of St John the Baptist and the Lombard summer palace complex at Monza and chapel of the same dedication, some twelve miles from the royal capital at Milan.[137] Particularly significant is king Perctarit's (671–88) construction of a magnificent gate close by the palace at Pavia. As we will see again for the Visigoths, it is difficult to imagine that such an expensive undertaking was unrelated to the king's ceremonial movements and their architectural backdrop.[138] The independently minded duchy of Benevento betrays a similar concern not long thereafter. That town's palace, church of Sancta Sophia and Golden Gate offer a combination redolent of the duke's Byzantine fervor and suggest that emulation of imperial monarchy was not confined to Lombard kings.[139] Taken together, topography and the historical record evince consistent traces of royal concern with ceremonial and provide the framework within which we can view the rare vestiges of victory practices among the Lombards.

The earliest demonstrable concern of a Lombard king for the Roman trappings of victory comes from a nineteenth-century find of unknown archaeological context in the Val di Nievole (Prov. Lucca).[140] A gilded bronze helmet plate or visor inscribed with the name of king Agilulf (591–615) preserves the earliest known portrait of a Germanic ruler seated on a throne (fig. 12);

---

[137] Paul Deacon, *Hist. Lang.*, 4, 21, Bethmann–Waitz 123.17–124.5. For the Constantinopolitan installations, Janin, *Cple byz.*, pp. 139–40, 446–9, and *Églises*, pp. 426–9. See esp. K.H. Krüger, *Königsgrabkirchen der Franken, Angelsachsen und Langobarden bis zur Mitte des 8. Jahrhunderts*, Münstersche Mittelalter-Schriften, 4 (Münster, 1971), pp. 346ff.

[138] Paul Deacon, *Hist. Lang.*, 5, 36, Bethmann–Waitz, 156.30–1; cf. Bullough, 'Urban change', p. 90, n. 25, and Krüger, *Königsgrabkirchen*, p. 371.

[139] The Golden Gate is mentioned ca. 752–6 in a Beneventan act, ed. C. Troya, *Codice diplomatico Langobardo dal DLXVIII al DCCLXXIV con note storiche, osservazioni e dissertazioni*, 4 (Naples, 1854), 179–82, here 182; cf. A. Chroust, *Untersuchungen über die Langobardischen Königs- und Herzogsurkunden* (Graz, 1888), pp. 200–1. On the political context in general, H. Belting, 'Studien zum beneventanischen Hof im 8. Jahrhundert', *DOP*, 16 (1962), 141–93.

[140] See O. von Hessen, *Secondo contributo alla archeologia Longobarda in Toscana* (Florence, 1975), pp. 90ff. Cf. H. Roth (ed.), *Kunst der Völkerwanderungszeit*, Propyläen Kunstgeschichte, Supplementband 4 (Frankfurt, 1979), no. 101, pp. 178–9 (O. von Hessen).

Figure 12. Agilulf visor (see pp. 289–93)

Agilulf is making the gesture of *adlocutio*, familiar from imperial iconography.[141] His feet rest on a support and, in a most unimperial detail, he clasps his sword in his lap. He does not wear a crown. Agilulf's long hair, moustache and long, pointed beard proclaim his non-Romanness. The accompanying inscription identifies him:

DN
AG
IL
V[...

to the left, RĘGI to the right.[142] Behind him stand two bodyguards, holding lances and shields and wearing helmets quite similar to the reconstructed seventh-century helmet of Sassanian derivation found at Niederstötzingen.[143] The central figures are flanked by two winged Victories, holding horns – cornucopia for

---

[141] Schramm, *Herrschaftszeichen und Staatssymbolik*, 1, 319 and 231.

[142] von Hessen, *Secondo contributo*, p. 93 with pl. 29b. Judging by the photo, the damaged segment affects only the right inscription, where space would allow the restitution DN/ AG/ IL/ V[L/ F], probably without a Latin case ending. Agilulf's bare head suggests that at the time the plate was executed, Lombard rulers had not yet adopted the crown as an emblem of power, particularly since the artist was so scrupulous in executing the D.N. title, the throne, long hair, and other details.

[143] Roth, *Völkerwanderungszeit*, pl. 267; cf. p. 296 (M. Schulze).

some, drinking horns for others – and inscribed standards.[144] The Victories introduce to the king two sets of figures with out-stretched hands and bent knee, apparently proceeding from the towers or city-symbols which end each side of the visor. The right-hand suppliant is bearded and has been identified as a Lombard while the left-hand suppliant appears to be clean shaven and has been viewed as a Roman. Each is followed by a seemingly clean shaven person, carrying what look like decorated helmets or helmet-crowns surmounted by crosses.

Art historians do not agree on what is being shown. According to Wessel, the plate shows the triumph of Agilulf over his rebel-lious dukes who are performing the feudal gesture of *immixtio manuum*. Following von Hessen, it may show Agilulf's accession, with crowns brought to him by his Roman and Lombard subjects.[145] Both agree that the composition is inspired by similar Byzantine scenes of the homage of subject or vanquished peoples to the emperor, a scene which had been given monu-mental form as recently as Justinian's Brazen House mosaic.[146] As far as contemporary imperial ceremonies are concerned, the closest parallel would be the presentation of the symbols of victory to the enthroned emperor, as for instance when Totila's headdress was laid at Justinian's feet after the victory of the Byzantines and their Lombard allies over the Goths in 552. The possibility that the king who staged his son's accession in the Milanese circus may have lifted a page from imperial victory celebrations cannot be excluded. Surely the fact that, beyond the king's name, the only other writing on the piece is the word VICTVRIA, inscribed twice on the Victories' standards, is not without significance. The kind of iconographical model, the contemporary parallel of imperial ritual, the gestures of submission of Roman and barbarian alike, the king's majesty, the intermediary position and gestures of the Victories and the outright statement of their

144 K. Wessel, 'Ikonographische Bemerkungen zur Agilulf-Platte', *Festschrift Johannes Jahn zum XXII. November MCMLVII* (Leipzig [1958]), pp. 61–7, here 63, and von Hessen, *Secondo contributo*, p. 94. Note that horn-shaped goblets were popular with the Lombards: N. Åberg, *Die Goten und Langobarden in Italien* (Uppsala, 1923), pp. 132–3, and that drinking bouts were a prominent part of legendary Lombard victory celebrations: Paul Deacon, *Hist. Lang.*, 1, 23, Bethmann–Waitz, 61.8–10.
145 Wessel, 'Agilulf-Platte', pp. 64–5; von Hessen, *Secondo contributo*, p. 96.
146 Wessel, 'Agilulf-Platte', pp. 62–3; von Hessen, *Secondo contributo*, p. 94.

standards, even the drinking horns seem to add up to one conclusion: the relief proclaims the king's victory. Whether the scene was meant to commemorate a particular ceremony along the lines of the arrival of the Roman symbols of victory or whether it was intended as a symbolic depiction of Agilulf's quality as victor and ruler of Roman and barbarian alike is not easy to determine. Both are possible. In either case, the essential conclusion remains the same: the metalworker adapted an imperial iconographic schema to project king Agilulf's victory on the visor of what must have been a very splendid helmet.

But iconography does not exhaust this witness's testimony: we have still to address the problem of the original object's function. How else can we determine the *audience* of this neat piece of dark-age propaganda? The visor's subject points clearly to production in Agilulf's milieu, if not at the royal court itself.[147] At the same time, it has been noted that no evidence suggests this was Agilulf's helmet. Indeed, the reported provenance argues against this identification.[148] How then does a lavish helmet, conspicuously associated with the king but apparently not made for his personal use, fit with what we know of migration-era Germanic society?

The most obvious answer is that the Val di Nievole helmet was a royal gift, a prime example of that lordly open-handedness for which early Germanic society felt the high esteem which is clear to any reader of Beowulf.[149] Indeed, the Anglo-Saxon poet cites precisely king Beowulf's gifts of helmets and mail shirts as evidence of his good rulership, which his followers rewarded by their disloyalty.[150] Gifts of *arma* were part and parcel of Lombard rulership.[151] Von Hessen has suggested that this helmet was a gift

---

[147] von Hessen, *Secondo contributo*, p. 97; cf. Wessel, 'Agilulf-Platte', p. 61.

[148] von Hessen, *Secondo contributo*, p. 97. Agilulf died at Milan. Various traditions place his grave at Monza or Pavia, while Milan cannot be excluded. That still leaves us far from Val di Nievole. See Krüger, *Königsgrabkirchen*, p. 338, n. 3.

[149] On the helmet as a probable gift, von Hessen, *Secondo contributo*, p. 97. Personal retainers in early Germanic societies expected to receive arms from their lord, whence the law codes' regulations on their disposition upon termination of service: *Codex Euricianus*, 310–1, on *arma* received from patrons by *bucellarii* or (private) *saiones*, ed. K. Zeumer, *MGH. Leges Visigothorum* (1902), 18.18–26 and 19.18–21; cf. *Lex Visigothorum*, 5, 3, 1–2, *ibid.*, 216.17–20 and 217.10–11.

[150] *Beowulf*, 2868–9; cf. 2811, Wrenn, 200 and 199.

[151] Paul Deacon, *Hist. Lang.*, 1, 24, Bethmann–Waitz, 61.14–62.11.

from Agilulf to one of the Lombard dukes, but the precise identity of the likely recipient cannot of course be determined.[152] Another possibility is that Agilulf gave the helmet to one of his personal retainers, a possibility comforted by the consideration that the visor may have belonged to a Niederstötzingen-type helmet, for Agilulf's guards are shown with precisely this kind of headgear.[153] The man, whoever he was, on whom Agilulf may have bestowed such a splendid gift quite likely came from his own elite. For we can be certain the message of the king's victory was intended for the helmet's user, not for the unhappy enemy who would have been dead before he got close enough to discern the message on the Lombard warrior's brow.

One other shaft of light falls on the Lombards and victory in the Roman style, thanks to Paul the Deacon's rather detailed account of king Cunincpert's (678–700) struggle against the usurpation of Alahis, duke of Trent and Brescia.[154] An anecdote reveals that Byzantine triumphal customs were not foreign to seventh-century Lombard battlefields. When Cunincpert's troops confronted the rebel forces, the king proposed hand-to-hand combat with the duke, so as to spare both armies. Cunincpert's followers were overcome with fear for their king and their cause and prevailed on him to send Seno, a deacon from Pavia, in his place. After Alahis had made short work of the hapless cleric, he ordered what was clearly a customary observance among the Lombards: Seno was to be decapitated and his head raised on a spear while the army chanted 'Thanks be to God'. Of course as soon as he saw the head, Alahis recognized the trick.[155] Both liturgical thanksgiving

---

152 von Hessen, *Secondo contributo*, p. 97.

153 So von Hessen, *Secondo contributo*, pp. 91–2. This is contradicted by W. Kurze, 'La lamina di Agilulfo: usurpazione o diritto?', *Atti del 6° congresso internazionale di studi sull'alto medioevo*, 2 (Spoleto, 1980), 447–56, here 451–2, who observes that the visor is slightly larger and has a smaller nose piece than comparable helmets. That one of the rivets damaged the inscription leads him to the hypothesis that the plate was conceived for another use and then reused as a helmet visor, a possible but not inescapable deduction.

154 On the usurpation, see in general L.M. Hartmann, *Geschichte Italiens im Mittelalter*, 2, 1 (Gotha, 1900). pp. 266ff; cf. G. Fasoli, *I Langobardi in Italia* (Bologna, 1965), pp. 139ff.

155 Paul Deacon, *Hist. Lang.*, 5, 40, Bethmann–Waitz, 159.27–160.28, esp. 160.27–8: 'Cumque caput eius amputari praecepisset, ut, levato eo in conto, "Deo gratias" adclamarent, sublata casside, clericum se occidisse cognovit.' It was then that Alahis

on the battlefield and the triumphal display of a vanquished enemy's head are familiar features of late Roman military practice and both are obviously at home among the Lombards. What seems new and particularly repugnant to modern spectators is their conflation into one observance.

Ultimately, Cunincpert was victorious. To mark his success, he celebrated a triumphal entry into the capital, presumably through the magnificent gate his father had built.[156] Though the ceremony's details are not recorded, the appropriation of Byzantine army customs on the battlefield suggests that similar influences shaped the king's entry. Moreover, triumphal entries may also have been staged by the kingdom's unruly dukes.[157]

Finally, Cunincpert's success over Alahis also shows that here, as elsewhere in the twilight of antiquity, the cult of saints had become enmeshed in Lombard victory practices. After the rebel's defeat, the king founded a monastery of St George on the site of the fateful battle. The choice of the monastery's location argues strongly for its establishment as a thanksgiving foundation to St George for his presumed intervention on the king's behalf.[158] At any rate, this is the earliest attestation of a custom whose most famous example occurs several centuries later in William the Conqueror's Battle Abbey. Like the Roman commanders against whom they fought, Lombard rulers rewarded their celestial battle

---

made a memorable, if unusual, battlefield vow, which Paul has carefully recorded for posterity: 'Tale itaque nunc facio votum, ut, si mihi Deus victoriam iterum dederit, quod unum puteum de testiculis impleam clericorum', *ibid.*, 160.30–1.

[156] Paul Deacon, *Hist. Lang.*, 5, 41, Bethmann–Waitz, 161.20–1, is laconic, perhaps because of the work's unfinished state: '...ipse vero regnator cum omnium exultatione et triumpho victoriae Ticinum reversus est'. As Schneider, *Königswahl*, p. 49, n. 242, emphasizes, this is the concluding sentence of Book Five. Paul's list of *capitula* suggests that he intended to dwell on the ceremony at greater length: 'Item bellum Cunicperti [*sic*] et Alahis, et de victoria Cunincperti, et quomodo triumphans Ticinum ingressus est', Bethmann–Waitz, 141.32–3. On Paul's authorship of the *capitula*, *ibid.*, p. 25.

[157] Paul Deacon, *Hist. Lang.*, 5, 10, Bethmann–Waitz, 149.19–23, on the son of Grimuald, duke of Benevento (647–62) and his victory over the Byzantine army of Constans II (641–68): '...Romuald vero, patrata de inimicis victoria, Beneventum triumphans reversus est patrique gaudium et cunctis securitatem, sublato hostium timore, convexit'. Cf. Sicco's intended triumph, in Erchempert of Monte Cassino's ninth-century *Historia Langobardorum Beneventanorum*, 10, ed. G. Waitz, *MGH.SRL*, (1878), 238.19–28 concerning the siege of 821.

[158] Paul Deacon, *Hist. Lang.*, 6, 17, Bethmann–Waitz, 170.20–1.

patrons with earthly gifts. But once again, the adoption of earlier custom includes adaptation, for no instance has yet come to light when a victorious late antique commander singled out the very site of battle and bloodshed for a victory endowment.[159]

The pattern of celebration is maintained by a rare literary endeavor from the same period. Around 698, a certain Stephen composed a rhythmic Poem on the Synod of Pavia to honor the synod and king Cunincpert. The king's victory over rebels, including Alahis, finds a prominent place in Stephen's description of the royal qualities.[160]

Two general points need to be made about Lombard royal ritual in general and victory practices in particular. The first is that the earliest systematic development occurs in the reign of Agilulf and Theudelinda. To this period dates the Agilulf visor – which may reflect a ceremony derived from imperial ritual – the constructions at Monza and celestial patronage reminiscent of Constantinople as well as the elevation of a royal heir in the circus of Milan. This is the period of the peace treaty with the empire; it is also, following the short reign of Theudelinda's first husband, a period of consolidation of the monarchy after the anarchy of the interregnum of 574–84.[161] That the bulk of otherwise attested victory observances occur during the reaffirmation of royal authority after a defeated rebellion offers an important clue to the motivation behind such displays. What is known of Lombard royal ritual indicates that its primary objective was to enhance the monarchy's prestige and that imitation of the Roman emperor was a viable means of doing this. The historical context which we

[159] On Byzantine victory endowments, see above, Ch. 6, n. 6: cf. Ch. 2, n. 133. For military cults in the Lombard kingdom, cf. the army's standard showing the image of St Michael: Paul Deacon, *Hist. Lang.*, 5, 41, Bethmann–Waitz, 161.7–10; on the cult, G.P. Bognetti, *L'età longobarda*, 3 (Milan, 1968), 333; on the cult's Byzantine origin, W. von Rintelen, *Kultgeographische Studien in der Italia Byzantina. Untersuchungen über die Kulte des Erzengels Michael und der Madonna di Costantinopoli in Süditalien*, Archiv für vergleichende Kulturwissenschaft, 3 (Meisenheim, 1969), pp. 42ff. John the Baptist also interceded for the Lombard armies: *Hist. Lang.*, 5, 6, Bethmann–Waitz, 146.21–147.8, as well as the curious interpolation at 4, 21, 123.30–1 and 124.18–26. Cf. Krüger, *Königsgrabkirchen*, pp. 347 and 441.
[160] *Carmen de synodo Ticinensi*, ed. K. Strecker, *MGH.Poet.*, 4.2 (1923).728–31, esp. str. 5, *ibid.*, 729.
[161] On the peace treaty, Hartmann, *Geschichte*, 2, 1, 116ff; on the *interregnum* and restoration, Schmidt, *Ostgermanen*, pp. 596–603; cf. Fasoli, *Longobardi*, pp. 61ff.

have argued for the Agilulf visor, as well as the social dichotomy of Romans and Lombards in the early history of the kingdom, hints that the audience for these efforts lay largely *within* the ranks of the newcomers themselves. Competition between king and dukes may have played a significant role in both groups' recourse to elements of eastern *Staatssymbolik*.

This internal focus of Lombard royal prestige elucidates a second major point: as early as the Agilulf visor and as late as the struggle between Cunincpert and Alahis, Lombard appropriation of Byzantine victory customs is characterized as much by adaptation as by adoption. But perhaps the most significant Lombard contribution to the ancient victory conceptions occurs in their most ancient extant historical narrative, the anonymous 'Origin of the People (*gens*) of the Lombards'. According to a tradition current in the first half of the seventh century, the pre-settlement Lombards emerged as an ethnic unit named 'Langobarbi' only with their first great victory, when Wodan granted them a crushing defeat of the Vandals. The victoriousness of the Lombards was bound up with and emblematized their awareness of their emergence as a unique people. Rather than characterizing an individual, like Augustus, or an institution, like the late Roman imperial office, victory has now become what Jordanes had hinted for the Goths: a characteristic of a tribe. We have taken another step into the Middle Ages.[162]

---

[162] *Origo gentis Langobardorum*, 1, Waitz, 2.21–3.5. A century later, Paul would retell the story in the *Hist. Lang.*, 1, 8, Bethmann–Waitz, 52.11–53.7; although he dismisses the story of Wodan and Frea, he considers the victory over the Vandals as historical fact. In Fredegar, *Chronicae*, 3, 65, ed. B. Krusch, *MGH.SRM*, 2 (1888).110.18–21, this sequence becomes a victory cry of the Lombards. Cf. K. Hauck, 'Lebensnormen und Kultmythen in germanischen Stammes- und Herrschergenealogien', *Saeculum*, 6 (1955), 186–223, here 207–14, and R. Wenskus, *Stammesbildung und Verfassung. Das Werden der frühmittelalterlichen Gentes* (Cologne, 1961), pp. 487–8.

8

The king's victory in Visigothic Spain

The Goths who settled as federates in the territory around
Toulouse in 418 had known late Roman civilization at first hand
for more than a generation and had long undergone its influence
from across the *limes*.[1] Late antique culture and society made a
powerful impact on them during the Tolosan period, when a
Visigothic king could develop an acquaintance with Latin
literature and Romans rose high in royal service, when even
Euric's (466–84) 'national' ethnic legislation was impregnated
with Roman principles and practice. Perhaps precisely because
they were Germanic islands in a Roman sea, the Goths clung to
their customs, dress, language and Arian confession, and their
kings came to enforce a policy of separateness which extended
from religion to intermarriage with the Roman majority.[2] For
this they paid the price in 507, when their army and their kingdom
collapsed under attack from Clovis and what later sources portray as well-timed Catholic propaganda. Thanks to Ostrogothic
intervention, the Visigoths retained their southernmost possessions and slowly began to reorganize their power in the Iberian
peninsula. Under Leovigild (568–86), the barriers between Goth
and Roman started to diminish: the ban on miscegenation was
explicitly lifted and some movement toward theological compro-
mise appeared.[3] The conversion of his son Reccared to orthodoxy

---

[1] On this period, see Wolfram, *Goten*, pp. 207ff. Cf. M. Rouche, *L'Aquitaine des
Wisigoths aux Arabes, 418–781. Naissance d'une région* (Paris, 1979), pp. 19ff, which
unfortunately came into my hands too late to be used in a systematic fashion.
[2] Wolfram, *Goten*, pp. 256ff and 287ff. On the *Codex Euricianus*, P. D. King, *Law and
society in the Visigothic kingdom* (Cambridge, 1972), pp. 8ff.
[3] K. Schäferdiek, *Die Kirche in den Reichen der Westgoten und Suewen bis zur Errichtung der*

was followed by that of the Gothic church and elite. Although the details are difficult to discern, the first half of the seventh century saw the two ethnic groups becoming increasingly indistinguishable, as the Gothic language and traditional costume vanished from the Iberian peninsula.[4] The development of Visigothic royal ceremonial reflects one facet of this process of acculturation.

I. ROYAL CEREMONY AND VISIGOTHIC KINGSHIP

Kingship among the Visigoths developed in dialogue with their wanderings through the Roman empire.[5] The emergence of an ambitious monarchy and attendant institutions settled in the capital of Toulouse created traditions which influenced the kingdom's second incarnation in Spain. As the ruler acclamations recorded by Spanish church councils attest, the rhetoric of royal power surrounding the sacral monarchy of the late sixth and seventh centuries has rightly been characterized as 'theocratic'.[6] Whether royal rhetoric was embodied in ritual display is more complex. There is universal agreement that Leovigild – whose reign marked a decisive turn in the power and prestige of the Visigothic monarchy – developed royal ceremonial. Claude has correctly observed, however, that it has not thus far been possible to demonstrate that Visigothic court ceremonies imitated those of Constantinople.[7] The analysis of Visigothic victory celebrations will supply a definitive resolution to this problem. A second difficulty concerns the long-term development of royal ceremonial. A celebrated passage in Isidore of Seville's History of the Goths has made axiomatic among specialists that a throne, royal robes and, consequently, court ceremonial, were adopted only under Leovigild.[8] The problem is that this account contradicts Sidonius

---

westgotischen katholischen Staatskirche, Arbeiten zur Kirchengeschichte, 39 (Berlin, 1967), pp. 189ff, and King, *Law*, pp. 13–15. E.A. Thompson, *The Goths in Spain* (Oxford, 1969), pp. 58–9 is more sceptical of Leovigild's intentions.
[4] E.g. Thompson, *Spain*, pp. 108–9, 151–2, 314; D. Claude, *Geschichte der Westgoten* (Stuttgart, 1970), pp. 62 and 85ff; King, *Law*, pp. 18–19.
[5] Wolfram, *Goten*, pp. 169ff, and idem, 'Gotisches Königtum', pp. 5ff.
[6] King, *Law*, pp. 23ff.
[7] D. Claude, *Adel, Kirche und Königtum im Westgotenreich*, Vorträge und Forschungen, Sonderband, 8 (Sigmaringen, 1971), p. 67.
[8] *Ibid.*, p. 62, with n. 36; K. F. Stroheker, *Germanentum und Spätantike* (Zurich, 1965),

Apollinaris' fifth-century description of king Theoderic II (453–66) in the audience hall of his palace at Toulouse. According to Sidonius, the king sat on a throne (*sella, solium*) during audiences. He was flanked by armed bodyguards who stood inside the chancel barrier separating the throne area from the rest of the room, but outside the curtain which veiled the ruler.[9] That this arrangement was only part of Theoderic's accoutrements of majesty follows from Sidonius' account of royal banquets. The couches and hangings were imperial purple or festive white, while the meals themselves were characterized by 'Greek elegance ..., public ceremony (*pompa*), private diligence and royal discipline'.[10] More than a century before Leovigild and even before king Euric's break with the empire, a Visigothic ruler flaunted symbols of royal power.

It has recently been suggested that it may not be necessary to scrap Isidore's account, nor even to hypothesize the total disappearance of royal trappings in the disaster of 507.[11] Isidore says that Leovigild was the first to sit on a throne, dressed in a royal

---

p. 143; Thompson, *Spain*, p. 57; King, *Law*, p. 12, etc. Isidore, *Historia Gothorum, Wandalorum, Sueborum* (51), ed. C. Rodríguez Alonso, Fuentes y estudios de historia leonesa, 13 (Leon, 1975), p. 258.5–10: 'Aerarium quoque ac fiscum primus iste auxit, primusque inter suos regali ueste opertus solio resedit, nam ante eum et habitus et consessus communis ut genti, ita et regibus erat. Condidit autem ciuitatem in Celtiberia, quam ex nomine filii Recopolim nominauit. In legibus quoque ea quae ab Eurico incondite constituta uidebantur correxit...'. Note that the passage occurs only in the short recension and the MSS contaminated by it. Rodríguez's study of the MS tradition led to the restoration of the MS 'communis...genti' for Mommsen's 'communis...populo'. The new reading accentuates the ethnic connotation: cf. Rodríguez, p. 333, s.v. 'gens'.

9 *Ep.*, 1, 2, 4, ed. A. Loyen, 2 (Paris, 1970), 6. The letter probably dates from 455–60: *ibid.*, p. xiii. Claude, *Adel*, p. 62, n. 36, notes the passage but considers it metaphorical and of little weight (however the same passage is used as evidence on court personnel, *ibid.*, pp. 67–8, with n. 70). The letter seems to be portraying an idealized 'Stoic' or philosopher king who is characterized by moderation (e.g. *ibid.*, 1, 2, 6, p. 6). The presence of trappings of majesty contradicts this ideal and only lends credence to the description. On the Visigothic palace at Toulouse, C. Brühl, *Palatium und Civitas. Studien zur Profantopographie spätantiker civitates vom 3. bis zum 13. Jahrhundert*, 1, *Gallien* (Cologne, 1975), pp. 195–200.

10 *Ep.*, 1, 2, 6, Loyen 2.6: 'uideas ibi elegantiam Graecam...publicam pompam, priuatam diligentiam, regiam disciplinam'.

11 This interpretation was first published by Reydellet, *Royauté*, pp. 532–3. The same conclusion was reached by myself, without knowledge of Reydellet's translation: 'Victory and its celebration in the Byzantine empire and the Barbarian kingdoms, A.D. 476–1000', Diss., 2 (Louvain, 1979), 338–40.

robe, 'inter suos'. While the traditional interpretation of these words presumes the translation 'first of the Visigoths to sit...', they could easily signify the first to do so 'among his own people', as opposed to Hispano-Romans and foreigners. What Isidore may in fact mean is that, until Leovigild's time, the kings eschewed a Roman-inspired monarchical style of conduct toward their own kind and that Leovigild was the first to impose on the Visigoths the same kind of ceremonial strictures which governed Roman behavior in the same circumstances. Such an interpretation would square with what is known of Leovigild's determination to tame the Gothic aristocracy, as well as with his first steps toward placing Goths and Romans on an equal footing.[12]

The monarchy's ceremonial evolution did not stop there. Unction, for instance, was introduced into royal investitures sometime before 672, possibly between 621 and 642.[13] A trend toward codification emerges from the closely related domain of the capital's sacred ritual. In 633 the bishops assembled at Toledo laid down guidelines for the ceremonies inaugurating a national council.[14] Just over a decade later, another assembly spelled out the occasional obligation of nearby bishops to reside in the capital, for 'deference to the prince, and the honor of the royal throne, as well as the consolation of the metropolitan'.[15] This obligation likely entailed ceremonial duties.[16] The content of the capital's liturgical service-books dovetailed with certain royal ceremonies, and they continued to be revised down to the time of bishop Julian (680–90), whose hand has been detected in the *ordo* for the celebration of a council.[17] All this points to Toledo's continued preoccupation with ritual. Even leaving aside liturgical pro-

---

[12] Claude, *Adel*, pp. 80–9; cf. King, *Law*, p. 13; Reydellet, *Royauté*, pp. 533–4.

[13] King, *Law*, pp. 48–9, with n. 5.

[14] IV Tol. 1, ed. J. Vives et al., *Concilios visigóticos e hispano-romanos*, España cristiana, Textos, 1 (Barcelona, 1963), 189–90.

[15] VII Tol. 6, Vives, 256: 'Id etiam placuit, ut pro reverentia principis ac regiae sedis honore vel metropolitani civitatis ipsius consolatione convicini Toletanae urbis episcopi, iuxta quod eiusdem pontificis admonitionem acceperint, singulis per annum mensibus in eadem urbem debeant conmorari.'

[16] Cf. the subscriptions of Isidore of Seville and Innocent of Merida, *Decretum Gundemari regis de ecclesia Toletana*, ed. Vives, 406, who came 'pro occursu regio'.

[17] C. Munier, 'L'*Ordo de celebrando concilio* wisigothique. Ses remaniements jusqu'au Xe siècle', *Revue des sciences religieuses*, 37 (1963), 250–71, here 259 and 261. On Julian's work on various liturgical books, Felix, *Vita Iuliani* (*BHL*, 4554), 11, *PL*, 96.450A–B;

cessions, ritualized ostentation continued to play a significant role in public life outside the capital in a town like Merida, the economic capital of sixth-century Spain.[18] King Reccared, for instance, condemned a Gothic conspirator who had taken asylum in the church of St Eulalia to the humiliating penalty of walking in front of a mounted deacon of that shrine, from St Eulalia's into town and up to the bishop's palace.[19] Bishop Masona was so rich that he furnished his church's slaves with *olosericae chlamydes*, silk capes of the type which served as uniforms in the imperial administration. The slaves are reported to have made a splendid show as they walked in front of Masona en route to the Easter procession, 'just as if they were escorting a king'.[20] It is revealing that the man so enamored of late Roman pomp was an ethnic Goth and Leovigild's contemporary.[21] Public spectacles continued to be staged in some arenas of Gothic Spain as late as the first quarter of the seventh century and perhaps beyond.[22] Clearly, some sectors of Hispanogothic society remained alive to forms of ritual display and ceremony which prolonged the patterns of late antique public life.

---

cf. M.C. Díaz y Díaz, 'Literary aspects of the Visigothic liturgy', *Visigothic Spain: new approaches*, ed. E. James (Oxford, 1980), pp. 61–76.

[18] On the economic role of Merida, X. Barral i Altet, *La circulation des monnaies suèves et visigotiques. Contribution à l'histoire économique du royaume visigot*, Beihefte der *Francia*, 4 (Munich, 1976), pp. 111 and 123; cf. R. Collins, 'Merida and Toledo: 550–585', *Visigothic Spain*, pp. 189–219, here 207.

[19] *Vitae patrum Emeretensium (BHL*, 2530), 5, 11, 19, ed. J.N. Garvin (Washington, D.C., 1946), 244.92–9; cf. 5, 11, 20, Garvin, 244.103–7.

[20] *Ibid.*, 5, 3, 12, Garvin, 196.50–5: 'coram eo quasi coram rege incederent'.

[21] L.A. García Moreno, *Prosopografía del reino visigodo de Toledo*, Acta salmanticensia, Filosofía y letras, 77 (Salamanca, 1974), no. 435.

[22] The major Roman cities were of course endowed with circuses and theaters, the life-spans of which remain to be determined: *The Princeton encyclopedia of classical sites* (Princeton, 1976), pp. 115 (Merida), 616–17 (Nîmes), 883 (Tarragona), 927 (Toledo). Although the amphitheater at Tarragona was already occupied by a church in the sixth century (H. Schlunk and T. Hauschild, *Die Denkmäler der frühchristlichen und westgotischen Zeit*, Hispania antiqua (Mainz, 1978), pp. 160–1), some kinds of spectacles were still taking place: *Epistolae wisigothicae*, 7, ed. J. Gil, *Miscellanea wisigotica*, Anales de la Universidad hispalense, Filosofía y letras, 15 (Seville, 1972), 15.7–9; cf. García Moreno, *Prosopografía*, no. 565. Animals apparently intended for spectacles ('qui ad istadium fortasse servatur') are still mentioned by an 'antiqua' preserved in Ervig's Code of 681 and going back at least to Reccesvinth: *Lex Vis.*, 8, 4, 4, Zeumer, 332.8–9; cf. King, *Law*, p. 202, n. 3.

Once in a while, we catch a fleeting glimpse of power's public display as it was shaped by royal ceremonial. But it is rarely possible to go beyond the naked observation of a ceremony's existence to the essential problems of origin, development, ritual form and intent, historical context and meaning. In most cases, the church played an eminent role. Coronations and royal appearances at national church councils top the list of recorded ceremonies.[23] Even after a brief absence, the king's return to the *urbs regia* of Toledo was routinely marked by a *susceptio*.[24] His wars came to be the focus of public prayer, his military movements were punctuated with liturgical services and his birthday was celebrated by the seventh-century church.[25] And he celebrated his victories.

2. ROYAL VICTORY CELEBRATIONS

To read Isidore of Seville's detailed account of the classical Roman triumph, one would never guess that victory celebrations were a fixture of contemporary public life. But as his own words suggest, his was a bookish, antiquarian concern: 'There was a Roman custom...' or 'Writers often confuse these terms...'.[26] Yet we have a description of one king's triumph, gold coins were issued announcing or commemorating various victories and the bishops of Spain hailed their kings as victors or triumphators.

[23] For coronations, C. Sánchez Albornoz, 'La *ordinatio principis* en la España goda y postvisigoda', *Cuadernos de historia de España*, 35–6 (1962), 5–36; cf. R. Collins, 'Julian of Toledo and the royal succession in late seventh-century Spain', *Early Medieval Kingship*, ed. P.H. Sawyer and I.N. Wood (Leeds, 1977), pp. 30–49. For the church councils, *Ordo de celebrando concilio*, 11, Munier, 267–8.

[24] *Liber ordinum*, ed. M. Férotin, *Le Liber ordinum en usage dans l'église wisigothique et mozarabe d'Espagne du Vᵉ au XIᵉ siècle*, Monumenta ecclesiae liturgica, 5 (Paris, 1904), 155.27–156.14.

[25] On military services, see below. Birthday services are attested by the hymn *In natalitio regis*, ed. C. Bluhme, *Analecta hymnica medii aevi*, 27 (1897), 269. Cf. M.C. Díaz y Díaz, *Index scriptorum latinorum medii aevi Hispanorum*, 1, Acta salmanticensia, Filosofía y letras, 13 (Salamanca, 1958), no. 341.

[26] *Etymologiae*, 18, 2, 4 and 3 respectively, ed. W.M. Lindsay, 2 (Oxford, 1911). As Isidore admits, at least part of his discussion is derived from Suetonius' lost *Prata*; cf. J. Fontaine, *Isidore de Séville et la culture classique dans l'Espagne wisigothique*, 2 (Paris, 1959), 749. The derivations of *tropaeum* and *triumphus* seem to come from Servius, *Commentarii in Vergilii carmina*, ad *Aen.* 10, 775, ed. G. Thilo and H. Hagen, 2 (Leipzig, 1883–4), 466.28–467.3.

Only the dim outlines of the evolution of Visigothic victory celebrations are discernible today, but they begin in the kingdom of Toulouse and continue practically to the eve of the Islamic invasion. At almost every point, the debt to imperial practice is patent. On the literary level a Roman poet could casually dip into the stock of imperial conventions to praise an early Visigothic queen's unvanquished literary patronage.[27] On a ceremonial one, the victorious Visigoths celebrated the suppression of a Roman revolt in Tortosa by staging a traditional parade of the head of the man they called 'usurper'.[28] The treatment inflicted on a Frankish count by the Visigothic defenders of Carcassonne in 585 suggests the custom outlived the kingdom of Toulouse by many decades.[29]

Visigothic rulers adopted the punishment traditionally inflicted on enemies of the imperial throne. Early in Reccared's reign, the count Argimund was convicted of scheming against the king. He was 'decalvated', suffered amputation of the right hand and was led around Toledo on an ass, to instruct the citizens of the fate which awaited 'servants who were haughty to their masters', a verse which, applied as it is to an aristocratic Goth, offers a sinister commentary on the style of monarchy espoused by Leovigild's successor.[30] The horrible rite's imperial inspiration is manifest; the connection with the East is emphasized by the fact that the technical term (*pompizare*) designating the parade of infamy

---

27 Sidonius Apollinaris, *Ep.*, 4, 8, 5, Loyen, 2, 129; cf. *Ep.* 8, 3, 3, Loyen, 3 (Paris, 1970), 87.
28 *Chronicorum caesaraugustanorum reliquiae*, a. 506, ed. T. Mommsen, *MGH.AA*, 11 (1894).222. On the revolt see Thompson, *Romans and barbarians*, p. 193; cf. R. de Abadal i [D'Abadal y] de Vinyals, *Dels Visigots als Catalans*, 1 (Barcelona, 1969), 42–5 and *PLRE*, 2, 869 'Petrus 25'.
29 Gregory of Tours, *Hist.*, 8, 30, Krusch–Levison, 394.2–6.
30 John Biclar, *Chronicon*, ed. J. Campos, *Juan de Biclaro, Obispo de Gerona, su vida y su obra* (Madrid, 1960), 99.380–3, or T. Mommsen, *MGH.AA*, 11 (1894).219.38–220.3. The hexameter, noted by Levison, (*MGH.SRM*, 5, 525, n. 6), 'et docuit famulos dominis non esse superbos', does not appear to be a citation of a surviving work: cf. O. Schumann, *Lateinisches Hexameter-Lexikon. Dichterisches Formelgut von Ennius bis zum Archipoeta*, 2, *MGH*. Hilfsmittel, 4 (Munich, 1980), 189. Is it John's 'final touch' or an echo of the parade's original *titulus*? On Argimund, García Moreno, *Prosopografía*, no. 19. Opinions differ on the exact meaning of *decalvare* and its equivalents, e.g. E. Kaufmann, 'Über des Scheren abgesetzter Merowinger Könige', *Zeitschrift der Savigny-Stiftung für Rechtsgeschichte, Germanistische Abteilung*, 85 (1955), 177–85; Av. Cameron, 'How did the Merovingian kings wear their hair?' *Revue belge de philologie et d'histoire*, 43 (1965), 1203–16, here 1203, and King, *Law*, p. 90, n. 5.

here – and elsewhere in Hispanogothic Latin – appears to be a Greek loan word.[31] Nearly a century later the custom lived on, since a similar parade introduced king Wamba's triumphal entry into the same city.[32]

Royal military success seems also to have been celebrated in provincial centers. Early in Reccared's reign, duke Claudius' victory over an uprising proved the king's wisdom in abandoning the ancestral religion of the Goths. The reverse of gold coins issued at Merida which hail Reccared as PIVS VICTOR may commemorate the event.[33] The same bishop who had outfitted his slaves to look like a royal escort organized a liturgical service honoring the victory. It was followed by a procession of hymn-singing and hand-clapping faithful and their shepherd to the church of St Eulalia.[34] Like the ancients, that is the Israelites, the citizens of Merida celebrated in the open air, intoning Moses' triumphal chant. The long-standing association of the Exodus canticle and Christian military victory – an association which can be traced as far back as Eusebius and the Milvian bridge and was maintained in a sixth-century provincial celebration of emperor Anastasius' victory – made it an apt chant for the occasion.[35] Its aptness was not lessened by the Mozarabic liturgy's use of the canticle for the Christian victory feast par excellence, that of Christ over death, so that the citizens singing these verses in the streets may well have been echoing chants heard inside their churches during Eastertide.[36] A similar chant figured at thanks-

---

[31] Other uses of *pompizare*: *Continuatio Isidori hispana*, a. 750 (aera = A.D. 712), ed. T. Mommsen, *MGH.AA*, 11 (1894).354.8 and a. 767 (= A.D. 729), Mommsen, 360.29–32. The usual form in Greek texts is πομπεύω, but πομπιάζω is attested in Modern Greek and glossary material: C. Du Cange, *Glossarium ad scriptores mediae et infimae graecitatis*, 1 (Lyons, 1688), 1200–1, s.v. πομπεύω.

[32] Julian of Toledo, *Historia Wambae regis*, 30, ed. W. Levison, *MGH.SRM*, 5 (1910). 525.9–20.

[33] G.C. Miles, *The coinage of the Visigoths of Spain, Leovigild to Achila II*, Hispanic Numismatic Series, 2 (New York, 1952), pp. 119 and 223ff.

[34] *V. pat. Emer.*, 5, 12, 5–6, Garvin, 246.21–30.

[35] *Ibid.*, 5, 12, 7, Garvin, 246.30–247.38. For the destruction of Pharaoh and the Milvian Bridge, e.g. Eusebius, *H.e.*, 9, 9, 8, Schwartz, 2.830.12–21; Severus of Antioch cites Exodus 15.2–4 in his hymn for the defeat of Vitalian: Brooks, 711. The story is at home in the Visigothic liturgy of war, e.g. the 'Missa de hostibus', *Lib. ord.*, Férotin, 444.14–21.

[36] In the Mozarabic liturgy for the vigil of Easter, a prayer for the prince is followed by a reading from Exodus 13.18–15.2 or 20–1: *Lib. ord.*, Férotin, 220.15–25 and *Liber*

giving services marking the delivery of Saragossa from siege and the defeat of the usurper Froja. This, at any rate, appears to be the implication of bishop Taio's (ca. 651–83) allusion to a non-Vulgate form of Exodus 15.6 and 7, when describing these events to Quiricus, bishop of Barcelona:

God destroyed him with his right hand; he drove him from his tabernacle, and his root from the land of the living, *so that rightly we sang to the Lord*: Dextera tua, Domine, percussit inimicum et per multitudinem virtutis tuae contrivisti adversarios nostros.[37]

Liturgical celebrations of royal victory might be viewed as a natural counterpart to the services which local authorities organized to marshal the kingdom's spiritual forces in favor of the king's triumph. The bishops convened at Merida in 666 laid down their contribution to the king's campaigns. Each bishop was to celebrate one Mass a day for the king's victory, so long as the king was at war. They were to entreat God that 'safety be granted to all by the Lord and that victory be bestowed on him [the king] by almighty God'.[38] The Visigothic votive Mass for the king gives an idea of what the proper of such services sounded like. The eucharistic prayer (*inlatio*) beseeches God to grant the king three things: peace, the crushing of internal enemies and subjugation of external ones, and a long life. Nor were these special services the only time when the Hispanogothic population prayed for royal victory. Like other Christian liturgies of the early medieval successor states, that of Spain included annual prayers for the king's military success.[39]

---

commicus, ed. F.J. Perez de Urgel and A. González y Ruiz Zorilla, 2, Monumenta Hispaniae liturgica, 3 (Madrid, 1950), 367–70. Exodus 15.6–7 figured in a Matins responsory in the cathedral office for Eastertide: L. Brou and J. Vives, ed., *Antifonario visigótico mozárabe de la catedral de León*, 1, Monumenta Hispaniae sacra, ser. lit., 5 (Barcelona, 1959), 293.

[37] *Sententiae*, praef. 3, *PL*, 80.728C: 'Destruxit eum dextera sua Deus, et evellit de tabernaculo suo, et radicem ejus de terra viventium, ut rite Domino psalleremus...'. On Taio and Quiricus, García Moreno, *Prosopografía*, nos. 592 and 584 respectively; on the work, Díaz y Díaz, *Index*, no. 207.

[38] Emer. 3, Vives 327: 'ut salus cunctis a Domino tribuatur, et victoria illi ab omnipotenti Deo concedatur'.

[39] E.g. the prayer for peace and curbing of the barbarians in the Mozarabic Easter Vigil service, *Lib. ord.*, Férotin, 220.9–17.

The most important Visigothic victory celebration featured the king himself. Triumphal entries may not have been infrequent occurrences in the public life of the Hispanogothic capital. Although the sole description comes from Julian of Toledo's gushing account of how king Wamba repressed a usurpation in 673, this History is but one of three surviving historiographical works from Visigothic Spain, and the only one to describe a royal campaign in any detail. The very allusiveness with which Julian treats the triumphal entry, insisting as he does only on the misery of the captives, suggests that the rest of the ceremony was not unfamiliar to his audience.[40] The fact that Wamba's building activities in the capital included the adornment of one or more gates with sculpture and commemorative inscriptions indicates a lasting concern with the architectural backdrop of such ceremonies.[41] A compelling argument against the uniqueness of the celebrations of 673 comes from a service marking the king's triumphant return from war, preserved in what might be called the Visigothic liturgy's 'pontifical', the *Liber ordinum*.[42] The victory celebrations of 673 were no more likely a unique occurrence than the other major ceremony which Julian alone describes: the king's investiture and unction. This suggests that other sources' allusions to royal 'triumphs' or the victorious returns of kings to the capital may in fact concern similar ceremonies. Such allusions occur as early as Leovigild's successful attack on the Byzantine possessions of Baza and Malaga in 570 and his son's repulse of a Frankish invasion fifteen years later.[43] Another ceremony could have celebrated the conclusion of the civil war triggered by the conversion to Catholicism and usurpation of Leovigild's other

[40] Julian makes this point at the end of c. 29, just before the description and again, right after it, with the work's concluding words: *Hist. Wamb.*, 29, Levison, 525.5–8 and 30, 525.20–526.4.
[41] *Cont. Isid. hisp.*, Mommsen, 348.16–36; cf. J. Vives, *Inscripciones cristianas de la España romana y visigoda*, Monumenta Hispaniae sacra, ser. patr. 2, 2nd edn (Barcelona, 1969), 125, no. 361.
[42] *Lib. ord.*, Férotin, 154–5; see below.
[43] John Biclar, *Chron.*, Campos, 80.51–2, or Mommsen, 212.14–15: '...victor solio redit'. Cf. P. Goubert, 'L'administration de l'Espagne byzantine', *RÉB*, 3 (1945), 127–42, and 4 (1946), 70–134, here 4, 89 and 95, as well as Thompson, *Spain*, p. 321 with n. 4. Reccared's victory: Biclar, *Chron.*, Campos, 93.255–63; Mommsen, 217.19: 'victor ad patrem patriamque redit'.

son, Hermenegild.[44] Isidore says that king Sisebut (612–21) 'twice triumphed with felicity' over Byzantine forces, while Suinthila (621–31) enjoyed an 'increased glory of triumph' because he finally drove the imperial government from Spain.[45] Toledo probably witnessed a victory celebration under king Chintila (636–39/40). Others have followed Thompson's deduction that provisions of the Fifth Council of Toledo (636) – which prays that the king will triumph – mirror an unknown revolt.[46] A year and a half later, Chintila convened a new council in the capital. It alludes to the king's military success and its celebration in the intervening period. The meeting is dated by means of a formula which is unique in Visigothic documents, to the 'second year of the aforesaid prince *and triumphator* in Christ'.[47] The bishops evoked a triumphal parade when they enumerated the king's benefactions: they recalled how, through God, he had restored peace, how he had 'led charity back' to them, 'as if it were a prisoner'.[48] And, in their concluding prayer the bishops no longer wished that the king might enjoy a triumph; they prayed instead that his triumph might be long lasting.[49] A generation later, in 673, king Wamba marked his victory over a usurper with rites in

---

[44] Both sides made great efforts to propagandize their success in this civil war: J.N. Hillgarth, 'Coins and chronicles: propaganda in sixth-century Spain and the Byzantine background', *Historia*, 15 (1966), 438–508, here pp. 501ff. Moreover, Gregory of Tours refers to the *vilis vestis* with which Hermenegild was dressed before Leovigild took him to the capital: *Hist.*, 5, 38, Krusch–Levison, 245.11–15. This was customary for prisoners in a triumphal parade: Julian, *Hist. Wamb.*, 30, Levison, 525.10.

[45] *Hist.*, 61, Rodríguez Alonso, 272.6–9: 'De Romanis...bis feliciter triumphauit', and 62, 276.8–16: 'auctamque triumphi gloriam prae ceteris regibus felicitate mirabili reportauit'.

[46] All or nearly all the canons are directed against a threat to the throne: Thompson, *Spain*, pp. 181–2; Claude, *Adel*, p. 102; Barral, *Circulation*, p. 109; H.H. Anton, 'Der König und die Reichskonzilien im westgotischen Spanien', *Historisches Jahrbuch*, 92 (1972), 257–81, here 266.

[47] VI Tol. praef., Vives, 233: 'anno praefati principis et triumfatoris in Christo secundo'.

[48] VI Tol. 16, Vives, 244: 'ipse enim auctore Deo nobis pacem, ipse quasi cabtivam reduxit caritatem...'.

[49] VI Tol., Vives, 246: 'donet ei Dominus ut obtimo principi diuturnum in seculum triumphum...'. Note too that VI Tol. 17, Vives 244–5 adds one detail to the disqualifications of candidates to the throne as stated 18 months earlier (V Tol. 3–4, Vives 228): 'nullus sub religionis habitu detonsus aut turpiter decalvatus'. For decalvation and the parade of infamy, cf. the penalties inflicted on Argimund or Paul.

the field before the assembled army and a triumphal entry into the capital.[50]

Joined with the evidence of the Mozarabic liturgy, Julian of Toledo's account of this triumph offers a fairly detailed picture of how a seventh-century 'barbarian' king went to war and celebrated his victory. Like contemporary imperial armies, Hispanogothic troops followed into battle the symbol and source of victory, the great golden war cross and reliquary of their king.[51] This insignia featured in a special service developed by the Toledan church for the king's departure for war; a similar rite honored his triumphal return. Since the rubrics are lacking for the latter service, and since we can presume some parallelism between the two, it is worth looking at the former in some detail.[52]

Both services were staged in the same place, the 'Praetorian' Church of the Apostles Peter and Paul, located somewhere on Toledo's outskirts.[53] The *profectio bellica* ceremony began when the king arrived at the church's threshold. Like the emperors, he was censed there by the clergy. Two deacons performed this rite, while the rest of the clergy awaited the procession in the choir, except for the party who would carry the royal ensign. They were

---

[50] Julian, *Hist. Wamb.*, 27 and 30, Levison, 522.12–16 and 525.9–526.4. Cf. Thompson, *Spain*, pp. 219ff and Claude, *Adel*, pp. 157ff.

[51] Thus the rebels in Nîmes expected the insignia of Wamba among the besieging troops: Julian, *Hist. Wamb.*, 16, Levison, 515.29–516.5; cf. Claude, *Adel*, pp. 65–7 who argues on the basis of this passage for a special royal war standard and mentions the possibilities of a banner or streamer. The solution lies in the *profectio bellica* service, *Lib. ord.* Férotin, 152.8–11: 'et leuat crucem auream, in qua lignum beate Crucis inclusum est, que cum rege semper in exercitu properat...'. Note that Gregory I had sent a relic of the true cross to Reccared in 599: *Reg.*, 9, 229, Norberg, 810.129–30; cf. Frolow, *Relique*, p. 184, no. 41.

[52] On the circumstances of the transcription of Silos, Arch. 4 (A) (18 May 1052) and its use of a MS reflecting the seventh-century rituals of the Praetorian Church, *Lib. ord.*, Férotin, pp. xviiff. M.C. Díaz y Díaz, 'El latin de la liturgia hispanica. Notas introductorias', *Estudios sobre la liturgia mozarabe* (Toledo, 1965), pp. 55–87, here pp. 79–80, has a sensitive literary analysis of the 'Deus exercituum'; his dating of the *profectio* text is, however, inadmissible, since it presumes that Wamba was the first anointed king: cf. King, *Law*, pp. 48–9, with n. 5.

[53] The church is cited 'in suburbio Toletano': XII Tol. 4, Vives, 390. It was the site of a number of councils in the second half of the seventh century, as well as at least two coronations (Wamba and Egica): *Lib. ord.*, Férotin, pp. 150–1, n. 1; Julian, *Hist. Wamb.*, 4, Levison, 503.12–13 and n. 6.

all dressed in white.[54] The king entered the church and prostrated himself in silent prayer. As he arose, a biblical verse was sung: 'May God be on your journey and may his angel attend you' (Tobit 5.21).[55] The Lord God of Hosts was then entreated to grant victory and make the prince a triumphator. A threefold blessing for a safe campaign followed this prayer.[56] After the first series of blessings, a whole new sub-ceremony began, during which the royal ensign and the army's standards were solemnly presented to their bearers. A deacon walked to the altar and lifted up the king's golden war cross, which he brought to the bishop. After washing his hands, the prelate accepted the cross reliquary and handed it to the king who passed it to the priest (*sacerdos*) charged with carrying the ensign. As soon as the king's fingers touched the sacred standard, the chorus broke into an antiphonal chant derived from the Wisdom of Solomon:

> *Ant.:* Take from the hand of the Lord impartial
> judgement as a helmet, and let all creation be
> armed for vengeance against your enemies.
> *Vers. I:* Take up the invincible shield of
> justice. For vengeance.
> *Vers. II:* For your power was given you by the
> Lord and your strength from the Most High.
> For vengeance.[57]

[54] *Lib. ord.*, Férotin, 149.42–150.3. It is worth noting that the task of deacons in seventh-century Spain fell to the patriarch himself in tenth-century Constantinople: Constantine VII, *De cer.*, 1, 1, Vogt, 1.22.3 and Treitinger, *Oströmische*, pp. 70–1. The *profectio* as we have it may actually be an expansion of an earlier, simpler rite, since a surprising aside in the rubric indicates that participants expected it to end after the first blessing: 'Post haec *non statim* absoluitur', *Lib. ord.*, Férotin, 152.8, where 'absoluitur' refers, of course, to the deacon's dismissal (cf. *ibid.*, 153.28). The implication would be that the antiphonal sub-ceremony was added to the *profectio* sometime before 711.

[55] *Lib. ord.*, Férotin, 150.4–8: 'Sit deus in itinere uestro, et angelus eius comitetur uobiscum.'

[56] *Ibid.*, 150.11–151.12; 151.14–152.7.

[57] *Ibid.*, 152.7–22: 'ANT. Accipe de manu Domini pro galeo iudicium certum, et armetur creatura ad ultionem inimicorum tuorum [cf. Wisdom 5.19 and 18]. VERSUS I: Sume scutum inexpugnabile equitatis [Wisdom 5.20]. Ad ultionem. II. Quoniam data est uobis potestas a Domino et uirtus ab Altissimo [Wisdom 6.4]. Ad ultionem.' The personalization of the enemies ('tuorum') reflects the usual form of this verse in the Spanish liturgy and bears comparison with the Peshitta version: *Vetus latina*, 11.1, *Sapientia Salomonis*, ed. W. Thiele (Freiburg, 1981), 340–1, app.

The standard-bearers (*unusquisque*) approached the altar one by one and received their standards (*bandus*) from a priest (*sacerdos*) standing behind the altar. Meanwhile, the chorus stretched out the service with eight more verses, each one punctuated by the refrain 'For vengeance against your enemies'. As soon as the last standard-bearer had walked out of the church, the chorus intoned a Gloria and repeated the antiphon. The elaborate blessing which closed the ceremony focused on the king's war cross and fused the theology of Christ's victory over death with the king's victory over his enemies.[58] When the bishop finished it, the deacon dismissed the gathering, using the ancient formula which seems so ironic to a modern observer: 'In the name of our Lord Jesus Christ, go in peace', answered by a rousing 'Thanks be to God!' The king kissed the bishop and anyone else he chose and left the church, preceded by deacons carrying his standard and chanting 'O Lord God, power of my salvation, cover my head in the day of battle.'[59] Suitably reinforced, the ruler mounted his horse and the royal party moved off to war.

The prayers naturally touched on royal victory. Harmony must reign in the army for the king to triumph.[60] The antiphonal chant during the delivery of the battle standards cites Psalm 120 and predicts that the king will perform the *calcatio colli*, an allusion which was far from gratuitous.[61] The great pontifical blessing that concludes the ceremony strikingly formulates a Christocentric sacrality which permeated kingship and combat. Just as it had once served Christ's triumph, the sacred wood would preside over the forthcoming battle and champion the king's victory. The path to battle which began in the Praetorian church was destined to end there as well. The prayer insists:

Through the victory of the holy cross may you both successfully complete the journey begun here and bring back to us flourishing proofs of your triumphs. – Amen.[62]

---

[58] *Lib. ord.*, Férotin, 152.23–153.27.

[59] *Ibid.*, 153.28–40. The antiphon is from Psalm 139.8: 'Domine Deus, uirtus salutis mee, obumbra caput meum in die belli.'   [60] *Lib. ord.*, Férotin, 150.17–151.3.

[61] *Ibid.*, 152.30–1: 'Negabunt te inimici tui, et tu eorum colla calcabis': Deuteronomy 33.29.

[62] *Lib. ord.*, Férotin, 153.21–3: 'Vt per uictoriam sancte Crucis et ceptum abhinc iter feliciter peragatis et florentes ad nos triumphorum uestrorum titulos reportetis.'

Table 3. *Comparison of rubricated 'profectio' with texts for king's return from war, Praetorian church*

Departure service	Return service
1. King censed at threshold	[King censed at threshold]
2. King enters; prostrate; (silent prayer)	[King enters; prostrate; silent prayer]
3. First verse; prayer: 'Deus exercituum'	Prayer: 'Rex Deus'; Our Father
4. Blessing I	Blessing I
5. Handing over of battle cross and army standards; antiphonal prayer of ten verses; repetition	[Kiss of peace?] Two prayers: 'Deus cui subiacent' and 'Te inuocamus'
6. Gloria	—
7. Blessing II	Blessing II
8. Dismissal	[Dismissal]
9. Kiss of peace	—
10. Departure for war	[Departure for triumphal parade]

Clearly, the anticipated thanksgiving service at the campaign's end would parallel the *profectio*:

As we send you forth with the kiss of peace, by which we bid you farewell from here, let us, on your successful return (*feliciori reditu*), welcome you back in this very place with acclamations (*laudibus*) of victories.[63]

This explicit statement underscores the implicit parallelism of the king's liturgical departure and his triumphant return. Table 3 exploits this parallelism by fitting the texts from the homecoming service into the framework established by the *profectio* rubrics. Elements in brackets are supplied hypothetically on the basis of the *profectio* rubrics.

Once the indispensable and conventional elements of greeting and dismissal are added, the texts of the return service fit rather well into the ritual framework laid out in the departure service. The most significant discrepancy is that the return omits a long antiphonal prayer. This probably indicates that the *regressus* lacked a time-consuming ritual transaction like the solemn return of the

---

[63] *Ibid.*, 153.24–6: 'Qualiter in osculo pacis, quo uos abhinc uale facientes deducimus, feliciori reditu in hoc loco cum uictoriarum uos laudibus receptemus.'

standards to the altar.[64] Compared with the *profectio*, the texts of the return service are rather bland. The theme of peace plays a prominent role.[65] But the prayers do offer insight into how far this successor society had assimilated the ideology of imperial civiliz-ation: the triumphant army of the Visigoths beseeched God to banish 'barbarian wars'. Yesterday's barbarians had come to consider themselves the champions of civilization.[66]

These services set the spiritual tone for war; an incident from Wamba's expedition illustrates it. As the loyalist forces headed for insurgent Gaul, some troops started to pillage their own territory and, God forbid, fornicate with the locals. Wamba was quite unsettled by their behavior. War, he is supposed to have said, is divine judgement; certainly, the liturgy comforted him in this thought.[67] How could he go to divine judgement in an impure state? Citing Eli's chastisement (1 Samuel 4.17–18), the king declared that, if only his army could remain pure, 'there can be no doubt we will triumph over the enemy'.[68] After inflicting a most bizarre punishment on the offenders, he kept strict watch over his troops' morals and headed on to certain victory. Like Heraclius' prescriptions for the Byzantine army half a century earlier, Wamba's purification of his tainted troops was considered the condition for victory.[69]

---

[64] Army standards may not have been kept in the church in times of peace. It would, at any rate, have been surprising if the standards were returned to the church before the triumphal parade into the city. Cf. above, Ch. 6, 2.

[65] *Lib. ord.*, Férotin, 154.12–13, and 155.7–11 and 20–4.

[66] *Ibid.*, 155.8–11: 'et amoue clementer barbarica bella'. The same text occurs in the prayer 'Ad pacem' of the votive Mass for kings, *ibid.*, 295.13–17.

[67] Julian, *Hist. Wamb.*, 10, Levison, 510.7–11; cf. *Lib. ord.*, Férotin, 152.17–18.

[68] Julian, *Hist. Wamb.*, 10, Levison, 510.11–15: '...si purgati maneamus a crimine, non dubium erit, quod triumphum capiamus ex hoste'.

[69] *Ibid.*, 510.1–16: he had the guilty parties circumcised. The punishment seems to have no parallel in the *Lex Visigothorum*. It is probably to be explained by the anti-Semitism rampant in some sectors of Visigothic society (cf. S. Katz, *The Jews in the Visigothic and Frankish kingdoms of Spain and Gaul*, Monographs of the Mediaeval Academy of America, 12 (Cambridge, Mass., 1937), pp. 11ff and esp. 16–17; cf. B. Blumenkranz, *Juifs et chrétiens dans le monde occidental, 430–1096*, Études juives, 2 (Paris, 1960), pp. 105ff, and B.S. Bachrach, *Early medieval Jewish policy in western Europe* (Minneapolis, 1977), pp. 5ff and 18–19). The particular ignominy associated with such a penalty is indirectly confirmed by a late interpolation in the *Lex Vis.*, 12, 2, in fine, Zeumer, 463.3–34, a highly obscure title dealing with insults and outrage. If someone calls another 'circumcized' and it is not true, the first person shall suffer 150 lashes in public, the maximum punishment foreseen in this title.

The campaign was crowned with success. After what the victor's panegyrist portrays as a fairly easy victory, Nîmes capitulated and the usurper duke Paul was dragged from the amphitheater, his last refuge. On 4 September 673, the vanquished pretender and his key followers appeared before the king for the second time.[70] This time the scene had been more carefully prepared than two days earlier, when Paul had been brought to Wamba in the first flush of victory. Now king Wamba was properly ensconced in the royal throne and the rebels weighted down with shackles. In the presence of the Visigothic army, the symbolic ritual of victory was performed: '...after the custom of the ancients, [Paul], with bent back, placed his neck under the royal footsteps'.[71] There can be no doubt about the character of this symbolic gesture: Wamba performed on the usurper the ritual trampling of total victory, the *calcatio colli*, just as Heraclius had before and Justinian II would after him.

After the symbolic act of victory came the judicial one. In front of the same audience, the evidence concerning the usurpation was laid out. Paul himself testified to his unprovoked act of treason, laying full blame on the devil.[72] The written and signed oaths of allegiance, as well as the relevant texts of the Law of the Visigoths and the Fourth Council of Toledo were produced. Finally the judges arrived at a foregone conclusion: Paul and his helpers were condemned to death, and their property confiscated, although the judges left open the possibility of a royal commutation of the death penalty to judicial blinding.[73] In fact, Wamba was unable or unwilling to apply even this mitigated punishment and the penalty was further reduced to decalvation.[74]

---

[70] Julian, *Hist. Wamb.*, 27, Levison, 522.12–13; cf. *ibid.*, 24–5, 520.20–521.14.

[71] *Ibid.*, 27, 510.11–14: '...antiquorum more curba spina dorsi vestigiis regalibus sua colla submittit...'. For the 'antiqui' there are three different possibilities, of which the first seems to me the most likely: Old Testament figures (cf. e.g. Joshua 10.24–5; Psalm 8.8, 46.4, 109.1; Deuteronomy 33.29); the Roman emperors; or, earlier Visigothic kings.

[72] *Iudicium in tyrannorum perfidia promulgatum*, 1, ed. W. Levison, *MGH.SRM*, 5 (1910). 533.19–22.

[73] *Ibid.*, 6–7, Levison, 533.22–535.10. On the Visigothic conception of treason, F.S. Lear, *Treason in Roman and Germanic law* (Austin, 1965), pp. 143ff, and King, *Law*, pp. 40ff.

[74] Julian, *Hist. Wamb.*, 27, Levison, 522.16–17; cf. *ibid.*, 30, 525.10.

The army was then dismissed and the royal party and prisoners headed back to the capital.[75] Julian's description of the triumphal entry that ensued is explicit but incomplete, for, in his efforts to dramatize the miserable fate of would-be usurpers, he dwells only on the pitiful spectacle of the captives in the parade. Near the fourth milestone from the royal city, Paul and his associates were prepared for the seventh-century Spanish version of the parade of infamy and triumphal entry. Their heads were shaved or scalped, their beards shaved off and their footgear removed.[76] They were dressed in filthy rags and seated on camels, a beast considered symbolically appropriate to their humiliation.[77] The pretender preceded his subordinates and was decked out in a mock crown.[78] With the population standing to either side of the road, the cortege entered the capital. The rest of the triumph ceremony was so obvious to his readers that Julian didn't even bother to mention the king's presence in the parade.[79]

Like the parade of infamy inflicted on conspirators or the custom of leading the way to war with a golden battle reliquary of the true cross, the Visigothic monarch's triumphal celebrations are clearly patterned on those of contemporary Constantinople. This tells us much about the cultural orientation of the Visigothic monarchy and its subjects and much about the spell cast by the Byzantine emperor, even in the grim years of the seventh century. But a careful consideration of who watched Wamba's ritual trampling, and an examination of how related Visigothic victory customs came into being, are even more interesting. They illuminate the social conditions which fostered the development of royal authority's symbolism in early medieval Spain.

---

[75] *Ibid.*, 29, Levison, 524.25–525.2. [76] *Ibid.*, 30, Levison, 525.9–12.

[77] *Ibid.*, Levison, 525.11–12 and 525.16–20. Note that 'camelorum vehiculis' (*ibid.*, 525.11) does not mean 'in carts pulled by camels' (Thompson, *Spain*, p. 226). In Visigothic Latin, 'vehiculum' is almost always a lofty way of referring to a transport animal, e.g. *Passio Eulaliae Emeretensis* (BHL, 2700), ed. A. Fabrega Grau, *Pasionario hispánico*, 2, Monumenta Hispaniae sacra, ser. lit., 6 (Barcelona and Madrid, 1953–5), 69.11: 'vehiculo publico' glossed 'mulione'; cf. 2.47 and *Vit. patr. Emer.*, 5, 11, 19, Garvin, 244.94–6, etc.

[78] Julian, *Hist. Wamb.*, 30, Levison, 525.12–16.

[79] Present he was though: *ibid.*, 29, Levison, 525.5–6.

3. THE SOCIAL CONTEXT OF VISIGOTHIC VICTORY CELEBRATIONS

Stroheker long ago voiced the hypothesis that Leovigild's revamping of royal ritual was directed against the Gothic aristocracy.[80] A closer examination of Wamba's ritual trampling of the defeated usurper and its audience confirms and deepens this view. Julian's account identifies the audience for Paul's ritual trampling and public judgement in some detail. It comprised, on the one hand, the powerful sector of the aristocracy directly associated with the palace (*seniores palatii*), as well as the king's elite military retainers known as *gardingi* and the lower ranks of palace personnel, the *palatinum officium*.[81] On the other, the scene was witnessed by the Visigothic field army which, precisely in this period, was assuming a protofeudal social profile. As Sánchez Albornoz, Diesner and García Moreno have shown, the field army by this time chiefly comprised the kingdom's grandees, the landed magnates, accompanied by their large personal followings of free and unfree retainers, serving under the direct command of their *patronus*.[82] The scene outside Nîmes indicates that Wamba was essentially concerned with glorifying his complete victory, not to the population of the reconquered town, or even that of the capital – he could have saved the *calcatio* as well as the public judgement for later – but to the most powerful men of the kingdom, the aristocracy, as represented by the *seniores palatii* and the magnates serving in the army, before they were dismissed and returned to their homes.[83] It cannot be forgotten that, but a few

---

[80] *Germanentum*, pp. 142–3.

[81] Julian, *Hist. Wamb.*, 27, Levison, 522.14–15 and, more explicitly, *Iudicium*, 5, Levison, 533.11–13.

[82] C. Sánchez Albornoz, 'La pérdida de España. El ejército visigodo: su proto-feudalización', *Cuadernos de historia de España*, 43–4 (1967), 5–73; H.J. Diesner, 'König Wamba und der westgotische Frühfeudalismus', *JÖB*, 18 (1969), 7–35, esp. 12ff and 23ff, as well as his *Westgotische und langobardische Gefolgschaften und Untertanenverbände*, Sitzungsberichte der sächsischen Akademie der Wissenschaften, Phil.-hist. Kl. 120, 2 (Berlin, 1978), pp. 7–19; L.A. García Moreno, 'Estudios sobre la organización administrativa del reino visigodo de Toledo', *Anuario de historia del derecho español*, 44 (1974), 5–155, here 75ff; cf. his *El fin del reino visigodo de Toledo* (Madrid, 1975), pp. 147–8 and 188–90.

[83] Julian fails to precisely identify the site. That it was not in Nîmes follows from the description of the *Hist. Wamb.* and the *Iudicium*, which imply that the site was

months earlier, duke Paul had been a trusted member of this same elite and, indeed, that the king himself had been raised from their ranks only a year before. By witnessing the ritual of total victory and participating in the trial of their captive peers, the *seniores* and magnates expressed the consensus of the Visigothic elite that the usurper's bid for supreme power had failed and that his defeat was indeed a victory for the king and his fellow aristocrats, even as they consented in the infamy which stripped aristocratic status from their former peers.[84] The new king and the king-makers agreed, for the time being, on Wamba's success and worthiness to hold the royal office.

This observation takes us to the heart of the exercise of royal power in seventh-century Spain: its insecurity. Perhaps the dominant feature of the development of Visigothic rulership between Leovigild and the Islamic conquest – insofar as the meager evidence allows of generalization – was the unending struggle for supremacy between the royal ambitions of new-made kings and a truculent aristocracy's appetite for power. The 'Gothic disease', *morbus Gothicus* as Fredegar calls it, was rampant among an aristocracy with a pronounced penchant for ignoring the rhetoric of sacral kingship and murdering, dethroning or otherwise replacing their rulers.[85] One statistic spells out the trend with chilling clarity: of the seventeen Visigoths who are known to have claimed the royal office in the seventh century, six were certainly deposed and four more very probably suffered the same fate.[86] In

---

spacious enough to accommodate the entire army. The likely setting is suggested by Julian's casual remark on the prince's whereabouts on the day after the *calcatio* (cf. 523.9): *Hist. Wamb.*, 27, Levison, 523.15–16: 'Nam et religiosus princeps eminus a Neumasense urbe in plana cum exercitu consistebat. Illic castra posuit...'.

[84] The *Iudicium* records with care those present: 5, Levison, 533.11–18, in which Wamba conjures Paul to contend with him 'in hoc conventu fratrum meorum'; cf. *ibid.*, 7, 534.24–535.1: 'hoc omnes communi definivimus sententia'. That the rebels lost their privileged social status follows from the later restoration of their nobility: cf. Thompson, *Spain*, pp. 233–4.

[85] Fredegar, *Chron.*, 4, 82, Krusch, 162.22–163.12. See in general, Claude, *Adel*, pp. 204ff; García Moreno, *Fin*, pp. 140ff.

[86] Counted as follows: certainly deposed or assassinated: Liuva II (601–2/3), Witteric (603–9/10), Suinthila (621–31), Tulga (639–42), Paul (673), Wamba (672–80); very probably deposed or assassinated: Sisebut (612–21), Reccared II (621), Iudila (631?–33), Suniefrid (692?–3?); completed their reign and died a natural death: Gundemar (609/10–12), Sisenand (631–6), Chintila (636–39/40), Chindasvinth (642–53), Reccasvinth (653–72), Ervig (680–7), Egica (687–702).

fact, not ten years after his victory over one aristocrat, Wamba, the triumphator of 673, would fall victim to another and a national council would restore full nobility, privileges and property to all surviving participants in Paul's usurpation.[87] It is hard to avoid suspecting a link between the prolific internal challenges the Visigothic aristocracy created for those it made king and these rulers' efforts to raise themselves above their former peers and demonstrate the totality of their own victory over a dissident noble. In this respect, it cannot be overlooked that the fullest account of a victory celebration comes from the court history of the suppression of yet another internal challenge to royal authority, particularly since that work explicitly claimed as its audience the youthful warriors of the country.[88] Given the social profile of lay literacy as well as that of the army in Visigothic Spain, the audience for Julian's account of the triumph was probably no less distinguished than that of the ritual trampling.[89] The social context of Wamba's victory celebrations can be verified and extended thanks to three related but independent developments. They are evidenced by numismatics and canon law and reveal how internal challenges to the monarchy crystallized other customs related to royal victory.

The conversion of Leovigild's eldest son Hermenegild to orthodox Christianity, his usurpation, alliance with Constantinople and the four years of civil war that ensued, must have unleashed great stresses in the upper echelons of Visigothic society. As controversial as some details may yet be, Hillgarth's work in particular has made clear that Leovigild matched his military response to the usurpation with a political one whose traces can still be read in his coinage. For the first time, Visigothic gold coins propagandized specific acts in the king's exercise of power: his victories over the rebel forces. The reverse legend CVM D(E)O OPTINVIT SPALI announced the fall of Hermenegild's capital Seville and the divine favor which attended such a success.[90] Other key victories were hailed with coin reverses like +PIVS

---

[87] XIII Tol. 1, Vives, 415–16; cf. Thompson, *Spain*, pp. 233–4.

[88] Julian, *Hist. Wamb.*, 1, Levison, 501.8–10.

[89] Díaz y Díaz, 'Literary Aspects', pp. 74ff, considers that church services were basically intelligible only to the clergy: but cf. P. Riché, *Éducation et culture dans l'Occident barbare, VI*ᵉ*–VIII*ᵉ *siècles*, 3rd edn (Paris, [1973]), pp. 300–10.

[90] Miles, *Coinage*, p. 191, no. 31(a).

EMERITA VICTOR, signaling the recovery of the peninsula's economic center, while CORDOBA BIS OPTINVIT saluted the final collapse of resistance.[91] In other words, the first issues of Visigothic coinage proclaiming the king's victory were forged in the crucible of internal strife.

For whom were these messages of royal victory minted? An essential clue comes from the metal in which they were struck: gold. As Bellinger has noted of Byzantine gold issues and Barral reaffirmed for the economic context of early medieval Spain: '... the government is largely indifferent to the opinion of the general public and chiefly concerned only with ... the aristocracy'.[92] The emergence of this victory custom in Visigothic Spain was triggered by an internal challenge to the ruler, and again the aristocracy was the primary target.

Victory coinage continued to be struck intermittently after Leovigild's time, although the legends quickly became stereotyped. Reccared's issues touted VICTORIA or the king's quality of VICTOR. One group of tremisses struck at Merida has tentatively been linked with the same victory for which Masona staged a thanksgiving procession.[93] Both king Sisebut and Suinthila issued at the Galician town of Lugo coins which display the VICTOR epithet, and both issues have been connected with campaigns in that region.[94] Chindasvinth's reign (642–53) was characterized by the repression of insurrections and he too seems to have called himself a VICTOR on a coin bearing the Merida mintmark.[95] Egica's (695–702) issues at Toledo and at the Galician

---

[91] *Ibid.*, pp. 195–7, nos. 39–41; cf. p. 194, no. 38; and *ibid.*, pp. 190–1, no. 30; cf. Thompson, *Spain*, p. 72.

[92] A.R. Bellinger, 'The coins and Byzantine imperial policy', *Speculum*, 31 (1956), 70–81, here 71; cf. A.P. Kazhdan, 'Certain traits of imperial propaganda in the Byzantine empire from the eighth to the fifteenth centuries', *Prédication et propagande au moyen âge: Islam, Byzance, Occident* (Paris, 1983), pp. 13–28, here 13; cf. Barral, *Circulation*, pp. 69, 74, etc. on the contrast between coin denominations and price levels.

[93] Miles, *Coinage*, p. 119 and pp. 224ff, no. 93.

[94] *Ibid.*, pp. 136–7 and 271, no. 205; pp. 298–9, no. 246. Suinthila's VICTOR issue at 'EBORA', i.e., Elvora, mod. Évora is given doubtful authenticity: *ibid.*, pp. 292–3, no. 234(b).

[95] Miles, *Coinage*, p. 343, no. 331. For aristocratic insurrection under him, see, in addition to Fredegar, *Chron.*, 4, 82, Krusch, 162.22–163.12, Barral's hypothesis on the motive for the burial of the great La Grassa hoard, ca. 649–53 or 653–4: *Circulation*, pp. 121 and 124.

mints of Braga and Túy (Tude) testify to a development whose significance has not been adequately appreciated. Hitherto, victory epithets appeared only on the less important side of the coins, the reverse.[96] Two important innovations were made simultaneously in the capital's coinage. The old invocation 'In the name of the Lord' was replaced by a christological one 'In the name of Christ': +N +PI NM.[97] At the same time, the victory epithet was transferred from the reverse and became part of the royal title itself: EGICA REX VICTOR.[98] The father of the last ruler of Visigothic Spain probably faced more than one uprising by insurgent aristocrats and, less than a decade after Egica's demise, a feuding elite would invite the Arab invasion. Given the king's efforts to shore up the monarchy's prestige and victorious quality in another domain, a connection between the new royal title and the repression of high-level dissidence is not altogether unlikely.

If the medium of Visigothic victory issues indicates the social level of their audience, the mintmarks of certain series suggest a further resolution of their focus, particularly when place of issue is correlated with circulation patterns. Barral's analysis of peninsular hoards reveals a fairly intensive circulation of the coinage *within* rather narrow regional boundaries. Down to the time of Wamba, only money struck at Merida and Toledo could be expected to break this pattern routinely and carry its message to the kingdom's far reaches, thanks to these centers' dominant role in the economy.[99] This explains victory coins minted there but raises the question of why Leovigild, Reccared, Sisebut, Suinthila and Egica issued similar coins at rather eccentric locales like Lugo, Túy, or Braga, which would not have been the peninsula's most densely populated areas. The answer may lie in regional military activities, for it has been suggested that the proliferation of mints must sometimes have been connected with payments to the army.[100] In

---

[96] Visigothic minters remained aware of the distinction: Miles, *Coinage*, p. 32; Barral, *Circulation*, p. 121.

[97] Cited from one of the clearest examples: Miles, *Coinage*, p. 396, no. 437(f); cf. *ibid.*, p. 37.

[98] E.g. Miles, *Coinage*, p. 396, no. 437(b); p. 404, nos. 452 and 453 (x). This title should be added to the evidence assembled by Wolfram, *Intitulatio*, I, pp. 62ff and 70ff.

[99] Barral, *Circulation*, pp. 70, 157 and 159.

[100] García Moreno, 'Estudios', pp. 97ff and 113ff, and esp. his pointed observation that the only Visigothic coinage ever minted at Italica was connected precisely with

other words, there is some reason to think that the local issue of victory coinage was addressed to the same audience as king Wamba's ritual humiliation of duke Paul.

The citation of the Fourth Council of Toledo during Paul's trial is a measure of the role of the Spanish bishops and their pronouncements in the political life of the kingdom. This impact can be studied thanks to the extensive records of church councils preserved in the *Collectio hispana*.[101] The legal framework of these meetings, like the custom of acclaiming the secular power, was taken over from the practice of the later Roman empire.[102] Customarily, each council's records begin with a prayerful preamble and conclude with a thanksgiving text. Even under the Arian kings, these liminary statements had included a certain amount of well-wishing for the Gothic prince.[103] The conversion of the monarchy to orthodoxy naturally upped the ante, beginning with the remarkable acclamation of Reccared at the Third Council of Toledo in 589.[104] But it took nearly fifty years and nine more councils before the bishops' prayer and praise for the prince addressed the issue of royal victory. The prelates convened at the Fifth Council of Toledo in 636 prepared a document in which all or nearly all the canons concern attempts to overthrow the new king Chintila. As has been noted, the conclusion that these provisions mirrored an ongoing usurpation attempt has met with wide acceptance. For the first time in the history of Visigothic conciliar legislation, the bishops added to their concluding acclamations a new kind of wish, one which entreated God to grant the king 'triumph over his enemies'.[105] This innovation would be echoed by four more of the surviving fourteen councils which followed it. Again, an internal challenge to the monarchy

---

Leovigild's reconquest of that city. For some tentative indications of population distribution, see P. de Palol, 'Demography and archaeology in Roman Christian and Visigothic Hispania', *Classical Folia*, 23 (1969), 32–114, Maps I, III, IV and VI; cf. pp. 35ff.

[101] See e.g. A. van Hove, *Prolegomena ad Codicem iuris canonici* (Mechelen, 1945), pp. 280–1.

[102] J. Orlandis, 'Lex in confirmatione concilii', *La iglesia en la España visigótica y medieval* (Pamplona, 1976), pp. 185–221; cf. rectifications in M. McCormick, *Revue d'histoire ecclésiastique*, 77 (1977), 371–2.

[103] *Ibid.*, p. 369.   [104] III Tol., Vives, 116–17.

[105] V Tol. 9, Vives, 230: 'Donet ei [*correxi*] Dominus de inimicis triumfum...'.

provoked the birth of a new, trend-setting victory custom. The bishops at the Sixth Council of Toledo prayed in 638 that Chintila's triumph might prove a lasting one.[106] The synod held at Merida in 666 regulated the performance of diocesan services for victory during the king's campaign, a measure which must reflect a period of conflict.[107] Accordingly, the bishops left a record of their collective prayer that the king would be victorious and bend the enemies' necks to his dominion.[108] King Ervig convoked the Twelfth Council of Toledo only twelve weeks into his reign. Although nothing is known of armed opposition to his accession, the king's wholesale concessions to the church and aristocracy evidence an insecure hold on the throne, and the prelates publicly prayed that he might appear the unconquered conqueror of enemies.[109] Even though the record is nearly blank in the closing decades of Visigothic history, the reign of Egica was certainly marked by ever increasing tensions with the nobility: a usurper issued coins mintmarked Toledo, a primate of Spain was implicated in a plot to murder the king, and Egica's son was forced to cancel many of his father's policies and penalties.[110] The prayer for the king's victory inserted in the Council of Saragossa (691) leaves plenty of room for civil strife:

May He consolidate his [the king's] reign in peace through many cycles of years and may He preserve both the race (*gentem*) and the entire fatherland in tranquility and may Christ's victorious right hand make him ever victor against the opposing host.[111]

Usurpation triggered the first performance of victory prayers during a Spanish council. Although little is known concerning the circumstances of the succeeding assemblies which pronounced

---

106 Above, n. 49.   107 Emer. 3, Vives, 327–8. Cf. Thompson, *Spain*, p. 210.
108 Emer., Vives 325: '... sicque eum de suis hostibus reddat victorem ut suorum inimicorum colla ditioni eius subdat gratia sua favente...'.
109 XII Tol. 13, Vives, 400. Cf. Thompson, *Spain*, pp. 232ff.
110 On Suniefrid's usurpation, Miles, *Coinage*, p. 37, cf. 405; Thompson, *Spain*, p. 244. Egica was remembered for his persecution of 'the Goths', that is, the Gothic aristocracy: *Cont. Isid. hispana*, Mommsen, 349.30–1; cf. *ibid.*, 350.30–351.4, for his son's abandonment of his policies.
111 III Caesaraug. 5, Vives, 480.1: '...ut ipse regnum eius in pace sub multimoda annorum curricula solidet gentemque et universam patriam in tranquilitate conservet, et contra hostem adversum victrix Christi dextera victorem efficiat semper...'.

similar prayers, it is not impossible that civil strife continued to condition their performance through the next half century. One further consideration reinforces this connection; it is particularly relevant to the bishops' prayers for king Egica's victory in 691.

Within two years of the Saragossa meeting and two decades before the kingdom's final agony, the Sixteenth Council of Toledo devised the last recorded measures aimed at shoring up a tottering monarchy and invoking divine power against its adversaries. The bishops who gathered in the capital in the spring of 693 had their hands full and the context of conspiracy and usurpation permeates their pronouncements. No less a figure than Sisibert, bishop of Toledo and primate of Spain, was condemned, deposed and excommunicated for his plot to topple and murder Egica and a number of prominent men.[112] The penalties for perjuring the oath of allegiance and the Fourth Council of Toledo's triple anathema against usurpers were reasserted and repeated,

because transgression of the oath has become stoutly rooted and the savage custom has become prevalent of plotting against our princes, in order to murder the prince or deprive him of the royal dignity.[113]

In this highly charged atmosphere, the bishops passed a decree reinforcing the spiritual defense of the monarchy by instituting perpetual daily Masses throughout the peninsula. These services would beseech the Lord to ensure that the subjects' good will toward the king increase with every passing day, 'while the efforts of those who resist be smashed by the power of His right hand'.[114] This time a measure designed to enhance royal success by spiritual means was formulated and promulgated in the immediate aftermath of an aborted usurpation.

On three separate occasions, then, from the early, middle and late period of Visigothic Spain, practices related to obtaining or

---

112 XVI Tol. 9, Vives, 507–9; cf. Thompson, *Spain*, pp. 244–5 and García Moreno, *Prosopografía*, no. 252.

113 XVI Tol. 10, Vives, 509–12, here 509: '...tamen quia et iurandi transgressio valide inolevit et machinandi contra principes nostros consuetudo saeva percrebuit, quo aut nece diversa princeps interimatur aut regni dignitate privetur...'. Cf. the royal *tomus, ibid.*, 487.

114 XVI Tol. 8, Vives, 507: '...adversantium eorum conamina virtute suae dexterae confringantur...'.

magnifying royal success were triggered by and focused on internal challenges to the monarchy. The testimony of the coins and councils is wholly concordant with what can be discerned of the social context of the celebration marking Paul's defeat. This is all the more remarkable if it is remembered that civil war did not monopolize the military activity of Visigothic kings, who also fought with the Franks, Byzantines and Basques. The Hispano-gothic monarchy was characterized by instability and unceasingly confronted a powerful aristocracy. To buttress their own power and differentiate their new-found status from the aristocracy out of which they had ascended, Visigothic kings possessed no universally recognized qualification like the dynastic tradition of their northern neighbors. In no small measure, the Visigoths' reliance on Byzantine models and rich development of *Staatssymbolik* were conditioned by an acute form of the social drama which so dominated early medieval rulership, the competition between a powerful aristocracy and an ambitious, unstable monarchy.

4. THE RHETORIC OF VICTORY

The problem of unrest and internal subversion found a distinct echo in the rhetoric of victory. Visigothic writers were not content with the empty repetition of earlier conventions; they tailored them to the current conditions of rulership. Thus king Chindasvinth's prologue to the law on treason emphasized the damage done the kingdom by disloyalty; in his time, he says, the king was more often obliged to take up arms to crush his own subjects than to repel foreign enemies.[115] When his son prefaced his promulgation of the Law of the Visigoths, he adopted the very terms and concepts of royal victory to the final cause of royal legislation and echoed the royal obsession with dissidence.[116] This introductory section is entitled 'That the Law triumphs over enemies' and argues that law is the ultimate source of royal victory.[117] Thanks to the law, the 'plague of quarrels' can be banished from the kingdom and the army will advance to battle

---

[115] *Lex Vis.*, 2, 1, 8, Zeumer, 53.13–54.7.

[116] King, *Law*, p. 21, has emphasized the value of this kind of theoretical statement for understanding the Visigothic legislator's mentality. On the date, *ibid.*, p. 18.

[117] *Lex Vis.*, 1, 2, 6, Zeumer, 42.1.

confidently, more sure of victory over external enemies for the certainty that there is nothing to fear from internal ones. The people who have been cemented together by the oil of peace – here clearly internal peace – and the wine of law stand undefeated against their enemies. Men whose laws are equitable fight harder, and the prince's battle will be more successful if it is preceded by domestic justice.[118]

Just as the modesty of the prince is the temperance of the laws, so harmony of the citizens is victory over the enemy. For from the mildness of the princes arises the disposition of the laws; from the disposition of the laws, the arrangement of morals; from the arrangement of morals, the harmony of citizens; from the harmony of citizens, triumph over enemies.[119]

In this fashion, the lawmaker continues, the good prince can hope to possess internal peace (*suam pacem*), void the foreign quarrel (*alienam litem*) and, before arriving at the crowning glory of eternal life, he can be celebrated both as a rector among his citizens and a victor among his enemies.[120]

The acuteness of high-level dissidence was reflected with exceptional candor by the liturgy's prayers. Thus the votive Mass for the king:

...we entreat you, greatest Father, that you ever guard with your invincible aid our glorious Prince King N. whom you have caused to reign in this life, and that his wishes be pleasing in your eyes. Give peace in his days, grant safety, confer quiet, *crush his internal adversaries*, subject his external enemies to his rule... .[121]

The themes of the royal legislator recur in very straightforward fashion in one of the prayers intoned during the *profectio bellica*

---

[118] *Ibid.*, Zeumer, 42.2–11.

[119] *Ibid.*, Zeumer, 42.13–16: 'sicut ergo modestia principum temperantia est legum, ita concordia civium victoria est hostium. Ex mansuetudine etenim principum oboritur dispositio legum, ex dispositione legum institutio morum, ex institutione morum concordia civium, ex concordia civium triumphus hostium.'

[120] *Ibid.*, Zeumer, 42.16–20.

[121] *Lib. ord.*, Férotin, 295.25–32: 'Per quem te etiam, summe Pater, exposcimus, ut gloriosum principem nostrum *Illum* regem, quem in presenti seculo regnare fecisti, tuo inuicto semper tuearis auxilio, eiusque uota sint in tuis oculis placabilia. Des in diebus eius pacem, concedas salutem, dones quietem, internos eius aduersarios conteras, externos inimicos dicioni eius subicias...'.

service: 'Through your concession, O Lord, let him [the king] have strong armies, *faithful dukes, agreeing minds*, so that he might overcome the enemy with valor...'.[122]

The insistence of monarchy and church on royal victory makes readily understandable that willing subjects responded in kind. A petitioning monk could address his letter to the king, who 'triumphs and reigns in unconquered faith'.[123] A Gothic count living in a distant corner of the realm concluded a letter consoling king Gundemar (609/10–12) on the death of his queen with a prayer that the felicity of the king's glory might be preserved through unceasing triumph and the defeat of all adversity.[124] Seventh-century poetry dedicated to the king fastens on his victory in much the same fashion, as an element of polite intercourse – at least that is as near an appreciation as is possible in our ignorance of the precise political conjuncture when such works were composed.[125] Late in the kingdom's history, Julian of Toledo adapted the victory conceit to his personal plea for even harsher persecution of the Jews.[126]

A close link between the monarchy and historical writing is rather characteristic of the early Middle Ages. In this respect, it may be wondered whether there was more in the way of victory celebration to Visigothic society's version of this relationship. The connection of the History of Wamba with the suppression of Paul's rebellion is patent.[127] Fontaine has uttered the suspicion

---

122 *Ibid.*, 150.17–151.2: 'Habeat, te concedente, Domine, exercitus fortes, duces fidos, concordes animos, quo ualeat uirtute superare aduersos...'. An unnoticed editorial comment of Isidore of Seville underscores this point, when he adds to his source that Leovigild was successful in restoring the monarchy, 'studio quippe exercitus concordante...'. *Hist.*, 49, Rodríguez Alonso, 252.5–6. For the comparison with Biclar, *ibid.*, p. 89.

123 Tarra, from a monastery near Merida, to Reccared, 'gloriose triumphanti et inuicta fide regnanti', *Ep. wisig.*, 9, Gil, 28; cf. Thompson, *Spain*, p. 103. On Tarra, G. Kampers, *Personengeschichtliche Studien zum Westgotenreich in Spanien*, Spanische Forschungen der Görresgesellschaft, 2, 17 (Münster, 1979), p. 67, no. 240.

124 *Ep. wisig.*, 15, Gil, 43.33–5.

125 E.g. *Oratio pro rege*, no. 20, ed. F. Vollmer, *MGH.AA*, 14 (1905), 275.1–6 (cf. Díaz y Díaz, *Index*, I, 59); Eugenius, *Libellus carminum*, Vollmer, 263.1–264.6, as well as the anonymous poems on virtues and vices assigned to the seventh century (Díaz y Díaz, *Index*, I, 68, no. 236), e.g., no. 19, Vollmer, 275.1–6.

126 *De comprobatione sextae aetatis*, praef., ed. J.N. Hillgarth, *CCL*, 115 (1976). 148.117–20.

127 The tendency of the *Hist. Wamb.* is spelled out in the title-incipit which dates from

that the final triumph over the Byzantines was not foreign to the genesis of Isidore's History of the Goths.[128] And a hexameter lauding the parade of infamy inflicted on a rebel against Reccared closes John Biclar's Chronicle.[129]

Two works related to these histories and whose titles are suggestively parallel even qualify as a kind of literature of victory: Isidore's Praise of the Province of Spain and Julian's Revilement of the Despicable Province of Gaul.[130] They share the device of apostrophe: the argument directly addresses a personified province. Isidore concludes on a triumphal note befitting the final defeat of Byzantine forces in Spain. First Roman power desired and espoused her but, after many victories won throughout the world, the Gothic *gens* carried Spain off and loved her.[131] If the bishop of Seville imagined Spain as a desirable woman, the bishop of Toledo portrays Gaul as a wayward one, as an insane ingrate, who is rightly subjugated by the main force of the victorious 'army of the Spaniards'. These passages testify to more than seventh-century male chauvinism: in both cases victory is assigned not to the sole ruler of the Visigoths, but to the *gens* or army.[132]

The trend whose first hints are discernible in Gothic Italy and increasingly prominent among the Lombards became a significant element in Visigothic conceptions of military success. The *gens* or ethnic unit rivals and even surpasses the ruler as the agent and embodiment of victory. Isidore's History of the Goths furnishes

---

Wamba's lifetime: 'In nomine sanctae trinitatis incipit historia excellentissimi Wambae regis de expeditione et victoria, qua revellantem contra se provinciam Galliae celebri triumpho perdomuit', Levison, 501.4–7; on the date, *ibid.*, n. 1.

[128] J. Fontaine, *Revue des études latines*, 55 (1977), 601.

[129] Above, n. 30.

[130] On the MS authority for the title of Isidore's *Laus*, Rodríguez Alonso, pp. 58–9. For Julian's I have preferred the explicit, *Insultatio*, 9, Levison, 529.30, to the incipit since *vilis* seems out of place as an epithet of the *storicus*, i.e. Julian himself: Levison, 526.6.

[131] *Laus Spaniae*, Rodríguez Alonso 170.26–30. On the metaphor, J. Fontaine and J.N. Hillgarth, *La storiografia altomedievale*, 1, Settimane 17 (Spoleto, 1970), 350–1.

[132] Note that in Isidore, the old tag 'aurea Roma caput mundi' becomes (unconsciously?) 'aurea Roma caput *gentium*': Rodríguez Alonso, 170.26–7, and it is the 'Gothorum florentissima gens' who enjoy victory throughout the world and abscond with Spain: *ibid.*, 170.28–9. The trend is even more pronounced in Julian. He generally speaks of the victors of Gaul (e.g., *Insultatio*, 1, Levison, 526.7; 7, 528.19; 8, 529.10; 'exercitus Spanorum' or 'Spani', *ibid.*, 7, Levison, 528.15–18; 528.20–1; 8, 528–9, *passim*).

the most outstanding example. The early Goths had rebuffed Roman patronage and named their own ruler because they had triumphed over the empire.[133] Reccared's conversion had permitted him to elevate the entire *gens* through the trophy of faith.[134] The success of the king and the new faith against the Franks is transformed into a collective victory of the Goths.[135] Even a Gothic defeat is made into proof of the entire people's extraordinary victoriousness.[136] The best illustration of the pattern comes from the highly compressed résumé of the History found in Isidore's Recapitulation. A comparison of the long version's view of Visigothic victory over Rome with its condensation in the Recapitulation shows a surprising result: the condensation is twice as long as the original. The latter reads:

Sicque urbs cunctarum gentium uictrix Gothicis triumphis uicta subcubuit eisque capta subiugataque seruiuit.[137]

While the abbreviation goes:

Quibus [sc. Gothis] tanta extitit magnitudo bellorum et tam extollens gloriosae uictoriae uirtus ut Roma ipsa uictrix omnium populorum subacta captiuitatis iugo Gothicis triumphis adcederet et domina cunctarum gentium illis ut famula deseruiret.[138]

To the deeply rooted and widely diffused propaganda of the Roman empire's eternal victory, the young Gothic kingdom offered a new and different ideological response. It derived from and mirrored the old ideology, but it was infused with new meaning. The new content reflects the circumstances of an early medieval aristocracy which had risen from the double spring of a late Roman provincial elite and Germanic upper class deeply shaped by its experience of imperial civilization.

---

133 *Hist.*, 12, Rodríguez Alonso, 190.2–10.   134 *Ibid.*, 52, 260.8–11.
135 *Ibid.*, 54, Rodríguez Alonso, 262.1–263.9.
136 Thus Jerome's dry 'Romani Gothos in Sarmatorum regione uicerunt', *Chron.*, Helm, 233, becomes Isidore's 'Constantinus...ingentique certamine [Gothos] uix superatos ultra Danuuium expulit, de diuersis gentibus uirtutis gloria clarus, sed de Gothorum uictoria amplius gloriosus. Quem Romani senatu adclamante publica laude prosecuti sunt, quod tantam gentem uicerit...'. Rodríguez Alonso, 178.13–17.
137 *Ibid.*, 15, 194.11–14.
138 *Recapitulatio*, 67, Rodríguez Alonso, 284.4–7.

9

From late antique to early feudal society: Frankish victory celebrations

Fourth-century Gaul experienced at first hand the pomp of the Roman emperors. Four centuries later, another kind of emperor and his court would travel through the French countryside, claiming to be their successor. In some respects, the outward trappings of his authority resembled those of fourth-century rulers, but this was due as much to conscious archaism as to uninterrupted continuity. Some of his *Staatssymbolik*, while of imperial cachet, was more modern in substance and style, and not a little of this can be traced to the Byzantine provincial civilization of Italy. Some of the ways in which the new emperor manifested and exercised his power were inherited from his Merovingian predecessors. What little is known of their victory celebrations illuminates the challenges the Merovingians confronted in the sixth and early seventh centuries. But the long-haired kings were already well on their way to puppet status when the first irrefutable evidence of a Frankish liturgy of victory appears. Under the Carolingians, the pace of development quickened in this area and in that of court ceremonial, particularly in the 790s. In both instances, a new concern with the Frankish army looms large.

By and large, the best information on Merovingian kings and their doings comes from the sixth century, thanks to Gregory of Tours, Venantius Fortunatus, Procopius and Agathias. Data on royal ceremonies dwindles as the Frankish kings faded from the center stage in the course of the next century. There is, moreover, next to nothing in the way of court historiography, and even a talented 'provincial' observer like Gregory of Tours tended to record royal ceremonies only when they impinged on his own and

St Martin's concerns.[1] But numerous, if vague, contemporary allusions to 'royal ornament' or 'pomp' attest that Frankish kings did indeed seek symbolic means of distinguishing themselves from their subjects.[2]

The Gallo-Roman society which the first Merovingians ruled remained sensitive to patterns of public deportment inherited from the past, and Clovis and even his father appreciated at least some elements of the late antique upper crust's life-style.[3] Early in the sixth century, the bishop of Arles made a scathing remark on his parishioners' eagerness to bend the knee and bow the head when asking a favor of the earthly king, his representative or even any magnate ('ab aliqua potenti persona').[4] Decades later, the bishops convened at Mâcon tried to resolve the social controversy generated by the clerical claim of precedence over secular grandees ('saeculares honorati').[5] At every public encounter, the clergy's

[1] The only time Gregory draws anything like a detailed picture of royal ceremonial is during king Gunthram's visit to Orleans in July 585. Typically, he begins by noting that the king arrived there on the feast of the *Ordinatio S. Martini* (4 July): *Hist.*, 8, 1, Krusch–Levison 370.12–14. The only *adventus* of Clovis described in any detail is that at Tours (cf. below). The nature of his historical curiosity in both instances is illuminated by his slight deformation of Clovis' order forbidding the army from taking fodder and water from the Tours area 'pro reverentia beati Martini' (*Hist.*, 2, 37, Krusch–Levison 85.8–9). The surviving edict from 507–11 does show that Clovis tried to win favor by preventing his troops from ravaging church holdings, but no mention is made of St Martin: ed. A. Boretius, *MGH.Capit.*, 1 (1883). 1–2.
[2] E.g. 'regio cultu', 'culto [sic] regale', 'regali ordine', or 'regalis pompa': Fredegar, *Chron.* 3, 20, Krusch, 101.6; 4, 53, 146.27; 4, 59, 150.22; 4, 71, 156.27; *Liber historiae Francorum*, 40, ed. B. Krusch, *MGH.SRM*, 2 (1888).310.16; Venantius Fortunatus, *Carmina*, 6, 5, 216, ed. F. Leo, *MGH.AA*, 4.1 (1881).142. The expression continues in use in the Carolingian era, often in the obvious meaning of 'with royal insignia', e.g., *Ann. Bert.*, a.865, Grat, Vielliard and Clémencet, 122.
[3] On the social continuity of the Roman elite in the area south of the Loire, Stroheker, *Germanentum*, pp. 192–206, and *Der senatorische Adel im spätantiken Gallien* (Tübingen, 1948); M. Heinzelmann, *Bischofsherrschaft in Gallien. Zur Kontinuität römischer Führungschichten vom 4. bis 7. Jahrhundert. Soziale, prosopographische und bildungsgeschichtliche Aspekte*, Beihefte der Francia, 5 (Munich, 1976). For the cultural situation, Riché, *Éducation*, pp. 220ff. Something of Childeric's attitudes can be deduced from his grave furnishings: K. Böhner, 'Childerich von Tournai', *Reallexikon der germanischen Altertumskunde*, 4 (1981), 440–60, esp. 458–9. Cf. Clovis' request for a cithara-player–vocalist from Theoderic: Cassiodorus, *Var.*, 2, 41, 4, Fridh, 92.33–7.
[4] Caesarius of Arles, *Sermo 77*, 3, ed. G. Morin, *CCL*, 103 (1953).320. The similarity Morin notes with Severus of Antioch, *Sermo 53*, does not include this passage, to judge by the French tr.: ed. and tr. R. Duval, *Patrologia orientalis*, 4 (1908).42.
[5] The canon concerns clerics 'down to the lower grade of honor'. That the bishops are responding to a controversy may be deduced from their bothering to legislate and

preeminence was to be expressed by the grandee's bow; if both individuals happened to be mounted, the layman needed only to remove his hat and salute the cleric. If, however, the cleric was on foot, the grandee was required to dismount immediately and pay the churchman 'due honor' (*debitus honor*). Although we may wonder whether episcopal legislation really transformed the pattern of public encounters in late sixth-century Gaul, the symbolic gestures concretizing the respective social status of clergy and grandees were sufficiently significant for the bishops to back them with the threat of excommunication.[6]

The social group which promulgated this kind of ruling on public precedence was dominated by the old senatorial aristocracy's self-conscious progeny, or at least men who called themselves such.[7] The same men who attempted to force on their lay counterparts public acknowledgement of clerical priority presided over a remarkable deployment of flamboyant rituals expressing their power and influence. It is not surprising, given the ecclesiastical bias of surviving records, that we should be informed of their contribution to this area of public life. Can it be an accident that the Gallican custom of parading a new bishop in a sedan chair evokes precisely the most prestigious ritual open to senators of the fifth- and sixth-century imperial capitals, the inaugural processions of the ordinary consulate?[8] These prelates never allowed the traditional pomp of their solemn entries to falter: from the sixth century down to the Carolingians and

---

their statement that it is only appropriate 'causis singulis honestum terminum dare': *Concilium matisconense, a. 585*, 15, ed. C. De Clercq, *CCL*, 148A (1963).246.264–5. On the term *honoratus*, H. Grahn-Hoek, *Die Fränkische Oberschicht im 6. Jahrhundert. Studien zur ihrer rechtlichen und politischen Stellung*, Vorträge und Forschungen, Sonderband, 21 (Sigmaringen, 1976), pp. 74ff and 122ff.

6 *Matisc. a. 585*, De Clercq, 246.264–81.

7 Heinzelmann, *Bischofsherrschaft*, pp. 243ff; cf. however, F.D. Gilliard, 'The senators of sixth-century Gaul', *Speculum*, 54 (1979), 685–97.

8 Episcopal enthronement entailed being carried about the city: Gregory, *Hist.*, 2, 23, Krusch–Levison 68.33–4 (cf. *ibid.*, 586.7, for the morphology). More details in Eddius Stephanus, *Vita Wilifredi* (*BHL*, 8889), 12, ed. W. Levison, *MGH.SRM*, 6 (1913).206.15–207.4. On episcopal appropriation of non-episcopal insignia, see the classic study of T. Klauser, 'Der Ursprung der bischöflichen Insignien und Ehrenrechte', *Gesammelte Arbeiten*, pp. 195–211. Such displays included acclamations: Venantius Fortunatus, *Vita Germani*, (*BHL*, 3468), 63, ed. B. Krusch, *MGH.SRM*, 7 (1920).410.14–16; cf. Hauck, 'Randkultur', pp. 38ff.

beyond, the episcopal *adventus* flourished north of the Alps.[9] Bishops celebrated their *natalis*, and failure of subordinates to perform the ancient obligation of courtesy or *salutatio* to their lordly patron could trigger severe consequences.[10] The liturgy itself gave them power over the crowd and played up episcopal authority and prestige: when an imposter holy man rode into Paris and incited the crowd to stage counter-processions in competition with those of the resident prelate, it was a grave matter indeed.[11]

As might be expected, the evidence shrinks when it comes to the bishops' lay counterparts. Even so, the secular magnates' love of public display and flamboyant gestures have left unmistakable traces. If lay grandees were indifferent to externalizations of power and rank, why did the bishops have to buttress clerical pretensions with excommunication? And it is certain that, like their imperial predecessors, the officers of Frankish kings continued to enjoy traditional perquisites like the *adventus* ceremony, not only on the shores of the Mediterranean, where such survivals might be expected, but in far away Brittany as well.[12] On a lower social

---

[9] Hauck, 'Randkultur', pp. 37ff. Hauck's evidence may be expanded as follows: Cyprian, Firminus and Viventius, *V. Caesarii* (*BHL*, 1508–9), 26, Morin, 306.6–12; cf. *ibid.*, 43, 313.21–3; *Vita Genouefae* (*BHL*, 3335), 11, ed. B. Krusch, *MGH.SRM*, 3 (1896).219.1–2; Gregory, *Liber vitae patrum*, 5, 2, ed. W. Arndt and B. Krusch, *MGH.SRM*, 1.2 (1885).678.34–679.1; Venantius Fortunatus, *Vita Severini Burde-galensis* (*BHL*, 7652), 3, ed. W. Levison, *MGH.SRM*, 7 (1920).220.7–221.4; *Vita Amandi Traiectensis* (*BHL*, 332), 21, ed. B. Krusch, *MGH.SRM*, 5 (1910).444.14–18; Stephanus Africanus, *Vita Amatoris Autissiodorensis* (*BHL*, 356), 28, ed. *AASS*, Maii I (1680).58C; *Vita Aniani Aurelianensis* (*BHL*, 473), 6, ed. B. Krusch, *MGH.SRM*, 3 (1896).111.15–19; *Vita Gaugerici Cameracensis* (*BHL*, 3286), 7, ed. B. Krusch, *MGH.SRM*, 3 (1896).654.11–14; *Vita Audoini Rotomagensis* (*BHL*, 750), ed. W. Levison, *MGH.SRM*, 5 (1910).560.10–561.5. Examples of Carolingian episcopal *adventus*: *Narratio clericorum Remensium*, ed. A. Werminghoff, *MGH. Conc.*, 1.2 (1908).809.5–810.17; Sedulius Scottus, ed. L. Traube, *MGH. Poet.*, 3 (1896).176–7; *Annales Xantenses*, a. 866, ed. B. von Simson, *MGH.SRG* (1909).24.31–4. Another common form of *adventus* was that of saints' relics: N. Gussone, 'Adventus-Zeremoniell und Translation von Reliquien. Victricius von Rouen, De laude sanctorum', *FMS*, 10 (1976), 125–33; cf. M. Heinzelmann, *Translationsberichte und andere Quellen des Reliquienkultes*, Typologie des sources du moyen âge occidental, 33 (Turnhout, 1979), pp. 70ff.

[10] Thus Gregory, *Hist.*, 5, 49, Krusch–Levison, 263.16–19, where Riculf's failure to come to Gregory is the symbolic last straw in his presumption.

[11] *Ibid.*, 9, 6, Krusch–Levison, 418.3–420.2.

[12] Marseilles: *ibid.*, 6, 11, 281.15–26; cf. Hauck, 'Randkultur', pp. 37ff, and K. Selle-Hosbach, 'Prosopographie Merowingischer Amtsträger in der Zeit von 511. bis 613.', Diss. (Bonn, 1974), pp. 108–9, no. 118; Brittany: Gregory, *Hist.*, 10, 9,

level, as late as Procopius' day, some mysterious elements of the old imperial forces stationed in Gaul were reported to have maintained their specific identity, standards and customs 'right down to their shoes'.[13] And it is not likely that ethnic Franks shunned Gallo-Roman zest for the traditional trappings of success. A Constantinopolitan observer went so far as to claim that the only difference in the life-style of Franks and Gallo-Romans lay in their national dress and language.[14]

The monarchy which sought to govern such a society could ill afford to ignore its values and customs. In keeping with the patchwork political fabric of Merovingian Gaul, whose single name conceals a complex web of towns and local elites, the consensus between sixth-century ruler and ruled was constantly exemplified by the *adventus* ceremony.[15] The quintessentially Merovingian institution of the 'royal circuit' or *circuitus regis* of a wandering monarchy became so essential a trait of rulership that a seventh-century Frank assumed its roots reached into the Roman past.[16] The king's contact with local elites continued in the banquets which attended his progress, and sixth-century Merovingians more than once delighted their new subjects with

Krusch–Levison, 492.10–12; cf. Selle-Hosbach, *Prosopographie*, p. 85, no. 81. The anonymous author (s. viii?) of the *V. Aniani Aurelianensis* (*BHL*, 473), 3, Krusch, 109.10–12, was still quite familiar with the kind of *adventus* ceremony he thought appropriate to a sixth-century official. The continuity of ceremonial entries for lay officials is shown by Gospel readings from eighth-century Francia 'In adventum iudicum' (Luke 18.18–30): T. Klauser, *Das römische Capitulare Evangeliorum. Texte und Untersuchungen zu seiner ältesten Geschichte*, Liturgiewissenschaftliche Quellen und Forschungen, 28, 2nd edn (Münster, 1972), p. 171, no. 350.

[13] Procopius, *Bella*, 5, 12, 13–19, Haury, 2.64.23–65.24; cf. E. Zöllner, *Geschichte der Franken bis zur Mitte des sechsten Jahrhunderts* (Munich, 1970), pp. 51ff.

[14] Agathias, *Hist.*, 1, 2, 3–4, Keydell, 11.10–18. Cf. Av. Cameron, 'Agathias on the early Merovingians', *Annali della Scuola normale superiore di Pisa*, 3rd ser., 37 (1968), 95–140, here 113, who tends to downplay the accuracy of Agathias' testimony. It should be noted that sixth-century national clothing styles dissolved into a predominantly Roman and regional one in Burgundian territory: J. Werner, 'Die romanische Trachtprovinz Nordburgund im 6. und 7. Jahrhundert', *Von der Spätantike zum frühen Mittelalter. Aktuelle Probleme in historischer und archäologischer Sicht*, Vorträge und Forschungen, 25 (Sigmaringen, 1979), pp. 447–65.

[15] See Hauck, 'Randkultur', pp. 34ff. Cf. N. Coulet, 'De l'intégration à l'exclusion: la place des juifs dans les cérémonies d'entrée solennelle au Moyen Age', *Annales. Économies, sociétés, civilisations*, 34 (1979), 672–81.

[16] Fredegar, 4, 59 mentions a royal *circuitus* 'regio cultu' in 630–1, Krusch, 150.22. For the Roman roots, see the remark on Titus, *ibid.*, 2, 36, 61.10–11.

royal munificence in the form of circus shows.[17] For the Franks, royal power found symbolic expression in the king's audience and the annual assemblies of grandees and kings, the Marchfield.[18] Ceremonial informed the great events in the life of the dynasty: largess signaled and memorialized to the populace the birth of an heir, and his baptism was a solemn occasion of state.[19] Specific rituals were devised for the new king's elevation while dynastic marriages were celebrated with due pomp.[20] Links between ruler and ruled were tightened with oaths and prayers reinforced them, while the end of earthly power was demarcated by the funeral customs which have recently attracted scholarly attention.[21]

[17] Examples of royal banquets and their social significance: Gregory, *Hist.*, 7, 27, Krusch–Levison, 345.19–346.10; 8, 1, 370.19–371.9; 8, 2–5, 372.3–374.21; 9, 11, 426.8–16; 9, 30, 441.1–13. Cf. Caesarius of Arles, *Sermo* 74, 3, Morin, 308, and *Sermo* 187, 3, *CCL*, 104 (1953).764 (although which king is not clear); Venantius Fortunatus, *Carm.*, 10, 3, Leo, 232.13–14, and 10, 9, 243.69ff. Is there a connection with the Frankish legal status of *convivae regis* held by certain Romans? Cf. *Pactus legis Salicae*, 41, 8, ed. K.A. Eckhardt, *MGH.Leges*, 1.4.1 (1962).157 and e.g., W. Schlesinger, 'Herrschaft und Gefolgschaft in der germanisch-deutschen Verfassungsgeschichte', *Herrschaft und Staat im Mittelalter*, Wege der Forschung, 2 (Darmstadt, 1956), pp. 135–90, here 169. Banquets have been identified as an element of status in the Frankish aristocratic life-style: F. Irsigler, *Untersuchungen zur Geschichte des frühfränkischen Adels*, Rheinisches Archiv, 70 (Bonn, 1969), pp. 248ff. For circus shows: Gregory, *Hist.*, 5, 17, Krusch–Levison, 216.13–14; Procopius, *Bella*, 7, 33, 5, Haury, 2.442.17–22.

[18] See in general G. Waitz, *Deutsche Verfassungsgeschichte*, 2, 2, 3rd edn (Berlin, 1882), 183ff; L. Levillain, 'Campus Martius', *Bibliothèque de l'École des chartes*, 107 (1947–8), 62–8; B. Bachrach, 'Was the Marchfield a part of the Frankish constitution?', *Mediaeval Studies*, 36 (1976), 178–85; cf. Zöllner, *Franken*, pp. 129–31.

[19] Birth of an heir: Gregory, *Hist.*, 6, 23, Krusch–Levison, 290.20–2. Manumissions on such occasions were ordered with sufficient regularity to warrant the establishment of legal formulas: *Collectio Marculfi*, 2, 52, ed. K. Zeumer, *MGH.Form.* (1882), 106; cf. 1, 39, 68.11–17. Baptism: *V. Amandi* (BHL, 332), 17, Krusch, 442.4–9, seems to indicate that the 'army' was present. Krusch places the baptism in 630, while the *V. Amandi* has been dated to the late seventh or early eighth century: E. De Moreau, 'La Vita Amandi prima et les fondations monastiques de S. Amand', *AB*, 67 (1949), 447–64, here 447–9. The *Vita*'s account is at variance with Fredegar, 4, 62, Krusch, 151.19–20, but whether or not Amandus participated in the baptism has little significance for the story's ceremonial background. Cf. Gregory, *Hist.*, 6, 27, Krusch–Levison, 295.1–6, on the celebrations at Paris for Theoderic's baptism in 583.

[20] Investitures: Schneider, *Königswahl*, pp. 192ff; for royal weddings, e.g. Venantius Fortunatus, *Carm.*, 6, 1, Leo, 124.15–125.24; Fredegar, 4, 53, Krusch, 146.27–147.2.

[21] Oaths: Zöllner, *Franken*, pp. 127–8; prayers: E. Ewig, 'La prière pour le roi et le royaume dans les privilèges épiscopaux de l'époque mérovingienne', *Mélanges offerts à Jean Dauvillier* (Toulouse, 1979), pp. 255–67. Cf. the dramatic story of king Gunthram, Gregory, *Hist.*, 7, 8, Krusch–Levison 331.1–10; cf. *ibid.*, 8, 4, 373.10–11,

Since most of the evidence comes from the sixth century, it is tempting to conclude that royal ceremonial followed the *rois fainéants* into oblivion. But the disproportionate role of a Gregory of Tours' testimony cautions against such a deduction. In fact, at least rudimentary royal ritual accompanied the kings down to the eve of the Carolingian coup. Sources favorable to the new dynasty emphasize precisely that the last Merovingians had to be content with the ceremonial functions of royalty, while the Carolingians possessed real power. Puppet kings might continue to receive foreign legations and furnish the 'species dominantis', but they were merely pronouncing the words dictated by the mayors of the palace.[22] Childeric III (743–52), last of the Merovingians, continued to make annual appearances at the Marchfield. The Chronicle of Lorsch paints a vivid picture of his performance, ensconced in a throne and surrounded by the army, accepting the customary gifts and promulgating the assembly's decisions, before abandoning the scene to the real power-brokers.[23]

Most of these ceremonies helped define the king's relations with various socially significant groups of subjects, whether they were the Gallo-Roman aristocrats and populations of the sixth-century towns or the whole Frankish elite assembled for a royal baptism or Marchfield. Much of the raw material for such ceremonies lay ready to hand in the aristocratic milieux of late Roman Gaul and the ancestral traditions of the Franks. And yet some degree of imperial influence cannot be denied, for instance when the same king who celebrated circus shows at Paris and Soissons was blamed for introducing the Byzantine punishment of blinding into France.[24]

---

and below, section 2. Funerary customs: A. Erlande-Brandenburg, *Le roi est mort. Étude sur les funérailles, les sépultures et les tombeaux des rois de France jusqu'à la fin du XIIIe siècle*, Bibliothèque de la société française d'archéologie, 7 (Paris, 1975), pp. 5–7, 32–6, 133–48, and Krüger, *Königsgrabkirchen*, pp. 3off.

[22] Einhard, *Vita Karoli magni*, 1, ed. G. Waitz and O. Holder-Egger, *MGH.SRG*, 6th edn (1911), 3.10–13.

[23] *Ibid.*, 3.21–33; H. Schnorr von Carolsfeld, 'Das *Chronicon Laurissense breve*', *Neues Archiv*, 36 (1911), 15–39, here 28.

[24] Gregory, *Hist.*, 6, 46, Krusch–Levison, 321.1–5.

I. MEROVINGIAN VICTORY CELEBRATIONS

Clovis' father Childeric was buried with his trusty steed but still insisted on depicting himself as a Roman general. As their very names suggest, the first Merovingians were first and foremost successful Germanic warlords. But the forms with which they celebrated their success bear the clear imprint of the Roman empire's eternal victory. If, as most historians believe, Gregory of Tours' account of Clovis' visit to Tours in 508 is substantially reliable, the ceremony marking that occasion forms the obligatory starting point of any consideration of Merovingian victory celebrations. As Hauck has clearly and correctly emphasized, the event as a whole must be viewed as a victory festival. This understanding is implicit in Gregory's description, for the parade story follows the winter operations in which Clovis mopped up what Visigothic resistance remained after the great victory of 507. Gregory himself explicitly confirms this interpretation elsewhere in his History.[25]

The ceremony's immediate political context has been pretty well clarified by Hauck and others. The conqueror and new Germanic ruler was heading north to Paris after his drive into the heart of the Visigothic kingdom and the fall of Toulouse and Angoulême.[26] The visit to Tours not only consecrated Clovis' victory over the Gallo-Romans' old Germanic overlord, it ritually manifested the new relation between the newest barbarian ruler and his subjects. As such, the arrival from Constantinople of a diploma (*codicelli*) granting Clovis the Roman dignity of honorary consul was particularly welcome, since it placed the emperor's seal of approval on the new state of affairs.[27]

[25] On Childeric's horse, K. Böhner, 'Childerich', p. 455. On his name, W. Jungandreas, *ibid.*, pp. 440–1; on Clovis's, idem, 'Chlodwig', *Reallexikon der germanischen Altertumskunde*, 4 (1981), 478; cf. in general, Wallace-Hadrill, *Kingship*, pp. 18–20. On Clovis at Tours, see Hauck, 'Randkultur', pp. 44 and 54; Gregory, *Hist.*, 2, 37–8, Krusch–Levison, 87.13–89.6; *ibid.*, 10, 9, 531.17–532.1: 'Huius tempore Chlodovechus rex *victor* de caede Gothorum Turonus *rediit*.' Gregory's own succinct characterization of the entry is a precious clue to the ceremonial reality behind jejeune phrases like 'victor rediit' or 'victor intravit' in early medieval historiography.

[26] Gregory, *Hist.*, 2, 37, Krusch–Levison, 88.10–13.

[27] T. Mommsen, *Gesammelte Schriften*, 6 (Berlin, 1910), 426; R. Guilland, 'Études sur l'histoire administrative de l'empire byzantin. Le consul, ὁ ὕπατος', *Byz.*, 24 (1954), 545–78, here 565–7; J. Deér, 'Byzanz und die Herrschaftszeichen des Abendlandes', *BZ*, 50 (1957), 405–36, here 410–11.

Ritually speaking, the event consisted of a ceremonial entry and parade into the city. According to Gregory, it began outside the walls at St Martin's.[28] In the basilica, Clovis dressed in a purple tunic and put on the *chlamys*, a standard element of the imperial administration's uniform. To this he added a 'diadem'.[29] He then mounted his horse and rode in procession into the city and the Cathedral of St Gatien, throwing gold and silver to the inhabitants who lined his route.

Because of Gregory's description of the dignity and largess, the ceremony at Tours has often been viewed in terms of the *processus consularis*, the inaugural procession of a consul. Yet at best it was a bastardized version of that ceremony for, if it included a largess, it lacked the most visible and characteristic element of contemporary consular parades in Ravenna, Rome and Constantinople: the procession in the *sella curulis*. Furthermore, the distinction between an honorary consulate and the ordinary consulate would scarcely have escaped an informed contemporary of senatorial background.

Much closer in fact to the external form of the parade at Tours was the triumphal entry. And, despite the imperial overtones Gregory and modern scholars perceive in this act, the most precise correspondence of the Tours ceremony seems not to be with imperial triumphal entries, which were of decidedly reduced importance in the public life of contemporary Constantinople, but with the provincial ceremonies staged by victorious imperial generals to mark their successes. The triumph parade on horseback, the conclusion of the procession at a local sanctuary, even the festive *sparsio* of cash to win the hearts and minds of a newly

---

[28] Gregory, *Hist.*, 2, 38, Krusch–Levison, 88.15–89.5; on the sixth-century topography: Brühl, *Palatium*, pp. 105–8 and map, facing p. 104.

[29] Gregory, *Hist.*, 2, 38, Krusch–Levison, 89.1–2. Gregory's account does not mention whether the insignia themselves came from Constantinople with the *codicelli* of appointment, but the imperial government often dispatched such objects with the dignities conferred on satellite rulers, e.g. Procopius, *Bella*, 2, 15, 2, Haury, 1.215.26–8; 3, 25, 3–6, 1.412.17–413.8; 3, 25, 7–8, 1.413.8–15; *Aed.*, 3, 1, 18–23, Haury, 4.85.5–29. An unnoticed parallel to Clovis' appointment occurred in the last quarter of the seventh century, when Maurus received the title ὕπατος (consul) along with authority over Byzantine refugees from Sirmium: *Miracula Demetrii* (BHG, 516z–523), 292, Lemerle, 1.229.32–230.10; cf. comm., 2 (Paris, 1981), 151–62. On the *chlamys*, see J. Ebersolt, *Mélanges d'histoire et d'archéologie byzantines* (Paris, 1917), pp. 53–6.

subjugated town all recall the victory celebrations not of Constantinople, but of imperial commanders operating in the provinces.[30]

The message of the ceremony is even clearer than its source. For the second time in forty years, a new Germanic overlord – whose savage elimination of opponents would have been no less obvious to Gallo-Roman contemporaries than it was to their descendants two generations later – was establishing his control over the town and its Roman population.[31] He was doing so as the military victor and he availed himself of the indigenous ritual form expressive of that reality. Its specific shape lent that procession an unambiguous political content, calculated to appeal to Clovis' audience, the local Roman population of Tours.

Ethnic foreigner though he might be, the king enjoyed the approval of the Roman emperor and flaunted some of a loyal imperial servant's external trappings. In contrast to the old rulers, he shared his new subjects' religion and made a pointed show of his veneration for the local patron and hierarchy by beginning his parade at St Martin's and ending it at the cathedral. Even more tangible appreciation was expressed by his votive offering of Gothic – and Arian – booty to the great saint.[32] Cynics not swayed by the new barbarian's delicate spirituality would surely have had difficulty remaining indifferent to the appeal of liberally distributed cold, hard cash. At Tours, the founder of the Merovingian kingdom utilized the traditional Roman ritual forms derived, at least in part, from provincial victory celebrations to build a new political consensus, to win the approval of the foreign majority he hoped to govern.[33]

The regime that began with a victorious entry likely did not entirely dispense with such celebrations in succeeding decades, but the evidence is sparse. One may have marked Theoderic II's victory over Chlothar and his entry into Paris in 604; another is

---

[30] See above, Ch. 6, 3. A very close parallel is Belisarius' triumphal entry into newly subjugated Syracuse on the last day of his consulate, when he also distributed largess to his troops and the population: Procopius, *Bella*, 5, 5, 18–19, Haury, 2.27.19–28.5.

[31] Brühl, *Palatium*, p. 100.   [32] Hauck, 'Randkultur', pp. 46ff.

[33] Was Tours unique? It was not the only or even the most important town Clovis needed to win over to the new order. Because of Gregory's Tours-centered vision, his silence on similar ceremonies at other towns on Clovis' itinerary is not an argument against the possibility. Moreover, Clovis made precisely the same sort of ostentatious gifts to St Hilary of Poitiers: Hauck, 'Randkultur', p. 46.

implied by a late story concerning Fredegund.[34] The same source shows that the late Roman custom of head display was thought to be current among seventh-century Franks and called for no comment early in the eighth.[35]

Clovis' grandson Theudebert I (534–47/48) showed interest in imperial victory prerogatives and it is no coincidence that Gallo-Romans enjoyed prominence at his court.[36] His chancellery was aware of imperial titulature's niceties and the king himself was reportedly vexed by Justinian's assumption of the victory cognomen *Francicus*.[37] Frankish irritation at Byzantine victory customs was matched by the sensation caused at Constantinople when Frankish kings took the initiative of issuing gold coinage in their own names.[38] The precarious nature of Merovingian gold issues and the increasing proportion of *tremisses* in sixth-century hoards suggest that *solidi* issues may have been as closely connected with royal prestige and propaganda as with economic policy.[39] Theudebert certainly struck gold coins which departed from the usual pseudo-imperial barbarian issues and displayed propagandizing messages. The obverse of one gold *solidus* discovered in modern-day Belgium gives Theudebert's name and royal title, while the reverse has the unusual slogan PAX ET LIBERTAS.[40] Another *solidus* preserved in several examples shows a fairly typical pseudo-imperial reverse, the legend VICT AUCCCI and a standing Victory. The obverse, however, presents an imperial-style portrait which may have been modeled on that of Anastasius. It is surrounded by the startling legend DN THEODEBERTVS VICTOR (fig. 13). The issue seems to have celebrated

---

[34] Fredegar, 4, 26, Krusch, 131.4: 'Theudericus victur Parisius ingreditur'; a similar ceremony at a royal palace seems to be the setting imagined for the story about the meeting of Fredegund and Chilperic in the early eighth-century *Lib. hist. Franc.*, 31, Krusch, 292.25–293.26.

[35] *Lib. hist. Franc.*, 40, Krusch, 313.20–314.2.

[36] Irsigler, *Untersuchungen*, pp. 105–6.

[37] See Theudebert's letter to Justinian (547): *Epistolae austrasicae*, 18, ed. W. Gundlach, *MGH. Epist.*, 3 (1892). 131.29–30, for epistolary etiquette; cf. Childebert to Maurice (584), *ibid.*, 25, 138.21–2. For *Francicus*, Agathias, *Hist.*, 1, 4, 3, Keydell, 14.6–11.

[38] Procopius, *Bella*, 7, 33, 5, Haury, 2.442.18–22.

[39] P. Le Gentilhomme, 'Le monnayage et la circulation monétaire dans les royaumes barbares de l'Occident (V^e–VIIIe siècle)', *Revue numismatique*, ser. 5, 7 (1943), 45–112, here 100–1.

[40] M. Prou, *Les monnaies mérovingiennes*, Catalogue des monnaies françaises de la Bibliothèque nationale (Paris, 1892), pp. 14–15, no. 55, pl. I, 21.

Figure 13.   Gold *solidus* of king Theudebert (enlarged; see pp. 338–9)

Theudebert's Italian campaign of 539.[41] The form chosen to commemorate this success underscores the Merovingians' reliance on traditional Roman means of glorifying their rulership.

King Gunthram, who ruled Burgundy from 561 to 592, appears to have alluded to some unidentified military success on a coin whose reverse has been interpreted as REGIA VICTORIA.[42] Chlothar II (584–629) finally scrapped the old pseudo-imperial reverse and replaced it with a memorial to his own accomplishments, in the form of the legend VICTVRIA CHLOTARI. This coin was issued by the mint at Marseilles and was the first of that city to displace the old imperial inscription.[43] It is particularly significant because it may well have been struck in honor of the Merovingians' last recorded victory celebration. Chlothar could not have issued coinage at Marseilles before he defeated Brunichildis and reunified the partitioned kingdom in 613, so there is a good chance that the *solidi* and *tremisses* hailing Chlothar's victory proclaimed the major success of his reign, the unexpected victory over Brunichildis which transformed him from a petty kinglet into the master of Gaul. The disaffection and defection of her leading magnates had brought a swift and violent end to Brunichildis' last civil war for control of Gaul.[44] The ruthless old queen was delivered into the hands of her nephew Chlothar at Renève on the Vingeanne River.[45] After he had tortured her for

[41] Prou, *Monnaies*, pp. 10–15, nos. 39, 41–2, 46, 49, 51, 54, 56. Cf. Le Gentilhomme, 'Monnayage', pp. 98ff.

[42] Prou, *Monnaies*, pp. xxxvii–xxxviii.

[43] *Ibid.*, pp. 303–4, nos. 1380–7, pl. 23, 1–4.

[44] R. Buchner, *Die Provence in merowingischer Zeit. Verfassung, Wirtschaft, Kultur* (Stuttgart, 1933), pp. 11–12; E. Ewig, 'Die fränkischen Teilungen und Teilereiche (511–513)', *Spätantikes und fränkisches Gallien. Gesammelte Schriften (1952–1973)*, I, Beihefte der Francia, 3 (Munich, 1976), pp. 114–71, here 149–50.

[45] B. Krusch, *MGH.SRM*, 2.141, n. 5; cf. J.M. Wallace-Hadrill, ed. and tr. *The Fourth Book of the Chronicle of Fredegar with its continuations* (London, 1960), p. 35.

three days, the king celebrated his victory in a fashion which has by now become grimly familiar. Brunichildis was placed on a camel's back and paraded in front of the army, on her way to the executioner. The parade of infamy seems to have been motivated by the queen's role in the murders of ten Merovingian kings.[46]

Comparison of the earliest and latest victory celebrations points up the transformations in Merovingian politics and society over the intervening century. Clovis' triumphal entry into Tours celebrated the establishment of a new regime and the favorable relations it desired with its new subjects. Chlothar's marked the suppression of a civil war and the triumph of the queen's aristocracy over their lord. Setting and audience had changed dramatically. Clovis' ceremony had appealed to a Gallo-Roman town and its patron saint; Brunichildis' ritual humiliation was performed in front of the Frankish army which, like its Visigothic counterpart, was increasingly dominated by the great magnates and their followings.[47] The ceremony had left behind the urban setting of the early sixth century and moved into the countryside, where it played to the only audience that counted in the seventh century: the aristocracy. Thirty years before the onset of the era of do-nothing kings, the dominant actors of the last Merovingian century had already occupied the stage and foreshadowed the future. Yet for all the novelty of the setting, the ritual form remained typically late Roman.

Gallo-Romans responded to their kings' concern with promoting an awareness of their victories; in so doing, they sometimes availed themselves of traditional forms and formulas, even when expressing new realities. Clovis' reign in particular came to be surrounded with an aura of victory. In his lifetime, a bishop would defend himself before his peers by insisting that he had only acted on the orders of that king, the 'triumphator gentium'.[48] After his

---

[46] Fredegar, 4, 42, Krusch, 141.27–142.5; *Lib. hist. Franc.*, 40, Krusch, 310.16–311.7; *Auctarium [Isidorianum] a. 624*, 8, ed. T. Mommsen, *MGH.AA*, 11 (1894).490.19–23; Jonas, *Vita Columbani* (*BHL*, 1893), 1, 29, ed. B. Krusch, *MGH.SRG*, (1905), 219.23–220.3; Sisebut, *Vita Desiderii* (*BHL*, 2148), 21, ed. B. Krusch, *MGH.SRM*, 3 (1896).639.6–12.

[47] B.S. Bachrach, *Merovingian military organization, 481–751* (Minneapolis, 1972), pp. 89–90, 124ff.

[48] *Ep. aust.*, 3, Gundlach, 114.18. The context suggests that Remigius' use of the victory epithet may have been a subtle reminder to his detractors that he was ill equipped to thwart the will of the victorious barbarian.

death, the reputation would stick: the authors of the Life of Caesarius of Arles continued to remember the late ruler as 'the most victorious king', and king Theudebert took great pride in his father's victories when writing to the Roman emperor.[49] In 567, a group of bishops assembled at Tours could still refer to him as 'the most unvanquished king'.[50] The memory of Clovis and his victories had taken on a dynastic tinge by this time. Gregory of Tours and king Gunthram looked back on Clovis and his sons as the fountainhead of the dynasty's victories.[51] In other words, the king's victory was tailored to the dynastic reality of the sixth century. That the Merovingians came to view themselves as possessing a kind of dynastic right to victory is consistent with Venantius Fortunatus' praise of their triumphal lineage.[52] This family notion of victory did not entirely displace more traditional expressions. Like their counterparts in Visigothic Spain, another assembly of bishops may have had a specific victory and its celebration in mind when they hailed their king as 'the most clement prince, the most unvanquished in proofs of triumph Lord King Childebert'.[53] A contemporary poet easily tailored the tags of the old imperial ideology of victory to Clovis' descendants: the dynastic marriage of Sigibert and Brunichildis in 566 was not merely going to promote harmony between the Frankish and Visigothic kingdoms: it was expected to produce 'victorious concord'.[54] Sigibert was 'illustrious with excellent triumphs' yet humble, despite his many victories.[55] The panegyric which

---

[49] *V. Caesarii (BHL*, 1508–9), 1, 28, Morin, 306.31; *Ep. aust.*, 18, Gundlach, 132.5–7; cf. ibid., 20, 133.6–13.

[50] *Conc. Tur. a. 567*, 22, De Clercq, 189.411–12.

[51] Gregory, *Hist.*, 5, praef., Krusch–Levison 193.10–12; cf. 8, 30, 395.8–11. See in general on the Merovingians and their passion for various sources of victory, J.M. Wallace-Hadrill, *The long-haired kings and other studies in Frankish history* (London, 1962), pp. 169ff.

[52] Venantius Fortunatus, *Carm.*, 6, 2, Leo, 131.27–132.34.

[53] *Conc. Aurel. a. 549*, praef., De Clercq, 148.6–7: 'clementissimus princeps domnus triumphorum titulis inuictissimus Childeberthus rex'. The most recent military expedition recorded by Gregory (*Hist.*, 3, 29, Krusch–Levison, 125.10–126.5) was the campaign against the Visigoths some years earlier, but we are not very well informed on events of this period.

[54] 'Victrix concordia': *Carm.*, 6, 1, Leo, 129.141. Cf. W. Meyer, *Der Gelegenheitsdichter Venantius Fortunatus*, Abhandlungen der königlichen Gesellschaft der Wissenschaften zu Göttingen, Phil.-hist. Kl. n.F. 4, 5 (Berlin, 1901), pp. 12–13.

[55] *Carm.*, 6, Ia, Leo, 129.7–130.20.

commemorated the Synod of Berny in 580 proclaimed the old theme that the enemies who sought to wound the king merely provided an occasion for royal success. To the dismay of would-be rebels and various foreign enemies, Chilperic was at hand, 'nomine victoris'.[56]

2. THE LITURGY OF VICTORY IN FRANCIA

No less than their imperial and barbarian colleagues, the rulers and ruled of early medieval Francia imagined that faith was a prime ingredient in military success. Gregory of Tours stated the theme in connection with Clovis' conversion and the dynasty.[57] King Gunthram reportedly uttered the same idea, Venantius Fortunatus elaborated on it and the pope himself wrote to Brunichildis and Chlothar II to reassure them on this account.[58] Since the murderous Merovingians rarely lived up to Christian ideals, even by sixth-century lights, it is no wonder that a high price was set on sure-fire victory producing relics from the East or powerful prayers for victory.[59]

Frankish kings' concern for prayer on their behalf is amply attested. An anecdote in Gregory of Tours shows a troubled king Gunthram getting up and soliciting the prayers of the faithful at Mass.[60] The royal precept which appointed Desiderius to the see of Cahors in 630 ordered the new prelate to pray for his king and his church.[61] And the exhortation to prayer 'for the kingdom's

---

[56] *Ibid.*, 9, 1, Leo, 202.51–2; 203.69–82. Meyer, *Gelegenheitsdichter*, p. 114, thought that the words 'nomine victoris' indicated that Chilperic bore *victor* as an official title, but the context will not bear that burden. Triumphal themes remained useful when addressing Merovingian kings. E.g. Aurelian, bishop of Arles, writing to Theudebert I ca. 546–8, *Ep. aust.*, 10, Gundlach, 125.11–15 and 30–2, on the king's ethical triumph; cf. Desiderius of Cahors, *Ep.*, 1, 3, ed. D. Norberg, Studia latina stockholmensia, 6 (Stockholm, 1961), 15.1–3. Note the application of like formulas to Desiderius himself, *ibid.*, 2, 11, 59.1–4 and 2, 14, 66.1–4.

[57] E.g. *Hist.*, 2, 37, 86.12–16; 3, praef. 97.2–5; cf. Wallace-Hadrill, *Kingship*, p. 31 for the same development in Britain.

[58] Gregory, *Hist.*, 8, 30, Krusch–Levison, 395.8–12 and 14–16; Venantius, *Carm.*, 9, 1, Leo, 201.51–2. Gregory I, *Reg.*, 11, 49, Norberg, 948.18–949.30; 11, 51, 951.30–3.

[59] Gregory, *Hist.*, 7, 31, Krusch–Levison, 350.6–351.17. Cf. Queen Radegundis' explanation of her negotiations with the emperor for relics of the true cross: Baudonivia, *Vita Radegundis* (BHL, 7049), 16, ed. B. Krusch, *MGH.SRM*, 2 (1888).388.11–15; cf. Frolow, *Relique*, pp. 179–80.

[60] Gregory, *Hist.*, 7, 8, Krusch–Levison, 331.1–10.

[61] Preserved in the later *Vita Desiderii* (BHL, 2143), 13, ed. B. Krusch, *MGH.SRM*, 4

stability' (*pro estabiletate rigni*) or the 'king's security' (*incolomitas rigis*) recurs again and again in the royal privileges preserved from the seventh and eighth centuries.[62] Prayers were particularly appropriate when the royal well-being was threatened by warfare. Like Clovis' triumphal parade, like, too, the church which performed them, the idea of such services was an inheritance of late antiquity. Yet for all this emphasis on divine favor as expressed in royal victory, Gregory and the others have left no hint of large-scale services in time of war, of a *profectio bellica* ceremony similar to that of the Visigoths or Byzantines. What we do find is the persistence of some old customs on a purely local level.

Particularly telling in this regard is the spiritual defense of cities by means of the *circuitus murorum*, the liturgical procession around the walls of a beleaguered town, which was so familiar a feature in the public life of the provinces and capitals of the later Roman empire. Gregory of Tours claims that, early on, the Franks were innocent of such ceremonies. When besieging Saragossa in 541, they saw women dressed in black with ashes in their hair, wailing as they walked around the city walls. The Franks concluded that the Spaniards were casting some evil spell on them. Only the interrogation of a local peasant convinced them that this was no superstitious magic but a holy ceremony to protect the city.[63] Saints' lives nonetheless delight in depicting the salvation of Gaulish cities from barbarian onslaught thanks to their bishops' performance of the *circuitus*. Thus Bazas was supposed to have been saved from Arian attack by a procession featuring the relics of John the Baptist.[64] Early in the sixth century, it was claimed, the bishop of Clermont had delivered his city through a psalm-singing procession around the walls matched by vigils and fasting. A Merovingian preacher did not hesitate to remind his flock of

(1902).572.7–12; on the date and reliability, Wattenbach–Levison, *Geschichtsquellen*, p. 127; cf. *Coll. Marc.*, 1, 6, Zeumer, 46.22–4. On the problem in general, Krüger, *Königsgrabkirchen*, pp. 476ff, and Ewig, 'Prière'.

[62] Exx. from Dagobert I (632–3) to Chilperic II (717): P. Lauer and C. Samaran, *Les diplômes originaux des Mérovingiens* (Paris, 1908), pp. 5, 6–7, 13, 17, 19, 23, 26–7.

[63] Gregory, *Hist.*, 3, 29, Krusch–Levison, 125.11–126.4.

[64] Gregory, *In gloria martyrum*, 1, 12, ed. B. Krusch, *MGH.SRM*, 1.2 (1885).675.11–14. A later tradition credited Anianus with saving Orleans by the same method, early in the sixth century: *V. Aniani (BHL, 473)*, 9, Krusch, 114.18–21.

litanies' power against the Goths.[65] Late in the seventh century, bishop Leodegarius prepared his city for siege with a three-day fast and a procession along the ramparts, led by a cross and relics, during which each of Autun's gates was sanctified with prostrations and special prayers.[66]

By these accounts, local echelons played the decisive role in preserving such ceremonies. This view finds confirmation in the fact that the rare references to prayers for rulers in time of war give Merovingian kings little part in their organization. The nun Baudonivia cites as an example of the cloistered queen Radegunda's (ob. 587) piety that, in time of civil war, she prayed for *all* the protagonists. As abbess, she commanded her community to pray 'for their stability', echoing the phraseology of royal privileges.[67] In other words, a sixth-century royal monastery's special services in time of war were organized on the sole initiative of the house's superior. An Irish ascetic was infuriated by the suggestion that he pray for king Theudebert II's victory at the battle of Tolbiac. Characteristically, the idea had come not from the royal court but from St Columban's simple-minded Frankish servant.[68]

A miserable scrap of parchment from Reichenau proves that by the early eighth century, special services for the king's victory had gained sufficient currency to warrant the codification of appropriate texts, in which Frankish priests beseeched the 'Lord God, Creator of All, Terrible and Strong' to 'grant victory to the kings of the Franks' over their rebels, as He had once delivered Israel from Egypt.[69] A similar note was sounded in another eighth-

---

[65] Gregory, *Liber vitae patrum*, 3, 2, Krusch, 675.11–14; Eusebius 'Gallicanus', *Collectio homiliarum*, 25, 2 and 3, ed. F. Glorie, CCL, 101 (1970).296.40–6.

[66] *Passio Leodegarii* (BHL, 4849–50), 23, ed. B. Krusch, MGH.SRM, 5 (1910).304.2–6.

[67] *V. Radegundis* (BHL, 7049), 10, Krusch, 384.29–31. Cf. the biographer of Eligius of Noyon (ob. 660), who emphasized the apostolic origin (cf. 1 Timothy 2.2) of the bishop's habit of praying day and night for the *salus patriae, quies ecclesiarum* and *pax principum*: *Vita Eligii* (BHL, 2474–6), 1, 38, ed. J. Ghesquière, *Acta sanctorum Belgii selecta*, 3 (1785).225, and 2, 8, ed. B. Krusch, MGH.SRM, 4 (1902).701.11–14.

[68] Jonas, *Vita Columbani* (BHL, 1898), 1, 28, Krusch, 218.15–219.5. Columban's violent opposition to this 'stultum ac religione alienum consilium' is out of step with his age and harkens back to the archaic attitudes of the fourth century. This may be an authentic echo of the Patrician tradition. Cf. St Patrick, *Epistola ad Coroticum*, 9, ed. R.P.C. Hanson, SC, 249 (Paris, 1978), 142.4–9.

[69] Karlsruhe, Landesb. Cod. Aug. CCLIII (CLA, 8 (1959), 1100), ed. A. Dold and A. Baumstark, *Das Palimpsestsakramentar im Cod. Aug. CXII*, Texte und Arbeiten, 1, 12

century service from the so-called 'Bobbio Missal'. Here, an untitled Mass was added to what seems to be the work of an elderly priest, living in some place of secondary importance.[70] United in prayer, the faithful entreated God to defend 'our prince'. As once He had saved Abraham and his servants with a tremendous triumph (Genesis 14.14ff), 'so He vivifies, saves, guards, preserves our prince, ever victor against all enemies.'[71] The Mass's second collect deepens the Old Testament parallel by a comparison with Moses' battle against Amalek (Exodus 17.18ff), 'whence we beseech you, O Lord, and, on this day, with devoted minds we pour out our prayers to you, for the benefit of your faithful servant and our prince N., and for his entire army, that You, through the right hand of Your power, O Lord, may bid him always be a victor with triumph over all his enemies, as You once helped Moses...'.[72] The 'Post nomina' prayer pursues the plea for divine help: any who dares oppose the prince will languish under his feet as quickly as Jericho fell to Joshua. Just as David once procured peace for Israel by killing Goliath, so, the prayer 'Ad pacem' hopes, may the king reign resplendent and in peace for countless years, 'universis devictis undeque gentibus'.[73]

Such texts assure us that, despite the silence of all other sectors of evidence, efforts to insure and magnify the king's victory did not

---

(Beuron, 1925), 37: 'prista Francorum rigibus uicturiam...'. Palaeography suggests the MS was copied in the first half of s. viii; the plural 'kings' means the prayer was composed or adapted in 718–19 at the latest.

[70] Paris, B.N. lat. 13246, J.W. Legg, *The Bobbio Missal. A Gallican Mass-Book. Facsimile*, Henry Bradshaw Society, 53 (London, 1917), f.251v–253r; ed. E.A. Lowe, *The Bobbio Missal. A Gallican Mass-Book*, Henry Bradshaw Society, 61 (London, 1924), 64–5, etc. Cf. *CLA*, 5 (1950), 653.

[71] The Mass is without title in the MS; Mabillon called it 'Missa pro principe', cf. Lowe, *Bobbio Missal*, 151, n. 2; citation from *ibid.*, no. 492, 151.24–26: '...ita princepem nostrum semper uictorem contra cunctus aduersarius uiuificit, psaluit, tuçatur, conseruit'. E. Ewig, 'Zum christlichen Königsgedanken im Frühmittelalter', *Spätantikes*, 1, 3–71, here 42, n. 181, wonders whether there is a connection between the text's insistence on *princeps* and Charles Martel. Cf. *ibid.*, p. 20, where the piece is tentatively associated with the thought world of the seventh century.

[72] *Bobbio Missal*, no. 493, 151.33–152.8: '...Unde domine te supleces deprecamur tibique deuotis mentibus in hac die fundemus preces. pro fidele famulo tuo. princepeque nostro ill. adque pro huniuerso exercito illius. ita eum. domine per dexteram uirtutes tui. contra omnes aduersarius semper esse iubeas cum triumpis uictorem. sicut condam auxiliatus es Moysen...'.

[73] *Ibid.*, no. 494 and 495, Lowe, 152.17–24 and 30–4.

completely cease in the last century of Merovingian dominion. Victory remained an essential trait of rulership, even for puppet kings who no longer led their people to war. New, ecclesiastical measures designed to produce victory were devised in circumstances which escape us. The constant wear and replacement of liturgical texts means that the sources of most of these rare witnesses to the late Merovingian liturgy of victory will not be recovered. But the deluxe codex known as the 'Missal of the Franks' (Vat. reg. lat. 257), copied in the first half of the eighth century and once kept in the royal abbey of St Denis, shows that the imperial provinces' creative role had not yet ceased. Like most surviving representatives of the local Gallican liturgical tradition, the Missal is a kind of mixed bag. Although the formulas' structure is considered Gallican, much of the content harkens back to the prestigious liturgies of Byzantine Rome.[74] The votive Mass for the king is not inconsistent with the Reichenau and Bobbio pieces. The Preface makes an emotional appeal ('As prostrate suppliants, with all our hearts, we entreat...') to the Lord to use the power of His majesty to crush those who dare to oppose the Franks.[75] The 'Hanc igitur' insists that the Mass is intended 'pro salute et incolomitate vel statu regni Francorum', recalling once again the phraseology of royal privileges.[76] The third collect asks God to assist the 'princes of the kingdom of the Franks, so that they might be clement by Your tranquility, ever victors by Your power'.[77] Perhaps there is only one surprise to these prayers for Frankish victory: comparison with the Gelasian tradition shows that they have been lifted from the Roman liturgy. The late antique prayer of a prestigious provincial center for the Roman state's perpetual victory has been adapted to local circumstances, the words 'Romani nominis inimici' and 'Romani regni' replaced with 'kingdom of the Franks'.[78]

These texts tell us only that men and women prayed for the

[74] *CLA*, I, 103; L.C. Mohlberg et al., *Missale Francorum*, Rerum ecclesiasticarum documenta, series maior, fontes 2, 2 (Rome, 1957), p. 63 and tables 41–59.
[75] Mohlberg, no. 76, 20.35–21.3.
[76] *Ibid.*, no. 77, 21.8–12.
[77] *Ibid.*, no. 71, 20.14–16: '...Francorum regni adest principibus, ut tua tranquillitate clementis, tua semper sint uirtute uictores'.
[78] No. 76, 20.35–21.3; cf. *Liber sacramentorum Romanae aecclesiae ordinis anni circuli*, ed. L.C. Mohlberg et al., Rerum ecclesiasticarum documenta, series maior, fontes 4

victory of the Merovingian kings and that some of their prayers were derived from the old services for the victory of the Roman empire. They do not tell us when, why, or under what circumstances they did so, although the stories of Radegunda and Columban imply that the performance of such prayers was largely a local affair. This changes with the Carolingians. The king or his entourage came to assume an unmistakable role in developing and organizing new military services aimed at procuring victory. Local initiative is superseded by an attempt at centralized direction. Secondly, the focus of the services widens, in that the army is more directly involved. Whereas the late Merovingian texts were suitable for performance in monasteries and cathedrals far from the scene of battle, new services are performed by and for the Frankish army on campaign.

In the late eighth century, the outset of campaigns was sacralized by a special ceremony for which there is no clear Merovingian antecedent. The Frankish *profectio bellica* is chiefly known from a votive Mass 'In profectionem hostium eontibus in prohelium': 'Mass on the Departure of the Troops for those who are Going to Battle' which occurs in the Sacramentary of Gellone, a manuscript (Paris, B.N. lat. 12048) representing the 'Eighth-Century Gelasian' tradition of the Frankish liturgy, i.e. the first stage in the romanization of the local services.[79] In contrast to the other prayers already examined and as the title itself suggests, the army dominates this service. God is asked to grant light to His army, to send His angel to His foreordained people; the service is performed for the 'victory and preservation of Your army' (*pro exertitus tui uictoria custodiaque*).[80] The Mass is full of references to the army's imminent victory over the 'infidel barbarians'.[81] The Frankish king is not even mentioned until the closing lines of the third collect, and direct prayer for him does not appear until the

---

(Rome, 1960), no. 1485, 215.15–16, and *Miss. Franc.*, no. 71, Mohlberg, 20.14–16. Cf. *Lib. sac.*, no. 1488, Mohlberg, 215.26–7: 'Romani regni adesto principibus'. On the substitution of 'Frank' for 'Roman', Tellenbach, *Reichsgedanke*, pp. 19ff.

[79] Ed. A. Dumas and J. Deshusses, *CCL*, 159 (1983).431–4. Cf. Kantorowicz, 'Advent', pp. 54–5. On the sacramentary: *CLA*, 5, 617; *CLLA*, 855, and B. Moreton, *The Eighth-Century Gelasian Sacramentary. A study in tradition* (Oxford, 1976), pp. 187–91.

[80] No. 2750, Dumas, 431.1–4; no. 2755, 432.12–13.

[81] E.g. no. 2750, Dumas, 431.9–11; no. 2751, 431.1–9; 2752, 431.1–13, etc. Barbarians: no. 2752, 431.3; no. 2753, 432.2–3.

but these refs don't contain any refs to FRANKISH kings/people &c. (PTO)

following prayer.[82] Does this mean that the *profectio bellica* service was developed independently of the royal court and its influence?

Palaeographers and liturgists have illuminated the historical context in which the Sacramentary of Gellone was transcribed; their conclusions bear directly on this question. The sacramentary's rich decoration is indicative of its intended recipient's prestige. It was copied in the closing decade of the eighth century or the opening years of the next, quite probably by David, of the monastery of Holy Cross at Meaux. Specific liturgical features indicate a very close link with the royal court. Within a few years the book came to Gellone where, as an ex-libris suggests, it probably arrived with the monastery's founder. This man was none other than count William of Toulouse, Charlemagne's relative and an important member of the royal entourage, who was closely identified with the conquest of the Spanish March. In other words, by both its content and its codicological provenance, the Sacramentary of Gellone and the *profectio bellica* service it contains bear the unmistakable stamp of the royal court.[83]

The Sacramentary of Angoulême (Paris, B.N. lat. 816) may have been composed at the Frankish court in Aquitania around 800; it offers concordant testimony on the new military spirituality of the last decade of the eighth century. It too belongs to the 'Eighth-Century Gelasian' tradition and contains a 'Missa pro re⟨ge⟩ in die belli contra paganos', perhaps intended for wars against the Saracens or Basques.[84] The collect implores the eternal Trinity to deliver 'Your Christian people from the oppression of the *gentes*', as it once saved the sons of Israel from the Egyptians, and to grant victory to the royal servant of Christendom.[85] The Secret develops the parallel of Moses, Aaron and the Franks, asking God to free the king and his army from the 'terror of the tyrants', so that the Franks might return from battle with

---

[82] No. 2752, Dumas, 431.11–12; no. 2753, Dumas, 432.8–9; cf. 432.2.

[83] See J. Deshusses, *CCL*, 159A (1981).xx–xxi; cf. C.R. Baldwin, 'The scriptorium of the Sacramentary of Gellone', *Scriptorium*, 25 (1971), 3–17. On William, e.g. P. Wolff, 'L'Aquitaine et ses marges', *Karl der Grosse*, 1, 269–306, here 277.

[84] *CLLA*, 860; cf. Moreton, *Eighth-Century*, pp. 192–3; diplomatic ed. P. Cagin, *Le sacramentaire gélasien d'Angoulême* (Angoulême, n.d.), f. 167recto–167verso, nos. 2307–10.

[85] F. 167recto, no. 2307.

348

exultation.[86] The Preface beseeches the Lord to succor his servant and his army against the perfidious pagans, just as he once helped Abraham. He must send his angel to protect the Franks, who will return home 'triumphantes de victoria'.[87] The Postcommunion prayer evokes the salvation of Israel through God's manna; in like manner, God will intervene to spare the Franks from heavy casualties.[88] The God of the Frankish army was close indeed to that of ancient Israel and the liturgy provided the link.[89] Once again, the king shares the liturgical limelight with his army, even though the Mass's rubric emphasizes the royal intention.

The posterity, and therefore the influence, of this kind of text has been questioned by Kantorowicz. That the Gellone Sacramentary is the sole surviving eighth-century witness to the *profectio bellica* service led Kantorowicz to assume its archaic character and subsequent disappearance; at most a segment of the Mass might have survived as a vague '*Oratio pro exercitu*'.[90] So long as a proper philological and theological analysis is lacking, it is impossible to speculate on the origin of such texts, although it has already been noted that there is no clear evidence of their use under the Merovingians. There is, however, evidence on their posterity. Alcuin and Sedulius Scottus, to name only two thinkers in the mainstream of Carolingian culture, both referred to the necessity of prayer on such occasions.[91] More importantly, it is risky to argue for a narrow diffusion or disappearance of an attested votive text on the sole basis of rarity in extant early Carolingian manuscripts because the representativeness of surviving codices is, in this respect, quite problematic.[92] And in fact, this particular

---

[86] *Ibid.*, no. 2308.   [87] F. 167recto–167verso, no. 2309.

[88] F. 167verso, no. 2310.

[89] See e.g. E.H. Kantorowicz, '*Laudes regiae*'. *A study in liturgical acclamations and medieval ruler worship*, University of California publications in history, 33 (Berkeley, 1946), pp. 56ff; cf. E. Ewig, 'Zum christlichen Königsgedanken', pp. 42ff.

[90] 'Advent', p. 55.

[91] Alcuin, *Ep.*, 25, ed. E. Dümmler, *MGH.Epist.*, 4 (1895).66.15–18, writing to Riculf on the occasion of the latter's departure on campaign; cf. 'Benedictio pro iter agentibus', ed. E. Moeller, *CCL*, 162A (1971), no. 1881. Nicholas I, *Responsa*, 35 (JL, 2812), ed. E. Perels, *MGH.Epist.*, 6 (1925).581.28–35.

[92] Liturgical MSS were mostly used on a daily basis and so deteriorated more rapidly than other kinds of MSS. The 'Eighth-Century Gelasian' is usually considered the most significant service book of the realm around the turn of the eighth century. In 831 the inventory of the sacristy at Centula lists 19 or 14 'Gelasiani', generally identified as texts of the 'Eighth-Century' variety. If this is true, either quantity – the

ceremony did survive the ninth century, since a blessing for *profectio bellica* occurs in the Pontifical of Sens (Leningrad, G.P.B. Q.v.I, no. 35), an under-studied service book assigned to the early tenth century.[93] A useful parallel is the tradition of formal blessings of the Frankish army, which can also be traced back to the reign of Charlemagne. Again the 'Eighth-Century Gelasian' has preserved a blessing 'super regem et populum' whose content suggests the army's presence; Leo III lent papal prestige to the custom when he said prayers for the Frankish Ost, massed at Paderborn to attack the Saxons.[94] Such prayers for the army crop up with increasing frequency in liturgical books from the ninth century's last decades.[95]

A further parallel offers the additional advantage of re-connoitering one part of the path by which early Carolingian war liturgies came to influence the spiritual trappings of later medieval armies. In the course of the ninth century, the drive for liturgical authenticity fostered the displacement of the 'Eighth-Century Gelasian' sacramentaries and their war texts by the Hadrianum

---

fonds of only one large monastery – is more than double the number of surviving MSS from the whole empire: C. Vogel, *Introduction aux sources de l'histoire du culte chrétien au moyen âge*, Biblioteca degli Studi medievali, 1, 2nd edn (Spoleto, 1975), pp. 58–67 and 79, no. 259. A similar conclusion is suggested by the 'Ninth-Century Gregorian Sacramentary' which must once have existed in sufficient numbers to cover the altars of Carolingian Europe: some 35 MSS survive intact: J. Deshusses, *Le sacramentaire grégorien. Ses principales formes d'après les plus anciens manuscrits*, 1, Spicilegium friburgense, 16 (Fribourg, 1971), p. 34.

[93] From f. 95 verso, transcribed by A. Staerk, *Les manuscrits latins du V⁰ au XIII⁰ siècle conservés à la Bibliothèque impériale de Saint-Pétersbourg*, 1 (St Petersburg, 1910), 169, in preference to E. Moeller, *CCL*, 162, nos. 567–8, based on an early modern copy of the original.

[94] Ed. E. Moeller, *CCL*, 162, no. 721, attested in three MSS of s. viii^ex–ix^in, including the sacramentaries of Angoulême and Gellone and one of s. ix–x; *Liber pontificalis*, ed. L. Duchesne, 2 (Paris, 1892).6.6.

[95] Thus in the 'Leofric Missal' (Oxford, Bodl. Libr. Bodl. 579 [2675], *CLLA*, 950), the original layer of which has been assigned to s. ix (Arras?), ed. F.E. Warren (Oxford, 1883), p. 230, the *Oratio super militantes*: (inc. 'Deus perpetuitatis auctor, dux uirtutum omnium cunctorumque hostium uictor'); cf. the blessing *Quando contra paganos pugnandum est*, Moeller, *CCL*, 162, no. 568, and the *Oratio pro exercitu*, M. Andrieu, *Les 'Ordines Romani' du haut moyen âge*, 1, Spicilegium sacrum Lovaniense, Etudes et documents, 1 (Louvain, 1931), p. 57. The best general account of Carolingian military practices of this sort remains A.M. Koeniger, *Die Militärseelsorge der Karolingerzeit. Ihr Recht und ihre Praxis*, Veröffentlichungen aus dem kirchenhistori-schen Seminar, 4, 7 (Munich, 1918), pp. 44–61.

version of the Gregorian sacramentary. Since this Roman liturgical book lacked some of the texts a Frankish priest required for his everyday liturgical duties, it was soon fitted with various additions. The most famous of these, the so-called 'Alcuinian' or 'Aniane' Supplement, incorporated the more common Roman propers for 'Masses in Time of War'.[96] Even so, the style of war liturgy embodied by the 'Eighth-Century Gelasians' did not disappear from the altars of the West. Ninth- and tenth-century liturgical manuscripts illustrate the 'new' Roman liturgy's inadequacies and the way local material worked its way back into the Gregorian books, through the process which would ultimately lend the medieval 'Roman' liturgy its 'classical' shape.[97] From the second half of the ninth century on, special wartime 'Masses Against the Pagans' were inserted on a fly leaf or blank space, or incorporated into the votive Mass sections of these books, in what is obviously a liturgical response to the depredations of the Northmen and Saracens.[98]

Among the most significant witnesses to this process are half a dozen sacramentaries showing various degrees of interrelation. Vat. lat. 377 contains scraps of a north Italian sacramentary assigned to the second half of the ninth century, including a 'Missa contra paganos'. Except for the Preface, this text is identical to the corresponding piece in the celebrated Sacramentary of Senlis (Paris, B. Ste Geneviève 111), thought to have been copied in the abbey of St Denis, ca. 880. Two sacramentaries from Tours also used the same texts as Senlis.[99] One of the Tours books offers as well a remarkable 'Mass for Imminent Barbarian Persecution' which beseeches God to liberate his faithful followers 'from the present calamity of Northmen'.[100] The Sacramentaries of St Vaast (Cambrai, B.M. 162 and 163, s. ix²) and Echternach (Paris,

---

[96] Ed. J. Deshusses, *Sacramentaire grégorien*, 1.441–4.

[97] See e.g. Vogel, *Sources*, pp. 82ff.

[98] In addition to the prayer from the Tours Sacramentary cited hereafter, see the variant ending to the prayer 'Parce, domine parce', reported by Tellenbach, *Reichsgedanke*, p. 70, no. 5.

[99] *CCLA*, 809, ed. K. Gamber, 'Oberitalienisches Sakramentarfragment', 353–76, here 370; in St Geneviève 111 (*CLLA*, 745), f. 137recto where the rubric reads 'Missa contra infestatione paganorum'. For the texts, cf. the edn of the Tours sacramentaries, Paris, B.N. lat. 9430 and n. acq. lat 1589 in J. Deshusses, *Le sacramentaire grégorien*, 2, Spicilegium Friburgense, 24 (Fribourg, 1979), 164, nos. 2564–6.

[100] *Ibid.*, 165.3–4, no. 2572.

B.N. lat. 9433, s. ix^ex) share a 'Mass against the Pagans', while the ninth-century part of the Leofric Missal presents yet another combination under the same rubric.[101] The Sacramentary of Arles (Paris, B.N. lat. 2812) preserves a text which proves the posterity of the 'Eighth-Century Gelasian's' version of the liturgy of war. Its 'Missa pro persecutione paganorum' is nothing other than a late ninth- or early tenth-century reworking of the Angoulême Sacramentary's 'Mass for the King on the Day of Battle'.[102] By the time the threat diminished, this kind of service was solidly entrenched in post-Carolingian liturgical usage. Thus the tenth-century Sacramentary of Fulda (Göttingen, Univ. Cod. theol. 231, ca. 975) included both a 'Missa pro rege et exercitu eius' and one 'ad comprimendas gentium feritates'.[103]

The Sacramentaries of Angoulême and Gellone indicate that, by the 790s, the royal entourage promoted new services directly involving the army and aimed at obtaining victory. Their testimony receives splendid confirmation from the court itself. A new kind of liturgical preparation for battle was introduced to the Frankish army no later than September 791 and very possibly in that year. It included both votive Masses, undoubtedly of the kind found in the Sacramentaries, and litanic processions. The laconic court record, the 'Royal Annals of the Franks', are a little more loquacious than usual in documenting the army's decision to spend three days on the bank of the Enns River so that the troops could stage special services entreating divine assistance against the Avars:

> ... with God's help they reached the aforesaid region of the Avars. They hurried to the Enns and there decided to celebrate litanies and Masses; they requested God's help for the safety of the army and the aid of Our Lord Jesus Christ and for victory and vengeance over the Avars.[104]

---

[101] St Vaast, ed. Deshusses, *Sacr. grég.*, 2.164–5, nos. 2567–9; cf. B.N. lat. 9433 (*CLLA*, 920), f. 219recto–219verso; *Leofric Missal*, Warren, p. 185–6.

[102] See below, n. 251.

[103] Ed. A. Richter and A. Schönfelder, *Sacramentarium Fuldense s. X*, Quellen und Abhandlungen zur Geschichte der Abtei und Diözese Fulda, 9 (Fulda, 1912), 221, nos. 1934–8, and 223–4, nos. 1956–9. Another example is the late tenth-century Lorsch Sacramentary, which has two Masses 'ubi gens contra gentem surgit', L. Eizenhöfer, 'Das Lorscher Sakramentar im Cod. Vat. Pal. lat. 495', *Die Reichsabtei Lorsch. Festschrift zum Gedenken an ihre Stiftung 764*, 2 (Darmstadt, 1977), 129–69.

[104] *Annales regni Francorum*, a. 791, Kurze, 88: '... cum Dei adiutorio partibus iamdictis

The novelty of the army service in 791 is underscored by the fact that some two decades later, when a member of the imperial entourage updated the latinity and historical vision of the old Royal Annals, the need for description was no longer felt: it now sufficed to say that a three-day supplication took place for the successful outcome of the war.[105] Even more significantly, Charlemagne himself took the trouble to write to his wife from the Enns and tell her about the services. The king described in detail how the ceremonies were performed and requested that the queen and his *fideles* arrange for similar services at the palace. Now Fastrada had previously wintered with the king and his army and there would have been little need for the letter's circumstantial account if such litanic services had been a standard feature of contemporary military life.[106] The evidence of the liturgical manuscripts and the Enns ceremony are completely independent and this makes their convergent testimony on the new development all the more eloquent. The reasons for the new departure in the army's liturgy of war are not completely clear. The new services by and for the army fall in a period in which the king was experimenting with wide-scale litanic services in times of crisis.[107] The army itself was changing, as Charlemagne sought to develop the newly prestigious royal vassals into an elite force of heavy cavalry.[108] Another factor may have contributed to the form and nature of the service. Only one campaign earlier, Franks and

---

Avarorum perrexerunt. Ad Anisam vero fluvium properantes ibi constituerunt laetanias faciendi per triduo missarumque sollemnia celebrandi; Dei solatium postulaverunt pro salute exercitus et adiutorio domini nostri Iesu Christi et pro victoria et vindicta super Avaros'. On these Annals and the court, Wattenbach–Levison, *Geschichtsquellen*, p. 247ff.

[105] *Annales qui dicuntur Einhardi*, a. 791, ed. F. Kurze, *MGH.SRG*, (1895), 89: 'Ibi supplicatio per triduum facta, ut id bellum prosperos ac felices haberet eventus...'.

[106] Ed. E. Dümmler, *MGH.Epist.*, 4 (1894).528.28–529.7; cf. M. McCormick, 'The liturgy of war in the early Middle Ages: crisis, litanies and the Carolingian monarchy', *Viator*, 15 (1984); on Fastrada and the army, S. Abel and B. Simson, *Jahrbücher des fränkischen Reiches unter Karl dem Grossen*, 2nd edn, 1 (reprint, Berlin, 1969), 476.   [107] McCormick, 'Liturgy', pp. 8ff.

[108] F.L. Ganshof, 'À propos de la cavalerie dans les armées de Charlemagne', *Académie des inscriptions et belles-lettres. Comptes rendus*, Année 1952, 531–6, esp. 535–6, and 'Das Lehnswesen im fränkischen Reich: Lehnswesen und Reichsgewalt in karolingischer Zeit', *Studien zum mittelalterlichen Lehenswesen*, Vorträge und Forschungen, 5 (Lindau, 1960), pp. 37–49, here 43–4; Charlemagne's letter itself contains a rare explicit reference to the participation of royal vassals: Dümmler, 528.26–7.

Lombards had fought against a Byzantine expeditionary force in Calabria, and there can be little doubt that this army observed the liturgical preparation for combat traditional in the imperial forces. It was probably as a result of this Franco-Lombard victory that Sisinnius, the reputed brother of the patriarch of Constantinople, came to Charles' court as a prisoner.[109] At the same time Byzantine Istria came under Frankish control and Charlemagne's letter to Fastrada mentions that duke John of Istria had played a decisive role in the first phase of the operations of 791, which had been launched by the king's son from Frankish Friuli.[110] The liturgical nature of the service points in the same direction, for its litanic character hints that it emulated the Byzantine army's traditional 'Kyrie eleisons' before combat. In fact, a source of unimpeachable character proves that Frankish armies prepared for battle with the same prayer as the Byzantines. The Old High German *Ludwigslied* was composed in the aftermath of king Louis III's (*ob.* 5 August 882) defeat of the Vikings at Saucourt on 3 August 881 and describes how the Franks prepared to attack the Northmen:

> Ioh alle saman sungen 'Kyrrieleison'.
> Sang was gisungan, Uuig was bigunnan....[111]

As the *Ludwigslied* suggests, the services of 791 became part and parcel of Carolingian military practice in the ninth century. Thus, in 841, the armies of Charles the Bald and Louis the German performed fasts and prayer services on the eve of the fateful encounter of Fontenoy-en-Puisaye.[112] The following March, the same kings attended Mass at St Castor's before crossing the Moselle to attack Lothar's army.[113] A hostile Hincmar of Reims insinuated the cause of defeat when he described how Charles the

---

[109] O. Bertolini, 'Carlomagno e Benevento', *Karl der Grosse. Lebenswerk und Nachleben*, ed. W. Braunfels, 1 (Düsseldorf, 1965), 609–71, here 653 and 658.

[110] R.J.H. Jenkins et al., Constantine VII Porphyrogenitus, *De administrando imperio*, 2, *Commentary* (London, 1962), 118–20; cf. J.F. Böhmer, E. Mühlbacher et al., *Die Regesten des Kaiserreichs unter den Karolingern 751–918*, ed. C. Brühl and H.H. Kaminsky, Regesta imperii, 1, 2nd edn (Hildesheim, 1966), no. 315. For 790 as an unusual year without a campaign, *Ann. r. Franc.*, a. 790, Kurze 86.

[111] *Ludwigslied*, ed. E. von Steinmeyer, *Die kleineren althochdeutschen Sprachdenkmäler* (Berlin, 1916), 86.47–8.

[112] Nithard, *Historiarum libri IV*, 2, 10, ed. P. Lauer, Classiques de l'histoire de France au moyen âge, 7 (Paris, 1926), 70.

[113] *Ibid.*, 3, 7, Lauer, 114.

Bald's men laughed at Louis the Younger and his *comites* as they began to fast and perform litanies shortly before the battle of Andernach.[114] In 894, king Arnulf ordered a Mass before storming Bergamo and, when he decided to subject Rome to the same treatment, he and his men called for a one-day fast.[115]

Armies and kings which expended such effort to secure success could not fail to thank the divine author of victory after the battle. Some of the Masses beseeching God for victory allude to thanksgiving after the battle's successful completion, and toward the middle of the ninth century, Sedulius Scottus touted proper thanksgiving for victory as a typical trait of the ideal prince.[116] The Royal Annals' wording intimates that the Frankish army staged some kind of thanksgiving service after the campaign which had begun with the litanies on the Enns River.[117] The double victory over the Avars five years later was certainly the occasion for a victory service. Theodulf of Orleans wrote a poem in which he urged Charlemagne to give thanks to God and generous gifts to the church and, in fact, the king did both, celebrating a thanksgiving service at Aachen and dispatching a large part of the booty to Rome.[118] In 801, the Frankish army led by Louis the Pious held a service to thank God for his help in reconquering Barcelona and the custom was maintained throughout the ninth century, for instance after a victorious campaign against Brittany in 817 and following a successful crossing of the

---

[114] *Ann. Bert.*, a. 876, Grat, 207. Hincmar was particularly displeased with Charles at that time because of the Ansegisus affair: J. Devisse, *Hincmar, archevêque de Reims, 845–882*, 2 (Geneva. 1976), 810–17.

[115] *Annales Fuldenses, Continuatio Ratisbonnensis*, a. 894, ed. F. Kurze, *MGH.SRG*, (1891), 123, and a. 896, Kurze, 127; cf. *ibid.*, 130, on the role of fasting in the Bulgar king's victory. Cf. too the account of the traditional services with which pope Leo IV encouraged the defenders of Ostia in 850, replete with transcriptions of the prayers composed for the occasion: *Lib. pont.*, Duchesne, 2.118.11–21.

[116] *Sacr. Gell.*, nos. 2750, Dumas, 431.9–11; 2755, Dumas, 432.21–3; Sedulius Scottus, *De rectoribus christianis*, 17, ed. S. Hellmann, Quellen und Untersuchungen zur lateinischen Philologie des Mittelalters, 1, 1 (Munich, 1906), 80–4.

[117] *Ann. r. Franc.*, a. 791, Kurze, 88: 'ad propria reversi sunt, magnificantes Deum de tanta victoria'.

[118] Theodulf, *Carm.*, 25, ed. E. Dümmler, *MGH.Poet.*, 1 (1881).484.33–6. Cf. *Ann. r. Franc.*, a. 796, Kurze, 98, 'peracta Deo largitori omnium bonorum gratiarum actione'. The subject of Carolingian votive offerings would reward further study. On these events, Böhmer–Mühlbacher, *Regesta*, no. 3281 (= letter 1).

Seine in the spring of 841.[119] Spiritual measures were decreed for the victorious armies after the terrible carnage of Fontenoy, in praise of the divine judgement revealed by the battle, on behalf of the souls of the fallen brethren, and so that God would continue to help and protect the victors in the future.[120] King Arnulf ordered a victory service on the spot when he crushed the Northmen by the banks of the Dyle in 891.[121]

Arnulf's celebration offers the most explicit evidence on the liturgical form developed for the army's thanksgiving. A litanic procession was staged on the battlefield. Knowingly or not, the king imitated Theodosius II by personally leading the procession. Although the annalist's account is not devoid of ambiguity, his statement that the king sang 'praises (*laudes*) to God', hints that the famous *laudes regiae* may have been chanted during the procession.[122] This would not be inconsistent with the possibility that the *laudes regiae* were used during the empire-wide supplications for victory and divine succor staged by Charlemagne and his successors.[123] Furthermore, Sedulius Scottus' description of the ideal prince specifically mentions *laudes hymnidicae* as an appropriate thanksgiving for his victory.[124] The services which accompanied the triumphal entries of Carolingian kings into conquered cities point in the same direction, for they too were marked by 'hymns and *laudes*' or '*laudes hymnidicae*'.[125] Certainly the triumphant tone of these prayers, with their acclamation-like supplication for the life and victory of the Frankish king and his army, matched the occasion.[126]

---

[119] 'Astronomer', *V. Hludowici imperatoris*, 13, ed. G.H. Pertz, *MGH.SS*, 2 (1829). 613.12–18; cf. Ermoldus Nigellus, *In honorem Hludowici*, 1, 566–9, ed. E. Faral, Classiques de l'histoire de France au moyen âge, 14 (Paris, 1932), 46; *ibid.*, 3, 1750–2, Faral, 132; Nithard, *Hist.*, 2, 6, Lauer, 56.

[120] *Ibid.*, 3, 1, Lauer, 82.

[121] *Ann. Fuld.*, a. 891, Kurze, 120–1; cf. Böhmer–Mühlbacher, *Regesta*, no. 1865a.

[122] *Ann. Fuld.*, a. 891, Kurze, 120–1, 'Eodem in loco...die...Kal...laetanias rex celebrare praecipit; ipse cum exercitu laudes Deo canendo processit, qui talem victoriam suis tribuit...'.

[123] McCormick, 'Liturgy', p. 23.

[124] *Rect. christ.*, 17, Hellmann, 84.9–11.

[125] *Chron. Laur. breve*, Schnorr von Carolsfeld, 31; cf. *Ann. Fuld.*, a. 774, Kurze, 9; 'Astronomer', *V. Hlud.*, 13, Pertz, 613.15–18.

[126] Kantorowicz, '*Laudes regiae*', p. 32 (cf. p. 73), seems to suppose a very unmedieval rigor of terminology. Note that the conclusion of the 'Missa in profectione hostium'

Händel among others has accustomed moderns to the performance of a 'Te deum' to celebrate a victory. The Carolingians
used the great hymn on various occasions of state and they seem to
have been the first to adopt it as a song of triumph.[127] There is a
hitherto unrecognized citation of the 'Te deum' in Abbo's account
of the Northmen's siege of Paris in 885–6. At one point, the relics
of St Germain were trotted out to encourage the Frankish
defenders. When the assault had been repelled, the relics were
transported back to the Basilica of St Stephen, while the people
intoned a 'Te deum'.[128]

The Carolingians expanded Merovingian precedent in the cult
of military relics. Every medievalist is familiar with the etymology of the royal 'chapel' from the *capella* of St Martin, with
which campaigning Frankish kings sought to guarantee their
victory.[129] The veracity of the ninth-century etymology is
underscored by an eighth-century canonical ruling which excluded the clergy from military expeditions, but specifically excepts
those required for the troops' spiritual needs and 'carrying the
relics (*patrocinia*) of the saints'.[130] A century later, monks still

[handwritten: et dicant: sanctus, sanctus]

appears to refer to the opening words of the Gallo-Frankish *laudes* 'Christus vincit,
Christus regnat, Christus imperat': 'Vt cum ipsos ad propria[m] in pace[m] feceris
reduci, *te uictorem* quasi uno one *laudent*. . .' *Sacr. Gell.*, no. 2755, Dumas, 432.21–3. B.
Opfermann, *Die liturgischen Herrscherakklamationen im Sacrum Imperium des Mittelal-
ters* (Weimar, 1953), pp. 72–82, lists eight examples of his 'Type I' (Kantorowicz's
'Gallo-Frankish Type'), of which six are from the second half of the ninth century.

[127] S. Žak, 'Das Tedeum als Huldigungsgesang', *Historisches Jahrbuch*, 102 (1982), 1–32.

[128] Abbo of Paris, *Bella Parisiacę urbis*, 2, 308–13, ed. H. Waquet, Classiques de l'histoire
de France au moyen âge, 20 (Paris, 1942), 89, esp. 311–12, where 'praecelsa "Te"
reboantes/ Voce: "Deum te laudamus dominumque fatemur"' obviously refers
to the great hymn's opening words 'Te deum laudamus, te dominum confitemur';
the citation peremptorily invalidates Waquet's aberrant translation. On the St
Stephen's Basilica, Brühl, *Palatium*, p. 16, n. 112.

[129] Walafrid Strabo, *De exordiis et incrementis quarumdam in observationibus ecclesiasticis
rerum*, ed. A. Knöpfler, Veröffentlichungen aus dem kirchenhistorischen Seminar, 1
(Munich, 1899), 100–1. On this and the other sources, all of which are connected to
St Gall, J. Fleckenstein, *Die Hofkapelle der deutschen Könige*, 1, MGH. Schriften, 16
(Stuttgart, 1959), pp. 10ff, and J. van den Bosch, *Cappa, Basilica, Monasterium et le
culte de saint Martin de Tours. Étude lexicologique et sémasiologique*, Latinitas
Christianorum primaeva, 13 (Nijmegen, 1959), pp. 7ff.

[130] Boniface, *Ep.*, 56, ed. M. Tangl, *MGH.SRG*, 2nd edn (1955), 99.24–100.2. Cf. F.
Prinz, *Klerus und Krieg im früheren Mittelalter. Untersuchungen zur Rolle der Kirche
beim Aufbau der Königsherrschaft*, Monographien zur Geschichte des Mittelalters, 2
(Stuttgart, 1971), pp. 8ff.

served as standard-bearers (*signiferi*).[131] By the reign of Charles the Bald, Frankish kings had gone a step further and adopted the Byzantine and Visigothic practice of leading their armies into battle behind a cruciform war ensign.[132]

The rapid development of services of supplication and thanksgiving for the Frankish army seems remarkable. But they must be viewed as part of a broader pattern of development, in which Frankish kings sought to use the liturgy to strengthen their links with their subjects and harness the spiritual forces of the latter to their own undertakings in times of crisis. Ultimately, special litanic services by the population in times of crisis went back to the Roman empire and the more advanced successor states, like those of the Visigoths and Ostrogoths; a specific variant, the *circuitus murorum*, had continued to flourish locally in Gaul under the Merovingians. Whether the Carolingians created an institution new to Francia or breathed life into an old one, the change is clear enough. Charlemagne's father Pippin III was the first Frankish ruler to show interest in organizing litanic services on a broader scale, perhaps drawing his inspiration from the crisis litanies of Byzantine Rome and the exhortation of St Boniface. Special local services for the king's victory entered Charlemagne's experience no later than the Italian campaign of 774, when pope Hadrian ordered litanic prayers – three hundred kyries – to be performed by the city of Rome's religious every day, for the remission of Charles' sins and 'plentiful victories'.[133] A year after the introduction of army litanies, Charles attempted to assuage an angry God by arranging large-scale prayer services and fasts throughout his kingdom. Prayers for the army assumed a significant place in this liturgy of crisis, and services of supplication ultimately took root in the local administrative routines of Carolingian Europe.[134]

---

[131] Thus the monk Hadhemarus mentioned by the 'Astronomer', *V. Hlud.*, 13, Pertz, 612.33–4. See in general, Schramm, *Herrschaftszeichen*, 2, 674–88.

[132] Nithard, *Hist.*, 2, 6, Lauer, 56: 'dum...classisque appropinquare videretur, crucem in qua juraverant et Karolum ut cognoverunt, relicto littore protinus fugerunt'. I take this to mean that Charles' battle cross contained a relic (of the true cross?) which had provided a *res sacra* for the perjured oath of fidelity. A dozen years later, Louis II had a witness swear 'super sanctam ac venerabilem dominicam crucem suam', Frolow, *Relique*, p. 219.

[133] *Codex Carolinus*, 51 (JL, 2413), ed. W. Gundlach, *MGH.Epist.*, 3 (1892).570.14–21.

[134] McCormick, 'Liturgy', pp. 14–15. Further evidence for this has just been brought

Like the litanic services offered by the Carolingian army, the staging of supplication services by noncombatants implies a parallel arrangement to thank God and insure his continued favor once victory was won or famine overcome.

Local thanksgiving services for Frankish victories were certainly mounted by the church of Rome in the eighth and ninth centuries.[135] On a grander scale, Cathwulf wrote to Charlemagne after the conquest of the Lombards, spicing his famous letter of congratulations with exhortation. Of the two suggestions concerning the celebration of this victory, one urged the king to offer thanksgiving with 'all his armies' and 'his entire kingdom'.[136] In similar fashion, the rhythmic poem which hailed the victories of 796 called on all Christians to give thanks to God for the great success.[137] These suggestions were not empty flourishes of fawning courtiers, for, on at least one occasion, empire-wide services seem to have been organized to thank God for a great victory conferred on Frankish arms. They took place just five years before the first recorded army litanies and again involved the city of Rome.

Late in 785 or early in 786, Charles wrote to Hadrian I to inform the pope of his most recent victories and the 'conversion' of the Saxons. At the same time, he asked the pope to organize services honoring this great success, for the 'stability' of royal victory.[138] Hadrian arranged the celebration of litanies throughout the

---

to light by D. Misonne, 'Mandement inédit d'Adventius de Metz à l'occasion d'une incursion normande (mai–juin 867)', *Revue bénédictine*, 93 (1983), 71–9.

135 E.g. *Cod. Carol.*, 50 (JL, 2409), Gundlach, 570.3–8; *ibid.*, 67 (JL, 2431), 594.38–595.3; *ibid.*, 89 (JL, 2473), 626.17–21; Nicholas I, *Ep.*, 60 (JL, 2722), Perels, 372.4–9.

136 Ed. E. Dümmler, *MGH.Epist.*, 4 (1895).502.42–503.1: '... pro his modis beatitudinem nocte et die com omnibus exercitibus tuis da gloriam Deo regi regnorum et gratiarum acciones com omni regno tuo ...'. Cf. on this document H.H. Anton, *Fürstenspiegel und Herrscherethos in der Karolingerzeit*, Bonner historische Forschungen, 32 (Bonn, 1968), pp. 75–9.

137 *Carmen de Pippini regis victoria avarica*, ed. O. Holder-Egger and G. Waitz, in Einhard, *Vita Karoli*, *MGH.SRG*, 6th edn (1911), 43: 'Nos fideles Christiani/Deo agamus gratiam ...'.

138 Charlemagne's letter is lost, but the contents are easily reconstructed from Hadrian's reply: *Cod. Carol.*, 76 (JL, 2451), Gundlach, 608.8–10: 'Illud autem, quod vestra regalis intimavit excellentia: ut in uno mense vel in una die pro huiuscemodi opias [sic], scilicet stabilitatis vestrae victoriae, laudes Deo gerentes canere una vel duas ferias letanias peragere ...'.

territories subject to him for the forthcoming 23, 26 and 28 June. In this way, the pope outdid the king, for Charles had only requested a day or two of litanies; moreover Hadrian suggested that the ceremonies be extended over the entire empire.[139] By timing the victory celebration to conclude on the vigil of St Peter's feastday, the pope underscored the role of Peter in Frankish victory and capitalized on the cult of the apostle.[140] That the celebration of 786 was not unique is suggested by the survival of a model for letters in which a bishop notifies the ruler of the performance of thanksgiving services and psalters for the ruler's safety following a campaign.[141] In 839, a legation arrived in Ingelheim from Constantinople. Among other things, it announced Theophilus' recent victory over his foreign enemies and conveyed the emperor's request that Louis the Pious and his subjects celebrate thanksgivings for the Byzantine triumph. The Frankish annalist is silent on Louis' response.[142]

The intersection of liturgy, war and victory spawned another custom under the Carolingians, the second victory practice referred to by Cathwulf. The victorious king was urged to found a new liturgical feast in honor of the Trinity, the angels and all the saints and to further order that the feasts of St Michael and St Peter be specially observed in his kingdom, for himself and for the army of the Christians.[143] It is not known if Charlemagne acted on Cathwulf's recommendation, but Cathwulf was surely referring to a liturgical custom familiar to the Franks.

In 1937, Bischoff uncovered a series of dry-point annotations added to specific dates in St Willibrord's Calendar (Paris, B.N. lat. 10837), by an eighth-century insular hand. A number of entries beginning 'pugna. . .' were quickly identified as decisive battles in the career of Charles Martel. With these were mixed a saint's day and obits, including an attested but erroneous death date for Charles Martel.[144] Specialists have yet to explain why the battle

---

[139] *Ibid.*, 608.10–22.
[140] On the development of the Frankish cult: E. Ewig, 'Der Petrus- und Apostelkult im spätrömischen und fränkischen Gallien', *Spätantikes und fränkisches Gallien*, 2 (Munich, 1979), 318–54.
[141] *Formulae Merkelianae salicae*, 55, ed. K. Zeumer, *MGH.Form.* (1882), 260.26–8.
[142] *Ann. Bert.*, a. 839, Grat, 30; cf. Lounghis, *Ambassades*, pp. 167–8.
[143] Dümmler, 504.24–9.
[144] *CLA*, 5, 606a, from Echternach; B. Bischoff, 'Über Einritzungen in Handschriften

dates were entered into a liturgical document. A historical impulse is not perhaps the easiest explanation, for no effort was made to record the year: indeed, Samaran and Levillain thought the calendar notes were excerpted from some lost annals.[145] The best clue to the purpose behind these notes comes from their context, a liturgical calendar, i.e. an annual list of potential liturgical celebrations. The non-battle entries all look to be liturgical anniversaries.[146] Viewed in the light of Cathwulf's testimony, the *pugna* annotations also seem to reflect the liturgical commemoration of eighth-century battles.

Further research is needed before the scope of this custom becomes clear, but it is likely that the manuscript calendars of eighth- and ninth-century Francia conceal more such humble notes, whether in dry-point or in ink. It is already possible to show that the Echternach document is not alone, for the calendar contained in a sacramentary from Lorsch (Vat. Pal. lat. 485), copied at that monastery in the second half of the ninth century, offers additional evidence unnoticed by its editor.[147] Louis the Younger's victory over Charles the Bald at Andernach on 8 October 876 is commemorated in a second hand, using the solemn letter forms of rustic capital:

---

des frühen Mittelalters', *Mittelalterliche Studien. Ausgewählte Aufsätze zur Schrift-kunde und Literaturgeschichte*, 1 (Stuttgart, 1966), 88–92, here 92, n. 23; W. Levison, 'À propos du Calendrier de S. Willibrord', *Revue bénédictine*, 50 (1938), 37–41; L. Levillain and C. Samaran, 'Sur le lieu et la date de la bataille dite de Poitiers de 732', *Bibliothèque de l'École des chartes*, 99 (1938), 243–67, and the critical remarks of F. Lot, 'Études sur la bataille de Poitiers de 732', *Revue belge de philologie et d'histoire*, 26 (1948), 35–59.

[145] Levillain and Samaran, 'Lieu', p. 257. If the annotator had desired to leave a historical record, he could have turned to the paschal tables for A.D. 684–759 found in lat. 10837: cf. Lowe, *CLA*, 5, 606a, and, on paschal tables and eighth-century historical writing, M. McCormick, *Les annales du haut moyen âge*, Typologie des sources du moyen âge occidental, 14 (Turnhout, 1975), pp. 15ff; 22ff.

[146] Bischoff, 'Einritzungen', p. 92; on such notices, see, e.g. N. Huyghebaert, *Les documents nécrologiques*, Typologie des sources du moyen âge occidental, 4 (Turnhout, 1972), p. 35.

[147] *CLLA*, 1582, ed. J.E. Gugumus, 'Die Lorscher Kalendarien in Cod. Palat. Lat. 485 und 499 der Vatikanischen Bibliothek', *Jahrbuch für das Bistum Mainz*, 8 (1960), 286–321. On the MS, see B. Bischoff, 'Lorsch im Spiegel seiner Handschriften', *Die Reichsabtei Lorsch. Festschrift zum Gedenken an ihre Stiftung 764*, 2 (Darmstadt, 1977), 7–128, here 46–7.

VII ID [Octobr.] BELLA INTER. CAROLO ET HLUDO-
UUICO[148]

Particularly significant for the intent behind the annotation is the
fact that the same hand used the same script to note an event which
had occurred only a few weeks earlier and which was almost
certainly the object of liturgical commemoration in the imperial
abbey of Lorsch: the death of king Louis the German (28 August
876).[149]

A dry annotation does not tell a lot about the nature of the
commemoration. It is not, for example, impossible that some
battle notices might have been intended for prayers for the rest of
casualties' souls, whether the engagement was a success or not.[150]
But a grant of Charles the Bald proves that some anniversaries
were surely intended as liturgical commemorations of victory. On
19 September 862, the king of West Francia gave a villa in the
region of Paris to the monastery of St Denis. The endowment was
to pay for four commemorations: Charles' birthday, and the
anniversaries of his elevation, marriage and his great victory of
15 January 859, when he had unexpectedly triumphed over
his brother's invasion.[151]

3. CAROLINGIAN COURT CEREMONIAL AND THE KING'S VICTORY

There is little scholarly consensus on the nature and history of
Carolingian court ceremonial. Schuberth has maintained, for
instance, that it was of Byzantine inspiration and was introduced

---

[148] Vat. Pal. lat. 485, f. 10verso. Cf. Bischoff, 'Lorsch', p. 46.

[149] Vat. Pal. lat. 485, f. 9verso: 'V KL [Sept.] MIGRAVIT AD XPM /
HLVDOVVICVS REX'. The notice has been erased. Bischoff, 'Lorsch', p. 46
appears to have misinterpreted this *obit*, referring to it as that of Louis the Younger
(20 January 882). The correct identification reinforces his deduction of a *terminus
ante quem* in 876 (not 875!).

[150] This seems to be the implication of the note 'Pessimum bellum de gentibus' added to
Vat. Pal. lat. 485, f. 9recto, III NON. [Iul.] in a Caroline hand. The custom took root
on a local level, as evidenced by the annual commemoration of the delivery of the
monastery of Lobbes from the Magyars in 955, celebrated there on 2 April: M.
Coens, *Recueil d'études bollandiennes*, Subsidia hagiographica, 37 (Brussels, 1963),
p. 252.

[151] Ed. A. Giry, M. Prou and G. Tessier, *Recueil des actes de Charles II le Chauve, roi de
France*, 2 (Paris, 1963), no. 256, 55.15–27.

in 757, while Riché has claimed that Charlemagne and Louis the Pious generally shunned ceremonial of Byzantine origin.[152] Much work needs to be done before the historical development of Carolingian court ceremonial and its various sources become clear. A provisional evaluation suggests that here, as in the liturgy of war, the Carolingians built on Merovingian precedent, systematizing or expanding local customs and occasionally adapting one or another element from the Byzantine provinces or capital.

Several considerations argue for an underlying continuity of royal ritual. Some Merovingian rituals and symbols of power, Einhard's *species dominantis*, certainly survived until the coup. It is not unlikely that they were taken over by the new masters of the throne, since the usurper's need for a cachet of authenticity and legitimacy drove the ruler to invent another ritual of investiture, sacring.[153] And it is difficult to imagine that the same rulers and advisers who stirred a thorough renewal of the divine liturgy remained totally indifferent to the symbolism of the king's public life.[154] Some elements of a ceremonial of prestige were certainly in place within the first twenty-five years of Carolingian rule, while more and more show up in the increasingly abundant sources of the 780s and 790s.[155] By the 820s, it is even possible to discern the outlines of an organizational apparatus behind court

[152] D. Schuberth, *Kaiserliche Liturgie. Die Einbeziehung von Musikinstrumenten, insbesondere der Orgel, in den frühmittelalterlichen Gottesdienst*, Veröffentlichung der Evangelischen Gesellschaft für Liturgieforschung, 17 (Göttingen, 1968), pp. 114–26; P. Riché, 'Les représentations du palais dans les textes littéraires du haut moyen âge', *Francia*, 4 (1976), 166–71, here 166.

[153] From a vast bibliography, see C. Erdmann, *Forschungen zur politischen Ideenwelt des Frühmittelalters*, ed. F. Baethgen (Berlin, 1951), pp. 52ff; C.A. Bouman, *Sacring and crowning. The development of the Latin ritual for the anointing of kings and the coronation of an emperor before the eleventh century*, Bijdragen van het Instituut voor middeleeuwse geschiedenis der Rijksuniversiteit te Utrecht, 30 (Groningen, 1957); P.E. Schramm, *Kaiser, Könige und Päpste. Gesammelte Aufsätze zur Geschichte des Mittelalters*, 2 (Stuttgart, 1968), 140ff; J. Nelson, 'Inauguration rituals', *Early Medieval Kingship*, ed. P.H. Sawyer and I.N. Wood (Leeds, 1977), pp. 50–71, esp. 56ff and J. Jarnut, 'Wer hat Pippin 751 zum König gesalbt?' *FMS*, 16 (1982), 45–57.

[154] See the references in McCormick, 'Liturgy', p. 2, n. 5.

[155] Among early ceremonies, in addition to the sacring of 756 and the ritual deployed for the papal visit (*Lib. pont.*, Duchesne, 1.447.10–18), cf. the commendation of Tassilo at the annual assembly of 757: F.L. Ganshof, *Qu'est-ce que la féodalité?*, 3rd edn (Brussels, 1957), pp. 46–7, or the triumphal entry into Pavia in 774 discussed below.

ceremonies: an usher, a choirmaster and a Master of the Door-keepers all contributed to the smooth functioning of imperial processions.[156]

Another factor to be borne in mind when evaluating Frankish ceremonial development comes from Carolingian attitudes toward Constantinople, the perennial embodiment of rulership in the grand tradition. They were complex and, in their political expression at least, underwent several about-faces in the century and a half of the dynasty's unchallenged authority, ranging from projects of dynastic marriage and military alliance to outright conflict.[157] But this should not blind us to the fact that the Frankish kings tacitly surrounded themselves with a distinctly Byzantine luxury and even adopted certain elements of the Byzantine life-style. In this they probably followed their later Merovingian predecessors.[158] It is not uncommon for scholars to point to the outcry over Charles the Bald's Byzantine regalia at the council of Ponthion in 876, although it is usually overlooked that the chief criticism comes from the court of Charles' archrival.[159] But Charlemagne himself donned Byzantine costume twice in his life. His private quarters were served by eunuch chamberlains of which one at least was Greek, and Louis the Pious would do likewise.[160] Perhaps we need not insist on Charles' plunging into the baths with over a hundred of his grandees and bodyguards or

---

[156] Ermoldus Nigellus, *Hon. Hlud.*, 4, 2280–97, Faral, 174–6; cf. G. Waitz, *Deutsche Verfassungsgeschichte*, 3, 3rd edn (Berlin, 1883), 505–6 and B. Simson, *Jahrbücher des fränkischen Reichs unter Ludwig dem Frommen*, 2 (reprint, Berlin, 1969), 243.

[157] A thorough, general examination of Carolingian–Byzantine relations is much needed. O. Harnack, *Das karolingische und das byzantinische Reich in ihren wechselseitigen politischen Beziehungen* (Göttingen, 1880), and A. Gasquet, *L'empire byzantin et la monarchie franque* (Paris, 1888), pp. 227ff, are outdated. Individual points have fared much better, as exemplified by W. Ohnsorge, *Abendland und Byzanz. Gesammelte Aufsätze zur Geschichte der byzantinisch-abendländischen Beziehungen und des Kaisertums* (Darmstadt, 1958), or P. Classen, 'Karl der Grosse, das Papsttum und Byzanz'; Lounghis, *Ambassades*, and O. Mazal, *Byzanz und das Abendland. Ausstellung der Handschriften- und Inkunabelsammlung der österreichischen Nationalbibliothek. Handbuch und Katalog* (Graz, 1981). W. Berschin, *Griechisch-lateinisches Mittelalter* (Bern, 1980), 130ff, is valuable for the intellectual aspect.

[158] H. Vierck, 'Chelles', *Reallexikon der germanischen Altertumskunde*, 4 (1981), 425–30.

[159] *Ann. Fuld.*, a. 876, Kurze, 86.

[160] Einhard, *V. Karoli*, 23, Holder-Egger and Waitz, 28.5–7; Theodulf of Orleans, *Carm.*, 25, 87–92, ed. E. Dümmler, *MGH.Poet.*, 1 (1881).493; Einhard, *Translatio Marcellini et Petri* (*BHL*, 5233), 4, 1, ed. G. Waitz, *MGH.SS*, 15.1.256.40–2.

the role of the baths in his decision to build a palace at Aachen, even though this kind of installation remained almost emblematic of the Byzantine way of life. He also owned a silver table with a map of Constantinople on it, while his son's court enjoyed an organ – a chiefly ceremonial instrument – assembled by George the Venetian.[161] The influence of Charles' daughters on the life and loves of his court is well known, but it is sometimes forgotten that Rotruda was coached in the language and customs of the imperial court by a Byzantine envoy, the eunuch notary Elissaios.[162] While these things scarcely sufficed to turn a Frank into a Byzantine, they do show that appreciation of and even intimacy with Byzantine civilization were factors to be reckoned with at the Carolingian court.

By the late eighth century, not a few elements of late antique public life were gone forever. Circus races and their rituals, the daily promenades of aristocrats and their retinues through the town market, finely shaded rituals of greeting at chance encounters, were now things of northern Gaul's past. No small part of the causes of such change is to be sought in the decay of the cities. Nonetheless, the first stirrings of renewed life in Carolingian towns were heralded by the growing frequency of recorded arrival ceremonies. In the late eighth and ninth centuries, the Frankish ruler's movements about his kingdom were punctuated by ceremonies of *valedictio* or *profectio* from one place and *adventus* at another. Even so, many of these arrival ceremonies were staged in a non-urban setting, in the Frankish empire's great monasteries.[163]

This last point underscores the unique role of the church, which acted as a kind of institutional archipelago of late antique ideas,

---

[161] Einhard, *V. Karoli*, 22 and 23, Holder-Egger and Waitz, 27.13–21 and 40.17–21; *Transl. Marc. et Petri*, 4, 11, Waitz, 260.16–17; cf. Walafrid Strabo, *De imagine Tetrici*, 137–8, ed. E. Dümmler, *MGH.Poet.*, 2 (1884). 374.

[162] Theophanes, A.M. 6274, De Boor, 455.23–5; cf. Dölger, *Regesten*, no. 339.

[163] *Profectio*: *Ann. r. Franc.*, a. 787, Kurze, 76; liturgical evidence might include the common blessing for departing travelers 'Prosperum iter faciet vobis', Moeller, *CCL*, 162A, no. 1881, as well as the Mass texts of the Aniane supplement to the ninth-century Gregorian, ed. Deshusses, *Sacr. grég.*, 1.438–9, nos. 1317–19. Theodulf of Orleans composed a poem for such an occasion: *Carm.*, 32, Dümmler, 523–4; on the *adventus*, Kantorowicz, 'Advent', pp. 40ff and P. Willmes, *Der Herrscher-'Adventus' im Klöster des Frühmittelalters*, Münstersche Mittelalter-Schriften, 22 (Münster, 1976).

life-style, language and ritual, scattered across the broad expanse of Frankish dominion. It introduces a major difference between Carolingian and contemporary Constantinopolitan ceremonial. Although eastern ritual left generous room for liturgical elements, nonetheless the principal organizers and not a few settings of Byzantine victory celebrations remained secular. In Francia, ritual was first and foremost sacred ritual. The clergy dominated the administrative and, at times, even the executive structures of government, and it would have been surprising if they had not had a hand in royal ritual.[164] This is shown by the ceremonies themselves which display debts to parallel ecclesiastical rites. Carolingian royal investitures, for instance, reveal borrowings from the consecration of bishops.[165] And, for an imperial divestiture, no better ritual framework came to a Frankish mind than the act of public penance.[166] If the alliance of Frankish church and Carolingian power lent much of secular ritual a liturgical cachet, its chief setting is also indicative of how the situation of a Carolingian prince differed from that of his eastern colleagues. A quick glance at some of the most important staged events in Carolingian history confirms the shift to a highly defined audience heralded by the humiliation of Brunichildis.

Leaving aside for a moment the ceremony at Rome in 800, it is clear that, by and large, the main acts in the kingdom's political life coincided with general assemblies of the Frankish grandees: Charlemagne's coronation of Louis as coemperor in 813, Louis' promulgation of the *Ordinatio imperii* in 817, or the public penance and divestiture of Louis at Soissons, which occurred in connection with the general assembly held at Compiègne. An exception proves the rule: Charlemagne's coronation at Rome may have been stage-managed by the local clergy and it was certainly far from the Frankish heartland, but the audience inevitably included

---

[164] That the royal *capellani* were associated with all activities of rulership involving blessing or writing, including the *scola cantorum*, argues in this direction: cf. J. Fleckenstein, *Hofkapelle*, 1, 91–4. So does the fact that some state ceremonies (e.g. the presentation of a treaty and acclamation of Charles the Great by Byzantine ambassadors, *Ann. r. Franc.*, a. 812, Kurze, 136), were staged in the chapel of Our Lady at Aachen.

[165] Bouman, *Sacring*, pp. 116–17 and 129ff.

[166] L. Halphen, 'La pénitence de Louis le Pieux à Saint-Médard de Soissons', *A travers l'histoire du moyen âge* (Paris, 1950), pp. 58–66.

the grandees of the Frankish army.[167] The reason for the coincidence of general assemblies and big political events lies in a facet of Carolingian rulership illuminated by Tellenbach, the continual shaping and reshaping of a political consensus between kings, courtiers, and magnates.[168] Even were a given ceremony to take a particularly Byzantine ritual form, it would occur in a uniquely Frankish institutional framework.

Frequently the yearly assembly was held at or near a royal palace, which thereby served as the main stage for royal self-representation.[169] It was there that the king, like his Merovingian predecessors, received the *dona annualia* of his subjects or performed the Frankish ceremony of the *commendatio manuum*.[170] There the ruler held audiences for delegations from within the Frankish dominions or without and the Frankish grandees could witness their king's pomp and ostentatious wealth during the festive crown-wearings which accompanied the celebration of Mass on Sundays and high holy days.[171] Like the dynasty they

---

[167] This is clear from *Lib. pont.*, Duchesne, 2.7.21–2: 'omnes iterum congregati sunt' which plainly refers back to the audience of Leo III's oath-taking, immediately before: *ibid.*, 7.13–14; cf. 7.4–7.

[168] G. Tellenbach, 'Die geistigen und politischen Grundlagen der karolingischen Thronfolge. Zugleich eine Studie über kollektive Willensbildung und kollektives Handeln im neunten Jahrhundert', *FMS*, 13 (1979), 184–302.

[169] On the one at Aachen, e.g. W. Schlesinger, 'Beobachtungen zur Geschichte und Gestalt der Aachener Pfalz in der Zeit Karls des Grossen', *Studien zur europäischen Vor- und Frühgeschichte* (Neumünster, 1968), pp. 258–81, and L. Falkenstein, 'Zwischenbilanz zur Aachener Pfalzenforschung', *Zeitschrift des Aachener Geschichtsverein*, 80 (1970), 7–71.

[170] One description is Hibernicus Exul, *Carm.*, 2, ed. E. Dümmler, *MGH. Poet.*, 1 (1881). 396.1–8; cf. Hincmar's advice for royal conduct during these assemblies: *De ordine palatii*, 7, ed. T. Gross and R. Schieffer, *MGH. Fontes iuris germanici antiqui in usum scholarum*, 3 (1980). 90.575–94.619; on commendation, Ganshof, *Féodalité*, pp. 46–7; cf. pp. 22–3.

[171] Audiences granted to Franks: Candidus, *Vita metrica Aegilii* (BHL, 2441), ed. E. Dümmler, *MGH.Poet.*, 2 (1884). 103.10–104.23; Agobard of Lyons, *Ep.*, 4, ed. E. Dümmler, *MGH.Epist.*, 5 (1899). 164.28–36; ecclesiastics observed strict precedence on such occasions, as is indicated by Hincmar's care in noting his exact position during an audience with Louis the German: *Episcoporum relatio*, ed. A. Boretius and V. Krause, *MGH.Capit.*, 2 (1898). 466.10–11. One of the rare occasions on which Charlemagne wore a richly decorated sword was during the reception of foreign legations: *V. Kar.*, 23, Holder-Egger and Waitz, 28.5–7; cf. Theodulf, *Carm.*, 25, Dümmler, 485.57–8; Thegan, *Vita Hludovici imperatoris*, 9, ed. G. Pertz, *MGH.SS*, 2 (1829). 593.6–11, and the contrasting tale of Notker the Stammerer, *Gesta Karoli*, 2, 6, ed. H.F. Haefele, *MGH.SRG*, n.s., 12 (1962).56–7.

displaced, the Carolingians played up their power and prestige in the key moments of their earthly existence, from baptism to funeral.[172] Even the ruler's amusement could take the form of a *Festkrönung* when, accompanied by his great men, he went out on the royal hunt, *sollemni more*.[173] Something of the character of these ceremonies and the limited nature of their audience can be deduced from the fact that most Carolingian palaces shunned what urban centers there were in the empire.[174] Unless it coincided with annual assemblies, the royal ritual which occurred in the palace was limited in focus to the narrow but influential sector of society composed of resident prelates, great officers, lower clergy occupied with the humdrum tasks of a limited administration, as well as visiting aristocrats and foreigners.[175] This explains as well the significance of ceremonies staged in front of the army, like Lothar's submission and reconciliation with his father.[176] Although all Franks were theoretically subject to

---

Charlemagne also wore the bejewelled sword for church processions: Einhard, *V. Kar.*, 23, Holder-Egger and Waitz, 28.5–7; cf. 'Astronomer', *V. Hlud.*, 28, Pertz, 621.40–1. Lothar used the procession of the feast of the Assumption to demonstrate his reconciliation with Theutperga: *Ann. Bert.*, a. 865, Grat, 122; cf. Adventius of Metz, *Ep.*, ed. E. Dümmler, *MGH.Epist.*, 6 (1925). 235.21–4. The most complete description is Ermold, *Hon. Hlud.*, 4, 2280–317, Faral, 174–8; cf. *Ad Pippinum*, 1, 25–38, Faral, 204. See in general C. Brühl, 'Fränkischer Krönungsbrauch und das Problem der Festkrönungen', *Historische Zeitschrift*, 194 (1962), 265–326, and K.U. Jäschke, 'Frühmittelalterliche Festkrönungen? Überlegungen zu Terminologie und Methode', *Historische Zeitschrift*, 211 (1970), 556–88.

172 Baptism: Agnellus, *Lib. pont. Rav.*, Holder-Egger, 338.10ff. On royal funerals: Erlande-Brandenburg, *Roi*, pp. 7–12, 60ff.

173 A crowned Charlemagne, riding a richly decorated horse, could turn the hunt into a political spectacle involving his family and assorted aristocrats: *Karolus Magnus et Leo papa*, 137–325, ed. E. Dümmler, *MGH.Poet.*, 1.369–74, or H. Beumann, F. Brunhölzl et al., *Karolus magnus et Leo papa. Ein Paderborner Epos vom Jahre 799*, Studien und Quellen zur westfälischen Geschichte, 8 (Paderborn, 1966), 68–82, on which document see D. Schaller, 'Das Aachener Epos für Karl den Kaiser', *FMS*, 10 (1977), 134–68 and 'Interpretationsprobleme in Aachener Karlsepos', *Rheinische Vierteljahrsblätter*, 41 (1977), 160–79, here 169ff. Cf. Ermold, *Hon. Hlud.*, 4, 2362–437, Faral, 180–4. The element of display explains why some royal hunts are qualified as 'sollemni more', e.g. *Ann. r. Franc.*, a. 819, Kurze, 152, or Einhard, *Trans. Marc. et Petri*, 2, 6, Waitz, 247.26–8.

174 See e.g. P. Riché, *Daily life in the world of Charlemagne*, tr. J.A. McNamara (n.p., 1978), p. 41.

175 J. Fleckenstein, 'Karl der Grosse und sein Hof', *Karl der Grosse*, 1, 24–50; cf. Riché, *Life*, pp. 89ff.

176 Thegan, *V. Hlud.*, 55, Pertz, 602.24–34, who carefully notes that Louis was

military service, specialists agree that the brunt of warfare fell on the shoulders of the better off and the royal vassals, who could afford the heavy expense of cavalry warfare in the Frankish style.[177] The levy of the king's vassals and the presence of the magnates meant that the Ost provided a significant opportunity to project the king's power, wealth and piety, whether or not the concentration of the troops coincided with the annual assembly, as it frequently did down to the reign of Louis the Pious.[178]

Victory was an essential characteristic of Carolingian kingship as it was portrayed in art, literature and ceremony. As even the humble entries in the Willibrord calendar suggest, military success – and the booty it entailed – played a decisive role in the rise of the new dynasty and the coalescence of most of the aristocracy around it. The Merovingian tradition of dynastic victory was taken over with a vengeance. The family's historiography, embodied, for instance, in the *Annales Mettenses priores*, and its art, exemplified by the lost frescoes of the Ingelheim palace, reiterate this theme, while court poets echo it.[179] It would be a tedious task to catalogue the numerous references to the ruler's victory spread throughout the abundant panegyrical material produced by the Carolingian renewal.[180] But it must be noted that poems began to be written to celebrate specific victories, although nothing is as yet known of the circumstances of their performance. In this category fall the anonymous 'Rhythm on the Avar Victory', Sedulius Scottus' charming piece 'On the Slaughter of the Northmen' or the vernacular *Ludwigslied*.[181] A symbol

---

enthroned in an open tent on top of a rise in a large field, so the whole army could witness the scene, 'ubi eum exercitus omnis contemplari potuit'.

[177] F.L. Ganshof, 'L'armée sous les Carolingiens', *Ordinamenti militari in Occidente nell'alto medioevo*, 1, Settimane, 15 (Spoleto, 1968), 109–30, here 111–15; K.F. Werner, 'Bedeutende Adelsfamilien im Reich Karls des Grossen', *Karl der Grosse*, 1, 83–142, here 122; J.F. Verbruggen, 'L'armée et la stratégie de Charlemagne', *Karl der Grosse*, 1, 420–36, here 421 and 426–7.

[178] Ganshof, 'L'armée', pp. 116–17.

[179] *Annales Mettenses priores*, ed. B. von Simson, *MGH.SRG* (1905), 1.4 and 9; 3.11; 5.2; 6.15–16; 11.29; 12.27; 13.17. The family is 'invictissima parentum prosapia', *ibid.*, 3.13–14. On the frescos at Ingelheim, Ermold, *Hon. Hlud.*, 4, 2156–63, Faral, 164.

[180] See the survey of material in F. Bittner, *Studien zur Herrscherlob in der mittellateinischen Dichtung*, Diss. (Würzburg, 1962), pp. 35ff.

[181] *Rhythmus*, Holder-Egger and Waitz; Sedulius Scottus, *Carm.*, 2, 45, Traube, 208–9; *Ludwigslied*, von Steinmeyer.

of royal authority like Charlemagne's lead seal, as well perhaps as that of his namesake, propagated the idea of royal victory in hexameter form: 'Let there be glory for Christ and victory for king Charles!'[182]

The ideology of royal victory spilled over into the ruler's ceremonial life, most notably the royal investiture. Charles the Bald's coronation as ruler of the *regnum Lotharii* at Metz on 9 September 869 is one of the rare instances for which there is a detailed and reliable description.[183] After the unction and crowning, the bishops handed the king a palm branch and a royal scepter. The accompanying prayer expounded the palm's message of victory on earth and in heaven.[184] That the palm was placed on the same ceremonial level as the royal scepter emphasizes the role of victory in the Carolingian idea of the ruler.[185] Alcuin had referred to palm branches in his allusion to a triumphal welcome for Charlemagne and, in keeping with late antique tradition, that king had been welcomed into Rome by children waving palm branches, during the final campaign against the Lombards. But more recent developments helped place the palm in Charles the Bald's hand. Ninth-century popes had been sending palm branches to Frankish kings at least since 853.[186] The branch was probably meant to be carried by the ruler in the palace liturgy's Palm Sunday procession, and the papal letters accompanying the palms emphasize their symbolism of both ethical and military triumph.[187] The papal and liturgical connection underpinned the

<hr/>

[182] P.E. Schramm, *Die Zeitgenössischen Bildnisse Karls des Grossen*, Beiträge zur Kulturgeschichte des Mittelalters und der Renaissance, 29 (Leipzig, 1928), pp. 20ff: + GLORIA SIT XPO REGI VIC[TORIA CARLO]; cf. 'Drei Nachträge zu den Metallbullen der Karolingischen und Sächsischen Kaiser', *Deutsches Archiv*, 24 (1968), 1–15, esp. 5ff.

[183] *Ordo coronationis Karoli II in regno Hlotharii II factae*, ed. A. Boretius and V. Krause, *MGH.Capit.*, 2.456–8; cf. Wattenbach–Levison, *Geschichtsquellen*, p. 504.

[184] Boretius–Krause, 457.28–30.

[185] Cf. comm. of Schramm, *Herrschaftszeichen*, 2, 410–12, and *Der König von Frankreich. Das Wesen der Monarchie vom 9. zum 16. Jahrhundert*, 2nd edn, 1 (Weimar, 1960), 28–32.

[186] For Leo IV, see JL, 2626. In February 875, John VIII alluded to the custom's ancientness: JL, 3007, ed. E. Caspar, *MGH.Epist.*, 7 (1928). 302.28. There seems to be no evidence for the custom in the *Cod. Carol.* or the letters of Gregory I.

[187] John VIII to Charles the Bald (JL, 3079; 13 February 877), Caspar, 31.31–4; to Charles III (JL, 3345; 29 March 881), Caspar, 245.30–2. Stephen V to Charles III (JL,

appearance of this symbolic object in Charles the Bald's coronation at Metz.

Victory imagery was not confined to one aspect of the coronation of 869. At the crucial moment of anointment, God was entreated to bless Charles as He had once blessed the victorious rulers of the Old Testament and to make him an ever victorious triumphator over all enemies, visible and invisible.[188] The same prayer was used again for the crowning of Louis the Stammerer in December 877.[189]

Although no early *ordines* have survived, it is clear that the role of victory imagery in Carolingian coronations went back to the eighth century. Thus the 'Royal Blessing When There is an Elevation to the Realm' preserved by an 'Eighth-Century Gelasian' sacramentary stresses the parallel between the modern kings of the Franks and the ancient heroes of Israel. God is asked to grant spiritual and material blessings to the king and his realm and to make him 'a most powerful protector of the fatherland', as well as a 'most powerful triumphator of kings for the oppression of rebels and pagan nations'.[190]

A number of poems associated with the royal *adventus* survive from the ninth century. Some at least seem to have been recited during the ceremony, so that they furnish unique insight into the meaning learned Carolingians attached to the king's epiphany in his towns and monasteries.[191] One of their most prevalent themes is royal victory. Thus a poem ascribed to Theodulf of Orleans hailed Louis the Pious at Tours, 'victor on land and sea' and trampler of the wicked nations that failed to bend their knee to his power.[192] Jonas of Orleans developed the same theme during a

---

3427, March 887), ed. E. Caspar, *MGH.Epist.*, 7 (1928).340.7–9. On the liturgy of the Palm Sunday procession, H. Leclercq, *DACL*, 14, 2 (1928), 2063–4.

[188] *Ordo cor.*, Boretius–Krause 457.4–12.

[189] *Ibid.*, 462.23–6.

[190] 'Regalis benedictio quando elevatur in regno', *Sacr. Angoul.* f. 130recto, Cagin, no. 1857, cited here from E. Moeller, *CCL*, 162A. 769, no. 1882d: '. . . ut sit fortissimus protector patriae . . . atque . . . fortissimus regum triumphator hostium ad opprimendas rebelles et paganas nationes'.

[191] Kantorowicz, 'Advent', pp. 38–41. Cf. O.G. Oexle, 'Die Karolinger und die Stadt des heiligen Arnulf', *FMS*, 1 (1967), 250–364, here 302ff.

[192] Theodulf, *Carm.*, 77, Dümmler, 578, 1.1 and 5.1–4. On the doubtful attribution, J. Szövérffy, *Weltliche Dichtungen des lateinischen Mittelalters. Ein Handbuch*, 1 (Berlin, 1970), 482.

visit of Louis and his son Lothar to his see.[193] In similar circumstances, Sedulius Scottus saluted Charles the Bald's 'doxa triumphalis'; Charles and Louis are 'fulmina belli', guaranteeing that the Christian people remains unvanquished. It is only appropriate that the poet wishes that they may ever enjoy victory, 'pompa' and trophies.[194] The association between royal visits and victory was so strong that a late ninth-century versifier at St Gall who had to welcome a son of Louis the German and who seems to have been at a loss for the young ruler's victories, saved the day with the theme of dynastic victory. Before and after each verse, the welcoming choir chanted 'Hail, Scion of most unvanquished kings!'[195]

The first Carolingian kings frequently led their armies on campaign, after which they headed for the palace to winter. Contemporary writers qualify the ruler's return with words like 'cum magno triumpho' or 'cum gloria triumphi'.[196] Not every use of like expressions may be ascribed to literary flourish. For instance, in late March 798, Alcuin responded to Charlemagne's invitation to join him in the green meadows of Saxony for scriptural delights. Seeing that the verdant fields were infested with hostile Saxons, the aging scholar begged to be excused from enjoying the king's beatitude in the land of the Philistines. He would rather enjoy it in Jerusalem, i.e. the vision of peace, 'where God's temple is being constructed by the art of the most wise Solomon'.[197] The allusion fits the chapel of the Virgin at Aachen,

---

[193] Theodulf, *Carm.*, 37, Dümmler, 529, 4.1–4. For the ascription to Jonas, D. Schaller, 'Philologische Untersuchungen zu den Gedichten Theodulfs von Orléans', *Deutsches Archiv*, 18 (1962), 13–91, here 27–8.

[194] Sedulius Scottus, *Carm.*, 2, 12, Traube, 180.5; *Carm.*, 2, 15, Traube, 183.9, 14 and 21; cf. too *Carm.*, 2, 25, Traube, 190.4 and 9–10, 191.39–40. Cf. R. Düchting, *Sedulius Scottus. Seine Dichtungen* (Munich, 1968), pp. 63–4 and 70–2.

[195] 'Salve proles regum invictissimorum': *Sylloge codicis Sangallensis CCCLXXI*, no. 8, ed. P. von Winterfeld, *MGH.Poet.*, 4.1 (1899).323.1; cf. W. Bulst, 'Susceptacula Regum. Zur Kunde deutscher Reichsaltümer', *Corona Quernea. Festschrift K. Strecker*, MGH. Schriften, 6 (Stuttgart, 1941), pp. 97–135, here 103–5.

[196] A few examples from many: Charlemagne's return from the final Lombard campaign 'cum magno triumpho', *Ann. r. Franc.*, a. 774, Kurze, 40, *Ann. Ein.*, a. 774, Kurze, 68; according to the *Annales Maximiani*, a. 791, Charles returned from the Avar campaign of that year to Regensburg 'cum triumphi gloria', ed. G. Waitz, *MGH.SS*, 13 (1881). 22.11–12.

[197] Alcuin, *Ep.*, 143–5, Dümmler, 227–35, on the circumstances, Böhmer–Mühlbacher, *Regesta*, no. 346. Citation from *Ep.*, 145, Dümmler, 235.7–8. The

and it is there that Alcuin, adapting a liturgical phrase, desired to come to greet 'the triumph of your glory, with palm branches and singing children'. The elaborate metaphor intimates the king would be met by some sort of welcoming ceremony.[198] This is seconded by the Chronicle of Moissac when it mentions that Louis the Pious returned from a successful campaign in Brittany, 'cum triumpho gloriae'. Another contemporary coincidentally drops the fact that, on this occasion, foreign legations participated in the *occursus* which welcomed the ruler to the palace at Herstal.[199] No less a figure than John Scot Eriugena composed a poem on Christ the victor of the devil and Charles the victor of Louis to celebrate what seems to have been Charles the Bald's triumphal *reditus* after the unexpected success over his brother near Laon in 859, the same event enshrined in Charles' victory endowment at St Denis.[200] But, compared to the evidence available on other aspects of Carolingian rulership, these occasions do not cut an imposing figure: the return of the victorious Frankish king to his palace did not develop into a widely resonant ceremony. One reason may be the decentralization of Carolingian society, with its far-flung aristocracy, and the lack of a settled capital. Such returns fell outside the most important institutional framework of Carolin-

---

allusion fits both the Biblical tone of these letters and what is known of the chapel's rough state of completion in 798: e.g. G. Bandmann, 'Die Vorbilder der Aachener Pfalzkapelle', *Karl der Grosse*, 4, 424–62, here 425, n. 7.

[198] *Ep.*, 145, Dümmler, 235.5–6: 'Ut... liceat mihi cum ramis palmarum et pueris cantantibus occurrere triumpho gloriae vestrae... et dicere: "Benedictus dominus Deus, qui adduxit et reduxit David dilectum cum prosperitate et salute ad servos suos"'. Cf. the antiphon *ad primam* for the proper of Palm Sunday in the monastic office. Palms figure prominently in Carolingian victory conceptions and were actually used, in keeping with late antique tradition, during Charlemagne's *adventus* at Rome in 774: *Lib. pont.*, Duchesne, 1.497.2–3. Alcuin alludes to them in his wish for Charlemagne's triumphant return from Italy in 800: *Versus ad Carolum imperatorem*, 75–80, ed. E. Dümmler, *MGH.Poet.*, 1.257, in which the first lines are again a liturgical allusion (cf. E. Moeller, *CCL*, 162A, no. 1881). See also above, nn. 185–7.

[199] *Chronicon Moissacense*, ed. G.H. Pertz, *MGH.SS*, 1.315.15–18; 'Astronomer', *V. Hlud.*, 13, Pertz, 624.3–7; cf. Böhmer–Mühlbacher, *Regesta*, no. 671f and, on Herstal: A. Gauert, 'Zum Itinerar Karls des Grossen', *Karl der Grosse*, 1, 307–21, here 320.

[200] John Scot Eriugena, *Carm.*, 2, ed. L. Traube, *MGH.Poet.*, 3 (1896). 527–9, esp. 528.55–62. Cf. M. Cappuyns, *Jean Scot Erigène. Sa vie, son oeuvre, sa pensée* (Louvain, 1933), p. 59–67; Böhmer–Mühlbacher, *Regesta*, no. 1436e.

gian royal ritual: the greater part of the potential audience had already returned to their estates when the Ost had been dismissed at the end of the campaign.

It would be wrong, however, to infer that Carolingian kings had no use for triumphal entries. When they did, the evidence confirms what has already been said about the character and context of their kind of royal ritual. The surrender of Pavia in 774 marked the end of the Lombard kingdom's independence and the annexation of vast new territories to the Frankish domains. On the day after the surrender, Charlemagne staged a triumphal entry into the city, to the sounds of 'hymns and *laudes*'. The magnates and lesser lights of the Frankish expeditionary force were richly rewarded for their service, when the king distributed the treasury of king Desiderius.[201]

A quarter-century later, Frankish forces had nearly exhausted Barcelona's resistance and the field commanders summoned young Louis, the twenty-two-year-old king of Aquitania, under whose auspices the Frankish dream of subjugating Septimania was finally reaching fulfillment. As his biographer noted, the young ruler's prestige could only benefit from presiding over the fall of so famous a town.[202] Louis posted guards as soon as the city surrendered, but he 'postponed his entry until he could organize the consecration to God's name of a victory so long desired and finally attained, with an appropriate service of thanksgiving'.[203] The description of the next day's triumphal entry is close enough to that of Pavia to suggest that the same ceremonial pattern was observed in both cases. Louis' biographer continues:

The next day, therefore, the king and army passed through the city gate with solemn pomp and *laudes hymnidicae*, preceded by the priests and clergy. He continued in procession to the church of the Holy and most

---

[201] *Chron. Laur. breve*, Schnorr von Carolsfeld, 31, 'cum hymnis et laudibus ingrediens'. Cf. *Ann. Fuld.*, a. 774, Kurze, 9.

[202] 'Astronomer', *V. Hlud.*, 13, Pertz, 613.6–7; note that *Ann. r. Franc.* do not allude to the triumphal entries of 774 and 801. On the siege of Barcelona, E. Levi-Provençal, *Histoire de l'Espagne musulmane*, 1, 2nd edn (Leyden, 1950), 178–82.

[203] 'Astronomer', *V. Hlud.*, 13, Pertz, 613.12–14: '... ipse autem ab eius ingressu abstinuit, donec ordinaret, qualiter cum digna Deo gratiarum actione cupitam atque susceptam victoriam eius nomini consecraret'.

Victorious Cross, to celebrate a service of thanksgiving to God, for the victory the Lord had divinely granted.[204]

The procession was opened by the clergy, presumably decked out with processional crosses, censers and the like. Behind them came the king and his army. As at Pavia, the audible aspect of the ceremony was dominated by the singing of *laudes hymnidicae*, of liturgical texts whose name suggests a connection with the *laudes regiae*. The cumulative effect of these circumstances was to transform the Frankish triumphal entry into a liturgical procession of litanic quality, in which the churchly element prevailed. Why were these events marked by a solemn ceremony, when royal returns to the palace have left so few traces? Several factors contributed to making the victories at Barcelona and Pavia worthy of a triumphal entry. The populations of both places belonged to or stemmed from successor kingdoms in which triumphal entries by victorious kings had been a typical element of *Staatssymbolik*. The inhabitants may well have expected some such symbolic gesture. Both acts marked a decisive military conquest and the formal annexation of a new territory and its inhabitants into the allegiance of the Frankish king. The liturgical procession into the city symbolized the new situation, much as it had long before when Clovis entered Tours. Finally, and perhaps most importantly, the indispensable partners and foils of royal authority were well represented on both occasions, thereby furnishing the king with the politically significant audience required for a successful ceremony: the Frankish army, comprising magnates, royal vassals and assorted followers.

Carolingian kings did not always lead their armies in person. This fact helps account for the sudden revival of a victory custom which, as has been seen, was deeply rooted in early Byzantine military routine, the dispatch and presentation to the ruler of symbols of success won in his name. The 790s again witness important innovation. As king and court began to take on a more sedentary character, conditions ripened for the custom's

---

[204] *Ibid.*, 613.15–18: 'Antecedentibus ergo eum in crastinum et exercitum eius sacerdotibus et clero, cum sollempni apparatu et laudibus hymnidicis portam civitatis ingressus, et ad aecclesiam sanctae et victoriosissimae Crucis, pro victoria sibi divinitus conlata gratiarum actiones Deo acturus, est progressus'.

reappearance. Early in 796, duke Heiric of Friuli sent booty taken from the Avar ring to Charles at Aachen, while the king's son later brought more spoils in person.[205] The royal annalist's account of a delegation from Asturia suggests that the court was aware of the imperial custom of receiving 'symbols of victory' from field commanders. In 798, Alfonso II sent ambassadors to Charles with a report on his successful raid against Muslim-held Lisbon. The annalist calls the gifts brought by the envoys *insignia victoriae*, implying that Alfonso was acting under Carolingian authority. This distortion is quite in keeping with Frankish pretensions to universal rule.[206] The implication was sufficiently clear that the revisor of the Royal Annals was at pains to modify the original account in such a fashion that the reader would not deduce that Charlemagne claimed some special power over the Asturian king.[207] The following year, the Frankish force which defeated the Saracens menacing the Balearic islands notified Charlemagne of his distant success by dispatching the enemy standards to the court, where they were presented to the king.[208] Wido, prefect of Brittany, got on the bandwagon and presented Charles with the weapons of the various 'dukes' who had surrendered to him; each sword was engraved with the owner's name.[209] The triumphal audiences continued after Charlemagne's return from the imperial coronation. Following Louis' triumphal entry into Barcelona, he sent the city's governor and appropriate booty to his father. The prisoner arrived at the imperial court and was presented to Charlemagne on the same day as the rebel commander of Chieti, which had just surrendered to a Frankish siege.[210] The importance

---

[205] *Ann. r. Franc.*, a. 796, Kurze, 98; *Ann. Ein.*, Kurze, 99.

[206] *Ann. r. Franc.*, a. 798, Kurze, 104; cf. Böhmer–Mühlbacher, *Regesta*, no. 347c. On Frankish pretensions and reality: H. Löwe, 'Von den Grenzen des Kaisergedankens in der Karolingerzeit', *Deutsches Archiv*, 14 (1958), 345–74, here 350.

[207] *Ann. Ein.*, a. 798, Kurze, 105: '... legati Hadefonsi regis ... munera deferentes, quae ille de manubiis ... regi mittere curavit, Mauros videlicet *septem* cum *totidem* mulis atque loricis, *quae licet pro dono mitterentur, magis tamen* insignia victoriae *videbantur*', where italics indicate the revisor's additions to the text of the *Ann. r. Franc.*

[208] *Ann. r. Franc.*, a. 799, Kurze, 108; cf. *Ann. Ein.*, Kurze, 109, and Böhmer–Mühlbacher, *Regesta*, no. 350h.

[209] *Ann. r. Franc.*, a. 799, Kurze, 108.

[210] The presentation of the captive commanders overshadowed the gifts of booty, which are entirely omitted by *Ann. r. Franc.*, a. 802, Kurze, 116; but cf. Ermold, *Hon. Hlud.*, I, 572–647, Faral, 46–50; Böhmer–Mühlbacher, *Regesta*, no. 374e.

Louis and the court attached to this kind of presentation is confirmed by the fact that the mission was entrusted to Bego, Louis' closest friend, who was destined to become his son-in-law and count of Paris.[211] The court's eagerness to magnify the dynasty's success explains why, a few years later, Louis with no little fanfare presented to his father the keys of Tortosa, even though the Frankish army's operation against that city was anything but a total victory.[212]

Although the custom of presenting the ruler with the symbols of success became rarer in the next half-century, so did Carolingian victories. It did not disappear. In 865, count Robert the Strong successfully engaged the Northmen and transmitted the captured enemy standards and weapons to his sovereign, Charles the Bald.[213] The very next year a scandal erupted in Italy when emperor Louis II learned that the Bulgar king had escaped an ambush thanks to his new religion and, as a sign of gratitude, sent his arms to the pope. Louis was furious and ordered the pope to turn the arms over to him.[214]

The sudden reappearance of delegations of socially important individuals bearing the symbols of a commander's victory to the king is doubly significant. On one hand, it shows that the Roman legacy of the ruler's implication in every victory won in his name, regardless of his personal involvement, was alive at the Frankish court late in the eighth century. It is certainly noteworthy that this new victory custom appears just a few years before the imperial coronation. On the other, it seems symptomatic of the new importance of person to person relations in the structure of Carolingian government. Charlemagne in particular had developed a network of personal loyalties, often symbolized by an explicit relationship of vassalage, into a primary tool for running a very rudimentary apparatus of government. By the time of his

---

[211] Ermold, *Hon. Hlud.*, 1, 578, Faral, 46; on Bego, see the references assembled in Wattenbach–Levison, *Geschichtsquellen*, p. 318, n. 85.

[212] 'Astronomer', *V. Hlud.*, 16, Pertz, 615.15–18. On the chronology and true nature of the operations: Levi-Provençal, *Espagne*, pp. 182–4.

[213] *Ann. Bert.*, a. 865, Grat, 122.

[214] The pope complied only in part: *ibid.*, a. 866, Grat, 134. King Arnulf sent 16 *signa* taken from the Northmen at Louvain to Bavaria 'in testimonium', but the precise meaning of this gesture is not clear: *Ann. Fuld., Cont. Ratisp.*, a. 891, Kurze, 120–1; cf. Böhmer–Mühlbacher, *Regesta*, no. 1865a.

successor, at the latest, the link between ruler and official was regularly reinforced by the special personal tie of vassalage. And, for Charlemagne and his successors, vassalage was first and foremost a military institution.[215] In this context, the royal annalist's distorted presentation of king Alfonso's dispatch of booty deserves a second look. His depiction of the event takes on a new significance if it is viewed in the light of Einhard's unwarranted assertion that the Asturian king insisted on being portrayed as Charlemagne's *proprius*, or, as the term has been translated by a specialist, as his vassal.[216]

The glorification of the king's victory manifested by this kind of triumphal audience has also left traces in written communications between ruler and ruled. Because so many letters addressed to Carolingian kings have survived, an analysis of the spread of victory conceptions in epistolary etiquette allows an interesting test of the patterns perceived in other kinds of evidence. It is to a happy initiative of Charlemagne that we owe a thorough record of papal letters to Charles Martel, Pippin and Charles himself. In 791, the king commanded that the decaying letters from the popes and 'from the empire' (*de imperio*, i.e. Byzantium) be transcribed on parchment.[217] The chronology of victory concepts developed by papal scribes in correspondence with the Frankish kings differs according to their position in the documents' structure. Throughout the eighth century, the papal chancellery remained sensitive to the victory ideology's imperial overtones and avoided triumphal epithets when addressing communications to the Frankish king. This is because the precise form of address was a delicate issue, the subject of handbooks of epistolary etiquette like the papal *Liber diurnus*, or the memorandum on foreign powers' style of address and the values of corresponding gold bulls produced by the Byzantine bureaucracy of the tenth century.[218] For fear of his

215 Ganshof, 'Lehnswesen'.
216 Einhard, *V. Kar.*, 16, Holder-Egger and Waitz 19.3–6. Cf. Löwe, 'Grenzen', pp. 350–1. Translation of *proprius*: J.F. Niermeyer, *Mediae latinitatis lexicon minus* (Leyden, 1976), p. 864, s.v.
217 See the preface to the collection, *Cod. Carol.*, Gundlach, 476.1–20; the letters from the empire are of course lost.
218 L. Santifaller, *Liber Diurnus. Studien und Forschungen*, ed. H. Zimmermann, Päpste und Papsttum, 10 (Stuttgart, 1976); for the Byzantine memorandum, *De cer.*, 2, 48, Reiske, 686.5–692.2.

own sovereign's reaction, the exarch of Italy once refused to use any address at all when he wrote to Charlemagne.[219]

For the first Carolingian kings, the popes did not use the style laid out by the *Liber diurnus* for letters to kings. Rather, address and subscription were derived from the model for a patrician, in keeping with Stephen II's concession of this title to Pippin and his sons.[220] The only Roman document to infringe on the principle confirms the rule, for it was not officially issued by the papal chancellery. In 757, the 'Entire Senate and Whole Entirety of People of the God-Preserved City of Rome' addressed Charlemagne's father as 'The Most Excellent and Most Distinguished Lord and Divinely Appointed Great Victor, Pippin, King of the Franks and Patrician of the Romans'.[221] They concluded with a well-developed victory wish, that God might send His angel to vanquish the king's enemies, extend his boundaries and grant him victory.[222]

Charlemagne's imperial coronation removed Roman reluctance. The change in the ruler's status entailed the resurrection of a victory titulature derived from that sported by the emperors of late antiquity and which emphasized the ancient 'victor and triumphator' couplet. Papal missives were now addressed 'To the Most Pious and Most Serene Lord, Victor and Triumphator, Son, Lover of God and Our Lord Jesus Christ, Charles Augustus'. Like the concluding subscription which echoes the biblical and late Roman *calcatio* imagery, this address derives directly from the *Liber diurnus* style of imperial address.[223] But there is more.

---

[219] Leo III, *Ep.* 7 to Charlemagne (JL, 2526, 11 November 813), ed. K. Hampe, *MGH.Epist.*, 5 (1899). 99.3–8.

[220] *Liber diurnus*, Foerster, 181.25–6 (royal address); from 755, the address is a modified form of the one for patricians, *ibid.*, 181.15–16; cf. the identical subscription *ibid.*, 181.17–18. On the title, L. Halphen, *Charlemagne et l'empire carolingien*, 2nd edn (Paris, 1968), p. 37.

[221] *Cod. Carol.*, 13, Gundlach, 509.5–8: 'Domino excellentissimo atque precellentissimo et a Deo instituto magno victori Pippino, regi Francorum et patritio Romanorum, omnis senatus atquae universa populi generalitas'.

[222] *Ibid.*, 510.28–32.

[223] 'Domino piissimo et serenissimo victori atque triumphatori filio amatori dei et domini nostri Iesu Christi, Karolo Augusto', e.g. JL, 2529 (A.D. 809), ed. K. Hampe, *MGH.Epist.*, 5 (1899).66.33–5; cf. *Liber diurnus*, Foerster, 181.2–4, and Deér, 'Vorrechte', pp. 42–3.

The reserve of pre-800 addresses contrasts with the texts. As early as 757–8, the pope referred to Pippin as 'victor king'.[224] In 760, the Frank was hailed as the 'most victorious and excellent king' for the first time, and a similar qualification was applied to his sons.[225] It may have been in connection with a campaign in Saxony that 'triumphatorissimus' begins to appear in 779–80.[226] Some eight years later, a new element was introduced, perhaps in response to Frankish success against the Byzantines or the Avars. The king's victory was crystallized into a new formula of majesty, and victory became a regular royal attribute along the lines of 'your excellency' or 'your serenity': Charlemagne was referred to as 'your royal victory, illustrious in triumphs'.[227] In other words, papal reserve when addressing letters to the Carolingians reflected the *de iure* situation, while the same letters' text mirrored the *de facto* alliance.

Another area of Italy with connections to nearby Byzantine outposts provided the first preserved epistolary address which adopted the victory ideology. It is only more significant for the intimate relations of its author with the Frankish court. A letter from Paulinus after his appointment as patriarch of Aquileia greeted his friend Charlemagne as the 'Catholic and ever Glorious Triumphator in Christ', in what may be an allusion to the very Avar campaign of 791 which first witnessed battle supplications.[228] The same hand was at work in the Council of Friuli's acts, where Charles and his son received the old imperial epithet

---

[224] JL, 2335, *Cod. Carol.*, 11, Gundlach, 504.35–6; 505.4; 505.7; 507.14; JL, 2336 (April–May 757), *ibid.*, 12, 508.5; JL, 2338 (A.D. 758), *ibid.*, 17, 511.19.

[225] 'Victoriosissime eximieque rex': JL, 2344 (April 760), *Cod. Carol.*, 18, Gundlach, 519.31; JL, 2353 (763), *ibid.*, 26, 530.30; JL, 2380 (769–70), *ibid.*, 44, 559.1.

[226] JL, 2428 (779–80), *Cod. Carol.*, 64, Gundlach, 591.13; JL, 2434 (May–September 781), *ibid.*, 70, 600.19; JL, 2440 (782), *ibid.*, 72, 603.11 and 23; JL, 2438 (April 781 to April 783), *ibid.*, 73, 604.19, etc. On the campaigns see S. Abel and B. Simson, *Jahrbücher des fränkischen Reiches unter Karl dem Grossen*, 2 (reprint, Berlin, 1969), 633ff and 639ff.

[227] 'Vestra regalis in triumphis praecelsa victoria', JL, 2467 (788–9), *Cod. Carol.*, 85, Gundlach, 621.28; JL, 2480, *ibid.*, 86, 622.25; same formula in a different sense: JL, 2473, *ibid.*, 89, 626.14–15.

[228] 'Catholico semperque in Christo inclyto triumfatori', *Ep.*, 15, ed. E. Dümmler, *MGH.Epist.*, 4.517.4–5. Cf. Abel-Simson, *Jahrbücher*, 2, 20ff. On Paulinus and the court, F. Brunhölzl, *Geschichte der lateinischen Literatur des Mittelalters*, 1 (Munich, 1975), 250–1.

familiar from the Latin-speaking provinces and early barbarian kings of Italy: 'the most unvanquished princes'.[229] Paulinus forged another variation when he wrote to Charles in the year of the imperial coronation.[230] A few years after that, the archbishop of Milan also applied the *invictissimus* formula.[231]

The intimate connection between victory and the imperial office cannot be forgotten, particularly since the first penetration of victory addresses north of the Alps dates from the months immediately preceding the imperial coronation and is due to a close friend of Paulinus. About a year before the crowning, when triumphal audiences were becoming a regular occurrence at the court, Alcuin reflected the general ambience and hailed the king as 'greatest victor'; a few months before the imperial dignity, Charles had become 'the most outstanding triumphator' and 'greatest and most unvanquished triumphator and most clement rector of kingdoms'.[232] The impact of papal usage cannot be overlooked either. It is difficult to imagine that papal prestige did not contribute to the appearance of the 'victor and triumphator' couplet in a letter of Leidrad, archbishop of Lyons to Charlemagne; the influence is unmistakable in Agobard's formulation of 816.[233]

Victory addresses occur most often in the imperial years of Charlemagne and the reign of Louis the Pious. The increasing visibility of victory addresses came to influence the imperial titulature itself. As Schlesinger has pointed out, Charlemagne's chancellery used both the *invictissimus* title and the 'victor and triumphator' couplet in the *intitulatio* of a most important document, the 806 *Divisio regni*, which determined the distribution of territories after Charlemagne's decease.[234] In 816, Louis

[229] 'Invictissimi principes', *Concilium Foroiuliense*, ed. A. Werminghoff, *MGH.Conc.*, I (1906). 179.8.
[230] *Ep.* 17, Dümmler, 523.1–3.
[231] Ed. A. Boretius, *MGH.Capit.*, 1.247.25–6.
[232] *Ep.* 163 (ca. 799), Dümmler, 263.6: 'victoris maximi'; *Ep.* 197 (ca. 4 April 800), Dümmler, 325.19–20: 'praestantissimo triumphatori'; *Ep.* 202 (800), 335.5–7: 'maximo atque invictissimo triumphatori atque clementissimo regnorum rectori'.
[233] *Epistolae variorum*, 29, ed. E. Dümmler, *MGH.Epist.*, 4.540.30–1; Agobard, *Ep.* 1, Dümmler, 153.5–7, 'Christianorum religiosissimo, benignorum benignissimo, mansuetorum tranquillissimo, *Christi amatori* ideoque *victori ac triumphatori piissimo augusto* . . .'.
[234] *Divisio regni*, ed. A. Boretius, *MGH.Capit.*, 1.126, *app.*: 'Imperator Caesar Karolus

the Pious was using a victory title in his correspondence, calling himself 'The most glorious Louis, Victor by celestial gift, ever Augustus', perhaps in reference to successes against the Slavs and Basques that spring. The passing fashion was reflected by the council convened at Aachen that year, for it adopted the same title for the emperor.[235] Other church councils followed suit. In 825 Louis was 'most victorious'; in 829 and 836 he was more than once hailed as *invictissimus*.[236] Victory titles kept pace in correspondence sent to the emperor.[237] But the next big step came from Lothar's chancellery and refers to Louis the Pious. From December 822 to April 833, during Lothar's co-empire with his father, the ruler of Italy's acts began 'In the name of Our Lord Jesus Christ Eternal God, Lothar Augustus, son of the Most Unvanquished Lord Emperor Louis'.[238] Lothar's revolt against his father put a provisional end to chancellery use of the title.[239] In the disorders which followed Louis' death, victory addresses became scarcer, without disappearing altogether.[240]

rex Francorum invictissimus et Romani rector imperii pius felix victor ac triumphator semper augustus'. Cf. W. Schlesinger, 'Kaisertum und Reichsteilung. Zur *Divisio regnorum* von 806', *Zum Kaisertum Karls des Grossen*, pp. 116–73, here 125–7, where he also argues for the title's derivation from the Donation of Constantine.

235 'Gloriosissimus Hludowicus superno munere victor semper augustus', ed. A. Werminghoff, *MGH.Conc.*, 1.458.14–15; cf. Böhmer–Mühlbacher, *Regesta*, no. 612a; cf. *Concilium Aquisgranense a. 816*, ed. Werminghoff, *MGH.Conc.*, 1.312.16–17 and 313.21: 'victoriosissimo principe'.

236 *Libellus synodalis Parisiensis*, ed. A. Werminghoff, *ibid.*, 481.1–2; *Episcoporum ad Hludowicum imperatorem relatio*, ed. A. Boretius and V. Krause, *MGH.Capit.*, 2.27.24–5; *Concilium Parisiense a. 829*, ed. A. Werminghoff, *MGH.Conc.*, 2.667.12–13; *Praeceptum synodale*, *ibid.*, 683.34–5; *Concilium Aquisgranense a. 836*, *ibid.*, 705.2–3.

237 Agobard, *Ep.* 7 (826–7), Dümmler, 182.14–15; Venerius of Grado, *Epistolae variorum*, 10–11, ed. E. Dümmler, *MGH.Epist.*, 5.313.30–2 and 314.24–5; Clergy of Mainz, *Ep. var.* 18, *ibid.*, 324.30–1.

238 'In nomine domini nostri Iesu Christi dei aeterni, Hlotharius augustus invictissimi domni imperatoris Hludouuici filius', T. Schieffer, *MGH.Diplomata Karolinorum*, 3 (1968), nos. 1–12; cf. G. Tessier, *Diplomatique royale française* (Paris, 1962), p. 87, and M. Hein, 'Die Kanzlei Kaiser Lothars I.', *Neues Archiv*, 39 (1914), 281–325, here 282ff.

239 Cf. however, Lothar's reference to Charlemagne, 'Karolo invictissimo' 29 August 842, Scheiffer, 180.34.

240 E.g. Heiric of Auxerre to Charles the Bald, ed. L. Traube, *MGH.Poet.*, 3 (1896). 428.1–2.

From about the middle of the century, papal usage began to influence royal epithets anew. There is not much evidence on papal forms of address for rulers, since most of the documents are known only from register copies or extracts. But in the texts of such letters, the 'most unvanquished' theme begins to dominate imperial victory epithets in papal correspondence from Leo IV's (847–55) reign.[241] At precisely the same time, *invictus* and its derivatives emerged as regular epithets of majesty in the official papal biographies composed under Leo and his successors.[242] The papal usage did not escape the bishops of Francia: within a quarter-century, the victory title was adopted as an epithet of Charles the Bald in the dating formula of the synod of Ponthion, the very occasion on which Charles made ceremonial waves by his Byzantine behavior.[243]

The eastern Frankish court kept its eye on Charles' conduct in 876.[244] In the wake of papal usage and Ponthion, *invictissimus* began to crop up in the *signum* and dating formulas of privileges issued by the chancellery of king Carloman (876–9) between 877 and 879.[245] It occurs once in the twenty-four extant diplomas of Louis the Younger.[246] By the end of the century, the epithet was becoming entrenched in the *signum* of Arnulf the Bastard's charters and even showed up in his dating formulas.[247] Out of this east Frankish chancellery usage would emerge the Ottonian formula *signum...invictissimi*.[248]

The spread of victory conceptions in epistolary etiquette again illustrates the creative role of Italy and the papacy in the

---

[241] JL, 2626 (February–March 853), ed. A. von Hirsch-Gereuth, *MGH.Epist.*, 5 (1899). 588.78; JL, 3006 (874–5), ed. E. Caspar, *MGH.Epist.*, 7 (1928). 302.11; JL, 3099 (May 877), *ibid.*, 51.24–5; JL, 3146 (May 878), *ibid.*, 89.4–5, etc.

[242] *Lib. pont.*, Duchesne, 2.87.24–5; 141.3; 151.28, etc.

[243] Ed. A. Boretius and V. Krause, *MGH.Capit.*, 2.351.7.

[244] *Ann. Fuld.*, a. 876, Kurze, 86.

[245] 20 November 877 to 8 July 879, ed. P. Kehr, *MGH. Dipl. stir. Kar.*, 1 (1934). 298.37 and 324.33.

[246] 22 November 879, *ibid.*, 351.17.

[247] From 1 April 888 to 13 December 898: P. Kehr, *MGH. Dipl. stir. Kar.*, 3 (1940). 30.21 and 258.24; date formula: 27 November 887 to 9 October 891, *ibid.*, 2.29 and 137.22.

[248] See, e.g. Conrad I, 5 July 918 (date formula), ed. T. Sickel, *MGH. Diplomata regum et imperatorum Germaniae*, 1 (1879–84). 32.37; Henry I, 7 January 932, *ibid.*, 66.40; 9 May 935, *ibid.*, 72.3; Otto I, 13 September 936 (date), *ibid.*, 90.31; 4 November 936, *ibid.*, 93.24, etc.

development of ruler symbolism north of the Alps. In the eighth and ninth centuries, papal custom influenced the epistolary usage of ruler and ruled in Francia. The changing nature of papal addresses underscores once again how, for the papacy, Charlemagne's imperial coronation marked a decisive turning point. Finally, it appeared that chancellery adoption of victory titles tended to follow trends at work outside the court, rather than vice versa.

CONCLUSION

The earliest victory celebration of a Merovingian king was a lesson in romanization, the last provided insight into the aristocracy's growing power. Both reflected the appropriation and adaptation of traditional forms of celebration inherited from the later Roman empire. Some of the differences between Carolingian and Merovingian victory celebrations are due to the differences in the historical and social circumstances of the two dynasties, as well as the distance covered by a developing society and rulership over three centuries. In the sixth century, the application of the victory ideology to the Frankish kings was in one way an attempt at domestication, an effort to translate into old terms the realities of new political power. These terms had the advantage of being familiar to the Gallo-Romans and, we may think, impressive to the Franks. When the Carolingians rediscovered these terms and usages, the ethnic dilemma was long since past. The new kings had to refurbish the prestige of a monarchy which had lost its luster, bolster their standing among the aristocrats over whom they presided, strengthen their authority over newly conquered territories, foster the revival of ancient literary, liturgical, and artistic forms. They had to exercise their power through new social and military institutions, hints of which may be detected in royal victory customs. And, above all, they turned to the church.

Perhaps the most significant finding is that the new involvement of the ruler and his entourage in obtaining and celebrating royal victory peaked in the decade preceding the imperial coronation. On this point the liturgical manuscripts, ritual innovation for the army, triumphal audiences and letters addressed to the king agree. This suggests that the royal entourage's conception of the king's victorious quality helped pave the way for the fateful events of Christmas Day 800. It testifies to a lively interest in royal *Staatssymbolik* in the years leading up to them.

Triumphal returns to the palace elicited scant attention from contemporary writers. But, in an interesting parallel to the first imperial coronation, triumphal entries were staged by Frankish kings in their Mediterranean territories. Nonetheless, the liturgy now served as the primary vehicle for obtaining and manifesting the king's victory, completing a development begun under the Roman empire four centuries earlier. Triumphal audiences asserted the king's role in distant victories and the presentation of the symbols of victory reaffirmed his personal ties to his commanders. In the course of the ninth century, Carolingian chancelleries experimented with victory titles, reflecting in this the epistolary etiquette of the king's correspondents.

By and large, the Carolingians avoided aping the customs of the court of Constantinople, although they were doubtless aware of them and even influenced by them. Rather, they created out of indigenous ceremonial, traditions and ancient literary forms; they eclectically appropriated some imperial customs and transformed them. The whole was powerfully cemented by the haughty self-awareness and ethnicity of victory echoed so loudly in a document like the prologue of the *Lex Salica*.[249]

The most striking aspect of Carolingian court ritual is its liturgical content and character, which far outstrip even the medieval court of Constantinople. The next is the way Carolingian ritual is fitted into a specifically Frankish institutional and social context. Another important point concerns what borrowing did take place. Not a little of that can be traced to Italy, parts of which would remain a provincial outpost of Byzantium for some time to come. Much of the borrowing involved Rome, the prestige of the pope and the prince of the apostles. But Frankish fascination with Peter does not diminish the fact that, down to the reign of Hadrian I, Rome was in spirit and in fact a provincial town of the eastern empire.[250] In one sense, Rome's creative role

---

[249] *Lex Salica. 100 Titel-Text*, Prologue, 1 and 4, ed. K.A. Eckhardt, *Germanenrechte*, n.F. (Weimar, 1953), 82.3–84.6 and 88.3–90.4, on which see Kantorowicz, 'Laudes regiae', pp. 58–9.

[250] P.E. Schramm, 'Die Anerkennung Karls des Grossen als Kaiser. Ein Kapitel aus der

in forming Carolingian court culture ought to be viewed as a particularly distinguished example of the wider phenomenon, the fascination the Byzantine provinces exercised on their barbarian neighbors.

The liturgy of war and imperial diplomatic point the way to a problem which lies outside our scope, the Ottonian reception of the Carolingian contribution to the afterlife of the Roman empire's eternal victory. A final avatar in the ancient ideology's transformation which emerges in the second half of the ninth century will serve as an excellent concluding point to this enquiry, for it announces an even more important development. New social and political trends triggered by a disintegrating Carolingian empire were destined to demonstrate once again the infinite flexibility of the ancient tradition of triumphal rulership. In this regard the Sacramentary of Arles (Paris, B.N. lat. 2812) which was probably copied at Lyons early in the ninth century is most telling. A Carolingian hand of the late ninth or early tenth century added a 'Missa pro persecutione paganorum' on a fly leaf. The prayers of this supplementary Mass are identical to those found in the Sacramentary of Angoulême's 'Mass for the King on the Day of Battle', with a slight but significant exception. In the service for victory over the pagans as it was heard in the cathedral of late Carolingian Arles, the officiant no longer prayed for the king's success. Instead he substituted the vaguer words 'thy servants'.[251] In the context in which it was performed, the prayer for 'thy servants' can only refer to the real rulers of Arles, the powerful bishop and the count or his representatives.[252] Some two centuries earlier, the services intended to secure the Byzantine emperor's

---

Geschichte der mittelalterlichen Staatssymbolik', *Historische Zeitschrift*, 172 (1951), 449–515; Deér, 'Vorrechte', passim, and P. Classen, '*Romanum gubernans imperium*', *Zum Kaisertum Karls des Grossen*, pp. 4–29.

[251] (*CLLA*, 744), f. 1verso: 'Sempiterna trinitas Deus . . . gratuletur hecclesia' (cf. *Sacr. Angoulême*, no. 2307); 'Omnipotens sempiterne deus nostras . . . ad propria remeare' (*ibid.*, no. 2308); 'Quos celesti, domine, dono saciasti . . . gratulari solacio' (cf. *ibid.*, no. 2310). For the evidence of the sacramentary's use at Arles, *Catalogue général des manuscrits latins* [de la Bibliothèque Nationale], 3 (Paris, 1952), 105.

[252] On the count's authority and its transformations at Arles in the ninth and tenth centuries, see J.R. Poly, *La Provence et la société féodale (879–1166). Contribution à l'étude des structures dites féodales dans le Midi* (Paris, 1976), pp. 40ff; cf. *ibid.*, p. 6, on the military activity of archbishop Rolland.

victory had been adopted and adapted to insure the military success of the Frankish kings. Now, as royal authority melted away in the upheavals of the ninth century, the local authorities of a moribund Carolingian empire quietly fashioned to their own use the Mass for royal victory and assumed the liturgical trappings of royal power. The poetry of ceremony mirrors the sacramentary's testimony on the devolution of the victory ideology. Sedulius Scottus, for example, turned his talents to a theme whose application would have been unthinkable in the world which produced the vocabulary and genre he manipulated: the victory of his bishop, Halitgar of Liège who, resplendent with the sword of salvation, crushed the rebel Viking and dampened the field with carnage.[253] To the powerful count of Friuli and 'victor inormis', Sedulius did not hesitate to apply the selfsame epithet he used for the sovereign: *doxa triumphalis*.[254] The liturgy, poetry and ceremonial of victory were now applied to the new territorial potentates destined to supplant Carolingian supremacy and set the tone for medieval civilization.

[253] *Carm.*, 2, 8, Traube, 176.15–16 and 177.21–32; cf. Düchting, *Sedulius Scottus*, pp. 53–4, with the suggestion that this piece was set to music.
[254] *Carm.*, 2, 39, Traube, 202.3–4; cf. 203.45–8; *Carm.*, 2, 67, Traube, 220–1, esp. 221.7–8. Cf. Düchting, *Sedulius Scottus*, pp. 132–4.

Epilogue

Though symbolism of state had clustered around the ruler's victory since the establishment of the Roman empire, the fourth century brought change and fresh vigor. For half a millennium thereafter, this symbolism contributed much to the conceptions and public manifestations of rulership among the empire's heirs in East and West. But because this enquiry moves within such broad geographic and chronological limits, its findings on rulership, government and society inevitably possess a provisional character.

Three main conclusions deserve mention right away. First, seizing the legacy of three hundred years of imperial victory ideology, the rulers of the Constantinian empire presided over a renaissance of triumphs and triumphal rulership. Its aftereffects reached far into the Middle Ages, both eastern and western. Not infrequently, the intensity of the celebration was inversely related to the significance of the victory. Threats from within and without provoked defiant assertions of imperial invincibility – sometimes forceful enough to skew contemporaries' perceptions of the situation's gravity. Official bluster and entrenched attitudes cushioned the realization that, in the West, the days of the Roman empire were numbered.

In part, the second conclusion is methodological. Despite a large measure of continuity from the fourth to the eleventh century, the shape of imperial victory celebrations changed incessantly: there was no such thing as a 'typical' Byzantine triumph ceremony. Assembled from a large repertory of symbolic gestures, each performance responded to the specific needs of the moment. Every description of a triumph opens a window on a scene of great freshness, and its surprising details are linked to its historical context, concrete and immediate, in late Roman and Byzantine civilization. Tracking various changes over the ceremony's long-term development has shown how ceremonies reflect larger trends in a society's development.

The third conclusion concerns the destiny of victory ideology in the western successor societies. Thanks no doubt to the lasting prestige and power of Constantinople, the collapse of imperial authority in the West had little effect on this destiny. When Germanic rulers celebrated victory, late Rome and Byzantium profoundly shaped the public manifestation of their kingship. To cite only two examples, the Visigothic triumph ceremony and Charlemagne's epithets 'victor ac triumphator' reveal how powerfully a specifically Roman tradition could appeal to the early medieval West.

The history of victory celebrations raises questions on certain broad developments in late antique and early medieval civiliz-ation. From the end of the fourth century, for example, the victory ceremony tended to shift from the streets into the circus. Though future research on the later Roman circus may further clarify this change, it is already evident that the new setting changed the emperor's role in the victory celebration. By appearing in the imperial loge and receiving the homage of the victorious general and defeated enemies, the supreme victor and triumphator remained the ceremony's focus and final cause. His position in the imperial box nevertheless removed him from the defilement of bloodshed and the potential responsibility for defeat. At a time when a professional army of mercenaries found less favor with a population burdened by heavy taxes and requisitions, the triumphant emperor in his loge kept a certain distance from the troops. Moreover, this form of celebration offered the general a measure of celebrity, even if – as the case of Belisarius shows – it could also underline the general's subordi-nation to the ultimate triumphator. In any event, by combining a political spectacle with a popular form of mass entertainment, the authorities of a declining empire guaranteed a sizable audience, if not full credence, for their message.

Although the more traditional form of victory celebration probably persisted alongside this new form of extravaganza, it attracted less attention. In the eighth century, however, as the army again paraded in the streets of Constantinople, the pendulum began to swing in the opposite direction. Circus celebrations still served as a setting for imperial triumphs into the eleventh century, but they were again paralleled and sometimes replaced by parades through the streets. Both forms of triumph might include a celebration – for example, a banquet or reception – intended for a more select body of participants. And both forms indicate that the emperor's subordinates gained a new centrality in the ceremonies: from the eighth century to the eleventh, victorious generals frequently played the leading role. In medieval Constantinople, that is, commanders commonly infringed on the imperial monopoly of victory. As these subordinates often succeeded in dominating one of Byzantium's great political ceremonies, one should reconsider the usual assumption that the Byzantine monarchy preserved the absolute character of the later Roman state. When the emperor celebrated a triumph over a rebellious aristocrat, he increasingly relied more on symbolic punishment than on real penalties, apart from confiscation. If the middle Byzantine monarchy's growing tolerance of aristocratic dissidence seems to differ from late Roman practice, it does resemble royal attitudes in the medieval West, where a great lord often treated with his rebellious magnates, fined them, and restored them to his favor.

Here we confront another methodological – or even epistemological – problem. The sources' vision of victory celebrations and, to some extent, the staged events themselves, gradually shifted their focus from the masses to an elite. In the fourth, fifth and sixth centuries the emperors conveyed their message of victory primarily to the urban audience of the streets and circus, whereas later emperors like Theophilus or Basil I began their celebration with the empire's elite and concluded it with a banquet for the bureaucracy. Certainly, late Roman emperors did not spurn their senators, bureaucrats and bishops. But their emphasis on the circus suggests that, in those centuries, the public display of rulership was geared to the crowd. In short, late Roman rulership looks mass-oriented, whereas that of the early Middle Ages, and not only in Byzantium, looks more to the elite, through whom the ruler hoped – indeed was forced – to govern.

The imperial provinces played two roles in the destiny of triumphal rulership: one within the empire, one beyond its borders. In the empire's internal development, their significance appears to have changed over the centuries. The provincial towns of late antiquity witnessed local victory celebrations. These provincial festivals were intended to spread news of imperial success, display loyalty to a triumphant emperor or honor a victorious regional commander. But from the eighth century to the eleventh, when Basil II celebrated his victory over the Bulgars in Athens as well as Constantinople, little is heard from the provinces. An obvious conclusion suggests that the economic and social vitality of provincial life sagged during these centuries. But perhaps this is too simple. It is scarcely coincidental that, during this period, Byzantine generals enjoyed great triumphal honors in the capital. The provinces also reinforce evidence from the capital that the most prevalent and potent form of *imitatio imperii* occurred not outside the imperial frontiers, but within them, as imperial officers looked up the hierarchical ladder and tried to pattern their own ritual deportment after what they saw at the top.

The twin pillars of imperial power in the provinces, the army and the church, relayed the message of imperial victory. But they also served as forces for innovation in imperial victory celebrations. Military ceremonial apparently influenced the rite of presenting captive enemy leaders to the victorious emperor. It might be suspected as well behind the grim rituals involving the heads of vanquished rebels, for similar displays can be traced back to Julius Caesar's time, when they were used for mutineers.[1] Victory celebrations also tapped the Christian thought world and its public expression in the liturgy. The first clear conjunction of Christian celebration and imperial victory appears late in the fourth century. And, although a symbolic gesture like the *calcatio colli* had a long history in classical civilization, the sound of Psalm 90 reverberating around Justinian II, Leontius and Apsimar shows Christianity could reinforce an ancient tradition. But the actual integration of liturgical practices into imperial victory parades – or at least, those which derived from the ancient Roman triumph – is first attested only in Heraclius' reign. Before that,

---

[1] T. Mommsen, *Römisches Strafrecht* (Leipzig, 1899), p. 913.

specifically Christian practices tended to remain distinct from secular observances. Even Justinian's visit to Theodora's tomb in the Holy Apostles' during the triumph of 559 is as much an ostentatious act of personal devotion as a public synthesis of Christian worship and ancient ceremony. In other words, although we can trace the first steps in the christianization of imperial victory rituals back to the fourth century, the shift was protracted through three centuries.

When victorious Burgundian or Lombard troops raised a toppled ruler's head on a lance, they paid homage to the victory customs of the late Roman army. When Visigothic or Frankish bishops organized large-scale supplications for their kings' military success, they marched in the footsteps of the imperial church. At other times, the channels are less distinct, but the imperial model's influence remains unmistakable. Temporally, the contribution of contemporary imperial victory conceptions and practices to the West's nascent monarchies clustered in the fifth through the seventh centuries. Precisely in this era the new societies established monarchies and made their first efforts at state building. Both the empire's power and its hold on the minds of these kings and their Roman subjects were greatest in this period. It was also, roughly speaking, the era during which Constantinople could still realistically claim more than simple leadership as a regional power. All the Mediterranean kingdoms, even those about which the least is known, adopted and adapted imperial victory customs and concepts. There can be little doubt that the central role of victory in the imperial idea and the many forms it took helped fashion the image of rulership in the new societies. But this imitation of empire raises in turn further questions: its causes and its nature.

In the Albertini Tablets, the Pomptine Marsh inscriptions and royal panegyrics, we see Roman subjects taking the initiative and applying to their Germanic kings the imperial trappings of victory. Much like the development of the imperial cult under the principate, this 'imperialization' of the Germanic kings came, at least in part, from below. With this adoption of imperial victory ideology, the Roman population itself integrated its foreign kings into the prestigious traditions of the past and voiced its newfound loyalties. Theoderic's medallion, Huniric's arenga or Clovis' parade at Tours show the other side of the coin. The same process moved in the opposite direction, for by manipulating traditional forms and presenting himself as one of 'them', the ruler created a favorable climate for consensus between Germanic ruler and Roman ruled.

But the bolstering of royal prestige required more than simply winning over the Roman population, for the turbulent careers of early Germanic rulers show the weakness of kingship among the newcomers to Mediterranean civilization. The Agilulf visor or Argimund's parade of infamy at Toledo offer the same lesson: by exploiting the trappings of imperial victory, the new rulers burnished their prestige and power in the eyes of their Germanic followers as well as their Roman subjects. Hence the paradox that imperial power enjoyed high esteem among those credited with its destruction. Though the crises of the late sixth and seventh centuries shook royal and imperial authority alike, the imperial ritual model continued to celebrate the defeats of usurpers and regicides. When legitimacy was in question, Byzantium provided reassurance.

This was nowhere truer than in Visigothic Spain. There, an ambitious monarchy and a powerful aristocracy shared a deep, if implicit, appreciation for the civilization and political institutions of Constantinople. At the same time, the competition between monarchy and aristocracy fostered the royal imitation of Byzantium.

Only in its early phase did the kingdom of the Franks adhere to the pattern of the other *regna*. The written sources suggest that royal appropriation of imperial ceremonial forms peaked in the sixth and early seventh centuries. After the initial decades of the seventh century, the paucity of evidence on royal victory celebration – apart from the ambiguous testimony of some later liturgical manuscripts – severely hinders judgement on subsequent borrowings from the imperial model.[2] When the clouds lift under the first Carolingian kings, we find a court which, if surprisingly 'oriental' in some aspects of its life-style, relied

---

[2] Krüger, *Königsgrabkirchen*, pp. 481ff thinks he detects a diminishing Merovingian fascination with Constantinople in the course of the seventh century. But Vierck, 'Chelles', points in the opposite direction; the jury is still out.

nonetheless on the local traditions of Frankish Gaul, augmented by borrowings from Byzantine Italy. Eighth-century Franks rarely looked to contemporary Constantinople for the symbolic forms of their public life. Their debts to the imperial tradition differed from those of the first kingdoms. In their coins, seals and titles, the early Carolingians commonly turned away from eighth-century Constantinople and toward a more distant imperial past.[3] In part, Italian influence on Francia explains this. And in part, the aura of Byzantine power was still tarnished in precisely those decades when Frankish dominion reached its apogee. Eighth-century Franks found in the fourth and fifth centuries the new model of rulership which they sought. Only in the course of the ninth century did a resurgent Byzantium begin to change that. It is no accident that the first Carolingian to don Byzantine imperial robes in Francia did so during the successful reign of Basil I. Franks and Visigoths differed markedly in their receptivity to Byzantine state symbolism and correspondingly in their broader cultural orientation. Note for example that in Spain some Goths took Roman or even distinctly Byzantine names, while Romans tended to maintain their traditional ones. In Francia, the opposite tendency prevailed and Germanic names gained a clear upper hand.[4] At any rate, Carolingian appropriation or renewal reflected new developments in Frankish society and military institutions. So much so, in fact, that customs like special propitiatory services for royal victory took on a life of their own and were in turn usurped by the territorial powers that emerged out of a collapsing Carolingian empire.

Between the sixth and the ninth centuries, two parallel developments in East and West have contradictory implications worthy of note. In the liturgy of victory, the transformation of Roman liturgical texts makes explicit what was implied when western armies and churches developed special war supplications. Here, the imperial church led the way and furnished western rulers with a tool for state building. The final appraisal of this connection must await a thorough philological and liturgical analysis of the Latin texts. Once the approximate date and circumstances of

[3] Classen, '*Romanum gubernans Imperium*', p. 23.
[4] See now H. Ebling, J. Jarnut and G. Kampers, 'Nomen et gens', *Francia*, 8 (1980), 687–745.

origin emerge and the corresponding evidence for the orthodox liturgical tradition has been assembled and evaluated, a comparison may be attempted. Nonetheless, some parts of the story seem evident: Leo the Deacon's tenth-century account of Tzimisces' departure service strikingly resembles the seventh-century *profectio bellica* of Visigothic kings, whose royal ceremonial owed so much to Constantinople. In general the barbarian kingdoms of the seventh century may preserve distant echoes of developments in Byzantium which, because so few Byzantine sources survive from this period, are attested at home only later.[5] This may be another instance.

Imitatio imperii, does not, however, explain all parallels. From the seventh century, both Germanic and Byzantine rulers increasingly sought to impress their power and majesty on their aristocrats, rather than on their more humble subjects. Here, Mediterranean-wide transformations constitute rather than explain the link. Differently stated, parallel developments in sibling societies may trigger parallel consequences.

These similarities correspond to certain continuities. For all their differences, some aspects of tenth- and eleventh-century Byzantine ceremonial remain true to the letter, if not the spirit, of the late Roman model. No doubt, the imperial government's tradition and routines show much continuity. Still, for its own political, social and cultural aims, the Byzantine ruling class stridently asserted that continuity and thereby magnified and distorted it.[6] Though western rulers borrowed from this tradition, prior to 800, none claimed to incarnate it as Constantinople did.

In both East and West, victory seemed the prerogative of a particular people. Yet, western notions of victory's ethnicity diverged from eastern ones. Granted, the late Romans perceived themselves as a society which uniquely enjoyed victory, and Byzantine acclamations echoed that conception. But the various Germanic peoples stressed more vigorously the ethnic monopoly

---

[5] First noted by R.S. Lopez, 'Byzantine law and its reception by the Germans and the Arabs', *Byz.*, 16 (1942–3), 445–61, in connection with customary law in Byzantium.

[6] H. Ahrweiler, *L'idéologie politique de l'Empire byzantin* (Paris, 1975), pp. 48–50. Cf. patriarch Nicholas I's reproach to Symeon of Bulgaria, for writing abusively 'to those who are by divine sanction entrusted with the only empire which God has fixed indissoluble on earth', *Ep.* 25, ed. and tr. R.J.H. Jenkins and L.G. Westerink, *CFHB*, 6 (Washington, D.C., 1973).178.105–7; cf. 178.97–100.

on victory. Lombards, Goths and Franks all celebrated victory as a special privilege of their own ethnos. One can neither disprove nor demonstrate that these claims grew out of ancient Germanic conceptions. But even when – witness an Isidore of Seville – the new peoples' Latin historiographers boasted the ethnicity of victory, they had once again reacted to the enduring myth of the Roman empire's eternal victory.

Bibliography of cited primary sources

Abbo of Paris, *Bella Parisiacę urbis*, ed. H. Waquet, Classiques de l'histoire de France au moyen âge, 20 (Paris, 1942).

Adventius of Metz, *Epistolae*, ed. E. Dümmler, *MGH.Epist.*, 6 (1925) and D. Misonne, *Revue bénédictine*, 92 (1983), 71–9.

Agathias, *Historiarum libri v*, ed. R. Keydell, *CFHB*, 2 (Berlin, 1967).

Agnellus, *Liber pontificalis ecclesiae Ravennatis*, ed. A. Testi Rasponi, *Rerum italicarum scriptores*, 2.3 (Bologna, 1924) and O. Holder-Egger, *MGH.SRL* (1878).

Agobard of Lyons, *Epistolae*, ed. E. Dümmler, *MGH.Epist.*, 5 (1899).

Aistulf, *Leges*, ed. F. Bluhme, *MGH.Leges*, 4 (1868).

Album municipal de Timgad, ed. A. Chastagnol, Antiquitas, 3, 22 (Bonn, 1972).

Alcuin, *Carmina*, ed. E. Dümmler, *MGH.Poet.*, 1 (1881).
 Epistolae, ed. E. Dümmler, *MGH.Epist.*, 4 (1895).

Ambrose of Milan, *Oratio de obitu Theodosii*, ed. O. Faller, *CSEL*, 73 (1955).
 Epistolae, *PL*, 16.
 Expositio euangelii secundum Lucam, ed. M. Adriaen, *CCL*, 14 (1957).

Ammianus Marcellinus, *Res gestae*, ed. C.U. Clark (Berlin, 1910–15).

Anastasius Bibliothecarius, *Theophanis Chronographiae versio latina*, see Theophanes, *Chronographia*.

Andrieu, M. (ed.), *Les 'Ordines Romani' du haut moyen âge*, Spicilegium sacrum Lovaniense, Études et documents, 11, 23–4, 28–9 (Louvain, 1931–61).

Annales Bertiniani, ed. F. Grat, J. Vielliard and S. Clémencet, Société de l'histoire de France, 470 (Paris, 1964).

Annales Fuldenses, ed. F. Kurze, *MGH.SRG*, (1891).

Annales Maximiani, ed. G. Waitz, *MGH.SS*, 13 (1881).

Annales Mettenses priores, ed. B. von Simson, *MGH.SRG*, (1905).

Annales qui dicuntur Einhardi, ed. F. Kurze, *MGH.SRG*, (1895).

Annales Ravennates, ed. B. Bischoff, in B. Bischoff and W. Köhler, *Medieval Studies in Memory of A. Kingsley Porter*, 1 (Cambridge, Mass., 1939), 125–38.

Annales regni Francorum, ed. F. Kurze, *MGH.SRG* (1895).

Annales Xantenses, ed. B. von Simson, *MGH.SRG* (1909).

Anonymous Ravennate, *Cosmographia*, ed. J. Schnetz, *Itineraria romana*, 2 (Leipzig, 1940).

Anonymus Byzantinus, Περὶ στρατηγικῆς, ed. H. Köchly and W. Rüstow, *Griechische Kriegsschriftsteller*, 2 (Leipzig, 1855).

Anthologia graeca, ed. P. Waltz et al. (Paris, 1928–).

Anthologia latina, ed. F. Bücheler and A. Riese, 1.1 (Leipzig, 1894).

Antifonario visigótico mozárabe de la catedral de León, ed. L. Brou and J. Vives, Monumenta Hispaniae sacra, ser. lit., 5 (Barcelona, 1959).

Arethas, *Opera minora*, ed. L.G. Westerink (Leipzig, 1968–72).

Arnulf I, *Diplomata*, ed. P. Kehr, *MGH.Dipl. stir. Kar.*, 3 (1940).

Asterius of Amasea, *Homiliae*, ed. C. Datema (Leyden, 1970).

'Astronomer', *Vita Hludowici imperatoris*, ed. G.H. Pertz, *MGH.SS*, 2 (1829).

Athanasius of Alexandria, *Historia Arianorum*, ed. H.G. Opitz, *Athanasius Werke*, 2.1 (Berlin, 1935–41).

Michael Attaleiates, *Historia*, ed. I. Bekker (Bonn, 1853).

Auctarium [Isidorianum] a. 624, ed. T. Mommsen, *MGH.AA*, 11 (1894).

Augustine, *De ciuitate dei*, ed. B. Dombart and A. Kalb, *CCL*, 47–8 (1955).

Avitus of Vienne, *Opera*, ed. R. Peiper, *MGH.AA*, 6.2 (1883).

Baudonivia, *Vita Radegundis* (*BHL*, 7049), ed. B. Krusch, *MGH.SRM*, 2 (1888).

Benedictio in profectione bellica, ed. A. Staerk, *Les manuscrits latins du Ve au XIIIe siècle conservés à la Bibliothèque impériale de Saint Pétersbourg*, 1 (St Petersburg, 1910), 169.

Beowulf, ed. C.L. Wrenn, 3rd edn (London, 1958).

Bobbio Missal, ed. E.A. Lowe, Henry Bradshaw Society, 61 (London, 1924).

Boethius, *Philosophiae consolatio*, ed. L. Bieler, *CCL*, 94 (1957).

Boniface, *Epistolae*, ed. M. Tangl, *MGH.Epistolae selectae* (reprint, 1955).

Brightman, F.E. (ed.), *Liturgies Eastern and Western* (Oxford, 1896).

Caesarius of Arles, *Sermones*, ed. G. Morin, *CCL*, 103–4 (1953).

Calendar of Lorsch, ed. J.E. Gugumus, *Jahrbuch für das Bistum Mainz*, 8 (1960), 286–321.

Candidus, *Vita metrica Aegilii* (*BHL*, 2441), ed. E. Dümmler, *MGH.Poet.*, 2 (1884).

Capitulare euangeliorum Vat. Pal. lat. 46, ed. T. Klauser, *Gesammelte*

Arbeiten zur Liturgiegeschichte, Kirchengeschichte und christlichen Archäologie, JAC, Ergänzungsband, 3 (Münster, 1974).

Capitulare euangeliorum, ed. T. Klauser, Liturgiewissenschaftliche Quellen und Forschungen, 28, 2nd edn (Münster, 1972).

Carloman, *Diplomata*, ed. P. Kehr, *MGH.Dipl. stir. Kar.*, 1 (1934).

Carmen de Pippini regis uictoria auarica, ed. O. Holder-Egger and G. Waitz, see Einhard, *Vita Karoli*.

Cassiodorus, *Chronicon*, ed. T. Mommsen, *MGH.AA*, 11 (1894).

Orationum reliquiae, ed. L. Traube, *MGH.AA*, 12 (1894).

Variae, ed. Å. Fridh, *CCL*, 96 (1973).

Cathwulf, *Epistola ad Karolum*, ed. E. Dümmler, *MGH.Epist.*, 4 (1895).

Cecaumenus, *Strategicon*, ed. G.G. Litavrin (Moscow, 1972).

Cedrenus, *Synopsis historiarum*, ed. I. Bekker (Bonn, 1838–9).

Charlemagne, *Diuisio regni*, ed. A. Boretius, *MGH.Capit.*, 1 (1883).

Epistola ad Fastradam, ed. E. Dümmler, *MGH.Epist.*, 4 (1895).

Charles the Bald, *Diplomata*, ed. A. Giry, M. Prou and G. Tessier (Paris, 1943–63).

Nicetas Choniates, *Historia*, ed. J.A. van Dieten, *CFHB*, 11.1 (Berlin, 1975).

Chronica Gallica a. 452, ed. T. Mommsen, *MGH.AA*, 9 (1892).

Chronica minora byzantina, ed. P. Schreiner, *CFHB*, 12 (Berlin, 1975–9).

Chronicon Laurissense breue, ed. H. Schnorr von Carolsfeld, *Neues Archiv*, 36 (1911), 15–39.

Chronicon Moissacense, ed. G.H. Pertz, *MGH.SS*, 1 (1826).

Chronicon paschale, ed. L. Dindorf (Bonn, 1832).

Chronicorum caesaraugustanorum reliquiae, ed. T. Mommsen, *MGH.AA*, 11 (1894).

Chronographus a. 354, ed. T. Mommsen, *MGH.AA*, 9 (1892), and A. Degrassi, *Inscriptiones Italiae*, 13.2 (1963).

Claudian, *Carmina*, ed. T. Birt, *MGH.AA*, 10 (1892).

Codex Carolinus, ed. W. Gundlach, *MGH.Epist.*, 3 (1892).

Codex Euricianus, ed. K. Zeumer, *MGH.Leges Visigothorum* (1902).

Codex Theodosianus, ed. T. Mommsen and P. Krüger (Berlin, 1905).

Collectio auellana, ed. O. Günther, *CSEL*, 35 (1895–8).

Collectio Marculfi, ed. K. Zeumer, *MGH.Formulae* (1882).

Concilia Galliae, ed. C. De Clercq, *CCL*, 148–148A (1963).

Concilia visigothica, ed. J. Vives et al., España cristiana, Textos, 1 (Barcelona, 1963).

Concilium in Trullo, ed. P.P. Joannou, *Discipline générale antique*, 1.1 (Grottaferrata, 1962).

Concilium Nicaenum II, ed. J.D. Mansi, *Sacrorum conciliorum noua et amplissima collectio*, 12–13 (Florence, 1766–7).

Concilium Serdicense, ed. C.H. Turner, *Ecclesiae occidentalis monumenta iuris antiquissima*, 1.2.3 (Oxford, 1930).

Constantine VII Porphyrogenitus, *Contio ad duces exercitus orientalis*, ed. R. Vári, *BZ*, 17 (1908), 75–85.

   De administrando imperio, ed. and tr. G. Moravcsik and R.J.H. Jenkins, Dumbarton Oaks Texts, 1, 2nd edn (Washington, D.C., 1967).

   De ceremoniis aulae byzantinae, ed. J.J. Reiske (Bonn, 1829), and A. Vogt (Paris, 1935–9).

   De thematibus, ed. A. Pertusi, Studi e testi, 160 (Vatican City, 1952).

   On Imperial Expeditions (Περὶ βασιλικῶν ταξειδίων), ed. J.J. Reiske, see *De ceremoniis*.

Constantius II, *Epistola ad senatum*, see Themistius.

Consularia Constantinopolitana, ed. T. Mommsen, *MGH.AA*, 9 (1892).

Continuatio Isidori hispana, ed. T. Mommsen, *MGH.AA*, 11 (1894).

Corippus, *In laudem Iustini augusti minoris*, ed. and tr. Av. Cameron (London, 1976).

   Iohannidos libri viii, ed. J. Diggle and F.R.D. Goodyear (Cambridge, 1970).

Corpus iuris ciuilis, ed. P. Krüger and R. Schöll (Berlin, 1928–9).

Cyprian, Firminus, Viventius, Messianus and Stephen, *Vita Caesarii Arelatensis* (*BHL*, 1508–9), ed. G. Morin, *S. Caesarii episcopi Arelatensis opera omnia*, 2 (Maredsous, 1942).

Cyril of Alexandria, *Epistolae*, ed. E. Schwartz, *ACO*, 1.1.1 (1927).

Cyril Scythopolitanus, *Vita Sabae* (*BHG*, 1608), ed. E. Schwartz, Texte und Untersuchungen, 49.2 (Leipzig, 1939).

Darrouzès, J. (ed.), *Épistoliers byzantins du Xe siècle*, Archives de l'Orient chrétien, 6 (Paris, 1960).

De rebus bellicis, ed. R. Ireland, B.A.R. International series, 63 (Oxford, 1979).

Desiderius of Cahors, *Epistolae*, ed. D. Norberg, Studia latina Stockholmensia, 6 (Stockholm, 1961).

Dio Cassius, *Historiae Romanae*, ed. U.P. Boissevain (Berlin, 1895–1931).

Dioscorus of Aphrodito, *Carmina*, ed. E. Heitsch, *Die griechischen Dichterfragmente der römischen Kaiserzeit*, 1 (Göttingen, 1961).

Dold, A. and Baumstark, A., *Das Palimpsestsakramentar im Cod. Aug. CXII*, Texte und Arbeiten, 1, 12 (Beuron, 1925).

Dracontius, *Satisfactio*, ed. F. Vollmer, *MGH.AA*, 14 (1905).

XII panegyrici latini, ed. R.A.B. Mynors (Oxford, 1964).

Eddius Stephanus, *Vita Wilifredi* (*BHL*, 8889), ed. W. Levison, *MGH.SRM*, 6 (1913).

Einhard, *Translatio Ss. Marcellini et Petri* (*BHL*, 5233), ed. G. Waitz,

MGH.SS, 15.1 (1887).

Vita Karoli magni, ed. O. Holder-Egger and G. Waitz, *MGH.SRG*, 6th edn (1911).

Ennodius of Pavia, *Opera*, ed. F. Vogel, *MGH.AA*, 17 (1885).

Epistolae austrasicae, ed. W. Gundlach, *MGH.Epist.*, 3 (1892).

Epistolae Theodericianae uariae, ed. T. Mommsen, *MGH.AA*, 12 (1894).

Epistolae uariorum [*aeui Carolini*], ed. E. Dümmler, *MGH.Epist.*, 4 (1895).

Epistolae wisigothicae, ed. J. Gil, *Miscellanea wisigotica*, Anales de la Universidad hispalense, Filosofía y letras, 15 (Seville, 1972).

Epitome de Caesaribus, ed. F. Pichlmayr and R. Gründel (Leipzig, 1966).

Erchempert of Monte Cassino, *Historia Langobardorum Beneventanorum*, ed. G. Waitz, *MGH.SRL* (1878).

Ermoldus Nigellus, *Carmina*, ed. E. Faral, Classiques de l'histoire de France au moyen âge, 14 (Paris, 1932).

Εὐχολόγιον τὸ μέγα περιέχον τὰς τῶν ἑπτὰ μυστηρίων ἀκολουθίας, ed. Sp. Zervos, 5th edn (Venice, 1885).

Eugenius of Toledo, *Libellus carminum*, ed. F. Vollmer, *MGH.AA*, 14 (1905).

Eunapius, *De sententiis*, see *Excerpta historica*.

Eusebius of Caesarea, *Vita Constantini* (*BHG*, 361x), ed. F. Winkelmann, GCS [57] (Berlin, 1975).

   Historia ecclesiastica, ed. E. Schwartz, GCS, 9 (Leipzig, 1903–9).

Eusebius 'Gallicanus', *Collectio homiliarum*, ed. F. Glorie, *CCL*, 101–101B (1970–1).

Eustratius, *Vita Eutychii* (*BHG*, 657), PG, 86.

Eutropius, *Breuiarium*, ed. H. Droysen, *MGH.AA*, 2 (1879).

Evagrius, *Historia ecclesiastica*, ed. J. Bidez and L. Parmentier (London, 1898).

Excerpta historica iussu imp. Constantini Porphyrogeniti confecta, ed. U.P. Boissevain, C. De Boor and T. Büttner-Wobst (Leipzig, 1903–10).

Excerpta Valesiana, ed. J. Moreau and V. Velkov, 2nd edn, (Leipzig, 1968).

Felix, *Vita Iuliani Toletensis* (*BHL*, 4554). *PL*, 96.

Ferrandus of Carthage, *Vita Fulgentii* (*BHL*, 3208), ed. G. Lapeyre (Paris, 1929).

Fiebiger, O. and Schmidt, L., *Inschriftensammlung zur Geschichte der Ostgermanen*, Kaiserliche Akademie der Wissenschaften, Wien, Phil.-hist. Kl., Denkschriften 60.3, 70.3, 72.2 (Vienna, 1917–44).

Florentinus, see *Anthologia latina*.

Formulae Merkelianae salicae, ed. K. Zeumer, *MGH.Form.* (1882).

Fredegar, *Chronicae*, ed. B. Krusch, *MGH.SRM*, 2 (1888).

Fulgentius of Ruspe, *Ad Trasamundum regem*, ed. J. Fraipont, *CCL*, 91 (1961).

Gamber, K. (ed.), 'Ein oberitalienisches Sakramentarfragment des M–Typus', *Sacris erudiri*, 13 (1962), 367–76.

Gelasius, *Historia ecclesiastica*, ed. G. Loeschke and M. Heinemann, GCS, 28 (Leipzig, 1918).

'Genesius', *Regum libri IV*, ed. A. Lesmüller-Werner and I. Thurn, *CFHB*, 14 (Berlin, 1978).

Gennadius, *De uiris inlustribus*, ed. E.C. Richardson, Texte und Untersuchungen, 14.1 (Leipzig, 1896).

George, *Vita Theodori Syceotae* (*BHG*, 1748), ed. A.-J. Festugière, Subsidia hagiographica, 48 (Brussels, 1970).

George the Monk, *Chronicon*, ed. C. De Boor (Leipzig, 1904).

Georgius Continuatus, [Redaction A], ed. I. Bekker (Bonn, 1838) and E. Muralt (St Petersburg, 1859); [Redaction B], ed. V.M. Istrin, *Khronika Georgiya amartola v drevnem slavyanorusskom perevode*, 2 (Petrograd, 1922).

George Pisides, *Carmina*, ed. A. Pertusi, Studia patristica et byzantina, 7 (Ettal, 1959).

Gerontius, *Vita Melaniae iunioris* (*BHG*, 1241), ed. D. Gorce, SC, 90 (Paris, 1962) and (*BHL*, 5885), ed. M. Rampolla del Tindaro (Rome, 1905).

Gesta episcoporum Neapolitanorum, ed. G. Waitz, *MGH.SRL*, (1878).

Michael Glycas, *Annales*, ed. I. Bekker (Bonn, 1836).

Goar, J. (ed.), *Euchologion, sive rituale Graecorum*, 2nd edn (Venice, 1730).

Gregory I, *Dialogi*, ed. A. de Vogüé, SC, 251, 260, 265 (Paris, 1978–80).

    Registrum, ed. P. Ewald and L.M. Hartmann, *MGH.Epist.*, 1 (1887), and D. Norberg, *CCL*, 140–140A (1982).

Gregory, *Vita Basilii iunioris* (*BHG*, 263), *AASS*, Mart. 3 (1865).

Gregory Abū'l Faraj (Bar Hebraeus), *Chronography*, tr. E.A. Wallis Budge (Oxford, 1932).

Gregory of Nyssa, *Contra Eunomium*, ed. W. Jaeger, *Opera*, 1, 2nd edn (Leyden, 1960).

Gregory of Tours, *Historiarum libri X*, ed. B. Krusch and W. Levison, *MGH.SRM*, 1.1 (1951).

    In gloria martyrum, ed. B. Krusch, *MGH.SRM*, 1.2 (1885).

    Liber uitae patrum, ed. W. Arndt and B. Krusch, *MGH.SRM*, 1.2 (1885).

Harun Ibn Yahya, tr. A.A. Vasiliev, *Seminarium kondakovianum*, 5 (1932), 149–63.

Heiric of Auxerre, *Carmina*, ed. L. Traube, *MGH.Poet.*, 3 (1896).

Herodian, *Historiae*, ed. C.R. Whittaker (Cambridge, Mass., 1969–70).

Hibernicus Exul, *Carmina*, ed. E. Dümmler, *MGH.Poet.*, 1 (1881).

Hincmar of Reims, *De ordine palatii*, ed. T. Gross and R. Schieffer, *MGH. Fontes iuris germanici antiqui in usum scholarum*, 3 (1980).

Hydatius, *Chronicon*, ed. A. Tranoy, SC, 218–19 (Paris, 1974).

Hymnus in natalitio regis, ed. C. Blume, *Analecta hymnica medii aevi*, 27 (1897).

Ignatius, *Vita Nicephori patriarchae* (*BHG*, 1335), ed. C. De Boor, *Nicephori... opuscula historica* (Leipzig, 1880).

Inuentio et depositio uestis B.V.M. in Blachernis (*BHG*, 1058), ed. C. Loparev, *VV*, 2 (1895), 581–628.

Isidore of Seville, *Etymologiae*, ed. W.M. Lindsay (Oxford, 1911).
  Historia Gothorum, Wandalorum, Sueborum, ed. C. Rodríguez Alonso, Fuentes y estudios de historia leonesa, 13 (Leon, 1975).
  Laus Spaniae, ibid.

Januarius Nepotianus, *Epitome Valerii Maximi*, ed. C. Kempf (Leipzig, 1888).

Jerome, *Chronicon*, ed. R. Helm, GCS, 47, 2nd edn (Berlin, 1956).
  Epistolae, ed. I. Hilberg, *CSEL*, 54–6 (1910–18).

John VIII, *Epistolae*, ed. E. Caspar, *MGH.Epist.*, 7 (1928).

John of Antioch, *De insidiis*, see *Excerpta historica*.

John of Biclar, *Chronicon*, ed. J. Campos (Madrid, 1960) and T. Mommsen, *MGH.AA.*, 11 (1894).

John Chrysostom, *Expositiones in Psalmos*, PG, 55.
  Homiliae in Kalendas, PG, 48.
  Homiliae in Matthaeum, PG, 57.
  Homiliae in statuas, PG, 49.

Ps. Chrysostom, *Comparatio regis et monachi* (*CPG*, 4500), PG, 47.

John of Ephesus, *Historia ecclesiastica*, tr. E.W. Brooks, *Corpus scriptorum christianorum orientalium, Scriptores Syri*, series 3, 3 (Louvain, 1936).

John Lydus, *De magistratibus populi Romani*, ed. R. Wünsch (Leipzig, 1903).

John Malalas, *Chronographia*, ed. L. Dindorf (Bonn, 1831), and the Slavonic version, tr. M. Spinka and G. Downey (Chicago, 1940).

John of Nikiu, *Chronicle*, tr. R.H. Charles (London, 1916).

John Scot Eriugena, *Carmina*, ed. L. Traube, *MGH.Poet.*, 3 (1896).

John of Thessalonica, *Miracula S. Demetrii* (*BHG*, 499–516), ed. P. Lemerle (Paris, 1979).

Jonas, *Vita Columbani* (*BHL*, 1893), ed. B. Krusch, *MGH.SRG*, (1905).

Jordanes, *De summa temporum uel origine actibusque gentis Romanorum*, ed. T. Mommsen, *MGH.AA*, 5.1 (Berlin, 1882).
  Getica, ibid.

Flavius Josephus, *De bello Iudaico*, ed. B. Niese and J. von Destinon, *Opera* (Berlin, 1887–94).

Joshua Stylite, *Chronicle*, tr. W. Wright (Cambridge, 1882).

Julian the Apostate, *Opera*, ed. J. Bidez (Paris, 1932–60).

Julian of Toledo, *De comprobatione sextae aetatis*, ed. J.N. Hillgarth, *CCL*, 115 (1976).

   Historia Wambae regis, Insultatio uilis prouinciae and *Iudicium*, ed. W. Levison, *MGH.SRM*, 5 (1910).

Julius 'Paris', *Epitome Valerii Maximi*, ed. C. Kempf (Leipzig, 1888).

Karolus magnus et Leo papa, ed. E. Dümmler, *MGH.Poet.*, 1 (1881), or H. Beumann, F. Brunhölzl et al., Studien und Quellen zur westfälischen Geschichte, 8 (Paderborn, 1966).

Lactantius, *De mortibus persecutorum*, ed. J. Moreau, SC, 39 (Paris, 1954).

Lauer, P. and Samaran, C. (eds.), *Les diplômes originaux des Mérovingiens* (Paris, 1908).

Laurent, V., *Le Corpus des sceaux de l'empire byzantin* (Paris, 1963–81).

Leo I, *Sermones*, ed. A. Chavasse, *CCL*, 138–138A (1973).

Leo III, *Epistolae*, ed. K. Hampe, *MGH.Epist.*, 5 (1899).

Leo IV, *Epistolae*, ed. A. von Hirsch-Gereuth, *MGH.Epist.*, 5 (1899).

Leo III the 'Isaurian', *Ecloga*, ed. L. Burgmann, Forschungen zur byzantinischen Rechtsgeschichte, 10 (Frankfurt, 1983).

Leo VI, *Book of the Eparch*, ed. J. Nicole, reprint I. Dujčev, Τὸ ἐπαρχικὸν βιβλίον (London, 1976).

   Oratio funebris de patre, ed. A. Vogt and I. Hausherr, *Orientalia christiana*, 26 (1932), 5–79.

   Tactica, ed. R. Vári (Budapest, 1917–22), and *PG*, 107.

Leo Deacon, *Historiae*, ed. C.B. Hase (Bonn, 1828).

Leo Syncellus of Synades, see J. Darrouzès.

Leofric Missal, ed. F.E. Warren (Oxford, 1883).

Leontius, *Vita Ioannis Eleemosynarii* (*BHG*, 886) ed. H. Gelzer (Freiburg, 1893).

Lex salica. 100 Titel-Text, ed. K.A. Eckhardt (Weimar, 1953).

Lex Visigothorum, ed. K. Zeumer, *MGH. Leges Visigothorum* (1902).

Libanius, *Opera*, ed. R. Foerster (Leipzig, 1903–27).

Liber commicus, ed. F.J. Perez de Urgel and A. González y Ruiz Zorilla, 2, Monumenta Hispaniae liturgica, 3 (Madrid, 1950).

Liber diurnus, ed. H. Foerster (Bern, 1958).

Liber historiae Francorum, ed. B. Krusch, *MGH.SRM*, 2 (1888).

Liber ordinum, ed. M. Férotin, Monumenta ecclesiae liturgica, 5 (Paris, 1904).

Liber pontificalis, ed. T. Mommsen, *MGH.Gesta pontificum Romanorum* (1898), and L. Duchesne (Paris, 1886–92).

Liber sacramentorum Romanae aecclesiae ordinis anni circuli, ed. L.C. Mohlberg et al., Rerum ecclesiasticarum documenta, series maior, fontes 4 (Rome, 1960).

Liutprand of Cremona, *Opera*, ed. J. Becker, *MGH.SRG*, (1915).

Lothar I, *Diplomata*, ed. T. Schieffer, *MGH.Diplomata Karolinorum*, 3 (1968).

Ludwigslied, ed. E. von Steinmeyer, *Die kleineren althochdeutschen Sprachdenkmäler* (Berlin, 1916).

Lupus Protospatharius, *Annales*, ed. G.H. Pertz, *MGH.SS*, 5 (1844).

Macrobius, *Commentarii in Somnium Scipionis*, ed. I. Willis, *Opera*, 2 (Leipzig, 1970).

Marcellinus Comes, *Chronicon*, ed. T. Mommsen, *MGH.AA*, 11 (1894).

Marius of Avenches, *Chronica*, ed. T. Mommsen, *MGH.AA*, 11 (1894).

Mark, *Vita Porphyrii* (*BHG*, 1570), ed. H. Grégoire and M.A. Kugener (Paris, 1930).

Martin I, *Epistola ad Constantem II*, ed. J.D. Mansi, *Sacrorum conciliorum noua et amplissima collectio*, 10 (Florence, 1764).

Matthew of Edessa, *Chronique*, tr. E. Dulaurier, Bibliothèque historique arménienne (Paris, 1858).

Mauricius, *Strategicon*, ed. G.T. Dennis, *CFHB*, 17 (Vienna, 1981).

John Mauropous, *Opera*, ed. P. de Lagarde (Göttingen, 1882).

Maximus of Turin, *Sermones*, ed. A. Mutzenbecher, *CCL*, 23 (1962).

Τὸ μέγα ὡρολόγιον, ed. M.I. Saliveros (Athens, n.d.).

Michael II and Theophilus, *Epistola ad Hludowicum*, ed. A. Werminghoff, *MGH.Conc.*, 1.2 (1908).

Michael Italicus, *Opera*, ed. P. Gautier, Archives de l'Orient chrétien, 14 (Paris, 1972).

Miracula Artemii (*BHG*, 173), ed. A. Papadopoulos-Kerameus, *Varia graeca sacra* (St Petersburg, 1909).

Miracula Demetrii (*BHG*, 516z–523), ed. P. Lemerle (Paris, 1978).

Miracula Theclae (*BHG*, 1718), ed. G. Dagron, Subsidia hagiographica, 62 (Brussels, 1975).

Missale Francorum, ed. L.C. Mohlberg et al., Rerum ecclesiasticarum documenta, series maior, fontes, 2, 2 (Rome, 1957).

E. Moeller (ed.), *Corpus benedictionum pontificalium*, *CCL*, 162– (1971–).

Narratio antiquior miraculi B.V.M. in obsidione (*BHG*, 1061), ed. L. Sternbach, *Analecta Avarica* (Cracow, 1900).

Narratio clericorum Remensium, ed. A. Werminghoff, *MGH.Conc.*, 1.2 (1908).

Nicephorus I, *Antirrheticus*, *PG*, 100.

Breuiarium, ed. C. De Boor (Leipzig, 1880).

Nicephorus, *Praecepta militaria*, ed. Yu. A. Kulakovsky, Zapiski imperatorskoy akademii nauk, ser. 8, po istor.-filol. otdeleniyu, 8, 9 (St Petersburg, 1908).

Nicholas I, *Epistolae*, ed. E. Perels, *MGH.Epist.*, 6 (1925).

Nicholas I Mysticus, *Epistolae*, ed. R.J.H. Jenkins and L.G. Westerink, *CFHB*, 6 (Washington, D.C., 1973).

Nithard, *Historiarum libri IV*, ed. P. Lauer, Classiques de l'histoire de France au moyen âge, 7 (Paris, 1926).

Notitia prouinciarum et ciuitatum Africae, ed. M. Petschenig, *CSEL*, 7 (1881).

Notker the Stammerer, *Gesta Karoli*, ed. H.F. Haefele, *MGH.SRG*, n.s. 12 (1962).

Oikonomides, N. (ed.), *Les listes de préséance byzantines des IXe et Xe siècles*, Le monde byzantin (Paris, 1972).

Ordo coronationis Karoli II in regno Hlotharii II factae, ed. A. Boretius and V. Krause, *MGH.Capit.*, 2 (1897).

Oratio pro rege, ed. F. Vollmer, *MGH.AA*, 14 (1905).

Ordo de celebrando concilio, ed. C. Munier, *Revue des sciences religieuses*, 37 (1963), 250–71.

Origo gentis Langobardorum, ed. G. Waitz, *MGH.SRL* (1878).

Orosius, *Historia aduersum paganos*, ed. C. Zangemeister, *CSEL*, 5 (1882).

Pactus legis Salicae, ed. K.A. Eckhardt, *MGH.Leges*, 1.4.1 (1962).

P. Maspéro, *Papyrus grecs d'époque byzantine*, ed. J. Maspéro (Cairo, 1911–16).

P. Oxyrhynchus, ed. B.P. Grenfell et al. (London, 1898–).

Παρεκβολαί, ed. J.A. de Foucault, *Strategemata* (Paris, 1949).

Paschale Campanum, ed. T. Mommsen, *MGH.AA*, 9 (1892).

Passio X martyrum (*BHG*, 1195), *AASS*, Aug. 2 (1735).

Passio Eulaliae Emeretensis (*BHL*, 2700), ed. A. Fabrega Grau, *Pasionario hispánico* 2, Monumenta Hispaniae sacra, ser. lit. 6 (Barcelona, 1953–5).

Passio Leodegarii (*BHL*, 4849–50), ed. B. Krusch, *MGH.SRM*, 5 (1910).

Passio XLII martyrum Amoriensium (*BHG*, 1209), ed. V. Vasil'evsky and P. Nikitin, *Zapiski imperatorskoi akademii nauk, Otdelenie istoricheskikh nauk i filologii*, Ser. 8, 7, 2 (St Petersburg, 1905).

St Patrick, *Epistola ad Coroticum*, ed. R.P.C. Hanson, SC, 249 (Paris, 1978).

Paul Deacon, *Historia Langobardorum*, ed. L. Bethmann and G. Waitz, *MGH.SRL* (1878).

Paul Silentiary, *Descriptio S. Sophiae*, ed. P. Friedländer (Leipzig, 1912).

Paulinus, *Vita Ambrosii (BHL*, 377), ed. M. Pellegrino, Verba seniorum, n.s. 1 (Rome, 1961).

Paulinus of Aquileia, *Epistolae*, ed. E. Dümmler, *MGH.Epist.*, 4 (1895).

Peter Patrician, *De sententiis*, see *Excerpta historica*.

Philetus Synadenus, *Epistolae*, see J. Darrouzès.

Philostorgius, *Historia ecclesiastica*, ed. J. Bidez, GCS, 21 (Leipzig, 1913).

Philotheus, *Cleterologium*, see N. Oikonomides.

Photius, *Bibliotheca*, ed. R. Henry (Paris, 1959–77).

   Homiliae, ed. B. Laourdas, Παράρτημα, Ἑλληνικά, 12 (Thessalonica, 1959).

Polemius Silvius, *Laterculus*, ed. A. Degrassi, *Inscriptiones Italiae*, 13.2 (1963).

Priscian, *De laude Anastasii imperatoris*, ed. E. Baehrens, *Poetae latini minores*, 5 (Leipzig, 1883).

Proclus of Constantinople, *Homiliae*, PG, 65.

Procopius of Caesarea, *Opera*, ed. J. Haury and G. Wirth (Leipzig, 1962–4).

Procopius of Gaza, *In imperatorem Anastasium panegyricus*, ed. C. Kempen (Bonn, 1918).

Prosper Tiro, *Epitoma chronicon*, ed. T. Mommsen, *MGH.AA*, 9 (1892).

Additamenta ad Prosperum Havniensia, ed. T. Mommsen, *ibid.*

Prudentius, *Carmina*, ed. M.P. Cunningham, *CCL*, 126 (1966).

Michael Psellus, *Chronographia*, ed. E. Renauld (Paris, 1926–8).

Rufinus, *Historia ecclesiastica*, ed. T. Mommsen, GCS, 9 (Leipzig, 1903–9).

Sabas, *Vita Joannicii (BHG*, 935), ed. J. Van Den Gheyn, *AASS*, Nov. 2.1 (1894).

Sacramentarium gelasianum s. VIII [of Angoulême], ed. P. Cagin (Angoulême, n.d.).

Sacramentarium Fuldense s. X, ed. A. Richter and A. Schönfelder, Quellen und Abhandlungen zur Geschichte der Abtei und Diözese Fulda, 9 (Fulda, 1912).

Sacramentarium Gellonense, ed. A. Dumas and J. Deshusses, *CCL*, 159–159A (1983).

Sacramentarium gregorianum s. IX, ed. J. Deshusses, *Spicilegium Friburgense*, 16 and 24 (Fribourg, 1971–9).

Sacramentarium Laurissense, ed. L. Eizenhöfer, *Die Reichsabtei Lorsch. Festschrift zum Gedenken an ihre Stiftung 764*, 2 (Darmstadt, 1977), 129–69.

Sacramentarii fragmentum Vat. lat. 377: See K. Gamber.

Scriptor incertus de Leone Armenio, ed. I. Bekker (Bonn, 1842).

John Scylitzes, *Synopsis historiarum*, ed. I. Thurn, *CFHB*, 5 (Berlin, 1973).

Scylitzes Continuatus, ed. I. Bekker (Bonn, 1839).

Sebeos, *Histoire d'Héraclius*, tr. F. Macler (Paris, 1904).

Sedulius Scottus, *Carmina*, ed. L. Traube, *MGH.Poet.*, 3 (1896).
  De rectoribus christianis, ed. S. Hellmann, Quellen und Untersuchungen zur lateinischen Philologie des Mittelalters, 1, 1 (Munich, 1906).

Servius, *Commentarii in Vergilii carmina*, ed. G. Thilo and H. Hagen (Leipzig, 1881–1919).

Severus of Antioch, *Opera*, ed. and tr. R. Duval, *Patrologia orientalis*, 4 (1908); E.W. Brooks, *ibid.*, 7 (1911); M. Brière, F. Graffin and C.J.S. Lash, *ibid.*, 36 (1972).

Sickel, T. (ed.), *Diplomata regum et imperatorum Germaniae*, 1 (1879–84).

Sidonius Apollinaris, *Opera*, ed. A. Loyen (Paris, 1960–70).

Sisebut, *Vita Desiderii* (*BHL*, 2148), ed. B. Krusch, *MGH.SRM*, 3 (1896).

Socrates, *Historia ecclesiastica*, PG, 67.

Ps. Sophronius, *Vita Cyri et Ioannis* (*BHG*, 469), *PG*, 87.3.

Souda, *Lexicon*, ed. A. Adler (Leipzig, 1928–38).

Sozomen, *Historia ecclesiastica*, ed. J. Bidez and G.C. Hansen, GCS, 50 (Berlin, 1960).

Stephanus Africanus, *Vita Amatoris Autissiodorensis* (*BHL*, 356), ed. *AASS*, Maii 1 (1680).

Stephen V, *Epistolae*, ed. E. Caspar, *MGH.Epist.*, 7 (1928).

Stephen, *Carmen de synodo Ticinensi*, ed. K. Strecker, *MGH.Poet.*, 4.2 (1923).

Stephen Deacon, *Vita et miracula Stephani iunioris* (*BHG*, 1666), *PG*, 100.

Στρατηγικὰ παραγγέλματα, ed. J.A. de Foucault, *Strategemata* (Paris, 1949).

Suetonius, *De vita caesarum*, ed. M. Ihm (Leipzig, 1908).

Sulpicius Severus, *Vita Martini* (*BHL*, 5610), ed. J. Fontaine, SC, 133–5 (Paris, 1967–9).

Sylloge codicis Sangallensis CCCLXXI, ed. P. von Winterfeld, *MGH.Poet.*, 4.1 (1899).

Symeon Magister, *Chronographia*, ed. I. Bekker (Bonn, 1838).
  Epistolae, see J. Darrouzès.

Symmachus, *Opera*, ed. O. Seeck, *MGH.AA*, 6.1 (1883).

Synaxarium Constantinopolitanum, *AASS*, *Novembris*, *Propylaeum* (1902).

Synesius of Cyrene, *Hymni et opuscula*, ed. N. Terzaghi (Rome, 1939–44).
  Epistulae, ed. A. Garzya (Rome, 1979).

Tablettes Albertini, Actes privés de l'époque vandale (fin du Ve siècle), ed. C. Courtois et al. (Paris, 1952).

Tacitus, *Annales,* ed. H. Furneaux (Oxford, 1896–91).

Taio of Saragossa, *Sententiae, PL,* 80.

Tellenbach, G. (ed.), *Römischer und christlicher Reichsgedanke in der Liturgie des frühen Mittelalters,* Sitzungsberichte der Heidelberger Akademie der Wissenschaften, Philos.-hist. Kl. 1934–5, 1 (Heidelberg, 1934).

Tertullian, *Opera,* ed. E. Dekkers et al., *CCL,* 1–2 (1954).

Thegan, *Vita Hludowici imperatoris,* ed. G.H. Pertz, *MGH.SS,* 2 (1829).

Themistius, *Orationes,* ed. H. Schenkl et al. (Leipzig, 1965–74).

Theodore Lector, *Historia ecclesiastica,* ed. G.C. Hansen, GCS [54] (Berlin, 1971).

Theodore Studite, *Epistulae, PG,* 99.

Theodosius Grammaticus, *Carmen,* ed. S.P. Lampros, Ἱστορικὰ μελετή-ματα (Athens, 1884).

Theodulf of Orleans, *Carmina,* ed. E. Dümmler, *MGH.Poet.,* 1 (1881).

Theophanes, *Chronographia,* ed. C. De Boor (Leipzig, 1883–5).

Theophanes Continuatus, ed. I. Bekker (Bonn, 1838).

Theophylactus Simocattes, *Historiae,* ed. C. De Boor and P. Wirth (Leipzig, 1972).

Theosterictus, *Vita Nicetae (BHG,* 1341).

Trempelas, P.N. (ed.), Αἱ τρεῖς λειτουργίαι κατὰ τοὺς ἐν Ἀθήναις κώδικας., Texte und Forschungen zur byzantinisch-neugriechischen Philologie, 15 (Athens, 1935).

Triodion, PG, 92.

Troya, C. (ed.), *Codice diplomatico Langobardo dal DLXVIII al DCCLXXIV con note storiche, osservazioni e dissertazioni,* 4 (Naples, 1854).

Typicon of the Great Church, ed. J. Mateos, Orientalia christiana analecta, 165–6 (Rome, 1962–3).

Uspensky Tacticon, see N. Oikonomides.

Vegetius, *Epitoma rei militaris,* ed. C. Lang (Leipzig, 1885).

Venantius Fortunatus, *Carmina,* ed. F. Leo, *MGH.AA,* 4.1 (1881).

Vita Germani (BHL, 3468), ed. B. Krusch, *MGH.SRM,* 7 (1920).

Vita Seuerini Burdegalensis (BHL, 7652), ed. W. Levison, *MGH.SRM,* 7 (1920).

Victor of Vita, *Historia persecutionis Africanae prouinciae,* ed. M. Petschenig, *CSEL,* 7 (1881).

Vita Amandi Traiectensis (BHL, 332), ed. B. Krusch, *MGH.SRM,* 5 (1910).

Vita Aniani Aurelianensis (*BHL*, 473), ed. B. Krusch, *MGH.SRM*, 3 (1896).

Vita Antonii iunioris (*BHG*, 142), ed. A. Papadopoulos-Kerameus, Συλλογὴ παλαιστινῆς καὶ συριακῆς ἁγιολογίας, 1, Pravoslavnyi Palestinskii sbornik, 57 (St Petersburg, 1907); *Additamentum*, ed. F. Halkin, *AB*, 62 (1944), 187–225.

Vita Audoini Rotomagensis (*BHL*, 750), ed. W. Levison, *MGH.SRM*, 5 (1910).

Vita Danielis stylitae, ed. H. Delehaye, Subsidia hagiographica, 14 (Brussels, 1923).

Vita Desiderii (*BHL*, 2143), ed. B. Krusch, *MGH.SRM*, 4 (1902).

Vita Elias iunioris (*BHG*, 580), ed. G. Rossi Taibbi, Testi e monumenti, Testi 7 (Palermo, 1962).

Vita Eligii (*BHL*, 2472–6), ed. J. Ghesquière, *Acta sanctorum Belgii selecta*, 3 (1785), and B. Krusch, *MGH.SRM*, 4 (1902).

Vita Euthymii (*BHG*, 651), ed. P. Karlin-Hayter, Bibliothèque de Byzantion, 3 (Brussels, 1970).

Vita Gaugerici Cameracensis (*BHL*, 3286), ed. B. Krusch, *MGH.SRM*, 3 (1896).

Vita Genouefae (*BHL*, 3335), ed. B. Krusch, *MGH.SRM*, 3 (1896).

Vita Georgii Amastridos (*BHG*, 668), ed. V.G. Vasil'evsky, *Trudy*, 3 (St Petersburg, 1915).

Vita Nicholae Studitae (*BHG*, 1365), *PG*, 105.

Vitae patrum Emeretensium (*BHL*, 2530), ed. J.N. Garvin (Washington, D.C., 1946).

Vita Pauli iunioris (*BHG*, 1474), ed. H. Delehaye, *AB*, 11 (1892), 19–74.

Vita Symeonis stylitae iunioris (*BHG*, 1689), ed. P. van den Ven, Subsidia hagiographica, 32, 1 (Brussels, 1962).

Vita Theodorae imperatricis (*BHG*, 1731), ed. W. [= V. E.] Regel, *Analecta Byzantino-Russica* (St Petersburg, 1891).

Vita Theophano imperatricis (*BHG*, 1794), ed. E. Kurtz, *Zapiski imperatorskoi akademii nauk*, s. 8, *po istor.-filol. otdeleniyu*, 3, no. 2 (St Petersburg, 1898).

Vives, J., *Inscripciones cristianas de la España romana y visigoda*, Monumenta Hispaniae sacra, ser. patr. 2, 2nd edn (Barcelona, 1969).

Walafrid Strabo, *Carmina*, ed. E. Dümmler, *MGH.Poet.*, 2 (1884).

　　De exordiis et incrementis quarumdam in observationibus ecclesiasticis rerum, ed. A. Knöpfler, Veröffentlichungen aus dem kirchenhistorischen Seminar, 1 (Munich, 1899).

William of Puglia, *La geste de Robert Guiscard*, ed. M. Mathieu (Palermo, 1961).

Nicephorus Callistus Xanthopoulos, *Historia ecclesiastica*, *PG*, 146.

Yahya Ibn Sa'id of Antioch, *Histoire*, tr. A.A. Vasiliev, *Patrologia orientalis*, 23 (1932).

Zachary Rhetor, *Historia ecclesiastica*, tr. E.W. Brooks, *Corpus scriptorum christianorum orientalium*, Scriptores Syri, 3,5–6 (Versio) (Louvain, 1924).

Zeno, *Henoticon*, ed. E. Schwartz, *Codex Vaticanus gr. 1431, eine antichalkedonische Sammlung aus der Zeit Kaiser Zenos*, Abhandlungen der bayerischen Akademie der Wissenschaften, Philos.-philol. und hist. Kl., 32, 6 (1927).

John Zonaras, *Epitome historiarum*, ed. T. Büttner-Wobst (Bonn, 1897).

Zosimus, *Historia noua*, ed. F. Paschoud (Paris, 1971–), and L. Mendelssohn (Leipzig, 1887).

Select bibliography of secondary sources

This list is not intended as a general guide to the literature. It is meant only to aid the reader by supplying the full reference for those studies which are repeatedly cited in non-consecutive chapters.

Balsdon, J.P.V.D., *Life and leisure in ancient Rome*, New York, 1969.
Barnes, T.D., *Constantine and Eusebius*, Cambridge, Mass., 1981.
Bury, J.B., 'The Ceremonial Book of Constantine Porphyrogennetos', *English Historical Review*, 22 (1907), 209–27 and 417–39.
  History of the later Roman empire from the death of Theodosius I to the Death of Justinian, London, 1923.
  The imperial administrative system in the ninth century, London, 1911.
Cameron, A., *Circus factions. Blues and Greens at Rome and Byzantium*, Oxford, 1976.
  Porphyrius the Charioteer, Oxford, 1973.
Chastagnol, A., *Les fastes de la préfecture de Rome au Bas-Empire*, Études prosopographiques, 2, Paris, 1962.
  La préfecture urbaine à Rome sous le Bas-Empire, Publications de la Faculté des lettres et sciences humaines d'Alger, 34, Paris, 1960.
Classen, P., 'Karl der Grosse, das Papsttum und Byzanz: Die Begründung des karolingischen Kaisertums', *Karl der Grosse. Lebenswerk und Nachleben*, 1, Düsseldorf, 1965, 537–608.
Dagron, G., 'L'empire romain d'Orient au IVe siècle et les traditions politiques de l'hellénisme. Le témoignage de Thémistios', *TM*, 3 (1968), 1–242.
Deér, J., 'Die Vorrechte des Kaisers in Rom (772–800)' [2nd edn], *Zum Kaisertum Karls des Grossen*, ed. G. Wolf, Wege der Forschung, 38, Darmstadt, 1972, pp. 30–115.
Dölger, F., *Regesten der Kaiserurkunden des oströmischen Reiches von 565–1453*, Munich, 1924.
Frolow, A., *La relique de la vraie croix. Recherches sur le développement d'un culte*, Archives de l'orient chrétien, 7, Paris, 1961.

Gascou, J., 'Les institutions de l'Hippodrome en Égypte byzantine', *Bulletin de l'Institut français d'archéologie orientale*, 76 (1976), 185–212.

Grabar, A., *L'empereur dans l'art byzantin. Recherches sur l'art officiel de l'empire d'Orient*, Publications de la Faculté des lettres de l'Université de Strasbourg, 75, Paris, 1936.

Grierson, P., and Bellinger, A.R., *Catalogue of the Byzantine Coins in the Dumbarton Oaks and in the Whittemore Collection*, Washington, D.C., 1966–.

Guilland, R., *Recherches sur les institutions byzantines*, Berliner byzantinistische Arbeiten, 35, Berlin, 1967.

Hahn, W., *Moneta Imperii Byzantini. Rekonstruktion des Prägeaufbaues auf synoptisch-tabellarischer Grundlage*, Vienna, 1973–.

Halkin, L., *La supplication d'action de grâces chez les Romains*, Bibliothèque de la Faculté de philosophie et lettres de l'Université de Liège, 128, Paris, 1958.

Hauck, K., 'Von einer spätantiken Randkultur zum karolingischen Europa', *FMS*, 1 (1967), 3–93.

Jones, A.H.M., *The later Roman empire: a social, economic and administrative survey*, Norman, 1964.

Kampers, G., *Persongeschichtliche Studien zum Westgotenreich in Spanien*, Spanische Forschungen der Görresgesellschaft, 2, 17, Münster, 1979.

Kantorowicz, E.H., 'The "King's Advent" and the enigmatic panels in the doors of Santa Sabina', *Selected Studies*, Locust Valley, 1965, pp. 37–75.

Karayannopulos, J., *Das Finanzwesen des frühbyzantinischen Staates*, Sudosteuropäische Arbeiten, 52, Munich, 1958.

Klauser, T., *Gesammelte Arbeiten zur Liturgiegeschichte, Kirchengeschichte und christlichen Archäologie*, JAC, Ergänzungsband, 3, Münster, 1974.

Kneissl, P., *Die Siegestitulatur der römischen Kaiser. Untersuchungen zu den Siegerbeinamen des ersten und zweiten Jahrhunderts*, Hypomnemata, 23, Göttingen, 1969.

Kollwitz, J., *Oströmische Plastik der theodosianischen Zeit*, Studien zur spätantiken Kunstgeschichte, 12, Berlin, 1941.

Krüger, K.H., *Königsgrabkirchen der Franken, Angelsachsen und Langobarden bis zur Mitte des 8. Jahrhunderts*, Münstersche Mittelalter-Schriften, 4, Münster, 1971.

Kruse, H., *Studien zur offiziellen Geltung des Kaiserbildes im römischen Reiche*, Studien zur Geschichte und Kultur des Altertums, 19, 3, Paderborn, 1934.

Lounghis, T.C., *Les ambassades byzantines en Occident depuis la fondation des états barbares jusqu'aux Croisades (407–1090)*, Athens, 1980.

MacCormack, S.G., *Art and ceremony in late antiquity*, The transformation of the classical heritage, 1, Berkeley, 1981.

McCormick, M., 'Odoacer, emperor Zeno and the Rugian victory legation', *Byz.*, 47 (1977), 212–22.

Mango, C., *The Brazen House. A study of the vestibule of the imperial palace of Constantinople*, Copenhagen, 1959.

Matthews, J.F., *Western aristocracies and imperial court, A.D. 364–425*, Oxford, 1975.

Ostrogorsky, G., *Geschichte des byzantinischen Staates*, Handbuch der Altertumswissenschaft, 12, 1, 2, 3rd edn, Munich, 1963.

Platner, S.B., and Ashby, T., *A topographical dictionary of ancient Rome*, London, 1929.

Petit, P., *Libanius et la vie municipale à Antioche au IVe siècle après J.-C.*, Paris, 1955.

Reydellet, M., *La royauté dans la littérature latine de Sidoine Apollinaire à Isidore de Séville*, Bibliothèque des Écoles françaises d'Athènes et de Rome, 243, Rome, 1981.

Rösch, G., *'Ονομα βασιλέως. Studien zum offiziellen Gebrauch der Kaisertitel in spätantiker und frühbyzantinischer Zeit*, Byzantina vindobonensia, 10, Vienna, 1978.

Schlesinger, W., 'Über germanisches Heerkönigtum', *Das Königtum. Seine geistigen und rechtlichen Grundlagen*, Vorträge und Forschungen, 3, Constance, 1956.

Schneider, R., *Königswahl und Königserhebung im Frühmittelalter. Untersuchungen zur Herrschaftsnachfolge bei den Langobarden und Merowingern*, Monographien zur Geschichte des Mittelalters, 3, Stuttgart, 1972.

Schmidt, L., *Geschichte der Wandalen*, 2nd edn, Munich, 1942.

Schramm, P.E., et al., *Herrschaftszeichen und Staatssymbolik. Beiträge zur ihrer Geschichte vom dritten bis zum sechszehnten Jahrhundert*, MGH, Schriften, 13, Stuttgart, 1954–78.

Stein, E., *Histoire du Bas-Empire*, ed. J.R. Palanque, Paris, 1959–49.

Thompson, E.A., *Romans and barbarians. The decline of the western empire*, Madison, 1982.

Treadgold, W., 'The chronological accuracy of the Chronicle of Symeon the Logothete for the years 813–845', *DOP*, 33 (1979), 159–97.

Treitinger, O., *Die oströmische Kaiser- und Reichsidee nach ihrer Gestaltung im höfischen Zeremoniell*, Jena, 1938.

Wallace-Hadrill, J.M. *Early Germanic kingship in England and on the Continent*, Oxford, 1971.

Wolfram, H. 'Gotisches Königtum und Römisches Kaisertum von Theodosius dem Grossen bis Justinian I.', *FMS*, 13 (1979), 1–28.

Zum Kaisertum Karls des Grossen, see Deér.

Descriptive list of figures

Figure 1 (p.38). Rome, Arch of Constantine, East side, A.D. 315 (courtesy of Deutsches Archäologisches Institut Rom)

Relief showing Constantine's triumphal entry into Rome on 29 October 312, after his victory over Maxentius. Various units of the victorious army are parading through the Campus Martius, flying vexilla and dragon standards on their way into the city. At the extreme right, the parade enters the Arch of Domitian; to the left, in the place of honor at the parade's end, Constantine emerges from the city side of the Porta Flaminia. He is seated in a four-wheeled carriage, pulled by the traditional four horse team. See Chs. 2, 1 and 3, 1 and 2.

Figures 2–5 (pp. 52–5). Paris, Musée du Louvre, inv. 4951, sixteenth century (Photo: cliché des Musées Nationaux)

One of several early modern drawings of the reliefs of Constantinople's lost fourth-century triumphal columns. This one may depict sculptures from the column of Arcadius, showing the triumphal entry of Fravitta, Master of Both Services, into New Rome. Figure 2 shows the procession's conclusion, with three captured barbarian leaders in a parade of infamy: they straddle camels and have their arms bound behind their backs. Figure 3 shows the commander's group as it enters what seems to be a city gate. Figures 4 and 5 depict the opening segment of the parade, barbarian prisoners escorted by victorious Roman soldiers. See Ch. 2, 2.

Figure 6 (p. 57). Merseburg, Archiv des Domkapitels, Cod. 202, eleventh century (courtesy of Kurt Weitzmann)

Fragmentary medieval copy of lost fifth-century consular annals of Ravenna. In an era of usurpation, the traditional triumphal display of defeated pretenders' heads became a disturbingly common feature of imperial ceremonial and propaganda. Pictured here are the heads of the usurpers Jovinus and Sebastian, and that of their brother Sallustius. They

416

figured in a victory celebration staged by the court of Ravenna in A.D. 412. See Chs. 2, 2 and 3, 1.

Figure 7 (p. 139). Washington, D.C., Dumbarton Oaks Collection, A.D. 778–80 (enlarged; courtesy of Dumbarton Oaks)

The obverse of this gold *nomisma* issued at Constantinople under Leo IV and Constantine VI may represent the triumph celebrated by the theme commanders at the Sophianae Palace in the capital's Asian suburbs (late 778). During the ceremony, Leo and his infant son were enthroned in a σένζος. The coin may have been struck for the largess distributed during the victory celebration. See Ch. 4, 2.

Figure 8 (p. 145). Madrid, Biblioteca Nacional, Cod. Vitr. 26–2, fol. 37recto ('Madrid Scylitzes'), twelfth century, Sicily? (Photo: Biblioteca Nacional)

The miniature accompanying Scylitzes' account of Michael II's triumph over Thomas the Slav at Adrianople in October 823 depicts the *calcatio colli*, the traditional late Roman gesture of total victory over vanquished usurpers. See Ch. 4, 3.

Figure 9 (p. 149). Washington, D.C., Dumbarton Oaks Collection, A.D. 830/1–42 (enlarged; courtesy of Dumbarton Oaks)

This copper *follis* was probably issued at Constantinople, perhaps in connection with Theophilus' triumphs over the Arabs. The innovative obverse has a half-portrait rather than the traditional bust. This allowed the designer to depict the emperor's *loros* as well as the triumphal headdress or *tufa*. The reverse legend, written in Greek in the usual Latin characters, echoes the triumphal message: 'You conquer, O Augustus Theophilus!' See Ch. 4, 3.

Figure 10 (p. 172). Madrid, Biblioteca Nacional, Cod. Vitr. 26–2, fol. 172verso, twelfth century (Photo: Biblioteca Nacional)

This illustration of Scylitzes' account of John Tzimisces' spectacularly ostentatious act of humility shows the triumphal entry into Constantinople in 971, after the emperor's victory over the Russians and Bulgarians. The parade's focal point was a captured icon of the Virgin and the Bulgarian regalia. These Tzimisces placed in a wagon and followed on horseback into the capital, in order to stress his own modesty and divine approval of his actions.

Figure 11 (p. 183). Madrid, Biblioteca Nacional, Cod. Vitr. 26–2, fol. 224verso, twelfth century (Photo: Biblioteca Nacional)

The eunuch *sebastophorus* Stephen Pergamenus is shown in the place of honor at the end of the triumphal parade (contrary to the mistaken implication of the Greek caption), riding the traditional white horse. The triumph celebrated Stephen's defeat of the usurper George Maniaces, whose head was displayed for a second time in this procession, held at Constantinople between March and July 1043. The victorious official celebrated his triumph in imperial fashion, as the itinerary led through the capital's bazaar to the church of the Chalke, where Constantine IX Monomachus and the two purple-born empresses were enthroned. See Ch. 4, 6.

Figure 12 (p. 290). Florence, Museo nazionale del Bargello, A.D. 591–615.

This remarkable adaptation of a traditional Roman triumphal scheme is the earliest known portrait of an enthroned Germanic ruler. The gilded helmet visor shows two winged Victories presenting Roman and Germanic suppliants to the triumphant king of the Lombards. He is depicted with the long hair and beard characteristic of his people, without a crown, and grasps a sword as the symbol of his authority. The word 'VICTORY' is inscribed on each of the standards carried by the Victories. The damaged inscription around the king's head completes the legend 'TO OUR LORD KING AGILULF'. The king may have presented the helmet to one of his followers. See Ch. 7, 4.

Figure 13 (p. 339). Paris, Bibliothèque Nationale, Département des médailles, A.D. 534–54 (Photo: Bibliothèque Nationale)

The obverse of this gold *solidus* imitates imperial issues but shows the Merovingian king Theudebert in the military uniform of Roman emperors, including the triumphal *tufa*. The legend avoids the royal title and reads: 'OUR LORD THEUDEBERT THE VICTOR'. See Ch. 9, 1.

Index

The Latin loan-words of the Byzantine administration appear in this index under their Latin form, when both Greek and Latin forms have been used in the text. Greek technical terms occur at their place in the English alphabet.*

*I am grateful to Magda Jabbour for her generous help in data-processing the text of this index.

390, softens punishment, 146, 186–8,
and imperial banquets, 105, 105n109;
Italo-Roman, 276, 279, attachment to
ceremonial, 269, uses victory
ideology for Ostrogothic kings, 281;
Lombard: and Roman luxury goods,
285; Visigothic, 300, 303, 315,
321n110, 327, 393, love of
ceremonial, 301, and royal
ceremonial, 315, restored, 317;
Merovingian, 340, senatorial and
bishops, 330, concern with
ceremonial, 329–32, and royal
ceremonial, 332–40; Carolingian, 374,
375, 384, and royal ceremonial,
366–9; *see also* audience, ceremonial;
retainers; senate
Aristomachus, 191n10
Arithmos, 163
Arius, 238; *see also* Arians
Arles, 386; *see also* Sacramentary of
Armeniacus, 22; *see also* cognomina
Armeniakon, theme, 137, 142, 151n68;
rebels, 258
arms, armor, 87, 136, 166, 253n106,
292, 292n149, 377; *see also* helmet;
shield; spear; sword
army: imperial, 16, 41, 93, 96, 113, 126,
152, 169, 180, 185, 229, 252, 259, 389,
395; and triumphs, 15, 86–7, 135,
138–41, 147–8, 150, 158, 161, 165,
181, 226, 390, 416; ceremonies, 17,
48, 97, 98, 144, 155, 391, for officers,
255, for Roman client, 255n113; and
cognomina devictarum gentium, 115;
influence, 286, 391–2; liturgy, 107,
239n34, 241, 242, 244–52, 256;
martyrdom, 251–2; parade grounds,
28; political unrest, 141, 244n54;
purity, 244, 250–1; relics, 245, 247;
and Thomas the Slav, 146;   royal:
394; Ostrogothic, 269, 275, 276;
Visigothic, 308, 313, 314, 325n122,
326, 340, liturgy, 308–12, purity, 312,
payments, 319, social profile, 315–7;
Merovingian, 334, and ceremonial,
333n19, 340; Carolingian, 328, 350,
384, triumphal entries, 374–5, and
ceremonies, 366–7, 368–9, 375,
liturgy, 347–56, 358, 359, 360;

medieval, 244, 259, 350, 352; *see also*
audience; booty; cavalry;
commanders; costume; tagmata;
themes
Arnulf, 355, 356, 377n214, 383
Arras, 350n95
Arslanhane, 174n174
Artabasdus, usurper: 134, 140, 186, 194;
strategos of the Anatolikon, 137
Artopolia, 215, 217n135, 219; *see also*
Arch of
asecretis, 193n23, 200
Ashod, 195n29
ἀσφάλεια, 224
assemblies, general: Carolingian and
ceremonial, 366–9
asses, 146, 177, 303; seated upon
backwards, 135, 144, 181, 186; *see also*
camels
Assumption, procession, 368n171
Astronomer, *Vita Hludovici Pii*, 374
Asturia, 376
Athalaric, 269n45, 269n46, 271n54;
ethical triumph, 275
Athaulf, 109, 119
Athens, 141, 178, 391
Attalus, 56, 58n76, 86n27, 98, 99, 119,
123
Attila, 60
audience: for imperial ceremonial, 7,
105, 198n43, participation by
command, 200; for triumphs, 64,
aristocratic 66, 67, 70, 71, 88, 132,
390, mass or urban, 16, 85–90, 128,
164–5, 174, 204, 389–90, military,
138–9, 144–6; victory bulletins, 192,
193, 195;   for royal ceremonial:
Ostrogothic, 269–70, 271–2, 278,
propaganda, 282–3; Lombard,
propaganda, 292–3, 296; Visigothic,
triumph, 313, 315–18, victory
coinage, 318–20, propaganda, 306;
Merovingian, Clovis' triumph, 337;
Clothar II, 340; Carolingian, 366–9,
triumphs, 374–5; late Roman,
Byzantine, early medieval compared,
390, 395; *see also* ceremonial
audiences, receptions: imperial, 147, 148,
150, 204n71, 212–220, 221, 227;
victorious commanders, 69, 151, 158,

447

Past and Present Publications

General Editor: PAUL SLACK, *Exeter College, Oxford*

Family and Inheritance: Rural Society in Western Europe 1200–1800, edited by Jack Goody, Joan Thirsk and E.P. Thompson

French Society and the Revolution, edited by Douglas Johnson

Peasants, Knights and Heretics: Studies in Medieval English Social History, edited by R.H. Hilton

Towns in Societies: Essays in Economic History and Historical Sociology, edited by Philip Abrams and E.A. Wrigley

Desolation of a City: Coventry and the Urban Crisis of the Late Middle Ages, Charles Phythian-Adams

Puritanism and Theatre: Thomas Middleton and Opposition Drama under the Early Stuarts, Margot Heinemann

Lords and Peasants in a Changing Society: The Estates of the Bishopric of Worcester 680–1540, Christopher Dyer

Life, Marriage and Death in a Medieval Parish: Economy, Society and Demography in Halesowen 1270–1400, Zvi Razi

Biology, Medicine and Society 1840–1940, edited by Charles Webster

The Invention of Tradition, edited by Eric Hobsbawm and Terence Ranger

Industrialization before Industrialization: Rural Industry and the Genesis of Capitalism, Peter Kriedte, Hans Medick and Jürgen Schlumbohm[†]

The Republic in the Village: The People of the Var from the French Revolution to the Second Republic, Maurice Agulhon[†]

Social Relations and Ideas: Essays in Honour of R.H. Hilton, edited by T.H. Aston, P.R. Coss, Christopher Dyer and Joan Thirsk

A Medieval Society: The West Midlands at the End of the Thirteenth Century, R.H. Hilton

Winstanley: 'The Law of Freedom' and Other Writings, edited by Christopher Hill

Crime in Seventeenth-Century England: A County Study, J.A. Sharpe[†]

The Crisis of Feudalism: Economy and Society in Eastern Normandy c. 1300-1500, Guy Bois[†]

The Development of the Family and Marriage in Europe, Jack Goody

Disputes and Settlements: Law and Human Relations in the West, edited by John Bossy

Rebellion, Popular Protest and the Social Order in Early Modern England, edited by Paul Slack

Studies on Byzantine Literature of the Eleventh and Twelfth Centuries, Alexander Kazhdan in collaboration with Simon Franklin[†]

The English Rising of 1381, edited by R.H. Hilton and T.H. Aston

Praise and Paradox: Merchants and Craftsmen in Elizabethan Popular Literature, Laura Caroline Stevenson

The Brenner Debate: Agrarian Class Structure and Economic Development in Pre-Industrial Europe, edited by T.H. Aston and C.H.E. Philpin

Eternal Victory: Triumphal Rulership in Late Antiquity, Byzantium and the Early Medieval West, Michael McCormick[†]

East-Central Europe in Transition: From the Fourteenth to the Seventeenth Century, edited by Antoni Mączak, Henryk Samsonowicz and Peter Burke[†]

[†]Co-published with the Maison des Sciences de l'Homme, Paris

453

Past and Present Publications

Small Books and Pleasant Histories: Popular Fiction and its Readership in Seventeenth-Century England, Margaret Spufford★
Society, Politics and Culture: Studies in Early Modern England, Mervyn James
Horses, Oxen and Technological Innovation: The Use of Draught Animals in English Farming 1066-1500, John Langdon

★Published only as a paperback

Frankish / Carol. liturgy [?]

454